Praise for *Diversity at Work: The Practice of Inclusion*

"Experts provide clear guidance on how to design and implement initiatives that will truly connect and engage diverse individuals in the workplace."
Ann Marie Ryan, Ph.D., professor, Michigan State University and past president, SIOP

"A must read for leaders who want to understand both the academic background and practical D&I approaches to driving systemic change."
Candi Castleberry-Singleton, Chief Inclusion and Diversity Officer, University of Pittsburgh Medical Center

"Comprehensive and data informed, yet personal and practical, this is a must-read book for those interested in both the science and practice of diversity and inclusion in the workplace. Perfect to jump start a discussion with the managers in your organization or for teaching a class to the managers of the future!"
Ana Mari Cauce, Ph.D., provost and professor, University of Washington

"Brilliant! The editors and contributors deliver penetrating insight into today's meaning of diversity and inclusion."
Manny Gonzalez, CEO, National Society of Hispanic MBAs

"This book succeeds not just in combining theory with practice but also in bringing together a variety of different approaches and disciplines. The writers are the best in the field and they refresh our knowledge whilst challenging our thinking."
Binna Kandola, Ph.D., OBE, senior partner, PearnKandola, and former chair, Division of Occupational Psychology, British Psychological Society

"This impressive volume fills an important gap in the diversity and inclusion literature by bringing together research and practice. The contributors—from both academia and practice—have the depth of experience, insight, and credibility that make this volume especially valuable for both audiences."
Nancy DiTomaso, Ph.D., vice dean, Rutgers Business School; author, *The American Non-Dilemma: Racial Inequality without Racism*

The Professional Practice Series

The Professional Practice Series is sponsored by The Society for Industrial and Organizational Psychology, Inc. (SIOP). The series was launched in 1988 to provide industrial and organizational psychologists, organizational scientists and practitioners, human resources professionals, managers, executives, and those interested in organizational behavior and performance with volumes that are insightful, current, informative, and relevant to *organizational practice*. The volumes in the Professional Practice Series are guided by five tenets designed to enhance future organizational practice:

1. Focus on practice, but grounded in science
2. Translate organizational science into practice by generating guidelines, principles, and lessons learned that can shape and guide practice
3. Showcase the application of industrial and organizational psychology to solve problems
4. Document and demonstrate best industrial and organizational-based practices
5. Stimulate research needed to guide future organizational practice

The volumes seek to inform those interested in practice with guidance, insights, and advice on how to apply the concepts, findings, methods, and tools derived from industrial and organizational psychology to solve human-related organizational problems.

Previous Professional Practice Series volumes include:

Published by Jossey-Bass

The Professional Practice Series

Diversity at Work: The Practice of Inclusion

Bernardo M. Ferdman, *Editor*

Barbara R. Deane, *Associate Editor*

A Wiley Brand

Published by Jossey-Bass
A Wiley Brand
One Montgomery Street, Suite 1200, San Francisco, CA 94104-4594—www.josseybass.com

For additional copies/bulk purchases of this book in the U.S. please contact 800–274–4434.

Wiley books and products are available through most bookstores. To contact Wiley directly call our Customer Care Department within the U.S. at 800-274-4434, outside the U.S. at 317-572-3985, fax 317-572-4002, or visit www.wiley.com

Wiley publishes in a variety of print and electronic formats and by print-on-demand. Some material included with standard print versions of this book may not be included in e-books or in print-on-demand. If this book refers to media such as a CD or DVD that is not included in the version you purchased, you may download this material at http://booksupport.wiley.com. For more information about Wiley products, visit www.wiley.com.

Library of Congress Cataloging-in-Publication Data

Diversity at work: the practice of inclusion / Bernardo M. Ferdman, editor, & Barbara R. Deane, associate editor.
    1 online resource. – (The professional practice series)
  Includes index.
  Description based on print version record and CIP data provided by publisher; resource not viewed.
  ISBN 978-1-118-41782-9 (pdf) – ISBN 978-1-118-41515-3 (epub) – ISBN 978-0-470-40133-0 (cloth) 1. Diversity in the workplace.   2. Corporate culture.   I. Ferdman, Bernardo M. II. Deane, Barbara.
  HF5549.5.M5
  658.3008–dc23

                                        2013027688

Printed in the United States of America

HB Printing   10 9 8 7 6 5 4 3 2 1

Contents

List of Tables, Figures, and Exhibits

Tables

Figures

Exhibits

Foreword

From our perspective, diversity and inclusion (D&I) represent some of the core values of the fields of I-O psychology and organization development (OD). As a result, as scientist-practitioners we have a dual responsibility both to dimensionalize and research these constructs to continue to build our understanding of them, and to assist others in driving these values deep into the business and people strategies of the organizations in which we work and consult. Given the ubiquity of the war for talent, with its increasing emphasis on shifting demographics and generational differences in the workplace and on concepts such as global thinking, learning agility, and cultural dexterity, it is no wonder that D&I have become the epicenter of the talent management agenda of many prominent and forward-thinking organizations today.

That said, if D&I are indeed at the center of talent management and at the forefront of many corporate sustainability efforts, where then are the explicit linkages to the fields of I-O, OD, and human resource management (HRM)? This was the question we asked ourselves several years ago during one of our annual Professional Practice Series Editorial Board planning meetings at the annual conference of the Society for Industrial and Organizational Psychology (SIOP). After years of having experienced D&I efforts at PepsiCo as being at the core of our HR agenda, we wondered why they were not more fully integrated with the fields of I-O, OD, and HR in general. As we discussed with Bernardo Ferdman (who was one of our board members at the time), there was little in the literature directly linking the different fields of practice, aside from some key early efforts such as the original volume by Susan Jackson and Associates in the early 1990s, even though many of the philosophical underpinnings and workplace practices of D&I overlap and have a shared heritage with I-O and OD efforts. Despite some more recent targeted efforts in the field to create these connections (for example, see recent focal articles in the *Industrial-Organizational Psychologist: Perspectives on Science and Practice*), there remains no single definitive source that effectively integrates D&I efforts with the fields of I-O, OD, and HRM. That is, until now.

This volume you hold in your hands, *Diversity at Work: The Practice of Inclusion*, represents a needed comprehensive and holistic approach to bridging the gap in the literature between these different but related fields. Bernardo Ferdman and his coeditor, Barbara Deane, have moved the needle forward with this addition to the Professional Practice Series by incorporating perspectives from both academics and practitioners across multiple disciplines to focus not just on the concepts of D&I (recognizing both old and new dimensions), but also on the actual application or practice of inclusion in the workplace. In many ways it represents the next step in the combined evolution of D&I and I-O.

Starting with the introduction of new frameworks for conceptualizing inclusion (that is, going beyond diversity alone, which is a notion that some organizations continue to struggle with), we are then presented with a range of different individual and organizational perspectives or lenses on the practice of inclusion as integrated specifically with key areas of I-O as well as other related disciplines in psychology and business. Some of the topics here focus on inclusion as applied to personal identity, communication, leadership, organizational culture, human resource management, organization development, work group climate, and corporate strategy. The volume then includes a discussion of some important aspects of practice in the world of D&I, such as benchmarking D&I efforts across different organizations, future trends in the field, and insightful case studies from a variety of chief diversity officers and practitioners.

As with any effort of this magnitude, it is important to recognize all the work that has gone into the development and execution of this edition. A heartfelt thank-you to Bernardo and Barbara for delivering an excellent volume in the series. Thanks also to our editorial team (Dave W. Bracken, Michael M. Harris, Allen I. Kraut, Jennifer Martineau, Steven G. Rogelberg, John C. Scott, Carol W. Timmreck, and of course Bernardo M. Ferdman) for their original feedback on Bernardo's proposal. Thanks as well to our successor, Allen Kraut, and his editorial team (Seymour Adler, Neil R. Anderson, Neal M. Ashkanasy, C. Harry Hui, Elizabeth B. Kolmstetter, Kyle Lundby, William H. Macey, Lise M. Saari, Handan Sinangil, Nancy T. Tippins, and Michael A. West) for keeping the momentum going during their tenure with the series. Finally, thanks to Matt Davis at Jossey-Bass for helping keep the process on track, as always.

D&I is a critically important topic to organizations in general and a core value of I-O and OD in particular. In our opinion, it has not yet been given the full attention or level of integration it deserves in the I-O arena. This important volume serves to close that gap. Although it has been some years in the making, the topic is as significant and timely as it ever was, and we are very pleased to see it finally completed. We enjoyed working with Bernardo in the early formation of the book concept and outline and watching it continue to develop all the way through the various phases of the effort. In many ways it is ironic that this volume represents our last as Professional Practice Series Editors and Allen Kraut's final volume, as we all feel like we have been actively involved, invested, and engaged in the outcome. And isn't that what being inclusive is all about? Enjoy!

September 2013

ALLAN H. CHURCH
JANINE WACLAWSKI
Original series editors for this volume

Preface

Diversity at Work: The Practice of Inclusion

Bernardo M. Ferdman and Barbara R. Deane

Much has been said and written—especially in recent years—about diversity at work. The idea that people vary on a range of identity and cultural dimensions and that this diversity matters for organizations and society is now widely accepted and discussed, not only in industrial-organizational (I-O) psychology, in human resources, in management, and in related fields, but also in the world at large.

We have learned a great deal about the role of diversity in organizations and about the interactions in the workplace among individuals and groups with different social identities and backgrounds; increasing scholarly and practical effort has been applied to describing the dynamics of these relationships and to documenting ways to manage them productively. In part, this is because intergroup relations often can be problematic; indeed, much diversity scholarship and practice has focused on the problems associated with diversity and on ways to avoid or surmount them. This has been important and generative work. In today's and tomorrow's societies and workplaces, it is imperative to reduce and prevent invidious bias and discrimination, to eliminate negative conflicts, to avoid waste, to increase fairness, and to take better advantage of all possible resources, in ways that ideally result in creativity, innovation, and better outcomes for more people, for their organizations, and for society as a whole.

Yet, working with and managing diversity in ways that are productive, healthy, growthful, and empowering—for both individuals and organizations—often remains an elusive goal. How can groups and organizations best use and benefit from the diversity that is inevitably present in and around them? What can individuals, leaders, and organizations do to work with diversity not simply as a reality that must be addressed, but rather as an opportunity and a gift? How might diversity truly be put to work on our individual and collective behalf? What can individuals, leaders, and organizations do to make this happen?

In this book, we present a fresh perspective and approach to understand and benefit from diversity. We focus on *inclusion*—and specifically *the practice of inclusion*—as a fundamental approach for benefitting from diversity, in a way that works for everyone, across multiple dimensions of difference. Inclusion involves creating, fostering, and sustaining practices and conditions that encourage and allow each of us to be fully ourselves—with our differences from and similarities to those around us—as we work together. To be inclusive, these practices and conditions should also permit and elicit everyone's full contributions to the collective (Ferdman, 2010; Ferdman & Sagiv, 2012), in a virtuous cycle that is beneficial both for individuals and the larger groups and/or organizations to which they belong (as well for their various social identity groups). The *practice of inclusion* is what individuals, leaders, and organizations do to bring this experience and process to life. Essentially, our claim, as documented and supported throughout this book, is that the practice of inclusion permits applying the collective wisdom regarding diversity—developed through theory, research, application, and experience—and does so in a way that focuses on recognizing and realizing the positive contributions of diversity. Rather than assuming diversity is a problem to be solved, practitioners of inclusion assume that it is a rich resource to be tapped and enjoyed.

This view is in evidence today to some degree—as seen, for example, in the typical pairing of the terms *diversity* and *inclusion*, as in Chief Diversity and Inclusion Officer, or Office of Diversity and Inclusion. But it is a perspective that evolved over time, as the field developed, and it is in many ways still in its infancy. In 1992, SIOP published *Diversity in the Workplace: Human Resources Initiatives*, by Susan Jackson and Associates, as the second volume of its then newly launched Professional Practice Series, in which this current volume now takes its place. Jackson's book exemplified the goal of the series, which is to provide practitioners in organizations—particularly I-O psychologists, HR professionals, managers, executives, and others who address human behavior at work—with resources, insights, information, and guidance on how to address key organizational issues by applying the best of what organizational psychology has to offer. *Diversity in the Workplace* combined the voices of scholars and practitioners to document effective ways to conceptualize and address the challenges of diversity. Along with other work emerging at the time (for example, Cox, 1993; Cross, Katz, Miller, & Seashore, 1994; Ferdman, 1992, 1994; Fernandez, 1991; Jamieson & O'Mara, 1991; Loden & Rosener, 1991; Morrison, 1992; Thiederman, 1990; Thomas, 1990; Thompson & DiTomaso, 1998; Triandis, Kurowski, & Gelfand, 1994) produced by both academics and practitioners, Jackson's book provided some theory and structure, grounded in psychology and related fields, for the emerging field of diversity in organizations. From an initial focus on addressing historical inequities, targeting oppression, and bringing the promise of civil rights to the workplace—with a primary emphasis on gender, race, ethnicity, and sometimes cultural and national origin, and combined with the goal of preparing for demographic shifts in the workforce and increasing globalization—the field developed to incorporate attention to reaping the potential business benefits of diversity of various types, both visible and invisible, including sexual orientation, ability status, age, social class, religion, life experience, and a myriad of other dimensions.

More than twenty years after Jackson's (1992) book, knowledge about both the role and dynamics of diversity in organizations and the practice of diversity management has dramatically developed and expanded. Many of the challenges posed by Jackson and her collaborators remain, but they are no longer seen as unusual or new—they have become part of the "normal" work of organizations. For example, recruitment, retention, and assessment that account for diversity are now focal topics in I-O psychology and human resource management, thanks in part to the efforts of pioneers such as Jackson and the contributors to her volume. At the same time, attention to diversity has become a global phenomenon, and the dimensions of diversity that matter have expanded and become more complex and nuanced. With globalization, new forms of exchange and collaboration have proliferated across cultural boundaries of all sorts. I-O psychologists and diversity practitioners are often asked to help global organizations navigate, in both broad and systematic ways, through the tensions associated with difference. Beyond addressing these tensions, professionals find themselves supporting organizations in a time of shrinking resources and great competition and must seek proactive ways to ensure that all people's contributions can be used effectively and wisely for the benefit of the organization and its many stakeholders.

Given these trends, and in line with work grounded in what has become known as positive organizational scholarship and with new insights on multiple identities and their intersections across a range of dimensions of diversity, the concept and practice of inclusion provide a frame to permit addressing the dynamics of diversity in more complex, expansive, and productive ways. Through an inclusion lens, we can continue to incorporate our prior insights regarding diversity and also highlight the practices needed so that individuals, groups, and organizations can truly benefit from that diversity. Through an inclusion lens, we can attend to the complexity of individual experience and identity, without losing sight of intergroup relations, intercultural dynamics, and systemic processes and structures.

Today, then, the cutting edge of diversity practice for organizations addresses the challenge of inclusion—the degree to which organizations and their members are able to fully connect with, engage, and utilize people across all types of differences. Diversity can provide advantages only when it is combined with fundamental changes in individual behaviors and attitudes, group norms and approaches, and organizational policies, procedures, and practices that result in people feeling appreciated, valued, safe, respected, listened to, and engaged—both as individuals and as members of multiple social identity groups. This is the work of inclusion, which is both theoretically and practically different from diversity. Inclusion is a key driver and basis for reaping diversity's potential benefits.

Nevertheless, theory and practice have not kept pace with the needs of organizations to attend to diversity and its implications, particularly in regard to inclusion, in spite of the growing use of the term. I-O psychologists, human resource professionals, managers and executives, and related practitioners need clearer guidance regarding best practices for inclusion. This book provides practitioners with an understanding of and a way to navigate the new challenges posed by the need for inclusion amidst diversity, a challenge that has yet to be taken up in a systematic way by the bulk of I-O psychologists, or with any consensual definition or approach by the bulk of practitioners. The book's key premise is that inclusion is a core element for leveraging the advantages of diversity at the individual, interpersonal, group, organizational, and societal levels. To elaborate on this premise, we provide a state-of-the-art perspective on inclusion and its practice: what it is and how it is manifested in individual and collective behavior and in organizational practices (Chapter 1), how it can be created and fostered (Chapters 2 through 13), how it can be applied in a variety of settings (Chapters 14 through 19), and what this means for the future of the field (Chapters 20 through 23).

This volume is unique for practitioners because it provides an applied focus while emphasizing the lens and grounding provided by research and theory in industrial and organizational psychology and related fields. It contains a reliable compendium of information and experiences on the practice of inclusion from topic experts, including internal and external change agents and academics. By including and combining the perspectives of both scholars and practitioners, the book not only provides a bridge between I-O psychology and related fields to the practice of inclusion in organizations but also exposes both sets of professionals to each other's thinking and work. In putting this volume together, we sought to exemplify the value and practice of inclusion, in particular by incorporating a range and variety of voices, approaches, and styles. The thirty-four authors of the book's twenty-three chapters represent not only I/O psychology but also other areas of psychology as well as various other fields, including management, leadership, intercultural communication, social work, and public policy. The authors live, work, or have extensive experience in over ten countries and span a range of identities on various dimensions.

Our illumination of inclusion is consistent with the growing emphasis on positive organizational scholarship and practice.

A focus on eliminating invidious forms of discrimination, while important, is insufficient. There is growing recognition by scholars and practitioners that great benefits can be derived for organizations and their members by focusing on excellence, strengths, and vitality. Attending to and practicing inclusion permits organizations and their members to proactively replace discrimination with a much more positive and productive approach that can serve to release potential and result in more optimal outcomes for all.

Audience

This book is intended for a broad range of readers. Seasoned practitioners seeking a textured and well-founded compendium of cutting-edge approaches grounded in theory, research, and experience, as well as novices seeking to understand what diversity and inclusion at work are all about, together with everyone in between, will find a great deal of relevant and useful knowledge in these pages. For example, professionals (whether internal or external to an organization) who must plan, design, and/or implement an inclusion initiative or who want to learn more about such initiatives will find this book indispensable. Additionally, this book will be useful to managers and executives as they work to define and carry out strategic initiatives related to diversity and inclusion.

Thus industrial-organizational and consulting psychologists, HR professionals, organization development (OD) practitioners, management consultants, training professionals, and diversity and inclusion leaders, practitioners, and consultants will all benefit from the range of material presented in the book's chapters. Organizational leaders and practitioners, whether specializing in diversity and inclusion or not, will be able to find a great deal of useful information and applicable suggestions. Finally, instructors and graduate students in I-O and consulting psychology, HR, OD, organizational behavior, management, business administration, public administration, and social work are also an intended audience for the book, which can be used as a text for courses focused on diversity or as a supplementary text for courses on organizational behavior, organization development, human resource management, and related courses.

Overview of the Book

This volume addresses the key issues in framing, designing, and implementing inclusion initiatives in organizations and in developing individual and collective competencies for inclusion, with the goal of fully benefiting from diversity. The chapters are grouped into five major parts, covering foundational frameworks, individual and interpersonal perspectives and practices, organizational and societal perspectives and practices, applications, and integrative reflections and commentaries.

Part One, "Frameworks for Understanding Inclusion," introduces the concept of inclusion and effective ways to communicate about it in organizations. In Chapter 1, Bernardo Ferdman tackles defining inclusion and explains how it connects to diversity, yet differs from it; he also develops a multilevel systemic framework for inclusion that links the psychological experience of inclusion to interpersonal, group, organizational, and societal practices, norms, and values. In Chapter 2, Robert Hayles provides another essential framework: how to communicate about diversity and inclusion so that a broad audience sees their benefits, using a developmental model that encourages a strategic and tailored approach to communicating about inclusion.

Part Two, "Individual and Interpersonal Perspectives and Practices," addresses the work that individuals, including leaders, must do to foster inclusion for themselves and others. In Chapter 3, Bernardo Ferdman and Laura Morgan Roberts explore how individuals can include themselves, especially their multiple identities, and how they can bring more of their whole selves to work. In Chapter 4, Ilene Wasserman moves into the interpersonal realm and argues that effective and inclusive communication involves a relational responsibility to create shared meaning. She explores new competencies and processes to minimize destructive conflict and to leverage diversity so that it is mutually beneficial. In Chapter 5, Janet Bennett continues in the interpersonal realm with the concept of intercultural competence. Pointing to cognitive, affective, and behavioral skills and characteristics, Bennett contends that this competence not only supports effective interaction in a variety of cultural contexts but also can be developed to enhance inclusion. Her chapter exposes readers to the field of intercultural communication, a body of knowledge and practice quite relevant to diversity and inclusion. In the final chapter of Part Two, Chapter 6, Plácida Gallegos calls for a new type of leadership—inclusive leadership—which she describes as a relational approach that fosters authentic relationships and models courage and humility. This chapter serves as a bridge to Part Three, because inclusive leadership is a key component for translating inclusion across levels of analysis.

The seven chapters of Part Three, "Organizational and Societal Perspectives and Practices," explore a range of approaches that organizations can use to practice inclusion systematically and systemically. In Chapter 7, Mary-Frances Winters introduces a model (the *inclusion equation*) that depicts four interrelated variables for creating and sustaining inclusive organizational cultures. In Chapter 8, Lynn Offermann and Tessa Basford address inclusive HR management and show how successful organizations advance inclusion in a variety of ways, in the process changing how they manage and develop their people. In Chapter 9, a team of authors from PepsiCo—Allan Church, Christopher Rotolo, Amanda Shull, and Michael Tuller—delve into inclusive organization development by focusing on four OD processes: organizational and employee surveys, 360-degree feedback, performance management, and talent management. Each process is explored with extensive examples of how it was addressed at PepsiCo. In Chapter 10, Lize Booysen describes how to develop leaders to foster inclusive behavior and practice, and she explains how leadership development can be done more inclusively. In Chapter 11, Lisa Nishii, from an academic background, and Robert Rich, from a practitioner background, share their conceptualization of inclusive climates and provide details on how to design change efforts to foster such inclusive work climates. In Chapter 12, Karsten Jonsen and Mustafa Özbilgin describe various models for global diversity management based on evidence from a number of field studies of practitioners. The final chapter in Part Three, Chapter 13, by Michàlle Mor Barak and Preeya Daya, examines how, using what the authors call *corporate inclusion strategies,* organizations can and should go well beyond corporate social responsibility to extend inclusion to their surrounding communities and societies.

Part Four, "Key Application Issues and Domains," incorporates six chapters; each addresses the practice of inclusion in a particular context or provides a key application tool or perspective. In Chapter 14, Julie O'Mara describes a very useful framework and tool she co-developed, the Global Diversity and Inclusion Benchmarks, which organizations can use to determine the level of inclusive best practices they are using. In Chapter 15, Effenus Henderson, chief diversity officer at Weyerhaeuser, explains the details of his company's multiyear strategy to build a more diverse and inclusive culture, as well as its inclusive leadership training program. In Chapter 16, Kumea Shorter-Gooden, now chief diversity officer at the University of Maryland, addresses the goals and key components necessary to create diverse and inclusive higher educational settings, and shares examples from her experience in her previous role as the chief diversity officer of Alliant International University. In Chapter 17, Carolyn Lukensmeyer, Margaret Yao, and Theo Brown describe how America*Speaks*, a leading organization in the deliberative democracy movement, practices inclusion in all aspects of its efforts to engage diverse citizens in dialogue and decision-making about complex issues that affect them at local, state, and national levels. Alan Richter, in Chapter 18, examines how a global organization, UNAIDS, has worked to build a culture of inclusion in its workplace and in the societies where they operate. Finally, in Chapter 19, Charmine Härtel, Dennis Appo, and Bill Hart, authors representing diverse experiences, share a case study of how Rio Tinto pioneered a new organizational approach to include aboriginal contractors, both socially and economically, in the Pilbara region of Australia.

In Part Five, "Moving Forward," the book concludes with four chapters that provide overall reflections on the practice of inclusion, each from a different perspective. In Chapters 20, 21, and 22, key thought leaders—Michael Wheeler, a well-regarded corporate diversity officer and practitioner; Angelo DeNisi, a prominent I-O psychologist; and Stella Nkomo, a noted diversity scholar—reflect on the value of the book, the field as a whole, and the challenges they see for practitioners going forward. Finally, in Chapter 23, we share our comments about the book's themes and our experience in editing it, implications for the practice of inclusion, and thoughts about the future of the field.

Acknowledgments

A book such as this reflects the efforts and contributions of many people. Indeed, a key tenet of inclusion is that we cannot accomplish great work alone, and this book is no exception. In particular, we would like to thank the contributors to the volume, who not only shared their ideas and expertise but were also willing to go above and beyond to be responsive to our many editorial demands. We very much appreciate the contributions of Jennifer Habig, who initially was to be a partner in this project and was instrumental in helping to formulate the initial book proposal and outline, before she had to take a different path for her career and education. Sergio Valenzuela-Ibarra, Liz Barat, Maggie Sass, and Sarah Maxwell provided Bernardo with helpful and productive research assistance for the project at various stages. Allan Church and Janine Waclawski, our Professional Practice Series editors, provided ongoing encouragement and insights and have been kind and responsive, for which we are grateful; we also appreciate the input on the original proposal provided by the rest of Allan and Janine's editorial board. We owe much appreciation to the subsequent series editor, Allen Kraut, who took a special interest in this volume and inspired (as well as cajoled, prodded, and encouraged) us to keep it moving and get it done. The rest of Allen's editorial board—Seymour Adler, Neil R. Anderson, Neal M. Ashkanasy, C. Harry Hui, Elizabeth B. Kolmstetter, Kyle Lundby, William H. Macey, Lise M. Saari, Handan Sinangil, Nancy T. Tippins, and Michael A. West— provided useful input on an updated proposal and outline for the book. Matt Davis, the acquisitions editor at Wiley, was both patient and insistent at the right times; Ryan Noll, his editorial assistant, made sure that we got all the final pieces right; and Kristi Hein, our copy editor, carefully and brilliantly made sure to catch and help us address errors, ambiguities, and inconsistencies both large and small. The members of the Diversity Collegium, some represented among the chapter authors and others not, have been consistently supportive, cheering us forward and providing input, ideas, and connections whenever requested. Our greatest debt and gratitude is reserved for our life partners and for our children (and Barbara's grandchildren), who provided both support and distraction, and primarily meaning; they encouraged us to stick with it when we thought we couldn't and pulled us away when we couldn't stop, and they made sure that each of our lives is full of all that makes inclusion worthwhile in the first place.

March 2013   Bernardo M. Ferdman
San Diego, California
Barbara R. Deane
Seattle, Washington

References

Cox, T. H., Jr. (1993). *Cultural diversity in organizations: Theory, research, and practice.* San Francisco: Berrett-Koehler.

Cross, E. Y., Katz, J. H., Miller, F. A., & Seashore, E. W. (Eds.). (1994). *The promise of diversity: Over 40 voices discuss strategies for eliminating discrimination in organizations.* Burr Ridge, IL: Irwin.

Ferdman, B. M. (1992). The dynamics of ethnic diversity in organizations: Toward integrative models. In K. Kelley (Ed.), *Issues, theory and research in industrial/organizational psychology* (pp. 339–384). Amsterdam, Netherlands: North Holland.

Ferdman, B. M. (Ed.). (1994). *A resource guide for teaching and research on diversity.* St. Louis, MO: American Assembly of Collegiate Schools of Business.

Ferdman, B. M. (2010). Teaching inclusion by example and experience: Creating an inclusive learning environment. In B. B. McFeeters, K. M. Hannum, & L. Booysen (Eds.), *Leading across differences: Cases and perspectives—Facilitator's guide* (pp. 37–50). San Francisco: Pfeiffer.

Ferdman, B. M., & Sagiv, L. (2012). Diversity in organizations and cross-cultural work psychology: What if they were more connected? (Focal article). *Industrial and Organizational Psychology: Perspectives on Science and Practice, 5*(3), 323–345. doi:10.1111/j.1754-9434.2012.01455.x

Fernandez, J. P. (1991). *Managing a diverse workforce: Regaining the competitive edge.* New York: Lexington.

Jamieson, D., & O'Mara, J. (1991). *Managing workforce 2000: Gaining the diversity advantage.* San Francisco: Jossey-Bass.

Jackson, S. E. & Associates (1992). *Diversity in the workplace: Human resources initiatives.* New York: Guilford.

Loden, M., & Rosener, J. B. (1991). *Workforce America! Managing employee diversity as a vital resource.* Homewood, IL: Business One Irwin.

Morrison, A. M. (1992). *The new leaders: Guidelines on leadership diversity in America.* San Francisco: Jossey-Bass.

Thiederman, S. (1990). *Bridging cultural barriers for corporate success: How to manage the multicultural workforce.* New York: Lexington.

Thomas, R. R., Jr. (1990). From affirmative action to affirming diversity. *Harvard Business Review, 68*(2), 107–117.

Thompson, D. E., & DiTomaso, N. (Eds.). (1998). *Ensuring minority success in corporate management.* New York: Plenum.

Triandis, H. C., Kurowski, L. L., & Gelfand, M. J. (1994). Workplace diversity. In H. C. Triandis, M. D. Dunnette, & L. M. Hough (Eds.), *Handbook of industrial and organizational psychology* (Vol. 4, pp. 769–827). Palo Alto, CA: Consulting Psychologists Press.

The Editors

Bernardo M. Ferdman, Ph.D., consults, writes, speaks, teaches, and conducts research on diversity and inclusion, multicultural leadership, Latinos/Latinas in the workplace, and bringing one's whole self to work. He is full professor in the Organizational Psychology Program at the California School of Professional Psychology of Alliant International University, where he has taught since 1993, and a leadership and organization development consultant with almost three decades of experience. Dr. Ferdman works with organizational leaders and employees to foster inclusion, to develop and implement effective ways of using the talents and contributions of every member of the organization, and to build multicultural and cross-cultural competencies on the part of individuals, teams, and the whole organization, as well as to inspire individuals to find their own voice and make their full contribution. Ferdman earned his Ph.D. in psychology from Yale University and his A.B. from Princeton University, and he is a Board Certified Coach. He has published and presented widely in the areas of diversity, inclusion, leadership, and Latino identity, and conducts research on the assessment of inclusion and on its antecedents and consequences. Ferdman is a SIOP Fellow and a Fellow of three other divisions of the American Psychological Association, a Charter Fellow of the International Academy for Intercultural Research, a member of the Diversity Collegium (a think tank of diversity practitioners), and a network associate with America*Speaks*. He served as president of the Interamerican Society of Psychology, as well as chair of the Academy of Management's Gender and Diversity in Organizations Division and chair of its Diversity and Inclusion Theme Committee. In 1991, Ferdman received the Gordon Allport Intergroup Relations Prize, and in 2011, the Ph.D. Project Management Doctoral Student Association recognized him with its Trailblazer Award. Ferdman, a native

Spanish speaker with a great deal of international experience, lives in San Diego, California, with his family, where he is involved in various community activities, including co-chairing the San Diego Latino-Jewish Coalition, and previously served as trustee of the San Diego Repertory Theatre.

Barbara R. Deane, M.A., is a writer, editor, consultant, and speaker on diversity and inclusion and cross-cultural business issues. She is editor-in-chief for DiversityCentral.com and the Cultural Diversity at Work Archive, an online database of articles, tools, and resources. Deane cofounded *Cultural Diversity at Work,* one of the first national and international publications on workforce diversity, in 1988. She is the author of more than one hundred articles on topics related to workforce diversity, diversity management, intercultural communication, cultural differences, and inclusion. She is also vice-president of The Gil Deane Group, Inc., a Hispanic and woman-owned firm in Seattle, Washington, that provides consulting and training services on domestic and international diversity, inclusion, and intercultural effectiveness to Fortune 500 companies, government agencies, and not-for-profit organizations. Deane is the cofounder of the NW Diversity Learning Series, a collaborative venture on the part of progressive companies and organizations to build a diversity education resource in the Greater Seattle Area. The Series, now under new management, continues its fifteenth year in 2013. Deane now offers the Diversity Learning Series model (DLS) as a limited-term licensing opportunity for other cities and metropolitan regions. She has a bachelor's degree, cum laude, in organizational communication from The Ohio State University, and a master's degree from the University of Washington, where she specialized in interpersonal and intercultural communication. Deane is a member of the board and coordinator of The Diversity Collegium, a think tank of internal and external diversity professionals based in the United States, Canada, Switzerland, and South Africa. Deane lives in Seattle, where she enjoys her extended family and being actively engaged with Bailadores de Bronce, a Mexican folkloric dance group. She speaks Spanish fluently and has lived in Mexico for several extended periods.

The Authors

Dennis Appo, Ph.D., (of the Mamu People) was the first Aborigine to be awarded a Ph.D. in the business faculty at the University of Queensland. He has over two decades of experience writing and contributing to Australian Aboriginal policy and working with Aboriginal communities across Australia. Dr. Appo is recognized internationally for his extensive pioneering of indigenous issues into the management arena at universities, and for government policy work aimed at developing indigenous communities within Australia and New Zealand. He is one of the very few Aborigines in Australia who have been involved in constructing indigenous paradigms for management education. He has made significant contributions to the available research on indigenous Australians—in particular, the juxtaposition of Anglo-Australian and indigenous Australian values, beliefs, and behaviors, with a particular focus on the social, legal, political, and economic context of cross-cultural perspectives.

Tessa E. Basford, Ph.D., earned her doctorate in industrial/organizational psychology from the George Washington University. Through her research, Dr. Basford contributes to advancements in our understanding of leadership, followership, diversity, and impression management. Her work appears in the *Journal of Leadership, Journal of Leadership and Organizational Studies,* and *Journal of Management and Organization,* among other outlets. She frequently presents her research at conferences of the Society for Industrial and Organizational Psychology and the American Psychological Association.

Janet M. Bennett, Ph.D., is executive director of the Intercultural Communication Institute (ICI) and director of the ICI/University of the Pacific Master of Arts in Intercultural Relations program.

Her Ph.D. is from the University of Minnesota, where she specialized in intercultural communication and anthropology. For twelve years Dr. Bennett was chair of the Liberal Arts Division at Marylhurst College (now Marylhurst University), where she developed innovative academic programs for adult degree students. As a trainer and consultant, she designs and conducts intercultural competence and diversity training for colleges and universities, corporations, NGOs, government, and social service agencies. She teaches courses in the training and development program at Portland State University and has published many articles and chapters on the subjects of developmental "layered" intercultural training and adjustment processes. She co-edited *The Handbook of Intercultural Training* (3rd edition) and recently authored the chapter "Cultivating Intercultural Competence: A Process Perspective" for *The SAGE Handbook of Intercultural Competence*. Bennett is currently editing *The SAGE Encyclopedia of Intercultural Competence*.

Lize Booysen, Ph.D., is a full professor of leadership and organizational behavior at Antioch University, teaching in its Ph.D. in Leadership and Change program. Dr. Booysen is an internationally recognized scholar in the field of diversity, race, gender, and leadership, an executive coach, and a management consultant. She holds a doctorate in business leadership from the University of South Africa, as well as master's degrees in clinical psychology, research psychology, and criminology, all with distinction. Booysen is also adjunct faculty at the Center for Creative Leadership (CCL) in Greensboro, North Carolina, and has been involved in the twelve-nation Leadership across Differences (LAD) research project steered by CCL. She also participated in the GLOBE sixty-five-nations research project on leadership, national culture, and organizational practices, steered by Wharton Business School at the University of Pennsylvania. Booysen recently served as chair of the Business Leadership Member Interest Group of the International Leadership Association (ILA). Prior to joining Antioch in 2009, Booysen was full professor at the Graduate School of Business Leadership (SBL), University of South Africa since 1992. She served on the SBL board of directors from 1999 to 2006 and held the portfolios of Director of Human Resources Development and Academic Director and Research Manager at the SBL.

Theo Brown has more than thirty-five years of experience as an organizer, administrator, and facilitator for organizations that work to educate citizens and get them more involved in efforts to improve society. He has worked for dozens of local, state, national, and international organizations that focus on issues relating to social justice, human rights, political reform, peace, and conflict resolution. Since 1998, he has been a senior associate with America*Speaks*, where he has supervised recruitment for many different projects. He has helped to organize large America*Speaks* 21st Century Town Meetings on a range of issues in New York City; Washington, DC; New Orleans; Los Angeles; Albuquerque; Dallas; and many other cities around the country. Brown has a bachelor's degree from Baylor University and a master's degree from Duke University Divinity School. For fifteen years he was an adjunct professor at the University of Southern California's Washington Semester Program and later taught for four years in the Washington Semester Program at American University.

Allan H. Church, Ph.D., is VP of Global Talent Development for PepsiCo, where he is responsible for leading the talent management and people development agenda for the enterprise. Previously he spent nine years as an external OD consultant with Warner Burke Associates, and several years at IBM. Concurrently, he has served as an adjunct professor at Columbia University, a visiting scholar at Benedictine University, and past chair of the Mayflower Group. Dr. Church received his Ph.D. in organizational psychology from Columbia University. He is a Fellow of the Society for Industrial and Organizational Psychology, the American Psychological Association, and the Association for Psychological Science.

Preeya Daya, Ph.D., is a senior lecturer in human resources (HR) and organizational behavior at the University of Cape Town's Graduate School of Business (in South Africa). She joined the GSB following an international corporate career in HR, in which her focus was on enhancing business performance through transforming HR and organization development initiatives, including diversity and inclusion, leadership, performance management, employee engagement, and human resource information systems. Dr. Daya is an advisory board member in the GSB's

Women in Leadership Program and holds a senior consulting position at the Achievement Awards Group, where she optimizes and designs HR business solutions for clients through her research in this field. Through her research and industry alliances, Daya is passionate in her pursuit to enhance organizational and institutional excellence through strategic engagement and utilization of people. She completed her undergraduate degree in HR and specialized in organizational behavior for her master's and Ph.D. degrees. Daya's research focuses on understanding diversity and inclusion in emerging market contexts and on building tools for creating more inclusive workplaces. Her second research interest relates to employee engagement/disengagement and organizational culture.

Angelo DeNisi, Ph.D., is the Albert Harry Cohen Chair in Business Administration at Tulane University's A. B. Freeman School of Business. He previously served on the faculties of Texas A&M University, Rutgers University, University of South Carolina, and Kent State University. Dr. DeNisi's research interests include performance appraisal, expatriate management, and work experiences of persons with disabilities; his research has been funded by the Army Research Institute, the National Science Foundation, and several state agencies. He has published more than a dozen book chapters, several books, and more than sixty articles in refereed journals, most of them in top academic journals such as *Academy of Management Journal, Academy of Management Review, Journal of Applied Psychology, Journal of Personality and Social Psychology*, and *Psychological Bulletin*. DeNisi's research has been recognized with awards from the OB and OCIS Divisions of the Academy, and SIOP named him the cowinner of its 2005 Distinguished Scientific Contribution Award. He also serves or has served on a number of editorial boards, including *JAP, AMJ*, and *AMR*, and as editor of the *Academy of Management Journal*. DeNisi is a Fellow of SIOP, the American Psychological Association, and the Academy of Management. He has served as chair of both the OB and HR Divisions of the Academy of Management and as president of the Academy.

Plácida V. Gallegos, Ph.D., is a professor in the School of Human and Organizational Development at Fielding Graduate University and has conducted research in the areas of transformational leadership, career development of women and people of color, and creating inclusive organizations. She is also an organization development consultant who has spent the past thirty years engaged in supporting diverse individuals, groups, and organizations in thriving and achieving optimal outcomes. Dr. Gallegos' work spans a wide range including corporations, non-profits, educational institutions, and government agencies. In her consulting work, she has led large change projects and partnered with executives to develop sustainable interventions that align with their values and with their business and organizational objectives. Gallegos designs and conducts workshops, presentations, and interventions based on sound assessment practices and customization to fit clients' needs and goals. Rather than emphasize an "expert" model when working with leaders, she operates on the philosophy of true partnership wherein the client organization or individuals are fully engaged in each step of the change effort. Gallegos has published widely on interpersonal and intercultural communication, leadership development, and building inclusive cultures that support the full engagement of all employees.

Bill Hart, M.B.A. (University of Chicago), is currently vice president of Global Marketing at Cliffs Natural Resources and has over twenty-five years' local and international experience across the resources sector. Prior to joining his current employer, he held the position of general manager communities at Rio Tinto Iron Ore. Hart's involvement with managing agreements with the Traditional Owners of the Pilbara began in 2006.

Charmine E. J. Härtel, Ph.D., is management cluster leader and chair of Human Resource Management and Organisational Development for UQ Business School at the University of Queensland. Dr. Härtel is a registered member of the College of Organizational Psychologists (Australia), Fellow and past president of the Australian and New Zealand Academy of Management, and chair-elect of the Gender and Diversity in Organizations Division of the Academy of Management. She has won numerous awards internationally for her research, including five awards for innovation in organizational practice. Härtel is recognized internationally as a leading expert in the areas of diversity management, ethical leadership development, and workplace well-being. Her pioneering work on the characteristics of positive work environments has identified a number of the individual, group, and organizational drivers of exclusionary and toxic work environments along with the leadership and human resource management strategies and practices to turn such situations around. Her work appears in thirteen books, over sixty book chapters, and eighty-six refereed journal articles. Härtel earned her Ph.D. in industrial and organizational psychology at Colorado State University.

V. Robert Hayles, Ph.D., effectiveness/diversity and inclusion consultant, assists people and organizations in becoming more effective. He has served more than 150 clients in the private, public, and civic sectors in more than fifteen different countries. Dr. Hayles was formerly vice president, human resources and diversity, with Pillsbury. His human resource responsibilities included tax, treasury, and technology and his worldwide diversity role covered Pillsbury, Green Giant, Häagen-Dazs, and GrandMet Foods Europe. Prior to that position, Hayles was director, human resources, for the Pillsbury Technology Center. Before joining Pillsbury he was manager, valuing differences, at Digital Equipment Corporation for Sales, Services, Marketing, and International. Other previous positions include associate professor of engineering administration at George Washington University; director, research and human resources at the Office of Naval Research; and research scientist at Battelle's Human Affairs Research Center. Hayles was the first behavioral scientist to manage the U.S. Department of Navy Technology Base, with an annual budget of more than $1 billion. He has an undergraduate degree in the behavioral and physical sciences, a doctorate in psychology, and postgraduate education in business. Hayles was the 1996 chair of the board of directors, American Society for Training and Development. He is co-author of *The Diversity Directive: Why Some Initiatives Fail and What to Do about It* (McGraw-Hill, 1997).

Effenus Henderson, as chief diversity officer for Weyerhaeuser Company (based in Federal Way, Washington), advises the CEO and senior management team on diversity, inclusion, and affirmative-action-related matters. An internationally recognized diversity thought leader, Henderson has been invited by numerous companies and organizations to share his expertise. He addressed members of the General Assembly of the United Nations on intercultural and interreligious diversity and advised members of the United Nation's Alliance of Civilizations and Global Compact on emerging issues. In 2010, he was appointed to the advisory board of the Global Dialogue Foundation, Melbourne, Australia. Named as one of the top diversity officers in corporate America by Diversity Best Practices/Working Mother Media, Henderson received its first Diversity Officer Leadership Award in 2007. In 2011, *Black Enterprise* magazine named him as one of the Top Executives in Diversity for his outstanding business achievements. In 2011, Henderson became co-chair of a Diversity and Inclusion Standards Project (with co-chair Cari Dominguez, former head of EEOC) sponsored by the Society of Human Resources Management to develop an ANSI-approved standard for chief diversity officer competencies, diversity programs, and diversity metrics. A graduate of North Carolina Central University and Stanford University's Executive Program, Henderson is married to Helen Skinner Henderson and is the father of three sons, Kevin, Justin, and Marcus.

Karsten Jonsen, Ph.D., is a research fellow in organizational behavior at IMD, Switzerland. Before coming to IMD in 2002 he held European management positions in the IT industry. He earned an M.Sc. in economics from CBS in Copenhagen, an MBA from ESCP-EAP in Paris, France, and a Ph.D. from the University of Geneva. Dr. Jonsen's research interests and publications cover a variety of issues in cross-cultural business, including workforce diversity, gender, team performance, virtual teams, stereotyping, globalization trends, research methodology, career mobility, Generation Y, and cross-cultural communication. Jonsen has served as advisor to large corporations in the field of workforce diversity and is the winner of the 2010 Carolyn Dexter Award for best international research paper at the Academy of Management.

Carolyn J. Lukensmeyer, Ph.D., is the first executive director of the National Institute for Civil Discourse at the University of Arizona. She previously served as founder and president of

America*Speaks*, where she made her mark as an innovator in deliberative democracy, public administration, and organization development. Under Dr. Lukensmeyer's leadership, America*Speaks* earned a national reputation as a leader in the field of deliberative democracy and democratic renewal. The organization has success-fully applied its 21st Century Town Meeting process to a number of health care-related topics, including state-wide health care reform in California and Maine and the national childhood obesity epidemic. Prior to founding America*Speaks*, Lukensmeyer served as consultant to the White House Chief of Staff from November 1993 through June 1994, as the deputy project director for manage-ment of the National Performance Review (NPR), on Vice President Al Gore's reinventing government task force, and as chief of staff to Governor Richard F. Celeste of Ohio from 1986 to 1991. She also led her own successful organization development and man-agement consulting firm for fourteen years. In this capacity, she worked with public and private sector organizations on four con-tinents. Lukensmeyer holds a doctoral degree in organizational behavior from Case Western Reserve University.

Michàlle Mor Barak, Ph.D., is the Lenore Stein-Wood and William S. Wood Professor in Social Work and Business in a Global Society at the University of Southern California, with a joint appointment at the School of Social Work and the Marshall School of Business. A principal investigator on several large research projects, Dr. Mor Barak has published extensively in the areas of global diversity and inclusion and has authored numerous articles and books. Her research was funded by national and international founda-tions and corporations, including TRW-Aerospace and Defense, Nike, Edison, the Rockefeller Foundation, and the Wellness Foundation. Mor Barak has received various awards of distinction, including a Fulbright award, the Lady Davis award, the University of California Regents Award, and the Franklin C. Sterlin Distin-guished Faculty Award for Research and Scholarship. She has been invited to give keynote addresses and received grants to lead several prestigious conferences around the world, including the Rockefeller Foundation's award to lead an international confer-ence on global workforce diversity in Bellagio, Italy, and the Bor-chard Foundation's grant to lead a global think tank of scholars in France. Mor Barak's most recent book, *Managing Diversity: Toward a Globally Inclusive Workplace* (3rd edition, 2013), received accolades and favorable reviews in academic journals from several disciplines, both nationally and internationally; it was named an Outstanding Academic Title in 2006 by *Choice,* a publication of the Association of College and University Libraries, and received the prestigious George Terry Book Award from the Academy of Management for "the most significant contribution to management knowledge."

Lisa H. Nishii, Ph.D., is an associate professor in the Human Resource Studies department at the ILR School, Cornell University. She holds a Ph.D. in organizational psychology from the University of Maryland and a B.A. in economics from Wellesley College. Dr. Nishii's most active body of research includes multilevel projects on diversity and inclusion, in which she examines the confluence of climate, leader characteristics, and group demography on group processes, group performance, and individual outcomes. She has received substantial grants from the U.S. Department of Labor, the U.S. Department of Education, and the SHRM Foundation for her research. Her research suggests that the "value in diversity" emerges only in inclusive environments, in which subgroup disparities are minimized and there are strong norms for people to cultivate cross-boundary relationships. Nishii actively publishes in top-tier management journals, including *Academy of Management Review, Academy of Management Journal, Journal of Applied Psychology,* and *Personnel Psychology.* She serves on the editorial boards of *AMJ, AMR, JAP, Journal of Management,* and *Organizational Psychology Review.* She is also serving a three-year term on the executive committee of the Academy of Management's Human Resources Division, and is part of the leadership rotation to be division chair for the Gender and Diversity in Organizations Division.

Stella M. Nkomo, Ph.D., is a professor in the Department of Human Resource Management at the University of Pretoria in South Africa. She received her Ph.D. in human resource management from the University of Massachusetts, Amherst. Dr. Nkomo's internationally recognized research on race and gender and diversity in organizations has been published in several journals including *Academy of Management Review, Academy of Management Learning and Education, Academy of Management Executive, Journal of Organizational Behavior, Journal of Applied Behavioral Science, Organization, Journal of Occupational and Organizational Psychology, Strategic Management Journal, Work and Occupations,* and *Sex Roles.* She is associate editor for *Organization: The Critical Journal of Organization, Theory and Society* and the *British Journal of Management.* Nkomo is the co-author of two books: *Our Separate Ways: Black and White Women and the Struggle for Professional Identity* (Harvard Business School Press, 2001) and *Courageous Conversations: A Collection of Interviews and Reflections on Responsible Leadership by South African Captains of Industry* (Van Schaik Publishers, 2011). Nkomo received the 2009 Sage Scholarly Contributions Award from the Academy of Management's Gender and Diversity in Organizations Division for her research on gender and diversity in organizations.

Lynn Offermann, Ph.D., is professor of industrial and organizational psychology in the Department of Organizational Sciences and Communication and the Department of Management, George Washington University. Her research focuses on leadership and followership, teams, organizational processes and influence, and diversity issues. Dr. Offermann is a Fellow of the Society for Industrial and Organizational Psychology, the American Psychological Association, and the Association for Psychological Science, and her work has appeared in the *Journal of Applied Psychology, American Psychologist, Academy of Management Journal, Leadership Quarterly, Harvard Business Review, Journal of Cross-Cultural Psychology, Human Performance, Journal of Applied Social Psychology,* and the *Journal of Occupational Health Psychology,* among other outlets. Offermann holds a Ph.D. in applied social psychology from Syracuse University.

Julie O'Mara, president of O'Mara and Associates, an organization development consulting firm, serves clients in several sectors and specializes in leadership, managing diversity, and fostering inclusion. O'Mara is considered a pioneer for her work in D&I, having been engaged in numerous successful initiatives with major clients. She is active in several organizations and often collaborates with others to advance the field. A former national president of the American Society for Training and Development, O'Mara was instrumental in developing professional competencies for the training and development field. She has received several awards for her leadership and diversity work and has taught at University of California Berkeley Extension, John F. Kennedy University, and Golden Gate University. Along with seventy-nine expert panelists, she and Alan Richter are co-authors of *Global Diversity and Inclusion Benchmarks*. O'Mara is also co-author of *Managing Workforce 2000: Gaining the Diversity Advantage*, a best seller published by Jossey-Bass in 1991, and author of *Diversity Activities and Training Designs*, published by Pfeiffer in 1994.

Mustafa Özbilgin, Ph.D., is professor of organizational behavior at Brunel Business School in London, UK, and co-chair of Diversity and Management at University of Paris Dauphine. He researches in the field of equality, diversity, and inclusion at work from comparative and relational perspectives. Dr. Özbilgin's research is published in journals such as the *Academy of Management Review*, *Academy of Management Learning and Education*, *British Journal of Management*, *Human Relations*, *Journal of Vocational Behavior*, and *Social Science and Medicine*. He has authored or edited more than ten books and is the editor-in-chief of the *British Journal of Management* and the editor of the book series Equality, Diversity, and Inclusion (Emerald Press). Özbilgin is the founder of an international conference series, Equality, Diversity, and Inclusion. He earned his Ph.D. in social sciences at the University of Bristol.

Robert E. Rich has been a practitioner of action research for almost forty years. His early work was done with Fred and Merrelyn Emery, Eric Trist, and later William Foote Whyte and Davydd Greenwood. Rich retired from Cornell's School of Industrial and Labor Relations in 2005 after a long affiliation with its well-known Program for Employee and Workplace Systems (PEWS). He continues his practice through the Ithaca Consulting Group on a part-time basis.

Alan Richter, Ph.D., is president of QED Consulting, a twenty-five-year-old company based in New York. He has consulted to corporations and organizations for many years in multiple capacities, primarily in the areas of leadership, values, diversity and inclusion, culture and change. Dr. Richter is the creator of many successful training tools such as the award-winning *Global Diversity Game,* the *Global Diversity Survey*—a self-assessment tool that measures how we deal with difference—and the *Global Leadership Survey,* a leadership style self-assessment tool. He is also co-author, with Julie O'Mara, of *Global Diversity and Inclusion Benchmarks.* Richter has worked closely with many multinational organizations in both the private and public sectors in Africa, Asia, Europe, and the Americas. He has also been a presenter at many conferences in the United States, Africa, Asia, and Europe. Richter is on the board of the South African Chamber of Commerce in America. He has an M.A. and a B.A.B.Sc. from the University of Cape Town, and a Ph.D. in philosophy from Birkbeck College, London University.

Laura Morgan Roberts, Ph.D., is professor of psychology, culture, and organization studies in Antioch University's Ph.D. in Leadership and Change Program. She has served on the faculties of several business schools, including Harvard, Georgia State University, and AVT in Denmark. Dr. Roberts' research and teaching focus on increasing personal and professional alignment by constructing, sustaining, and restoring positive identities at work. She has published her work on authenticity, identity, image management, diversity, strengths, and value creation in her edited book, *Exploring Positive Identities and Organizations* (Roberts and Dutton, Eds., Taylor & Francis, 2009), and in numerous articles, book chapters, and case studies. Roberts earned her B.A. in psychology from the University of Virginia and her M.A. and Ph.D. in organizational psychology from the University of Michigan.

Christopher T. Rotolo, Ph.D., is the senior director of Organization Measurement & Assessment for PepsiCo, where his team is responsible for PepsiCo's core survey research processes, such as the Organization Health survey, On Boarding survey, and Exit Survey, as well as PepsiCo's enterprise-wide high-potential assessment process and competency modeling. Prior to joining PepsiCo, he managed the Leadership Strategy and Research team at IBM. Dr. Rotolo has also served in government and external consulting roles and is an adjunct professor in New York University's I-O

Psychology master's program. Rotolo earned his Ph.D. in industrial/organizational psychology at Old Dominion University in Norfolk, Virginia.

Kumea Shorter-Gooden, Ph.D., was appointed the first chief diversity officer and associate vice president at the University of Maryland, College Park in January 2012. Formerly, she served as associate provost for international-multicultural initiatives at Alliant International University, as professor and coordinator of the Multicultural Community-Clinical Psychology Emphasis Area at the Los Angeles campus of the California School of Professional Psychology, and as director of the student counseling center at the Claremont Colleges. Dr. Shorter-Gooden is co-author of *Shifting: The Double Lives of Black Women in America* (HarperCollins, 2003), a winner of the 2004 American Book Awards. A Fellow of the American Psychological Association, Shorter-Gooden has presented and published on African American women and identity, psychotherapy with diverse populations, and multicultural and diversity issues in higher education. Shorter-Gooden is a consulting editor for *Professional Psychology: Research and Practice* and for *Cultural Diversity and Ethnic Minority Psychology*, and a member of the editorial board of *Consulting Psychology Journal*. She received a bachelor's degree *magna cum laude* from Princeton University with its first class of women, and earned a Ph.D. in clinical/community psychology from University of Maryland, College Park.

Amanda C. Shull, Ph.D., is manager of Talent and Organization Capability at Guardian Life. Her primary responsibilities include managing employee engagement, succession planning, performance management, and select leadership development programs. Prior to joining Guardian, Dr. Shull was manager of Organization and Management Development at PepsiCo, where she managed all organization-wide employee feedback surveys and leveraged survey results to drive action. Previously, Shull held positions as a survey consultant at Sirota and internal roles at New York Life and Morgan Stanley. She completed her Ph.D. in social-organizational psychology at Teachers College, Columbia University. She continues to teach as an adjunct faculty member at Columbia University.

Michael D. Tuller, Ph.D., is a manager at PepsiCo with the enterprise Organization and Management Development team. He plays a key role in the execution and management of the organization's 360-degree feedback processes as well as several other organizational feedback processes, including the MQPI, Hogan personality assessment, and a targeted development "check-in" tool. Dr. Tuller received his Ph.D. in I/O psychology from the University of Connecticut and is a member of SIOP.

Ilene C. Wasserman, Ph.D., founder and president of ICW Consulting, has over thirty years of experience in organizational consulting, strategic planning, change management, leadership development, and executive coaching. As founder and president of ICW Consulting, Dr. Wasserman helps leaders and teams throughout organizations leverage multiple dimensions of domestic and global diversity by enhancing communication and collaboration. Her approach is appreciative, based on the principles that we transform organization cultures through engaging the whole system, and that the culture of organizations is created and perpetuated in the stories people tell and live and through organizational structures and processes. Wasserman received her Ph.D. in human and organization development from Fielding Graduate University. She also holds master's degrees in both counseling psychology and social work from Washington University and a bachelor's degree in human development from Cornell University. She is a member of the Board of Governors of the Center for Creative Leadership, where she chairs the Research, Innovation, and Program Development Committee. She also co-chairs the Human Relations Commission for Lower Merion Township in Pennsylvania. Wasserman is a member of the Taos Institute and NTL and is a Fellow of the Kurt Lewin Center.

Michael L. Wheeler has been recognized internationally for leadership roles throughout his career. He has written and published extensively on the topic of diversity, has been cited in newspapers around the world, and has appeared on *Larry King Live*. He was named a "Pioneer in Diversity" by *Diversity Journal*. Charged with leading Omnicom Media Group's diversity strategy in the role of Chief Diversity Officer, Wheeler brings twenty years of experience providing expertise to government, not-for-profit, and Fortune 500 companies. Prior to joining Omnicom Media Group, Michael founded OEStrategies, Inc., and was previously a program director for the Conference Board, where he launched their first executive Council on Workforce Diversity, their annual Diversity Conference and Workshops, and their diversity research area of expertise. He wrote various pioneering reports on diversity published by the Conference Board and has published in *Harvard Business Review* and *BusinessWeek*. Wheeler currently serves on the Society for Human Resources Management's national committee for establishing standards and competencies for the diversity executive role. In the past, he was adjunct professor for the Graduate School of Management, New School University. Wheeler earned a B.A. in organizational communication, California State University and an M.S. in human resources management, Milano Graduate School of Management, New School University.

Mary-Frances Winters is president and founder of the Winters Group, a twenty-nine-year-old organization development and diversity consulting firm, and specializes in research, strategic planning, training, and public speaking with an emphasis in ethnic and multicultural issues. Prior to founding the Winters Group in 1984, she was affirmative action officer and senior market analyst at Eastman Kodak Company, where she worked for eleven years. Among her many awards and distinctions, Winters was named a diversity pioneer by *Profiles in Diversity Journal* in August 2007. A life member of the board of trustees of the University of Rochester, Winters has served on the boards of the Greater Rochester Metro Chamber of Commerce and United Way of Greater Rochester, and on the National Board of the Girl Scouts of the U.S.A. She has served as a mentor for the Emerging Leaders Program sponsored by the Centers for Leadership and Public Affairs at Duke University and the University of Cape Town, South Africa. Winters is a frequent contributor to *USA Today*'s Forum column on workplace and diversity issues. She has been published in the *International Personnel Management Association Newsletter, Profiles in Diversity Journal, DiversityInc Magazine, Executive Excellence Magazine,* the Society of Human Resource Management's *Mosaics* newsletter, and *EMA Reporter*. Winters is the author of three books: *Only Wet Babies Like Change: Workplace Wisdom for Baby Boomers, Inclusion Starts With "I,"* and *CEO's Who Get It: Diversity Leadership from the Heart and Soul.*

Margaret Yao is deputy vice president for the Department of Administration and Finance for the Millennium Challenge Corporation (MCC). MCC is an innovative and independent U.S. Government foreign aid agency that fights global poverty through the promotion of sustainable economic growth. Prior to joining MCC, Yao ran her own organization change consulting practice of fifteen years, where she led federal, state, and local government agencies and non-profit organizations to innovative performance solutions. Blending federal and private-sector management experience, she led organizational turnarounds, strategic planning, collaborative interagency service delivery, and public deliberation. Yao's work achieved national best-practice recognition in performance-based accountability in government and state and local innovation and team awards for her clients. She is published in *Memos to the President: Management Advice from the Nation's Top Public Administrators* (2001). While at the Office of Management and Budget from 1991 to 1995, Yao helped to establish the President's Management Council (PMC), worked toward passage of the Government Performance and Results Act (GPRA), and received "reinventing government" and other leadership awards. Prior to joining OMB, Yao pursued her interest in management and innovation first as a staff reporter for the *Wall Street Journal* and later as cofounder of an automotive innovation company. She earned an M.B.A. from the University of Texas at Austin, where she was a University Fellow and a Sord Scholar, and a B.A. in economics from the University of Michigan. Yao lives in Washington, D.C., where she volunteers in her community and tries to improve her Mandarin.

Part One

Frameworks for Understanding Inclusion

CHAPTER ONE

The Practice of Inclusion in Diverse Organizations

Toward a Systemic and Inclusive Framework

Bernardo M. Ferdman

In the last twenty years or so, organizations have considerably expanded attention to diversity at work; this has been accompanied by growth not only in the number and range of diversity practitioners, but also in the interest in diversity shown by organizational and other psychologists, by specialists in organizational behavior and human resources, and by other scholars, researchers, and practitioners. What is the role of diversity at work? How can organizations and their leaders best manage and leverage the range of differences in the workforce in ways that lead to positive outcomes for the organizations, their members, and other stakeholders? What conditions can maximize the benefits of diversity? These and similar questions permeate both practitioner and academic discussions on diversity.

Research and practice suggest that *diversity*—the representation of multiple identity groups and their cultures in a particular organization or workgroup—by itself may not necessarily result in positive benefits without the presence of additional conditions. *Inclusion* has emerged as a core concept in relation to diversity; in particular, it is now considered by diversity practitioners as a key approach to benefit from diversity (see Ferdman & Deane, Preface) and is in many ways at the forefront of contemporary diversity practice. Yet how inclusion relates to diversity, what inclusion is, and how it operates are not always clear or precisely specified. In this chapter, after briefly discussing its relationship to diversity, I develop the concept of *inclusion* and its various facets, as well as its manifestation in individual and collective behavior and in organizational practices.

Inclusion involves how well organizations and their members fully connect with, engage, and utilize people across all types of differences. In this chapter, I argue that the core of inclusion is how people experience it—the psychological *experience of inclusion*, operating at the individual level (and often collectively as well). This experience of inclusion is facilitated and made possible by the behavior of those in contact with the individual (such as coworkers and supervisors), by the individual's own attitudes and behavior, and by the values, norms, practices, and processes that operate in the individual's organizational and societal context. Thus inclusion can involve each and all of the following: an individual or group experience; a set of behaviors; an approach to leadership; a set of collective norms and practices; or a personal, group, organizational, or social value.

The terms *diversity* and *inclusion* are now often used together and inextricably bound—as in "diversity and inclusion (D&I) practice" (for example, Hays-Thomas & Bendick, 2013), "Office of Diversity & Inclusion" (for example, http://www.opm.gov/policy-data-oversight/diversity-and-inclusion), or "chief diversity and inclusion officer"; indeed, one can often see *D&I* used as a singular noun. In many ways, diversity and inclusion are now often treated almost like two sides of the same coin. Yet in spite of (or perhaps because of) this usage, the distinctions and relationships between them are not always sufficiently specified. Related to this, there has been a great deal of work focusing on diversity, but much less on inclusion. Because there is a growing area of professional practice in organizations commonly referred to as diversity and inclusion (or D&I), more conceptual and practical clarity regarding what *inclusion* means and how it can be cultivated in diverse organizations and groups will be helpful not only in providing more coherence to this growing field, but also in establishing a foundation for more effective practice and a basis for empirically testing its assumptions.

Inclusion as the Key to Diversity's Benefits

What is the connection of diversity and inclusion? Why are they tied so closely together? To varying degrees, diversity is a fact of life in work groups and organizations. Inclusion is grounded in what we do with that diversity when we value and appreciate people *because of* and not in spite of their differences, as well as their similarities. More important, it involves creating work contexts in which people are valued and appreciated as themselves and as integrated and complex—with their full range of differences and similarities from and with each other. Essentially, inclusion is a way of working with diversity: it is the process and practice through which groups and organizations can reap the benefits of their diversity.

Diversity at Work

What makes diversity so important? On the one hand, much of the focus in the field of diversity in organizations has been on reducing or eliminating undesirable, unfair, and illegal bias and discrimination and on increasing equity and social justice (Ferdman & Sagiv, 2012). On the other hand, many theorists, researchers, and practitioners (for example, Davidson, 2011; Ely & Thomas, 2001; Ferdman & Brody, 1996; Mor Barak, 2011; Page, 2007) have emphasized the benefits that individuals, groups, organizations, and societies can derive from diversity. This understanding forms the foundation for many organizational diversity initiatives.

In the United States and elsewhere, much of the focus on and work on diversity in organizations began in the context of efforts to expand social justice and civil rights across lines of race, gender, age, disability, and other dimensions of identity that had often formed (and in many cases continue to form) the basis for systematic exclusion and discrimination. As societies and organizations expanded the degree to which members of previously excluded groups were represented in different institutions, in different types of jobs, and at various hierarchical levels, issues of authenticity and effectiveness became more important. In many cases, members of previously excluded groups were not willing (or able or allowed) to assimilate to dominant norms and styles as a price of admission or promotion; in other cases, the quantity of newer members made intergroup differences more notable; and in still other cases, people who were already members but had needed to blend in and perhaps submerge aspects of themselves to be accepted began to be more willing to "come out" regarding previously hidden differences. These processes have meant that, as diversity has become more discussed, recognized, and valued, we seem to find and see more and more of it, along a greater number of dimensions.

Simultaneously, it became clearer that these differences, when viewed and managed as potential assets, could bring substantial benefits to organizations. Because diversity is not simply about supposedly superficial demographic facts or labels, but rather about identities, cultures, and the varied meaning and ways of thinking about and approaching situations that these represent (Ferdman, 1992; D. A. Thomas & Ely, 1996), theorists and practitioners developed descriptions of organizations that treated differences more positively. Cox (1991), for example, distinguished among monocultural, plural, and multicultural organizations, and R. R. Thomas (1990) discussed the importance of creating work environments "where no one is advantaged or disadvantaged . . . [and] where 'we' is everyone" (p. 109). Miller and Katz (1995), based on earlier work by Bailey Jackson and others, described a path from exclusive to inclusive organizations. Holvino (1998; see also Holvino, Ferdman, & Merrill-Sands, 2004) described the differences and transitions between monocultural exclusionary organizations, transitional compliance-focused organizations, and finally truly multicultural organizations, which "seek and value all differences and develop the systems and work practices that support members of every group to succeed and fully contribute" (Holvino et al., 2004, p. 248). Similarly, D. A. Thomas and Ely (1996) described what they called the "learning and effectiveness paradigm" or later the "integration and learning perspective" (Ely & Thomas, 2001) for addressing diversity in organizations; this approach involves viewing and treating cultural and other identity-based differences as resources from which the whole organization can benefit and learn, rather than as something to be ignored for the purpose of avoiding discrimination or highlighted solely for the purpose of accessing niche markets.

In spite of the many arguments for the benefits of diversity at work (for example, Cox & Blake, 1991; Stahl, Mäkelä, Zander, & Maznevski, 2010), scholars have also pointed out that diversity can be associated with negative outcomes. Mannix and Neale (2005), for example, reviewed research on diversity in teams. They summarized the premise of their work as follows: "[T]here has been a tension between the promise and the reality of diversity in team process and performance. The optimistic view holds that diversity will lead to an increase in the variety of perspectives and approaches brought to a problem and to opportunities for knowledge sharing, and hence lead to greater creativity and quality of team performance. However, the preponderance of the evidence favors a more pessimistic view: that diversity creates social divisions, which in turn create negative performance outcomes for the group" (p. 31). Based on their review of relevant theory and research, Mannix and Neale concluded that, in general, identity-based differences—those based on gender, age, race, and ethnicity, for example—tended to result in more negative effects on group functioning; in contrast, what they called "underlying differences"—those grounded in characteristics such as education or functional background—were more likely to result in performance benefits, but only by carefully managing group process. They conclude that the key to effects of diversity on group performance is most likely to be found in the context and in a more nuanced understanding of the processes involved. Other reviewers (for example, Horwitz & Horwitz, 2007; S. E. Jackson & Joshi, 2011; van Knippenberg & Schippers, 2007) also report mixed results with regard to the effects of diversity in work groups on a range of processes and outcomes, including communication patterns, conflict, cohesion, commitment, turnover, creativity, innovation, and performance. Similarly, Kochan et al. (2003), in a series of studies over five years investigating the connections of business performance with gender and racial diversity, found that the effects of diversity on performance were not consistent and in part appeared to depend on the organizational context and group processes.

In sum, it is clear from both research and practice that more diversity does not, by itself, necessarily lead to more positive outcomes for groups and organizations. Simply representing a greater variety of differences in an organization or group is not a magical path toward greater performance, for example. The frameworks mentioned earlier, proposed by Cox, by Holvino, by Miller and Katz, and by D. A. Thomas and Ely, all take this into account and describe the type of organizational cultures and group processes that are more likely not only to incorporate and value greater diversity, but also to derive its benefits. In these accounts, it is not the presence of diversity by itself but rather how it is addressed that leads to positive outcomes.

Building on this perspective, Ferdman, Avigdor, Braun, Konkin, and Kuzmycz (2010) proposed that, rather than treating diversity as a predictor of performance, it may better be viewed as a moderator of the relationship between the group's approach to differences—and more specifically inclusion—and its outcomes; in this approach, inclusion is seen as the key factor increasing performance, with the relationship expected to be stronger in more diverse groups, in which the presence of more varied resources makes inclusion especially useful. Whether or not inclusion is a predictor (see Ferdman et al., 2010), a moderator (see Nishii & Mayer, 2009), or both, it has become clearer that it is quite critical in the context of diversity. This view of inclusion as a fundamental practice for realizing the benefits of diversity in groups and organizations is addressed in the next section.

Inclusion as Essential to Support and Work with Diversity

Although scholars have only recently begun to highlight inclusion as a focal construct in understanding diversity and its possible outcomes, diversity practitioners began doing so somewhat earlier (along with a few researchers, such as Mor Barak; see, for example, Mor Barak & Cherin, 1998, and Mor Barak, 2000a). In 1995, for example, Miller and Katz's (1995) path model highlighted the importance of inclusion, and Marjane Jensen (1995) developed a list of key behaviors for inclusion to support diversity; beginning in 1996, their consulting firm, the Kaleel Jamison Consulting Group, supported the design and implementation of Dun & Bradstreet's Inclusion Initiative (see Gasorek, 2000). Also in 1996, Ferdman and Brody pointed out various models of inclusion in the context of different rationales for diversity initiatives, and in 1999, Davidson highlighted the idea that "[i]f diversity initiatives address ways of building structural and psychological inclusiveness for organizational members, they are more likely to be successful" (p. 174). Miller and Katz's 2002 book, *The Inclusion Breakthrough: Unleashing the Real Power of Diversity*, highlighted ways of doing this through systemic change in organizations, including new competencies on the part of leaders and members, and policies and practices to encourage, enable, and support these behaviors. They forcefully summarized the connection of diversity and inclusion this way: "If an organization brings in new people but doesn't enable them to contribute, those new people are bound to fail, no matter how talented they are. *Diversity without inclusion does not work*" (p. 17, italics in original).

Davidson (1999) aptly pointed out how members of organizations can have a different "expectation of being included" on the basis of their varying histories of oppression or privilege. In other words, members of more dominant groups, historically, have generally been more likely to expect that they will be able to join groups and organizations, and that once they have joined, they will be fully accepted and made to feel that they are equal and valued participants. Inclusion, in the sense described by Miller and Katz, has always been more likely for members of more powerful groups.

This connection of inclusion to inequality and the hierarchical aspects of intergroup relations in a societal and organizational context is quite important because it reminds us of some of the original goals of diversity initiatives related to addressing societal inequities and systematic discrimination. In other words, the roots of inclusion are intertwined with those of diversity in organizations, and it is in this connection that inclusion derives its power. Whether the focus of an inclusion initiative is on first making sure that there is broad and equitable representation of multiple groups at various levels of an organization, or whether such an effort extends to addressing how differences and similarities in the now more diverse organization are viewed and treated, as well as to how the members of multiple groups experience the workplace, it is important to not lose sight of the underlying values and the intergroup context for the initiative.

Indeed, Pless and Maak (2004) addressed inclusion as an ethical imperative for diversity management. They grounded their analysis on what they called the founding principle or moral basis for inclusion—"mutual recognition" of humans for each other—which incorporates *emotional recognition, solidarity* and *legal and political recognition*" (p. 131, italics in original). For Pless and Maak, "*legal and political recognition*" includes equality, particularly with regard to freedom and the rights of organizational citizenship. They argue that these types of recognition are developed through "reciprocal understanding, standpoint plurality and mutual enabling, trust, and integrity" (p. 129), which together support development and maintenance of an "intercultural moral point of view" (p. 131). Their analysis points out that noticing differences and being open to them are insufficient "especially if intellectual traditions induce people to find the one right way" (p. 133); what is necessary is what they call "standpoint plurality," which involves creating processes, in light of what are typically unequal power distributions in groups and organizations, to foster true dialogue that allows consideration of all points of view, including those that may be marginalized in less inclusive contexts.

To further understand the connections and differences between the concepts of diversity and inclusion, Roberson (2006) surveyed human resource officers in fifty-one large public companies and asked them for their definitions of both inclusion and diversity. Through content analyses, Roberson found that "definitions of diversity focused primarily on differences and the demographic composition of groups or organizations, whereas definitions of inclusion focused on organizational objectives designed to increase the participation of all employees and to leverage diversity effects on the organization" (p. 219). Specifically, respondents described diversity in terms of "the spectrum of human similarities and differences" and conceived of diversity in organizations primarily as representation of people across this spectrum. Her respondents described inclusion, in contrast, as "the way an organization configures its systems and structures to value and leverage the potential, and to limit the disadvantages, of differences" (p. 221).

In sum, the concept of inclusion has developed as a way to capture and communicate how people and organizations must be and what they must do to benefit from diversity, both individually and collectively. Focusing on inclusion not only allows doing diversity work that emphasizes reducing negative and problematic processes—such as those grounded in prejudice, discrimination, and oppression—but also fosters a positive vision of what might replace those undesired behaviors, policies, and systems. The concept of inclusion also allows and encourages practitioners to simultaneously take into account and address multiple dimensions of diversity; inclusion recognizes the various ways in which people are different—particularly on the basis of socially and culturally meaningful categories, many involving systematic patterns of intergroup inequality—and at the same time facilitates approaches that view these categories as coexisting in whole people. Rather than focusing on individuals as representatives of only one group at a time and on one identity at a time, an inclusion lens highlights multiplicity and integration, in the context of empowerment and equality. Inclusion allows and encourages us to learn about, acknowledge, and honor group-based differences while at the same time treating each person as unique and recognizing that every identity group incorporates a great deal of diversity (Ferdman, 1995; Ferdman & Gallegos, 2001).

Inclusion has also become a key approach for working with diversity because it is global and it is scalable. It works for everyone. People—across cultures and across identities—resonate to inclusion. Inclusion can be less polemical and political than some other approaches—particularly those focused on ensuring representation, such as affirmative action, or those focused on specific group identities or "protected" groups—but it does not negate or undermine those approaches; rather, it complements them and provides a lens and practices that can help make them more successful. Indeed, when people understand and work toward inclusion, as both a value and a practice, they can become energized and more excited about diversity and about eliminating invidious bias and discrimination. They can discover new and previously unexplored connections with other people across multiple dimensions of difference and learn valuable perspectives and skills that are personally beneficial as well as helpful to their workgroups and organizations.

The challenge for both practitioners and scholars, then, is to develop clarity about what inclusion is in the context of diverse workplaces, a topic that I now turn to.

What Is Inclusion? A Multilevel Perspective

Inclusion at work has to do with *how* organizations, groups, their leaders, and their members provide ways that allow everyone, across multiple types of differences, to participate, contribute, have a voice, and feel that they are connected and belong, all without losing individual uniqueness or having to give up valuable identities or aspects of themselves. Inclusion involves recognizing, appreciating, and leveraging diversity so as to allow members of different cultural and identity groups—varying, for example, across lines of ethnicity, race, nationality, gender, age, sexual orientation, ability/disability, cultural background, and many other dimensions—to work together productively without subsuming those differences and, when possible, using those differences for the common good (Ferdman, 2010).

Inclusion also means reframing both what it means to be an insider in a work group or organization and who gets to define that. Rather than treating membership and participation as a privilege granted by those traditionally in power to those previously excluded—often with assimilation to established norms as a condition of full acceptance—inclusive practices redefine who the "we" is in an organization or work group so that all have the right to be there and to have an equal voice, both in managing the boundary and in defining (and redefining) norms, values, and preferred styles for success (Ferdman & Davidson, 2002a; Miller & Katz, 2002). This can be challenging because in many cases it requires ongoing reexamination of previously accepted or taken-for-granted ways of working and interacting. It means developing skills and practices for collectively reevaluating notions of what (and who) is "normal," appropriate, and expected in ways that incorporate more voices and perspectives, many of those unfamiliar or uncomfortable for those previously in power.

The practice of inclusion is dynamic and ongoing: because inclusion is created and re-created continuously—in both small and large ways—organizations, groups, and individuals cannot work on becoming inclusive just once and then assume that they are done; it is a recursive and never-ending approach to work and life.

In this section, I review concepts of inclusion in diverse organizations in the context of an emergent framework for the practice of inclusion that spans multiple levels of analysis and incorporates multiple voices and perspectives.

Toward a Systemic Inclusion Framework

The concept of inclusion can be quite simple. Many people can quickly describe, for example, what it feels like when they are being included and how that contrasts with exclusion. In many of my workshops (see, for example, Ferdman, 2011), I ask participants to think about and then describe to a neighbor a situation at work or elsewhere in which they have felt fully present, engaged, and included; in most cases, the immediate positive energy in the room is quite palpable, and participants are very quickly involved in animated conversations about their inclusion experience, which they can easily recall and recount.

Essentially, people often see inclusion as synonymous with a sense of belonging and participation. Schutz (1958) considered inclusion (along with control and affection) to be a central interpersonal need—albeit varying in intensity across individuals—and described it as comprising the desire to belong, to feel important, and to feel cared about. Baumeister and Leary (1995), based on a review of theoretical and empirical literature, described a basic human need to belong as a "powerful, fundamental, and pervasive motivation" (p. 497). Fiske (1994, cited in Levine & Kerr, 2007) saw belonging as a core social motive supporting people's ability to be part of and contribute to groups.

Inclusion is also complex. It can be conceptualized and operate at multiple levels, including the individual, interpersonal, group, organizational, and societal, and may be experienced differently by different individuals and in different situations (Ferdman & Davidson, 2002b). A straightforward focus simply on belonging can be deceptive, because it can hide many of the subtleties and nuances of inclusion and its practice, and it may not necessarily address the intergroup aspects of inclusion that are most relevant in the context of diversity. Focusing solely on individuals' motivation to belong does not fully address how group or social identities play a part in the dynamics of inclusion (and exclusion). I may, for example, be part of a work group in which I feel valued, heard, and treated as an equal, full, and important member, but to achieve this, perhaps I had to change important aspects of how I communicate to become more like other members of the group, or perhaps I decided to change my name so that it would be easier for my fellow group members to pronounce, or perhaps I am reluctant to reveal aspects of myself that are quite important to me but that I believe may be misunderstood or not valued by my colleagues.

Some of this complexity is addressed by Shore, Randel, Chung, Dean, Ehrhart, and Singh (2011), in their review of theory and research on inclusion and diversity in work groups. They base their approach on Brewer's (1991) optimal distinctiveness theory, which indicates that, in general, people look for a balance between being subsumed into a larger social unit and also standing out within that unit with regard to their unique social identities. According to Brewer's theory, everyone needs to feel sufficiently connected to others, so as to be accepted and to belong, and also sufficiently individuated and different, so as not to be absorbed. Shore et al. conclude that inclusion exists when individuals' simultaneous needs for belonging and uniqueness can both be satisfied (in the context of being "an esteemed member of the work group," p. 1265). Their approach is useful because it highlights the importance of considering the interplay of multiple social identities in individual experience. In other words, my experience is typically related not just to one of my identities (such as being a man, a professor, or a middle-aged person) but also to the unique configuration of all of my identities (Ferdman, 1995).

Another key aspect of its complexity has to do with the frame of reference for defining what constitutes inclusion. Say an organization or person decides that they would like to become more inclusive. What defines whether a particular organizational practice or individual behavior is inclusive? I believe that, ultimately, it should be based on whether or not those affected by the practice or behavior feel and are included. At the core, and particularly from a psychological perspective, inclusion needs to be conceptualized phenomenologically—in other words, in terms of people's perceptions and interpretations. A set of objective facts cannot necessarily determine whether inclusion exists; it must be assessed based on the experience of those involved; therefore it could vary from person to person and situation to situation. In a study related to this point, Stamper and Masterson (2002) found that how many hours employees worked and how long they had been in the organization—which the researchers referred to as "actual inclusion"—were not associated with how much the employees perceived themselves to be "insiders" in the organization.

Inclusion is also not static or a one-time achievement; because it is created anew in each situation (Ferdman & Davidson, 2002b) through the relationship of the individual with the surrounding social system, inclusion involves a dynamic and interrelated set of processes, as depicted in Figure 1.1. In other words, "inclusion

Figure 1.1. Inclusion as a Systemic and Dynamic Process

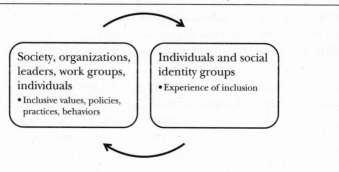

is a momentary, even evanescent creation, which depends on the particular people and the particular situation involved. At the same time, the behavior and attitude of the moment may not mean much without a history and a future, without a structure and system around them that give them the appropriate meaning and weight" (Ferdman & Davidson, 2002b, pp. 83–84). **It is in this sense that inclusion is a *practice*—an interacting set of structures, values, norms, group and organizational climates, and individual and collective behaviors, all connected with inclusion experiences in a mutually reinforcing and dynamic system.** Individuals, groups, organizations, and even societies adopt values and policies and engage in practices geared toward fostering inclusion; when these result in individual and collective experiences of inclusion, then those approaches can be considered to be inclusive. As more people and groups experience inclusion, they are more likely to have a shared sense of what it takes to create more inclusion for themselves and others and to incorporate this learning into the ongoing processes and practices of the groups and organizations of which they are a part. This will in turn increase confidence that the behaviors, policies, and practices are indeed inclusive, in a recursive and ongoing virtuous cycle.

Inclusion at Multiple Levels

This framework (Figure 1.1) can be further analyzed to consider the various levels at which inclusion can be conceptualized, assessed, and practiced, as shown in Figure 1.2. It is important to consider multiple levels of analysis in conceptualizing inclusion because, even though individual experience plays a key role in assessing inclusion's existence or potency, that alone is not sufficient. For example, an individual may say that she has not faced discrimination and that, on the contrary, she feels very included in her work group. But that may not be the case for other people who share one or more identity groups with her. To understand inclusion at the group level, we would need to assess how common her experience is within her work group as well as among others sharing some of her identities. It may also be possible that she is not aware of discrimination or patterns of participation that

Figure 1.2. Systems of Inclusion: A Multilevel Analytic Framework

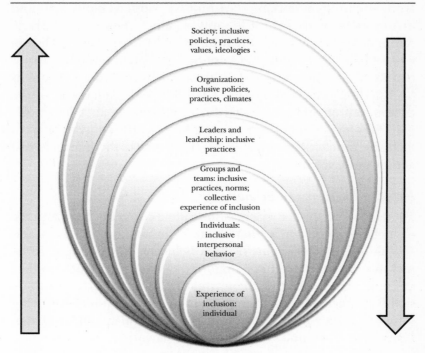

Society: inclusive policies, practices, values, ideologies

Organization: inclusive policies, practices, climates

Leaders and leadership: inclusive practices

Groups and teams: inclusive practices, norms; collective experience of inclusion

Individuals: inclusive interpersonal behavior

Experience of inclusion: individual

objectively exist. If we are talking about a young African American woman, is her experience similar to that of other African American women and/or other young people? Additionally, fostering inclusion experiences requires particular behaviors on the part of leaders and other work group members, as well as suitable policies and practices in the organization. Moreover, it is more likely that experiences of inclusion will be noticed and valued and that the vocabulary for describing and sharing them will be developed in the context of inclusive practices and climates of inclusion. To fully practice inclusion, we need to simultaneously consider and address these multiple levels (depicted in Figure 1.2).

Individual Experience

As discussed previously, the foundation for inclusion is individual experience. At the individual level, I have defined the *experience of inclusion* as the degree to which individuals "feel safe, trusted, accepted, respected, supported, valued, fulfilled, engaged, and authentic in their working environment, both as individuals and as members of particular identity groups" (Ferdman, Barrera, Allen, & Vuong, 2009, p. 6). In this view, I experience inclusion when I believe not only that I am being treated well individually, but also that others who share my identities and those groups as a whole "are respected, honored, trusted, and given voice, appreciation, power, and value" (Ferdman, Barrera, et al., 2009, p. 6).

These experiences of inclusion both lead to and stem from inclusive practices at other levels—particularly the interpersonal and group levels.

Inclusive Interpersonal Behavior

To help create this experience, individuals can engage in a range of inclusive behavior as they relate to others around them and can also be the recipients of such behavior. For example, to be inclusive, I can seek others' opinions, be curious about who they are and what matters to them, treat them in ways that to them signify respect, and work with others to arrive at jointly satisfying solutions rather than impose my approach or direction. (Later, I give more examples of inclusive behavior; see also Bennett, Chapter 5, and Wasserman, Chapter 4, this volume.)

Group-Level Inclusion

Groups create inclusion by engaging in suitable practices and establishing appropriate norms, such as treating everyone with respect, giving everyone a voice, emphasizing collaboration, and working through conflicts productively and authentically. Additionally, it is possible to consider the collective experience of inclusion in the group in terms of the aggregate of individuals' experiences (Ferdman, Avigdor, et al., 2010), again framing it as a construct grounded in perception and interpretation—in this case at the group level. For example, I worked with a client to develop an assessment of employees' perceptions of inclusion and then was able to compare their overall sense of being included as a function of various identity categories, such as gender, ethnicity, sexual orientation, type of job, unit, and location.

Inclusive Leaders and Leadership

Leaders play an important role in fostering inclusion (see Booysen, Chapter 10; Gallegos, Chapter 6, this volume; also Chrobot-Mason, Ruderman, & Nishii, 2013, and Wasserman, Gallegos, & Ferdman, 2008), and one can identify critical practices to that effect. Beyond the interpersonal behaviors that everyone can put into practice, leaders have additional responsibilities, including holding others accountable for their behavior and making appropriate connections between organizational imperatives or goals—the mission and vision of the organization—and inclusion. Beyond the particular practices of individual leaders, the approach to leadership that is preferred or valued in an organization also plays an important role in the practice of inclusion. For example, leadership may emphasize a positive approach that is strengths-based and looks for ways to bring out the potential contributions of as many people as possible. In many ways, inclusive leadership is the linchpin for inclusion at other levels of the multilevel framework; it can facilitate (and perhaps even be considered a key part of) inclusion in groups, organizations, and societies, as well as help translate and spread inclusion across these levels.

Inclusive Organizations

Organizational policies and practices play a critical role in fostering a climate of inclusion and provide a context in which individual behavior and leadership are displayed, cultivated, and interpreted. This level of analysis is perhaps the one that has received the most attention on the part of both scholars and practitioners (see Church, Rotolo, Shull, & Tuller, Chapter 9; Nishii & Rich, Chapter 11; Offermann & Basford, Chapter 8; O'Mara, Chapter 14; and Winters, Chapter 7, this volume; also Kossek & Zonia, 1993, and Holvino, Ferdman, & Merrill-Sands, 2004). The organization's culture—its values, norms, and preferred styles—as well as its structures and systems, provide the container in which individuals interact and interpret their experience. Holvino et al. (2004) described an inclusive organization as one where "the diversity of knowledge and perspectives that members of different groups bring . . . has shaped its strategy, its work, its management and operating systems, and its core values and norms for success; . . . [and where] members of all groups are treated fairly, feel and are included, have equal opportunities, and are represented at all organizational levels and functions" (p. 249). Inclusive policies and practices to achieve this can be incorporated in most if not all of the organization's systems, including, for example, how work is organized and done; how employees are recruited, selected, evaluated, and promoted; how, by whom, and on what bases decisions are made, implemented, and evaluated; and how the organization engages with the surrounding community and other stakeholders.

Inclusive Societies

Finally, these experiences, behaviors, policies, and practices all occur in the context of broader societal frameworks, including policies, practices, values, and ideologies that may or may not be supportive of inclusion (see Jonsen & Özbilgin, Chapter 12; Lukensmeyer, Yao, & Brown, Chapter 17; and Mor Barak & Daya, Chapter 13, this volume). For example, in the United States, as in other societies, there have been many debates about whether it is valuable or appropriate for individuals and groups to remain culturally distinct within the larger society (Ferdman & Sagiv, 2012). Communities and societies (as well as international organizations) can take proactive steps to promote inclusion. Inclusive communities and societies incorporate values and practices that encourage individuals and groups to maintain and develop their unique identities and cultures while continuing to fully and equally belong to and participate in the larger community.

Conceptualizing Inclusion . . . Inclusively

The multilevel perspective described in the previous section provides a framework for organizing and developing some clarity among the many descriptions and definitions of inclusion that have begun to appear in both academic and applied work. Because the concept of inclusion can be so broad and encompass so many aspects, it can sometimes unfortunately appear that the term is not quite precise. Yet, when we sort the concepts and definitions according to their focus and level of analysis, I believe that a much clearer and useful picture can emerge. In Table 1.1, I present many of these conceptualizations, sorted both by level of analysis and by year of publication.

The perspectives on inclusion listed in Table 1.1 are important not only because they represent a historical overview of the development and application of the concept, but also because viewing them together and in juxtaposition helps highlight key themes regarding an emergent comprehensive inclusion framework.

One such emergent theme is that there are many useful definitions of inclusion, all of which make sense in some context. I would argue that it is not necessary or even productive to arrive at one single definition of inclusion, because ultimately the suitability of a particular version of the concept will depend on our frame of reference, our purpose, and our level of analysis. At the same time, if we are to advance the field, it may be helpful and perhaps is even imperative that both practitioners and scholars seek to be clearer and more specific about how their particular or preferred approach fits into the larger system or framework of inclusion, and at which level(s). Particularly when seeking to generalize from research, but also from one applied setting to another, considering the particular operationalization of inclusion that is involved can also be helpful.

This requires knowing more about and acknowledging what others are doing and saying; being precise, where possible, about one's own perspective; and describing (or at least being aware of) how one's position or view relates to that of others. This point is somewhat analogous to the practice of inclusion itself, in that inclusion is grounded in the idea that we are all better off—collectively and individually—with a broader range of interdependent and mutually reinforcing contributions and perspectives. Bailey Jackson (1994) eloquently described it this way: "My attempts to construct a vision of a multicultural system were extremely frustrating until I realized it is impossible for me or any other single person to construct such a vision of a multicultural organization, community, society, or other social system. . . . To create a vision of a multicultural system, a diversity of perspectives must be represented in a group of people who are engaged in a

Table 1.1. Concepts of Inclusion

Level of Analysis	Concept	Source
Individuals	"Inclusiveness encourages individuals of all identity groups to contribute all their talents, skills, and energies to the organization, not merely those that could be tolerated or accepted within a narrow range of monocultural style and expectations."	Miller and Katz, 1995, p. 278
	Inclusion is "the degree to which individuals feel part of critical organizational processes," indicated by their access to information and resources, work group involvement, and ability to influence decision making.	Mor-Barak and Cherin, 1998, p. 48
	Inclusion is "the degree to which an employee is accepted and treated as an insider by others in a work system." Used "three inclusion indicators: (1) decision-making influence, that is the influence that an employee has over decisions that affect him/her or the work that s/he does . . . ; (2) access to sensitive work information, that is the degree to which an employee is kept well-informed about the company business objectives and plans; and (3) job security, that is the likelihood that an employee will retain his/her job."	Pelled, Ledford, and Mohrman, 1999, p. 1014–1015
	"One's experience of inclusion in the collective is a powerful determinant of action. . . . One's sense of feeling included is most critical because it strengthens affective commitment to the organization. If one feels included, one perceives oneself as psychologically linked to the organization, experiencing the successes and failures of the organization as one's own."	Davidson, 1999, p. 172

There is "a range of aspects of the experience of inclusion, such as feeling validated, accepted, heard, and appreciated; using one's talents and making a difference (including being part of something that is working and doing a meaningful task); having some work autonomy; receiving feedback; having one's input solicited and used; involvement in collaboration; openness for dialogue; and wanting to learn from others. . . . [W]hile there are commonalities or general themes in terms of what people experience as inclusion—feeling valued, respected, recognized, trusted, and that one is making a difference—not everyone experiences these in the same way."

Ferdman and Davidson, 2002b, p. 81

Inclusion is "an individual's collective judgment or perception of belonging as an accepted, welcomed and valued member in the larger organization units, such as a work group, department, and overall organization."

Hayes and Major, 2003, p. 5

Defines "belonging" as having two related aspects: "The first is social connection or affiliation, including bonds of love, friendship and shared purpose, as well as the basic ability to communicate and relate to others. . . . The second aspect is social acceptance, which enables a person to be with and among others with a sense of comfort and entitlement, or in short, a sense that she belongs and that she has a rightful place in the world."

Hubbard, 2004, p. 218

"Workplace Social Inclusion . . . captures the extent to which employees have informal social ties with others at work and feel as if they belong and are socially included by others in their workplace."

Pearce and Randel, 2004, p. 84

"Inclusion represents a person's ability to contribute fully and effectively to an organization."

Roberson, 2006, p. 215

"An organization is inclusive when everyone has a sense of belonging; feels respected, valued and seen for who they are as individuals; and feels a level of supportive energy and commitment from leaders, colleagues and others so that all people—individually and collectively—can do our best work."

Miller and Katz, 2007, p. 2

Continued

Table 1.1. Continued

Level of Analysis	Concept	Source
	"We define the *experience of inclusion* in a workgroup as individuals' perception of the extent to which they feel safe, trusted, accepted, respected, supported, valued, fulfilled, engaged, and authentic in their working environment, both as individuals and as members of particular identity groups"	Ferdman, Barrera, et al., 2009, p. 6
	"[I]nclusion involves both being fully ourselves and allowing others to be fully themselves in the context of engaging in common pursuits. It means collaborating in a way in which all parties can be fully engaged and subsumed, and yet, paradoxically, at the same time believe that they have not compromised, hidden, or given up any part of themselves. Thus, for individuals, experiencing inclusion in a group or organization involves being fully part of the whole while retaining a sense of authenticity and uniqueness."	Ferdman, 2010, p. 37
	"We define inclusion as the degree to which an employee perceives that he or she is an esteemed member of the work group through experiencing treatment that satisfies his or her needs for belongingness and uniqueness."	Shore, Randel, Chung, Dean, Ehrhart, and Singh, 2011, p. 1265
Leaders	"Managers and leaders routinely use a variety of techniques, such as encouraging informal social interaction and creating and maintaining strong organizational cultures, to help people feel a part of the whole organization."	Davidson, 1999, p. 172

Continued

	Leader inclusiveness: "words and deeds by a leader . . . that indicate an invitation and appreciation for others' contributions. Leader inclusiveness captures attempts by leaders to include others in discussions and decisions in which their voices and perspectives might otherwise be absent."	Nembhard and Edmonson, 2006, p. 947
	"Building a culture of inclusion involves a new set of leadership qualities and skills including flexibility, fluidity, self-awareness and mindfulness, courage, and the capacity to be vulnerable in a powerful way."	Wasserman, Gallegos, and Ferdman, 2008, p. 180
Groups	"Inclusive groups encourage disagreement because they realize it leads to more-effective solutions and more-successful adaptations to a changing environment. Instead of pressuring members to leave their individual and cultural differences outside, inclusive groups ask everyone to contribute to the full extent of their being."	Miller, 1994, p. 39
	"Inclusion is the practice of embracing and using differences as opportunities for added value and competitive advantages in teamwork, product quality, and work output."	Katz and Miller, 1996, p. 105
	"[I]ncreasing inclusion would require developing the skills to allow ourselves and others to see more of the complete and complex picture of our intergroup realities, as these are expressed in our everyday collaborations. It is about allowing for both similarities and differences at both the individual and the group levels at the same time that we are joined together in a common endeavor. . . . [It is about avoiding fusion, in which I act as if we are the same, as well as avoiding disconnection, in which I believe and act as if we are completely different."	Ferdman and Davidson, 2004, p. 33–34

Table 1.1. Continued

Level of Analysis	Concept	Source
	"We define *Collective Experience of Inclusion* (Collective EOI) as the overall or additive sense of the extent to which people in a group feel accepted, engaged, safe, and valued—essentially the aggregated experience of inclusion across all individuals in a group."	Ferdman, Avigdor, et al., 2010, p. 16
	Members are "treated as . . . insider[s] and also allowed/encouraged to retain uniqueness within the work group."	Shore et al., 2011, p. 1266
	". . . from the perspective of the moral imperative, inclusion implies not only eliminating barriers to opportunity based on group differences but also supporting every individual to reach her or his full potential . . . without requiring assimilation."	Ferdman and Brody, 1996, p. 286
	"Inclusion as seen from the perspective of legal and social pressures primarily involves removing illegal barriers . . . or obstacles perceived to be unfair. . . . [This] approach tends to be primarily reactive . . ."	p. 287
Organizations and Complex Systems	"From the vantage point of business success, inclusion is about making sure the organization uses all productive capacity and potential to the full extent. . . . [It] is not limited to particular groups or categories of people. All individuals must be included in their full uniqueness and complexity."	p. 289

"Institutional and systemic bias can also serve as an impediment to cultivating an inclusive environment."

Davidson, 1999, p. 172

"The inclusive workplace is one that: values and uses individual and intergroup differences within its work force; cooperates with and contributes to its surrounding community; alleviates the needs of disadvantaged groups in its wider environment; collaborates with individuals, groups, and organizations across national and cultural boundaries."

Mor Barak, 2000b, p. 339

Inclusion addresses the degree to which (a) employees are valued and their ideas are taken into account and used, (b) people partner successfully within and across departments, (c) current employees feel that they belong and prospective employees are attracted to the organization, (d) people feel connected to each other and to the organization and its goals, and (e) the organization continuously fosters flexibility and choice, and attends to diversity.

Gasorek, 2000

"Experiences of inclusion result when policies, structures, practices, and norms of behavior are aligned in such a way that every member of a given collective (community, organization, or network) has a fair and equal opportunity to access the joint resources of that collective."

Davidson and Ferdman, 2002, p. 1

Continued

27

Table 1.1. Continued

Level of Analysis	Concept	Source
	"A culture of inclusion requires . . . a new set of actions, attitudes, policies, and practices designed to enable all people to contribute their energies and talents to the organization's success. Conflict becomes constructive debate. People are sought because they are different."	Miller and Katz, 2002, p. 16
	"Inclusion in multicultural organizations means that there is equality, justice, and full participation at both the group and individual levels, so that members of different groups not only have equal access to opportunities, decision making, and positions of power, but they are actively sought out *because* of their differences. In a multicultural, inclusive organization, differences of all types become integrated into the fabric of the business, such that they become a necessary part of doing its everyday work."	Holvino, Ferdman, and Merrill-Sands, 2004, p. 248 (italics in original)
	In an inclusive organization, "the diversity of knowledge and perspectives that members of different groups bring . . . has shaped its strategy, its work, its management and operating systems, and its core values and norms for success. . . . [M]embers of all groups are treated fairly, feel included and actually are included, have equal opportunities, and are represented at all organizational levels and functions." Diversity is woven "into the fabric of the organization."	p. 249

In a culture of inclusion, "differences are recognized, valued and engaged. Different voices are understood as being legitimate and as opening up new vistas; they are heard and integrated in decision making and problem solving processes; they have an active role in shaping culture and fostering creativity and innovation; and eventually in adding value to the company's performance. . . . [A culture of inclusion is] an organizational environment that allows people with multiple backgrounds, mindsets and ways of thinking to work effectively together and to perform to their highest potential in order to achieve organizational objectives based on sound principles. In such an environment different voices are respected and heard, diverse viewpoints, perspectives and approaches are valued and everyone is encouraged to make a unique and meaningful contribution."	Pless and Maak, 2004, p. 130–131
Inclusion is "the way an organization configures its systems and structures to value and leverage the potential, and to limit the disadvantages, of differences."	Roberson, 2006, p. 221
"Inclusion is the set of organizational norms and values that promote the development of an institutional culture in which diversity is valued and promoted and individuals feel empowered within an atmosphere of trust, safety, and respect. An inclusive work place is one that: accepts, values and utilizes individual and inter-group differences within its workforce. A warm and welcoming atmosphere eases the process of 'learning the ropes' for the new member and aids in making the member comfortable in the new group environment."	Future Work Institute, n.d., p. 6
"For us, a culture of inclusion recognizes, respects, values, and utilizes the talents and contributions of all the organization's people—current and potential—across multiple lines of difference [. . .]. In organizations with cultures of inclusion, people of all social identity groups have the opportunity to be present, to have their voices heard and appreciated, and to engage in core activities on behalf of the collective."	Wasserman, Gallegos, and Ferdman, 2008, p. 176

dialogical process. . . ." (p. 116). Building on Jackson's view, I believe that understanding of inclusion and its dynamics will be enhanced and deepened to the extent that those of us engaged in it share our views and approaches with each other and know about and build on each other's work. Because each of us holds just one or at most a few of the many jigsaw puzzle pieces necessary to build the full picture of inclusion, we must be able and willing to put in our piece(s), while at the same time being careful not to confuse our part with the whole picture.

In this sense, a prerequisite for inclusion that is not mentioned in the quotes is perhaps humility. To the extent that individuals—whether individual contributors or leaders—believe and accept that no one person can see, understand, and know everything, and then act accordingly by creating opportunities for learning and action based on multiple inputs, contributions, and perspectives, the likelihood of creating inclusion will be greatly enhanced.

A second key theme is that inclusion has both individual and collective components; in other words, it can be viewed as something that has to do with how individuals experience their life, work, and interactions, and it can also be looked at in terms of how social groups collectively experience the world. Both components are important for a complete picture of inclusion. In this context, inclusion involves growth and freedom, and eliminating the psychological, behavioral, and systemic barriers that can stand in the way. Addressing this at both the individual and collective levels, in the context of work groups and organizations, as well as society more generally, means attending both to the complex ways in which individuals are interconnected with (and in part defined by) social identity groups (see Ferdman & Roberts, Chapter 3, this volume) and to intergroup relations—how social identities play a role in individual and interpersonal situations as well as in organizations more generally. In prior work, I described it this way: "to create and increase inclusion, individuals must have appropriate competencies and demonstrate corresponding behaviors. Inclusion cannot exist without individuals who seek it and behave accordingly. At the same time, those individuals choose, display, and interpret their behavior and that of others in the context of organizational, intergroup, and socio-historical dynamics that are also very much part of the puzzle of inclusion" (Ferdman & Davidson, 2004, p. 36).

A final notable theme is that, even though the definitions provided are often framed in terms of workplaces, inclusion is a concept and practice that can more or less apply to everyone in all locations and social systems, across multiple differences; it is not limited to workplaces or to particular groups or types of diversity. Indeed, this is what makes inclusion in many ways quite easy for people to understand and particularly appealing as an approach to diversity. Because it is a concept that intuitively makes sense to people, however, it is relatively easy to focus on only one or some of the levels of system and ignore or even avoid the others, even when they may be quite important. For example, an organization can pay a great deal of attention to corporate policies that create barriers for certain groups more than others, but very little to how people actually treat each other every day. Or people in a workgroup can be extremely competent in handling multiple differences in ways that are quite satisfying to and very inclusive of all members, yet avoid any and all attention to whether or not they are fostering inclusion in a larger societal or organizational sense (for example, because their task or product is one that privileges particular societal groups over others). A systemic, dynamic, and inclusive perspective on inclusion incorporates attention to these and similar issues, as well as to ongoing learning over time.

Contributions from Inclusive Education and Social Inclusion

Although inclusion has recently gained prominence in connection with diversity in organizations, historically, the concept of inclusion was first developed and used extensively in the field of education, particularly of children with disabilities, and later expanded in relation to people with disabilities more generally. In the context of disability rights, inclusion has signified the perspective that people with disabilities should be able to fully participate in all aspects of society and its institutions. The Americans with Disabilities Act (ADA) in the United States and the United Nations Convention on the Rights of People with Disabilities (http://www.un.org/disabilities/convention/conventionfull.shtml) are both major examples of this approach and perspective.

In education, inclusion goes beyond notions of mainstreaming and integration, which privilege students without disabilities and consider those with disabilities as having "special needs." Rather, it refers to the rights of all students to participate fully in all aspects of the school and to have full access to education, without being separated from other students or being seen as less than others (see, for example, Bossaert, Colpin, Pijl, & Petry, 2013; Hick & Thomas, 2008). UNESCO, in a document emphasizing education as a basic human right for all people, defined inclusion "as a dynamic approach of responding positively to pupil diversity and of seeing individual differences not as problems, but as opportunities for enriching learning" (2005, p. 12). It goes on to describe inclusion "as a process of addressing and responding to the diversity of needs of all learners through increasing participation . . . and reducing exclusion within and from education. It involves changes . . . in content, approaches, structures and strategies, with a common vision . . . and a conviction that it is the responsibility of the regular system to educate all children" (p. 17). Particularly interesting and relevant here is the emphasis on changing the educational system and the school itself, rather than focusing on the children with "special" needs as the source or locus of problems or difficulties. In a similar way, inclusion in organizations is about creating work environments and processes that "work" for everyone, across all types of differences, rather than ones that emphasize assimilation.

A third and overlapping use of the term, *social inclusion*, is more typical in a larger societal context and from the vantage point of public policy, economics, political science, and sociology. Here the focus is on eliminating social exclusion as manifested in individual and particularly collective social disadvantages of poor or otherwise marginalized people in society—including those in the economic, political, health, housing, educational, labor, and similar arenas (see, for example, Atkinson & Marlier, 2010); social inclusion seeks to improve the material and economic conditions of such groups, as well as their full enfranchisement in society and their participation in its institutions. Boushey, Fremstad, Gragg, and Waller (2010) explain that "[s]ocial inclusion is based on the belief that we all fare better when no one is left to fall too far behind and the economy works for everyone. Social inclusion simultaneously incorporates multiple dimensions of well-being. It is achieved when all have the opportunity and resources necessary to participate fully in economic, social, and cultural activities which are considered the societal norm" (p. 1). The Australian Social Inclusion Board (2012) described social inclusion in this way: "Being socially included means that people have the resources, opportunities and capabilities they need to: Learn (participate in education and training); Work (participate in employment, unpaid or voluntary work including family and carer [*sic*] responsibilities); Engage (connect with people, use local services and participate in local, cultural, civic and recreational activities); and Have a voice (influence decisions that affect them)" (p. 12). This approach has elements that relate well with the practice of inclusion in diverse organizations, but it places less emphasis on individual experience, group processes, and interpersonal interactions, and more on social and economic policies and their effects.

Elements of Inclusion at Work

So far, I have presented various ways to conceptualize inclusion in the context of an emergent multilevel framework. From a practical perspective, the question then arises as to how to operationalize inclusion at each of these levels. What are the specific elements of inclusion? As exemplified in many of the quotes in Table 1.1, there are multiple ways to describe these, and the particular elements that are addressed can vary. In this section, I provide illustrative examples of such lists from my own research and consulting work as well as from other sources. First, I briefly discuss the importance of involving stakeholders in generating their own operational descriptions of inclusion, and I give an example of how this can be done.

Co-Constructing Inclusion

It is important to be specific about the elements of inclusion, especially in the context of inclusion initiatives, so that those involved can be clear about what is being addressed and what the goals are. My aim here, however, is not to provide a definitive list of all that the practice of inclusion encompasses, because rich descriptions are available in the academic and practitioner literature, and more important, as discussed earlier, these may vary from organization to organization or even from person to person.

Organizations and groups that wish to systematically embark on inclusion initiatives should carefully develop their own account of the specific ways that their current and prospective members and stakeholders experience inclusion, and of the behaviors, policies, and practices that foster those experiences, in the context of shared understanding of the concept of inclusion and its multiple facets. This is because lists of inclusive behaviors and practices will be most meaningful and useful when they are generated and discussed locally, among the people who will be involved in practicing those behaviors or benefiting from them, even if those lists are initially based on prior work. I suspect that inclusion that feels imposed will not be experienced as inclusion!

Another reason for developing one's own list of inclusion elements is that the process of creating localized operational definitions can itself provide a vehicle to begin practicing the very same desired behaviors and to test the expectation that they are the appropriate and best focus for an inclusion effort. For example, in one group, spending more time carefully listening to others may be an area that requires particular attention to foster more inclusion among its members. In another group, this may already be a behavior that is practiced well but other areas—such as making sure that those affected by decisions have a voice in making them, or increasing the group's skill in bringing out differences and handling conflict well—may need more attention. In yet other groups, the core inclusion issues may involve fairness and equity and their association to social identities, such as gender, race, or class. This understanding can be developed in the process of discovering the key issues for the group; at the same time, the group can test how it is doing in terms of acting on its expressed goals and values.

How can a group or organization generate its own detailed list of the elements of inclusion? Essentially, it can be done by involving key stakeholders in a process of describing their own experiences, perspectives, and hopes, and systematically combining the information generated to arrive at a collective picture of inclusion. Exhibit 1.1 provides examples of questions—generated using an appreciative inquiry approach—that can be adapted to engage individuals and groups in describing the specific behaviors and practices that they believe would result in more inclusion. (Prior to addressing these questions, it may be helpful to first spend some time discussing what participants consider inclusion to be.)

Exhibit 1.1. Questions to Generate and Co-Construct Descriptions of Inclusive Behavior and Inclusive Organizational Practices

- What behaviors—from yourself and from others—help *you* experience more inclusion?
- What behaviors help *others* around you experience more inclusion?
- Imagine that you've waved a magic wand and now everyone in the world behaves inclusively, in a way that brings inclusion to life in every encounter with others. What *inclusive behaviors* do you see around you?
- Imagine the most inclusive organization in the world, one in which everyone's talents, beliefs, backgrounds, capabilities, and ways of living—their uniqueness—is engaged, valued, and leveraged. What are one or two vital *inclusive organizational policies and practices* in that organization?

A few years ago, Frederick Miller and Christine Boulware brought together a number of practitioners and others interested in developing inclusion as a core idea for organizations and society. The result was the formation of a group called the Institute for Inclusion. In that context, a team composed of myself,

Judith Katz, Ed Letchinger, and C. Terrill Thompson—using a collaborative process of co-construction based on input from conference participants in response to questions very similar to those in Exhibit 1.1—created a list of inclusive behaviors and organizational policies and practices in three categories: (1) inclusive behaviors suitable for everyone, (2) inclusive behaviors for leaders, and (3) inclusive organizational policies and practices (Ferdman, Katz, Letchinger, & Thompson, 2009). Later, I give a summary of these lists; what is relevant here is the process we used, which can be adapted to different settings. Participants were first asked to generate individual responses to the questions. These responses were then compiled. Small groups were assigned to look for key themes and to assign behaviors and practices to one of the three buckets, as well as to add additional points as they saw fit. The working group took the material from the small groups and combined it into a document that was shared with everyone in the group, who then could provide additional suggestions, edits, and comments. The idea is to create a process that is itself inclusive and that permits generating an operational perspective for the practice of inclusion among those participating, a perspective in which everyone can feel ownership and see themselves reflected.

Elements of the Experience of Inclusion

In the context of developing and testing a measure of workgroup inclusion, my students and I (Ferdman, Barrera, et al., 2009; Hirshberg & Ferdman, 2011) defined the experience of inclusion, which, as discussed earlier, we conceptualized as involving feelings of safety, respect, support, value, trust, fulfillment, engagement, and authenticity within the workgroup. Based on that work, we can identify six key operational elements of the experience of inclusion and the associated issues, which are listed and described in Table 1.2. What is interesting about the elements and issues listed is that, while they cover a lot of ground, they are not necessarily all-encompassing; it may be possible in some contexts to produce lists that vary from the one here in terms of adding additional components or changing some of them to emphasize somewhat different issues. Nevertheless, the overall themes are likely to be quite similar.

Table 1.2. Elements of the Experience of Inclusion

Element	Examples of Issues Addressed
Feeling safe (self and group)	Do I feel physically and psychologically safe? Do I feel secure that I am fully considered a member of the group or organization? Can I move about and act freely (literally and figuratively)? Can I (and others like me) share ideas, opinions, and perspectives—especially when they differ from those of others—without fear of negative repercussions? Do I believe that others who share one or more of my identity groups are also safe from physical and/or psychological harm in the group or organization?
Involvement and engagement in the workgroup	Am I treated as a full participant in activities and interactions? Am I—and do I feel like—an insider? Do I have access to the information and resources that I need to do my work (and that others have)? Do I enjoy being part of the group or organization? Can I rely on others in my group or organization (and they on me)? Do I feel like we are part of the same team, even when we disagree? Can I (or people like me) succeed here?
Feeling respected and valued (self and group)	Am I (and others like me) treated in the ways I (they) would like to be treated? Do others in the group care about me (and people like me) and treat me (and them) as a valuable and esteemed member(s) of the group or organization? Am I trusted? Am I cared about? Are people like me trusted and cared about?
Influence on decision making	Do my ideas and perspectives influence what happens and what decisions are made? Am I listened to when weighing in on substantive issues?
Authenticity/ bringing one's whole self to work	Can I be truly myself around others in my group or organization? Do I need to conceal or distort valued parts of my identity, style, or individual characteristics? Can I have genuine conversations with others without needing to involuntarily hide relevant parts of myself? Can I be open, honest, and transparent about my ideas and perspectives? Can I make my contributions in ways that feel authentic and whole?

Continued

Table 1.2. Continued

Element	Examples of Issues Addressed
Diversity is recognized, attended to, and honored	Am I treated fairly, without discrimination or barriers based on my identities?
	Can I (and others) be transparent about and proud of my (our) social identities?
	Can we address differences in ways that lead to mutual learning and growth?
	Does the group or organization notice and value diversity of all types?

Note: Elements are adapted from Ferdman, Barrera, et al., 2009, and Hirshberg and Ferdman, 2011.

Building on this approach, I worked as an external consultant for a multinational corporation that wanted to generate a global inclusion survey. With my input, they created a four-item inclusion index, grounded in the organization's values and success factors, to assess employees' experience of inclusion. In addition to a global item assessing the individual's overall sense of being included, we also asked about how much the respondent felt that the company valued his or her unique contributions and strengths, to what degree the respondent believed that he or she (or others who are similar) could succeed at the company, and to what degree the respondent believed that he or she had equitable access to necessary information, tools, and resources. This index could then be statistically regressed on other items measuring inclusive behavior at other levels of analysis to discover the key drivers of inclusion in the organization, as well as compared across various demographic categories.

Elements of Inclusive Behavior

Inclusive behavior can be operationalized in a variety of ways, in part depending on who we are talking about. For example, there are behaviors that most people can practice in a range of situations as a way to build inclusion for themselves and others. There are additional behaviors that may be suited for particular settings; for example, in a work group. And there are behaviors that are associated with particular roles, especially that of leaders. Descriptions of inclusive behavior are particularly important because they can provide people with suggestions about what they can specifically do to foster inclusion.

Marjane Jensen (1995) was an early pioneer in explicitly listing behaviors for inclusion. Her list, later developed and expanded by Katz and Miller (2011), highlighted the importance of the following types of behavior for creating inclusion:

- Authentically greeting other people
- Fostering a feeling of safety
- Listening and understanding
- Communicating clearly and honestly
- Working through and learning from conflicts
- Seeking and listening to multiple voices and perspectives
- Noticing when exclusion occurs and intervening to address it
- Being intentional about individual and collective choices when working in groups
- Being courageous

In an application of this approach, The Hartford Financial Services Group (The Hartford, 2006) highlighted and stressed the following elements of inclusive behavior to its employees:

- Listen to all individuals until they feel understood
- Accept others' references as true for them
- Be honest and clear
- Build on each other's ideas and thoughts
- Take risks
- Speak up for oneself

Pless and Maak (2004) listed the following as key inclusive behaviors, based on a set of inclusion competencies:

- Showing respect and empathy;
- Recognizing the other as different but equal;
- Showing appreciation for different voices, e.g. by
  - Listening actively to them;
  - Trying to understand disparate viewpoints and opinions;

– Integrating different voices into the ongoing cultural discourse.
• Practising and encouraging open and frank communication in all interactions;
• Cultivating participative decision making and problem solving processes and team capabilities;
• Showing integrity and advanced moral reasoning, especially when dealing with ethical dilemmas;
• Using a cooperative/consultative leadership style [p. 140]

In the work to create a workgroup inclusion measure described earlier (Ferdman, Barrera, et al., 2009), we also developed an operationalization of inclusive behavior, based on the following categories:

• Creating safety
• Acknowledging others
• Dealing with conflict and differences
• Showing an ability and willingness to learn
• Having and giving voice
• Encouraging representation

Creating safety involves having and using clear ground rules for respectful behavior, avoiding belittling others, and speaking up about issues that matter to people and the organization. Acknowledging others involves not only greeting people but also recognizing contributions and asking for input, in a manner that also connects to coworkers in personal and human ways. Dealing with conflict means being able and willing to address it as it arises, developing skills for effectively working through and learning from conflict, and developing cultural competence for working with those who may think and behave quite differently. Being able and willing to learn includes such behaviors as asking for and providing feedback, sharing information, and using multiple perspectives to arrive at collaborative solutions. Voice-related behaviors involve speaking up and making one's full contributions to the group and organization, and providing opportunities for others to do so, as well as showing others that their contributions are valued; research by Major, Davis, Sanchez-Hucles, Germano, and Mann (2005) indicates that this can be done through both affective support, such as listening and being sympathetic, and instrumental support, such as helping with work responsibilities or switching schedules. Finally, encouraging representation means taking proactive steps to ensure that multiple voices and people of different identity groups and perspectives are present and involved. This last category includes many of the behaviors highlighted in traditional diversity initiatives that focus on making sure that groups and organizations actually incorporate diversity along multiple dimensions and across functions and hierarchical levels.

In working to develop a global inclusion survey with the company mentioned earlier, I used a similar perspective on inclusive behavior, but first I generated an overarching list of inclusion elements, which could then be translated into assessment items focused on specific groups. For example, participants rated their own inclusive behavior, that of members of their work group, that of their supervisors, and that of company leaders. The broad elements that we incorporated were collaboration/interdependence (feeling valued), fair and unbiased treatment, leadership and accountability, open communication, support, authenticity, trust, and work-life balance. We then ensured that there were items measuring the various elements for the different groups. Ratings of inclusive behavior could then be computed for the various groups (that is, self-ratings, work group ratings, supervisor ratings, and so on) as well as for each of the elements.

Finally, I turn to the work of the Institute for Inclusion (Ferdman, Katz, et al., 2009) introduced earlier. In that process, as mentioned, we generated two lists of inclusive behavior, one for everyone and one for leaders. The behaviors for everyone are those that anyone can practice to foster inclusion. Behaviors for leaders are complementary to those in the first list and are particularly geared for individuals holding positions of authority. The two lists are summarized in Table 1.3 (together with organizational policies and practices, which I discuss next).

Table 1.3. Inclusive Behaviors for Everyone and for Leaders; Inclusive Organizational Policies and Practices

Inclusive Behavior for Everyone

Acknowledge, connect, and engage with others.

Listen deeply and carefully.

Engage a broad range of perspectives.

Openly share information and seek transparency.

Be curious.

Lean into discomfort.

Increase self-awareness.

Be willing to learn and be influenced by others.

Be respectful and demonstrate fairness.

Foster interdependence and teamwork.

Inclusive Behavior for Leaders

Hold oneself and others accountable for creating an inclusive culture.

Invite engagement and dialogue.

Model bringing one's whole self to work, and give permission for and encourage others to do so.

Foster transparent decision making.

Understand and engage with resistance.

Understand and talk about how inclusion connects to the mission and vision.

Inclusive Organizational Policies and Practices

Create an environment of respect, fairness, justice, and equity.

Create a framework for assessing and implementing organizational policies and practices.

Build systems, processes, and procedures that support and sustain inclusion.

Enhance individual and collective competence to collaborate across cultures and groups.

Define organizational social responsibility (internally and externally).

Foster transparency throughout the organization.

Promote teamwork.

Create a diverse organization.

Foster continual learning and growth.

Source: Adapted from Ferdman, Katz, Letchinger, and Thompson, 2009.

Elements of Inclusion at the Organizational Level

At the organizational level, there are many practices organizations can adopt to create, foster, and sustain inclusion. Table 1.3 includes a broad list of these, generated by Ferdman, Katz, et al. (2009) using the process described earlier. Other detailed examples can be found in Holvino et al. (2004) and in various chapters in this volume, so I do not repeat those here. The key is for the organization to have a clear approach to inclusion and that this approach be translated into specific strategies, policies, and practices that can be observed and assessed. These practices should not only build inclusion systemically but also encourage leaders and all members of the organization to practice inclusion in their individual and collective behavior, both to support the overall culture of inclusion as well as to ensure that as many people as possible regularly experience inclusion.

One way to do this is to decide on the key dimensions of inclusion for the organization and how these can be addressed for each of the key dimensions, functions, or systems of the organization. In Figure 1.3, I present an Inclusion Assessment Matrix that my students and I (Ferdman, Brody, Cooper, Jeffcoat, & Le, 1995) developed almost two decades ago and that continues to be quite relevant. Across the top row we list the various systems of the organization, and down the left side we list the various dimensions of inclusion we identified at the time. For each of these dimensions of inclusion, we created illustrative general assessment questions or topics, which are also included in the figure.

Once the dimensions of inclusion are identified and defined, then they can be operationalized for the organization as a whole and for each of the relevant systems or functions of the organization.

Facing the Challenges and Paradoxes of the Practice of Inclusion

This chapter has covered much ground, and the book's other chapters provide a great deal of additional texture and rich perspectives and detail for the practice of inclusion. I conclude by

Figure 1.3. Organizational-Level Inclusion Assessment Matrix

Dimensions of Inclusion	Dimensions of the Organization									
	Socialization	Career planning	Recruitment, selection, promotion	Training and education	Performance appraisal	Reward systems	Work/life policies and practices	Communication	Measurement	Structural and informal integration
Openness	Openness: How much are variability, complexity, and ambiguity embraced? To what extent are the system and its boundaries open rather than hard? How acceptable is rigidity? Are there multiple solutions and many best ways? Is there a broad bandwidth of acceptance?									
Representation and voice	Representation/Voice: To what extent are differences, both apparent and not, attended to and represented across situations? Is there a critical mass of diverse members, with a mix of dimensions represented, in making decisions and benefiting from them?									
Climate	Climate: How valued do individuals and groups feel? Are they fully present, free to express themselves, accepted and integrated? How does it feel to be in the organization?									
Fairness	Fairness: To what extent do individuals and groups receive what they need and deserve? How much and in what ways is fairness considered? Are there mechanisms for resolving or addressing fairness? To what extent and in what ways has oppression and its effects (such as unearned privilege) been eliminated or reduced?									
Leadership and commitment	Leadership/Commitment: To what degree and in what ways are the strategies, vision, and mission of the organization connected to inclusion? How are resources allocated? How well do leaders model inclusion? How accountable and committed is leadership? How strategically is inclusion positioned and addressed? How central is inclusion to the core values and strategy of organization?									
Continuous improvement	Continuous Improvement: What is the capacity, ability, and mindset regarding necessary and possible improvement? How much and in what ways are employees empowered to be responsible for continuous improvement? What is the capacity to take advantage of all resources?									
Social responsibility	Social Responsibility: How much awareness is there of the world outside the organization? What is the vision of the organization as a member of a larger community? What kinds of contributions (such as time and resources) are made to societal needs?									

Source: Adapted from Ferdman, Brody, Cooper, Jeffcoat, and Le, 1995, *Inclusion Assessment Matrix,* unpublished document, California School of Professional Psychology, San Diego, CA.

WK	DATE	TOPICS	ASSIGNMENTS
8	Apr 12	Multicultural & international OD	Group case analysis outlines, due 10 am Group case analysis presentations READINGS: 1. Cummings & Worley, Chapter 17 2. Ferdman, B. M. (2014). Toward infusing diversity and inclusion as core elements of OD. *OD Practitioner, 46* (4), 44-46. 3. Holvino, E. (2014). Developing multicultural organizations: An application of the multicultural OD model. In B. B. Jones, B. B. & M. Brazzel (Eds.), *The NTL handbook of organization development and change: Principles, practices, and perspectives* (2nd ed., pp. 517-534). San Francisco: Wiley. 4. Litwin, A. H. (2014). Global OD practice: The legacy of colonialism and oppression. In B. B. Jones, B. B. & M. Brazzel (Eds.), *The NTL handbook of organization development and change: Principles, practices, and perspectives* (2nd ed., pp. 483-497). San Francisco: Wiley. 5. Johnson, H. H. (2013). A case of too much diversity? In H. H. Johnson, P. F. Sorensen, & T. F. Yaeger (Eds.), *Critical issues in organization development: Case studies for analysis and discussion* (pp. 251-260). Charlotte, NC: Information Age Publishing. 6. Yaeger, T. F. & Sorensen, P. F. (2013). Organization development's role when going global. In In H. H. Johnson, P. F. Sorensen, & T. F. Yaeger (Eds.), *Critical issues in organization development: Case studies for analysis and discussion* (pp. 283-292). Charlotte, NC: Information Age Publishing. OPTIONAL 7. Jackson, B. W. (2014). Theory and practice of multicultural organization development. In B. B. Jones, B. B. & M. Brazzel (Eds.), *The NTL handbook of organization development and change: Principles, practices, and perspectives* (2nd ed., pp. 175-192). San Francisco: Wiley. 8. Katz, J. H. & Miller, F. A. (2016). Leveraging diversity and inclusion for performance. In W. J. Rothwell, J. M. Stavros, & R. L. Sullivan (Eds.), *Practicing organization development: Leading transformation and change* (4th ed., pp. 366-375). Hoboken, NJ: Wiley. 9. Church, A. H., Rotolo, C. T., Shull, A. C., & Tuller, M. D. (2014). Inclusive organization development: An integration of two disciplines. In B. M. Ferdman & B. R. Deane (Eds.), *Diversity at work: The practice of inclusion* (pp. 260-295). San Francisco, CA: Jossey-Bass. 10. O'Mara, J. (2014). Global benchmarks for diversity and inclusion. In B. M. Ferdman & B. R. Deane (Eds.), *Diversity at work: The practice of inclusion* (pp. 415-430). San Francisco, CA: Jossey-Bass. 11. O'Mara, J., Richter, A., & 95 Expert Panelists (2016). Global diversity and inclusion benchmarks: Standards for organizations around the world. Available at 12. Jonsen, K., & Ozbilgin, M. (2014). Models of global diversity management. In B. M. Ferdman & B. R. Deane (Eds.), *Diversity at work: The practice of inclusion* (pp. 364-390). San Francisco, CA: Jossey-Bass.

9/10/07

Is inclusion still in the hands of those in power? PUB+ NC

What happens outside the organization?

Power Dynamics of Inclusion

very briefly discussing a few of the challenges of inclusion. Overall, the practice of inclusion involves being able to acknowledge, recognize, value, and work with diversity, in ways that benefit individuals, groups, organizations, and society, at multiple levels and across multiple identities. As discussed throughout this chapter, to do this well, we need to understand and engage with a good deal of complexity, while also making sure to address the essential and basic aspects of our common humanity and our needs for connection, consideration, respect, appreciation, and participation. Many of the challenges of inclusion involve attending to and engaging with seeming polarities or paradoxes, in the process of creating connections and practices that can work for everyone and allow everyone to work to their full potential. They also involve being willing to reexamine and test assumptions and to join with others with different perspectives and contributions so as to together weave an emergent and textured reality that none of us could have created or anticipated alone.

- **The practice of inclusion is about** *both* **everyday behavior** *and* **organizational and social systems.** The practice of inclusion addresses both micro *and* macro levels (and everything in between). Inclusion must occur in terms of individual experience and everyday interpersonal behavior, and also in terms of intergroup relations and patterns of experience at the level of complex organizational and societal systems. We need to make sure that inclusion is experienced not just by those who are most similar or most near to us, but also those who are different on key dimensions or who are not part of our proximal social system, such as those in other organizations, communities, and societies. Individual experience and interpersonal behavior, in the moment, are critical to inclusion, but so are addressing and redressing embedded and persistent systems of intergroup injustice and oppression (and the relationships among the two) in organizations and society.
- **The practice of inclusion is about** *both* **structures** *and* **processes**. To address inclusion, we need a dynamic perspective that attends to multiple processes over time. Inclusion is about patterns of behavior and experience in the context of relationships between individuals, between people and their

groups and organizations, and between groups. At the same time, the structures within which these dynamic relationships are created, enacted, interpreted, reproduced, and developed are also critical. Who is where in what parts of the system? What is the distribution of power? How is work organized? The answers to these and many similar questions are important for understanding the processual aspects of the practice of inclusion. How we treat each other, how we communicate, how we engage with others are all critical to inclusion as well, and over time can help change the structures within which these patterns occur. Indeed, the relationship between structure and process is perhaps much like that between a flowing river and its banks: the banks of the river certainly channel and shape where and how the river flows; yet, simultaneously, the flowing waters slowly and surely shape and change the river's seemingly solid and stationary banks.

○ **The practice of inclusion is about *both* comfort *and* discomfort**. In many ways, inclusion involves creating more comfort for more people, so that access, opportunity, and a sense of full participation and belonging are facilitated across a greater range of diversity than ever before, for the benefit of all. At the same time, practicing inclusion means distributing discomfort more equitably. Frederick Miller (1994) provocatively and creatively described it this way: "*Inclusion* turns *comfortable* upside out and inside down" (p. 39, italics in original). We need to move out of our individual and collective comfort zones, yet do so in a way that leads to growth, learning, and mutual and collective benefit.

Let me explain: It is not very difficult to behave inclusively with people with whom we are familiar or who are most like ourselves. Historically, however, this has happened in the context of exclusive organizations and groups. For example, once college students are able to get through the hazing typically imposed to be invited to join a fraternity or sorority, they can feel very much a part of the group. The problem is that inclusion of that type typically comes at a price: to experience inclusion, members of selective and therefore exclusive organizations or groups must assimilate to the dominant norms, styles, and practices, and subsume the ways in which they are different from the accepted or dominant ways of doing things. This means that those from less represented, less familiar, or less dominant groups and backgrounds will typically be more uncomfortable and less at ease than their colleagues.

In diverse groups, organizations, and societies, inclusion becomes both more important and more challenging and uncomfortable, because the key is to expand the experience of inclusion while maintaining and enhancing diversity. Essentially, the practice of inclusion requires becoming more comfortable with discomfort, both individually and collectively. More of us must be willing to take on the discomfort of being less than fully secure as we engage with each other to create inclusion. We must be willing to learn continuously and recognize that the practice of inclusion is never done; it requires ongoing alertness and engagement. As we notice and work across more and more types of diversity, this stance will be even more critical.

○ **The practice of inclusion is about *both* deriving practical benefits *and* about doing what is right and just.** Certainly, a key motivation for practicing inclusion is based on the premise that it will lead to tangible benefits for individuals, groups, organization, and societies. This assumption has begun to receive empirical support and is also based on existing and emergent theories and practical experience. At the same time, the practice of inclusion will be enhanced (and perhaps even greater benefits will be derived), if we simultaneously acknowledge that it is simply right, just, and moral.

Facing the challenges and paradoxes of the practice of inclusion will require ongoing learning and contributions from multiple perspectives and disciplines. It is an evolutionary journey and it will be very exciting to see how the emergent framework described here develops and changes as others add their voices and views to our collective understanding and practice.

Acknowledgments

I am greatly indebted to Barbara R. Deane and Sergio Valenzuela-Ibarra for very helpful comments on earlier versions of this chapter and for their support throughout the process of writing it. Barbara R. Deane in particular provided invaluable editorial advice, without which this would have been a much poorer chapter. Sergio, as well as Liz Barat, Sarah Maxwell, and Maggie Sass, provided valuable and much-appreciated research assistance at various points. I would also like to express my great appreciation to Derek Avery, Liz Barat, Victoria Barrera, Stacey Blake-Beard, Donna Blancero, Lize Booysen, Christine Boulware, Sari Brody, Catherine Buntaine, Chin-Chun Chen, Donna Chrobot-Mason, Dennis DaRos, Martin Davidson, Nancy DiTomaso, Angel Enriquez, Darcy Hanashiro, David Hayes-Bautista, Plácida Gallegos, Jeremy Hirshberg, Evangelina Holvino, C. Douglas Johnson, Judith Katz, Jennifer Habig, James A. Kimbrough, Ed Letchinger, Patrick McKay, Fred Miller, Michàlle Mor Barak, Stella Nkomo, Lisa Nishii, Kopitzee Parra-Thornton, Laura Morgan Roberts, Andrea Szulik, Kecia Thomas, Terrill Thompson, Cláudio Torres, Ilene Wasserman, Heather Wishik, and the late Marjane Jensen, as well as to my many other students, research collaborators, teachers, and consulting colleagues over the years, with whom I have had many conversations and from whom I've learned so much about inclusion. The many participants in my workshops have also been instrumental in teaching me about inclusion over the years, and I am very grateful to them for all they have shared.

References

Australian Social Inclusion Board. (2012). *Social inclusion in Australia: How Australia is faring* (2nd ed.). Canberra, Australia: Commonwealth of Australia. Retrieved from www.socialinclusion.gov.au

Atkinson, A. B., & Marlier, E. (2010). *Analysing and measuring social inclusion in a global context.* New York: United Nations Department of Economic and Social Affairs.

Baumeister, R. F., & Leary, M. R. (1995). The need to belong: Desire for interpersonal attachments as a fundamental human motivation. *Psychological Bulletin, 117*(3), 497–529.

Bossaert, G., Colpin, H., Pijl, S. J., & Petry, K. (2013). Truly included? A literature study focusing on the social dimension of inclusion in education. *International Journal of Inclusive Education, 17*(1), 60–79. doi:10.1080/13603116.2011.580464

Boushey, H., Fremstad, S., Gragg, R., & Waller, M. (2010, August). *Social inclusion for the United States*. Working Paper, Center for Economic Policy and Research, Washington, D.C. Retrieved from www .inclusionist.org.

Brewer, M. B. (1991). The social self: On being the same and different at the same time. *Personality and Social Psychology Bulletin, 17*(5), 475–482. doi:10.1177/0146167291175001

Chrobot-Mason, D., Ruderman, M. N., & Nishii, L. H. (2013). Leadership in a diverse workplace. In Q. M. Roberson (Ed.), *The Oxford handbook of diversity and work* (pp. 315–340). New York, NY: Oxford University Press.

Cox, T. H., Jr. (1991). The multicultural organization. *Academy of Management Executive, 5*(2), 34–47.

Cox, T. H., Jr., & Blake, S. (1991). Managing cultural diversity: Implications for organizational competitiveness. *Academy of Management Executive, 5*(3), 45–56.

Davidson, M. N. (1999). The value of being included: An examination of diversity change initiatives in organizations. *Performance Improvement Quarterly, 12*(1), 164–180.

Davidson, M. N. (2011). *The end of diversity as we know it: Why diversity efforts fail and how leveraging difference can succeed*. San Francisco: Berrett-Koehler.

Davidson, M. N., & Ferdman, B. M. (2002). The experience of inclusion. In B. Parker, B. M. Ferdman, & P. Dass (Chairs), *Inclusive and effective networks: Linking diversity theory and practice*. All-Academy symposium presented at the 62nd Annual Meeting of the Academy of Management, Denver.

Ely, R. J., & Thomas, D. A. (2001). Cultural diversity at work: The effects of diversity perspectives on work group processes and outcomes. *Administrative Science Quarterly, 46*(2), 229–273. doi:10.2307/2667087

Ferdman, B. M. (1992). The dynamics of ethnic diversity in organizations: Toward integrative models. In K. Kelley (Ed.), *Issues, theory and research in industrial/organizational psychology* (pp. 339–384). Amsterdam: North Holland.

Ferdman, B. M. (1995). Cultural identity and diversity in organizations: Bridging the gap between group differences and individual uniqueness. In M. M. Chemers, S. Oskamp, & M. A. Costanzo (Eds.), *Diversity in organizations: New perspectives for a changing workplace* (pp. 37–61). Thousand Oaks, CA: Sage.

Ferdman, B. M. (2010). Teaching inclusion by example and experience: Creating an inclusive learning environment. In K. M. Hannum,

L. Booysen, & B. B. McFeeters (Eds.), *Leading across differences: Cases and perspectives—Facilitator's guide* (pp. 37–50). San Francisco: Pfeiffer.

Ferdman, B. M. (2011). The inclusive workplace. In G. N. Powell, *Managing a diverse workforce: Learning activities* (3rd. ed., pp. 123–127). Thousand Oaks, CA: Sage.

Ferdman, B. M., Avigdor, A., Braun, D., Konkin, J., & Kuzmycz, D. (2010). Collective experience of inclusion, diversity, and performance in work groups. *Revista de Adminstraçao Mackenzie, 11*(3), 6–26. doi:10.1590/S1678–69712010000300003

Ferdman, B. M., Barrera, V., Allen, A., & Vuong, V. (2009, August). Inclusive behaviors and the experience of inclusion. In B. G. Chung (Chair), *Inclusion in organizations: Measures, HR practices, and climate.* Symposium presented at the 69th Annual Meeting of the Academy of Management, Chicago.

Ferdman, B. M., & Brody, S. E. (1996). Models of diversity training. In D. Landis & R. S. Bhagat (Eds.), *Handbook of intercultural training* (2nd ed., pp. 282–303). Thousand Oaks, CA: Sage.

Ferdman, B. M., Brody, S. E., Cooper, K. J., Jeffcoat, K. A., & Le, S. (1995). *Inclusion assessment matrix.* Unpublished document, California School of Professional Psychology, San Diego, CA.

Ferdman, B. M., & Davidson, M. N. (2002a). A matter of difference— Diversity and drawing the line: Are some differences too different? (Or: who's in, who's out, and what difference does it make?). *The Industrial-Organizational Psychologist, 39*(3), 43–46.

Ferdman, B. M., & Davidson, M. N. (2002b). A matter of difference— Inclusion: What can I and my organization do about it? *The Industrial-Organizational Psychologist, 39*(4), 80–85.

Ferdman, B. M., & Davidson, M. N. (2004). A matter of difference— Some learning about inclusion: Continuing the dialogue. *The Industrial-Organizational Psychologist, 41*(4), 31–37.

Ferdman, B. M., & Gallegos, P. I. (2001). Racial identity development and Latinos in the United States. In C. L. Wijeyesinghe & B. W. Jackson III (Eds.), *New perspectives on racial identity development: A theoretical and practical anthology* (pp. 32–66). New York: New York University Press.

Ferdman, B. M., Katz, J. H., Letchinger, E., & Thompson, C. (2009, March 9). *Inclusive behaviors and practices: Report of the Institute for Inclusion Behavior Task Force.* Presentation at the Institute for Inclusion 4th Conference, Arlington, VA.

Ferdman, B. M., & Sagiv, L. (2012). Diversity in organizations and cross-cultural work psychology: What if they were more connected?

Industrial and Organizational Psychology: Perspectives on Science and Practice, 5, 323–345. doi:10.1111/j.1754–9434.2012.01455.x

Future Work Institute (n.d.). *Inclusion: A journey in progress* (Hot Topics Research). Retrieved from http://www.futureworkinstitute.com.

Gasorek, D. (2000). Inclusion at Dun & Bradstreet: Building a high-performing company. *The Diversity Factor, 8*(4), 25–29.

The Hartford. (2006). *Diversity and inclusion.* Web page at www.thehartford.com, retrieved February 25, 2006.

Hayes, B. C., & Major, D. A. (2003, April). *Creating inclusive organizations: Its meaning and measurement.* Paper presented at the 18th Annual Conference of the Society for Industrial and Organizational Psychology, Orlando, FL.

Hays-Thomas, R., & Bendick Jr., M. (2013). Professionalizing diversity and inclusion practice: Should voluntary standards be the chicken or the egg? *Industrial and Organizational Psychology: Perspectives on Science and Practice, 6*(3), 193–205. doi: 10.111/iops.12033

Hick, P., & Thomas, G. (Eds.). (2008). *Inclusion and diversity in education.* Thousand Oaks, CA: Sage.

Hirshberg, J. J., & Ferdman, B. M. (2011, August 16). Leader-member exchange, cooperative group norms, and workplace inclusion in workgroups. In M. Shuffler, S. Burke, & D. Diaz-Granados (Chairs), *Leading across cultures: Emerging research trends from multiple levels.* Symposium presented at the 71st Annual Meeting of the Academy of Management, San Antonio, TX.

Holvino, E. (1998). *The multicultural organizational development model.* Unpublished training materials, Chaos Management, Brattleboro, VT.

Holvino, E., Ferdman, B. M., & Merrill-Sands, D. (2004). Creating and sustaining diversity and inclusion in organizations: Strategies and approaches. In M. S. Stockdale & F. J. Crosby (Eds.), *The psychology and management of workplace diversity* (pp. 245–276). Malden, MA: Blackwell.

Horwitz, S. K., & Horwitz, I. B. (2007). The effects of team diversity on team outcomes: A meta-analytic review of team demography. *Journal of Management, 33*(6), 987–1015. doi:10.1177/0149206307308587

Hubbard, A. (2004). The major life activity of belonging. *Wake Forest Law Review, 39*, 217–259.

Jackson, B. W. (1994). Coming to a vision of a multicultural system. In E. Y. Cross, J. H. Katz, F. A. Miller, & E. W. Seashore (Eds.), *The promise of diversity: Over 40 voices discuss strategies for eliminating discrimination in organizations* (pp. 116–117). Burr Ridge, IL: Irwin:

Jackson, S. E., & Joshi, A. (2011). Work team diversity. In S. Zedeck (Ed.), *APA handbook of industrial and organizational psychology* (Vol. 1, pp. 651–686). Washington, DC: American Psychological Association.

Jensen, M. (1995). *Eleven behaviors for inclusion.* Unpublished document. The Kaleel Jamison Consulting Group, Inc., Troy, NY.

Katz, J. H., & Miller, F. A. (1996). Coaching leaders through culture change. *Consulting Psychology Journal: Practice and Research, 48*(2), 104–114. doi:10.1037//1061-4087.48.2.104

Katz, J. H., & Miller, F. A. (2011). *12 behaviors for inclusion.* The Kaleel Jamison Consulting Group, Troy, NY. Downloaded from www.kjcg .com.

Kochan, T., Bezrukova, K., Ely, R., Jackson, S., Joshi, A., Jehn, K., . . . Thomas, D. A. (2003). The effects of diversity on business performance: Report of the diversity research network. *Human Resource Management, 42*(1), 3–21. doi:10.1002/hrm.10061

Kossek, E., & Zonia, S. (1993). Assessing diversity climate: A field study of reactions to employer efforts to promote diversity. *Journal of Organizational Behavior, 14,* 61–81.

Levine, J. M., & Kerr, N. L. (2007). Inclusion and exclusion: Implications for group processes. In A. W. Kruglanski & E. T. Higgins (Eds.), *Social psychology: Handbook of basic principles* (2nd ed., pp. 759–784). New York: Guilford Press.

Major, D. A., Davis, D. D., Sanchez-Hucles, J., Germano, L. M., & Mann, J. (2005). *IT workplace climate for opportunity and inclusion.* Paper presented at the 65th Annual Meeting of the Academy of Management, Honolulu.

Mannix, E., & Neale, M. A. (2005). What differences make a difference? The promise and reality of diverse teams in organizations. *Psychological Science in the Public Interest, 6*(2), 31–55.

Miller, F. A. (1994). Forks in the road: Critical issues on the path to diversity. In E. Y. Cross, J. H. Katz, F. A. Miller, & E. W. Seashore (Eds.), *The promise of diversity: Over 40 voices discuss strategies for eliminating discrimination in organizations* (pp. 38–45). Burr Ridge, IL: Irwin.

Miller, F. A., & Katz, J. H. (1995). Cultural diversity as a developmental process: The path from monocultural club to inclusive organization. In J. W. Pfeiffer (Ed.), *The 1995 Annual* (Vol. 2, Consulting, pp. 267–281). San Diego, CA: Pfeiffer.

Miller, F. A., & Katz, J. H. (2002). *The inclusion breakthrough: Unleashing the real power of diversity.* San Francisco: Berrett-Koehler.

Miller, F. A., & Katz, J. H. (2007). *The path from exclusive club to inclusive organization: A developmental process.* Retrieved from http://blogs .ces.uwex.edu/inclusiveexcellence/files/2011/11/Path-from-Exclusive-Club-to-Inclusive-Organization-Article.pdf.

Mor Barak, M. E. (2000a). Beyond affirmative action: Toward a model of diversity and organizational inclusion. *Administration in Social Work, 23*(3/4), 47–68.

Mor Barak, M. E. (2000b). The inclusive workplace: An ecosystems approach to diversity management. *Social Work, 45*(4), 339–352.

Mor Barak, M. E. (2011). *Managing diversity: Toward a globally inclusive workplace* (2nd ed.). Thousand Oaks, CA: Sage.

Mor Barak, M. E., & Cherin, D. A. (1998). A tool to expand organizational understanding of workforce diversity: Exploring a measure of inclusion-exclusion. *Administration in Social Work, 22*(1), 47–64.

Nembhard, I. M., & Edmondson, A. C. (2006). Making it safe: The effects of leader inclusiveness and professional status on psychological safety and improvement efforts in health care teams. *Journal of Organizational Behavior, 27*, 941–966. doi:10.1002/job .413.

Nishii, L. H., & Mayer, D. M. (2009). Do inclusive leaders help to reduce turnover in diverse groups? The moderating role of leader-member exchange in the diversity to turnover relationship. *Journal of Applied Psychology, 94*(6), 1412–1426. doi:10.1037/a0017190

Page, S. E. (2007). Making the difference: Applying a logic of diversity. *Academy of Management Perspectives, 21*(4), 6–20.

Pearce, J. L., & Randel, A. E. (2004). Expectations of organizational mobility, workplace social inclusion, and employee job performance. *Journal of Organizational Behavior, 25*(1), 81–98. doi:10.1002/ job.232

Pelled, L. H., Ledford, G. E., Jr., & Mohrman, S. A. (1999). Demographic dissimilarity and workplace inclusion. *Journal of Management Studies, 36*(7), 1013–1031.

Pless, N. M., & Maak, T. (2004). Building an inclusive diversity culture: Principles, processes and practice. *Journal of Business Ethics, 54*(2), 129–147. doi:10.1007/s10551–004–9465–8

Roberson, Q. M. (2006). Disentangling the meanings of diversity and inclusion in organizations. *Group and Organization Management, 31*(2), 212–236. doi: 10.1177/1059601104273064

Schutz, W. C. (1958). *FIRO: A three dimensional theory of interpersonal behavior.* New York: Holt, Rinehart & Winston.

Shore, L. M., Randel, A. E., Chung, B. G., Dean, M. A., Ehrhart, K. H., & Singh, G. (2011). Inclusion and diversity in work groups: A review and model for future research. *Journal of Management, 37*(4), 1262–1289. doi:10.1177/0149206310385943

Stahl, G. K., Mäkelä, K., Zander, L., & Maznevski, M. L. (2010). A look at the bright side of multicultural team diversity. *Scandinavian Journal of Management, 26,* 439–447.

Stamper, C. L., & Masterson, S. S. (2002). Insider or outsider? how employee perceptions of insider status affect their work behavior. *Journal of Organizational Behavior, 23*(8), 875–894. doi:10.1002/job.175

Thomas, D. A., & Ely, R. (1996). Making differences matter: A new paradigm for managing diversity. *Harvard Business Review, 74*(5), 79–90.

Thomas, R. R., Jr. (1990). From affirmative action to affirming diversity. *Harvard Business Review, 68*(2), 107–117.

UNESCO. (2005). *Guidelines for inclusion: Ensuring access to education for all.* Paris, France: United Nations Educational, Scientific and Cultural Organization.

van Knippenberg, D., & Schippers, M. C. (2007). Work group diversity. *Annual Review of Psychology, 58,* 515–541. doi:10.1146/annurev.psych.58.110405.085546

Wasserman, I. C., Gallegos, P. V., & Ferdman, B. M. (2008). Dancing with resistance: Leadership challenges in fostering a culture of inclusion. In K. M. Thomas (Ed.), *Diversity resistance in organizations* (pp. 175–200). Mahwah, NJ: Erlbaum.

CHAPTER TWO

Communicating About Diversity and Inclusion

V. Robert Hayles

Communicating about diversity and inclusion so that organizational members are inspired and engaged is challenging. Yet, like all successful initiatives, diversity and inclusion efforts gain more credibility and support when the communication strategy and tactics are well-crafted.

This chapter will help diversity and inclusion practitioners, human resource professionals, and leaders communicate in ways that affirm diversity, facilitate inclusion, and improve individual and organizational outcomes. The approach involves cognitive, affective, and behavioral (head, heart, and hand) components of communication and is grounded on current knowledge and practice in organization development. The materials describe how we can best communicate with the broadest possible audiences to nurture inclusion. My instrumental goal is to enhance the work of practitioners and researchers focused on inclusion. The ultimate goal is that they achieve better results.

My perspective comes from doing and managing research and working internally and externally as a practitioner. I weave these experiences together to help practitioners and researchers understand each other and advance their work. I hope to show the results of practitioners dancing well with researchers.

The Work

Other authors in this book present definitions of diversity and inclusion. In this chapter, diversity is taken to mean a mixture of "differences, similarities, and related tensions," as defined by Thomas (2004, p. 3). Inclusion is taken to signify the full participation of all relevant elements in that mixture. Although this chapter focuses primarily on inclusion, related practices like those promoting equal opportunity, affirmative action, equity, anti-bias, and diversity all contribute to progress on inclusion. No single approach is superior to another; the choice must be guided by the situation. Because inclusion is the least well-developed of these practices and the focus of this book, it gets more attention here. I refer to "the work" when indicating the preceding full constellation of practices.

Research and Practice-Based Models

In writing this chapter, I was motivated by a strong desire to see that what we have learned during the past several decades is implemented to get the best results. Much of what we know has been summarized in research- and practice-based models and approaches that focus on individual and organization development and change. Such research and practice together provide the basis for powerful tools that move organizations through predictable stages of development as they traverse the past, current, and desired future states. In the process of unfreezing, changing, and freezing described by Lewin (1947), individuals and organizations adapt in some predictable ways. Here I take a comprehensive approach that addresses cognition, affect, and behavior, more clearly expressed as head, heart, and hand. The goal of this chapter is to make communicating about the work more powerful by selectively drawing on the current knowledge base.

Structure of This Chapter

First, I briefly address why the facts are not adequate to persuade audiences to pursue inclusion. Second, I describe support for designing communication about this topic based on individual stages of development. Third, I address techniques that reduce bias and prejudice. Fourth, I provide communication approaches and content for advancing inclusion at different organizational stages of development. Finally, I give examples and information and point to resources regarding how to communicate in ways that are oriented to facts, feelings, and behavior, respectively.

Why Fact-Based Communication Is Not Enough

If one takes a purely cognitive approach to diversity and inclusion by defining terms and stating the desired outcomes, then fact-based communication should work. However, people and organizations are not driven by facts alone. Emotions also cause behavior. Therefore, a "just the facts" approach is insufficient. Some authors, such as Kochan et al. (2003), argue that diversity can have strong negative effects on performance. Others (such as Carfang, 1993; Corporate Leadership Council, 2003; Florida, 2005; Johansson, 2006; Ziller, 1972) argue for positive effects on performance. The most concise critique of such writings is to say that of course diversity alone does not cause better or worse outcomes. I strongly agree with researchers and practitioners like Ferdman, Barrera, Allen, and Vuong (2009; see also Ferdman, Avigdor, Braun, Konkin, & Kuzmycz, 2010) who make a compelling argument that inclusion facilitates a positive relationship between diversity and performance.

Diversity with inclusion can lead to better outcomes. I provide support for that belief throughout this chapter. Although I include a sample of data and studies regarding potential positive impacts, facts, even when true, are insufficient to motivate appropriate behavior. For example, we know that smoking, poor nutrition, inadequate hydration, skipping vacations, and being sedentary all have proven negative consequences. Even so, most of us do not always or even frequently behave in ways that reflect this knowledge. The same is true for advocating inclusion. Hearing about, believing in, or even knowing the benefits of diversity and inclusion do not consistently lead to supportive actions. Think of all the times a strong rationale for an initiative has been presented in your organization, followed by inaction. Positive actions and healthy outcomes require comprehensive and systemic approaches. How we communicate about diversity and inclusion is an influential element of this overall process.

The following section explains how to shape communication based on what we know about individual development.

Communication Based on Individual Development

To communicate effectively (that is, to influence attitudes and behaviors) with an individual it is useful to know where that person is situated according to several models of development. Some intercultural researchers and practitioners (such as M. J. Bennett, 1998) believe that human beings, as they grow and develop, move through predictable stages regarding how they deal with cultural diversity. Generally, when work that is characteristic of a given stage is completed, the individual then moves to the next stage. Regression occurs when work remains incomplete or life circumstances bring too much challenge. Understanding the concept of developmental stages allows professionals to choose the most effective messages for each person and situation. Skillfully selected messages facilitate continued growth toward the next stage.

Following, I briefly discuss models, concepts, and approaches to guide message selection. They are first: (1) identity models; (2) head, heart, hand; (3) unconscious competence; and (4) intercultural sensitivity. This group is followed by a set of additional approaches for reducing individual bias and prejudice: (5) contact hypothesis; (6) cognitive complexity; (7) cultural assimilator; (8) defeating bias; (9) psychotherapy; (10) meditation and mindfulness; and (11) communication in education and training.

Identity Models

These models address how individual identity or identities develop. Identity can pertain to ethnicity, race (as a social identity), gender, disability, age, culture, and more. Early stages in the development of an identity typically reflect ignorance or lack of awareness. In these stages individuals are not aware of who they are, or they have a very narrow view of their own identity; this sounds like "I am just an American," or "I'm just a woman." Middle stages show engagement and conflict: "I am an independent woman yet interdependent with my family while seeking more freedom and a broader definition of my roles." Advanced stages show integration or resolution: "I have multiple identities or components of my identity and am comfortable behaving in different ways as situations change."

From a practical standpoint, this is especially useful when communicating one-on-one or with a homogeneous group, assuming the communicator is sophisticated enough to apply this knowledge. When addressing more diverse groups, the speaker must cover the full range of stages. Communication directed at receivers in the early stages should focus on acknowledging who they are and on increasing self-awareness. For example, one can affirm the identity and acknowledge the contribution from that perspective, as in, "The contribution of many women is making us very successful." In the middle stages, facilitating nonjudgmental exploration of the issues can be helpful, as in, "I'm pleased to see both men and women participate in nurturing young talent." In the later stages, it is more useful to emphasize how that person can lead and contribute, as in, "We appreciate individuals like you, who can develop people who are different from you in significant ways."

Head, Heart, and Hand

In education, training, and development the head, heart, hand concept (Hayles & Russell, 1997) is often described as addressing cognitive, affective, and behavioral components. The approaches for the three aspects are as follows:

- Head: knowledge, data, factual information
- Heart: awareness, empathy, values, emotional understanding
- Hand: interpersonal interaction and communication skills

Comprehensive communication approaches for individuals and groups must involve all three components. My experience in designing, implementing, and evaluating diversity training confirms this belief (Hayles, 1996). It is also consistent with the social psychological literature on attitude and behavior change, which suggests that effective interventions regarding any two of the components will lead to progress on the third (Hayles, 1978). For example, if you love someone (affective) and they tell you that using their middle name will cause others to discriminate against them (cognitive information), you will probably comply (behavior) with their request to avoid using their middle name. Another example would be if you are (1) forced to treat another person respectfully with regard to the words and nonverbal messages you use (behavior), and (2) informed that if you use inappropriate words your organization will be sued and you will be disciplined (cognitive information), then (3) over time you will either change how you feel about that person or be inclined to leave the environment.

This works in part because of the positive feedback loop and psychological dynamics that can be created when we choose the appropriate words. It also works by facilitating consistency (or creating tension) among head, heart, and hand. Complicated questions about effective sequencing and speed of change remain to be answered. Based on my research and practice, I currently believe that all three components should be addressed to maximize the probability of creating inclusion. Until researchers can tell us more about sequence, I suggest starting with the most available and least threatening component. In most public situations this will mean head first, hand second, and heart last.

Unconscious Competence

Many experienced diversity and inclusion practitioners say that, in learning to be inclusive, people need to go from unconscious incompetence to conscious incompetence to conscious competence to unconscious competence (Howell, 1982; Tung, 1993). This process parallels similar models used regarding results and method of achievement, challenge and support, tasks and relationships, information known to self and known to others, and so on. From a practical standpoint, this means practitioners must help learners get feedback about unknowns, learning opportunities about what they need to know, and sufficient practice with feedback to internalize the expanding competence. Diversity competence supports the individual in creating inclusion. Although the research literature is not clear on this point, I believe that diversity practitioners must consistently make this connection between diversity competencies and inclusion.

Intercultural Sensitivity

Another model that describes stages of development in this arena is Milton Bennett's (1993) Developmental Model of Intercultural Sensitivity (DMIS). An excellent resource that guides application of the model was created by Janet Bennett (2006; see also Bennett, Chapter 5, this volume). She describes exactly what can be done or said to facilitate growth with respect to this model. There is also a psychometrically sound instrument developed by Milton Bennett and Mitch Hammer (Hammer, 1999) to measure individual development using this model. Although using an instrument provides greater accuracy in determining stages of development, one can also do an excellent job in applying it by using the model to make careful behavioral observations:

- Early-stage behavior demonstrates a denial that differences exist or even hostility to such differences. Training is not an effective intervention here. Clear communication of policies and guidelines with enforcement is best. Emphasizing the many similarities we share is also beneficial.
- Middle stages show a primary focus on similarities, such as telling an immigrant that they speak English as well as any American and suggesting that we treat others as we treat ourselves. Middle stages also show acceptance of some minor differences. Here one can begin to introduce nonthreatening differences and graduate to more significant ones. Learning more about the self (for example, identity, culture, beliefs, and values) is also helpful here.
- Advanced stages reflect curiosity about others, pursuit of new experiences, and the intention to treat others as they wish to

be treated. At these stages, it is healthy to provide opportunities (such as intense personal interactions and international travel) to learn about significant differences. More details to guide application can be found in J. M. Bennett (2006) and Hayles and Russell (1997, Chapter 3).

Other Approaches for Reducing Individual Bias and Prejudice

One of the goals of the work (equal opportunity, affirmative action, anti-bias, diversity, pluralism, inclusion, and so on) is to reduce negative attitudes and behaviors targeted at individuals and groups with diverse identities. Practitioners use many techniques to do so. Here I provide a brief description of a few of the many research- and evidence-based approaches for communicating in ways that reduce prejudice, bias, and accompanying negative behavior. Reducing bias makes it easier to create inclusive environments, but doing so is not sufficient to create inclusion. Additional processes addressed in other chapters of this book—such as accessing important identities (Chapter 3), creating a safe environment (Chapter 4), developing competencies (Chapters 5 and 6), and designing comprehensive diversity and inclusion initiatives (Chapters 7 to 11)—are also necessary. If one is designing programs, workshops, presentations, newsletter articles, video material, online content, e-learning, and the like, with a goal of reducing bias and prejudice, then applying the knowledge generated by some of the research noted here can enhance effectiveness.

The next six subsections note specific tools, concepts, and approaches selected to demonstrate the broad range of fields that contribute to inclusion.

Contact Hypothesis

By creating specific conditions for human interaction among and between members of different identity groups, prejudice can be measurably reduced (Allport, 1954; Amir, 1976; Dixon, Durrheim, & Tredoux, 2005; Hewstone, Caims, Voci, Hamberger, & Niens, 2006; Pettigrew, 2011; Pettigrew, Christ, Wagner, & Stellmacher,

2007; Shelton & Richeson, 2006). Allport (1954) thought that intergroup contact under favorable conditions could reduce prejudice, and he suggested policy changes to accomplish this. Amir developed a list of specific conditions for accomplishing this, including equal status and interdependent goals. Other scholars continued to contribute by refining the list, expanding applications, and getting more specific about how, when, and for whom the recommended conditions work. Pettigrew (2011) believes applications are lacking because social psychologists have "failed to make our work widely visible" (p. 147). Pettigrew also notes the expansion of the contact hypothesis literature to identities other than race, such as religion and ethnicity. I also know colleagues who apply this theory in the areas of generational diversity and people with disabilities.

A full chapter or book could now be written applying this knowledge to our work. For example, the entire volume 62, number 3, 2006 issue of the *Journal of Social Issues* is titled and devoted to "Reducing Prejudice and Promoting Social Inclusion: Integrating Research, Theory and Practice on Intergroup Relations." Based on all of the preceding citations and my own experience using the contact hypothesis, I note two specific application ideas:

○ To reduce prejudice by improving the conditions of contact, create as many of the following conditions as reasonably possible: Minimize status differences, emphasize interdependence, talk about goals shared by everyone, demonstrate the value of cooperation, show majority group members modeling positive contact with minority group members, and promote contact that is more than casual. To supplement this with our knowledge of how to develop intercultural sensitivity, the practitioner should begin with the most comfortable differences and work up to the least comfortable ones. As the differences become more challenging, incorporate more of the recommended conditions for contact. For example, start with differences in style (such as those highlighted by the Myers-Briggs Type Indicator) and later address issues like religion and sexual orientation.

○ Engage in indirect intergroup contact. Because contact with other ingroup members who have positive relationships with outgroup members is effective in reducing prejudice, this means that when your friends and colleagues have healthy interactions with others who are different, you also may experience a reduction in bias regarding those same different individuals and groups. One way to apply this knowledge is to show leaders, both live and using media venues, enjoying interactions with others who are different. This can facilitate the reduction of prejudice among participants in the organizations they lead.

Cognitive Complexity

Training participants in dealing with a broad range of relevant considerations (qualifications, experience, education, training, background, knowledge) and the interactions among such inputs helps them look beyond "surface" characteristics (such as race and gender) and behave in less prejudiced ways (Gardiner, 1972). Note that Gardiner takes the view that race and gender are surface characteristics. In applying this technique, I find it more useful to speak of physical appearance (color, sex characteristics, languages spoken, weight, height, age appearance, evidence of physical ability, and so on). This technique works by creating tension between potential stereotypes and actual skills, knowledge, and abilities. This is very similar to what Rokeach (1971) did to address negative attitudes by highlighting inconsistencies between validated facts and personal beliefs. Again, start with less contentious issues and work up to more volatile ones. When combined with other techniques noted in this chapter, I believe that communicating about complexity merits addition to the practitioner's toolkit.

Cultural Assimilator

In a cultural assimilator, participants are presented with many scenarios involving diversity (in paper and digital computer–based formats). The participant then selects, from a multiple-choice list, the behavior he or she believes to be correct or most effective. For example: When a German man meets an Asian-American woman in an American business setting, should he: (a) vigorously shake her hand, (b) kiss her on one cheek, (c) gently shake her hand, or (d) nod to acknowledge her presence? After individuals choose behavioral options in a wide range of situations involving cultural diversity and then receive feedback on the effectiveness of different choices, their real-time interaction skills measurably improve (Slobodin, 1972; Triandis, 1975). This approach has been used with both international cultural differences and social identity and cultural differences within the United States.

A variation on this theme is the use of games (such as *Ghetto, Starpower, Barnga,* and *Bafa Bafa*) to put the participant into roles simulating cultural differences, dominance, oppression, and subordination. The designers see these experiences as nurturing empathy and understanding. Rather than a simulated or virtual experience, Albert and Adamopoulos (1976) recommend immersing participants in real cultures that are different from their own. I see this latter technique as a high-risk, high-impact approach that should be considered only for individuals in or approaching advanced stages of individual development. Using it with individuals at earlier stages of development is likely to reinforce negative views of differences rather than educate the participant about similarities and differences.

Defeating Bias

Sondra Thiederman (2008) presents a comprehensive approach to defeating bias, grounded in selected recent research on human processes that lead to reduction in bias. Thiederman examined research on how the brain functions, evidence-based counseling, sociological research on intergroup violence, social psychological studies of beliefs and attitudes, and tools used to manage diversity in organizations. She shows how mindfulness, triage, understanding benefits, dissecting bias, and finding similarities can help us behave in less biased ways. Thiederman provides explicit details about how the path for each of these techniques leads to unbiased behavior.

Psychotherapy

By participating in evidence-based psychotherapy or other clinical diagnostic and therapeutic processes, individuals can become more personally and interpersonally competent. If the therapist has intercultural, diversity, inclusion, pluralism, multicultural, or related skills, the increased competence extends to interactions with those who are significantly different. Most diversity and inclusion professionals are careful not to label what they do as "therapy" of any kind. However, some of the leaders in our field are trained in the therapeutic disciplines and appropriately use those skills in their diversity and inclusion practices. Most of the professional associations with clinical arms now advocate evidence-based therapies. Some of the techniques used in such therapies filter into the practices of competent diversity and inclusion practitioners. They can be safe and appropriate. Included are principles for giving feedback, dealing with stereotypes, using "I" messages for effective communication, and guided cognitive breakdown processing of prejudices.

In diversity and inclusion, I believe we should move toward adopting a standard for our practices that is similar to the one operating in the clinical arena. Evidence-based practice standards have been in place there for more than a decade. They are grounded in qualifications imposed by science, standardized, replicable, and effective (Drake, 2001).

Meditation and Mindfulness

Moving out of the therapy arena, one relatively safe nonclinical technique for helping individuals gain insight into their biases and prejudices is to teach participants (volunteers only) how to meditate or be mindful. Significant effects have been demonstrated on avoiding unwanted thoughts (Winerman, 2011), reducing anxiety about dealing with people perceived as difficult (Price, 2011), focusing more on others and less on self (Azar, 2010), and improving interpersonal interactions and response flexibility (Davis & Hayes, 2012).

Communication in Education and Training

In many efforts to communicate about diversity and inclusion, a starting place is often to educate and train for at least tolerance of people, with an emphasis on differences. Enough research has been done now to know that this approach works for some learners but not others. In particular, this approach is less effective in reducing prejudice of high social dominance–oriented and right-wing authoritarian individuals (Esses & Hodson, 2006). Creating and emphasizing common ingroup identities is more effective for such individuals: for example, "we are all members of this group, qualified students for admission to this university, valued employees of this company, and/or citizens of this nation."

The process used to communicate or learn about commonalities and differences is also an important variable. Active learning is more effective than learning content from lectures and readings (Nagda, 2006). Active learning involves interactive processes that engage participants both as individuals and in groups (such as dialogue, action research, sharing personal stories, live encounters). Such two-way communication is more powerful in reducing bias than lectures, films, and readings. Interaction is more effective especially for issues that are complex and have emotional content, such as diversity and inclusion. Active learning of this type can reduce prejudice and also demonstrate inclusive practices.

Communication to Fit Organizational Stages of Development: A Generic Organization Development Diversity and Inclusion Model

Organizations also go through predictable stages of development with regression under stress or change (Hayles & Russell, 1997). This section describes generic stages of organization development specific to diversity, cultural competence, inclusion, and pluralism. Many practitioners and organizations have used developmental models of organizations to diagnose and guide the work of diversity and inclusion. This and the next section are designed to help practitioners know what to communicate within an organization at different stages of development. First, I describe a generic developmental model for organizations, with three stages. In the following section, I recommend communication approaches based on facts, values, and actions, suitable for each stage.

I have synthesized many of the models developed and used since the 1980s (for example, Cox, 1991; Holvino, Ferdman, & Merrill-Sands, 2004; Jackson & Holvino, 1988; Katz & Miller,

1988) and describe a generic one shortly. In general, these models describe early, middle, and later stages in the journey from less diverse and more exclusive to high-performing, diverse, and inclusive organizations. I provide a brief description of these stages, followed by recommended communication interventions for each stage. The suggested interventions are based on what I have learned and heard from colleagues regarding what works at each stage. The theoretically correct communication at the appropriate stage is projected to have a more positive impact on inclusion and thereby performance. This is offered in the context of very limited research on the effectiveness of any particular model. It is based on knowing many practitioners (and their models) and the externally visible results in the organizations involved. In other words, the recommendations that follow are based on synthesizing knowledge from theory and application.

The next sections discuss three different generic stages of development. To determine which stage an organization fits, a multifaceted assessment is important. This might include using internal data, focus groups, surveys, and tools such the Global Diversity and Inclusion Benchmarks (O'Mara, Chapter 14, this volume; O'Mara & Richter, 2011).

Early Stages

Words like *resistant, exclusive, passive, club,* and *segregated* describe the early stages. There is little visible diversity, and invisible diversity is typically undisclosed. Individuals who are members of certain groups need not seek entry. Intolerance and hostility are quite evident.

Effective communication designed to bring about change from the outside involves letters, emails, calls, complaints, articles and stories in the media, and threats of boycotts. Governments can speak of compliance and/or positive action (if such laws exist). Peer organizations in the same sector or region can tout lower risks and/or higher performance. At these stages it is often difficult for internal participants to be heard. Sometimes surveys and anonymous auditory or electronic channels can work. At this stage, internal leaders who support moving to inclusion must communicate to participants in their organization that behavioral change and new knowledge are required. Attitude change is beneficial although optional. Organizations directly or vicariously experiencing these pressures tend to move forward. Internal and external communication must be directed at getting the organization engaged with the appropriate diversity and inclusion work. As noted earlier in this chapter, at this stage more emphasis should be placed on similarities than on differences. The effort is likely to be more equal opportunity–oriented than diversity- or inclusion-oriented at this stage.

Middle Stages

Words like *tolerance, changing, responsive,* and *getting beyond reactive* describe these stages. Compliance continues to provide motivation. Internal complaints increase as internal participants begin to see signs of commitment to diversity and inclusion, with more hope for resolution. External litigation and threats decline as internal two-way communication increases. Employees who share common interests or characteristics often form networks or resource groups. The organization can now build on the fruits of equal opportunity, affirmative action, and equity efforts to begin more communication about diversity and inclusion.

In terms of communication, stories should be told about benefits (for example, higher quality recruitment, growing enrollments, profits, patents, shared benefits of organizational success, value to everyone of a diverse faculty and student body) that are clearly related to diversity and/or inclusion. It is also appropriate for leaders and practitioners to share failures (mistakes, turnover, losses, declines in enrollment, missed marketplace opportunities, and so on) that are clearly related to diversity and/or inclusion. It is during these stages that communication should emphasize differences as well as similarities. The work is now primarily diversity oriented. This is also the time to send messages acknowledging the need to continue to address bias and nurture the competencies required for success (such as diversity management, intercultural skills, emotional intelligence). The development of inclusion begins here.

Advanced Stages

Words like *respect, value-added, appreciation, inclusive,* and *transformation* describe these stages. Most organizations in these stages have been addressing diversity, pluralism, and possibly inclusion for at least a decade. They have also experienced regression to earlier stages at least once. Negative happenings are dealt with quickly and fairly. Leaders acknowledge when unfortunate things occur and talk about corrective action as well as learning and prevention. Sometimes private and public apologies are given. External recognition is frequent, and inclusion is a major theme as diversity is becoming an integral part of all business and human resource systems. Visible and invisible diversity are evident and seen as contributing to organizational performance and success via inclusion.

Effective communication shifts toward messages to reinforce progress, avoid regression, celebrate successes, take on new challenges, and institutionalize processes to remain in these higher stages. Annual reports include more implicit and less explicit diversity content. Diversity and inclusion are reflected in all communication materials. Links among diversity, inclusion, social responsibility, environmental sensitivity, sustainability, safety, and other important initiatives are visible. Inclusion is now occurring.

The next sections provide more examples of what to communicate, organized by head, heart, and hand.

Communication Addressing Facts, Feelings, and Behaviors

To present the most impactful rationales for doing this work, communication must be designed consistently with the knowledge presented earlier in this chapter. This applies when making the case to businesses, government agencies, nongovernmental organizations, educational institutions, religious institutions, families, service organizations, and more. Materials must touch head, heart, and hand and be sequenced to move individuals and organizations to more sensitive and inclusive stages of development.

The material that follows starts with facts (head), moves to feelings and values (heart), and closes with behaviors and actions (hand). It is intended for use by leaders, practitioners, and communication specialists.

Fact-Based Communication Examples

Fact-based content alone is not sufficient to motivate large-scale change. It remains necessary as a foundation to initiate the conversation, reaffirm a commitment to action, or simply respond "objectively" to resistance. When receivers continue to object to or resist diversity and inclusion after a compelling fact-based case for action has been presented, it is likely that resistance is grounded in fear of change, of loss of opportunity, of loss of status, of lack of required competence, or of people who are different (xenophobia). Practitioners must engage and pursue the basis for resistance to help the individual move forward. (For example, the resistance might be based in something as clear as "my White son did not get a scholarship but my minority neighbor's daughter got one." This is different from resistance based on deep-seated bigotry, lack of exposure, or other reasons.) I have learned this through both my own experience and consultation with colleagues, some of whom do confidential clinical work dealing with diversity and inclusion. Both I and these colleagues have been privy to candid conversations with individuals strongly opposed to what they think diversity and inclusion mean.

The following are descriptions of fact-based topics with annotations about resources and appropriate use at different stages of development. Again, it should be noted that sharing the same fact at different stages of development will have different results. Use developmental stages to guide the content of communication.

Demographics: Local, Regional, Global

Because fear often arises about demographic changes (stemming from immigration, variation in reproductive rates, and the like), this is not an effective topic for individuals and organizations in the early stages of development. The result will often be fear, disbelief, animosity, and resistance. In the middle and advanced stages, presenting information about current and future demographics can be beneficial. It must be presented in the context of education designed to develop diversity and inclusion competencies. Use politically neutral sources of information, such as www.vitalsigns.worldwatch.org, www.prb.org, www.100people.org, www.rand.org, and www.wilsonquarterly.com.

Benefits of Work-Life Balance

This topic can be used at almost any stage of personal development. It is threatening only when the organization is hostile to such balance. Studies report data that demonstrate a wide range of effects. Reducing work-family conflicts reduces employee use of mental health services (Graves, Ohlott, & Ruderman, 2007; Major, Klein, & Ehrhart, 2002; Siegel, Post, Brockner, Fishman, & Garden, 2005; Smillie, Yeo, Furnham, & Jackson, 2006); predictable time off increases job satisfaction (Ford, Heinen, & Langkamer, 2007); and flexible and compressed workweek schedules correlate positively with productivity, performance, job satisfaction, and lower absenteeism (Harris, 2007). In general, a strong case can also be made for broad work-life initiatives (Casper, Eby, Bordeauz, Lockwood, & Lambert, 2007; Friedman, Christensen, & DeGroot, 1998; Rapoport & Bailyn, 1996). Use these and similar facts to justify work-life programs.

Group Purchasing Power

The facts behind this concept are very compelling, particularly in retail or service organizations. The documented purchasing power of many groups can be persuasive and very motivating. Listing the groups with strong purchasing power is also another way to reinforce a broad and inclusive definition of diversity. I recommend providing information on groups such as older and younger generations, social identity groups (racial, multiracial, cultural, ethnic, gender, sexual orientation, religious, and so on), people with disabilities, and other groups that may suggest themselves.

Some organizations have fallen into the trap of following such information with statements that "we need members of each group to provide goods and services to members of these same groups." The result can be career-limiting for individuals allowed to serve only "their own people." Although the diversity within does facilitate serving the diversity without, a one-to-one relationship is not required. Competence is primary; choosing individuals who demographically mirror the customer is secondary. Understanding and being able to communicate with customers are elements of overall competence. One does not have to be a member of a certain community to competently serve that community. Indeed, one can be a member of a given community and still not be competent to serve that community. Therefore, when assessing candidates to serve a given population, the assessor must separate the skills to do so from membership in the culture. For example: "We need someone who speaks Thai and understands the culture to work in our division in Thailand," is preferable to "We are looking for a Thai person to work in our division in Thailand." This also prevents accusations of discrimination and communicates fairness to everyone.

Individuals and organizations that are in the earlier stages of development are vulnerable to just this trap because of their focus on eliminating discrimination against and giving opportunities to protected groups. They have yet to see protected class members as equal or even just different. Therefore making the case by citing purchasing power is recommended for middle and advanced stages of development. It is not recommended for early stages of development.

Individual, Group, and Organizational Performance

This heading merits an entire chapter or book. The relationships among diversity, inclusion, and performance form a very complex topic. My perspective is summarized here, along with a few citations to help readers build a custom rationale for their work. In general, organizations that make progress regarding diversity and inclusion also make correlated progress regarding outcomes such as financial performance, interpersonal competence of graduates, growing enrollments in higher education, accomplishment of mission (government and non-profit agencies), nurturing of talent for a global marketplace (professional associations), and more. There is a substantial and growing body of evidence supporting this assertion (Hayles, 2003). To prepare communication materials focused on this relationship, a suggested path is out-lined here.

Practitioners should start with the works of Hubbard (2008). He provides a framework for using the data within an organiza-tion to calculate the costs (education, training, salaries, benefits, and so on) of doing diversity and inclusion work and to measure the outcomes (sales, turnover, complaints, and so on) attributable to that work. In this process, practitioners should also use addi-tional measures like the ones noted earlier to determine the organization's stage of development (such as surveys, focus groups, or Global Diversity & Inclusion Benchmarks).

Next, the practitioner must understand at least some of the complexities in the relationships among diversity, inclusion, and performance. I maintain that managing the complexities well leads to a positive relationship. One of the complexities has to do with the conditions under which diversity can contribute to performance—conditions that create inclusion. Another pertains to the nature of the tasks that benefit from the presence of diver-sity. Yet another has to do with the specific types of diversity involved. There are obviously more complexities, but these are the major and better-known ones.

Conditions in Which Diversity Is an Asset

Scholars and researchers have made some progress in being able to specify the conditions that enhance the benefits of diversity, including the following:

- Diversity is more of an asset for complex rather than simple tasks (Ziller, 1972).
- Diversity works best when the required technical skills for the tasks are present and there is competent leadership, including diversity management competence (Thomas, 2010).
- Contact conditions that reduce bias and prejudice also nurture the benefits of diversity and facilitate inclusion (Cook, 1979).

Too often we expect instant results, so we stop the work too soon. We must allow adequate time to achieve the synergy made possible by diversity and nurtured by inclusion—as I learned, based on internal research I conducted at the Pillsbury Company. I investigated the time required for a diversity and inclusion initiative to demonstrate a significant positive correlation with financial performance, and I found that significance was absent at two years, present at five years, and very high at ten years.

Types of Tasks Performed Better by Diverse Groups

Research suggests that diverse groups are better than homogenous ones at general and creative problem solving (Ziller, 1972), personal growth and social skill development (Cook, 1979), dealing with conflict (Suinn, 2001), running a large business (Kanter, 1983), educating students for global business (Anderson, 2003), species survival (Lindsey, 1967), and investment decision making (Harrington, 2008). This list will continue to grow as researchers continue to study this issue.

Types of Diversity That Can Add Value

The knowledge base regarding specific types of diversity that arguably contribute to group performance continues to grow. Having read thousands of published and unpublished studies about diversity and inclusion, I generally ask the question, "For what types of diversity have you seen evidence of adding value to group performance?" My answer includes the following:

- Age (especially for male groups)
- Culture (particularly in multinational businesses)
- Degree source (where participants went to school)
- Gender (in investment groups and Fortune 500 companies)
- Human genetic pool diversity (based on survival rates in different geographies)
- Intelligence (of various types and levels)
- Job function (cross-functional team performance in corporate settings, especially manufacturing plants)
- Language (particularly to avoid marketplace translation errors)
- Myers-Briggs Type Indicator profiles (based on research I conducted at the Pillsbury Company)
- Personality (in numerous small groups that I facilitated as a consultant)

- Physical ability (in team sports)
- Political pluralism (based on the stability of different national political systems around the world)
- Race (as defined by the U.S. Census and reported in the *Wall Street Journal*)
- Sexual orientation (market expansions in the businesses of many clients)

Briefly, in situations in which optimal conditions are met (that is, inclusion is achieved), diverse team performance will tend to exceed homogeneous team performance. This supports Ferdman et al.'s (2010) view that diversity contributes to performance through inclusion. Communication using this argument can be used cautiously at early stages of organization development, heavily at middle stages, and only as needed at advanced stages of development. The user should be aware that in the earlier stages, personal resistance may surface based on emotions that cause a person to argue with the data. In the middle stages of development the practitioner must be sensitive to the possibility that members of particular groups might feel that their "difference" is being used by those in charge to achieve organizational goals (for example, using Latino images in advertisements to make sales in the Latino community). This is painful when those members do not feel valued or included. This reinforces the distinction between having diversity present but not included, and having diversity fully included. In more advanced stages, communication can shift from substantial rationales to continuing the learning and seeking ways to be more competent and effective.

Innovation and Creativity

In using this argument, one must be clear that diversity makes innovation possible. It does not guarantee it. Inclusion makes it even more probable (Ferdman et al., 2010).

Johansson (2006), Leung, Maddus, Galinsky, and Chiu (2008), Amabile and Khaire (2008), Graham (1993), Wheeler (2005), Corporate Leadership Council (2003), and Winters (2006) all provide excellent material reinforcing the general positive relationship between (1) diversity and inclusion and (2) innovation and creativity in organizations. On a larger scale, the results of Florida's empirical research in the United States (Florida, 2004) and around the globe (Florida, 2005), conducted over seven years and using multiple measures, make a strong case that having technology, diverse talent, and a welcoming climate leads to economic development and wealth creation. He found that regions with all three ingredients are notably more prosperous.

Communicating the idea that diversity with inclusion can lead to more innovation and creativity is appropriate for organizations in both the middle and advanced stages. Individual listeners in the early stages are often stuck in perspectives that see diversity as coming from minorities, immigrants, people with disabilities, or women. Bringing these groups into organizations can be costly (based on, for example, language issues, added restrooms, costs to build access) and perceived as negative (requiring change and adaptation). Listeners with this view are less able to see the potential benefits or investment value; they may even be hostile. Therefore do not use this case until you have gotten past the early personal and early organization developmental stages.

Marketplace Blunders and Successes

Ricks (1983, 1993) is a good source of documented blunders and successes that stem from cultural misunderstanding or understanding. Always check at least two sources before using a particular example. Even when the language is English, cultural differences can cause blunders. The British word *nappy* or *napkin* means "diaper." So you can imagine how Britons responded to an American commercial about napkins with the phrase that you "could use no finer napkin (*diaper*) at your dinner table." A commercial for cologne aimed at men in northern Africa showed a man and his dog in a rural setting. The advertiser was not aware that many northern African Muslims view dogs as unclean and/or symbols of bad luck. Exxon did well in Thailand with their brand symbol, the tiger. It was the perfect indicator of strength and power for that market. When possible, use internal examples, which are typically even more powerful than external ones.

This often humorous and delightful communication approach can be used for all stages of individual and organization development as long as examples of successes and blunders are diverse, relevant to your specific organization, free of stereotypes, and not offensive.

Recruitment and Retention

Organizations that have internal and external reputations for being preferred employers, best places to work, best schools for career preparation, best agencies for public servants, and so on find it easier to attract and retain the best talent. Such best talent will also be diverse. When examining lists of "best" places, give more credence to sources that get input from members of the organizations and have rational systems for validating their ratings and rankings. Some sources apply to specific social identity groups (such as generational groups by age, Blacks, Christians, Latinos, LGBT, people with disabilities, and women). Grant (1998); Wright, Ferris, Hiller, and Kroll (1995); Donkin (1995); and Gubman (1998) all describe a positive relationship between being a best place to work (in general) and organizational performance that is superior to the performance of lower-rated comparable firms. I believe that inclusion again provides the unspoken link between high-quality talent and superior performance.

Communicating about this aspect of the work requires being clear that being a great workplace contributes to organizational success through combining diversity with inclusion. Therefore we want to be a "best" place to work in order to reap the benefits for attracting diverse talent, retaining diverse members, and performing better than our peers. This argument can be used at all stages of organization development.

Feelings- and Values-Oriented Communication Examples

In this section I discuss communication content that appeals to the heart. It includes information about: (1) social justice, (2) fairness, (3) spirituality, (4) similarities among people, and (5) values and principles.

Social Justice

Part of the historical foundation for diversity and inclusion rests on work done under equal opportunity, employment equity, positive discrimination, and affirmative action. One label often applied to these approaches is social justice. In addition to appealing to personal values for social justice, we can note that among the Standard & Poor's 500, the 100 companies that most proactively broke barriers for women and minorities had stock returns that were more than double those for the one hundred companies that were least active along this line ("Equal Opportunity Pays," 1993). Companies that were more successful in implementing equal opportunity had better stock performance (Carfang, 1993). Even the *Economist* ("Affirmative Action," 1995) reported enhanced business performance for firms that successfully addressed equal opportunity. For practitioners, it can be useful to acknowledge the importance of social justice. Many individuals continue to feel strongly about this reason for the work. Being able to link social justice with organizational outcomes expands the receptive audience to those who may not see social justice as valuable in and of itself.

Although the preceding citations focus more on financial outcomes from a business perspective, Crosby and Clayton (2001), Pratkanis and Turner (1999); Aberson (2007); Harrison, Kravitz, Mayer, Leslie, and Lev-Arey (2006); Bell, Harrison, and McLaughlin (2000); and Holland (2003) speak to how attitudes about affirmative action are being changed through legal action, experiences with increasing diversity, and education. Collectively they make it clear that diversity and inclusion initiatives contribute to and benefit from social justice work.

Social justice arguments are best suited for the middle stages of individual and organization development. They are less effective with individuals and organizations in earlier stages of development and less necessary in advanced stages.

Fairness

Because fairness requires alignment of the head, heart, and hand, it is very difficult to achieve. When it happens, the benefits are clear and measurable (Brockner, 2006; Simons & Roberson,

2003). When fairness is not achieved, the losses can be significant, whether calculated as operating expense losses (one percent, demonstrated by Stuart, 1992) or as litigation costs. Achieving fairness requires dealing with fact and, most important, feelings.

For example, when a group that has been discriminated against begins to get equal treatment, the previously advantaged group experiences loss. The practitioner must first acknowledge the feelings of loss (anger, resentment, fear, and so on) for the previously advantaged group while touting the benefits of fairness to everyone, especially over time. This is difficult and necessary. Therefore using this argument requires addressing feelings first and then facts.

Spirituality

Capra (2000) sought an ultimate understanding of the universe through both modern physics and spirituality (mysticism). Both paths come to the same destination. Mystics often seek to experience it directly. Physicists try to measure it with instruments. Everything is composed of the same fundamental tiny particles or stuff, which has yet to be definitively described by physicists. Mystics describe a "unity" experience wherein one has a direct realization that everything in the universe is connected and composed of the same stuff. This point may be more relevant with scientists and engineers. For less technically inclined participants, human genetic facts can be helpful. Humans share more genetic similarities (greater than 99 percent) than differences (fewer than 1 percent). We are "one" at many levels and in many senses of the word. Harm to one harms all. The Deluxe Corporation captured this perspective in the tag line for its definition of diversity: "the power of many, the spirit of one."

Communication using spirituality as a rationale for inclusion is not for early stages or people who view spirituality negatively. It is for use only in the advanced stages, with people who understand that spirituality is not in conflict with religion or science, does not have a doctrine, and is open to everyone. Guillory (2000) provides an exploration of spirituality in the workplace, which he defines as our "inner consciousness" that is "the source of inspiration, creativity, and wisdom" (p. 33). The best organizations in the world will tap the urge to explore, create, and improve, which is strongest among high performers. Guillory sees spirituality at the root of that urge.

Similarities

Research on communicating about similarities among people in an organization in the training context (Paluck, 2006) indicates that movement toward at least accepting diversity may be nurtured by messages delineating and affirming similarities. Similarities include many potential dimensions (hobbies, families, experiences, ultimate ancestry, employers, and so on). The feelings that arise in the context of similarity are generally more positive than those that arise in discussions about differences. In terms of communication that nurtures change, begin with discussions of similarities, move to areas of difference that are least significant, and close with the value of many differences. This particular tactic is ideal for individuals and organizations in the early stages of development. It becomes less useful in the middle stages and unnecessary in the advanced stages.

Values and Principles

Communication about values and principles can inspire progressive behavior regarding diversity and inclusion. Most organizations have statements about their values, visions, principles, ethical standards, social responsibilities, public citizenship, and the like. Some even list diversity and/or inclusion as organizational values. Many organizations publicly recognized for excellence (such as General Electric) evaluate their leaders on how well they exhibit stated values. These performance evaluations include assessments of results achieved and the way (values-based) in which they were achieved. The way in which results were achieved explicitly includes how leaders and managers treat people. Diversity and inclusion practitioners must make sure that inclusive behaviors are part of these evaluations. This contemporary approach is grounded in classic organizational theories indicating that tasks and relationships are the two major variables determining successful management.

On a global scale, the Universal Declaration of Human Rights (United Nations, 1948) remains the secular state of the art for values-based communication supporting diversity, pluralism, and inclusion. Communication designed to facilitate agreement on values and principles such as those embodied in the Universal Declaration of Human Rights can be powerful for advancing inclusion in organizations and individuals in the middle and advanced stages of development.

Behavioral "Hand"-Oriented Communication Examples

Many people, particularly those relatively new to diversity and inclusion, request explicit guidance on how to behave around members of specific groups. Behavior that encourages inclusion is an important element even in some performance appraisal systems. Before addressing this directly, some context is required. When large numbers of people are asked about their requirements and preferences regarding words used and feelings conveyed, most respond as follows: When forced to choose between the correct words and a respectful tone or feeling, they will choose the respectful tone. When a respectful tone is not possible, then the correct words are required. If the question is posed more openly, respondents say they want correct words, appropriate behaviors, and a respectful tone. Therefore, telling individuals only how they should behave is very risky. Appropriate behavior that is not sincere often fails. Inappropriate behavior with a respectful tone and positive intent can frequently find temporary acceptance. Ultimately, both content and tone are important. Therefore practitioners must skillfully communicate about both behaviors and attitudes. This is potentially a very dangerous area for practitioners because no behavioral guidance is correct in *all* situations. Ultimately, we must help participants mature with respect to inclusion competencies and not depend on being told exactly what to do in each situation.

In this category, many resources and approaches are useful when applied in context of the preceding caveats. A few are examples are provided here.

Disability Etiquette

A quiz was developed to describe how to behave around people with disabilities ("Disability etiquette," 1995, pp. 40–41). It covers considerations such as how to guide a person who is blind or deal with a person in a wheelchair blocking one's view in a meeting.

Cross-Cultural and Intercultural Behavior

Publications or sources of explicit guidance for behavior include Intercultural Press (a publisher); *Culturegrams* from Brigham Young University (www.culturgrams.com); *Doing Business Internationally* (Training Management Corporation, 1997); *Black and White Styles in Conflict* (Kochman, 1981); and the Society for Intercultural Education Training and Research (SIETAR; http://www.sietar.org). These sources explain, for example, why pointing a finger can be helpful or an insult depending on where in the world you do so. They help explain why using one's left hand can be the basis for a rude or insulting communication in the Middle East, Africa, and other places. Kochman (1981) explains why Blacks and Whites have frequent miscommunication based on documented cultural differences. For example, a single word, *bad*, can have opposite meanings in Black and White contexts. A particular behavior—loudly proclaiming innocence when accused of a crime—can be interpreted in opposite ways in White and Black contexts.

Some understanding of appropriate behaviors in specific contexts can build at least some head and hand competencies that can be supplemented by heart skills.

Dance of Apology and Forgiveness

The most recognized application of this general approach to resolving intergroup tension occurred in South Africa. The truth and reconciliation process was skillfully orchestrated (Moyers, 1999) and facilitated admissions of guilt in a climate of forgiveness. This same generic process can be effective where there is a history of discrimination and individuals and organizations have reached at least the middle stages of development. To apply it in most parts of the world we should use a vocabulary that breaks the association with South Africa. That association can unnecessarily stimulate guilt, fear of retaliation among both parties, and resistance based on the idea of not being local. Therefore I recommend describing it as a *dance of apology and forgiveness.* In my opinion, when there is a history of intergroup conflict or discrimination, this is a powerful active step along the road to inclusion.

Conclusion

During the past few decades we have learned much about human and organizational behavior. In designing communication to create inclusion, we need to reflect that knowledge. Although differences are real and have measurable effects on how we interact, humans have far more similarities than differences. Differences are sources of both conflict and positive synergy. When diversity is present under specific conditions, inclusion occurs. Inclusion contributes to performance. Overly simplistic research has muddied those connections. The conditions that lead to inclusion and the specific differences that contribute to them are increasingly being demonstrated by researchers, scholars, and practitioners. As we competently apply this knowledge to our communication about inclusion, organizational outcomes will improve. That means less negative conflict, better-prepared students, improved service delivery, better and more enduring political decisions, more innovation, enhanced creativity, greater productivity, and stronger financial performance.

References

Aberson, C. (2007). Diversity experiences predict changes in attitudes toward affirmative action. *Cultural Diversity and Ethnic Minority Psychology, 13,* 285–294.

Affirmative action: A strong prejudice. (1995, June 17). *Economist,* p. 85.

Albert, R., & Adamopoulos, J. (1976). An attributional approach to culture learning: The culture assimilator. In R. Brislin (Ed.), *Topics in culture learning* (Vol. 4, pp. 53–60), Honolulu, HI: East-West Center.

Allport, G. W. (1954). *The nature of prejudice.* Reading, MA: Addison-Wesley.

Amabile, T., & Khaire, M. (2008). Creativity and the role of the leader. *Harvard Business Review, 86*(10), 100–109.

Amir, Y. (1976). The role of intergroup contact in change of prejudice and ethnic relations. In P. Katz (Ed.), *Towards the elimination of racism* (pp. 245–308). New York: Pergamon.

Anderson, N. (2003). Psychology as a health profession. *Monitor on Psychology, 34*(3), 9.

Azar, B. (2010). A reason to believe. *Monitor on Psychology, 41*(11), 52–55.

Bell, M. P., Harrison, D. A., & McLaughlin, M. E. (2000). Forming, changing, and acting on attitude toward affirmative action programs in employment: A theory-driven approach. *Journal of Applied Psychology, 85,* 784–798.

Bennett, J. M. (2006). *A developmental model of intercultural sensitivity.* Portland, OR: Intercultural Communication Institute.

Bennett, M. J. (1993). Towards ethnorelativism: A developmental model of intercultural sensitivity. In R. M. Paige (Ed.), *Education for the intercultural experience* (pp. 21–71). Yarmouth, ME: Intercultural Press.

Bennett, M. J. (1998). Intercultural communication: A current perspective. In M. J. Bennett (Ed.) *Basic concepts of intercultural communication: Selected readings* (pp. 1–34). Yarmouth, ME: Intercultural Press.

Brockner, J. (2006). Why it's so hard to be fair. *Harvard Business Review, 84*(3), 122–129.

Capra, F. (2000). *The Tao of physics. An exploration of the parallels between modern physics and eastern mysticism.* Boston, MA: Shambhala.

Carfang, A. (April 21, 1993). Equal opportunity and stock performance linked [News release]. Chicago, IL: Covenant Investment Management.

Casper, W. J., Eby, L. T., Bordeauzx, C., Lockwood, A., & Lambert, D. (2007). A review of research methods in IO/OB work-family research. *Journal of Applied Psychology, 92,* 28–43.

Cook, S. (1979). Social science and school desegregation: Did we mislead the Supreme Court? *Personality and Social Psychology Bulletin, 5,* 420–437.

Corporate Leadership Council (2003). *The business case for diversity.* Washington, DC: Corporate Executive Board.

Cox, T. H., Jr. (1991). The multicultural organization. *Academy of Management Executive, 5*(2), 34–47.

Crosby, F., & Clayton, S. (2001). Affirmative action: Psychological contributions to policy. *Analyses of Social Issues and Public Policy, 1,* 71–87.

Davis, D. M., & Hayes, J. A. (2012). What are the benefits of mindfulness? *Monitor on Psychology, 43*(7), 64–70.

Disability etiquette. (1995, April). *American Health,* pp. 40–41.

Dixon, J., Durrheim, K., & Tredoux, C. (2005). Beyond the optimal contact strategy: A reality check for the contact hypothesis. *American Psychologist, 60,* 697–711.

Donkin, R. (1995, February 8). Recruitment: Happy workers can generate high profits. *Financial Times,* p. 13.

Drake, R. E. (2001). Implementing evidence-based practices in routine mental health service settings. *Psychiatric Services, 52,* 179–182.

Equal opportunity pays. (1993, May 4). *Wall Street Journal,* p. 1.

Esses, V., & Hodson, G. (2006). The role of lay perceptions of ethnic prejudice in the maintenance and perpetuation of ethnic bias. *Journal of Social Issues, 62,* 453–468.

Ferdman, B. M., Avigdor, A., Braun, D., Konkin, J., & Kuzmycz, D. (2010). Collective experience of inclusion, diversity, and performance in work groups. *Revista de Administração Mackenzie, 11*(3), 6–26. doi:10.1590/S1678-69712010000300003

Ferdman, B. M., Barrera, V., Allen, A., & Vuong, V. (2009, August). Inclusive behavior and the experience of inclusion. In B. G. Chung (Chair), *Inclusion in organizations: Measures, HR practices, and climate.* Symposium conducted at the 69th Annual Meeting of the Academy of Management, Chicago, IL.

Florida, R. (2004). American's looming creativity crisis. *Harvard Business Review, 82*(10), 122–136.

Florida, R. (2005). *The flight of the creative class: The new global competition for talent.* New York: Harper Business.

Ford, M., Heinen, B., & Langkamer, K. (2007). Work and family satisfaction and conflict: A meta-analysis of cross-domain relations. *Journal of Applied Psychology, 92,* 57–80.

Friedman, S., Christensen, P., & DeGroot, J. (1998). Work and life: The end of the zero-sum game. *Harvard Business Review, 76*(6), 119–129.

Gardiner, G. (1972). Complexity training and prejudice reduction. *Journal of Applied Social Psychology, 2,* 326–342.

Graham, L. (1993). *The best companies for minorities.* New York: Plume.

Grant, L. (1998, January 12). Happy workers, high returns. *Fortune,* p. 81.

Graves, L., Ohlott, P., & Ruderman, M. (2007). Commitment to family roles: Effects of managers' attitudes and performance. *Journal of Applied Psychology, 92,* 44–56.

Gubman, E. (1998). *The talent solution: Aligning strategy and people to achieve extraordinary results.* New York: McGraw-Hill.

Guillory, W. A. (2000). *Spirituality in the workplace: A guide for adapting to the chaotically changing workplace.* Salt Lake City, UT: Innovations International.

Hammer, M. R. (1999). A measure of intercultural sensitivity: The intercultural development inventory. In S. Fowler & M. Fowler (Eds.) *The intercultural sourcebook* (Vol. 2, pp. 61–72). Yarmouth, ME: Intercultural Press.

Harrington, B. (2008). *Pop finance: Investment clubs and the new investor populism.* Princeton, NJ: Princeton University Press.

Harris, P. (2007). Flexible work policies mean business. *Training and Development, 61*(4), 32–36.

Harrison, D. A., Kravitz, D. A., Mayer, D. M., Leslie, L. M., & Lev-Arey, D. (2006). Understanding attitudes toward affirmative action programs in employment: Summary and meta-analysis of 35 years of research. *Journal of Applied Psychology, 91,* 1013–1036.

Hayles, R. (1978). Inter-ethnic and race relations education and training. In D. Hoopes, P. Pedersen, & G. Renwick (Eds.), *Overview of intercultural education, training and research* (Vol. 2, pp. 64–87). Washington, DC: Society for Intercultural Education, Training and Research.

Hayles, V. R. (1996). Diversity training and development. In R. L. Craig (Ed.), *The ASTD training & development handbook* (pp. 104–123). New York: McGraw-Hill.

Hayles, V. R., & Russell, A. M. (1997). *The diversity directive: Why some initiatives fail and what to do about it.* New York: McGraw-Hill.

Hayles, R. (2003, May). Strategies for change: Why proactively seek diversity? Cultural Diversity at Work Archive. Retrieved from www.diversitycentral.com

Hewstone, M., Cairns, E., Voci, A., Hamberger, J., & Niens, U. (2006). Intergroup contact, forgiveness, and experience of "the troubles" in Northern Ireland. *Journal of Social Issues, 62,* 99–120.

Holland, G. (2003, February 20). Hundreds file briefs in affirmative-action case. *Honolulu Advertiser,* p. A12.

Holvino, E., Ferdman, B. M., & Merrill-Sands, D. (2004). Creating and sustaining diversity and inclusion in organizations: Strategies and approaches. In M. S. Stockdale & F. J. Crosby (Eds.), *The psychology and management of workplace diversity* (pp. 245–276). Malden, MA: Blackwell.

Howell, W. S. (1982). *The empathic communicator.* Prospect Heights, IL: Waveland Press.

Hubbard, E. E. (2008). *The diversity discipline: Implementing diversity work with a strategy, structure, and ROI measurement focus.* Petaluma, CA: Global Insights Publishing.

Jackson, B. W., & Holvino, E. (1988). Developing multicultural organizations. *Journal of Religion and the Applied Behavioral Sciences, 9*(2), 14–19.

Johansson, F. (2006). *The Medici effect: What elephants and epidemics can teach us about innovation.* Boston, MA: Harvard Business School Press.

Kanter, R. M. (1983). *The change masters.* New York: Simon and Schuster.

Katz, J. H., & Miller, F. A. (1988). Between monoculturalism and multiculturalism: Traps awaiting the organization. *OD Practitioner, 20*(3), 1–5.

Kochan, T., Bezrukova, K., Ely, R., Jackson, S., Joshi, A., Jehn, K., . . . Thomas, D. (2003). The effects of diversity on business performance: Report of the diversity research network. *Human Resource Management, 42,* 3–21.

Kochman, T. (1981). *Black and White styles in conflict.* Chicago, IL: University of Chicago Press.

Leung, A., Maddus, W., Galinsky, A., & Chiu, C. (2008). Multicultural experience enhances creativity. *American Psychologist, 63,* 169–181.

Lewin, K. (1947). Frontiers of group dynamics. *Human Relations, 1,* 5–41.

Lindsey, G. (1967). Some remarks concerning incest, the incest taboo, and psychoanalytic theory. *American Psychologist, 22,* 1051–1065.

Major, V., Klein, K., & Ehrhart, M. (2002). Work time, work interference with family, and psychological distress. *Journal of Applied Psychology, 87,* 427–436.

Nagda, B. (2006). Breaking barriers, crossing borders, building bridges: Communication processes in intergroup dialogues. *Journal of Social Issues, 62,* 553–576.

O'Mara, J., Richter, A., et al. (2011). *Global diversity and inclusion benchmarks: Standards for organizations around the world.* O'Mara & Associates and QED Consulting. Retrieved from http://www.omaraassoc.com/pdf/GDIB_2011.pdf

Paluck, E. (2006). Diversity training and intergroup contact: A call to action research. *Journal of Social Issues, 62,* 577–595.

Pettigrew, T. F., Christ, O., Wagner, U., & Stellmacher, J. (2007). Direct and indirect intergroup contact effects on prejudice: A normative interpretation. *International Journal of Intercultural Relations, 31,* 411–425.

Pettigrew, T. F. (2011). SPSSI and racial research. *Journal of Social Issues,* *67,* 137–149.

Pratkanis, A. R., & Turner, M. E. (1999). The significance of affirmative action for the souls of White folk: Further implications of a helping model. *Journal of Social Issues, 55,* 787–815.

Price, M. (2011). Searching for meaning. *Monitor on Psychology, 42*(10), 57–61.

Public Affairs Television, Inc. (Producer) (1999). *Facing the truth with Bill Moyers* [Video]. Available from http://www.shoppbs.org

Rapoport, R., & Bailyn, L. (1996). *Relinking life and work: Toward a better future.* New York: Ford Foundation.

Ricks, D. (1983). *Big business blunders: Mistakes in multinational marketing.* Homewood, IL: Dow Jones-Irwin.

Ricks, D. (1993). *Blunders in international business.* Cambridge, MA: Blackwell Publishers.

Rokeach, M. (1971). Inconsistency highlighting to reduce prejudice: Long-range experimental modification of values, attitudes, and behavior. *American Psychologist, 26,* 453–459.

Simons, T., & Roberson, Q. (2003). Why managers should care about fairness: The effects of aggregate justice perceptions on organizational outcomes. *Journal of Applied Psychology, 88,* 432–443.

Shelton, J., & Richeson, J. (2006). Ethnic minorities' racial attitudes and contact experiences with White people. *Cultural Diversity and Ethnic Minority Psychology, 12,* 149–164.

Siegel, P., Post, C., Brockner, J., Fishman, A., & Garden, C. (2005). The moderating influence of procedural fairness on the relationship between work-life conflict and organizational commitment. *Journal of Applied Psychology, 90,* 13–24.

Slobodin, L. (1972). *Culture assimilators for interaction with the economically disadvantaged.* Urbana, IL: University of Illinois.

Smillie, L., Yeo, G., Furnham, A., & Jackson, C. (2006). Benefits of all work and no play: The relationship between neuroticism and performance as a function of resource allocation. *Journal of Applied Psychology, 91,* 139–155.

Stuart, P. (1992). What does the glass ceiling cost you? *Personnel Journal, 71*(11), 70–80.

Suinn, R. (2001). Documenting the positive case for affirmative action. *Analyses of Social Issues and Public Policy, 1,* 89–93.

Thiederman, S. (2008). *Making diversity work: 7 steps for defeating bias in the workplace.* New York: Kaplan Publishing.

Thomas, R. R., Jr. (2004, October 7). *Diversity management and affirmative action: Past, present and future.* Paper presented at Equity,

Affirmative Action and Diversity: From Past to Present to a Promising Future, 2004 Diversity Symposium, The Alliance, Landsdowne, VA. Retrieved from http://www.diversitycollegium.org/pdf2004/2004Thomaspaper.pdf

Thomas, R. R., Jr. (2010). *World class diversity management: A strategic approach.* San Francisco: Berrett-Koehler.

Training Management Corporation. (1997). *Doing business internationally: The resource book to business and social etiquette.* Princeton, NJ: Princeton Training Press.

Triandis, H. (1975). Culture training, cognitive complexity and interpersonal attitudes. In R. Brislin, S. Bochner, & W. Lonner (Eds.), *Cross-cultural perspectives on learning.* Thousand Oaks, CA: Sage.

Tung, R. L. (1993). Managing cross-national and intra-national diversity. *Human Resource Management, 32,* 461–477.

United Nations, General Assembly Resolution 217 A (III) of 10. (1948, December 10). *Universal Declaration of Human Rights.* Retrieved from http://www.unhcr.org/refworld/docid/3ae6b3712c.html

Wheeler, M. L. (2005, March). Diversity: The performance factor. *Harvard Business Review,* special advertising section, S1–S7.

Winerman, L. (2011). Suppressing the "white bears": Meditation, mindfulness, and other tools can help us avoid unwanted thoughts. *Monitor on Psychology, 42*(9), 44.

Winters, M. (2006). *CEOs who get it: Diversity leadership from the heart and soul.* Washington, DC: Diversity Best Practices.

Wright, P., Ferris, S., Hiller, J., & Kroll, M. (1995). Competitiveness through management of diversity: Effects on stock price valuation. *Academy of Management Journal, 38,* 272–287.

Ziller, R. C. (1972). Homogeneity and heterogeneity of group membership. In C. McClintock (Ed.), *Experimental social psychology* (pp. 385–411). New York: Holt, Rinehart and Winston.

Part Two

Individual and Interpersonal Perspectives and Practices

Creating Inclusion for Oneself: Knowing, Accepting, and Expressing One's Whole Self at Work

Bernardo M. Ferdman and
Laura Morgan Roberts

In an eloquent *New York Times* op-ed, K'naan (2012)—a singer and poet born in Somalia, raised in Canada, and now based in New York, whose song *Wavin' Flag* became one of the anthems for the 2010 FIFA World Cup—describes the pressures he felt from the American music industry to, as he put it, "change the walk of my songs" (p. SR7). Before he completed his third album, executives of his music label explained to K'naan how songs that are less anguished, more fun, and less focused on difficult subjects than his first two albums tend to get more radio air play, sell more, and be more successful in the United States. Without being told exactly what to do, K'naan nevertheless felt pressure— which he attributes mostly to himself—to conform for the sake of success and to, as his inner voice rationalized, "reach more people" (p. SR7).

In comparing his earlier and later work, he writes, "The first felt to me like a soul with a paintbrush; the other a body with no soul at all" (p. SR7), and he concludes by poetically explaining that one cannot successfully hide out as he temporarily tried to do: "while one can dumb down his lyrics, what one cannot do without being found out is hide his historical baggage. His sense of self. His walk. . . . I come with all the baggage of Somalia—of my grandfather's poetry, of pounding rhythms, of the war, of being an immigrant, of being an artist, of needing to explain a few things. Even in the friendliest of melodies, something in my voice stirs up a well of history . . ." (p. SR7). After using self-censorship to try to fit in and "walk like a prophet" (his metaphor for trying to be what others expected), K'naan found that his true strength came from his roots and his own walk. K'naan, like many others, discovered the dangers of suppressing key aspects of himself and the benefits of being authentic, of being fully himself, in his work. In the process, he first learned who he was and what was important to him; he then accepted these as things he did not want to give up, and found ways to express those identities and their associated values through his work, so as to strengthen both his output and himself.

Similar—albeit more ordinary—examples abound. One of us recalls a newly hired academic colleague who was afraid to tell her department chair that she was pregnant for fear of being seen as a less-than-serious assistant professor, and who suffered greatly as a result, both because she was not able to properly take care of her health throughout the pregnancy, and because she was constantly worried about being discovered; interestingly, her research focused in part on risk prevention. Participants in our workshops talk about wanting to feel like they really belong in their organizations and work groups, while at the same time struggling with dilemmas about how much to share with coworkers about various aspects of themselves, such as their culturally grounded experiences, their religious identities, or their families. Colleagues, relatives, or friends whose names are hard to pronounce for English speakers struggle with whether to adopt nicknames that are easier for coworkers to say or even with whether to change their names. Gay and lesbian people in organizations make choices daily about when and how, and whether, to come out to coworkers; even when their sexual orientation is known to their heterosexual coworkers, gay and lesbian individuals must continually make choices about how much information to share about their daily lives outside work. And many others, by trying to fit in or assimilate to their workplace in a range of ways, use up energy that could be spent more productively or lose valuable opportunities to draw on unique experiences or connections that could lead to innovation or creativity and otherwise add value to the organization and to their work groups.

Inclusive practices create environments in which a broader range of people can feel safe, accepted, valued, and able to contribute their talents and perspectives for the benefit of the collective. Much of the emphasis in diversity and inclusion work is on how organizations can effectively incorporate differences of various sorts, as well as on how individuals can better engage with dissimilar others without seeking to eliminate the differences. Given this, in discussing inclusion, the focus is typically on what organizations must do to be inclusive and how each of us can be more inclusive of others. Yet inclusion starts with oneself (Ferdman, 2007): knowing, accepting, and expressing one's whole self creates a platform for welcoming inclusion within one's organization. We believe that the ways in which we as individuals combine, manage, and express our multiple identities—in short, how we show up and express our full selves at work—is a key part of the dynamic process of inclusion. Thus the focus of this chapter is on the practice of self-inclusion, *bringing one's whole self to work*, as a fundamental component of inclusion overall.

Embracing Our Multiple Identities: The Foundation of Inclusion

Inclusion starts with our selves—recognizing and honoring the various components, characteristics, and identities that combine in each of us to make a whole person. To include others effectively and wholeheartedly, we first have to include ourselves; when we acknowledge the diversity of experiences, interests, and values that exist within ourselves, we are better equipped to notice and recognize the diversity around us in a more generative manner. Specifically, to be able to understand, engage, and value diversity at work and to effectively create inclusion for themselves and others, both leaders and employees must understand and appreciate all of their selves, without being required to compromise, hide, or give up any key part of what makes them who they are. Indeed, one could argue that being effective at work often involves a responsibility to be oneself, rather than using energy and resources trying to be someone different. Bell (2010), for example, in providing advice for women on including themselves and moving up in the corporate world, writes that "[i]n order to succeed you have to bring your whole self to the table. . . . [T]he higher you ascend, the more important it is to be authentic and comfortable with yourself. The finest, most accomplished, most effective leaders don't hide who they really are. In fact, the best leaders generally have a great deal of self-awareness and have learned from the . . . experiences that shaped their lives and enabled them to move ahead" (p. xiii).

Appreciating and using diversity for collective advantage involves recognizing, valuing, and leveraging the range of identities, perspectives, and approaches to work and life that are represented in any particular group or organization. In the same way, knowing about and engaging with one's full self (and its various components) is vital both to tapping into all of one's potential as well as to maximizing one's contributions in diverse groups and organizations.

Inclusion is deeper and more powerful than understanding or working successfully across multiple differences. At the individual level, it involves being able to connect to and integrate the various components of our identities, so as to experience ourselves more fully, as well as helping to create the conditions that can help others do this (Ferdman, 2007). Only when we are able to access and appreciate our full selves can we wholly experience inclusion, which means feeling that we are "safe, trusted, accepted, respected, supported, valued, fulfilled, engaged, and authentic in our working environment, both as individuals and as members of particular identity groups" (Ferdman, Barrera, Allen, & Vuong, 2009, p. 6). This *experience of inclusion* (Davidson & Ferdman, 2002; Ferdman & Davidson, 2002; Ferdman et al., 2009; Ferdman, Avigdor, Braun, Konkin, & Kuzmycz, 2010)—the psychological sense that we (and others who are like us) matter and that our voice and contributions are important—should be a fundamental goal of inclusion initiatives. The experience of inclusion helps us draw on our full resources and make our maximum contributions. Moreover, it provides a secure base and a model for how to respect the differences that others bring into the workplace.

To permit and encourage others to be fully themselves, we first need to be able to do that for ourselves. How can individuals do that? What are some approaches for being able to draw on more of our full selves at work and in our work in ways that foster integration, authenticity, engagement, and empowerment and that allow us to make our best contributions to our groups and organizations? In this chapter we address these questions, together with the following:

- What do we mean by *whole self*, and how does it connect to diversity and inclusion?
- How do multiple identities relate to inclusion?
- How can people access and use more of their relevant selves at work? What can people do to include themselves more (or to include more of themselves) and to feel and be more authentic at work?
- What is the responsibility of individuals to create inclusion for themselves and others?

Much of the literature on workplace diversity focuses on how people perceive and treat each other, on intergroup relations, and on structural aspects of organizations and society (Ferdman & Sagiv, 2012). These are core aspects of diversity and inclusion. Yet much of that literature does not directly address the internal phenomenology of inclusion—how people experience it psychologically—or the responsibilities of individuals with regard to including themselves. That is our focus here. We do want to highlight, however, that we do not see these as mutually exclusive issues, and our focus on the work of individuals is not intended to negate or minimize the critical importance of combating oppression, discrimination, and structural impediments to inclusion.

Views of the "Self"

The notion of *one's whole self* is at once simple and complex. Most individuals, when asked "Who are you?" or when they ask themselves "who am I?"—depending on the context—can answer quickly and without much reflection. They may, for example, describe their occupation, their values and beliefs, or their name and the names of their parents. They might focus on family roles (for example, parent, daughter) or their gender and hometown (for example, "I'm from New York," or "I'm a country girl"), or they might mention something about their typical behavior ("I like to play tennis") or personality ("I'm organized and persistent"). Yet our notions of "self" can also be quite layered and complex and are colored by culture and context (Ferdman, 1995, 2000, 2003).

The Self Incorporates Our Multiple Identities

A focal subject of much of psychology, the *self* is not static or fixed; rather, it is quite dynamic and develops over time, and incorporates not only descriptions, but also thoughts, feelings, intentions, and various other facets. In other words, when we speak of our whole self, we include and highlight our various identities—the labels and categories that situate us in a social world through the construction of defining characteristics and relationships with other entities—as well as the associated thoughts, feelings, and intentions (Roberts & Creary, 2012).

Identities are multifaceted; they encompass meanings that evolve from a range of sources, including group categories and memberships (for example, "Latino," "man," "Princetonian"), social roles ("mother," "customer," "neighbor"), self-narratives ("I persist in the face of difficulty," "I'm a reliable and dedicated friend"), reflected appraisals and interpersonal encounters ("My boss acknowledges that I'm a hard worker," "She understands how important my family is to me"), social structures ("rich" vs. "poor," "citizen," "undocumented"), individuating traits and characteristics ("extroverted," "tall"), and values ("democracy," "hard work") (for a review, see Roberts & Creary, 2012). They also include our views and beliefs about the groups we are part of and the cultural characteristics of those groups (Ferdman, 1990, 1995; Roberts & Creary, 2012). And each of us has particular accounts of how or why we came to be who we are (Ferdman, 2000) and how the various identities relate to each other.

For example, as management and leadership scholars both of us (Bernardo and Laura) study and write about diversity in organizations from a psychological perspective. We both participate actively in the Academy of Management meetings. We are both parents and spouses. We both engage in religious practices, but we are from different faith traditions. We enjoy teaching, consulting, mentoring, and researching. One of us lives on the U.S. West Coast; the other lives in the southeastern United States. And these are just a few of our many identities and characteristics.

Additionally, we each have particular ways to describe what it means to be part of each of these groups, and what cultural features tend to characterize them. Indeed, each of us has a different description even for identities that we share (such as "scholar"). These cultural identities—our views of the cultural features characterizing the groups we belong to, our feelings about those cultural features, and the degree of overlap we see between ourselves and "typical" members of these groups—can range from being quite idiosyncratic to being quite similar to those of others (Ferdman, 1995; Ferdman & Gallegos, 2001). Finally, each of us integrates our multiple identities in an individualized way and gives meaning to the intersections and relationships among the identities in the context of our particular life path and social history (Ferdman, 1995, 2000; Roberts & Creary, 2012).

The self, then, is indeed complex!

Divided Versus Integrated Selves

Later in the chapter, we discuss in additional detail some of the ways that even how we construct the notion of the "self" is very much culturally grounded. At this point, we highlight that individuals vary in the degree to which they view people's multiple identities as distinct and separable, or as part of an inseparable whole. For example, from some perspectives, it may be seen as wholly reasonable that a person could be primarily (or completely) a "corporate executive" from 8 in the morning until 6 in the evening, and then "mother" and "spouse" from 6 p.m. until 8 a.m., with the two identities not having much to do with each other. Other perspectives would see the two identities as inseparable, with both present and important to the individual at all times, albeit with differential salience. (By the way, were you surprised, even a bit, when you learned that the corporate executive is also a mother? To the degree that this reaction is typical, it highlights one of the problems that both lead to and are exacerbated by the splitting of such identities.)

Individuals who have identities that are stigmatized in some way and believe that these should be hidden may be particularly likely to keep their public or "self-at-work" and their private or "self-at-home" separate and even divided (Sedlovskaya, Purdie-Vaughns, Eibach, LaFrance, Romero-Canyas, and Camp, 2013). In a recent series of fascinating studies, Sedlovskaya et al. (2013) showed that, among people who have such stigmatized identities (for example, gay men and religious students at a secular university) those who actively hid those identities in public—compared to those who did not—made larger distinctions between their public and private selves. And, on average, those with greater public-private distinction experienced more psychological distress (such as depression-type symptoms). There was a cost associated with maintaining a divided self.

Boogard and Roggeband (2010) studied processes of inequality in the Dutch police force on the basis of gender, ethnicity, and organizational identity. They found that particular ways of splitting off identities—for example, emphasizing one's higher rank in the system rather than one's gender—could have the paradoxical effect of perpetuating gender-based inequality. This is because gender and rank were intertwined in the Dutch police force, as they are in many organizations around the world. Their findings can also be interpreted to suggest that there are more positive effects both for the individual and for the organization—in terms of highlighting and addressing inequality—to the extent that people claim more integrated and holistic identities.

In sum, then, I may experience more dilemmas regarding when and how it is permissible, advisable, or helpful to bring the various parts of my identity to my work role, and I may experience more pressure to split off parts of myself, to the degree that I hold or that my cultural environment holds the more fragmented view of the self—a view that is relatively common in North America, Western Europe, and similar cultural contexts—or to the degree that some or many of my identities may be seen negatively by others at work.

Whether or not we (or the people around us) believe that our various identities can be separated from each other in some way, these identities nevertheless coexist within the same person. Scholars who focus on identity have begun to refer to the interconnections among identities—especially those that are in some way stigmatized or treated unequally in society—as *intersectionality* (for example, Cole, 2009; Holvino, 2010). This perspective (see also Ferdman, 1995, 2003) emphasizes the interweaving of each person's various identities in the context of cultural, societal, and organizational contexts that privilege or give power to some groups over others (Gallegos & Ferdman, 2012). Learning more about how the various parts of our identities connect with and interact with each other in an integrated and holistic way to make us who we are, as well as understanding more about the relative privilege or power (or lack thereof) associated with our various identities (Davidson, Wishik, Ewing, & Washington, 2012; Ely, 1995), can help support development of a more integrated and whole sense of self that spans one's multiple identities. It can also contribute to processes leading to less inequality and greater inclusion in our work groups and organizations.

Bringing One's Whole Self to Work: What Do We Mean and Why Does It Matter?

In this section, we discuss the key aspects of inclusion in organizations that are communicated by the phrase *bringing one's whole self to work*, together with some of their applied implications. Our argument comprises four central assertions: (1) each of us has different degrees of awareness regarding our multiple identities and makes choices about how to express those identities in different situations, including at work (Roberts, 2005); (2) each of us, as well as our organizations, will derive important benefits when we can be more authentic, by connecting with and expressing more of our multiple identities at work; (3) doing this is challenging and demands a great deal of presence and attention, together with discretion and flexibility; and (4) our social and organizational contexts play an important role in either hindering or facilitating the likelihood that we will connect with and express the various facets of our selves at work. Although our choices are affected by our social environment, our values, and our beliefs, we believe that ultimately, when we can be authentic and draw on our full range of identities in an integrated and holistic way, we will be better off—and so will our work groups and organizations.

For example, based in part on the assumption that having to hide one's sexual orientation was damaging both to service members and to the military more generally, the United States recently repealed its "Don't Ask, Don't Tell" policy that had barred people who are openly gay, lesbian, or bisexual from serving in the U.S. armed forces. Sedlovskaya et al. (2013) cite a range of evidence showing that hiding one's identities can be associated with less psychological well-being. Bowen and Blackmon (2003) describe how individuals who believe that they can freely disclose their various identities at work—including those that may be less visible—in the context of a supportive climate are more likely to express their views on important organizational issues and to "engage in organizational voice" (p. 1408). One of us (Bernardo), in conducting workshops on this topic, often asks participants what benefits they anticipate for their organization when they bring more of their full selves to work; responses typically include a sense of feeling heard and connected, increased engagement and retention, higher morale, stronger connection to and desire to be at work, more loyalty to the company, more creativity and innovation, and more productivity. Both intuitively and based on theory, research, and social practice, self-inclusion can reduce negative outcomes and increase positive ones, in ways that are beneficial both for individuals and for organizations.

We Each Make Choices About How Much to Know and Be

So what meaning is carried by the concept of *bringing one's whole self to work?* First, the action word *bringing* indicates the notion of individual agency—the person's power to act in and on the world, including the power to choose who and how to be. We believe that individuals routinely make conscious and unconscious choices about how fully to embody and express the various facets of their identities in specific contexts and interactions. In particular, they consider how much to display or make salient certain components of their identity in particular situations (Bell & Nkomo, 2001; Bowen & Blackmon, 2003; Creed & Scully, 2000; Hewlin, 2003; Meyerson & Scully, 1995; Ragins, 2008; Roberts & Roberts, 2007; Stone-Romero, Stone, & Lukaszewski, 2006). For example, in the case of the pregnant woman mentioned earlier, she made a choice not to tell others at work about her pregnancy. Someone else may choose to be quite open about his religious beliefs, sexual orientation, and/or preferred sports teams, among many possible identities that he could highlight.

This type of choice may involve either specifically mentioning a particular aspect of one's identity to others or providing signals or cues regarding a particular identity (such as wearing a necklace with a religious symbol, putting a bumper sticker on one's car, or displaying a photograph of one's family in one's workspace). Note that this presumption of agency (or choice) and selective disclosure and expression of identities is grounded in a Western cultural context; in other cultural contexts, there may be less choice and/or less separation among identities. The presumption of agency also applies to emotional and attitudinal displays: bringing one's whole self correspondingly involves being honest and transparent about one's feelings and one's opinions, rather than keeping them hidden. (Later in the chapter, we acknowledge the necessity of wisdom, discretion, and respect for others when bringing more of one's identities, emotions, and beliefs into the workplace.)

These choices about *bringing one's whole self* should preferably emerge from self-awareness of our multifaceted identities and critical reflection on our own actions. How we think about and experience ourselves shapes whether or not we explicitly mention or highlight those identities to others. When we psychologically activate certain identities in our organizations, in the sense that we become consciously aware of them, we pay more attention to how (and whether) we might wish to draw on aspects of those identities—including associated experiences and perspectives—in work activities and interactions (Rothbard & Ramarajan, 2009). In other words, even before making choices regarding what to disclose to others about ourselves, the first step involves being clearer about the many identities that make us who we are, so that we can feel more whole and more empowered, including when we are at work—rather than split off from valued parts of ourselves.

For example, a former Olympic athlete, now working in an unrelated industry, may choose—consciously or unconsciously—not to note, mention, or even think about her athleticism or accomplishment while at work because it seems irrelevant in that context. Likewise, a manager in an organization who has extensive experience in a different domain outside of work—an amateur musician, for example—may not think about or make any connections between those activities and his role as a manager. Yet the creative talents associated with his musicianship and the leadership experience involved in heading a band may lend insight into how best to coordinate the work efforts of his team. Thus his team might benefit were he to bring more of his musician identity to his managerial work and identity.

Being inclusive of one's whole self, by attending to one's own multifaceted identities and related experiences and "bringing" them to work, can provide avenues for greater creative insight into one's work and can also foster a greater range of interpersonal relationships in diverse organizations (Dutton, Roberts, & Bednar, 2010). Thus we advocate being intentional in developing such self-awareness.

There is another benefit of self-awareness of one's multiple identities. People often prefer to think of themselves in individual terms, rather than seeing themselves in terms of their membership in social collectives (such as those based on gender, race, nationality, ethnicity, or religion); this is especially true for those who are part of the dominant or more powerful groups in society (Ferdman, 2007). By becoming aware of not only these particular dominant-group identities, but also one's full set of important identities, it becomes easier to both acknowledge our connections to these larger groups and at the same time continue to see ourselves as unique individuals. This is because each of us has a particular configuration of identities that, in large part, makes us who we are (Ferdman, 1995). So we can experience ourselves as unique individuals and at the same time also be more aware of how that individuality is grounded in a set of social identities.

In Figure 3.1, we illustrate an exercise that one of us (Bernardo) typically uses in workshops designed to encourage individuals to learn more about their multiple identities and the expressions or implications of these identities in the workplace (see also Ferdman, 2003; Hannum, McFeeters, & Booysen, 2010). In this exercise, participants are asked to list their multiple social identities and to reflect on them in various ways. This activity typically results in a greater sense of wholeness and new insights about oneself and about identity more generally. It also helps participants set the stage for exploring the possible relevance of these identities to their work, even when they previously had not seen or considered such connections.

More Wholeness and Authenticity Are Better

Our second assertion focuses on the *whole* self: individuals and organizations benefit from authentically including a wider (rather than narrower) range of multifaceted experiences, thoughts, perspectives, and attitudes at work. Why is this important? Inclusion, from this vantage point, is valuable because it brings a number of benefits, not just for groups and organizations but also for individuals who experience it. By experiencing inclusion, in the sense that they can access and contribute more of themselves, individuals are more likely to develop and grow in healthy ways that build on their strengths and to become more self-actualizing (Roberts, Dutton, Spreitzer, Heaphy, & Quinn, 2005). As we discussed earlier, they are also clearer about who they are and what matters to them and do not need to use energy to maintain a divided self.

Figure 3.1. Exploring the Sources of Our Identity

Some Sources of Our (Social) Identity

What Are the Sources of *Your* Identity?
List as many of your social (group-based) identities as you can

Ethnicity Job type   Academic/
Religion/spirituality   professional affiliation
        Health   Division, function in the
                                organization
    Education   Nationality
Physical/mental   Gender
    abilities   Family
Geographic factors   Sexual orientation
    Politics   Race   Color
    Phenotype/genetics   Professional identity
        Birth order   Class/economic status
    Language(s)   Age/cohort
        Life experiences Ability/disability

Exploring Our Identities at Work

Which of your identities and characteristics are the most obvious and/or important to others at work?

Which of your identities and characteristics, especially those that are important to you, are either relatively hidden or less known at work?

What identities do you see yourself acquiring, developing, or highlighting in the future? How/why are these identities important to you? How do they or can they make a difference for you and others at work?

How comfortable and/or uncomfortable are you in sharing more of yourself at work? Why? What conditions have helped or would help you share more?

What makes it easy or hard to share more of yourself at work?

When you think about being fully included and engaged at work, what does that look like for you? What behaviors from others and from yourself help you experience more inclusion? What behaviors do you believe help others around you experience more inclusion?

Source: Copyright 2013 by Bernardo M. Ferdman. Reprinted with permission.

Note: The first image is adapted from Ferdman, 2003. Copyright 2003 by Bernardo M. Ferdman.

Developing Our Best Selves

People continue to mature throughout their life span. For this reason, we take a developmental view of the whole self, rather than a static one, in which each individual takes a unique developmental path. Individuals who experience more inclusion—in the sense of experiencing more internal breadth and integration—will be more likely to develop in ways that can help them realize their potential, and in that way move toward becoming their reflected best selves (Roberts, Dutton, et al., 2005). This is because such individuals are more likely to follow their own developmental path, rather than one imposed externally or modeled on others who are very different.

The Reflected Best Self Exercise (RBSE)™, developed by researchers of the Center for Positive Organizational Scholarship (Ross School of Business, University of Michigan, Ann Arbor), is a valuable tool for helping people develop in ways that promote inclusion. The RBSE exercise involves soliciting examples of strengths-in-action from key constituents, such as family, friends, and/or coworkers, and then identifying the common patterns and themes that define one's reflected best self. (For detailed instructions, see http://www.centerforpos.org/the-center/teaching-and -practice-materials/teaching-tools/reflected-best-self-exercise). One of us (Laura) has facilitated this exercise with thousands of emerging and accomplished leaders across the globe. People are initially very resistant to the idea of focusing on their strengths as a platform for development; they would rather focus on and seek feedback about their weaknesses, to avoid being perceived as arrogant and to address what they deem to be their most urgent developmental challenges (Roberts, Spreitzer, Dutton, Quinn, Heaphy, & Barker, 2005). However, after experiencing this intense immersion in their own best-self moments, people begin to develop a clearer, more elaborate, and more refined understanding of their own potential to contribute to their workplaces, communities, and families in unique and valuable ways.

From an inclusion point of view, this emphasis on developing into one's reflected best self helps people to understand the critical connections between their strengths and weaknesses. It also reveals core themes in life that have surfaced during their best-self moments, creating a deeper sense of coherence between their past, present, and anticipated future. The intense exploration into one's reflected best self also requires examining various life experiences within and outside of the workplace; people are surprised to discover the consistency in how their friends, family, and coworkers perceive their contributions. Thus the fragmentation between the work and nonwork self is reduced as people realize that their best self is more consistent across contexts than they may have originally believed. To develop into one's best self, inclusion involves examining one's strengths and contributions across the span of one's life, both inside and outside the workplace.

This self-understanding also allows for learning the critical distinctions between one's best self, typical self, and worst self, given the acknowledgment that one's best self is an authentic, but not a constant, state of being. Identifying with one's best self also builds confidence, providing a secure base from which to confront the moments and situations in which we are less than our best selves (Roberts, 2007) and to develop concrete action plans to be at our best more often and to make our best selves even better (Roberts, 2013).

Committing to develop into our best self requires the courage to deviate from our own typical self, as well as from social expectations for who one should be or become. At our best, we actively engage our strengths and values in ways that enhance our own vitality and that also create value for the social systems in which we are embedded (Roberts, Dutton, et al., 2005). Often, these best-self moments call for positive deviance—standing out from the crowd and departing from the norm in honorable ways (Roberts, 2013). When I experience my environment as welcoming *all* of me, just as I am, then paradoxically, I may be more able to grow and change in healthier ways; the key is that I work to become *my* best self, grounded in who I am now, who I have been in the past, and my own aspirations and hopes, rather than trying to become someone else. Even when we are most likely to focus on fitting in and proving our legitimacy in our work roles and organizational memberships, we benefit from incorporating a broader range of our identities into our work. For example, Cable, Gino, and Staats (2013) found that incorporating best-self development into organizational socialization processes resulted in higher retention and performance outcomes; specifically, inviting organizational newcomers to describe their best selves and how they might engage their best selves to contribute to their employing organizations was more effective for promoting inclusion than was emphasizing the organization's identity or other typical socialization tactics that involve diminishing individuality for the sake of organizational conformity.

Role-Modeling and Leadership for Inclusion

Individuals with more access to themselves and their own identities and experience are also more likely to develop richer and deeper relationships with others (see, for example, Avolio & Gardner, 2005; Bushe, 2009; Shamir & Eilam, 2005). They are less likely to be stressed and more likely to experience psychological well-being (Sedlovskaya et al., 2013). They are more likely to be content with their work as well as to be effective and powerful in their roles. Finally, in being grounded in their own values, goals, and convictions, they are more likely to show courage and determination in the face of challenges and to be better able to support development of a more inclusive and better environment for others (Avolio & Gardner, 2005; Ferdman, 2007; George, 2003; Goffee & Jones, 2006). By serving as role models of integration and self-inclusion, such individuals can help create the kind of world that will be better for themselves and for others. As Mahatma Gandhi wrote, "if we desire that change, we must first change ourselves" (Gandhi, 1999, Vol. 24, p. 22) and "We but mirror the world. All the tendencies present in the outer world are to be found in the world of our body. If we could change ourselves, the tendencies in the world would also change. As a man changes his own nature, so does the attitude of the world change towards him. . . . We need not wait to see what others do" (Gandhi, 1999, Vol. 13, p. 241). In other words, it is unlikely that we can accept and value others unless we can first accept and value ourselves—including both our similarities to and differences from those around us.

Experiencing and Manifesting Authenticity

Ultimately, embodying Gandhi's charge requires *authenticity*. Authenticity is about being genuine, honest, centered, and consistent with one's values. Essentially, it is about being true to oneself by committing to a never-ending process of actively knowing and sharing one's experience. Bushe (2009), in his work on what he calls *clear leadership*, argues that a key to effective leadership is being able to access one's thoughts, feelings, and wants, as well as one's observations, and being able to share those with others when relevant.

While building on Bushe and others (Avolio & Gardner, 2005; Erikson, 1995; George, 2003; Goffee & Jones, 2006) in this chapter, we see authenticity as being broader than individual expression of personal beliefs, feelings, and experiences. Authenticity, as it relates to the practice of inclusion, also involves being clear about and true to the full range of who we are, not only as individuals but also as members of various social and cultural groups. In this sense, it can be helpful to recognize that we are shaped by our social identities and cultural backgrounds, and that for many of us, these are meaningful both symbolically and substantively (Ferdman, 1995, 1997). Once we do that, we then can begin to shape our own account of what it means to be part of these groups. Because there is great diversity within every social and cultural group, recognizing our cultural connections and social identities need not mean that we are stereotyping ourselves or advocating that we be seen simply or only in group terms. Indeed, each of us has a particular perspective on what it means to be a member of particular cultural groups and of a particular set of groups (Ferdman, 1995) and therefore has an individualized story to tell. At the same time, it is difficult to be fully authentic in a multicultural group, organization, or society without including these group-based identities in the picture in some way.

Beyond this, authenticity recognizes the inconsistencies in one's own behavior, takes responsibility for self-imposed failures, and embraces a holistic view of personal strengths and limitations that complement or undermine each other. For example, during the 2012 U.S. presidential election, President Barack Obama publicly acknowledged to the news media and general public (sometimes seriously, other times jokingly) that he was not at his best during his first televised debate against opponent Mitt Romney. Obama framed this debate performance as "having a bad night"; in so doing, he took responsibility for his own "failure," but he continued to maintain that this event did not define his capability or undermine his track record.

Authenticity also encompasses a commitment to share cultural experiences and cultural perspectives, which are associated with dimensions of difference related to social identities (Roberts, 2005). During the same 2012 campaign season, one of us (Laura) was teaching a leadership executive education course in Denmark on the U.S. election day, and she actively engaged these Danish leaders in a discussion of the social and political dynamics that influenced the election of the first African American president in the United States, as well as of the factors that influenced perceptions of his performance. In so doing, Laura brought her expertise as a diversity scholar, as well as her experience as an African American, female citizen of the United States to give her Danish students a different perspective on the U.S. presidential campaign. Laura followed this discussion with a lecture and case analysis of cross-cultural leadership and gender dynamics in European organizations. Thus authentic engagement was a theme for the entire day's discussions of global leadership. Authenticity involves giving voice to underrepresented perspectives and voices, shining light on marginalized groups, and making sense of teammates' competing commitments to different cultural traditions.

Authenticity Is Challenging and Requires Presence and Attention

Our third assertion is that bringing one's whole self is an effortful process that requires attention, discretion, and flexibility (Roberts, Cha, Hewlin, & Settles, 2009). We argued earlier that integration—experiencing oneself as a whole person with multiple identities, interests, and roles—has particular benefits; here we also suggest that there may be limits to the authentic expression of all the details and nuances of our identities, in the sense that we do not advocate necessarily or automatically being completely open to others at all times about all the facets of one's selves. At the same time, this need to be thoughtful and attentive should not preclude us from developing a more integrated sense of self.

For some people, accessing certain identities or values in a context where these are not accepted or where they may even be disdained can be jarring and problematic, at best, and in some cases even dangerous. In other cases, it can be inappropriate. We do not mean to suggest that one should always or even sometimes express the totality of one's thoughts and feelings at work.

"Bringing one's whole self" does not constitute the freedom to behave impulsively at work in ways that will be detrimental to other people in that environment—and likely harmful to oneself as well (Roberts et al., 2009). Rather, we advocate for a more strategic approach to self-inclusion, in which individuals increase alignment between internal experiences and external expressions of the most valued and valuable aspects of their identities at work (Roberts, 2007).

The challenge is that for many people the bias has been toward hiding and splitting off identities rather than toward integration. In many organizations, and for many people, there seems to be an assumption that one's nonwork identities are somehow not relevant or important at work. To support positive exploration of unexplored connections between one's work role and one's identities previously hidden or less salient at work, and particularly to explore how these and similar identities can be positively integrated with one's work identity, one of us (Bernardo) typically asks workshop participants to conduct appreciative interviews with each other in which the listener asks the speaker to describe a specific work situation in which she or he felt fully integrated and authentic and was also able to be particularly effective (see Exhibit 3.1). This activity is usually quite powerful for participants and can quickly fill a room with a great deal of excitement and energy. Beyond providing an opportunity to engage more deeply in challenging participants' prior assumptions about what belongs "inside" and "outside" the workplace, the activity also allows them to tell their own stories from their own perspective while receiving unconditional regard and interest from a work colleague or fellow participant.

Exhibit 3.1. Sharing Experiences of Inclusion and Success

Exercise: Exploring Our Best and Whole Selves at Work

Objective: To explore in depth an example of inclusion in your own experience, and to draw out implications for creating more inclusion for yourself and others.

Instructions to listener: Listen, be curious, and "bring out" the interviewee, on his/her own terms, rather than yours. Do not try to compare your experience with his/hers; rather, support your interviewee in exploring his/her identities through his/her own perspectives. If desired, jot down a few key quotes, themes, and examples from the "stories."

Questions:
1. What are one or two of your identities or parts of yourself that are very important to you yet not often particularly "up" for you or visible at work? Why is that part of yourself so important to you?
2. Now, describe a time, either at your current organization or in another work setting, when you felt particularly engaged with your work and with yourself. You felt and experienced yourself to be *effective, powerful, valuable, successful, authentic, energized, complete, proud, and fully ALIVE*. You and others valued your work, you contributed fully to your group/organization, AND you could be your "best" and "whole" self. What happened? What made you your "best self" in that situation? Who was involved? What did you feel? How did the parts of your self that you mentioned before show up and support you and your work? How did they integrate with the other parts of your identity?
3. Explore what it was that helped you to feel included:
   a. What did you do? How did it feel?
   b. What did others do? How did it feel?

Debriefing questions (for group): What was the experience like? Where was the energy? What was the feeling of releasing or disclosing? What are some insights/implications/learning/hopes?

Questions for further dialogue and/or reflection:
- What dilemmas have you experienced with regard to being more personally and culturally authentic at work? How have you handled these dilemmas?
- How can/should our cultural identities show up at work? Why?
- How will bringing more of our full selves and our culture to work help us, our colleagues, and our organizations?
- What stories can you share about any of these topics?

When we consider authenticity and self-expression in light of cultural and social identities, personal expressions, and critical reflection on one's own behavior, we bring to light some of the dilemmas and even paradoxes raised by the desire and imperative to bring all of one's self to work. Specifically, in finding effective and appropriate ways to be authentic, we need to figure out and decide when and how to address our individual connections to culturally and group-based experiences as well as when it may make sense to hold back. For example, for some men, part of their group experience may have been telling sexist jokes. We would not advocate for telling those jokes at work as a way to bring all of one's self and to create more authentic self-expression. In a different example, someone's identity outside of work may involve being a religious missionary; that person need not keep this missionary involvement a secret, yet it would be inappropriate to condemn coworkers' religious beliefs while on the job in a secular organization. In yet another example, a mid-level manager, who often finds herself disagreeing with her new boss's strategic plans, may struggle with determining when and how to express her concerns with his plans. In this circumstance, the need for diplomacy is clear; we advocate not undermining one's boss by gossiping about or sabotaging his plans, but rather being clear, specific, and direct in communicating how the specific concerns expressed are related to specific outcomes within one's own purview.

Being true to one's core values is the primary standard we advocate; other questions of inclusion can be considered based on their consistency with or contradiction of such values. These dilemmas are even more pointed for leaders, who have responsibility not only to include themselves but also to help make room for diversity and inclusion across the organization (Wasserman, Gallegos, & Ferdman, 2008). In this role, they must regularly make tactical and strategic choices about self-presentation that will enhance their own authenticity while creating an inclusive environment for others. For example, should I, as a manager, express my anxiety over tomorrow's executive staff meeting to members of my team? Should I raise my voice in anger with my boss (or even mention the feeling) for his (perceived) failure to support me in a cross-departmental meeting? Should I ask my administrative assistant how she and her children are dealing with their recent divorce? Should I invite my teammate to attend Bible study with me during lunch hour? Should I bring my same-sex significant other to the family picnic next weekend? Should I wear my favorite beer-can tie to work on dress-down day? Should I avoid telling my sales team the joke I just heard about a celebrity's sexual indiscretion?

Of course, sometimes core values can compete with each other; for example, I value having as much time with family as possible, but I also care about my job security, so I may not go home as early as I would like because it may put my job in jeopardy. By being clearer about my various identities and the commitments and values that each represents, I can then be more able to sort out what approach might make the most sense for me (and for others I care about). Moreover, I can be more discerning about the impact of my enacted values upon those around me when I choose to bring more of myself to work. And I may be better able to see how my choices are not always solely individual choices but may be grounded in one or more of my social identities. For example, some Latino leaders tell us that they find it relatively challenging to "toot their own horn"—to self-promote at work; for many of them, this is not simply an individual idiosyncrasy but reflects values grounded in cultural identity.

For us, then, a key part of authenticity involves learning how to manage one's effects on others and being able to engage effectively with the diversity present in one's environment, including one's work group. Each individual is responsible to learn that not everyone is like him or her. In this sense, then, part of including myself also involves being aware of my effect on others.

Work and Social Contexts Matter

Our fourth assertion addresses how the work context influences employees' experiences of inclusion: if certain aspects of identity are deemed less relevant or less valuable by an organization, industry, or profession, workers may be less likely—cognitively and behaviorally—to bring these aspects of their identity to work.

For instance, even though I may be clear that I am a parent, former athlete, or musician, the conditions of my work environment may make those aspects of my identity more or less salient in my own mind while I am at work.

Such messages are not always explicit. They can be communicated in a variety of ways, including by the way work gets done, by the types of interactions and processes that are typical or normative, and by the symbols and artifacts that are typically displayed in the workplace. In some organizations, for example, it may be quite normal and appropriate for a mother to nurse her newborn infant at her desk, while in others this would be unheard of and even grounds for dismissal. In some organizations, meetings may be scheduled for any time of the day or week including during hours that are presumably "off," or employees may be sent on long-distance assignments from one day to the next, without being asked first. In other organizations this would be considered inappropriate or extremely unusual, since it would be normative to check with the relevant individuals first.

To understand the dynamics of bringing (or not bringing) ourselves to work, we need to consider the systems of control, boundaries, containment, and prediction that often lead us to express only what we believe is normative, welcomed, or relevant in the work context. How much we reveal about ourselves and even how much we think about the different facets of our selves at work can depend, for example, on what we think the spoken and unspoken rules are for what is considered appropriate in that context. Being aware of these dynamics is important for all who wish to create more inclusion for themselves and others, and particularly so for leaders. Individually and with coworkers, creating inclusion for self and others involves ongoing reflection on the following questions: "How can we move to give each other and ourselves more permission and support for authenticity? How do we co-create contexts that engage more of ourselves at work?" Without such reflection, the process can at times be quite daunting; to the extent that we can create opportunities to collaborate on the processes of self-inclusion, the likelihood that it can occur and lead to benefits will be enhanced.

Earlier, we alluded to the cultural framing of the "self;" here, we elaborate on this and place the concept in a cultural context.

Sampson (1988) described the distinction between the *ensembled* or *relational self*—more common in collectivistic cultures such as those found in China, Africa, and Latin America—and the *autonomous self*, which is more common in individualistic cultures, such as those found in North America and Western Europe. Autonomous or self-contained views of the person construct the boundary between the self and others as firm, consider control over behavior and experience to reside solely in the person, and typically define self and nonself as mutually exclusive (Sampson, 1988). In contrast, ensembled views of the self construct the boundaries between self and nonself as more fluid, and even as overlapping, and consider that power and control over one's behavior does not fully reside in the individual but rather in the relationship of the individual and his or her environment (which includes important others).

The question of inclusion depends, then, on how we think of our "self" and how it is constituted—as ensembled or as autonomous. The dominant cultural assumption in the United States is that the self is autonomous and self-contained, and that we can therefore split ourselves up—for example, in different situations. From this perspective, one could be a parent in the evening and a professor by day, and the two do not have to have anything to do with each other. Many people in the United States conceive of the self as multiple, fragmented components that can be selectively featured, prioritized, or concealed and forgotten. In contrast, a notion of the ensembled self views our identities as very much connected to the groups and other people in our lives. From that perspective, our identities are constituted in relationship to others and in our various roles. In that view, being a parent and a professor cannot really be separated, even though the two roles are each in the foreground at different times. For those who hold an ensembled view of self, there is no choice in bringing the whole self, as there is no way to separate its various and interrelated components. And when such an individual works in an environment that seems to demand such splitting, it can be particularly stressful.

In both types of cultures, particularly in those settings that require more specialization, we see that people are more likely to split themselves up, as it were, and, when they go to work, to forget about aspects of themselves, when they do not see those identities as quite relevant to that situation. For example, I may be a parent at home, but my role as a parent may never come up at work, or it may be experienced as being in conflict with my role as professor or consultant (rather than an integral part of the role). This fragmentation can create dilemmas regarding whether, when, and how to bring my whole self—professor, consultant, *and* parent—to work. It can also make it more difficult for someone with that view of self to call upon parts of herself that could be important or helpful at work in some way yet do not seem immediately pertinent.

Given these dynamics, we believe that leaders and organizations have a responsibility to help create the conditions within which individuals can more fully include themselves. The study by Cable et al. (2013) that we referenced earlier provides specific examples of how leaders can help to create inclusion during socialization—the initial period of organizational membership—by inviting people to think about and discuss their personal identities and best selves. At the same time, each individual has a responsibility to take up the challenge of self-inclusion and to help create conditions that will allow others to be fully themselves as well. We often operate based on our assumptions about whether our whole self will be welcomed in a situation or an interaction. Yet our concerns about being rejected may lead us to miss the subtle cues or invitations that sharing more of ourselves can promote our own growth or can help to promote someone else's growth. In our workshops on authenticity, one of us (Laura) asks participants to discuss circumstances in which they wear "masks" at work, and their rationale for so doing. People respond that they wear masks because they often fear the presumed consequences of authenticity, assuming that people from different backgrounds will not understand their own perspectives, experiences, or interests. We discuss experiences in which these assumptions have proven false. We also discuss how people can respond to moments in which others (for example, dominant group members and/or bosses) disclose aspects of their own personal identities, in a way that creates a deeper authentic connection, without feeling forced to share more than what they feel comfortable sharing. It is our individual responsibility to be observant, take initiative, and be prepared to share different parts of ourselves when the opportunities present themselves. It is also our responsibility to respect others' decisions to disclose more or less than we choose to disclose in our workplaces. To the extent that more of us take personal responsibility to start on the path of becoming more integrated and whole and to also behave accordingly, it is more likely that the collective—those around us—will become similarly integrated and whole.

Toward Integration: Dilemmas and Challenges

Throughout this chapter, we have argued that it is helpful to be more integrated—first for ourselves, then for others. This leads to more open expression of thoughts, feelings, and intentions, and the ability to draw on more resources. What constitutes strategic and appropriate self-presentation and access? How do we move toward integration? As we have pointed out, we do not see bringing the whole self to work as being about "letting it all hang out" or sharing all aspects of oneself with others. Rather, this process involves sustaining commitment to understanding the complexity within ourselves and in others.

The Responsibility to Define and Express Ourselves

Bringing one's whole self to work is a process of self-definition. A key part of this involves our individual responsibility to understand our own cultural identity; in other words, to learn how our connections to rituals, practices, and perspectives are products of our cultural experience as well as our individual history (Ferdman, 1995). To what degree am I aware of how much my taken-for-granted assumptions about what is appropriate and normal are culturally grounded? And to what extent and in what ways am I able to express this awareness and these cultural connections? For example, I may have certain beliefs about privacy and individual expression—whether inside or outside of work—that come from the norms, values, and practices common in my identity groups. Or I may have views about the appropriateness of discussing one's dating partners at work—or about the need to do so. Similarly, groups can differ on what is considered safe and appropriate to share. If I can develop an awareness of what is going on inside me and why, and a willingness and skill to express and communicate it appropriately, I can be more likely to create a space not only in which I can more fully include myself, but also one in which others can do so for themselves. The key to this is developing skills for and practices to be able to share with others my needs, drivers, and perspectives—both as an individual and as a member of multiple identity groups.

Bringing one's whole self to work requires individuals to be accountable for their authenticity. Difficult choices of intrapersonal inclusion can confront us when we want to express, at work, certain aspects of our selves that we value but that are not typical or are even looked down on by others. That is, although a person may consider a particular aspect of identity to be critical to her self-definition, other people in the organization—its leaders, for example—may view it as insignificant, irrelevant, or even damaging to the dominant cultural practices. Choosing to express a nondominant aspect of identity at work will likely result in some degree of questioning and resistance by those who are less comfortable with that aspect of one's identity (Roberts et al., 2009). At the same time, doing so can make more visible the reality of diversity in that context and can serve at least to initiate a process of questioning and, hopefully, dialogue and learning. Choosing not to suppress but rather to "come out" with regard to such identities can ultimately strengthen individuals' capacity to contribute to the organization (Bowen & Blackmon, 2003). For example, one of us was recently approached at a workshop by a participant who explained that she was very uncomfortable with the expectation that she join in certain social events at work, because she believed that doing so was contrary to her religious convictions, and she also felt uncomfortable explaining her feelings and their bases to her colleagues and supervisor. Paradoxically, these events were designed with the goal of allowing coworkers to get to know each other better. In this type of situation, it may be more useful to the individual and to the group to take the risk of being more open.

Just as organizations that welcome inclusion should develop systems and strategies to manage resistance, individuals should do so as well. When we choose to bring more of our whole self to work, we are more likely to participate critically in life; as we do this, we learn to consider others' expectations and interpretations of who we are, but to reject these expectations and interpretations when they do not resonate with our own experiences (Heidegger, 1962; Shamir & Eilam, 2005). In this sense, when we decide how to display the most valued and valuable aspects of our identities at work, we also gain clarity about our own boundaries. We become clearer about our preferences for permeability, integration, or segmentation among the different facets of our life; we make this abstract conceptualization of boundaries more concrete through our choices of self-expression.

Being Our Imperfect Selves: Embracing Diversity, Inconsistency, and Humility

Inclusion can be uncomfortable when we have to coexist with differences that are unsettling! This is especially uncomfortable when we acknowledge the inconsistencies and differences among our own roles, identities, commitments, words, and deeds. To put forth our best self, we must recognize our multiple parts, including the imperfect parts of our complex selves. While some people may produce cutting-edge, innovative concepts for new product development, they may also lack sensitivity to deadlines and budget constraints. Others have a keen eye toward details, but may be frustrated by loosely defined visions that lack plans for implementation. Some of us may embrace change but have difficulty following through on long-term commitments. Others may thrive in front of audiences but crave the spotlight so voraciously that they consistently overshadow (or intentionally demean) others' equally valuable contributions. Bringing one's whole self to work involves being honest about these combinations of strengths and limitations, while recognizing that each of us is constantly developing and learning. This honesty enables diverse teams to complement one another's strengths, address limitations, and discover unique paths to thrive collectively.

Bringing one's whole self to work also means recognizing inconsistencies between our own espoused values and actions. Perhaps we consistently state that we value all of the members of our team, but we disproportionately allocate resources toward those who consistently support our own visions, at the expense of those who push back on our (seemingly brilliant) ideas. We must be honest about our ego-defensive routines so as to bring our vulnerability and awareness of insecurities into our work; this honesty is critical to override biases against those who differ from us (Ely, Meyerson, & Davidson, 2006). Recognizing these inconsistencies within ourselves can also help us show more grace toward ourselves and others when we notice that intentions and impact may contradict each other. In sum, we would like to avoid an overly glossy view of the whole self and how it promotes inclusion for groups, organizations, and societies. Bringing one's whole self should be motivated by the desire to become one's *best self,* and this involves the whole-hearted embrace of a multifaceted, imperfect, and yet valuable self.

Finally, bringing one's whole self to work requires humility. A key aspect of humility is that, at the same time that I claim my identities, I do not claim full ownership or definition of the groups those represent. For example, I may have a particular take on what it means to be Jewish, and can be proud and authentic about that, while recognizing that another Jew may have a different take on the same social identity. That way, I can be myself, grounded in my social identities, without placing myself and others in some kind of stereotypical bind.

In conclusion, the process and practice of inclusion begins with ourselves: identifying and affirming the multifaceted nature of our own self-concept and being strategic about how to engage various parts of ourselves to strengthen ourselves, our relationships, and our organizations. In this vein, inclusion requires concentrated effort and critical self-awareness; yet it is more rewarding and empowering to be ourselves than to expend our energy in trying to fragment and hide different parts of our identities when we fear they will not be embraced. In bringing our whole selves to work, we are able to focus our energy on fulfilling our potential and becoming our best selves.

References

Avolio, B. J., & Gardner, W. L. (2005). Authentic leadership development: Getting to the root of positive forms of leadership. *The Leadership Quarterly, 16,* 315–338.

Bell, E. L. J. E. (2010). *Career GPS: Strategies for women navigating the new corporate landscape.* New York: HarperCollins.

Bell, E. L. J. E., & Nkomo, S. M. (2001). *Our separate ways: Black and White women and the struggle for professional identity.* Boston, MA: Harvard Business School Press.

Boogaard, B., & Roggeband, C. (2010). Paradoxes of intersectionality: Theorizing inequality in the Dutch police force through structure and agency. *Organization, 17,* 53–75. doi:10.1177/1350508409350042

Bowen, F., & Blackmon, K. (2003). Spirals of silence: The dynamic effects of diversity on organizational voice. *Journal of Management Studies, 40,* 1393–1417.

Bushe, G. R. (2009). *Clear leadership: Sustaining real collaboration and partnership at work.* Boston, MA: Davies-Black.

Cable, D. M., Gino, F., & Staats, B. R. (2013). Breaking them in or eliciting their best? Reframing socialization around newcomers' authentic self-expression. *Administrative Science Quarterly, 58,* 1–36.

Cole, E. R. (2009). Intersectionality and research in psychology. *American Psychologist, 64*(3), 170–180.

Creed, W. E. D., & Scully, M. A. (2000). Songs of ourselves: Employees' deployment of social identity in workplace encounters. *Journal of Management Inquiry, 9,* 391–412.

Davidson, M. N., & Ferdman, B. M. (2002, August). The experience of inclusion. In B. Parker, B. M. Ferdman, & P. Dass (Chairs), *Inclusive and effective networks: Linking diversity theory and practice.* All-Academy symposium presented at the 62nd Annual Meeting of the Academy of Management, Denver.

Davidson, M. N., Wishik, H., Ewing, T., & Washington, S. B. (2012, August). *Social identity dominance: How we all live privileged identities (and what to do about it).* Workshop presented at the 72nd Annual Meeting of the Academy of Management, Boston.

Dutton, J. E., Roberts, L. M., & Bednar, J. (2010). Pathways for positive identity construction at work: Four types of positive identity and the building of social resources. *Academy of Management Review, 35,* 265–293.

Ely, R. J. (1995). The role of dominant identity and experience in organizational work on diversity. In S. E. Jackson & M. N. Ruderman

(Eds.), *Diversity in work teams: Research paradigms for a changing workplace* (pp. 161–186). Washington, DC: American Psychological Association.

Ely, R. J., Meyerson, D. E., & Davidson, M. N. (2006). Rethinking political correctness. *Harvard Business Review, 84*(9), 79–87.

Erikson, R. (1995). The importance of authenticity for self and society. *Symbolic Interaction, 18*(2), 121–144.

Ferdman, B. M. (1990). Literacy and cultural identity. *Harvard Educational Review, 60*, 181–205.

Ferdman, B. M. (1995). Cultural identity and diversity in organizations: Bridging the gap between group differences and individual uniqueness. In M. M. Chemers, S. Oskamp, & M. A. Costanzo (Eds.), *Diversity in organizations: New perspectives for a changing workplace* (pp. 37–61). Thousand Oaks, CA: Sage.

Ferdman, B. M. (1997). Values about fairness in the ethnically diverse workplace. [Special Issue: Managing in a global context: Diversity and cross-cultural challenges]. *Business and the Contemporary World: An International Journal of Business, Economics, and Social Policy, 9*, 191–208.

Ferdman, B. M. (2000). "Why am I who I am?" Constructing the cultural self in multicultural perspective. *Human Development, 43*, 19–23.

Ferdman, B. M. (2003). Learning about our and others' selves: Multiple identities and their sources. In N. Boyacigiller, R. Goodman, & M. Phillips (Eds.), *Crossing cultures: Insights from master teachers* (pp. 49–61). London: Routledge.

Ferdman, B. M. (2007). Inclusion starts with knowing yourself. *San Diego Psychologist, 22*(4), 1, 5–6.

Ferdman, B. M., Avigdor, A., Braun, D., Konkin, J., & Kuzmycz, D. (2010). Collective experience of inclusion, diversity, and performance in work groups. *Revista de Administração Mackenzie, 11*(3), 6–26. doi:10.1590/S1678-69712010000300003

Ferdman, B. M., Barrera, V., Allen, A., & Vuong, V. (2009, August 11). Inclusive behavior and the experience of inclusion. In B. G. Chung (Chair), *Inclusion in organizations: Measures, HR practices, and climate.* Symposium presented at the 69th Annual Meeting of the Academy of Management, Chicago.

Ferdman, B. M., & Davidson, M. N. (2002). A matter of difference— Inclusion: What can I and my organization do about it? *The Industrial-Organizational Psychologist, 39*(4), 80–85.

Ferdman, B. M., & Gallegos, P. I. (2001). Latinos and racial identity development. In C. L. Wijeyesinghe & B. W. Jackson III (Eds.), *New perspectives on racial identity development: A theoretical and practical anthology* (pp. 32–66). New York: New York University Press.

Ferdman, B. M., & Sagiv, L. (2012). Diversity in organizations and cross-cultural work psychology: What if they were more connected? (Focal article). *Industrial and Organizational Psychology: Perspectives on Science and Practice, 5*(3), 323–345. doi:10.1111/j.1754–9434 .2012.01455.x

Gallegos, P. V., & Ferdman, B. M. (2012). Latino and Latina ethnoracial identity orientations: A dynamic and developmental perspective. In C. L. Wijeyesinghe & B. W. Jackson III (Eds.), *New perspectives on racial identity development: Integrating emerging frameworks* (2nd ed., pp. 51–80). New York: New York University Press.

Gandhi, M. K. (1999). *The collected works of Mahatma Gandhi* (Electronic Book, 98 volumes). New Delhi: Publications Division Government of India. Available at www.gandhiserve.org

George, B. (2003). *Authentic leadership: Rediscovering the secrets to creating lasting value.* San Francisco: Jossey-Bass.

Goffee, R., & Jones, G. (2006). *Why should anyone be led by you? What it takes to be an authentic leader.* Boston, MA: Harvard Business School Press.

Hannum, K. M., McFeeters, B. B., & Booysen, L. (2010). Mapping your social identities. In K. M. Hannum, B. B., McFeeters, & L. Booysen (Eds.), *Leading across differences: Cases and perspectives* (pp. 183–192). San Francisco: Pfeiffer.

Heidegger, M. (1962). *Being and time* (J. MacQuarrie and E. Robinson, Trans.). London: SCM Press.

Hewlin, P. F. (2003). And the award for best actor goes to . . . : Facades of conformity in organizational settings. *Academy of Management Review, 28,* 633–656.

Holvino, E. (2010). Intersections: The simultaneity of race, gender and class in organization studies. *Gender, Work & Organization, 17*(3), 248–277. doi:10.1111/j.1468–0432.2008.00400.x

K'naan. (2012, December 9). Censoring myself for success. *New York Times,* p. SR7.

Meyerson, D., & Scully, M. (1995). Tempered radicalism and the politics of ambivalence and change. *Organization Science, 6*(5), 585–600.

Ragins, B. R. (2008). Disclosure disconnects: Antecedents and consequences of disclosing invisible stigmas across life domains. *Academy of Management Review, 33,* 194–215.

Roberts, L. M. (2005). Changing faces: Professional image construction in diverse organizational settings. *Academy of Management Review, 30,* 685–711.

Roberts, L. M. (2007). Bringing your whole self to work: Lessons in authentic engagement from women leaders. In B. Kellerman & D. L. Rhode (Eds.), *Women and leadership: The state of play and strategies for change* (pp. 329–360). San Francisco: Jossey-Bass.

Roberts, L. M. (2013). Reflected best self engagement at work: Positive identity, alignment and the pursuit of vitality and value creation. In I. Boniwell & S. David (Eds.), *The Oxford handbook of happiness* (pp. 767–782). New York: Oxford University Press.

Roberts, L. M., Cha, S. E., Hewlin, P. F., & Settles, I. H. (2009). Bringing the inside out: Enhancing authenticity and positive identity in organizations. In L. M. Roberts & J. E. Dutton (Eds.), *Exploring positive identities and organizations: Building a theoretical and research foundation* (pp. 149–169). New York: Routledge.

Roberts, L. M., & Creary, S. J. (2012). Positive identity construction: Insights from classical and contemporary theoretical perspectives. In K. Cameron & G. Spreitzer (Eds.), *The Oxford handbook of positive organizational scholarship* (pp. 70–83). New York: Oxford University Press.

Roberts, L. M., Dutton, J. E., Spreitzer, G. M., Heaphy, E. D., & Quinn, R. E. (2005). Composing the reflected best-self portrait: Building pathways for becoming extraordinary in work organizations. *Academy of Management Review, 30,* 712–736.

Rothbard, N., & Ramarajan, L. (2009). Checking your identities at the door? Positive relationships between nonwork and work identities. In L. M. Roberts & J. E. Dutton (Eds.), *Exploring positive identities and organizations: Building a theoretical and research foundation* (pp. 125–148). New York: Routledge.

Roberts, L. M., & Roberts, D. D. (2007). Testing the limits of antidiscrimination law: The business, legal, and ethical ramifications of cultural profiling at work. *Duke Journal of Gender Law & Policy, 14,* 369–405.

Roberts, L. M., Spreitzer, G., Dutton, J., Quinn, R., Heaphy, E., & Barker, B. (2005). How to play to your strengths. *Harvard Business Review, 83*(1), 75–80.

Sampson, E. E. (1988). The debate on individualism: Indigenous psychologies of the individual and their role in personal and societal functioning. *American Psychologist, 43,* 15–22. doi:10.1037/0003-066X.43.1.15

Sedlovskaya, A., Purdie-Vaughns, V., Eibach, R. P., LaFrance, M., Romero-Canyas, R., & Camp, N. P. (2013). Internalizing the closet: Concealment heightens the cognitive distinction between public and private selves. *Journal of Personality and Social Psychology.* doi:10.1037/a0031179

Shamir, B., & Eilam, G. (2005). "What's your story?" A life-stories approach to authentic leadership development. *The Leadership Quarterly, 16,* 395–417.

Stone-Romero, E., Stone, D., & Lukaszewski, K. (2006). The influence of disability on role-taking in organizations. In A. Konrad, P. Prasad, & J. Pringle (Eds.), *Handbook of workplace diversity* (pp. 401–430). Thousand Oaks, CA: Sage.

Wasserman, I. C., Gallegos, P. V., & Ferdman, B. M. (2008). Dancing with resistance: Leadership challenges in fostering a culture of inclusion. In K. M. Thomas (Ed.), *Diversity resistance in organizations* (pp. 175–200). Mahwah, NJ: Erlbaum.

CHAPTER FOUR

Strengthening Interpersonal Awareness and Fostering Relational Eloquence

Ilene C. Wasserman

> *Communication is about meaning . . . but not just in a passive sense of perceiving messages. Rather, we live lives filled with meanings, and one of our life challenges is to manage those meanings so that we can make our social worlds coherent and live within them with honor and respect. But this process of managing our meanings is never done in isolation. We are always and necessarily coordinating the way we manage our meanings with other people. (Pearce, 2012, p. 4)*

Recently, I was talking with a client about a strategic planning process to engage the whole organization that would, at the same time, impact people's everyday relationships. The CEO was committed to creating a more inclusive organization where everyone recognized his or her role in fulfilling the mission. He saw this process as "mission-critical." As we were reviewing the day's work over dinner, he turned to us and said: "Sometimes I feel like I am talking French and they are talking English." Given that this organization is located in the United States, his comment was both metaphorical and poetic. Each day, I am reminded that creating shared meaning that is coherent and coordinated requires a well-developed capacity to attend to others and to notice what patterns we are creating. We are in a constant process of choosing to engage in collaboration, conflict, or appreciation in our words and actions as we navigate our relationships. The challenge is to become aware of our choices and skilled in enacting the behaviors that lead to our intended outcomes.

The central questions I address in this chapter include:

- What interpersonal processes minimize destructive conflict and maximize the ability of dyads (and teams) to use their differences as a source of strength and effectiveness?
- What are the key competencies and tools, frameworks and practices for people to engage effectively across difference so as to leverage diversity for mutual benefit?
- How can these competencies be acquired, maintained, practiced, and developed?

This chapter describes what each of us can do, as we engage with each other, to enact inclusion. (I use the term *we* colloquially to refer to you, the reader, and me, the author, as I address the ongoing challenges and opportunities of inclusion.) I begin by addressing how we can be more competent with others—particularly those whose personal styles and cultural histories differ from our own. I articulate a shift in the notion of communication as primarily a process of transmitting meaning, to communication as an ongoing process of jointly creating meaning. This shift is consequential because it moves our attention from one person's responsibility to be clear, or the other's not getting it, to the shared and relational responsibility for clarity (McNamee & Gergen, 1999).

I then describe how key competencies for engaging effectively across differences may be acquired, practiced, and developed for mutual benefit and effectiveness. I offer specific tools for enhancing agility in noticing critical moments in relationships—those moments when not coordinating or connecting can be particularly consequential—and to intentionally make better choices in the next moment—choices that enhance our relationships with each other. Finally, I suggest processes that support interpersonal and relational practices for creating shared meaning.

Communicating in Global Context

As we engage across complex personal, positional, and cultural differences, both challenges and opportunities are created. (The term *culture* as used here refers to the attributes, heritage, beliefs, norms, and values of a group of people that are shared and largely learned.) The communication perspective provides a key lens for seeing these challenges and opportunities by highlighting patterns we create together and by providing tools for looking at those patterns together to enable us to shift and improve the quality of relationships that support more desired outcomes. Looking at the patterns we create together requires the capacity and agility to move back and forth between the first- and third-person perspective: from being in the conversation to looking at the conversation. After elaborating on the communication perspective, I further address this developmental capacity as critical to inclusive engagement with the complexity of our diverse social worlds and to fostering relational eloquence.

The Communication Perspective

There was a time when communication implied sending a message for another person to receive. If a message was not received, it was assumed that either the sender needed to be clearer in what was articulated or the receiver needed to be a better listener. In *Communication and the Human Condition*, W. Barnett Pearce (1989) coined a term: the *communication perspective* (p. 86). The communication perspective changes our notion of communication, from one of meaning being passed back and forth from one person to another—as if meaning were a tennis ball being lobbed between players—to something that people continuously make together. As seen from the communication perspective, meaning is influenced, in part, by the context of what came before and what follows. Each response refines and defines what has been said. For example, if I were to ask, "Would you do me a favor?" your response might vary based on the context of our relationship (including history, degree of intimacy and mutuality, cultural frame, and so on), or what preceded my request. In some cases, we might have a pattern of being there for each other, such that your automatic response would be "Sure!" In other cases, we might have a pattern of unfulfilled expectations; your response, in the context of a pattern lacking in mutuality, might be, "I am not sure I have the time." This response might create a pattern of reluctance. Or you might say: "*Again*?!" with an exasperated and annoyed tone. What pattern would that be creating? We make patterns all the time. Sometimes people make relationships and connections; sometimes we make insults or conflict; and often, we make incomplete meanings or misunderstanding.

It is quite common to take for granted what occurs in our everyday encounters. We may assume ease in understanding each other when we speak the same language and challenges when we do not. Yet I often hear people echo some version of what my client said: "Sometimes it feels harder to communicate with someone who speaks the same language!"

The Complexity of Meaning-Making in the Context of Differences

There are so many factors involved when considering meaning-making in the context of cultural differences that the process is often quite complex. When two people meet, each person brings a history that is influenced, in large part, by the story he or she has woven from personal experiences as well as the histories and cultures he or she has inherited. In this regard, Ferdman (2000) distinguishes between cultural identity at the group versus the individual level: "[C]ultural identity at the group level is the image shared by group members of the features that are distinctive or emblematic of the group. At the individual level, cultural identity is the reflection of culture as it is constructed by each of us" (p. 20). One implication is that even when we share a particular social identity with another person, we may each construct it differently in our personal narrative (Ferdman, 1995, 2003; see also Ferdman & Roberts, Chapter 3, this volume).

At the individual level, we bring multiple social group affiliations—among them gender, race, religion, ethnicity, nationality, education, sexual orientation, and age—to each encounter. We also bring narratives collected from our life experiences. The

**Figure 4.1. My Social Group Affiliations Influencing
This Chapter**

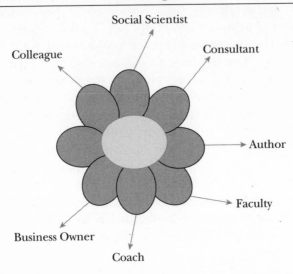

stories we have inherited and have lived are among the influences we call to the fore when we are connecting in the moment with each other. We may look at these influences as if they were petals of a daisy (Pearce, 1989). For example, the identity influences that are most pronounced for me as I write this chapter are my experience as a consultant to organizations, as a writer, as a social scientist, as a colleague, as a business owner, as a faculty member, and as a coach (see Figure 4.1).

Yet the petals on the metaphorical daisies of our encounters are not necessarily constant. As with the petals of an actual daisy, there are also aspects of my narrative that are in the background as I write this chapter, such as being a spouse, a mother, a friend, a Jewish woman, and a dog lover. At any moment—for example, when my daughter calls, or my dog needs a walk—one of those petals may shift into the foreground. Our narrative shifts in relationship to the social context and the particular relationship in which we are engaging. What might you label your own petals as you read this chapter? Note that, in Figure 4.2, your "daisy" stands in relationship to mine, because you are thinking about your identities as you engage with this text I have written.

Figure 4.2. Daisies in Relationship

More recently, the literature on social identity has expanded to include the ways in which our various group affiliations influence each other in how we narrate our stories. Holvino (2001), for example, indicates that "a poststructuralist approach to race, gender, and class is more interested in understanding the *intersectionality,* rather than the intersection of these dimensions of difference, emphasizing that the way in which the intersection is experienced and lived is dependent on particular circumstances and is always contextual and shifting" (p. 22, italics in the original). For example, we may both be women, but the value we place on ethnicity or religion may be qualitatively different and be consequential to how we narrate being a woman. The value of being middle-aged or over sixty varies by the contexts of culture and nationality (see also Ferdman, 1995, 2000; Holvino, 2010). Gallegos and Ferdman (2007, 2012; see also Ferdman & Gallegos, 2001) broadened this already complex picture, highlighting the contextual factors that influence identity, such as socioeconomic class, association or affiliation with the dominant culture, education, and other such factors.

The concept of intersectionality brings to the fore how identities are ranked in society and in our organizations and the associated power dynamics that therefore are at play in our interpersonal encounters. In one setting, one aspect of our identity may be central or dominant, whereas in another context or at another time the same aspect may be marginalized. For example, being multilingual has become highly valued in organizations that do business globally. Yet there was a time, not too long ago, when

Figure 4.3. Susan and Rosa

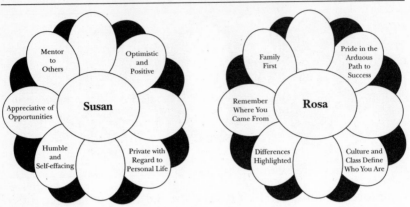

speaking Spanish at a company based in the United States was forbidden. Our identities are disadvantaged or privileged depending on the context.

In another example, I examine Susan and Rosa's relationship (see Figure 4.3). Susan is a senior manager of a medical technology organization. She expresses a lot of optimism and is committed not only to her own continued growth and development but to those of others as well. As an immigrant from China, she has had many opportunities and is eager to learn how she can help others. Rosa is a supervisor in the same organization. She rose through its ranks to a managerial position, having started as a janitor. Rosa was born in Puerto Rico and considers her success to be an important model for other Latinas. She often tells her story of her humble beginnings as a way to inspire others. As Rosa's mentor, Susan advised her not to tell people about her background, as it may make a bad impression. Rosa interprets Susan's advice as an insult. Susan wonders why Rosa doesn't value her advice. Without a conversation to explore how their differences are creating a misunderstanding, an episode that could be a rich learning opportunity can become one of mutual resentment.

The conceptualization of intersectionality informs how we understand the simultaneous influences of our multiple social group affiliations. We are continually combining these affiliations and identities in different ways, at different times, and in different relationships. With Susan and Rosa, it occurs in a mentoring relationship. Susan has positional power over Rosa. She may not realize that Rosa believes Susan's advice to be imposing judgment that it is not appropriate to share one's personal story. They are perpetuating a pattern of misunderstanding. Perhaps if Susan and Rosa were to step back and look at the pattern they are making and speak about what they prefer to create, they would have a different outcome. Their conversation also might help them recognize similar misunderstandings with other colleagues and, in some instances, family members.

The way the dimensions of our identity interact to narrate our relationship is in part a composite of our personal histories and in part a composite of the stories we tell about ourselves. Yet our stories are influenced by stories of others with whom we connect. Sometimes we are aware of how our stories change, but many times we are not. When I was working in Oklahoma, I thought about myself in terms of my role as a consultant, but once I opened my mouth, others defined me by where I was from, due to my New York accent. Once I realized how being a New Yorker influenced my encounters with others, I was able to take that into consideration. For example, I was attentive to how fast I spoke or what expressions I used. Our relationship with others is influenced not only by our stories of ourselves, but also by the stories we create about others, as well as the stories we create about the culture in which we live. At any given moment, we are some of, more than, all of, and just one of our particular affiliations or identities.

These multiple dimensions of diversity include personal traits, function or level, and cultural identity. One's personal and cultural history influences what one does, says, or enacts in any given moment and what others do, say, or enact in response based on their stories of their own histories and of yours. I may walk into a client's office with my story of myself as a consultant, and the client's first response to me might be influenced by her experience with White women of a certain age with a certain hairstyle. If her past experience with someone who looked like me was affirming, we have a head start! If it was negative, we have problems even before we open our mouths to speak. Either way, I might sense something in the client's response that I cannot quite understand. Working effectively with each other requires a well-developed capacity to attend to the continuous process of coordinating with each other. Given the multiple influences that are activated at any moment, we need guidance that supports a greater capacity to create shared meaning in the ongoing processes of relating.

The communication perspective suggests that meanings shift shape, changing from moment to moment. Pearce (1989, 2004) describes three interlocking realities we enact as we coordinate meaning: (1) coherence—that is, telling stories that help us make sense of our lives and help us know how to go on; (2) coordinating with others through a sequence of actions that seem logical and appropriate; and (3) mystery. Pearce (1989) defines mystery as, among other things, the "celebration of . . . ineffability" (p. 80), "the recognition of the limits of the stories in which we are enmeshed" (p. 84), and "a quality of experience of the human world, characterized by rapt attention, open-mindedness, [and] a sense of wonder" (p. 84). Pearce's allusions to mystery are from a positive frame; nevertheless, mystery in relationships, particularly with others whose social narratives are different from our own, can be disconcerting, even disorienting.

I have written about moments of dissonance (Wasserman, 2004) as being those times we find ourselves asking: "What just happened?" It may be that one asks about another's family as a way of warming up to a new business relationship, only to discover that asking such a question is considered either intrusive by the other person or even inappropriate in that person's culture. This is yet another version of one speaking French and another speaking English. Somehow, often through a visceral feeling, we realize we have crossed a line or broken some unspoken rule.

In some cultures, asserting a personal position or opinion is considered appropriate—even desirable—yet in other cultures, the value of group harmony takes precedence. We take our own norms for granted as the way things ought to be done. The response we choose to make—for example, standing out versus blending in with the group because that is what we have been encouraged to do—influences what we make in the next moment. Depending on what our taken-for-granted norms are, we may or may not find that behavior distasteful. When people relate across cultures, there are many opportunities for misunderstandings as they interpret others' behaviors and actions according to their own taken-for-granted frames of reference.

Think of the last time you were engaging with another and wished you could have pressed a rewind button to start all over again. You had the best of intentions, but somehow the other's response created a meaning wholly different from what you had anticipated or intended. Depending on the weight of the moment, such misunderstandings can have fleeting or profound implications.

Given how critical it is to foster positive relationships across differences in our daily lives, especially when the goal is inclusion, how can we develop our capacity to both pause and reflect while we are engaged with each other so as to make better choices about what we are making together? The communication perspective shifts our focus from the words themselves and their presentation to what we are making in the processes of relating. A friend of mine who is a neuropsychologist is also, in his spare time, an aspiring watercolorist. Recently he was selected to spend a year learning with a master artist. In his very first assignment, the master artist asked the student to paint a still life, with the caveat that the student was to attend to the relationship among the shapes rather than attend to the shapes themselves. Similarly, I invite you, in your next conversation, to consider attending to what is being made in the back-and-forth of the space between or among the two of you. If, for example, you are offering a colleague feedback, you can be creating trust and support, or you can be creating criticism and competition. As you look at what you are making in relationships, consider that what is emerging is something you are creating together. What happens next is a matter of choice in terms of how you listen and what you choose to say next. In any turn-by-turn process, you have the choice to assert your intentions and your being right, or you can do something different.

Capacity for Complexity

Looking at what we are making when we are engaged with each other requires the capacity to observe and reflect at the same time that we are engaged. This is a complex accomplishment. According to Kegan (1982, 1994), our capacity to look at the process of narrating rather than to be captured by our story is a developmental accomplishment. Constructive-developmental theory frames the process of development as an increasing capacity for complexity. This capacity involves the ability to distinguish and make that which is "subject"—that which we are identified with—into "object"—something we can look at, reflect on, and take responsibility for and integrate with some other way of knowing. It is not just having new ideas about things; rather, it is about coming to a new way of knowing how one knows. This is one of the opportunities offered by dialogue with another who is different. Kegan (2000) offers another example of the subject-object distinction, with regard to feelings. Typically, our language suggests that we have feelings. More often, however, our feelings have us. When engaging with another, we can be deterred by dissonance or we can pause and ask a question that shifts both of us to look at the dissonance and make sense of it together.

Kegan (1994) identifies five levels that distinguish ways of knowing. Levels 1 and 2 address ways of knowing from birth through childhood. At levels 1 and 2, there is no differentiation of self and other. At level 3, one can think abstractly and view one's own interests in the context of one's relationships. This shift typically manifests in adolescence and early adulthood. Although consequences are considered, typically at this stage the person is unable to reconcile conflicting points of view and may frame differences in beliefs and values in terms of polarities, such as right and wrong, or good people versus bad people. Those whose ways of knowing are at level 3 often limit their consideration of what is acceptable to those ideas that align with their own belief system. They are likely to judge quite harshly those whose perspectives or beliefs contradict their own. When encountering differences in relationships, this level manifests as holding an "us versus them" mindset, in which people "like us" are right and good and those who see or do things differently are seen as wrong or bad. A specific example of this could be one's culturally derived beliefs and behavior about timeliness; for some, being on time is a moral issue, while for others, relationships matter more than watching the clock.

When people hold competing views, whether about something mundane or something rather significant, and do not have the capacity to address the differences, the results can be destructive to creating and sustaining quality partnerships and ultimately inclusion.

Kegan (1994) calls the fourth level of cognitive complexity self-authoring. At this level, the person has the capacity to reflect, evaluate, and shift based on his or her own assessment, rather than depending on others to determine whether things are going well and what needs to be different. At level 4, one can take a meta-perspective of situations and therefore can view competing positions within a systemic framework that permits seeing the value of each. In the earlier example related to conceptions of time, one at this level would demonstrate the capacity for multiple, equally valid positions about the meaning of time and willingness to consider the other when apparent differences arise.

According to Kegan, few people achieve the capacity for the degree of complexity described by level 5, which is referred to as *trans-systemic*. At this level, one's perspective is considered incomplete, or as only one aspect of the fuller narrative. One's ways of knowing are open to being influenced by—and potentially enriched in consideration of—those of another.

Consider the capacity necessary for engaging another whose cultural rules and histories are different from our own. When we meet for the first time, we do not begin with a blank slate. We bring to our moment of meeting some history of attributions that may or may not facilitate a connection. For example, a leader introducing herself to her staff for the first time brings her own sense of self and story about who she is, who she has been, and her hopes for the potential of what she and her staff can do together. Her hopes are only as inspiring as what is measured by the response of her staff, then how she responds to them, and so forth. Each of us brings our own story of "people like us" whom we have known. One's story may be of an inspiring leader who was able to coalesce a group of individuals into a high-performing team. Another may bring a story of concern and doubt. These are but two possibilities for what we make together. In either case, we are never fully in charge of the narrative we aspire to create.

Knowing Ourselves and Each Other
Through Storytelling

Stories provide a scaffold to meaning that both enables and constrains relating. From the social construction perspective, social group identities are inherited and reproduced through stories—those we narrate about others, each other, and ourselves. These stories are continuously evolving and emerging at multiple levels, including the interpersonal, the intergroup, and the systemic. To strengthen our capacity to foster inclusion in our interpersonal relationships, it is important to coordinate the way we narrate our stories.

Imagine that you just left a meeting with five others. You run into another colleague who was supposed to be there but was pulled away for another meeting. She meets all of you in the cafeteria and asks what happened. One person talks about the style of the meeting. Another person talks about his feelings about the meeting. Yet another reiterates decisions made at the meeting, and another compares the meeting to what would have happened at her former job. The hierarchy model of meanings (Pearce, 2004) emphasizes the idea that there are multiple contexts within which communication acts occur: "communication occurs at several levels simultaneously, and . . . some of these stories function as contexts for other stories" (Pearce, 2007, p. 141). These contextual stories usually have to do with personal and group identities, with the relationships among the people in the situation, with the situation or communication act itself, and with the various organizations or cultures involved (Pearce, 2004).

Consider the implications in a performance review. Tom, the supervisor, may be focused on the individual, the position being reviewed, the economics of the organization, the developmental needs of this person in the context of the team, and other similar considerations. Yet Jeff, the person being reviewed, feels marginalized due to being the only person on the team who is over forty years old. Jeff hears all the feedback through the context of age and being on the margins, as that is most front and center for him. At first, Tom just keeps talking and hoping Jeff will understand. Jeff keeps responding, hoping that if he keeps explaining how his performance is affected by feeling marginalized, Tom will understand. Like many others, the two hope that if they keep talking, they will eventually connect. Instead, frustration builds. In this case, Tom notices that the conversation is out of sync, and he shifts from harping on the message to suggesting that they step back and look at their conversation. Doing so, they are able to name how they have been framing the conversation and recognize each other's points of view.

The stories we tell ourselves as we relate with others are complex. Although we engage hoping to foster shared meaning, there are many potentially unknown, untold, unheard, and even untellable stories that render our attempts to understand each other unfinished. Coordinating with others and creating coherence involves being attentive to what we are creating together, validating the stories we hearing, and exploring places that seem to be puzzling or mysterious.

Shifting to Relational Eloquence

Pearce (1989) distinguishes three forms of communication: monocultural, ethnocentric, and cosmopolitan. Each is a form of coordinating meaning in the process of relating. Monocultural communication implies "acting as if there were only one culture" (Pearce, 1989, p. 93). By treating the other as if he or she were the same as us, the unique qualities of the other are made to be invisible or are not valued. Ethnocentric communication "means viewing other cultures from the perspective of one's own" (p. 120) and references one's sense of *we* in relationship to and in contrast to *them*. Cosmopolitan communication is a quality of relating that demonstrates a commitment to coordinating meaning with another without denying the unique existence or humanity of the other, and without deprecating the other's way. It shifts attention to a commitment to relating, a social eloquence, rather than imposing oneself on another (Pearce, 1994).

Let's return to Susan and Rosa. Rosa places more emphasis on group identity and history; Susan emphasizes the rules of the organization's culture as primary to guide her actions, with her role as further refinement of what those actions might entail. Figure 4.4 depicts the contrasting hierarchies of meaning for Susan and for

Figure 4.4. Hierarchy Model: Susan and Rosa

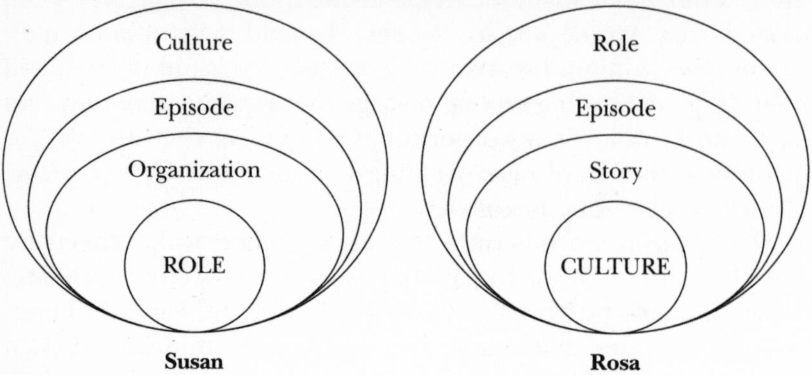

Note: For Susan, her role is the most defining context for their encounter. Second is the organization, third is the episode, and last is her culture. For Rosa, her culture is primary, her story is next, the episode is third, and her role is last.

Rosa. Susan views her role as the most defining context for their encounter. The next most important defining context for her is the organization, third is the episode, and last is her culture. In contrast, for Rosa, culture is primary, her story is next, the episode is third, and her role is last. Identifying the ways Rosa and Susan are missing each other required them to make a commitment to pause—and together look at how they were narrating their respective stories. Taking the opportunity to look at their different ways of ordering contexts and their consequent way of making meaning greatly enhanced their work relationship. Noticing their differences moved the quality of their relating from ethnocentric toward cosmopolitan communication.

Fostering interpersonal practices for inclusion involves the capacity to acknowledge others and to take the perspective of another without necessarily surrendering one's own perspective. Oliver (1996) describes systemic eloquence as the ability to make moment-by-moment choices about how we respond, especially in the face of the unexpected. *Systemic eloquence* highlights the relational commitments of attending to how one contributes to the experience of another. This includes being mindful of patterns of engaging that may interfere with relating and holding a commitment to collaboration while attending to the variety of contexts in which we are involved: "In calling such mindfulness *critical consciousness*, attention is drawn to the *interpretive act* and the opportunities it provides for reflection and reflexivity" (Oliver, 2004, p. 130, italics in the original).

The concept of relational eloquence (Wasserman, 2005) builds on Oliver's term to highlight the capacity involved in turning "the spotlight from the individualistic cognitive perspective (or what happens in my head) to the between or relational arena, or—what we make together" (p. 40). By looking at what we are making together, we are less likely to get caught up in making blame—and more apt to honor multiple perspectives.

The complexity of our encounters requires a degree of interpersonal competence, a capacity for complexity that may or may not have been part of our social skills education. The next section highlights frameworks and models that support interpersonal practices for inclusion.

Frameworks and Models That Support Interpersonal Practices for Inclusion

Interpersonal practices to support inclusion require both a commitment to engage with another who may see the world in a way different from one's own, and the capacity to do so. In this section, I discuss three frameworks that support interpersonal practices for inclusion—empathy, emotional and social intelligence, and mindfulness. This discussion is supported by three models—the daisy model, the hierarchy model, and the storytelling model (Pearce, 2004)—that can further support critical reflection in the service of inclusion. Together, these frameworks and models can help improve and sustain cosmopolitan communication—a commitment to coordinate meaning with others, particularly those whose way of framing things is significantly different from one's own. They are also essential in developing relational eloquence, the process of continuously expanding how one frames one's own story in relationship to the story of another (Wasserman, 2004), which involves broadening the context so that even conflicting narratives can be considered together. Here, I elaborate on how to use these models and frameworks to support inclusion through self-awareness and relational eloquence.

Empathy

In the early 1970s, Carl Rogers and Martin Buber engaged deeply in a series of dialogues to explore the connection between what Buber (1958) called an I-Thou relationship and what Rogers described as empathy. Through a series of intense public dialogues, they came to some shared definitions of empathy that clearly reflected their influence on one another. Buber (1947) wrote: "Empathy means, if anything . . . that this one person, without forfeiting anything of the felt reality of his activity, at the same time lives through the common event from the standpoint of the other" (pp. 114–115).

Rogers (1980) acknowledged shifting his definition of empathy from a state of being empathic to a process. According to him, empathy involves "entering the private perceptual world of the other and becoming thoroughly at home in it . . . being sensitive, moment by moment, to the changing felt meanings which flow in this other person, to the fear or rage or tenderness or confusion or whatever that he or she is experiencing. . . . It includes communicating your sensings [*sic*] of the person's world as you look with fresh and unfrightened eyes . . ." (p. 142).

In both of these frameworks of empathy, there is a sense that forming a connection with others consists of taking their perspective without necessarily changing one's own. Rather, one demonstrates the capacity to hold both. This is not easy when engaging others whose social worlds are informed by different forms of interpretation. More often, rather than an empathic process, the engagement with another whose social world is significantly different creates confusion and mystery. The next section expands this discussion with an overview of emotional and social intelligence.

Emotional and Social Intelligence

The concepts of emotional and social intelligence were mentioned in the literature as early as 1920, with Thorndike's definition of social intelligence as "the ability to understand and manage men and women, boys and girls—to act wisely in human relations" (p. 228). Emotional intelligence was initially defined by Peter Salovey and John Mayer (1990) as "the subset of social intelligence that involves the ability to monitor one's own and others' feelings and emotions, to discriminate among them, and to use this information to guide one's thinking and action" (p. 189, italics in original removed). They have since revised their definition to: "The ability to perceive accurately, appraise, and express emotion; the ability to access and/or generate feelings when they facilitate thought; the ability to understand emotion and emotional knowledge; and the ability to regulate emotions to promote emotional and intellectual growth" (Mayer & Salovey, 1997, p. 10). According to Mayer and Salovey (1997), emotional intelligence involves abilities that can be categorized into five domains: self-awareness, managing emotions, empathy, handling relationships, and motivating oneself. Goleman (1995) popularized the notion of emotional intelligence as a key personal and professional competency and identified its five components at work as motivation, empathy, social skills, self-awareness, and self-regulation (Goleman, 1998).

The popularization of emotional and social intelligence as core workplace competencies associates self-awareness and relational skills with being "smart." The expansion of the definition of intelligence to include self-awareness and relational skills thus values investing in interpersonal practices that support inclusion. Further, the various emotional intelligence assessment and feedback instruments invite the conversation that encourages development of the "observing self" (Deikman, 1982, as cited by Marlatt & Kristeller, 1999)—the capacity to note how we are thinking or feeling at any given time. I build on this concept of the observing self in the next section on mindfulness.

Mindfulness in the Face of Microaggressions

Siegel (2006), citing Kabat-Zinn (2005), defines mindfulness as "paying attention, in the present moment, on purpose, without grasping onto judgments. Mindful awareness has the quality of receptivity to whatever arises within the mind's eye, moment to moment" (p. 250). He goes on to indicate that, with mindful practices, "empathy, compassion, and interpersonal sensitivity seem to be improved. People who develop this capacity also develop a deeper sense of well-being and what can be considered a form of mental coherence" (Siegel, 2006, p. 250).

Mindfulness, a form of paying attention that originated in Eastern meditation practices (Nhất Hạnh, 1975), has become popular as a way of quieting our minds in the face of overstimulation. It has been described as "bringing one's complete attention to the present experience on a moment to moment basis" (Marlatt & Kristeller, 1999, p. 68) and as "paying attention in a particular way: on purpose, in the present moment, and nonjudgmentally" (Kabat-Zinn, 1994, p. 4). Mindfulness is considered a form of working out our reflective muscles to help us detach from triggers and move into inquiry.

In the course of the workday, there are potential triggers that challenge our capacity to engage with the fullness and expansiveness we have been discussing. Consider the following example: A group of senior leaders were enjoying a retreat designed for personal and professional development. Although there was a strong sense of camaraderie, the small group of women noted, among themselves, moments when their comments and guidance were unheard or not acknowledged. During a debrief of one of the activities, one of the women was encouraged by the others to voice the perception that on several occasions women's suggestions were passed over, only to be welcomed when later presented by a man. She went on to say that she frequently receives complaints from women in her organization that they do not feel recognized for their contributions and that frequently, someone from the nondominant culture makes a suggestion but it does not get heard until a person from the dominant culture reiterates the point.

The women in this example experienced a series of what has been referred to as microaggressions (Sue, 2010). Sue et al. (2007) describe microaggressions as "brief, everyday exchanges that send denigrating messages to people of color because they belong to a racial minority group. In the world of business, the term 'micro-inequities' is used to describe the pattern of being overlooked, underrespected, and devalued because of one's race or gender.

Microaggressions are often unconsciously delivered in the form of subtle snubs or dismissive looks, gestures, and tones. These exchanges are so pervasive and automatic in daily conversations and interactions that they are often dismissed and glossed over as being innocent and innocuous" (p. 273). Perpetrators of microaggressions—which can be targeted based on race, gender, or other social identities—are often unaware that they engage in such communications.

As we consider the scenario just described, what is the typical response to microaggressions at work? I have heard clients suggest that the choices they make are influenced by fear of reprisal, self-protectiveness, and concern for appearing to be the "victim." How does one determine when to speak up and how? How might one craft a response and frame the conversation to spark mutual curiosity to support mutual learning? The challenge is to notice when we are activated by fear or a sense of threat and to pause to look at our feelings, rather than, as Kegan (1982, 1994) would say, to be our feelings.

An additional way is to be on the lookout for the triggering event. Brookfield (1987) identified a trigger event that is perplexing or discomforting as the first of five stages of a transformational change process. Mezirow (1991, 2000) talks about a disorienting dilemma as the first stage of transformative learning. Cranton (1992) identifies confusion and withdrawal as stages in the transformational learning process. Transformative learning is the consequence of following the triggering event or the disorienting dilemma with critical self-reflection. In my research, I expanded this model to address how to transform patterns in relationships. Critical reflection in relationship with others was consequential to transform undesirable patterns of relating (Wasserman, 2004). This reflection process is important because those involved move from being solely in the dynamic to also looking at the dynamic together. Standing at the boundary together, we are more apt to pause, to ask questions, to seek the counsel of others, and to make sense together.

Having the presence of mind to pause and reflect takes practice. I liken that practice to working out. We work out to strengthen our muscles so we are strong and ready. This form of practice focuses on strengthening the reflective muscles. Strengthening the reflective muscles helps us to be awake to and to notice potential triggers and to respond at these critical moments with questions that prompt a stance of inquiry.

Models to Support Critical Reflection

The daisy model, the hierarchy model, and the storytelling model can be considered tools to support critical reflection with others. These tools help expand self-other awareness, so as to better understand each other and the dynamics at play in interpersonal interactions. Earlier in this chapter, I introduced the daisy model (Pearce, 2004), which can help identify the influences that are joining (or separating) us at any particular moment. In the example of the women experiencing the microaggressions, many came to their professions during a time when women experienced subtle discrimination on a regular basis. As a consequence of these experiences, some had strong inclinations to address these microaggressions and some had strong inclinations not to. Some had inclinations to raise a challenging conversation and some had strong desires to design generative conversation, the kind that generates new insights and possibilities. In that and similar situations, elaborating on the petals of the daisies of all involved, and in that way learning their respective histories and their hopes, can support shared meaning of the full range of differences and their implications.

The hierarchy of meaning (Pearce, 2004) emphasizes the idea that there are multiple contexts within which communication takes place. If the most important level of context to me is our relationship, and the most important level of context to you is being right, we will take very different approaches with each other. As with the earlier example (Susan and Rosa), standing back and naming those differences as well as identifying different priorities (such as when one is seeking shared understanding and another is seeking to be right) are critical to help guide us in how to go on together in constructive ways. As I noted earlier, the process of stepping back and observing their conversation together creates the possibility of viewing their different perspectives side by side.

Stories provide a scaffold to meaning that both enables and constrains relating. From the social construction perspective, social group identities are inherited and reproduced through stories—those we narrate about others, each other, and ourselves. These stories are continuously evolving and emerging at multiple levels, including the interpersonal, the intergroup, and the systemic. To strengthen our capacity to foster inclusion in our interpersonal relationships, it is important to coordinate the way we narrate our stories.

As noted earlier, people tell stories about themselves and their groups in an attempt to create coherence in their lives (Pearce & Pearce, 1998). The storytelling model provides a heuristic device for looking at all kind of stories and how they shape our process of meaning-making. There is storytelling about the stories that were lived together and the stories told or constructed by those involved. There are untold stories that, whether intentionally or unintentionally, do not present themselves. Because we cannot possibly hear everything, some stories go unheard while others are privileged. The stories we choose to tell are the ones that add meaning, and sometimes confusion, to our experiences. There are stories that are underdeveloped or eerily silent. There are stories that, in some contexts, are not allowed. For example, the storytelling about a hero is skewed toward amazing accomplishments. When honoring the hero, one may edit stories of shame. The different forms of stories provide a catalyst for inquiry to enrich and expand the stories we share and those we invite others to tell. In sharing our stories and inviting others to tell theirs, we are expanding how we know and understand each other and creating more inclusion.

In my work as a consultant and coach I often use these models as tools to guide the storytelling. As tools, these models expand the framing of the stories and the perspective or stance that the storytellers hold. Because meaning is created in our social relationships and is continuously produced in the processes of social interactions, changing our frames of reference, particularly in relationship with others who are different, is essential to support inclusion. Intentionally making space to hear the stories of those who are often marginalized enhances the quality of relating, enriches inclusion, and helps develop relational eloquence.

Summary

Changing our frames of reference, particularly in relationship with others who are different from us, requires a particular set of skills for engagement. First, it requires relational agility, or the capacity to move from talking at to dialogic engaging or being with. Second, it calls for the ability to critically reflect on one's taken-for-granted assumptions or frameworks and to view them as one of many possibilities. Third, it requires one to hold one's own perspective at risk of being changed in relationship with those of others (Buber, 1958; Wasserman, 2004).

Relational eloquence (Wasserman, 2005)—the capacity to shift our attention from the individualistic cognitive perspective to the relational arena—requires a quality of and deep capacity for attending to others. Self-awareness and relational eloquence are like muscles: they need to be exercised. We enhance our self-awareness and relational eloquence by looking at what we are making together: noticing how our past experiences influence our interpreting in the moment; noting how we are framing the beginning, middle, and end of the stories we tell; and being aware of what contexts we highlight. Our stories are not likely to be the same. Rather, our lives are enriched by the many stories we encounter.

This chapter has highlighted the frameworks and models that help us recognize the complexity that is present in the engagement of multiple sources of differences in our relationships. The following three summary points, drawn from my prior work (Wasserman, 2005) can provide guidance to support interpersonal awareness and relational eloquence when engaging complex interpersonal and intergroup differences:

○ "People want to be known. . . . The past must be acknowledged before moving on to the future. . . . Typically, those whose stories have been marginalized or muffled by the dominant discourse . . . are more present to their defining narratives than those whose story is echoed in the norms of everyday life" (p. 41).

○ "People want to name themselves. . . . [E]ach of us wants to define ourselves in relationship with others, rather than be defined by others. Often, in the effort to understand others, we attribute all of what we know about that group to them, disregarding what they ascribe to themselves" (p. 41). To promote inclusion, notice and make an effort to learn how others tell their story.

○ Relationships are strengthened when people have the opportunity to pause and reflect together. "The reflection process itself creates . . . opportunities that might otherwise be lost in the turn of the next moment. This is particularly significant when [those involved focus] on moments that are confusing or troubling. . . . When [people] engage these moments, the shared reflection is more likely to create [coherence and shared meaning]" (p. 42). In the process of group reflection prompted by questions that invite affirming narratives, each person's story of him- or herself expands when contextualized in relationship with the story of the other.

Relational eloquence involves the capacity to look at one's story along with another's (Wasserman, 2005). Strengthening interpersonal awareness and relational eloquence requires a deep commitment to pay attention and notice, to build the reflective muscles. This commitment is rewarded by the consequentiality of quality engagement. In making that engagement, we, together, make better and more inclusive social worlds.

References

Buber, M. (1947). *Between man and man* (R. G. Smith, Trans.). New York: Routledge.

Buber, M. (1958). *I and thou* (R. G. Smith, Trans.). New York: T and T Clark.

Ferdman, B. M. (1995). Cultural identity and diversity in organizations: Bridging the gap between group differences and individual uniqueness. In M. M. Chemers, S. Oskamp, & M. A. Costanzo (Eds.), *Diversity in organizations: New perspectives for a changing workplace* (pp. 37–61). Thousand Oaks, CA: Sage.

Ferdman, B. M. (2000). "Why am I who I am?" Constructing the cultural self in multicultural perspective. *Human Development, 43,* 19–23.

Ferdman, B. M. (2003). Learning about our and others' selves: Multiple identities and their sources. In N. Boyacigiller, R. Goodman, & M. Phillips (Eds.), *Crossing cultures: Insights from master teachers* (pp. 49–61). London: Routledge.

Ferdman, B. M., & Gallegos, P. V. (2001). Racial identity development and Latinos in the United States. In C. L. Wijeyesinghe & B. W. Jackson III (Eds.), *New perspectives on racial identity development: A theoretical and practical anthology* (pp. 32–66). New York: New York University Press.

Gallegos, P. V., & Ferdman, B. M. (2007). Identity orientations of Latinos in the United States: Implications for leaders and organizations. *Business Journal of Hispanic Research, 1*(1), 27–41.

Gallegos, P. V., & Ferdman, B. M. (2012). Latina and Latino ethnoracial identity orientations: A dynamic and developmental perspective. In C. L. Wijeyesinghe & B. W. Jackson III (Eds.), *New perspectives on racial identity development: Integrating emerging paradigms into racial identity models* (pp. 51–80). New York: New York University Press.

Goleman, D. (1995). *Emotional intelligence: Why it can matter more than IQ.* New York: Bantam.

Goleman, D. (1998). *Working with emotional intelligence.* New York: Bantam.

Holvino, E. (2001, June). *Complicating gender: The simultaneity of race, gender, and class in organization change(ing).* Center for Gender in Organizations Working Paper No. 14. Center for Gender in Organizations, Simmons Graduate School of Management, Boston, MA. Retrieved from Center for Gender in Organizations website:http://www.simmons.edu/som/docs/cgo_wp14_DNC.pdf

Holvino, E. (2010). Intersections: The simultaneity of race, gender, and class in organization studies [Special Issue: Gender and Ethnicity]. *Gender, Work and Organization, 17,* 248–277.

Kabat-Zinn, J. (1994). *Wherever you go, there you are: Mindfulness meditation in everyday life.* New York: Hyperion.

Kegan, R. (1982). *The evolving self.* Cambridge, MA: Harvard University Press.

Kegan, R. (1994). *In over our heads: The mental demands of modern life.* Cambridge, MA: Harvard University Press.

Kegan, R. (2000). What forms transforms? In J. A. Mezirow (Ed.), *Learning as transformation: Critical perspectives on a theory in progress* (pp. 35–70). San Francisco: Jossey-Bass.

Marlatt, G. A., & Kristeller, J. L. (1999). Mindfulness and meditation. In W. R. Miller (Ed.), *Integrating spirituality into treatment: Resources for practitioners* (pp. 67–84). Washington, DC: American Psychological Association. doi:10.1037/10327–004

Mayer, J. D., & Salovey, P. (1997). What is emotional intelligence? In P. Salovey & D. J. Sluyter (Eds.), *Emotional development and emotional intelligence: Educational implications* (pp. 3–31). New York: Basic Books.

McNamee, S., & Gergen, K. (1999). *Relational responsibility: Resources for sustainable dialogue.* Thousand Oaks, CA: Sage.

Mezirow, J. A. (1991). *Transformative dimensions of adult learning.* San Francisco: Jossey-Bass.

Mezirow, J. A. (2000). *Learning as transformation: Critical perspectives on a theory in progress.* San Francisco: Jossey-Bass.

Nhất Hạnh, T. (1975). *The miracle of mindfulness: An introduction to the practice of meditation.* Boston: Beacon.

Oliver, C. (1996). Systemic eloquence. *Human Systems, 7,* 247–264.

Oliver, C. (2004). Reflexive inquiry and the strange loop tool. *Human Systems, 15,* 127–140.

Pearce, W. B. (1989). *Communication and the human condition.* Carbondale: University of Illinois Press.

Pearce, W. B. (1994). *Interpersonal communication: Making social worlds.* New York: Harper Collins.

Pearce, W. B. (2004). The coordinated management of meaning. In W. B. Gudykunst (Ed.), *Theorizing about intercultural communication* (pp. 35–54). Thousand Oaks, CA: Sage.

Pearce, W. B. (2007). *Making social worlds: A communication perspective.* Malden, MA: Blackwell.

Pearce, W. B. (2012). Evolution and transformation: A brief history of CMM and a meditation on what using it does to us. In C. Creede, B. Fisher-Yoshida, & P. V. Gallegos (Eds.), *The reflective, facilitative, and interpretive practices of coordinated management of meaning: Making lives, making meaning* (pp. 1–21). Lanham, MD: Rowman & Littlefield.

Pearce, W. B., & Pearce, K. A. (1998). Transcendent storytelling: Abilities for systemic practitioners and their clients. *Human Systems, 9* (3–4), 167–185.

Rogers, C. R. (1980). *A way of being.* Boston: Houghton-Mifflin.

Salovey, P., & Mayer, J. D. (1990). Emotional intelligence. *Imagination, Cognition, and Personality, 9,* 185–211.

Siegel, D. J. (2006). An interpersonal neurobiology approach to psychotherapy: Awareness, mirror neurons, and neural plasticity in the development of well-being. *Psychiatric Annals, 36,* 248–256.

Sue, D. W. (2010). *Microaggressions in everyday life: Race, gender, and sexual orientation.* New York: Wiley.

Sue, D. W., Capodilupo, C. M., Torino, G. C., Bucceri, J. M., Holder, M. B., Nadal, K. L., & Esquilin, M. (2007). Racial microaggression in everyday life: Implications for clinical practice. *American Psychologist, 62,* 271–286.

Thorndike, R. K. (1920). Intelligence and its uses. *Harper's, 140,* 227–335.

Wasserman, I. C. (2004). *Discursive processes that foster dialogic moments: Transformation in the engagement of social identity differences in dialogue* (Doctoral dissertation). Available from ProQuest Dissertations and Theses database. (UMI No. 3168530)

Wasserman, I. C. (2005, August). Appreciative inquiry and diversity: The path to relational eloquence. *AI Practitioner: International Journal of Appreciative Inquiry,* pp. 36–43.

CHAPTER FIVE

Intercultural Competence: Vital Perspectives for Diversity and Inclusion

Janet M. Bennett

Being "global souls"—seeing ourselves as members of a world community, knowing that we share the future with others—requires powerful intercultural competence. Being effective domestically—seeking social justice, ensuring that privilege is shared—requires equally complicated skills. Such competence embraces globalization and seeks to reconcile the competing commitments to self and others, with the knowledge that this is profoundly difficult. It is grounded in the certainty that we cannot neglect either side of the equation, domestic or international.

The field of intercultural relations has evolved in the context of this demanding question: How can we address the vitality of globalization and yet resolve the domestic concerns we share? As we do so, how can we develop in ourselves the necessary mastery and concomitant humility required to be effective across cultures? And what is required to integrate an intercultural perspective with diversity and inclusion?

Definitions

As we develop this careful linkage between the intercultural world and the world of diversity and inclusion, definitions become all-important. Culture, as described here, refers to the learned and shared values, beliefs, and behaviors of a community of interacting people. In other words, members of a culture are likely to influence an individual's behavior when that person spends enough time interacting with them. Culture is dynamic, not static, and there are wide contextual variations within each group. These variations are enriched through communication. As Barnlund (1989) so aptly noted, "It is through communication that we acquire culture; it is in our manner of communicating that we display our cultural uniqueness" (p. xiv). The traditional definition of culture allows us to consider many of the well-known groups defined in diversity work as cultures, including nationality, ethnicity, gender, age, disability, sexual orientation, economic status, education, profession, religion, organizational culture, and any other cultural differences learned and shared by a group of interacting people. As we do so, it is vital to recognize that "culture is not a single variable but rather comprises multiple variables, affecting all aspects of experience. . . . Culture is a process through which ordinary activities and conditions take on an emotional tone and a moral meaning for participants. . . . Cultural processes frequently differ within the same ethnic or social group because of differences in age cohort, gender, political association, class, religion, ethnicity, and even personality" (Kleinman & Benson, 2006, pp. 1673–1674).

To the degree that each of these memberships is a part of an individual's identity, they comprise the multicultural self, that multilayered set of influences that intersect in complicated ways and relate importantly to who we are and to how others see us (see also Ferdman & Roberts, Chapter 3, and Wasserman, Chapter 4, this volume). Respect for the complexity of cultural identities is a prerequisite for understanding culturally influenced patterns of interaction. Further, it provides "the key to comprehending the juncture between global and domestic diversity. Although some people have histories that are far more extensive than others, and although some people carry unequal burdens of oppression or perquisites of privilege, they are all equal (but different) in the complexity of their cultural worldviews" (J. M. Bennett & M. J. Bennett, 2004, p. 150).

To a significant degree, this recognition of shared complexity can foster a mutual respect that opens dialogue between diversity and intercultural perspectives.

Intercultural Competence

This bridge between inclusion and intercultural approaches can best be built through a focus on *intercultural competence*, referring to the cognitive, affective, and behavioral skills and characteristics that support appropriate and effective interaction in a variety of cultural contexts. These attributes and abilities are often referred to as the "head, heart, and hand components" (Hayles & Russell, 1997; see Hayles, Chapter 2, this volume), or as a mindset, heartset, and skillset (J. M. Bennett, 2009b). This definition is the basis of the intercultural knowledge and competence rubric for assessing learning outcomes used by the Association of American Colleges and Universities (J. M. Bennett, as cited in Rhodes, 2010).

Kleinman and Benson (2006) imply that sometimes those who teach cultural competence hold the view that "culture can be reduced to a technical skill" (p. 1673). Rather, it should suggest that we educate ourselves and others to explore the complexity of cultural influences openly.

In recognition of the significant role that intercultural competence plays in global interchange, Deardorff (2009) has edited a collection of articles that explore the concept in a wide range of cultures and professional contexts, including a comprehensive overview by Spitzberg and Changnon (2009) of various competencies and the more widely recognized models that have been explored in the literature. Whether it is called "intercultural effectiveness" (Vulpe, Kealey, Protheroe, & Mac-Donald, 2001); "cultural intelligence" (Earley & Ang, 2003; Peterson, 2004; Thomas & Inkson, 2004); "global competence" (Bird & Osland, 2004; Hunter, White, & Godbey, 2006); "intercultural communication competence" (Byram, 2012; Collier, 1989; Dinges & Baldwin, 1996; Hammer, 1989; Kim, 1991; Spitzberg, 1994; Wiseman, 2002); "culture learning" (Paige, Cohen, Kappler, Chi, & Lassegard, 2002) or "intercultural competence" (Lustig & Koester, 2009), there is a fair consensus that we are describing the capacity to interact effectively and appropriately across cultures.

Inherently interdisciplinary, the academic exploration of intercultural competence spans sociology, business, linguistics, intercultural communication, counseling, social work, cultural geography, anthropology, and education. Various professional contexts promote intercultural competence to facilitate global leadership in the corporate world, culturally responsive teaching and learning at all levels of education, provision of culturally competent health care, development of culturally sensitive customer service, and even culturally appropriate tourism. Addressing the current focus on intercultural competence, there are dozens of assessment instruments that have been designed to measure knowledge, skills, and attitudes for needs assessment, coaching, program design, selection, and professional development (Intercultural Communication Institute, 2011).

Among the many competencies associated with being effective across cultures, cultural self-awareness is the key cognitive competency, curiosity is the key affective competency, and empathy is the key behavioral competency. I consider each of these in more depth.

Cognitive Competencies

Cultural self-awareness refers to our recognition of the cultural patterns that have influenced our identities and that are reflected in the various culture groups to which we belong, always acknowledging the dynamic nature of both culture and identity. This self-awareness of who we are culturally is a prerequisite for the development of intercultural sensitivity (J. M. Bennett, 2009a). Until I know that I am a multicultural person, with aspects of my identity influenced situationally by various cultures, I am less likely to understand why you are not just an inferior version of me. If I do not see you as a multicultural person, with an identity possibly influenced situationally by the cultural groups you belong to, I may observe that you do things differently; because I do them well, I may be left with the conclusion I am superior. It is this blinding filter that interferes with development of intercultural competence.

Other key cognitive competencies include knowledge of other cultures, of culture-general frameworks, and of culture-specific information. Culture-general frameworks refer to the patterns that may be used to explore any other cultures; culture-specific information focuses on the patterns that may exist in any one culture in which we are interested.

Knowledge of other cultures is a well-substantiated mediating influence in reducing prejudice and stereotypes but, interestingly enough, not necessarily the most effective way to counteract all the biases that we have been taught (Pettigrew, 2008; Pettigrew & Tropp, 2011). Pettigrew's meta-analytic research (2008) thoroughly explores numerous studies on how new knowledge of other culture groups affects attitudes; he concludes that "early theorists thought that intergroup contact led to learning about the outgroup, and this new knowledge in turn reduced prejudice. Recent work, however, reveals that this knowledge mediation does exist but is of minor importance. Empathy and perspective taking are far more important" (p. 190).

Affective Competencies

In the affective dimension, curiosity is often cited as the keystone of intercultural competence (Deardorff, 2006; Gregersen, Morrison, & Black, 1998; Mendenhall, 2001). Opdal (2001) describes curiosity as a sense of wonder, where "wonder is the state of mind that signals we have reached the limits of our present understanding, and that things may be different from how they look" (p. 33). Viewing curiosity as "unbridled inquisitiveness" in their research with global leaders, Gregersen et al. (1998) found that "inquisitiveness is the fuel for increasing their global savvy, enhancing their ability to understand people and maintain integrity, and augmenting their capacity for dealing with uncertainty and managing tension" (p. 23). In building a bridge between intercultural approaches and inclusion, curiosity would appear to be essential for accomplishing our goals.

Other core affective competencies include open-mindedness, tolerance of ambiguity, adaptability, and cultural humility. Although most of these characteristics are well-known, cultural humility is less frequently defined. Guskin (1991) refers to this way of being in the world as respecting the validity of other peoples' cultures, questioning the primacy of our own perspective, and recognizing that we may not know what is really going on!

Behavioral Competencies

In the behavioral dimension, empathy is the most frequently cited skill, along with the ability to listen, communicate, resolve conflict, manage anxiety, and develop relationships. Of these, empathy is the core competency, defined as "the imaginative intellectual and emotional participation in another person's experience" (M. J. Bennett, 1998, p. 207). In other words, empathy is an attempt to understand another person by imagining the individual's perspective. Especially in relating across cultures, this is not to be confused with imagining ourselves in the other person's position. That approach, labeled sympathy, is irrelevant when we find ourselves interacting with someone who does not share our worldview. For instance, it is an act of sympathy to feel sorrow and grief for the Japanese people after the horrendous earthquake and tsunami of 2011. It is an act of empathy to grasp the experience from their collective cultural perspective and understand how a group of people so traumatized would return millions of dollars of cash washed up on the shores of their country to fellow victims (Fujita, 2011). The usual context of intercultural relations—in which worldviews are not shared, language may obstruct, and deep values clash in our dialogues—requires empathy, not sympathy. As Goleman (1995) notes in his research on emotional intelligence, "all rapport . . . stems from emotional attunement, from the capacity for empathy" (p. 96). Although Pettigrew (2008) suggests that empathy may be the most significant mediator of prejudice reduction, it is certainly one of the more challenging competencies to develop, whether in global or domestic contexts.

Challenges and Opportunities in Integrating Intercultural and Inclusion

There has been occasional resistance to including intercultural relations in diversity and inclusion efforts. Interculturalists have been accused of *exotifying* other cultures, seeking the intriguing aspects of global cultures rather than facing powerful issues of discrimination at home. Some suggest that any effort to describe patterns in other culture groups is *essentializing*, suggesting that interculturalists attribute stereotypical characteristics to culture groups while ignoring wide variations and that such research must be contested. Others warn that research reifies cultural attributes in such a way as to deny the dynamic and contextual aspects of cultural interactions; they insist that this expresses a neocolonial point of view.

Suffice to say, most interculturalists acknowledge these important concerns and often employ social constructivist perspectives, confirming the notion that patterns exist in context, not as an immutable reality. The constructivist approach considers the role of the individual, the situation, and the society in the dynamic process of culture creation, particularly as it relates to the creation of shared meaning in interaction. With intercultural competence as the scaffolding, we can examine the issues of power and prejudice, of bias and discrimination, and bring to the surface the various privileges that allow certain cultural patterns to exist.

At the same time, the intercultural field recognizes the important research on cultural patterns that produces what Kochman and Mavrelis (2009) call a "cultural archetype," described as "a shared value, pattern, or attitude that insiders would accept as representative of a significant number of members of their group" (p. 6). They suggest that archetypes are "scientifically generated through the 'ethnographic process'" (p. 6), creating generalizations that are verifiable through the authoritative observations of ingroup members, always acknowledging that no hypothesized pattern applies to any single individual. Many professionals use the visual of a statistical normal curve, suggesting the notion that although there is a central tendency (a cultural pattern or archetype) for many cultural variables, there are outliers at either end of the curve: those individuals who for a variety of reasons do not fit the general pattern.

Although these challenges may present barriers to the integration of culture learning into diversity and inclusion, there are also compelling social realities that suggest a more unified approach is called for (J. M. Bennett & M. J. Bennett, 2004). First, the notion that domestic inclusion initiatives can be exported globally has now been identified as ethnocentric (Solomon, 1994). The content of domestic programs may be alien to other environments and cultures. Further, in practice the pedagogy, the cognitive styles, and the learning styles often defied the very nature of the goal (Yershova, DeJaeghere, & Mestenhauser, 2000); our inclusion initiatives were not inclusive. Although we often modified examples to export the training and development, the training design and implementation were often ill suited to the learning patterns in other societies.

Second, the artificial bifurcation of the training for corporate global transferees or international students and the diversity training at home left individuals unprepared for bridging cultures, whether on campus or at the workplace (Wentling & Palma-Rivas, 2000). International students were puzzled by diversity issues at their universities; study-abroad students imposed their American perspective on social issues as guests in other countries; and international corporate managers were befuddled by typical diversity standards in the organization as they related to gender, sexual orientation, and race. The supporters of diversity often didn't notice the barriers that the domestic point of view presented to those external to the American context.

Finally, the migration of refugees, immigrants, and transferees posed the question of "Who is ethnically diverse?" Is the recently arrived non–English speaking Chinese immigrant Asian American? Is she Asian? Is she American? Is her identity based on her passport culture? What about the Albanian man? Is he a White male? Is the Ghanaian global transferee an American African? A person of African descent? Is this biracial/bicultural student a member of one culture or the other? Or both? What is domestic? What is global? To neglect the inclusion of these diverse individuals hardly seems inclusive, and yet the domestic approach seldom emphasized the deep involvement of such individuals in the organization. Whether in education or the corporate context, despite high-quality domestic inclusion models, the global perspective has often been missing (Smith, García, Hudgins, Musil, Nettles, & Sedlacek, 2000; Williams, Berger, & McClendon, 2005), if not downright marginalized.

Further, there is no shortage of organization mission statements that urge the workforce or the campus to value, respect, and appreciate diversity (Meacham & Gaff, 2006). They offer suggestions of the outcomes to be achieved: greater productivity, better customer service or student satisfaction, competitive advantage, increased retention, global citizenship, community impact, increased market share, and effective management. However, few mission statements suggest that these outcomes would be more likely if the workforce developed intercultural competence and adapted to the cultural differences present in the organization. Instead, heartening statistics are offered regarding the existing affinity groups, the increase in diverse suppliers, and data on "compositional diversity" (Milem, Chang, & Antonio, 2005), all of which are obviously good things and often much easier to measure.

But rarely do these data include information on the complex participation of those from outside our national boundaries, nor are these groups widely acknowledged in diversity initiatives. The Workforce 2020 report summed up this lacuna succinctly: "The rest of the world matters" (Judy & D'Amico, 1997, p. 3). Intercultural competence is now more often integrated into diversity development as a bridge between traditional inclusion initiatives and international efforts (Carr-Ruffino, 2009; Gardenswartz & Rowe, 1998; Jamieson & O'Mara, 1991; Kochman & Mavrelis, 2009; Loden, 1996). Culture is indeed at the core of our work, both domestically and globally.

There are many ways in which intercultural skills can facilitate the goals of inclusion. For example, interviewing diverse applicants is frequently a culturally challenging task. Whether by exhibiting a "weak" handshake, downcast gaze, or effusive communication style, qualified candidates are often overlooked for lack of "fit." Further, efforts to counteract this bias tend to produce equality when equity is called for. A recent conversation with a large global employer outlined measures used to assure fair treatment: the use of identical questions, no follow-up questions, forty-five minutes maximum interview time, and restrictions to only over-the-phone (so nonverbal behavior couldn't corrupt the interview) and quantitative ratings of the applicant. Contrast this with a similar global employer who conducts three-day assessments on site, using multiple small group activities with a group of applicants observed by the interviewing team, various in-basket tasks, with multiple assessments of intercultural competence and personality. By varying the input to the assessment, the latter employer is more likely to have an inclusive selection process.

Interviewing is only one function of the organization that benefits from intercultural competence. Many of the primary goals of existing diversity and inclusion programs include a variety of functions that can be effectively supported by enhanced communication skills: recruitment and retention of members of underrepresented groups, management of a diverse workforce, productivity of multicultural teams, marketing across cultures, and development of a climate of respect for diversity in the organization, among others. The climate further improves when leaders are capable of conducting inclusive meetings, planning inclusive social events, and coaching and mentoring across cultures. This demands more than awareness, more than understanding; it requires adaptation built on the development of intercultural competence.

Training and Development of Intercultural Competence

While many disciplines share in the dialogue on intercultural competence, the perspective of intercultural communication is particularly useful in developing inclusive leadership in organizations and systems. Intercultural communication is the interactive process of creating shared meanings between or among people from different cultures. Often described in the past as the study of face-to-face interaction between individuals who have differing values, beliefs, and behaviors, intercultural communication now includes mediated communication as well; for instance, how culture impacts online learning or social networks (Edmundson, 2007). Intercultural communication focuses on what happens when individuals with contrasting patterns interact, how they create shared meaning, and how they express culture.

The remainder of this chapter focuses on the application of intercultural concepts and models for creating a bridge between diversity and inclusion and global diversity perspectives.

The Developmental Model of Intercultural Sensitivity

There are several models in the field of intercultural communication that are useful to the intercultural trainer and educator. Two that are pertinent to our work are the Developmental Model of

Figure 5.1. Developmental Model of
Intercultural Sensitivity (DMIS)

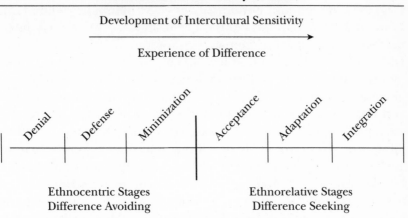

Source: Adapted from J. M. Bennett, 2009b, p. 100.

Intercultural Sensitivity (DMIS) (M. J. Bennett, 1986, 1993; J. M. Bennett & M. J. Bennett, 2004) and the support and challenge model (J. M. Bennett, 2009b).

When we are working on diversity and inclusion or global diversity, we are fundamentally exploring the individual's response to the experience of difference. When meeting a new Generation X employee with a different work ethic, how does the boomer manager react? When confronting a customer service representative from India, how does the American IT director respond? What happens on the diverse virtual team when one member appears to be taking credit for the team's accomplishment? In each of these situations, there is an opportunity for an interculturally effective or interculturally destructive outcome.

Much depends on the mindset the actors bring to the experience of difference. The DMIS suggests a predictable pattern of responses to difference based on the worldview the individual brings to the encounter with others. Moving from ethnocentric positions, where difference is avoided, to ethnorelative positions, in which difference is sought after, the model outlines six distinct mindsets that affect interactions with culturally different others, with each position suggesting particular competencies as developmental goals.

The DMIS supports a developmental design for training, education, coaching, and program design, allowing for precisely targeted interventions and initiatives (J. M. Bennett, 2009b; J. M. Bennett & M. J. Bennett, 2004). For instance, a human resource professional in a large global corporation was able to use the DMIS to assess the readiness level of each unit of the organization before she rolled out a diversity initiative for 150,000 employees. She was acutely aware that in one community there was curiosity and openness, and in another there would be resistance to the most basic interventions. She successfully planned her programming with an intentionally developmental design to avoid creating backlash. What this suggests is the wise application of Shepard's (1975) rules for change agents: "Start where the system is . . . never work uphill . . . don't build hills as you go . . . load experiments for success" (pp. 1–5). Essentially, the DMIS facilitates starting where the system is. For those interested in conducting an assessment of a specific audience, a psychometric instrument, the Intercultural Development Inventory (IDI), is available to measure these positions (Hammer, 2009; Hammer & Bennett, 2003; Paige, Jacobs-Cassuto, Yershova, & DeJaeghere, 2003).

Within the ethnocentric stages, there are three mindsets for avoiding difference: Denial of difference, Defense against difference, and Minimization of differences. The ethnorelative stages include three mindsets for seeking out differences: Acceptance of difference, Adaptation to difference, and Integration of difference.

The rest of this section briefly describes each mindset of the DMIS and notes the developmental task most appropriate for the readiness level of the audience.

When individuals live in blissful ignorance of the existence of differences and fail to see any relevance to their own lives, they may be viewing the world through a position of Denial. In the Denial mindset, the person has few categories for recognizing and construing culture. Having rarely experienced cultural differences, the person may observe a few superficial differences, see them as irrelevant, and, in any case, perceive that culture has little to do with life as it is lived in the world of Denial. In the workplace, this leaves the organization vulnerable to cultural surprises, whether in the form of low retention, constant conflict, unproductive teams, or grievances. There may be a climate of disregard or disrespect for differences. The developmental task is to introduce the individual to the existence of difference and its significance to the organization.

In the next position, after recognizing that differences do indeed exist, the person defends against difference by either denigrating others or assuming a superior posture. The Defense mindset is typically a polarizing position, taking an either/or stance, defending the person's own identity, culture group, race, gender, or other affinity groups against other perspectives. The Defense mindset also includes a variation labeled "reversal," in which people polarize against their own ingroup. This is often mistaken for intercultural sensitivity, because it appears to be a deep commitment to inclusion. But unfortunately that inclusion is accompanied by defense against the ingroup. For example, in a recent coaching session, a diversity trainer was horrified to discover she was in the Defense position on the Intercultural Development Inventory. When it became clear to her that her defense posture was against her own culture group, she blurted out, "That's right! I dread training these people every day!" Polarization still yields the us/them distinction, but the poles have merely changed. Within the organization, there may be efforts to undermine equal opportunity, attempts to make sure all employees conform to single cultural styles, half-hearted recruitment efforts, and expressions of outright prejudice. With this mindset, the developmental task is to emphasize similarity and identification with outgroup members. This is the only stage of intercultural competence where similarities are emphasized rather than differences. When individuals see others as part of their ingroup, for whatever reason, there is less anxiety and uncertainty, diminishing the perceived threat of contact (Gudykunst, 1995).

If the person begins to feel others are in some broad sense "just like me," the predominant mindset is Minimization of difference, where the emphasis is on physiological or psychological similarity. For example, people with this mindset might say "The only race is the human race!" or "It's all about personality types."

Sometimes the minimization is based on a presumed shared philosophy, such as a belief that everyone wants democracy or freedom. Any minor differences are construed through the person's own ethnocentric worldview and explained in terms of the ingroup culture, while any major differences are seen as potential threats to the minimization position. If the person thinks we are all alike in deep ways, and the outgroup member reveals a significant difference offensive to the ingroup's values, the person in Minimization is in danger of slipping back to Defense: "I thought you were like me, but I guess I was wrong. I can't tolerate your approach."

Within the organization, Minimization has several outcomes. First, there may be unconscious exercise of privilege. Second, there may be naïveté about how power gets exercised, with a self-congratulatory posture: "We don't see color." Third, in an effort to be equal and gain control over the organization's culture, there may be extreme emphasis on pressure for conformity to a dominant culture model, resulting in global team conflict and loss of diversity as a resource. Mentoring programs coach the norms of the ingroup; performance appraisals assess people based on ingroup patterns; promotions have a hidden criterion: "fit."

The developmental task is to acquaint these individuals with their own cultural patterns. Many intercultural professionals include such topics in their diversity work, such as nonverbal behavior, communication styles, values, interaction rituals, conflict styles, cognitive styles, and learning styles. (Topics such as identity development, stereotyping, privilege, gender, power, and prejudice are best promoted in the ethnorelative/difference-seeking mindsets.) These topics draw from many disciplines, but all are employed in the examination of meaning making.

If individuals are unaware they have a culture, it allows for the frame that everyone is the same—and, by the way, anyone who is truly different just hasn't learned yet how do it the right way. Cultural self-awareness, described earlier as the core cognitive intercultural competency, is the primary developmental goal for those with a Minimization mindset; that is, achieving recognition of one's own culture that demonstrates cultural humility.

Once a degree of cultural self-awareness has been attained, the DMIS suggests the person is moving from ethnocentrism to ethnorelativism, from difference avoiding to difference seeking. This position reflects a person who no longer sees the world through a filter of a single unexamined worldview but rather through a cultural filter that has been brought into consciousness. The position of Acceptance reflects this self-knowledge and fosters recognition and appreciation of cultural differences in behavior and values. With more complex categories for construing differences, people are now capable of beginning the process of exploring general contrasts between their own and other cultures. Building on the core affective competence of curiosity, this mindset promotes such exploration, which generally assumes a nonevaluative perspective for purposes of understanding. This does not imply a mindless cultural relativism, wherein all differences are perceived to be acceptable, but rather a thoughtful exploration of what the differences are before forming a judgment. In the organization, Acceptance promotes active efforts to recruit and retain a globally and domestically diverse workforce, in which managers are encouraged to recognize and value differences and to "talk the talk." However, they are not yet required to "walk the walk" or to adapt their own styles using effective intercultural skills. The group may resemble a rainbow, and the lunchroom may sound like the United Nations, but mutual efforts to actually adapt are not evident. The developmental task for this mindset is to refine the analysis of cultural contrasts, to recognize more complex patterns, and to use generalizations about cultural archetypes as testable hypotheses.

Based on this more complex analysis of culture, the individual is likely moving into the mindset of Adaptation, aware now that successful interaction across cultures is built on mutual adjustment of styles in order to create shared meaning. This developmental level is the appropriate mindset for managers, faculty, and anyone in the position of trying to engage others appropriately and effectively across cultures. It builds on the core intercultural competence skill of empathy—the powerful capacity to shift frames of reference, noted by Pettigrew (2008) as the primary mediator of prejudice and stereotype reduction. Within the organization, there are rewards for interculturally competent performance, and professionals see their roles as requiring constant attention to addressing intercultural development. This in turn leads to higher retention and becoming an employer of choice. Culture in all of its forms becomes a resource globally and domestically. The developmental task involves nurturing frame-of-reference shifting skills and cultivation of adaptation strategies.

Sometimes, when the adaptation process is intense over substantial time—such as several years of acculturation during an overseas sojourn outside the home culture, or constant pressure to adapt to a dominant culture—individuals reach the final position of the DMIS: the mindset of Integration. Not to be confused with the vernacular use of "integration," this mindset describes the capabilities of the bicultural or multicultural person who is able to readily shift into the frame of reference of two or more cultures, often with language fluency and equivalent cultural competence (J. M. Bennett, 1993). This state of dynamic-in-betweenness suggests the notion of fluid adaptation from one culture to another, in a movement similar to the Mobius strip or the infinity symbol (Yoshikawa, 1987). Although this is not an expected position for the majority of the workforce, it should be noted that those who have lived abroad, spent their childhood in other cultures, or currently live as immigrants, refugees, transferees, or underrepresented groups in a different society may have reached this developmental level. Within the organization, a mindset of Integration supports an overall climate of intercultural competence, wherein every action, policy, and issue is viewed through cultural filters. The corporate culture is therefore defined by its intercultural competence, not exclusively through a single national or ethnic identity. The organization is able to effectively leverage the resources represented by this mindset. The developmental task for individuals who have reached this position is continuing efforts to resolve their identity concerns.

The Challenge and Support Model

In addition to the DMIS, which allows us to structure interventions to address the developmental readiness of the group, the challenge and support model provides a systematic strategy for reducing threat (J. M. Bennett, 2009b). When we encounter The Other—the unfamiliar stranger in our world—things may be different from how we expect them to be. We may be confounded by our counterpart's agreeing to a deliverable he or she simply cannot deliver, or we may feel manipulated by the mysterious verbal circles painted by a colleague. We may have no precedent for this behavior and may be shocked by our own irritation. The result may be a teachable moment, a trigger event that provides us with a cultural learning opportunity (Osland, Bird, & Gundersen, 2007).

However, if that sudden exposure is too unpredictable or too anxiety producing, we may engage our flight response. There is a lengthy and substantial literature exploring the importance of reducing this anxiety and uncertainty during intercultural contact to manageable levels (Allport, 1954; Pettigrew, 2008; Pettigrew & Tropp, 2011). The anxiety/uncertainty management (AUM) theory puts forth the notion that both uncertainty (cognitive, involving knowledge and predictability) and anxiety (affective, involving emotional stability) must be carefully balanced so as not to exceed the maximum tolerable, while being over the minimal level to encourage learning (Gudykunst, 1995). In other words, how do our programs create just enough disequilibration to stimulate curiosity and culture learning, but not so much as to alienate participants, to "build hills as we go"?

Sanford (1966) proposes the notion of combining challenge and support in educational efforts, a notion that also proves useful in the intercultural context. Depending on a wide variety of factors, the professional administrating the program needs to examine, for each participant, which aspects of the context can provide support and which aspects present challenges. If the participants are overly supported, no learning takes place. If the participants are overly challenged, the individual flees the learning context and, of course, no learning takes place. In the intercultural context, depending on their culture and developmental worldview, participants may find certain content either very challenging or affirming of their experience. Diversity initiatives must balance challenge and support to maximize the opportunity of culture learning and culture contact (J. M. Bennett, 2009b).

By combining the DMIS and the challenge and support model, we can assess participant readiness and adjust the level of support and challenge. For instance, if we suspect that the group we are working with finds cultural difference quite challenging (from the

Denial or Defense mindset), we can create initial programming that is highly supportive in both content and methods. As a rule, the groups we engage are likely to have somewhat ethnocentric mindsets and therefore to find intercultural competence efforts challenging, at best, and quite threatening, at worst. Once the critical mass of participants has reached an Acceptance or Adaptation mindset, we can then intentionally and strategically increase the challenge; for instance, by moving to the powerful issues of prejudice, bias, and power.

For a long time, I have said "You can do diversity training any way you want, as long as it works." And this is still true; there is no absolute formula that will bond intercultural training and diversity work into a fail-safe package. However, in the absence of such an ideal model, using the intercultural tools that we have provides a theoretical rationale for why we do what we do—a posture that suggests high potential for effective work.

References

Allport, G. W. (1954). *The nature of prejudice.* Reading, MA: Addison-Wesley.

Barnlund, D. C. (1989). *Communicative styles of Japanese and Americans: Images and realities.* Belmont, CA: Wadsworth.

Bennett, J. M. (1993). Cultural marginality: Identity issues in intercultural training. In R. M. Paige (Ed.), *Education for the intercultural experience* (pp. 109–136). Yarmouth, ME: Intercultural Press.

Bennett, J. M. (2009a). Cultivating intercultural competence: A process perspective. In D. K. Deardorff (Ed.), *The SAGE handbook of intercultural competence* (pp. 121–140). Thousand Oaks, CA: Sage.

Bennett, J. M. (2009b). Transformative training: Designing programs for culture learning. In M. Moodian (Ed.), *Contemporary leadership and intercultural competence: Exploring the cross-cultural dynamics within organizations* (pp. 95–110). Thousand Oaks, CA: Sage.

Bennett, J. M., & Bennett, M. J. (2004). Developing intercultural sensitivity: An integrative approach to global and domestic diversity. In D. Landis, J. M. Bennett, & M. J. Bennett (Eds.), *Handbook of intercultural training* (3rd ed., pp. 147–165). Thousand Oaks, CA: Sage.

Bennett, M. J. (1986). A developmental approach to training for intercultural sensitivity. *International Journal of Intercultural Relations, 10*(2), 179–196.

Bennett, M. J. (1993). Towards ethnorelativism: A developmental model of intercultural sensitivity. In R. M. Paige (Ed.), *Education for the intercultural experience* (pp. 21–72). Yarmouth, ME: Intercultural Press.

Bennett, M. J. (1998). Overcoming the golden rule: Sympathy and empathy. In M. J. Bennett (Ed.), *Basic concepts of intercultural communication: Selected readings* (pp. 191–214). Yarmouth, ME: Intercultural Press.

Bird, A., & Osland, J. S. (2004). Global competencies: An introduction. In H. W. Lane, M. L. Maznevski, M. E. Mendenhall, & J. McNett (Eds.), *The Blackwell handbook of global management: A guide to managing complexity* (pp. 57–80). Malden, MA: Blackwell.

Byram, M. (2012). Conceptualizing intercultural (communicative) competence and intercultural citizenship. In J. Jackson (Ed.), *The Routledge handbook of language and intercultural communication* (pp. 85–98). New York: Routledge.

Carr-Ruffino, N. (2009). *Managing diversity: People skills for a multicultural workplace* (8th ed.). Needham Heights, MA: Pearson Custom.

Collier, M. J. (1989). Cultural and intercultural communication competence: Current approaches and directions for future research. *International Journal of Intercultural Relations, 13*, 287–302.

Deardorff, D. K. (2006). Identification and assessment of intercultural competence as a student outcome of internationalization. *Journal of Studies in International Education, 10*(3), 241–266.

Deardorff, D. K. (2009). *The SAGE handbook of intercultural competence.* Thousand Oaks, CA: Sage.

Dinges, N. G., & Baldwin, K. D. (1996). Intercultural competence: A research perspective. In D. Landis & R. S. Bhagat (Eds.), *Handbook of intercultural training* (2nd ed., pp. 106–123). Thousand Oaks, CA: Sage.

Earley, P. C., & Ang, S. (2003). *Cultural intelligence: Individual interactions across cultures.* Stanford, CA: Stanford University Press.

Edmundson, A. (2007). *Globalized e-learning cultural challenges.* Hershey, PA: Information Science.

Fujita, A. (2011, September 24). Honest Japanese return $78 million in cash found in quake rubble. *ABC News.* Retrieved from http://abcnews.go.com/international/honest-japanese-return-78-million-cash-found-quake/story?id=14322940

Gardenswartz, L., & Rowe, A. (1998). *Managing diversity: A complete desk reference and planning guide* (Rev. ed.). New York: McGraw-Hill.

Goleman, D. (1995). *Emotional intelligence: Why it can matter more than IQ.* New York: Bantam Books.

Gregersen, J. B., Morrison, A., & Black, J. S. (1998). Developing leaders for the global frontier. *Sloan Management Review, 40*(1), 21–32.

Gudykunst, W. B. (1995). Anxiety/uncertainty management (AUM) theory. In R. L. Wiseman (Ed.), *Intercultural communication theory* (International & Intercultural Communication Annual, Vol. 9, pp. 8–58). Thousand Oaks, CA: Sage.

Guskin, A. (1991). Cultural humility: A way of being in the world. *Antioch Notes, 59*(1).

Hammer, M. R. (1989). Intercultural communication competence. In M. K. Asante & W. B. Gudykunst (Eds.), *Handbook of international and intercultural communication* (pp. 247–260). Thousand Oaks, CA: Sage.

Hammer, M. R. (2009). The Intercultural Development Inventory: An approach for assessing and building intercultural competence. In M. Moodian (Ed.), *Contemporary leadership and intercultural competence: Exploring the cross-cultural dynamics within organizations* (pp. 203–218). Thousand Oaks, CA: Sage.

Hammer, M. R., & Bennett, M. J. (2003). Measuring intercultural sensitivity: The Intercultural Development Inventory. *International Journal of Intercultural Relations, 27*(4), 421–443. doi:10.1016/S0147-1767(03)00032-4

Hayles, V. R., & Russell, A. M. (1997). *The diversity directive: Why some initiatives fail and what to do about it.* New York: McGraw-Hill.

Hunter, B., White, G. P., & Godbey, G. C. (2006). What does it mean to be globally competent? *Journal of Studies in International Education, 10*(3), 267–285.

Intercultural Communication Institute. (2011). *Intercultural training and assessment tools* [data file]. Retrieved from http://www.intercultural.org/tools.php

Jamieson, D., & O'Mara, J. (1991). *Managing workforce 2000: Gaining the diversity advantage.* San Francisco: Jossey-Bass.

Judy, R. W., & D'Amico, C. (1997). *Workforce 2020: Work and workers in the 21st century.* Indianapolis, IN: Hudson Institute.

Kim, Y. Y. (1991). Intercultural communication competence: A system-theoretic view. In S. Ting-Toomey & F. Korzeny (Eds.), *Cross-cultural interpersonal communication* (International and Intercultural Communication Annual, Vol. 15, pp. 259–275). Thousand Oaks, CA: Sage.

Kleinman, A., & Benson, P. (2006). Anthropology in the clinic: The problem of cultural competency and how to fix it. *Public Library of Science Medicine, 3*(10), e294. doi:10.1371/journal.pmed.0030294

Kochman, T., & Mavrelis, J. (2009). *Corporate tribalism: White men/White women and cultural diversity at work*. Chicago, IL: University of Chicago Press.

Loden, M. (1996). *Implementing diversity*. Chicago, IL: Irwin.

Lustig, M. W., & Koester, J. (2009). *Intercultural competence: Interpersonal communication across cultures* (6th ed.). Boston, MA: Pearson/Allyn and Bacon.

Meacham, J., & Gaff, J. G. (2006). Learning goals in mission statements. *Liberal Education, 92*(1), 6–13.

Mendenhall, M. E. (2001). Introduction: New perspectives on expatriate adjustment and its relationship to global leadership development. In M. E. Mendenhall, T. M. Kuhlman, & G. K. Stahl (Eds.), *Developing global business leaders: Policies, processes, and innovations* (pp. 1–18). Westport, CT: Greenwood.

Milem, J. F., Chang, M. J., & Antonio, A. L. (2005). Making diversity work on campus: A research-based perspective. *Making excellence inclusive: Preparing students and campuses for an era of greater expectations*. Washington, DC: Association of American Colleges and Universities.

Opdal, P. M. (2001). Curiosity, wonder and education seen as perspective. *Studies in Philosophy and Education, 20*, 331–344.

Osland, J. S., Bird, A., & Gundersen, A. (2007, August). *Trigger events in intercultural sensemaking*. Paper presented at the 67th Annual Meeting of the Academy of Management, Philadelphia, PA.

Paige, R. M., Cohen, A. D., Kappler, B., Chi, J. C., & Lassegard, J. P. (2002). *Maximizing study abroad: A students' guide to strategies for language and culture learning and use*. Minneapolis, MN: University of Minnesota.

Paige, R. M., Jacobs-Cassuto, M., Yershova, Y. A., & DeJaeghere, J. (2003). Assessing intercultural sensitivity: An empirical analysis of the Hammer and Bennett Intercultural Development Inventory. *International Journal of Intercultural Relations, 27*(4), 467–486. doi:10.1016/S0147-1767(03)00034-8

Peterson, B. (2004). *Cultural intelligence: A guide to working with people from other cultures*. Yarmouth, ME: Intercultural Press.

Pettigrew, T. F. (2008). Future directions for intergroup contact theory and research. *International Journal of Intercultural Relations, 32*(3), 182–199.

Pettigrew, T. F., & Tropp, L. R. (2011). *When groups meet: The dynamics of intergroup contact*. New York: Psychology Press.

Rhodes, T. L. (Ed.). (2010). *Assessing outcomes and improving achievement: Tips and tools for using rubrics*. Washington, DC: Association of American Colleges and Universities.

Sanford, N. (1966). *Self and society: Social change and individual develop-ment.* New York: Atherton Press.

Shepard, H. A. (1975). Rules of thumb for change agents. *OD Practitio-ner, 7*(3), 1–5.

Smith, D. G., García, M., Hudgins, C. A., Musil, C. M., Nettles, M. T., & Sedlacek, C. A. (2000). *A diversity research agenda.* Washington, DC: Association of American Colleges & Universities.

Solomon, C. M. (1994). Global operations demand that HR rethink diversity. *Personnel Journal, 73*(7), 40–50.

Spitzberg, B. H. (1994). A model of intercultural communication com-petence. In L. A. Samovar & R. E. Porter (Eds.), *Intercultural communication: A reader* (7th ed., pp. 347–359). Belmont, CA: Wadsworth.

Spitzberg, B. H., & Changnon, G. (2009). Conceptualizing intercultural competence. In D. K. Deardorff (Ed.), *The SAGE handbook of inter-cultural competence* (pp. 2–52). Thousand Oaks, CA: Sage.

Thomas, D. C., & Inkson, K. (2004). *Cultural intelligence: People skills for global business.* San Francisco: Berrett-Koehler.

Vulpe, T., Kealey, D., Protheroe, D., & MacDonald, D. (2001). *A profile of the interculturally effective person* (2nd ed.). Quebec, Canada: Cana-dian Department of Foreign Affairs and International Trade, Centre for Intercultural Learning.

Wentling, R. M., & Palma-Rivas, N. (2000). Current status of diversity initiatives in selected multinational corporations. *Human Resource Development Quarterly, 11*(1), 35–60.

Williams, D. A., Berger, J. B., & McClendon, S. A. (2005). *Towards a model of inclusive excellence and change in post-secondary institutions.* Wash-ington, DC: Association of American Colleges and Universities.

Wiseman, R. L. (2002). Intercultural communication competence. In W. B. Gudykunst & B. Mody (Eds.), *Handbook of international and intercultural communication* (2nd ed., pp. 207–224.) Thousand Oaks, CA: Sage.

Yershova, Y., DeJaeghere, J., & Mestenhauser, J. (2000). Thinking not as usual: Adding the intercultural perspective. *Journal of Studies in International Education, 4*(1), 39–78.

Yoshikawa, M. J. (1987). Cross-cultural adaptation and perceptual development. In Y. Y. Kim & W. B. Gudykunst (Eds.), *Cross-cultural adaptation: Current approaches* (International and Intercultural Communication Annual, Vol. 11, pp. 140–148). Thousand Oaks, CA: Sage.

CHAPTER SIX

The Work of Inclusive Leadership
Fostering Authentic Relationships, Modeling Courage and Humility

Plácida V. Gallegos

> *The adaptive demands of our societies require leadership that takes responsibility without waiting for revelation or request. One may lead perhaps with no more than a question in hand. (Heifetz, 1994, p. 276)*

Theorists and practitioners have identified the problems associated with traditional views of leadership that have dominated the management literature (Bennis & Nanus, 1985; Chin, 2010; Ryan, 2006). Traditional models of leadership are guided by assumptions about individualism, meritocracy, and equal opportunity and often result in the use of dominance and coercion to get work done (Conger, 1990; Keleher et al., 2010). In their call for greater emphasis on intergroup boundary crossing, Ernst and Yip (2009) advocated shifting from organizational cultures that foster hierarchical structures to those that are more decentralized with more flexible structures that accommodate today's ever-increasing globalization and changing leadership landscape. Focusing on individuals and personalities represents a narrow slice of the complex phenomenon of leadership as it is practiced in these increasingly challenging times. The context of organizations today is one of ever-expanding diversity in which leadership happens across levels, roles, and cultures. This organizational landscape invites a different approach to leadership, as Heifetz and Laurie (1997) point out:

> Mobilizing an organization to adapt its behaviors in order to thrive in new business environments is critical. Without such change, any company today would falter. Indeed, getting people to do adaptive work is the mark of leadership in a competitive world. . . . [I]n order to make change happen, executives have to break a long-standing behavior pattern of their own: providing leadership in the form of solutions. . . . But the locus of responsibility for problem solving when a company faces an adaptive challenge must shift to its people. Solutions to adaptive challenges reside not in the executive suite but in the collective intelligence of employees at all levels, who need to use one another as resources, often across boundaries, and learn their way to those solutions [p. 124].

Although prominent leadership theories have evolved and increasingly reflect changing social contexts, they often still fail to incorporate issues of equity, diversity, and social justice in their conceptualizations (Chin, 2010, p. 150). Attention to diversity is more than measuring numerical representation of different groups in the ranks of leadership. We require a paradigm shift in our frameworks of leadership to incorporate how dimensions of diversity shape our understanding of leadership and influence styles of leadership and followership, and how bias influences the exercise of leadership (Thomas & Ely, 2002).

In this chapter, I describe how inclusive leadership is enacted across multiple levels of system, including the individual, relational, and organizational dimensions. To truly influence complex organizational circumstances, leaders and practitioners need to develop capacities to assess and intervene at each level strategically and sometimes simultaneously. I distinguish this view of inclusive leadership from more traditional models that are based on leadership being a specific designation or an individual responsibility. I elaborate on this perspective and provide examples of how inclusive leadership is a relational construct that is the consequence of mutual influence and collective adaptation to fluid environments.

Fundamentally, the workplace is a central location for relating and meaning making. Most of us want to make a difference in the lives of others and make our worlds better as a result of our contribution (Pearce, 2007). Taking leadership and utilizing our precious life energy for the betterment of the collective is at the root of inclusion and lies at the core of this chapter. While simple in some ways, paradoxically, the work of leadership is also fundamentally dangerous and fraught with potential difficulties. As Heifetz and Laurie (1997) point out, the greatest challenge for leaders is to focus on adapting to situations "when our deeply held beliefs are challenged, when the values that made us successful become less relevant and when legitimate yet competing perspectives emerge" (p. 124).

I also argue that inclusion goes far beyond merely developing "soft skills" of caring and compassion, to a need for courage and making tough decisions. Calling out incidents of structural inequity and making change to long-standing traditions and organizational practices needs to be part of a leader's toolkit if real and sustainable change is to be fostered (Kivel, 2002). The adaptive work of inclusion needs to be broad enough to encompass the heart and the head, and to develop strategies and practices that challenge dominant organizational paradigms and redress ways of being long held as sacrosanct.

As an organizational diversity consultant and researcher for the past thirty years, I have encountered many circumstances in which bold action was required to address deeply entrenched perspectives and patterns of behavior. More often subtle rather than blatant examples of exclusion called for nuanced understanding and willingness to engage resistance to change. I recall a particular example: the most senior leader insisted publicly that he and his all-White male management team understood the experiences of women and people of color and had no need to listen to the stories being shared by these marginalized groups. It took courage and considerable risk for consultants and employees to challenge his perspective while inviting formal leaders to become curious about what they might be missing. As a researcher and social psychologist, I could understand how the manager and his team assumed they shared the same experience as women and people of color. As a consultant, it was quite another challenge to engage them in expanding their perspectives while honoring their own values of equal opportunity and fairness. I have learned to bring humility to my organizational practice, especially when confronting subtle forms of bias and oppression. I realize that it is often not the intention of perpetrators to cause harm, just as my own intentions often do not align with my behaviors.

Leaders, as the shapers of the organization's culture, need to be the voice of a unified meta-narrative that supports a vision of an inclusive culture (Wasserman, Gallegos, & Ferdman, 2008). For this vision to be inclusive, it must be one that embraces the entire organization. The energy that lives in the stories of resistance holds great potential to support a culture of inclusion when transformed into shared narratives. Leaders who learn to "dance with resistance" model ways to support diversity and inclusion throughout the organization (Wasserman et al., 2008). In some ways it can be a relief to recognize that no one has all the answers when dealing with the vast array of heterogeneity in organizations. When we approach the task of leadership with humility, courage, and authenticity, all that is required is openness to learn and willingness to engage.

The Role of Leaders in Fostering Inclusive Cultures

Ferdman (2010) makes the important link between leadership and creating cultures of inclusion when he suggests that attention to inclusion pushes the envelope for leaders, because the required skill set involves an increasing capacity for complexity. This practice involves not only paying attention to how differences are managed in organizations but also supporting the conditions that increase the likelihood that those differences will be noticed, valued, and welcomed. As he describes it, "inclusion involves both being fully ourselves and allowing others to be fully themselves in the context of engaging in common pursuits. It means collaborating in a way in which all parties can be fully engaged and subsumed, and yet, paradoxically, at the same time believe that they have not compromised, hidden, or given up any part of themselves" (p. 37).

The process of becoming a more inclusive organization requires ongoing attention to the dynamic interplay of people and practices. In our previous writing, my colleagues and I drew on Heifetz's notion of being "on the balcony" while simultaneously being on the dance floor as one of the key competencies necessary in organizations (Wasserman et al., 2008). This ability to shuttle back and forth between the field of action and the view from above allows leaders to see patterns that emerge and constantly modify their actions to fit changing life conditions. In their seminal *Harvard Business Review* article, Heifetz and Laurie (1997) explain the importance of balancing these two vantage points:

> Leaders have to see a context for change or create one. They should give employees a strong sense of the history of the enterprise and what's good about its past, as well as an idea of the market forces at work today and the responsibility people must take in shaping the future. Leaders must be able to identify struggles over values and power, recognize patterns of work avoidance, and watch for the many other functional and dysfunctional reactions to change. Without the capacity to move back and forth between the field of action and the balcony, to reflect day to day, moment to moment on the many ways in which an organization's habits can sabotage adaptive work, a leader easily and unwittingly becomes a prisoner of the system. The dynamics of adaptive change are far too complex to keep track of, let alone influence, if leaders stay only on the field of play [Heifetz & Laurie, 1997, p. 125–126].

In developing and maintaining cultures of inclusion, actually considering alternative viewpoints on any issue or decision can be a daunting challenge. Inclusive leadership involves attention to the question, "Whose voices or perspectives might we be missing?" or asking "What are the limitations to the current ways we are seeing this issue?" Especially given that those at the table are typically acting in good faith, raising the possibility that they may be privileging certain perspectives (their own) over those not in the room can create tensions and intergroup conflict. Raising the questions and elevating these possibilities in spite of the challenges to be expected is the work of inclusive leadership.

Manifestations of Inclusive Leadership at Multiple Levels of System

To support the practice of inclusion, individuals need to be able to reflect on their multiple identities, attend to the identities of others, and develop the ability to communicate effectively across the boundaries of a wide range of differences in the context of complex organizational cultures (Ferdman & Roberts, Chapter 3, this volume; Wasserman, 2004). Individual and group differences are encountered in situations in which success may depend on the capacity to stand back far enough to be able to see and to intervene at interpersonal and institutional levels, simultaneously (Wasserman & Gallegos, 2009). Rather than relying on finding quick solutions, leadership is more productively focused on asking the right questions and acknowledging that diversity and inclusion are systemic challenges with no ready answers.

Individual Level of System

At the individual level, inclusive leadership demands cultural humility, courage, and tolerance for imperfection and ambiguity. Considerable awareness of one's own personal and professional background and biases is useful in developing greater facility to engage across differences. In training physicians to move beyond their expert orientation in clinical settings, Tervalon and Murray-Garcia (1998) differentiate between cultural competence and humility:

> Cultural competence in clinical practice is best defined not by a discrete endpoint but as a commitment and active engagement in a lifelong process that individuals enter into on an ongoing basis with patients, communities, colleagues and with themselves. This training outcome, perhaps better described as cultural humility versus cultural competence . . . is a process that requires humility as individuals continually engage in self-reflection and self-critique as lifelong learners and reflective practitioners. It is a process that requires humility in how physicians bring into check the power imbalances that exist in the dynamics of physician-patient communication by using patient-focused interviewing and care [p. 118].

Critical to the building of inclusion is reframing notions of leadership, from glorified and unrealistic expectations that leaders have the answers to the organization's challenges (Ancona, Malone, Orlikowski, & Senge, 2007) to a shared sense of responsibility. Given the wide range of differences present in most organizations in the United States and around the world, understanding all aspects of diversity or knowing how to deal with them becomes virtually impossible. The criteria for leading and following need to be transformed to address the ambiguous and emotionally charged situations in which we operate. Formal and informal leaders have to avoid the inclination to foster dependency rather than interdependence with followers. Heifetz and Linsky (2002) warn that, absent humility, leaders run the risk that "dependence can readily turn into contempt as the group discovers your mortal failings" (p. 170). Practicing inclusion in such volatile and unpredictable circumstances challenges leaders to be courageous in the face of uncertainty and constantly shifting landscapes. Remaining steadfast requires emotional stability and presence, which Heifetz and Linsky (2002) eloquently capture as follows: "Leading with an open heart means you could be at your lowest point, abandoned by your people and entirely powerless, yet remain receptive to the full range of human emotions without going numb, striking back, or engaging in some other defense" (pp. 227–228).

Much literature has focused on the value of leaders and organizations developing greater emotional intelligence (for example, Mayer, Salovey, & Caruso, 2008; Salovey & Mayer, 1990; Salovey & Sluyter, 1997). Goleman, Boyatzis, and McKee (2001) argue that emotional intelligence is the most important asset for leaders to master. The underlying assumptions of these frameworks is that becoming self-aware and sensitive to the emotional needs of others allows a person to choose from a wide range of behavioral choices to influence outcomes. The ability to attend to self and others simultaneously is difficult enough to muster when operating in one's own culture, but becomes exponentially more challenging when bridging across differences in race, gender, sexual orientation or nationality. Ruderman, Glover, Chrobot-Mason, and Ernst (2010; see also Ernst & Chrobot-Mason, 2011) have conducted extensive research that demonstrates the wide range of leadership practices found in organizations as leaders attempt to alleviate problems and threats associated with intergroup dynamics. Some individuals attempt to deal with these challenges by generating simplistic rules to guide behavior and training managers in how to perform accordingly. The results often fall short of the desired goals. Rather than creating comfort and safety, this approach comes across as lacking in authenticity and creates distance between groups. For example, during a recent consulting engagement in a manufacturing plant in southern California, some employee groups complained about other people's choice of music on the shop floor. In a knee-jerk attempt to end the problem, management initially banned all music. When production levels dropped, managers realized they needed to revisit their solution. A diverse team of employees was invited to join management in dialogue, leading to greater engagement across diverse groups, deeper learning about the others' preferences, and a creative solution.

Fortunately, when approached with sincere curiosity, a learning stance, and an open frame of mind, differences can be engaged to benefit the organization by providing multiple perspectives and innovative thinking (Hannum, McFeeters, & Booysen, 2010). A dramatic example from the law enforcement community demonstrates how gender differences are improving the effectiveness of police officers in potentially violent situations. A team of officers was dispersed to a domestic violence situation and approached the locked apartment where the victim was being held against her will. Utilizing their typical protocol, officers were preparing to break down the door to the apartment and storm in with guns blazing. The sole woman officer was finally able to get the attention of her male teammates in time to provide a safer alternative: she had obtained the key to the apartment from the building manager and the officers were able to enter the apartment without violence and de-escalate the situation. Although not always practiced in such a life-or-death situation, the principle of inclusion is fundamentally about building relationships that foster learning, engagement, and creativity. I now turn to how such relationships are created, maintained, and used in service of organizational inclusion.

Relational Level of System

What capacities are required to fully maximize the potential of relationships in diverse settings? The answers to this question are both simple and complex. They are simple in that similar behaviors are required to operate across any difference: listening well, practicing empathy, and being curious will serve to build relationships in most any situation (Wasserman & Gallegos, 2009). The complexity comes in because the application of these behaviors needs to take into account a wide array of variables that occur simultaneously with blinding speed and innumerable variation. Providing relational leadership in today's diverse organizations is anything but simple, as Wasserman and Blake-Beard (2010) note:

> Our interdependence means that leaders need to shift their focus from themselves as creating and transmitting leadership to being a leader who invites, considers, and incorporates other perspectives and new ways of making meaning in relation to those perspectives. . . . Traversing levels from individual to systems, taking up voice, reflection on experience, and welcoming others through a network of diverse developmental relationships are all aspects of this skill of moving between subject and object. These are the essential ingredients for leading well in today's complex organizational reality [p. 206].

Inclusive organizations are more likely to develop shared leadership at all levels, including individuals without formal roles as leaders. When people feel valued and respected, their sense of belonging increases along with their willingness to perform beyond expectations (Bass, 1985). Investing in building relationships across differences reaps benefits that contribute to greater engagement and higher performance (Hannum et al., 2010). It is essential, however, that relationships be based on the principles of authenticity if they are to foster trust and collaboration. Avolio and Gardner (2005) place authenticity at the root of all effective leadership. Although definitions vary, authentic leaders demonstrate awareness of self and context and are seen as "confident, hopeful, optimistic, resilient and high on moral character" (Avolio, Luthans, & Walumbwa, 2004, p. 4, as quoted by Avolio & Gardner, 2005, p. 321).

In the workplace, relationships are focused on shared goals and superordinate outcomes. Heifetz and Linsky (2002) stress the importance of reaching across boundaries and factions to create alliances and partnerships. These strategic connections increase the likelihood of accomplishing critical outcomes and marshalling personal and political power to get things done. This means investing time and energy to find and maintain diverse networks within and outside of one's organization.

In defining the practices of relational leaders, Geller (2009) identifies ways that a strong "web of connections" fosters shared commitment toward mutually defined goals. She emphasizes these six practices:

1. Acting "with communal intent fostering a collective identity,"
2. "A co-created and compelling vision aligns work activities with higher purpose and to the greater good."
3. "Dialogue is a process of discovery that promotes mutually responsive perspective sharing."
4. Responding "with flexibility and a resilient spirit to the myriad changes."
5. "Learning to think in new ways."
6. "Acting ethically" (pp. 189–190).

Intentionally creating diverse relationships challenges us to be aware of our preferences based on familiarity and history and to move beyond our comfort zones to seek out others from radically different backgrounds and work styles. Although most of us would agree with the value of extending our relational boundaries beyond our past experiences, actually achieving authentic relationships is neither easy nor comfortable. The impetus for courageously and authentically making the effort needs to be grounded in our passion for organizational outcomes that we cannot achieve by staying within our narrow boundaries of homogeneity.

Organizational Level of System

What then are the ways that inclusive leadership is best demonstrated and modeled across the organization? Being a relational leader who is mindful of inclusion requires being agile in alignment and coordination of meaning and action with others. As my colleagues and I have pointed out, "[c]reating and maintaining an inclusive culture is a complex and ongoing process that requires continuous self-examination and thoughtful reflection by leaders and all members of the organization" (Wasserman et al., 2008, p. 181). Specifically, we list and elaborate on four things leaders must do to foster cultures of inclusion:

- Explicitly define (and redefine) the boundaries and rules for acceptable behavior.
- Create the conditions for conversations to explore differences.
- Model and communicate an understanding of and valuing of (and comfort with) diversity.
- Be authentic and use personal experiences strategically [pp. 186–187].

Both adaptive and technical challenges face the leader of a diverse organization, and knowing which challenge is which is not always a simple matter (Wasserman et al., 2008). Unfortunately, many leaders confuse the two, such as when they address the problem of retaining women in leadership roles. If leaders approach this issue as simply a technical one, their response would likely be to increase efforts to recruit women into upper level positions. Furthermore, they might view information from exit interviews as providing the answer to the question of why women are leaving. The departing women executives are likely to respond to questions with palatable and safe explanations for their leaving, such as relocating to another area or having found another position that is more consistent with their long-term career goals. Women are less likely to speak to more sensitive issues, such as feeling excluded or experiencing overt acts of sexism on their teams, for fear of harming their relationship with the current organization. This is another case in which management needs to be "on the balcony," noticing the broader

patterns of hiring, promotions, and resignations before con-
cluding that the problems are unrelated to these more difficult
issues. An adaptive view of the situation would demand greater
introspection and provide the potential for a more comprehensive assessment of the problem and a more thoughtful, strategic approach. The organization might need to consider the
norms and behaviors that typify the current culture and inquire
as to how those practices may make it difficult for women to
find their voices or make their fullest contributions. Instead of
simply bringing in more women, only to have them leave
through the revolving door, the adaptive response might require
men (and sometimes women who have assimilated to the dominant styles) to consider their ways of being and identify
the need to change to make the workplace more amenable to
women's styles and contributions (Fletcher, 2010; Tannen,
2001).

Practices That Support Inclusive Leadership

What then should individual leaders and organizations attend
to if they wish to avoid the negative outcomes described thus
far in the chapter? Many organizations espouse support for
risk taking, outside-the-box thinking, and innovation. Inadvertently, however, they reward conformity, playing it safe, and
fitting in (Blancero, DelCampo, & Marron, 2007). Often, the
emotional work needed to develop positive relations across difference and to foster inclusive cultures is minimized. Along
these lines, Pittinsky (2010) draws an important distinction
between allophilia and xenophobia. He defines xenophobia
as "the general fear or hatred of those who are considered
to be in a different group than one's own" (p. 125). Often the
assumption is that groups are doomed to operate across the
chasm of negative emotions, based on their hard-wired predis-
positions to prefer their own groups and disdain those who are
different. The less well-known and possibly more useful concept
of allophilia relates to the work of inclusive leadership. This
concept is based on the development of liking and empathy
for others who are different, and it can be supported by actions

such as identifying common goals that bind people together and creating greater cohesion across groups. With attention to potential fault lines (Homan & Jehn, 2010; Ruderman & Chrobot-Mason, 2010) and possibilities, groups can be supported in learning new ways of being and caring that allow creativity to flourish.

Timing and managing the pace of change by recognizing the difficulties organizations face is also critical. Heifetz and Linsky (2002) remind us to pay attention to the subtle aspects that can accelerate or derail change efforts. Using the metaphor of an emotional roller coaster, they warn us that people will resist change unless we realize that we "are asking them to relinquish something—a belief, a value, a behavior—that they hold dear" (p. 116). An example in organizations facing culture change relates to the need to modify how to celebrate victories or holidays. As the workforce becomes increasingly diverse, assumptions of what is fun may need to shift from playing golf, going to football games, or visiting bars to more inclusive practices. When these historical ways of relating are identified as problematic for some individuals, the response can be to wonder "Why can't we have fun anymore?" In such situations, leadership is needed to frame such changes as expanding the repertoire of celebrations rather than putting a damper on the spirit of the organization or team. Involving a wider range of people and groups in determining new practices for celebration, rather than dictating from above, is more likely to gain buy-in and engagement from all associates and demonstrate creativity in adapting to changing conditions.

Providing the right combination of challenge and support (see Bennett, Chapter 3, this volume) becomes critical and relates to the importance of having an inclusive culture that fosters relationships of caring, empathy, and mutual support. The role of leaders involves "taking the heat with grace" (Heifetz & Linsky, 2002, p. 146) and can lead to deeper, stronger relationships based on mutual respect and the willingness to engage authentically in difficult moments. It is in the crucible of these difficult interactions that the organizational culture is built and the capacity to engage across differences is strengthened (Wasserman, Chapter 4, this volume).

Behavioral Manifestations of Inclusive Leadership

Researchers have consistently demonstrated that diverse teams make more creative decisions than homogeneous ones, with one important caveat (Hollander, 2009). Simply having diversity on a team alone does not automatically lead to desired outcomes of greater productivity or creative thinking. Concerted effort must be made to address exclusionary practices and intentionally maximize the diverse perspectives of each team member (Gardner, Gino, & Staats, 2012). When multicultural teams are developed and invested in, the return is manifold. Putting diverse bodies together does not automatically lead to diverse outcomes—it is necessary to have practices and competencies that support inclusion if the potential of diversity is to be tapped and amplified (Wyche, 2008). Again, this is where inclusive leadership comes into play. Leaders can pay attention to the wide range of styles, experiences, and values that diverse teams bring and can shine light on these differences to the advantage of the unit. Anticipating that valuing these differences will be more challenging than working within homogeneous teams, the leader can provide the support and resources for the team to engage in deeper dialogue and constructive conflict in service of establishing a cohesive environment where all can bring their best ideas to the table.

Traditional organizations rely heavily on hierarchical structures, which typically assume that those at the top of the management ladder have the answers and solutions to the major problems facing them (Hollander, 2009). When applied to inclusion, this model is particularly dysfunctional. When there is diversity represented at the lower and middle levels of the organization, senior leaders need to learn more from employees below them about what matters and what central issues are facing the business. An example of this "reversal" is the case of mentoring relationships across cultures and gender. When senior men from the dominant culture attempt to become mentors to younger women and people of color, the exchange between them becomes fraught with land mines as these leaders base their career advice on their own experiences without understanding the very different life experiences and worldviews of their mentees (Blake-Beard, 2009). For example, a mentor who is an older White male may have difficulty providing a young working mother seeking work-life balance with the support she needs to manage these competing commitments. If, however, he is truly interested in better understanding the experience of the younger woman, there is much he can learn from her that will serve him in working with employees who differ from him in significant ways. Rather than providing her with solutions, he can engage in inquiry and learn about structural and systemic barriers that exist for her and others that gets in the way of their being able to make their fullest contribution to the organization. The mentee can also demonstrate leadership in this situation by learning from her mentor more about the history of the organization and its norms and practices to better maneuver through the challenges she faces in achieving her career goals (Fletcher, 1999).

Table 6.1 offers behavioral manifestations of inclusive leadership across multiple levels of system to demonstrate the importance of attending to each level simultaneously. The need to notice and make choices about what is happening in the midst of all this complexity creates a developmental challenge that requires individual and organizational capacity to tolerate and embrace uncertainty. This challenge arises within the individual, between people in relationships, and in the context of systems designed to support the active involvement of all individuals and groups. For leaders and practitioners who want to further develop their capacities for inclusive leadership, the third column offers additional resources to pursue.

Conclusion

I recently attended a national conference on mentoring across difference and developing nontraditional leaders. Most of the emphasis of this program seemed to be on preparing White women and people of color to accommodate the dominant cultural norms of their organizations to achieve promotional opportunities and reach higher levels of success. As useful as some of

Table 6.1. Behavioral Manifestations of Inclusive Leadership

Level of System	Inclusive Leadership Practices	Resources
Individual	Take responsibility for your own learning and actions, rather than depending on a particular individual or single source. "Accept responsibility for your piece of the mess" (Heifetz & Linsky, 2002, p. 90).	Baxter-Magolda, Creamer, & Meszaros, 2010; Blake-Beard, 2009 Heifetz & Linsky, 2002; Heifetz, Linsky, & Alexander, 2009
	Have trusted advisors from different identity groups from whom you can seek feedback.	Blake-Beard, Murrell, & Thomas, 2007; Holvino, Ferdman, & Merrill-Sands, 2004; Johnson-Bailey & Cervero, 2004
	Recognize and explore your own identities and cultural orientations to be aware of when they complement or contradict the values and orientations of other groups and individuals.	Bhawuk & Munusamy, 2010; Chandler & Kram, 2005; Ferdman, 2003; also Ferdman & Roberts, Chapter 3, this volume, and Bennett, Chapter 4, this volume
	Expect to have your current assumptions challenged and invite these interactions as valuable moments that can lead to transformational learning and new insights. Make this an expectation of your team.	Keleher et al., 2010; Kivel, 2002 Gardner, Gino, & Staats, 2009; Ruderman, Glover, Chrobot-Mason, & Ernst, 2010

Table 6.1. Continued

Level of System	Inclusive Leadership Practices	Resources
	Be bold in addressing blatant and subtle acts of exclusion. Use these as opportunities for organizational learning rather than for compliance or punishment.	Miller & Katz, 2002
	Differentiate between stereotypes and real cultural differences and characteristics.	Ferdman & Cortes, 1991
Relational	Seek opportunities to mentor others and to be mentored, both within as well as across groups.	Blake-Beard, 2009
	Accept different work styles, communication styles, and relationship styles; allow for different ways of problem solving, leading, and getting work done.	Chandler & Kram, 2005
	Recognize intergroup fault lines	Homan & Jehn, 2010
	Recognize existing and implicit norms; continually examine and revise these to assure fit across cultures and subcultures and to minimize cultural bias.	Johnson-Bailey & Cervero, 2004; Pittinsky, 2005
	Provide tools and build skills to help diverse teams address conflict and value differences and to communicate clearly.	Geller, 2009; Wasserman & Blake-Beard, 2010

(Continued)

Table 6.1. Continued

Level of System	Inclusive Leadership Practices	Resources
	Intentionally involve a wide range of people and include diverse perspectives. Always look out for what/who might be missing and who else you may need to hear from, and consider possible blinders or unquestioned assumptions.	Hannum, McFeeters, & Booysen, 2010
	Increase direction, alignment, and commitment across groups focused on shared outcomes	Ely & Thomas, 2000
Organization/System	Establish a clear business case for valuing differences and communicate across the organization the specific business necessity and rationale for building inclusion, connecting initiatives to concrete business objectives and strategic plans.	Miller & Katz, 2002; O'Leary & Weathington, 2006
	Develop a vision of an inclusive culture that recognizes the added value of both between- and within-group differences.	Chrobot-Mason, D., Ruderman, Ernst, & Weber, 2011; Gallegos & Ferdman, 2007
	Be explicit about organizational norms and behaviors that support an inclusive culture for all employees.	Holvino, Ferdman, & Merrill-Sands, 2004

Table 6.1. Continued

Level of System	Inclusive Leadership Practices	Resources
	Identify "structural racism" and oppression beyond individual behaviors. Be willing and adept at naming exclusionary practices and behaviors.	Keleher et al., 2010; Ryan, 2006
	Review organizational policies and practices to eliminate subtle cultural biases, such as performance management systems that require active self-promotion in ways that may be culturally challenging for some groups such as Asians and Latinos.	Cox & Nkomo, 2001; Ferdman & Cortes, 1992; Gallegos & Ferdman, 2007; Wyche, 2008
	Provide quality educational opportunities to intentionally build organizational knowledge among all leaders and employees about the range of diverse cultures and identities.	Ferdman, 2010; Foldy, Rivard, & Buckley, 2009
	Create systems of accountability to hold leaders and employees responsible for practicing inclusion; provide support and incentives for best practices.	Bell & Nkomo, 2001; Hannum, McFeeters, & Booysen, 2010

these workshops and speakers might have been, what struck me most was what was missing from the agenda of this conference. Little attention was paid to recognizing and intentionally managing the organization's current culture. Often, silent yet powerful cultural forces are ignored to the detriment of all those who enter, especially for those from traditionally marginalized groups, such as women, LGBT, people with disabilities, and people from racial and ethnic groups in addition to Whites (Cox & Nkomo, 2001). Also missing from the agenda was consideration of the role of dominant group members in cocreating organizational dynamics. Too often, subordinate group members are assumed to be the ones who need to be modified or fixed to make them a better fit into the organizational norms, rather than questioning what needs to change to make the organization more inclusive for all. Why invest in recruiting and hiring diverse associates, only to reward them for conforming to institutional practices once they enter (Blancero et al., 2007)? Diversity initiatives need to instead include a process for preparing dominant group members to receive and maximize the diverse perspectives that these new entrants bring with them to the workplace. Marginalized groups need to step more fully into their leadership as well by demonstrating their value and courageously moving beyond real and perceived barriers to their full inclusion. If an organization is unable to reflect on its existing culture, it is less likely to take advantage of new ideas and multiple perspectives. Ultimately, organization development efforts to build inclusion need to focus on creating cultures that are expansive enough to incorporate the perspectives of all subgroups.

This chapter has focused on the development, fostering, and application of inclusive leadership. As noted in the sections of this chapter, inclusive leadership touches, and can be enacted at, all levels of an organization: individual, relational, and system-wide. Inclusive leadership must be reflected in behavior rather than platitudes. Unfortunately, many organizations today have gotten on the bandwagon of celebrating diversity and including language to that effect in their mission statements without doing the deeper work to make their organizational reality align with their aspirations. They—and particularly their leaders—need to pay attention to consistency between espoused values and demonstrable behavior in organizations. Words alone, unaccompanied by authentic and consistent behavior, cause more harm than good and have a demotivating impact on the workforce. Inclusion must be embedded in the fundamental culture of the organization and related to its day-to-day operations (Holvino, Ferdman, & Merrill-Sands, 2004; see also Nishii & Rich, Chapter 11; Offerman & Basford, Chapter 8; and Winters, Chapter 7, this volume).

What is at stake? What choices do organizations and their leaders have as they face a turbulent and unpredictable future? As comfortable as it might be to imagine a return to some fictitious "good old days," the past is gone, and it is unlikely that the future will bear any significant relationship to what is behind us. Our thinking and practice of leadership must be an ongoing developmental journey as life conditions demand that we expand, evolve, and transform. As Heifetz and Linsky (2002) remind us:

> Leadership is worth the risk because the goals extend beyond
> material gain or personal advancement. By making the lives of
> people around you better, leadership provides meaning in life.
> It creates purpose. We believe that every human being has
> something unique to offer, and that a larger sense of purpose
> comes from using that gift to help your organizations, families, or
> communities thrive. The gift might be your knowledge, your
> experience, your values, your presence, your heart, or your
> wisdom. Perhaps it's simply your basic curiosity and your
> willingness to raise unsettling questions [p. 3].

As described throughout this chapter, developing inclusive leadership is not for the faint of heart, and it requires long-term investment across the organization. The risks are worth taking; the rewards of inclusion far outweigh the costs. Building authentic relationships across difference involves overcoming layers of distrust and investing the time needed to develop working partnerships in unfamiliar circumstances. Inclusive leadership and cultures of inclusion hold great promise for new ways of relating, sense making, and creativity. The shift from cultures of individuality to collectivism, from isolation to collaboration, and from competition to mutuality can tap resources and energy needed to address the challenges to come. Fostering deeper relationships, modeling courage, and embracing our humanity with humility are key ingredients of inclusive organizations. As we embrace paradox, we move forward into the unknown, confident that we are building a foundation of partnership, continuous learning, and shared ownership that will carry us through any storm—together.

References

Ancona, D., Malone, T. W., Orlikowski, W. J., & Senge, P. M. (2007). In praise of the incomplete leader. *Harvard Business Review, 85*(2), 92–100, 108–117.

Avolio, B. J., & Gardner, W. L. (2005). Authentic leadership development: Getting to the root of positive forms of leadership. *Leadership Quarterly, 16,* 315–338.

Bass, B. M. (1985). *Leadership and performance beyond expectations.* New York: Free Press.

Baxter-Magolda, M. B., Creamer, E. G., & Meszaros, P. S. (2010). *Development and assessment of self-authorship: Exploring the concept across cultures.* Sterling, VA: Stylus Publishing.

Bell, E. L. J. E., & Nkomo, S. M. (2001). Gender and cultural diversity in the workplace. In L. Diamant & Lee, J. (Eds.), *The psychology of sex, gender and jobs: Issues and solutions* (pp. 249–273). Westport, CT: Praeger.

Bennis, W., & Nanus, B. (1985). *Leaders: The strategies for taking charge.* New York: Harper and Row.

Bhawuk, D. P. S., & Munusamy, V. P. (2010). Leading across cultural groups: Implications of self-concept. In K. Hannum, B. B. McFeeters, & L. Booysen (Eds.), *Leading across differences: Cases and perspectives* (pp. 155–162). San Francisco: Pfeiffer.

Blake-Beard, S. D. (2009). Mentoring as a bridge to understanding cultural difference. *Adult Learning, 20*(1–2), 14–18.

Blake-Beard, S. D., Murrell, A. J., & Thomas, D. A. (2007). Unfinished business: The impact of race on understanding mentoring relationships. In B. R. Ragins & K. E. Kram (Eds), *The handbook of mentoring* (pp. 223–247). Thousand Oaks, CA: Sage.

Blancero, D. M., DelCampo, R. G., & Marron, G. F. (2007). Hired for diversity, rewarded for conformity: Retaining Hispanic talent in corporate America. *Business Journal of Hispanic Research, 1*(1), 12–25.

Chandler, D. E., & Kram, K. K. (2005). Applying an adult development perspective to developmental networks. *Career Development International, 10*(6/7), 548–566.

Chin, J. L. (2010). Introduction to the special issue on diversity and leadership. *American Psychologist, 65*(3), 150–156.

Conger, J. A. (1990). The dark side of leadership. *Organizational Dynamics, 19*(2), 44–55.

Cox, T. H., Jr., & Nkomo, S. M. (2001). Race and ethnicity: An update and analysis. In R. T. Golembiewski (Ed.), *Handbook of organizational behavior* (pp. 255–286). New York: Marcel Dekker.

Ely, R. J., & Thomas, D. A. (2000). Cultural diversity at work: The effects of diversity perspectives of work group processes and outcomes. *Administrative Science Quarterly, 46*, 229–273.

Ernst, C., & Chrobot-Mason, D. (2011). *Boundary-spanning leadership: Six practices for solving problems, driving innovation, and transforming organizations.* New York: McGraw-Hill.

Ernst, C., & Yip, J. (2009). Boundary spanning leadership: Tactics to bridge social identity groups in organizations. In T. L. Pittinsky (Ed.), *Crossing the divide: Intergroup leadership in a world of difference* (pp. 89–99). Boston, MA: Harvard Business School Press.

Ferdman, B. M. (2003). Learning about our and others' selves: Multiple identities and their sources. In N. Boyacigiller, R. Goodman, & M. Phillips (Eds.), *Crossing cultures: Insights from master teachers* (pp. 49–61). London: Routledge.

Ferdman, B. M. (2010). Teaching inclusion by example and experience: Creating an inclusive learning environment. In B. B. McFeeters, K. M. Hannum, & L. Booysen (Eds.), *Leading across differences: Cases and perspectives—Facilitator's guide* (pp. 37–50). San Francisco: Pfeiffer.

Ferdman, B. M., & Cortes, A. (1992). Culture and identity among Hispanic managers in an Anglo business. In S. B. Knouse, P. Rosenfeld, & A. Culbertson (Eds.), *Hispanics in the workplace* (pp. 246–277). Thousand Oaks, CA: Sage.

Fletcher, J. K. (1999). *Disappearing acts: Gender, power, and relational practice at work.* Cambridge, MA: MIT Press.

Fletcher, J. K. (2010). Leadership as relational practice. In K. Bunker, T. Hall, & K. Kram (Eds.), *Extraordinary leadership: Addressing the gaps in senior executive development* (pp. 121–135). San Francisco: Jossey-Bass.

Foldy, E. G., Rivard, P., & Buckley, T. R. (2009). Power, safety and learning in racially diverse groups. *Academy of Management Learning & Education, 8*(1), 25–41.

Gallegos, P. V., & Ferdman, B. M. (2007). Identity orientations of Latinos in the United States: Implications for leaders and organizations. *Business Journal of Hispanic Research, 1* (1), 27–41.

Gardner, H. K., Gino, F., & Staats, B. R. (2012). Dynamically integrating knowledge in teams: Transforming resources into performance. *Academy of Management Journal, 55*(4), 998–1022.

Geller, K. (2009). Transformative learning dynamics for developing relational leaders. In B. Fisher-Yoshida, K. D. Geller, & S. A. Schapiro (Eds.), *Innovations in transformative learning: Space, culture, and the arts* (pp. 177–201). New York: Peter Lang.

Goleman, D., Boyatzis, R., & McKee, A. (2001). *Primal leadership: The hidden driver of great performance.* Boston, MA: Harvard Business School Publishing.

Hannum, K., McFeeters, B. B., & Booysen, L. (Eds.). (2010). *Leading across differences: Cases and perspectives.* San Francisco: Pfeiffer.

Heifetz, R. A. (1994). *Leadership without easy answers.* Boston, MA: Harvard University Press.

Heifetz, R. A., & Laurie, D. L. (1997). The work of leadership. *Harvard Business Review, 75*(1), 124–134.

Heifetz, R. A., & Linsky, M. (2002). *Leadership on the line: Staying alive through the dangers of leading.* Boston: Harvard Business School Press.

Heifetz, R. A., Linsky, M., & Alexander, G. (2009). *Practice of adaptive leadership: Tools and tactics for changing your organization and the world.* Boston, MA: Harvard Business School Publishing.

Hollander, E. P. (2009). *Inclusive leadership: The essential leader-follower relationship.* New York: Routledge.

Holvino, E., Ferdman, B. M., & Merrill-Sands, D. (2004). Creating and sustaining diversity and inclusion in organizations: Strategies and approaches. In M. S. Stockdale & F. J. Crosby (Eds.), *The psychology and management of workplace diversity* (pp. 245–276). Malden, MA: Blackwell.

Homan, A. C., & Jehn, K. A. (2010). Organizational faultlines. In K. Hannum, B. B. McFeeters, & L. Booysen, (Eds.), *Leading across differences: Cases and perspectives* (pp. 87–94). San Francisco: Pfeiffer.

Johnson-Bailey, J., & Cervero, R. M. (2004). Mentoring in Black and White: The intricacies of cross-cultural mentoring. *Mentoring & Tutoring: Partnership in Learning, 12*(1), 7–21.

Keleher, T., Leiderman, S., Meehan, D., Perry, E., Potapchuk, M., Powell, L. A., & Yu, H. C. (2010). *Leadership & race: How to develop and support leadership that contributes to racial justice.* Leadership for a New Era Series, Leadership Learning Community. Retrieved from

http://leadershiplearning.org/newpublication-how-develop-and
-support-leadership-contributes-racial-justice

Kivel, P. (2002). *Uprooting racism: How white people can work for racial justice.* Philadelphia: New Society.

Mayer, J. D., Salovey, P., & Caruso, D. R. (2008). Emotional intelligence: New ability or eclectic traits? *American Psychologist, 63*(6), 503–517.

Miller, F. A., & Katz, J. H. (2002). *The inclusion breakthrough: Unleashing the real power of diversity.* San Francisco: Berrett-Koehler.

O'Leary, B., & Weathington, B. (2006). Beyond the business case for diversity in organizations. *Employee Responsibilities & Rights Journal, 18*(4), 283–292.

Pearce, W. B. (2007). *Making social worlds: A communication perspective.* Malden, MA: Blackwell.

Pittinsky, T. L. (2005). Allophilia: A framework for intergroup leadership. In N. N. Huber & M. Walker (Eds.), *Emergent models of global leadership* [Building Leadership Bridges Series] (pp. 34–49). College Park, MD: International Leadership Association.

Pittinsky, T. L. (2010). Approaches to difference: Allophilia and xenophobia. In K. Hannum, B. B. McFeeters, & L. Booysen (Eds.), *Leading across differences: Cases and perspectives* (pp. 125–130). San Francisco: Pfeiffer.

Ruderman, M. N., & Chrobot-Mason, D. (2010). Triggers of social identity conflict. In K. Hannum, B. B. McFeeters, & L. Booysen (Eds.), *Leading across differences: Cases and perspectives* (pp. 81–86). San Francisco: Pfeiffer.

Ruderman, M. N., Glover, S., Chrobot-Mason, D., & Ernst, C. (2010). Leadership practices across social identity groups. In K. Hannum, B. B. McFeeters, & L. Booysen (Eds.), *Leading across differences: Cases and perspectives* (pp. 95–114). San Francisco: Pfeiffer.

Ryan, J. (2006). Inclusive leadership and social justice for schools. *Leadership and Policy in Schools, 5*, 3–17.

Salovey, P., & Mayer, J. D. (1990). Emotional intelligence. *Imagination, Cognition, and Personality, 9*, 185–211.

Salovey, P., & Sluyter, D. J. (1997). *Emotional development and emotional intelligence: Educational implications.* New York: Basic Books.

Tannen, D. (2001). *You just don't understand: Women and men in conversation.* New York: HarperCollins.

Tervalon, M., & Murray-Garcia, J. (1998). Cultural humility versus cultural competence: A critical distinction in defining physician-training outcomes in multicultural education. *Journal of Health Care for the Poor and Underserved, 9*(2), 117.

Thomas, D. A., & Ely, R. (2002). Making differences matter: A new paradigm for managing diversity. *Harvard Business Review*, 74(5), 33–66.

Wasserman, I. C. (2004). *Discursive processes that foster dialogic moments: Transformation in the engagement of social identity group differences in dialogue* (Doctoral dissertation). Retrieved from ProQuest Information & Learning (Accession number 2005–99018–175).

Wasserman, I. C., & Blake-Beard, S. (2010). Leading inclusively: Mindsets, skills and actions for a diverse, complex world. In K. Bunker, T. Hall, & K. Kram (Eds.), *Extraordinary leadership: Addressing the gaps in senior executive development* (pp. 197–212). San Francisco: Jossey-Bass.

Wasserman, I. C., & Gallegos, P. V. (2009). Engaging diversity: Disorienting dilemmas that transform relationships. In B. Fisher-Yoshida, K. D. Geller, and S. A. Schapiro (Eds.), *Innovations in transformative learning: Space, culture, and the arts* (pp. 155–175). New York: Peter Lang.

Wasserman, I. C., Gallegos, P. V., & Ferdman, B. M. (2008). Dancing with resistance: Leadership challenges in fostering a culture of inclusion. In K. M. Thomas (Ed.), *Diversity resistance in organizations* (pp. 175–200). Mahwah, NJ: Erlbaum.

Wyche, K. R. (2008). *Good is not enough: And other unwritten rules for minority professionals.* New York: Penguin Group.

Part Three

Organizational and Societal Perspectives and Practices

CHAPTER SEVEN

From Diversity to Inclusion: An Inclusion Equation

Mary-Frances Winters

For inclusion, you have to start with the heart and then move to the head. For authentic, sustainable, inclusive organizations, leaders have to "get it in their guts" and then commit to becoming competent so their behavior matches their intent.

—FORTUNE 100 FINANCIAL SERVICES CEO

In the past twenty-five years, the field of diversity and inclusion has become more sophisticated, both in its definitions and in articulating what the terms really mean. But multiple definitions of this burgeoning and complex discipline still abound, often leading to confusion and even controversy. As I pointed out in a prior review, "[d]iversity has evolved into a rather amorphous field, where the very word itself invokes a variety of different meanings and emotional responses" (Anand & Winters, 2008, p. 356).

Thought leader Dr. Roosevelt Thomas is credited with shifting the paradigm from complying with legal mandates to the business case for diversity. According to Thomas, the challenge of diversity was more than ensuring representation of historically under-represented groups. Data showed overwhelmingly that the careers of minorities and women plateaued, and few were breaking into higher-level positions (Thomas, 1990). He said the goal should be to "create . . . an environment where 'we' is everyone" (Thomas,

1990, p. 109). Thomas argued that we needed something else besides affirmative action: "That something else consists of enabling people, in this case minorities and women, to perform to their potential" (Thomas, 1990, p. 109).While he did not use the term *inclusion*, the definition commonly put forth is as Thomas articulated it: creating an environment in which everyone has the opportunity to reach his or her full potential.

It took almost a decade for Thomas's concept to become commonly referred to as *inclusion* and for it to become paired, routinely, as part of *diversity and inclusion.*

Distinguishing Inclusion from Diversity

Andrés Tapia, president of Diversity Best Practices and author of *The Inclusion Paradox*, offers a simple way of distinguishing between the definitions of diversity and inclusion: "Diversity is the mix. Inclusion is making the mix work" (Tapia, 2009, p. 12). Or, as others have defined the distinction: diversity is about counting heads; inclusion is about making heads count. Another way to distinguish between diversity and inclusion is to define diversity as a noun describing a state and inclusion as a verb or action noun, in that *to include* requires action. Expanding on these ideas, I define inclusion as creating an environment that acknowledges, welcomes, and accepts different approaches, styles, perspectives, and experiences, so as to allow all to reach their potential and result in enhanced organizational success.

Perhaps the most salient distinction between diversity and inclusion is that diversity can be mandated and legislated, while inclusion stems from voluntary actions. In an interview I conducted with a Fortune 100 CEO, he captured the distinction highlighted in this chapter's epigraph: that leaders must "get it in their guts" and then match their intent with their behavior.

Inclusion Is Harder to Achieve Than Diversity

Lack of advancement of historically underrepresented groups is the proverbial inclusion quandary. Twenty-five years ago, the common explanation was that these groups had less time in the workforce than White men. As more White women and people of color gained experience, the theory went, the inequities would self-correct. Lack of workforce experience is no longer a valid justification. Current evidence points to organizational cultural norms that unwittingly perpetuate exclusive behaviors as a key barrier to advancement. Achieving an inclusive culture is a complex endeavor, requiring deliberate examination of all aspects of the organization and a willingness to make changes to reduce the potential for bias that favors the dominant group.

As an example of the continued difficulty to achieve inclusion in organizations, a 2012 study conducted by the Center for Talent Innovation on the impact of sponsorship in advancing multicultural employees found that over one-third of African Americans and Hispanics and 45 percent of Asians reported a "need to compromise their authenticity" to conform to their company's standards of "demeanor or style." In addition, about one-fifth of Hispanics, one-third of African Americans, and 29 percent of Asians in the study reported that a "person of color would never get a top position at my company" (Hewlett, Jackson, Cose, & Emerson, 2012, p. 2).

Achieving an inclusive workplace for women is also challenging. Women make up half of the U.S. workforce yet as of this writing hold only 3.8 percent of Fortune 500 CEO positions and 4.0 percent of Fortune 1000 CEO positions (Catalyst, 2012). In 2009, Catalyst reported that almost 30 percent of Fortune 500 companies had no women executive officers at all, and less than 18 percent of companies had three or more women executive officers (Soares, Carter, & Combopiano, 2009).

Another compelling example is that, according to the *2010 Survey of Employment of Americans with Disabilities* ("Survey: Employers Not Doing Enough," n.d.), disability is included as part of their initiative by only two-thirds of companies surveyed that had diversity programs (70 percent of the total); only 18 percent of responding companies reported having education programs aimed at ensuring inclusive practices for people with disabilities.

Yet another example suggesting we have much work to do to achieve inclusion is the *Out and Equal Workplace Culture Report* (Harris Interactive, 2008), which tracked attitudes about LGBT workers in the U.S. from 2002 to 2008. This survey found that, in

2008, 42 percent of heterosexual respondents believed that LGBT people are treated fairly and equally, a proportion unchanged from 2002; 22 percent indicated that it would be very difficult to be openly gay, lesbian, bisexual, or transgender at their workplace. Fifty percent of LGBT adults reported hearing someone at their current or most recent job tell jokes about people who are gay, lesbian, bisexual, or transgender, and only 30 percent reported never having faced any workplace discrimination on the basis of gender identity or sexual orientation.

An innovative study conducted by Bendick and Egan (Bendick, 2008) pointed to a lack of inclusion as the *cause* of an organization's lack of diversity, and concluded that a lack of diversity is merely a *symptom* of the lack of inclusion. Based on a multiple-regression analysis of HR records for a large financial services company, key indicators for positive career advancement fell into two categories—demographic and professional (as shown in Exhibit 7.1). There was a higher likelihood of success at this company for people who were White and male, but also for those who had attended the "right" school, had military service, or had other characteristics or experiences that were more valued. While it has long been acknowledged that organizational norms often set up unwritten rules that favor the ingroup, Bendick (2008) and

---

Exhibit 7.1. Bendick and Egan Study Findings of Key Success Factors

Demographic Characteristics	Professional Characteristics
• White • Male • Age 36–55 • Grew up in US or EU • Native English speaker • Married with kids	• Degree from 20 "core" universities • Served in Marines • No degrees outside business • No experience in any other industry • With firm >10 years • No career shifts within the firm

Egan successfully isolated and quantified those factors for their client.

Developing Sustainable, Inclusive Organizational Cultures: The Inclusion Equation

While, as previously discussed, there is some consensus on the definition of inclusion (see also Ferdman, Chapter 1, this volume), the concept is open to widely varying behavioral interpretations. The specific behaviors and actions that exemplify inclusion are not consistent or well understood. Too often it is easier to perpetuate habitual exclusive practices rather than adopt new inclusive ones. To make the shift to an inclusive culture that will be sustainable over time requires a much broader and deeper approach than what has traditionally occurred in the name of diversity. Inclusion requires addressing both macro, systemic issues and ongoing micro behaviors that impact the experiences of individuals on a day-to-day basis. Inclusion also has to be driven both by top-down leadership and bottom-up engagement.

I created the inclusion equation to help depict the interrelated variables necessary to create and sustain inclusive cultures (see Figure 7.1). There are two broad components of the inclusion model it depicts: macro and micro inclusion practices. The two macro aspects focus on organizational culture and organizational systems. At the micro level, the model identifies individual cultural competence and emotional intelligence as the two core requirements to create and sustain inclusion. The components of the model are interdependent and work synergistically. When any one aspect is weak or absent, it severely inhibits the ability of an organization to effectively practice inclusion.

At the micro or individual level, inclusion or exclusion involves the day-to-day experiences that individuals have with managers and peers as well as outside vendors and suppliers. This is where microinequities as well as unconscious bias occur most often. The concept of *microinequities* was first introduced in 1973 by Mary Rowe (2008; see also Haslett & Lipman, 1997), who defined them as "small events which are often . . . hard-to-prove . . . often unintentional, frequently unrecognized by the

Figure 7.1. The Inclusion Equation

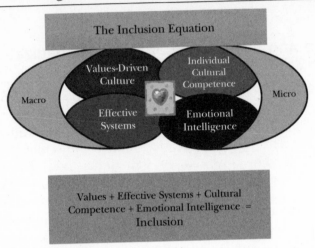

Source: Copyright © 2012, The Winters Group, Inc. Used by permission.

perpetrator, which occur wherever people are perceived to be 'different' " (Rowe, 2008, p. 45). Examples include names mistakenly left off a list, people inadvertently not being introduced at meetings (or erroneously introduced as someone else of the same race), and/or sending out invitations that may be insensitive to gays or women (for example, "Bring your wife"). Rowe (2008) contrasts these with *microaffirmations*, the small and sometimes hard-to-see behaviors that promote inclusion, such as "tiny acts of opening doors to opportunity, gestures of . . . caring, and graceful acts of listening" (p. 46). Unconscious bias is also a primary factor in the perpetuation of exclusive cultures. Unconscious bias can be defined as preferences based on perceptions, thoughts, feelings, and beliefs that are deeply hidden in our subconscious. Theorists believe that discrimination persists in society because we routinely act on our unconscious biases (see Ross, 2008).

Inclusion requires individuals to become culturally competent. As the first step, individuals must work on becoming aware of microinequities and their conscious as well as unconscious biases. The journey to becoming more culturally competent involves ongoing learning to develop the skills and abilities to recognize, accept, and adapt to cultural differences and similarities. I provide more detail on the role of cultural competence later in the chapter.

In the next section, I provide detailed examples of how the elements of the model work to either enhance or inhibit an inclusive culture.

Inclusion Equation Macro Element #1: Values-Driven Culture

Organizations today are beginning to link diversity and inclusion to the company's values. Here I cite two representative examples, as indicated on the companies' websites.

Microsoft's vision and strategy for the future:

> Diversity and inclusion are integral to Microsoft's vision, strategy and business success. We recognize that leadership in today's global marketplace requires that we create a corporate culture and an inclusive business environment where the best and brightest diverse minds—employees with varied perspectives, skills, and experiences—work together to meet global consumer demands. The collaboration of cultures, ideas, and different perspectives is an organizational asset and brings forth greater creativity and innovation [Microsoft, 2012, para. 1].

Dell's commitment to diversity and inclusion:

> Dell is committed to inclusion and diversity. Our mission is to succeed in the marketplace by fostering a winning culture of Dell employees who are highly talented, committed, reflective of our global customers and recognized as our greatest strength. Diversity is at the core of Dell's values and winning culture. It helps define the kind of company we are and aspire to be. Diversity initiatives tap additional talent, retain employees, strengthen relationships, improve our operating results and further our global citizenship efforts in the many communities we call home [Dell, 2012, para. 1–2].

Inclusion is a value, and as such must be inherent in and integrated into all aspects of an organization's culture. Values are the moral compasses that guide organizational behavior. Like other values that employees are expected to "live," inclusion must comprise a set of behaviors that are meaningful across a variety of backgrounds and cultures. In Exhibit 7.2, I list a useful set of such behaviors, adapted from Hubbard (2004).

Exhibit 7.2. Developing Inclusive Behaviors

Modify your listening skills
- Recognize and adapt to the variety of listening behaviors you will encounter among diverse employees.
- Recognize and adapt your own listening skills as necessary to understand diverse perspectives.
- Listen for value-based cultural assumptions, perceptions, and expectations.
- Observe behavior and monitor your interpretations and meanings.

Ask necessary and appropriate questions
- Learn about other views, work styles and assumptions, and needs. Encourage others to do the same.
- Be comfortable in asking questions about the preferred terminology, pronunciations, and so on.
- Be comfortable in asking if you have caused offense, and be open to understanding how to correct it or avoid it in the future.
- Ask for clarification of goals, directions, and instructions to ensure common understanding.

Shift the frame of reference when necessary
- Demonstrate an understanding that perceptions are relative.
- Demonstrate empathy and understanding for other values, attitudes, and beliefs; distinguish empathy from agreement.
- Be flexible in your approach to situations. There are many ways of doing things.

Manage conflict constructively
- Define the issues in the conflict and focus on interests, not positions.
- Make an effort to understand others' perspectives.
- Demonstrate an understanding of different cultural assumptions about what conflict is and alternative ways of dealing with it.
- Develop a collaborative ("win-win") problem-solving approach.

Recognize unconscious bias and stereotypes
- Know your own culture, why you believe what you believe, your history and early experiences that have shaped your value system.
- Be aware of and monitor your own unconscious biases and stereotypes.
- Ask people you trust to give you feedback on potential biases that you may not be aware of.
- Hold others accountable for their stereotypes.
- Learn to distinguish between individual difference and cultural difference.

Show respect for and interest in the other person
- Learn about the cultures of those around you (geography, customs, history, and so on).
- Be aware that humor is handled differently in different cultures. Something that you think is funny and harmless can be insulting to others.
- When talking with those who are more fluent in another language than yours, speak clearly (but not louder or slower) and ensure that there is shared understanding.

Strive to interact meaningfully with those you perceive as "different"
- Learn to feel and exhibit comfort with groups and individuals from other cultures (for example, spend time with people from diverse groups both at work and outside of work).
- Give cultural information about yourself freely when it is requested.
- Be open and accommodating to others' needs to gain information. Do not assume that they know what you know.

Strive to be nonjudgmental
- Continually ask yourself if you are making a value judgment about others, rather than recognizing that others might just do things differently that you.
- Remember that we are programmed to make snap judgments. Continuously work on this tendency in order to reduce such behavior.
- When judging others' cultural values and norms, refrain from using only your "yardstick."
- Continually check and recheck your perceptions about others.

Continued

Make decisions using a "cultural" lens
- When making decisions, ask yourself: does this work for most, or am I making assumptions based only on my own world view and cultural frame?
- Seek out the opinions of diverse people and test your assumptions.
- Integrate different world views into final decisions.

Source: Adapted from Hubbard (2004). Copyright 2004 by Edward E. Hubbard. Used with permission.

Living from the value of inclusion happens one action at a time, and often the little things, such as saying "Good morning," send a message of inclusion—or exclusion. Just like most values, inclusion is conceptually simple, but complex to implement consistently!

Inclusion Equation Macro Element #2: Inclusive Systems and Programs

At a systems level, human resource policies such as recruiting, onboarding, succession planning, high potential identification, leadership development, work-life balance, accommodations for differently abled employees, benefits, rewards and recognition, and performance systems all need to support the goal of inclusion, and many organizations' written policies do so today.

However, many large companies have launched robust diversity and inclusion initiatives, only to find their struggles continuing as a result of inconsistent implementation. Strong implementation depends on the intercultural capabilities of leadership (see Bennett, Chapter 5, and Gallegos, Chapter 6, this volume), which is responsible for interpreting and executing the policies, as well as on the extent to which those leaders are held accountable. I offer several examples of situations in which the policies are inconsistent with the practices.

Recruiting

From the HR policy perspective, a diversity strategy for recruiting may be in place, but individual recruiters sometimes systematically screen out candidates based on their own unconscious bias. Here is an example: University of Chicago professor Marianne Bertrand and MIT professor Sendhil Mullainathan sent 5,000 resumes to 1,250 potential employers and discovered that White-sounding names—such as Brendan, Gregg, Emily, and Anne—received 50 percent more responses than Black-sounding names like Tamika, Aisha, Rasheed, and Tyronne (Bertrand & Mullainathan, 2004). To ameliorate this problem, inclusive organizations ensure that their recruiters are some of the first to receive cultural competence training and education.

Work-Life Strategies

Work-life strategies offer another example. Many organizations claim to offer flexibility to support work-life balance. However, in conducting focus groups over the last few years for several clients, I discovered a consistent theme. Participants agreed the policies were in place, but they also said it would damage their careers to take advantage of them. Managers often subtly discouraged employees from taking time off or working from home. Once again, a policy may be in place, but without consistent implementation it cannot be considered inclusive. To shed light on the disconnect between the written work flexibility policy and its implementation, leaders of one client were shown the focus group results during a training session. Many of them were shocked at some of the sentiments expressed by employees. Another client chose to reinforce work-life policies by holding leaders accountable in their performance evaluations for the extent to which work-life balance was positively perceived by employees.

The rapid globalization of many companies also necessitates an inclusive approach to ensure that policies are adapted to different cultural norms. Many companies try to overlay U.S. policies around the world. However, as an example, Sodexo, a leading global quality-of-life services company headquartered in France, develops inclusion strategies country by country. The company's various diversity leaders do not "customize" French or U.S. policies, but rather start from scratch in each country, understanding the unique issues and then determining whether solutions that have been developed for one region can be tailored to another specific geographic region. If not, new diversity and inclusion initiatives are developed under the leadership of the country HR manager.

Programs such as mentoring, employee resource groups, and diversity councils that are integrated into an overall strategy can also be very effective in fostering and sustaining inclusion.

Mentoring

An examination of decades of employment statistics provided by companies to the federal government found that mentorships, particularly for Black women, were very effective in increasing diversity. Notably, they were much more effective in this regard than diversity training. In one example, mentoring increased Black women's numbers in management by 23.5 percent (Dobbin, Kalev, & Kelly, 2007).

What distinguishes inclusive mentoring programs from diversity mentoring programs is that inclusive programs are reciprocal, designed to acknowledge that the mentor learns as much from the mentee as the mentee from the mentor (see Gallegos, Chapter 6, this volume).

For one client, The Winters Group set up such a cross-cultural reciprocal mentoring program pairing senior leaders with someone different from themselves in some significant way. Each month the pair received a lesson on a different topic related to diversity and inclusion and met for a few hours to discuss the lesson. To her surprise, an African American female participant, who thought that as a Black woman she could not learn much more about diversity and inclusion, learned she had misconceptions about White men because she was seeing things only from her own world view. This shared learning experience at the micro level fostered greater intergroup inclusion in the organization.

"Reverse" mentoring programs are gaining in popularity. In this model the younger or underrepresented employee is set up to mentor a more seasoned leader. However, from my perspective this is still a one-sided concept and not as inclusive as one that acknowledges reciprocity.

Sponsorship

Studies have shown that sponsorship is an even more powerful concept than mentoring to create a climate in which more people can reach their full potential. Mentors provide advice; sponsors do so as well but also, more critically, serve as advocates: "They elevate a protégé's visibility within the corridors of power, win them key assignments and promotions, and place their own reputations on the line for a protégé's continued advancement" (Hewlett et al., 2012, p. 7). According to the study conducted by the Center for Talent Innovation (Hewlett et al., 2012), people of color continue to be undersponsored; only 8 percent of people of color (9 percent of African Americans, 8 percent of Asians, and 5 percent of Hispanics) have a sponsor, compared to 13 percent of Whites. A similar study conducted by the Center for Talent innovation in 2009 found that women are also undersponsored in corporations. Sponsorship requires a higher level of commitment than does mentoring. Sponsors have to be truly invested in their protégé's career and understand the organizational cultural barriers that they are helping their charge overcome.

To date, sponsorship has not been institutionalized in the same way that mentoring has been in many organizations. Sponsorship is often more informal and even secretive. Formalizing sponsorship as an inclusive practice can boost engagement and retention. According to the Center for Talent Innovation study (Hewlett et al., 2012), 53 percent of African Americans with a sponsor are satisfied with their rate of advancement, compared with 35 percent of those without sponsors. Similarly, 55 percent of Asians with a sponsor are content with their rate of advancement, compared with 30 percent of Asians without such support. In addition, people of color with sponsors are less likely than those without sponsors to leave the organization.

Diversity Councils

Diversity councils offer an effective means to drive inclusion. This was supported by results of DiversityInc's 2011 Top 50 Companies for Diversity survey, based on data from 535 organizations, which showed that "[c]ompanies with executive diversity councils have almost twice the number of Blacks, Latinos, and Asians, and 47 percent more women in senior management, than companies without executive diversity councils" ("How Effective Diversity Councils Get Results," 2011, para. 2).

Note that the DiversityInc survey focused on *executive* diversity councils. Well-meaning organizations often set up councils with a cross-section of employees at different levels in the organization in the name of inclusion. Often, visibly "diverse" employees are selected for the role. Such a method may promote diversity but may not be inclusive because councils comprising employees with no decision-making power cannot influence change in the organization. Participants become frustrated and often feel more excluded than included. The most effective approach to establishing inclusion councils is to set up an executive council and also divisional councils with employees at other levels to serve in advisory capacities.

Blue Cross Blue Shield of Michigan (BCBSM) devised an effective strategy to integrate inclusion at all levels, one "tier" at a time. In the first year of the diversity and inclusion initiative, Chief Diversity Officer Equilla Wainwright established a Diversity Leadership Council (DLC) comprising senior vice presidents from each business unit. They were charged with developing a three-year strategic plan for the enterprise. The group met monthly, was exposed to experiential education to enhance all members' cultural competence, and spent time developing the strategic plan.

The next stage involved identifying Champions, primarily middle managers, who would tailor and implement the enterprise-wide strategy divisionally. This new council of Champions had the Diversity Leadership Council members as advocates and resources to support them in the implementation of their plans.

Divisional plans focused on the more micro elements of inclusion, to ensure that the initiatives were cascading throughout the organization and executed by those closest to the issues. Measurable actions include incorporating diversity and inclusion into the agenda of every team meeting, requiring a diverse slate of candidates for every opening, encouraging participation in employee resource groups, devising strategies to ensure that more voices are heard, and increasing team involvement in the community.

BCBSM conducted enterprise-wide surveys (macro-level work) and focus groups to ensure inclusion in the process and also widely communicated progress to all employees, soliciting their input at every major juncture.

BCBSM's top-down and bottom-up approach has ensured that a critical mass of competent diversity advocates is seeding inclusion principles throughout the organization.

Employee Network Groups

Employee network, resource, or affinity groups can be instrumental in realizing inclusion. Sodexo's Employee Network Groups partner closely with Human Resources and the Office of Diversity to drive recruiting, professional development, and community outreach. They also partner with the market segments to support business growth. Sodexo not only encourages leader participation in network functions but also holds leaders accountable for supporting and participating in network events. Sodexo surveyed employee network group members and found that as a result of their participation, members were more engaged and more likely to say they will stay with the company.

In addition to conducting diversity and inclusion efforts within a company, employee resource groups (ERGs) can play a business role in providing information about the interests and needs of diverse market segments. For example, Macy's Hispanic ERG developed an electronic gift card specifically for the Hispanic market to recognize the *quinceañera*, a coming of age party for Latina girls (Jennifer Brown Consulting, 2010). And Prudential's GLBT ERG was instrumental in urging the company's multicultural marketing team to market to diverse segments, including the untapped LGBT market (Jennifer Brown Consulting, 2010). Employees feel valued and included when their opinions are sought and the company gains valuable insights to enhance marketing efforts: truly a win-win.

Programmatic inclusion efforts are most effective when they are simultaneously executed at the macro and micro levels. The Office of Diversity, HR, and senior leaders can ensure that policies are consistently followed, and employees should be engaged in providing feedback as to how well the policies are working for them day to day.

Employee Engagement Surveys

Employee engagement surveys can be an effective way to measure inclusion. Although inclusion is inherently more difficult to measure than diversity, it is not impossible to do so. Employee engagement surveys are very popular today and are used by most large organizations to understand the perceptions and attitudes of workers (see Church, Rotolo, Tull, & Shuller, Chapter 9, this volume). Employee engagement and inclusion are synergistic concepts. A 2005 Gallup Study (Wilson, n.d.) found that employee engagement was much more likely among respondents who perceived their companies as having a stronger diversity focus, compared to those who saw their companies as being in the lowest quartile for diversity focus (60 percent versus 11 percent); in the latter group, 38 percent were actively disengaged, whereas in the first group that was true of only 1 percent.

To measure inclusion, employee engagement surveys should be segmented by demographic and other characteristics to explore differences in attitudes and opinions. Many organizations today do analyze their data by different employee segments, but a large number have not yet made the connection between inclusion and engagement. To do this, employee engagement surveys should ask specific questions about inclusion, such as those in Exhibit 7.3, which are examples of those employed by

---

Exhibit 7.3. Sample Items to Assess Inclusion

- I think our CEO is committed to inclusion.
- I think that my immediate manager is committed to inclusion.
- I think leadership exhibits inclusive behaviors.
- I have the same opportunities for advancement as anyone else at XXX.
- I think that employees feel valued and respected for their unique contributions to XXX.
- I feel valued and respected for the unique contribution that I make to XXX.
- XXX's culture respects and values cultural differences.
- Work-life balance policies and practices allow me to balance my personal and work life effectively.

Source: The Winters Group. Used by permission.

The Winters Group as part of the surveys it conducts for clients. On one such survey conducted for a client, The Winters Group found a correlation of .78 between mean engagement scores and mean inclusion scores.

Segmenting the data by different demographic groups allows leaders to understand how perceptions of inclusion differ so that policies and practices can be adjusted to be more inclusive. Based on surveys conducted by The Winters Group over the years, in general, employees of color and White women, younger employees, and older employees have less favorable views of organizational inclusion practices. Perceptions of unfairness can lead to undesirable outcomes such as lower productivity, and higher turnover, which is costly to an organization. To effectively analyze results of an employee engagement survey, reviewers should be culturally competent enough to understand the reasons for some of the different opinions and recognize how deep-seated, long-standing perceptions about fairness may drive results.

Employee engagement data should be analyzed at the work unit level, holding unit managers accountable for survey results and for developing improvement strategies. Some organizations today have developed an inclusion index, and this measure becomes a part of the overall scorecard, which may also include other metrics such as hiring, promotions, manager involvement in diversity and inclusion initiatives, and termination metrics.

Inclusion Equation Micro Element #1: Cultural Competence

In my book *Inclusion Starts with I* (Winters, 2003), I assert that inclusion begins with the individual. An inclusion mindset often requires transforming the way individuals in the workforce think and behave. Eleanor Roosevelt sums up this sentiment for me in her book *You Learn by Living* (2011): "You must try to understand truthfully what makes you do things or feel things. Until you have been able to face the truth about yourself you cannot be really sympathetic or understanding in regard to what happens to other people" (p. 63).

Over the past twenty-five years, organizations have put substantial effort into training, especially for leaders, with the goal of shifting thinking and behavior to be more inclusive. However, in my observation, short-term training is inadequate to build skills and shift mindsets. Those with the power to drive inclusion must *want* to do it. No amount of coaching, coaxing, or coercion can convince the die-hard recalcitrant. Leaders have to believe in diversity and inclusion, either as part of an altruistic goal and/or because they truly believe that inclusion will enhance business success and in turn make them better off in some way.

Self-Reflection

Ultimately, inclusion will not be sustained by leaders who respond to diversity and inclusion initiatives as "check the box" exercises. Leaders need to think about and reflect on their day-to-day behaviors and how they might be perpetuating microinequities and unconscious bias. The Winters Group developed the following set of questions for leader reflection relative to inclusive behaviors:

- Do I understand my power as a leader, that those I lead are constantly looking for signals from me, both explicit and implicit, verbal and non-verbal?
- When it is time to form a team, do I tend to select the same people all the time?
- When I am in a meeting, does my body language send positive vibes to certain people and neutral or negative vibes to others?
- In one-on-one sessions, does my body language send micro-messages that are inconsistent with my words?
- Am I equally comfortable communicating with everyone on my team or do I find myself behaving differently with different members of the team? Do I know my source of discomfort?
- Do I have different relationships with people on my team? Is it obvious that I am closer and have more positive relationships with some rather than others?
- As I think about those on my team who are not performing as well as I think they could, are there messages that they may be getting from me which may be impacting their results?
- Does my tendency to minimize differences send a micro-message that I find others' uniqueness or individuality to be

unimportant? Does this lead to my devaluing of the individual and ultimately to lower engagement by that individual?

- Do I understand cultural differences related to communication styles and how certain gestures, words, body language may have different meanings to different groups? Do I respect these other styles as they may be exhibited by members on my team or do I send micro-messages that I expect conformity?
- When I interact with people who are different, do I find myself not exactly knowing what to say . . . not wanting to say the wrong thing and ending up feeling in the end that I had said the wrong thing?
- Am I aware of group dynamics among team members? What are the power dynamics? Where is the focus of leadership, both formal and informal? Who seems to be included/excluded? Why?
- Do I look for the signs that may say there is a disconnect between words, intent, and execution?
- How can I learn to be ever in tune with the micro-inequities that are occurring in my organization?

These questions can help leaders assess their willingness and capability to drive inclusion.

Measuring Cultural Competence

I believe that cultural competence is the linchpin to ensure inclusion. A focus solely on awareness and sensitivity training will not change behaviors and ways of thinking. To become culturally competent takes study, time, and practice. The first step is assessing one's current level of cultural competence.

The Winters Group uses the Intercultural Development Inventory (IDI; Hammer, 2010; Hammer & Bennett, 2003) to measure cultural competence (we typically use this term rather than *intercultural competence*, though we mean the same thing). The IDI, owned by Dr. Mitchell Hammer and IDI, LLC, and based on Milton Bennett's Developmental Model of Intercultural Sensitivity (DMIS; M. J. Bennett, 1986; J. M. Bennett & M. J. Bennett, 2004; see also Bennett, Chapter 5, this volume), is useful in providing a framework for understanding the developmental stages of cultural competence.

Hammer (2009) describes intercultural competence as reflecting "the degree to which cultural differences and commonalities in values, expectations, beliefs, and practices are effectively [understood,] bridged," (p. 3) managed, and leveraged in pursuit of an inclusive environment. The IDI provides a baseline for individuals and organizations to understand how they experience difference along a continuum from denial to adaptation. This self-awareness is the first step to learning how to be more culturally competent. Once individuals and organizations know where they fall along the continuum, it is then possible to shape learning and experiential interventions that help a person move along the continuum and develop greater competency.

Inclusion Equation Micro Element #2: Emotional Intelligence (EQ)

Modern management theory now widely accepts that effective leaders must possess more than technical expertise to engage employees and achieve business goals. Daniel Goleman, one of several emotional intelligence (EQ) theorists, asserted that one's EQ is a greater determinant of success than one's IQ (Goleman, 1995). Goleman identified the five domains of emotional intelligence or EQ as knowing your emotions, managing your own emotions, motivating yourself, recognizing and understanding other people's emotions, and managing relationships (that is, managing the emotions of others).

Lee Gardenswartz, Anita Rowe, and Jorge Cherbosque took emotional intelligence to another level by forming the Emotional Intelligence and Diversity Institute in 2004 to promulgate the connection between emotional intelligence and inclusion. They developed a model focused on introspection and self-governance, intercultural literacy, and social "architecting" (Gardenswartz, Cherbosque, & Rowe, 2010).

The Winters Group offers an eight-step personal journey model for individual introspection. It is a baseball card-sized reminder of the emotional commitment it takes to sustain inclusive behavior. It lists eight steps to inclusion constituting an individual's Personal Diversity Journey, as shown in Exhibit 7.4.

> **Exhibit 7.4. Steps in the Personal Diversity Journey**
>
> 1. **Know self first:** Who am I? What do I stand for? What makes "me" me?
> 2. **Value self:** What are my unique gifts? What is my best self?
> 3. **Acknowledge your prejudices:** In what ways do I exclude? How do I contribute to intolerance? What are my blind spots?
> 4. **Open yourself to change:** What are my opportunities to grow? To be my best self?
> 5. **Learn about others:** How are other individuals/groups different from me? How are they the same?
> 6. **Value differences:** How do differences enhance who I am and can become? What can I learn from differences?
> 7. **Include others:** Expand your circle to optimize diversity.
> 8. **Embrace personal growth:** Constantly ask yourself, Where am I now? Am I growing in my journey to be more inclusive? What do I need to change?
>
> *Source:* Copyright 2012 by The Winters Group, Inc. Used with permission.

As is inherent in these concepts and the required self-examination, the quest for inclusion is not possible without the willingness to be vulnerable and honest about oneself. Self-awareness and ongoing self-reflection are the foundation for enhancing cultural competence and one's ability to think and behave inclusively.

Summary

Diversity and inclusion are interconnected concepts. Many organizations, however, put most of their efforts into diversity, working to increase representation of historically underrepresented groups, and invest too little effort in creating a culture where all employees can thrive to enhance the achievement of organizational goals.

Fostering and nurturing inclusion must be embedded into an organization's normal business practices from top down and bottom up. Employees have to see, hear about, and, most important, experience inclusion regularly for it to be effective. Inclusion is accomplished when a critical mass of people inside an organization develops and implements policies and practices and rewards behaviors that lead to a sense of belonging, respect, and value. As described in the inclusion equation, inclusion will be sustained only when all of the elements are working synergistically, both at the micro (intercultural competence and emotional intelligence) and macro (systems and values) levels.

References

Anand, R., & Winters, M. F. (2008). A retrospective view of corporate diversity training: From 1964 to the present. *Academy of Management Learning & Education, 7,* 356–372.

Bendick, M. (2008, October 27). *Measure inclusion, not diversity!* Presentation at the Society for Human Resource Management Diversity Conference and Exposition, Atlanta, GA. Retrieved from http://bendickegan.com/pdf/BendickDiversityConf08.pdf

Bennett, J. M., & Bennett, M. J. (2004). Developing intercultural sensitivity: An integrative approach to global and domestic diversity. In D. Landis, J. M. Bennett, & M. J. Bennett (Eds.), *Handbook of intercultural training* (3rd ed., pp. 147–165). Thousand Oaks, CA: Sage.

Bennett, M. J. (1986). A developmental approach to training for intercultural sensitivity. *International Journal of Intercultural Relations, 10*(2), 179–196.

Bertrand, M., & Mullainathan, S. (2004). Are Emily and Greg more employable than Lakisha and Jamal? A field experiment on labor market discrimination. *American Economic Review, 94,* 991–1013.

Catalyst. (2012, November 18). *Women CEOs of the Fortune 1000.* Retrieved from http://www.catalyst.org/publication/271/women-ceos-of-the-fortune-1000

Dell (2012). *Workforce commitment: Advancing diversity and inclusion at Dell.* Retrieved from http://content.dell.com/us/en/gen/d/corp-comm/commitment

Dobbin, F., Kalev, A., & Kelly, B. (2007). Diversity management in corporate America. *Contexts, 6*(4), 21–28.

Gardenswartz, L. R., Cherbosque, J., & Rowe, A. (2010). Emotional intelligence and diversity: A model for differences in the workplace. *Journal of Psychological Issues in Organizational Culture, 1*(1), 74–84. doi:10.1002/jpoc.20002

Goleman, D. (1995). *Emotional intelligence: Why it can matter more than IQ.* New York: Bantam.

Hammer, M. R. (2009). *Intercultural Development Inventory v.3 individual profile report.* Retrieved from Intercultural Development Inventory website: http://www.idiinventory.com/pdf/idi_sample.pdf

Hammer, M. R. (2010). *IDI validity.* Retrieved from Intercultural Development Inventory website: http://www.idiinventory.com/pdf/idi _validity.pdf

Hammer, M. R., & Bennett, M. J. (2003, July). Measuring intercultural sensitivity: The Intercultural Development Inventory. *International Journal of Intercultural Relations,* 27(4), 421–443. doi:10.1016/ S0147–1767(03)00032–4

Harris Interactive. (2008). *Out and equal workplace culture report: Survey of workplace attitudes, 2002–2008.* Retrieved from Out & Equal Workplace Advocates website, http://outandequal.org/documents/ OE_workplace_culture_report.pdf

Haslett, B. B., & Lipman, S. (1997). Micro inequities: Up close and personal. In N. V. Benokraitis (Ed.), *Subtle sexism: Current practices and prospects for change* (pp. 34–53). Thousand Oaks, CA: Sage.

Hewlett, S. A., Jackson, M., Cose, E., & Emerson, C. (2012). *Vaulting the color bar: How sponsorship levers multicultural professionals into leadership.* New York: Center for Talent Innovation. Available at http:// www.worklifepolicy.org

How effective diversity councils get results. (2011, July 15). Retrieved from   http://www.diversityinc.com/diversity-management/how -effective-diversity-councils-get-results

Hubbard, E. E. (2004). *The manager's pocket guide to diversity management.* Amherst, MA: HRD Press.

Jennifer Brown Consulting. (2010). *Employee resource groups that drive business.* Retrieved from http://www.cisco.com/web/about/ac49/ ac55/docs/ERGreportEXTERNAL.pdf

Microsoft. (2012). *A vision and strategy for the future.* Retrieved from http://www.microsoft.com/about/diversity/en/us/vision.aspx

Roosevelt, E. (2011). *You learn by living: Eleven keys for a more fulfilling life* (50th Anniversary Edition). New York: Harper Perennial.

Ross, H. (2008). Proven strategies for addressing unconscious bias in the workplace. *CDO Insights,* 2(5), 1–18. Retrieved from www.cookross .com/docs/UnconsciousBias.pdf

Rowe, M. (2008). Micro-affirmations & micro-inequities. *Journal of the International Ombudsman Association,* 1(1), 45–48. Retrieved from https://www.fctl.ucf.edu/Events/WinterConference/2008/ content/Monday/microaffirmations.pdf

Soares, R., Carter, N. M., & Combopiano, J. (2009). *2009 catalyst census: Fortune 500 women executive officers and top earners.* Retrieved from http://www.catalyst.org/file/321/2009_fortune_500_census _women_executive_officers_and_top_earners.pdf

Survey: Employers not doing enough to hire people with disabilities [Blog post]. (n.d.). Retrieved from http://www.diversityinc.com/ diversity-and-inclusion/survey-employers-not-doing-enough-to -hire-people-with-disabilities

Tapia, A. T. (2009). *The inclusion paradox: The Obama era and the transformation of global diversity.* Lincolnshire, IL: Hewitt Associates.

Thomas, R. R. Jr. (1990). From affirmative action to affirming diversity. *Harvard Business Review, 68*(2), 107–111.

Wilson, D. C. (n.d.). When equal opportunity knocks: A Gallup survey reveals what workplace diversity really means to employees, managers, and the balance sheet. *Gallup Business Journal* [online]. Retrieved from http://businessjournal.gallup.com/content/223 78/When-Equal-Opportunity-Knocks.aspx

Winters, M.-F. (2003). *Inclusion starts with I.* Washington, DC: Renaissance Books.

CHAPTER EIGHT

Inclusive Human Resource Management

Best Practices and the Changing Role of Human Resources

Lynn R. Offermann and Tessa E. Basford

Human resource (HR) management is all about people at work—
how to recruit, train, and manage employees effectively in the
pursuit of an organization's strategic goals. As the people populat-
ing organizations have changed and the labor pool becomes
increasingly diverse, HR and its responsibilities have changed as
well. The rapidly shifting demographics of the workforce, both in
the United States and around the world, have created new challenges and opportunities for HR and for the organizations it
serves. In the United States, the workforce is becoming older,
more female, and more racially and ethnically diverse. Employees
often work alongside others who differ in sexual orientation,
speak another language, or may have a disability. Adding to this
complex landscape are potential dissimilarities in preferences
and job attitudes across generational cohorts of employees,
although at this point such differences have yet to be well validated empirically.

Awareness of the need for HR to successfully manage a diverse
workforce is not limited to United States. A recent survey conducted for the Society for Human Resource Management (SHRM)
across forty-seven countries (Society for Human Resource Management, 2010b) found that paying attention to workforce

diversity and inclusion issues is now a worldwide phenomenon, though strategies for defining, achieving, and managing diversity often differ significantly by country and region. Likewise, Klarsfeld's (2010) international examination of diversity management across sixteen countries highlights the broad range of initiatives currently being undertaken to promote fairness and equality in the global workplace. Around the world, different historical, religious, political, cultural, and social contexts shape the focus of diversity management practice. Despite wide recognition that effective diversity management can be achieved through appropriate HR strategies, the literature examining how diversity is managed through effective HR is very limited (Shen, Chanda, D'Netto, & Monga, 2009).

In this chapter, we address this gap by examining how diversity and inclusion are currently practiced in a sample of leading corporations recognized for their excellence in managing diverse workforces. Rather than focus heavily on particular interventions or programs, we more broadly examine how successful organizations advance inclusion through their culture, structure, and best practices, and how their experiences have changed the role of HR in their organizations.

In addition to surveying the literature from United States and abroad and talking to a variety of HR practitioners, we conducted in-depth interviews expressly for this chapter with senior HR leaders (including chief diversity officers and diversity managers) working in the area of diversity and inclusion. Interviewees represented five organizations widely viewed as successfully inclusive, all of whom were ranked among *DiversityInc*'s "Top 50" companies, including leaders from Ernst & Young, Marriott International, Time Warner Cable, Verizon Communications, and the Walt Disney Company. Many of these companies are also applauded by other sources, such as *Working Mother*'s "100 Best Companies" and the Human Rights Campaign's "Best Places to Work 2012" for employees identifying as lesbian, gay, bisexual, and transgender. These organizations vary widely by industry and diversity challenges, and all have experience operating in a variety of countries around the world. We believe their struggles and experiences can be instructive to practitioners interested in improving inclusiveness within their own companies. We also present their insight into persistent HR challenges, new future directions in diversity and inclusion practices, and implications of these changes for HR itself.

From Diversity to Inclusion

In the United States, many early diversity programs grew out of the civil rights movement, beginning with equal employment and affirmative action legislation in the 1960s and continuing as additional antidiscrimination laws were enacted throughout the 1990s. Tasked with ensuring fairness and equal treatment for protected classes of employees as defined by U.S. law, HR developed staffing, compensation, training, and other programs and policies that focused on employees and met legal compliance standards. Recently, as more companies have realized that sustainable competitive advantage comes through committed employees, HR has stepped up to the challenges of being a strategic business partner, working hand-in-hand with operations to deliver superior business results (Dessler, 2006). Current practice has expanded HR's focus even further to include reaching both inside and outside the firm to add value and help transform organizations to meet the demands of today's marketplace (Ulrich & Brockbank, 2005).

Unfortunately, decades of effort in United States directed at increasing equal opportunity and eliminating prejudice and discrimination have not been met with declines in reports of workplace discrimination. According to the U.S. Equal Employment Opportunity Commission (EEOC), the number of charges filed over the past ten years is actually on the rise. In fact, more than ninety-three thousand charges of discrimination were filed with the EEOC in 2009, of which over 66 percent related to race and gender (U.S. Equal Employment Opportunity Commission, 2010). Likewise, despite Australia's laws promoting fair employment, recently the country's military has faced serious allegations of sexism, prompting the Defense Minister to order Australia's Sexual Discrimination Commissioner to enact a "comprehensive review of the culture" of the armed forces (Siegel, 2011, p. A10).

However, formal charges may be just the tip of the discrimination iceberg. Organizational psychologists have become increasingly concerned that prejudice and discrimination have not disappeared but rather have gone "underground" and become more subtle and difficult to identify (Dipboye & Colella, 2005; Dovidio, Gaertner, Kawakani, & Hodson, 2002). Although less blatantly offensive than traditional manifestations of racism, these subtle "microaggressions" (Sue, 2010) can still send a clear message about unwelcomeness, harming the work performance, satisfaction, and retention of affected workers. Thus modern HR concerns extend far beyond following legislative guidelines on fair recruitment and promotion practices to include a more nuanced consideration of how the talents of a diverse workforce can best be leveraged for competitive advantage.

Little surprise, then, that with all these concerns diversity is now considered a separate discipline within HR (Society for Human Resource Management, 2010a). Within this HR discipline of diversity there are currently two different yet related approaches to the management of diversity, one of which continues to be called *diversity* and the other now being termed *inclusion* (Roberson, 2006; Shore, Randel, Chung, Dean, Ehrhart, & Singh, 2011). Diversity, defined as "the varied perspectives and approaches to work that members of different identity groups bring" (Thomas & Ely, 1996, p. 80), refers to the commonalities and differences among employees. While diversity is most frequently conceptualized in terms of observable characteristics, such as gender, race, disability, and age, it can also more broadly encompass less visible dimensions, such as education, national origin, family status, gender identity, generation, geographic background, language, life experiences, lifestyle, organizational function and level, religion, belief and spirituality, sexual orientation, and thinking patterns. Traditionally, HR in the United States has focused on this approach to diversity in its diversity management efforts.

More recently, HR practitioners have recognized that this conception of diversity tells only part of the story. Many organizations have shifted from attempting to minimize differences to striving to embrace them in order to realize the full potential of diversity (Thomas, 2004). However, the diversity or organizational demography of a workforce provides only the opportunity for greater creativity and innovation; it does not guarantee it.

For organizations to reap the full benefits of diversity, all members of heterogeneous workforces must feel included and accepted. Indeed, Shore et al. (2011) emphasize belongingness and uniqueness as the defining characteristics of an inclusive workgroup (see also Ferdman, Chapter 1, this volume). Similarly, Ferdman (2010) notes that "experiencing inclusion in a group or organization involves being fully part of the whole while retaining a sense of authenticity and uniqueness" (p. 37). This feeling of inclusion—manifested through perceptions of voice, fairness, and safety—may help employees and organizations experience the positive performance benefits of diversity (Ferdman, Avigdor, Braun, Konkin, & Kuzmycz, 2010).

Roberson's (2006) research provides support for making a distinction between diversity and inclusion. Surveying HR and diversity offices of fifty-one large public companies, Roberson found that their definitions of diversity focused on the demographic makeup of groups, while their definitions of inclusion emphasized the participation of all employees within an organization. HR has an important role to play in fostering both of these elements—diversity and inclusion—in that it has responsibilities in the attraction, selection, evaluation, promotion, and retention of diverse staff as well as in the creation of an organizational climate in which these diverse individuals can contribute and thrive.

Structure and Culture

Promoting diversity and inclusion involves establishing responsibility for these efforts and creating a supportive organizational culture. To advance diversity and inclusion in the workplace, HR must carefully attend to both structural and cultural elements of the organization. We address both of these in this section.

Establishing Responsibility for Diversity and Inclusion

Although responsibility for supporting diversity and inclusion falls to HR, ownership of these efforts is not always located structurally within the HR department. For example, Ernst & Young has found it advantageous to create a structure wherein the chief diversity officer (CDO) is a senior partner who reports directly to the head of all U.S. operations as well as coordinates with the head of the HR people team. This structure in some respects separates out issues of diversity from those of inclusion, with HR responsible for diversity compliance functions, such as recruitment and promotion, and the CDO dealing more directly with efforts to promote an inclusive climate and culture. In contrast, other companies have both diversity and inclusion more exclusively centralized within the HR chain of command, with designated CDOs reporting upward through their most senior HR leaders. Still other organizations have chosen not to separate inclusion responsibilities from mainstream HR jobs, instead charging all of HR to seek opportunities to expand diversity, promote inclusion, and interject diversity and inclusion into their various areas of responsibility. Verizon provides an example of yet another approach, which uses a model of shared accountability wherein accountability for diversity is spread throughout the business, as opposed to being housed solely in HR.

There are pros and cons to each of these approaches. Organizations may find it easier to coordinate all HR issues under a central HR function, assuming that HR has a good reputation within the organization and has a strong advocate for diversity and inclusion in the most senior HR position. As one interviewee noted, this centralized strategy may prevent diversity and HR leaders from competing for face time with key business leaders. On the other hand, giving diversity issues a direct line both to the operational top and to HR can send a strong message that these issues are not just niceties, but are strategic business concerns as well. Charging all of HR to act as "diversity leaders" has the potential either to fully integrate an inclusion focus throughout HR functions or—if HR staff are not well trained on how to effectively foster diversity and inclusion—to weaken inclusion efforts.

There is no one best way; any of these structures can potentially be successful. Rather, the structure must be aligned with the culture, challenges, and diversity issues faced by the particular firm, taking into consideration where the organization is in its diversity journey, the company's culture and processes, and its surrounding national culture. SHRM's (2010b) survey of forty-seven countries suggests that North American organizations tend to take a more centralized and prescriptive approach that is more likely to enforce diversity goals, whereas Western European and Asian companies often prefer a more decentralized approach. For example, SHRM's report cites the chief diversity officer of U.S.-based Merck pharmaceuticals as saying, "We look for meaningful and practical metrics to measure the success of each of our Diversity initiatives," whereas the HR director of a major conglomerate based in India noted, "We believe that Diversity cannot be forced within the organization. It has to evolve naturally" (p. 22).

Creating a Supportive Organizational Culture

Regardless of their differences in reporting structure, our sample of exemplary organizations reported striking similarities in the kind of inclusive culture they have created and the methods they use to maintain it. These organizations all invest heavily in supporting a culture of inclusion, understanding that the culture they seek does not just happen, and recognizing that it involves far more than simply achieving certain demographic numbers. For example, in keeping with their creative mission and identity, Disney is noted for creating a culture characterized by openness and acceptance of differences that promotes inclusiveness. Similarly, the other best practice organizations we studied also are known for having organizational cultures that embrace diversity and inclusion. Culture creation typically falls to senior organizational leadership, and it should come as no surprise that all of these organizations are headed by senior leaders who "get it" at a deep level. For example, Ernst & Young's CEO is also chair of Catalyst's board of directors. Marriott's CEO put it the following way: "Marriott International's commitment to diversity is absolute. It is the only way for us to attract and retain the very best talent available. It is the only way to forge the business relationships necessary to continue our dynamic growth. And it is the only way to meet our responsibilities to our associates, customers, partners, and stakeholders" (quoted in Hayes, 2004, p. 4).

So what characterizes a leader who "gets it"? Offermann and Matos (2007) recently presented a list of "Top Ten" similarities in best practices among leaders of successfully diverse organizations. Their findings suggest that these leaders view diversity as a business imperative, stand out front as diversity champions, take a broad view of high-potential employees, share unwritten rules, try different approaches, set high expectations for all staff, provide training as ongoing education, benchmark with other organizations but tailor practices to their own needs, are inclusive of all staff—both majority and minority group members—and learn from their diverse staff. Demonstrating these leadership practices sends a strong message to all staff that inclusiveness is a key part of the fabric of the organization's culture. In addition, Pittinsky (2010) argues that success as a leader in a diverse environment requires not only reducing prejudices but also promoting positive feelings about members of other groups, termed *allophilia.*

Successfully inclusive firms, such as those whose HR executives we interviewed, have mature and robust diversity programs. As one of Verizon's diversity managers put it, "Diversity and inclusion are part of the DNA here." A key component of that maturity is knowing how to align inclusion issues with the business needs inherent in the company. Although making the business case for diversity is sometimes problematic (Cañas & Sondak, 2008), organizations on the cutting edge of practice have been able to do so successfully. Diversity, in and of itself, is likely neither good nor bad for business (Kochan et al., 2003). However, given changing demographics, it is a fact of organizational life, and one that offers the opportunity for enhanced value if an organization is committed to maintaining a culture that promotes learning, cooperation, and fairness (Slater, Weigand, & Zwirlein, 2008; Weigand, 2007). Inclusiveness is not just something nice to do; it is imperative to the future success of the organization in a global marketplace (Thomas, 2004).

Because the diversity challenges of every organization differ, approaches to address them vary as well. Here again, the need to be responsive to different national cultures may explain why multinational organizations have tended to leave much of the implementation of diversity programs to managers at national and local levels. The first diversity question often faced by HR anywhere is, "What specific diversity issues are of major organizational concern?" The answers may differ by country, region within country, and particular organization. As noted by a diversity manager at Swedish auto manufacturer Volvo: "The Diversity work needs to be adjusted to the local context. . . . we need to find the Diversity dimensions that are important and relevant in each specific country . . . the local Diversity need becomes the point of departure for discussions within our Diversity and inclusiveness training for managers" (quoted in Society for Human Resource Management, 2010b, p. 21).

Nonetheless, for all of the companies we spoke with, working with diverse employees is considered to be a leadership competency that can be good for the bottom line as well as the right thing to do. That means engaging operational leaders across the organization in the tasks of managing a diverse workforce, rather than just assigning those duties to HR alone. All areas of the organization—from finance to IT—can and should be included in organization-wide diversity and inclusion efforts. However, it often falls to HR to identify and develop such operational champions.

As an example, Marriott's comprehensive and holistic culture wheel is illustrated in Figure 8.1, showing the company's structural approach to creating a positive climate for diversity through multiple integrated levers or, in their terminology, disciplines. The Workforce Diversity discipline highlights important areas for change that are especially sensitive to HR policies and practices, particularly employee attraction and engagement, leadership development, and training. Like some other best practice firms, Marriott's efforts are not restricted to its own employees; it reaches out to its communities to support diversity in suppliers, customers, and owners and franchisees as well. Accountability systems reside within the company's continent divisions and each of the global disciplines, which must work together collaboratively and cooperatively. Regional diversity and inclusion councils support the inclusion efforts of the business. Progress is reported up to a CEO-led Global Diversity & Inclusion Council, and ultimately to the board of directors' Committee for Excellence, which is chaired by a member of the board of directors and comprises other

Figure 8.1. Marriott's Holistic Culture Wheel

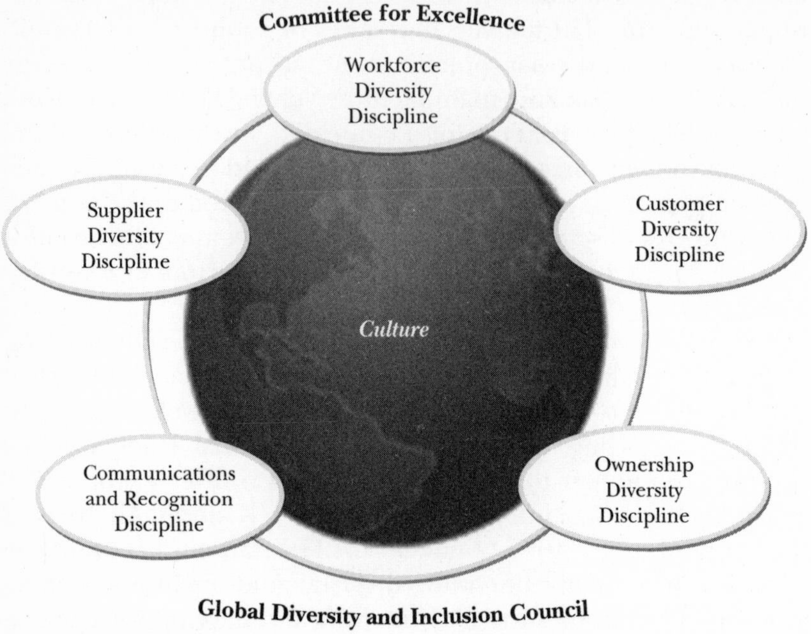

Committee for Excellence

Workforce Diversity Discipline

Supplier Diversity Discipline

Customer Diversity Discipline

Culture

Communications and Recognition Discipline

Ownership Diversity Discipline

Global Diversity and Inclusion Council

Source: Marriott International, 2010. Used with permission.

directors as well as members of company senior management. Permeating it all is a culture that sets for itself the goal of being the global leader for diversity and inclusion.

In sum, there are no easy answers for HR. For HR professionals wishing to succeed at "world-class diversity management," there is a need to shift perspectives, moving from viewing diversity as a one-time problem to be solved to recognizing it as a long-term challenge with real potential benefits (Thomas, 2010). Organizations that manage diversity and inclusion issues successfully have learned—sometimes through painful trial and error—what works for them and have tailored their approaches accordingly.

Best Practices

There is no shortage of suggestions for optimal HR practice in the area of diversity and inclusion, and one chapter certainly

Exhibit 8.1. Diversity and Inclusion Best Practices

- Develop a pipeline of diverse talent.
- Confront subtle discrimination.
- Leverage diversity to increase business performance.
- Develop accountability systems.
- Training, training, training.
- Use peer-to-peer influence.

cannot cover them all. Further, individual countries may possess unique HR challenges in addressing diversity and inclusion, such as seeking to reduce gender inequality in Pakistan, where Islamic values can conflict with gender equity (Klarsfeld, 2010), or being unable even to collect racial and ethnic data on employees in some European countries (Society for Human Resource Management, 2010b). On the other hand, some diversity and inclusion concerns have been proclaimed "global issues," as is the case with gender income equality (Shen et al., 2009) and workplace bullying (Einarsen, 2011).

The strategies summarized in Exhibit 8.1 and highlighted in the section that follows are those identified by our U.S.-based best practice organizations as the distinguishing features that are key to their success. These best practices are the prime levers these companies use to create cultures that support employees of all backgrounds, not just those from underrepresented groups. Although the U.S. organizations we sampled have a presence throughout the world and many of these strategies have been reported in a number of other countries, care should be taken in generalizing these practices to organizations based outside United States, in countries where culture, law, values, and tradition may require different approaches. Thus, whenever possible, we also present examples regarding best practices of other non-U.S.-based companies.

Developing the Pipeline

All of the HR leaders we interviewed recognize the importance of developing and maintaining a pipeline of diverse, high-quality talent. This best practice might at first appear to center more heavily on what we have termed *diversity* rather than on *inclusion* efforts. Indeed, one interviewee stressed the importance of a "critical mass" of diversity as necessary to allow inclusiveness discussions to take root. Kanter's (1977) classic work on tokenism highlights some of the difficulties that individuals from underrepresented groups face when their numbers fall below 15 percent: they are easily distinguishable from the mainstream of the workforce, their failures are often attributed to dispositional causes rather than to an unaccepting climate, and they often feel pressure to speak as representatives of their group rather than as themselves. Identifying diverse talent and attracting and hiring a diverse workforce have long been HR responsibilities and will continue to be so for the foreseeable future.

However, getting employees of diverse backgrounds in the door is just the beginning. As many organizations have discovered, it may be easier to recruit diversity than to keep it (Dreyfuss, 1990). Thomas (1990) notes that when staff who are members of minority groups leave, many companies blame HR selection strategies for failing to hire the right people and again attempt to recruit women and minorities without changing the company culture, only to fail again. Thus diverse recruitment alone will be insufficient to achieve diversity at all organizational levels; what is needed is a reassessment of how to change organizations to make them hospitable to the wide variety of people who populate them (Offermann, 1998).

As diversity increases in an organization's workforce, the need for a positive climate that encourages finding ways to use everyone's talents effectively becomes ever more apparent. While building diversity in the pipeline initially must involve acquiring staff of different backgrounds and growing "diversity in numbers," inclusiveness also needs to be stressed if an organization is to foster a healthy, effective pipeline of top-level diverse talent. A closer look at how organizations recognized for excellence in diversity and inclusion build and nurture their career pipelines through HR strategies reveals that both elements must be incorporated.

Although there is no one best way to develop and maintain diversity in the career pipeline, there are some particularly creative strategies. One example is Ernst & Young's Career Watch program, which has received well-deserved attention from other organizations seeking to model similar programs in their own workplaces. Ernst & Young started this program because it recognized that merely hiring workers who differed on some demographic characteristic from most others in the firm was not enough to ensure that they would progress upward in the organization or even remain in it at all. Thus, in Career Watch, newly hired female employees and employees of color are paired with high-level executives, who assume responsibility for monitoring their career paths and helping them identify and access the critical assignments they need to advance at the firm.

In addition to ensuring that managers consider a diverse slate of job candidates, Verizon places strong emphasis on recognizing the accomplishments of its employees, taking care to include workers of various backgrounds in these efforts. By highlighting the successes of members of its diverse staff, Verizon's HR team targets a number of objectives important in developing and maintaining a talent pipeline that reflects diversity. By featuring the accomplishments of promising employees in public advertisements and publications, Verizon's HR team shows that a variety of people can succeed at the company and, consequently, may attract more diverse talent to apply. This recognition may also enhance the featured employee's visibility within the company and hence increase the individual's chances for additional opportunities and promotion.

Similarly, Thomas (2004) has reported a number of strategies designed to foster diversity in the pipeline at IBM. For example, IBM is the home of the "five-minute drill," in which executives must be ready at any minute to discuss high-potential employees, and where there is a strong recognition that female and minority talent must be a focus in pipeline development. The company's interest in a pipeline that reflects diverse talent even extends to developing the next generation of future IBMers, as the company sponsors EXITE (EXploring Interests in Technology and Engineering) Camps that work with middle-school girls to encourage them to get involved in math and the sciences. Siemens, the German global electronics and engineering conglomerate, uses a similar strategy through programs aimed at getting young women interested in science and engineering careers by supporting women studying technology in universities, providing a Young Ladies Network of Technology, and even distributing mechanical toys to kindergartners to generate interest in engineering (Society for Human Resource Management, 2010b).

Confronting Subtle Discrimination

HR leaders working on the ground with issues of diversity and inclusion recognize that United States is not yet a "post-racial society" (Rachlinski & Parks, 2010), nor have other countries settled the diversity issues within their own borders. Though blatant expressions of discrimination appear to be declining, members of the HR teams of successfully inclusive organizations do not believe that prejudice is disappearing. Instead, they seem to agree with the many organizational psychologists who assert that prejudice is becoming more subtle, ambiguous, and difficult to identify with certainty (Dipboye & Colella, 2005; Dovidio et al., 2002). Nonetheless, many employees perceive it, with a recent study finding that 31.8 percent of a large sample of U.S. workers with disabilities reported subtle discrimination at work (Snyder, Carmichael, Blackwell, Cleveland, & Thornton, 2010). Similarly, a study of women managers and HR managers in Lebanon found that the majority of women described subtle processes of discrimination and favoritism, particularly in relation to their prospects for career advancement (Jamali & Abdallah, 2010). Likewise, the individuals we interviewed concurred with research showing that targets of subtle, implicit forms of discrimination can experience profoundly detrimental consequences (Sue, Capodilupo, & Holder, 2008). In addition, research has shown that discrimination can also negatively impact others in the organization who witness it, even without actually experiencing it themselves (Low, Radhakrishnan, Schneider, & Rounds, 2007).

Leading diversity practitioners now devote substantial time and attention to the concepts of "microinequities" (Rowe, 1990), "racial microaggressions" (Pierce, Carew, Pierce-Gonzalez, & Willis, 1978) and, more recently, the broader "microaggressions," which encompass behaviors directed at persons from a variety of underrepresented groups (Sue, 2010). Sue and his colleagues define *microaggressions* as "brief and commonplace daily verbal, behavioral, and environmental indignities, whether intentional or unintentional, that communicate hostile, derogatory, or negative racial slights and insults to the target person or group" (Sue et al., 2007, p. 273). At the lowest level of microaggressions, individual perpetrators may well be unaware that their words or actions are taken as offensive. Yet organizational researchers are starting to show the potentially detrimental effects of these subtle ways of withholding full inclusion, including the potential for reductions in motivation and retention (Basu, Basford, Offermann, Graebner, & Jaffer, 2010). In addition, discrimination stresses have also been associated with poorer mental health for minority group members (Noh, Kaspar, & Wickrama, 2007), which in turn may affect organizational health costs. Both Verizon and Ernst & Young are notable for placing strong emphasis in their training programs on these subtle forms of exclusion and their often discriminatory impact—Verizon as part of its Diversity Leadership Institute and Ernst & Young in its annual diversity training for partners at the firm. As part of diversity training, HR practitioners may find videotapes or common scenarios useful to illustrate subtle snubs or comments that could be perceived as devaluing, as these tools may help generate discussion about how to either extend or deny inclusion. To foster a truly inclusive environment, organizations need to understand that they must do far more than target explicit and overt manifestations of discrimination. Implicit biases can do just as much damage and may be far more pervasive, as they may be held and communicated even by well-meaning individuals (Sue, 2010).

Leveraging Diversity to Increase Business Performance

Successfully inclusive organizations not only have made a general business case for diversity; they also use their diversity creatively to enhance the performance of their organizations. Subscribing to Thomas and Ely's (1996) learning-and-effectiveness paradigm, these firms link diversity to the way they approach work. For instance, most U.S. best practice organizations have well-established employee resource groups (ERGs) whose roles have changed markedly since their inception. Initially established to increase socialization and networking opportunities for members of underrepresented groups, many ERGs have since stepped up to become valued strategic partners as well. For instance, a recommendation from IBM's people with disabilities task force to make its products accessible to a broader consumer base is expected to generate over a billion dollars of revenue (Thomas, 2004). Coca-Cola asks all its ERGs to compose an annual business plan that is presented to the president of its North American operations. When launching a new beverage product aimed at the Latino market, the company's Latino resource group helped market the product in the community, even accompanying the sales force to talk with customers about positioning the product for maximum sales (Frankel, 2008). Similarly, inclusiveness enabled Disney to capitalize on the new market opportunities presented by the increase in the Hispanic population, helping it identify and develop new consumer products associated with the traditional Latin American *quinceañera* coming-of-age celebration.

In addition to identifying new market prospects, a diverse workforce can aid in building strong external relationships with customers and communities, with employees more closely representing the demographics of the clients they serve. Also, as the face of the organization, diverse staff can attract additional diverse talent by illustrating with their presence and testimony that the company values different perspectives, thus giving HR a more diverse applicant pool from which to select. Further, there has been increasing interest in supplier diversity as well as internal staff diversity, with organizations recognizing their role in supporting diversity in their communities.

Developing Accountability Systems

Lack of accountability for results is viewed by our experts as one of the top reasons why most corporate diversity and inclusion efforts fail. Supporting this viewpoint, a recent SHRM report (2010b) emphasizes that accountability should be considered a best HR practice in fostering diversity and inclusion within organizations. Accountability requires careful attention to measurement in order to assess progress and determine areas for improvement. For example, a Coca-Cola representative noted,

"We have learned over time how to measure everything there is to measure and then report on it, which is the most important part" (Frankel, 2008).

Accountability for achieving inclusiveness should not just rest on the shoulders of the chief diversity officer; rather, it must be embedded within organizations' larger performance management systems (Gordon, 2010). Examining Marriott's system offers an excellent example. As shown in Figure 8.1, Marriott places strong emphasis on accountability systems, ensuring that diversity and inclusion goals do not get lost amid the many other demands placed on managers. Similarly, at IBM managing diversity is a core competency used to assess executive performance (Thomas, 2004), and U.K.-based Barclays bank also embeds equality and diversity into its performance management systems (Anonymous, 2002). Many organizations include it as a component of every manager's performance rating. For instance, at Verizon a portion of each executive's performance bonus is linked to how he or she manages diversity across all areas of the organization, including hiring, development, and promotion. In addition, both the company's and the business unit's success in utilizing diverse suppliers are considered. As a result, the performance bonuses of all Verizon management employees are affected by the extent to which senior management achieves their diversity targets. Further, at CSX, "The higher you go . . . the more stringent the requirement on you to be a coach and be inclusive or you will not get the compensation commensurate with your position, be it your base pay or merit increases, the bonus we pay every year or the long-term incentive program" (cited in Frankel, 2008, p. 38). In short, although the form of implementation varies, some type of accountability is a factor cited consistently as necessary to establish and maintain an inclusive organizational culture.

Training, Training, Training

Inclusiveness does not just happen. Inclusiveness-seeking organizations train, then train again. From Time Warner Cable's on-boarding program to Ernst & Young's partner workshops to Barclay's behavior-based programs (Anonymous, 2002), companies find their own strategies to best incorporate diversity and inclusion training into overall employee development. Cognizant that early diversity training efforts were sometimes associated with negative effects (Caudron, 1993), the organizations whose HR leaders we interviewed have learned from their own prior training successes and failures as well as those of their competitors. They have not merely mimicked others, but rather tailored training to match their own unique situations. For example, to maximize effectiveness, Disney customizes training to fit its organizational culture rather than adopting off-the-shelf programs. Evidence suggests that diversity training can positively impact employee emotional and behavioral reactions as well as perceived organizational outcomes (such as seeing diversity as an asset that can enhance company profits), both immediately after training and for some months thereafter (for example, DeMeuse, Hostager, & O'Neill, 2007).

The best organizations recognize that inclusiveness cannot be obtained without involving all levels of employees in diversity and inclusion initiatives (see also Nishii and Rich, Chapter 11, this volume). Engaging operational leaders in championing diversity and inclusion adds credibility. Their presence and participation in training events underscores their commitment to an inclusive workplace, and more organizations are adding this role in diversity training as a leadership responsibility (see, for example, Henderson, Chapter 15, this volume). Verizon takes this even a step further, bringing both managers and their staff together in diversity and inclusion programs as part of its Diversity Leadership Institute (DLI). One of several talent development programs, the intensive three-day program is open to employees identified as high potential. To ensure that DLI participants represent a diverse cross-section of employees, at least 60 percent of participants must be women or people of color. By receiving the same information together, both employees and their managers develop a shared basis for future discussions surrounding inclusion and can hold one another accountable for their commitments. Also, the shared structure of the program provides an opportunity for employees and managers to build stronger, deeper, more trusting relationships, something that our research (Basford & Offermann, 2009) indicates can foster employee feelings of being included and valued in their work environments.

Using Peer-to-Peer Influence

Although formal training is important, by itself it is insufficient to produce lasting change. Informative, engaging training can teach employees about the value of diversity and inclusion and help them develop techniques to better foster inclusive environments. However, when employees return to their everyday work contexts, they often fail to fully implement all that they learned in training. Making lasting behavioral changes to better promote inclusion in a diverse workplace requires conscious and continuous effort. Without post-training strategies established to remind and encourage employees to put their training into action, many workers may revert to their previous habitual behaviors.

Leading organizations recognize this risk and leverage peer-to-peer influence to foster lasting changes and improvements. For example, Ernst & Young's Leadership Matters program for firm partners stresses the importance of peer-to-peer influence in promoting a strong inclusive organizational culture. Partners attending the program engage in a dialogue on the topic and discuss strategies to help employees hold one another accountable for implementing inclusiveness training lessons in their work. Given high work demands, this is a rare opportunity for partners to share ideas and ensure that diversity issues are considered and aligned with business strategy. HR staff can serve a key role in designing and creating these kinds of creative training opportunities, as they should be especially sensitive to and knowledgeable about their own organizational context and culture.

Persistent Problems, Potential Solutions

Although our sample of organizations was selected for its noted successes with diversity and inclusion, none of these companies think that these efforts are anywhere near "done," or even that such a state will ever be possible. We now discuss some of the areas in which the executives we interviewed see sustained challenges that continue to demand attention, as well as some of the innovative ways they are trying to address them.

Balancing Diversity and Inclusion

As noted earlier, when these terms are used differentially in organizations, often diversity denotes group demographics, whereas
inclusion refers to participation by all. Several of our contacts
stated that, rightly or wrongly, *diversity* has come to be associated
predominantly with ethnicity and gender and that focusing solely
on these dimensions of difference may not be universally well-
received by other groups. Indeed, respondents to SHRM's recent
survey of 1,400 members found that a focus on ethnicity and
gender was considered the top weakness of the field (Society for
Human Resource Management, 2007). In contrast, the term *inclusion* implies a broader individual difference perspective that
embraces everyone, making it more acceptable to a wide range
of personnel without provoking backlash and defensiveness.
However, some practitioners worry that the underrepresentation
of certain groups may get lost in a focus on inclusiveness that fails
to acknowledge societal inequities in power, privilege, and opportunity. This concern may not be unfounded; the same SHRM
report (2007) noted that while the top priority of 96 percent of
surveyed diversity practitioners was creating a work environment
that allows everyone to fully contribute, only 54 percent of respondents listed appropriate representation of racial and ethnic groups
as extremely important. HR must continue striving to find the
difficult balance between engaging the broad spectrum of the
workplace through a culture of inclusiveness while still actively
promoting the hiring and participation of underrepresented
groups.

Giving Honest Feedback to People Different from Oneself

Managers in organizations paying even a minimum of attention
to inclusiveness know that they are responsible for developing all
of their staff. Nonetheless, sensitivity to diversity may itself generate concerns among managers about how staff members who are
different from themselves might receive negative feedback. Not
wanting to be seen as unsupportive of their diverse staff or even
fearing charges of discrimination, some managers withhold the

same kind of honest feedback they are comfortable giving to those more similar to themselves. In doing so, they deprive those different from themselves of the same opportunities to improve. One way Ernst & Young is addressing this problem is by not only training feedback-givers (managers) on how to provide feedback but also training nonmanagerial staff in how to receive feedback and why honest feedback can benefit them long-term. Knowing that recipients have been prepared to handle negative feedback constructively may make managers more open to sharing their honest assessment of areas for development and growth to all staff.

Occupational Group Segregation

Although an organization may be diverse overall, within certain occupational groups gender and race/ethnic segregation can remain. Certain occupations attract less diverse talent, causing some organizations to reach down even as far as middle school to encourage students from underrepresented groups to consider careers in these areas. For example, in 2009 Time Warner Cable made a commitment of $100 million to Connect a Million Minds, a five-year program designed to inspire students from all backgrounds to pursue careers in science, technology, engineering, and math. As noted earlier, Siemens also reaches out to young women to encourage them to consider engineering careers (Society for Human Resource Management, 2010b).

Current Economic Climate and Downsizing

Operating in the midst of a recession makes it difficult to change existing demographic distributions within organizations, as hiring is down overall. With layers of middle management reduced and few openings at senior levels, promotions that might have been forthcoming more quickly in prosperous times will be slower to materialize. This creates a particular problem for talented employees who become stalled in their anticipated career progression, resulting in frustration and sometimes organizational departure. In its Diversity Leadership Institute, Verizon addresses advancement concerns by having managers and their subordinate managers spend time in training together, working on the career development of the more junior manager. Building the relationship between managers at the two levels and establishing plans for the subordinate manager's growth and development can keep motivation high and expectations realistic.

Future Directions in Inclusive HR Practices

There is no shortage of work to be done in developing organizations as places where all different kinds of people can work together productively in a climate that promotes fairness and harmony. Having highlighted some of the practices used by leading organizations to ensure both diversity and inclusion in their workforces, we next share their views of key future directions for HR practitioners. Two particular areas of concern loomed large for the experts we spoke to: (1) maintaining the focus on diversity and inclusion they have worked so hard to develop and (2) expanding what they have learned about promoting inclusiveness into the global arena.

Maintaining Focus on Diversity and Inclusion

Maintaining focus on diversity and inclusion sounds as straightforward as continuing to "fight the good fight," but it is not that simple. In fact, previous success in advancing inclusiveness may actually make it even more difficult to sustain corporate attention. The tendency is for an organization to take a "been there, done that" view and assume that problems have been successfully addressed and they can move on to other concerns. Columnist Robert Samuelson observed a similar tendency in writing about the Deepwater Horizon oil spill. Describing how the disaster resulted at least in part from the previous success of underwater drilling, he noted, "It is human nature to celebrate success by relaxing" (Samuelson, 2010, p. A17).

In difficult economic times, concerns other than diversity and inclusion understandably occupy enormous collective attention. However, organizations that have been successful in making the business case for diversity may be better able to forestall cutbacks in the training and development activities that are often vulnerable in economic downturns. In fact, a recent survey by *DiversityInc* suggests, "Diversity's the differentiator in hard times," providing a competitive edge for organizations that is even more important when times are tough (Frankel, 2008, p. 22). Our experts stressed the need to keep inclusiveness on the organization's radar, reiterating the importance of vigilance and sustained efforts to remind, reinforce, and spread good practices throughout an organization.

Expanding the Global Focus

As our world shrinks, global diversity issues are now generating increasing HR focus and attention. HR practitioners in the United States have learned a great deal about creating inclusive workplaces, but the generalizability of these findings to other countries and cultures is questionable. What will or will not transfer from U.S. practice? What new issues must be addressed? Several of our contacts noted that some other parts of the world see diversity as an American problem with little relevance to them. While the truth of that view is suspect, the perception must be acknowledged and explored (see also Jonsen and Özbilgin, Chapter 12, this volume). Other HR leaders mentioned the efforts of countries such as Norway, which passed a law in 2003 requiring major companies to have at least 40-percent representation by women on their corporate boards. In moving toward effective corporate performance in international business, U.S. organizations likely have as much to learn as they have to teach—if not even more. Sensitivity to local needs and traditions around the world need to be balanced with U.S. corporate responsibilities for ethics and sustainability.

Successfully inclusive multinational organizations recognize the importance of broadening their diversity and inclusion efforts to include a greater focus on global diversity. As Marriott's vice president for talent management asserted in our interview, "We have to be seamless with the demographics of the planet." Indeed, all of our interviewees mentioned a shift toward concentrating more on both global and national concerns as integral components of their future diversity and inclusion efforts. Thomas

(2004) also uncovered a similar trend in his research at IBM, noting that IBM's Chief Diversity Officer Ted Childs had prioritized developing a global strategy to manage diversity concerns affecting the company across the world. Childs did not wish to impart a U.S.-centric approach when dealing globally with so many profoundly different cultures. Rather, he understood that diversity issues often vary across regions, from Europe's growing number of ethnic minorities to Asia-Pacific's many distinct cultures, with each posing unique challenges for organizational HR and diversity teams. Marriott also spoke of the need to adopt a "glocal" approach, employing a global mindset with localized delivery of products closely aligned with the needs of the local culture and marketplace.

We should not assume that organizations without an international physical presence are immune from the need to consider global diversity. Even U.S.-based employees now represent an astoundingly broad spectrum of cultural backgrounds and heritages. As one of the senior diversity managers we interviewed put it, "Even domestically, we need to think more globally." More and more, organizations need leaders who can engage in the mental processes and adaptive behaviors required to function effectively in workplaces that are populated by staff from a wide variety of backgrounds, skills that Offermann and Phan (2002) called culturally intelligent leadership (see also Gallegos, Chapter 6, this volume). Because most leadership theory has been created by and for people from highly individualistic cultures, care must be taken not to overgeneralize the practices recommended in those environments to other cultures whose values may be quite different. It is essential that both leadership theory and practice continue to be reexamined through the lens of culture (see Bennett, Chapter 5, this volume).

Changing Focus Changes HR

These and other challenges present continued opportunities for HR practitioners to assume the strategic lead in advancing both diversity and inclusion on a far broader basis than they ever have before. Focusing on diversity and inclusion can change HR in a number of ways, including the roles HR is expected to play and the skill set that HR practitioners must possess to be maximally successful.

In the past, HR struggled to be viewed as a strategic player deserving a seat at the table. Current recognition of the importance of the human factors—rather than merely the technological factors—in organizational success, coupled with the realities of diverse workforces that may span the globe, has given even more validation to the importance of HR having a strategic voice. If organizations are to achieve and sustain competitive advantage in a diversifying, globalizing market, HR needs to play an active, strategic role. In enacting this role, HR practitioners must continue to be sensitive as they work to mesh diversity and inclusion with operational needs. Encouraging HR staff to participate in training rotations in which they work in operational roles for a period of time, and/or welcoming operational staff rotating into HR roles, may help bridge the gap between HR and operations. HR needs a close, collaborative relationship with operations to give its voice strategic credibility.

Now, as they play a more strategic role, HR practitioners must view themselves as change agents as well as policy experts. As more emphasis is placed on creating organizational climates that support diversity and inclusion efforts, HR needs a thorough understanding of the processes of change and resistance that will help or hinder their efforts. Without changing the attitudes and behaviors of existing staff, efforts to attract and retain employees from underrepresented groups are doomed to failure. In addition to experiencing subtle discrimination, as cited earlier, underrepresented group members may suffer by being excluded from the informal social networks enjoyed by their colleagues. Some of our own recent work (Basford & Offermann, 2012) shows the importance of positive coworker relations in diverse workplaces, with these relationships enhancing the work motivation of workers in both lower- and higher-status job positions. Feeling excluded and disenfranchised is demotivating for everyone.

Further, the expanding global presence of many organizations, as well as the diversity of the workforce even among organizations located in a single country, challenge HR practitioners to adopt a global mindset in their work (Jeannet, 2000; Levy, Taylor, Boyacigiller, & Beechler, 2007). American companies attempting to implement U.S.-style diversity and inclusion practices outside the United States have experienced notable problems (see, for example, Ferner, Almond, & Colling, 2005). As discussed in SHRM's report (2010b), organizations in different countries may define diversity differently, have different views about how to diversify, focus on distinct key areas for increasing diversity, and adopt varying methodologies for doing so. Tensions between central control and local autonomy remain challenges for multinational organizations (Leung & Peterson, 2011), with HR practices and expectations varying by home culture. For example, Fenton-O'Creevy, Gooderham, and Nordhaug (2008) argue that U.S.-based multinationals more typically assume an internationally decentralized approach to HR than multinationals based in continental Europe or Japan. Thus HR practitioners are being challenged to learn about cultural and institutional characteristics in order to be successful, particularly because the use of HR practices such as performance appraisal, management training, and compensation systems can differ between headquarters and subsidiaries (Björkman, Fey, & Park, 2007).

Finally, HR must practice what it preaches. If HR itself is not diverse, or if it fails to create the kind of positive and inclusive climate worthy of emulation, it will have little credibility advocating the virtues of inclusion to others. For example, work with HR managers in Lebanon found that though they espoused gender diversity rhetoric, their words did not translate into generating employment targets for women, tracking their participation, measuring their satisfaction, or evaluating their career progression (Jamali & Abdallah, 2010), all activities that one might expect from an HR function that truly supported gender equity. As firms increasingly recognize the central role of employees in advancing profitability and continued organizational success, HR must be both a principled force insuring participation and equity of employees from all backgrounds as well as a key strategic partner. At Verizon, Vice-President of Talent Management & Diversity Al Torres says a fundamental role of HR diversity and inclusion practitioners is to be the "conscience of the organization," responsible for ensuring that their organization is keeping pace with the issues and needs of all staff in order to better serve their customers.

This is certainly a tall order, far beyond what any HR practitioner entering the field many years ago could ever have imagined. As global issues further expand the domain of diversity and inclusion, HR must take the lead in determining how to best approach diversity in all forms and in all geographic areas, both tactically and responsibly. It is indeed an exciting time of change for human resource management.

References

Anonymous. (2002). Success through inclusion: Equality and diversity at Barclays. *Human Resource Management International Digest, 10*(7), 9–12.

Basford, T. E., & Offermann, L. R. (2009, August). *Creating diversity-inclusive climates: What leaders can do.* Paper and poster presented at the 117th Annual Convention of the American Psychological Association, Toronto, Canada.

Basford, T. E., & Offermann, L. R. (2012). Beyond leadership: The impact of coworker relationships on employee motivation and intent to stay. *Journal of Management and Organization, 18,* 818–832. doi:10.5172/jmo.2012.2753

Basu, S., Basford, T. E., Offermann, L. R., Graebner, R., & Jaffer, S. (2010, April). Can leader behavior reduce perceptions of racial microaggressions at work? In L. R. Offermann (Chair), *Leadership and diversity: Science meets practice.* Symposium conducted at the 26th Annual Conference of the Society for Industrial and Organizational Psychology, Atlanta, GA.

Björkman, I., Fey, C. F., & Park, H. J. (2007). Institutional theory and MNC subsidiary HRM practices: Evidence from a three-country study. *Journal of International Business Studies, 38,* 430–446.

Cañas, K. A., & Sondak, H. (2008). *Opportunities and challenges of workplace diversity.* Upper Saddle River, NJ: Prentice-Hall.

Caudron, S. (1993). Training can damage diversity efforts. *Personnel Journal, 72*(4), 50–62.

DeMeuse, K. P., Hostager, T. J., & O'Neill, K. S. (2007). A longitudinal evaluation of senior managers' perceptions and attitudes of a workplace diversity training program. *Human Resource Planning, 30*(2), 38–47.

Dessler, G. (2006). *A framework for human resource management* (4th ed.). Upper Saddle River, NJ: Prentice-Hall.

Dipboye, R. L., & Colella, A. (2005). The dilemmas of workplace discrimination. In R. L. Dipboye & A. Colella (Eds.), *Discrimination at work: The psychological and organizational bases* (pp. 425–462). Mahwah, NJ: Erlbaum.

Dovidio, J. F., Gaertner, S. L., Kawakani, K., & Hodson, G. (2002). Why can't we all just get along? Interpersonal biases and interracial distrust. *Cultural Diversity and Ethnic Minority Psychology, 8,* 88–102.

Dreyfuss, J. (1990, April 23). Get ready for the new workforce. *Fortune, 121,* 165–181.

Einarsen, S. (2011, May). *Bullying and harassment at work: Recent developments in theory, research, and practice.* Paper presented at the 9th International Conference on Occupational Stress and Health, Orlando, FL.

Fenton-O'Creevy, M., Gooderham, P., & Nordhaug, O. (2008). Human resource management in U.S. subsidiaries in Europe and Australia: Centralization or autonomy? *Journal of International Business Studies, 39,* 151–166.

Ferdman, B. M. (2010). Teaching inclusion by example and experience: Creating an inclusive learning environment. In B. B. McFeeters, K. Hannum, & L. Booysen (Eds.), *Leading across differences: Cases and perspectives—Facilitator's guide* (pp. 37–49). San Francisco: Pfeiffer.

Ferdman, B. M., Avigdor, A., Braun, D., Konkin, J., & Kuzmycz, D. (2010). Collective experience of inclusion, diversity, and performance in work groups. *Revista de Administração Mackenzie, 11*(3), 6–26. doi:10.1590/S1678-6971201000030000

Ferner, A., Almond, P., & Colling, T. (2005). Institutional theory and the cross-national transfer of employment policy: The case of "workforce diversity" in U.S. multinationals. *Journal of International Business Studies, 36,* 304–321.

Frankel, B. (2008, November-December). Lessons learned from the *DiversityInc* Top 50. *DiversityInc,* 22–42.

Gordon, T. M. (2010, June 10). *Diversity and inclusion: A shock to the system. By system, I mean culture.* Invited address presented at the Workplace Diversity: Practice and Research Conference, George Mason University, Arlington, VA.

Hayes, C. (2004). Diversity leaders—Advancing business performance through diversity. *Black Enterprise.* Retrieved from http://findarticles.com/p/articles/mi_m1365/is_12_34/ai_n6169009

Jamali, D., & Abdallah, H. (2010). The challenge of moving beyond the rhetoric: Paradoxes of diversity management in the Middle East. *Equity, Diversity, and Inclusion: An International Journal, 29*(2), 167–185.

Jeannet, J. P. (2000). *Managing with a global mindset.* London: Prentice Hall.

Kanter, R. M. (1977). *Men and women of the corporation.* New York: Basic Books.

Klarsfeld, A. (2010). *International handbook of diversity management at work: Country perspectives on diversity and equal treatment.* Cheltenham, UK: Edward Elgar.

Kochan, T., Bezrukova, K., Jackson, S., Joshi, A., Jehn, K., Leonard, J., ... Thomas, D. (2003). The effects of diversity on business performance: Report of the diversity research network. *Human Resource Management, 42*(1), 3–21.

Leung, K., & Peterson, M. F. (2011). Managing a globally distributed workforce: Social and interpersonal issues. In S. Zedeck (Ed.), *APA handbook of industrial and organizational psychology* (Vol. 3, pp. 771–805). Washington, DC: American Psychological Association.

Levy, O., Taylor, S., Boyacigiller, N., & Beechler, S. (2007). Global mindset: A review and proposed extensions. In M. Javidan, R. Steers, & M. Hitt (Eds.), *Advances in international management: The global mindset* (pp. 13–50). Greenwich, CT: JAI Press.

Low, K. S., Radhakrishnan, P., Schneider, K. T., & Rounds, J. (2007). The experiences of bystanders of workplace ethnic harassment. *Journal of Applied Social Psychology, 37*(10), 2261–2297.

Noh, S., Kaspar, V., & Wickrama, K. A. S. (2007). Overt and subtle racial discrimination and mental health: Preliminary findings for Korean immigrants. *American Journal of Public Health, 97*(7), 1269–1274.

Offermann, L. R. (1998). Leading and empowering diverse followers. In G. R. Hickman (Ed.), *Leading organizations: Perspectives for a new era* (pp. 397–403). Thousand Oaks, CA: Sage.

Offermann, L. R., & Matos, K. (2007). Best practices in leading diverse organizations. In J. Conger & R. E. Riggio (Eds.), *The practice of leadership: Developing the next generation of leaders* (pp. 277–299). San Francisco: Jossey-Bass.

Offermann, L. R., & Phan, L. U. (2002). Culturally intelligent leadership for a diverse world. In R. E. Riggio, S. E. Murphy, & F. J. Pirozzolo (Eds.), *Multiple intelligences and leadership* (pp. 187–214). Mahwah, NJ: Erlbaum.

Pierce, C., Carew, J., Pierce-Gonzalez, D., & Willis, D. (1978). An experiment in racism: TV commercials. In C. Pierce (Ed.), *Television and education* (pp. 62–88). Thousand Oaks, CA: Sage.

Pittinsky, T. L. (2010). A two-dimensional model of intergroup leadership: The case of national diversity. *American Psychologist, 65*(3), 194–200.

Rachlinski, J. J., & Parks, G. S. (2010). Implicit bias, Election '08, and the myth of a post-racial America. *Cornell Law Faculty Publications, 178.* Retrieved from http://scholarship.law.cornell.edu/facpub/178

Roberson, Q. M. (2006). Disentangling the meanings of diversity and inclusion in organizations. *Group and Organization Management, 31*(2), 212–236. doi: 10.1177/1059601104273064

Rowe, M. P. (1990). Barriers to equality: The power of subtle discrimination to maintain unequal opportunity. *Employee Responsibilities and Rights Journal, 3*(2), 153–163.

Samuelson, R. J. (2010, June 7). Duped by success. *Washington Post,* p. A17.

Shen, J., Chanda, A., D'Netto, B. D., & Monga, M. (2009). Managing diversity through human resource management: An international perspective and conceptual framework. *International Journal of Human Resource Management, 20*(2), 235–251.

Shore, L. M., Randel, A. E., Chung, B. G., Dean, M. A., Ehrhart, K. H., & Singh, G. (2011). Inclusion and diversity in work groups: A review and model for future research. *Journal of Management, 37*(4), 1262–1289. doi:10.1177/0149206310385943

Siegel, M. (2011, April 21). Australia to review charges of sexism in its military. *New York Times,* p. A10.

Slater, S. F., Weigand, R. A., & Zwirlein, T. J. (2008). The business case for commitment to diversity. *Business Horizons, 51*(3), 201–209.

Snyder, L. A., Carmichael, J. S., Blackwell, L. V., Cleveland, J. N., & Thornton, G. C. III (2010). Perceptions of discrimination and justice among employees with disabilities. *Employee Responsibilities and Rights Journal, 22,* 5–19.

Society for Human Resource Management (SHRM). (2007). *State of Workplace Management Report.* Retrieved from http://www.shrm.org

Society for Human Resource Management (SHRM) (2010a). *Diversity.* Retrieved from http://www.shrm.org

Society for Human Resource Management (SHRM) (2010b). *Global diversity and inclusion: Perceptions, practices, and attitudes.* Retrieved from http://www.shrm.org

Sue, D. W. (2010). *Microaggressions in everyday life: Race, gender, and sexual orientation.* Hoboken, NJ: Wiley.

Sue, D. W., Capodilupo, C. M., & Holder, A.M.B. (2008). Racial microaggressions in the life experience of Black Americans. *Professional Psychology: Research and Practice, 39*(3), 329–336.

Sue, D. W., Capodilupo, C. M., Torino, G. C., Bucceri, J. M., Holder, A. M. B., Nadal, K. L., & Esquilin, M. (2007). Racial microaggressions in everyday life: Implications for clinical practice. *American Psychologist, 62*(4), 271–286.

Thomas, D. A. (2004). Diversity as strategy. *Harvard Business Review, 82*(9), 98–108.

Thomas, D. A., & Ely, R. J. (1996). Making differences matter: A new paradigm for managing diversity. *Harvard Business Review, 74*(5), 79–90.

Thomas, R. R., Jr. (1990). From affirmative action to affirming diversity. *Harvard Business Review, 68*(2), 107–117.

Thomas, R. R., Jr. (2010). *World class diversity management.* San Francisco: Berrett-Koehler.

Ulrich, D., & Brockbank, W. (2005). *The HR value proposition.* Boston, MA: Harvard Business School Press.

U.S. Equal Employment Opportunity Commission. (2010). *Charge statistics.* Retrieved from http://www.eeoc.gov/eeoc/statistics/ enforcement/charges.cfm

Weigand, R. A. (2007). Organizational diversity, profits and returns in U.S. firms. *Problems and Perspectives in Management, 5*(3), 69–85.

CHAPTER NINE

Inclusive Organization Development
An Integration of Two Disciplines
Allan H. Church, Christopher T. Rotolo,
Amanda C. Shull, and Michael D. Tuller

Introduction

Fundamentally, organization development (OD) is the implementation of a process of planned change for the purpose of organizational improvement (Waclawski & Church, 2002). From our perspective, OD reflects a normative or values-based approach to how organizations should function; it is grounded in the basics of social systems thinking, action learning, effective consulting and intervention skills, a well-rounded toolkit of tried and true practices and processes, and—perhaps most important—the integral use of data, feedback, or information obtained from employees at all levels to truly drive organizational transformation. While other OD practitioners may have entirely different definitions, and this has been heavily debated in the field (Church, 2001), for

Note. The authors would like to extend their thanks to Janine Waclawski for her input on the initial outline and for providing feedback on the manuscript for this chapter, Leslie Golay for her assistance in compiling the MayflowerGroup benchmark results, and Elona Pira and Jean McNulty of The Conference Board for their support in obtaining benchmark data from the Council of Talent Management Executives I and II.

the purposes of this chapter our approach to OD is a normative and data-driven one.

It is from this mindset that we approach the discussion of engaging in what could be called *inclusive organization development*—that is, the full integration of diversity and inclusion (D&I) messages, behaviors, practices, policies, and cultural indicators (that is, what we will collectively call the D&I perspective) into mainstream OD and related industrial-organizational (I-O) psychology-based efforts in organizations. While many HR organizations, such as the Conference Board and the Human Capital Institute, have fully embraced the D&I perspective and have regular conferences on the subject, this is not the case with many of the more specialized subdisciplines of HR-related practice. Although OD, D&I, and I-O as fields blossomed together culturally (at least in the United States) at essentially the same time during the 1960s, and in many ways they have very similar normative goals at their core (such as striving to create multicultural and inclusive organizations that value diversity and empowerment), they have as yet to fully integrate with each other in organizational practice. From an applied I-O psychology perspective, the only book to really focus on this area was Jackson and Associates (1992), in which the emphasis was primarily on diversity in the workplace, and D&I has only recently begun to enter into the lexicon of I-O conferences and general I-O related textbooks (for example, Levy, 2010). Although there have been texts dedicated to the construct of diversity, application and integration with specific areas of I-O-related practice has been lacking. The *American Psychologist* did run a special issue on diversity and leadership recently (Chin, 2010), but this is really only scratching the surface for applied organizational psychologists.

From an OD perspective, more progress has been made. Although many of the great "classic" texts of OD (for example, Burke, 1982; Cummings & Worley, 1993; French & Bell, 1990; Katz & Kahn, 1978; Schein, 1985) make no substantive mention whatsoever of any concepts related to D&I, in more recent editions the concepts have started to emerge in the subject index (for example, Cummings & Worley, 2009; McLean, 2006). However, we would argue that this still remains an area gravely lacking in focus in many texts. There have certainly been pockets of highly integrated activity among OD, HR, and D&I, including the work of Jackson and Hardiman (1994), with what they call multicultural organization development (MCOD); that of Holvino, Ferdman, and Merrill-Sands (2004) from a change management framework; that of others in business school contexts (for example, Kanter, 1977; Thomas & Gabarro, 1999); and some very interesting and personal articles published in the *OD Practitioner*, including a special issue in the spring of 2010 (Royal & Vogelsang, 2010). However, for the average OD professional, exposure to D&I-related concepts is likely limited.

Yet when we step back and think about the fundamental nature of a D&I change agenda—which many corporations clearly have taken on over the past decade, given shifting demographic trends and changes in generational differences, technology, and the global workforce (see Hankin, 2005; Karoly & Panis, 2004; Michaels, Handfield-Jones, & Axelrod, 2001; Zemke, Raines, & Filipczak, 2000)—we have to stop and wonder (1) what is the most effective means for practicing inclusive OD, and (2) what might some of the challenges or barriers be to such a seemingly natural integration of two fields that were both in some ways outgrowths of the progressive humanistic and social justice movements of the 1960s (for example, Brazzel, 2007; Jackson & Hardiman, 1994)? Our collective experience with organizational change efforts in general and specifically with the D&I agenda at PepsiCo and other organizations over the last decade indicates to us that practicing inclusive OD means applying a diverse and inclusive mindset and framework to every core HR, I-O, or OD process we are developing and deploying. In short, we believe that the only way to truly drive D&I as a transformational change effort is to fully integrate it into every aspect of one's assessment and development efforts. It should not be a standalone change effort nor perceived by employees as one (Holvino et al., 2004), but rather incorporated into all aspects of the organization to ensure a truly sustainable transformation to achieve a diverse and inclusive culture.

The Inclusive OD Paradox

As reviewed extensively elsewhere (for example, Church, 2001; Waclawski & Church, 2002), there are almost as many definitions

INCLUSIVE ORGANIZATION DEVELOPMENT

of the field of OD as there are individual practitioners, and unlike in other professions, such as medicine or law, anyone with any type of background or training can decide to call him- or herself an OD practitioner and begin doing OD work. While this has led some practitioners to call for changes in the field to ensure consistency of competency and approach, such as more accreditation or certifications, at its core OD remains reflective of one of its basic founding values: by its very nature it is an *inclusive field*. As a construct, inclusion involves being open to a variety of ideas and approaches; the toolkit of the OD practitioner certainly reflects that diversity of practice, background, and approach. That said, and as already noted, OD as a field has not entirely or overwhelmingly embraced the concept of creating a diverse and inclusive environment for others.

In fact, in a comprehensive OD values study conducted in the 1990s (Church, Burke, & Van Eynde, 1994) "diversifying the workplace" ranked eighteenth out of nineteen items in the humanistic factor dimension, and promoting business effectiveness as a factor overall was ranked higher as a general cluster of items. Although we suspect that those rankings might be very different today among practitioners, that result clearly indicates the inherent disconnect between OD as it approaches its own practice and professional membership criteria and what practitioners value regarding the methods and models they use in organizations. This does not mean that OD professionals do not seek diversity of thought and opinion in their data collection efforts during interventions—far from it—but their ultimate goal is seldom tethered to driving an inclusive environment (unless that is the expressed requirement from the client). Clearly this needs to change, and we hope that this chapter will prove useful to practitioners in driving more inclusive OD (and I-O related) interventions.

The purpose of this chapter, then, is to focus on how best to identify and use some of the key tools and processes available to the OD (and I-O) practitioner and on how to ensure that these integrate with and reinforce the overall D&I perspective at the broadest level. Although there are many areas and aspects of organizations on which we could focus (for example, the Burke-Litwin model, 1992, has twelve distinct dimensions), we decided to narrow the scope of this discussion to four key data-driven OD processes that most organizations have in place today in some form or fashion:

- Organization or employee surveys
- 360-degree feedback
- Performance management
- Talent management

Although corporate mission and values statements are critically important, as are training efforts and selection programs, here we emphasize OD interventions and processes that collect data and deliver feedback to drive change—particularly in light of (1) our contention that these are the most powerful tools for ensuring transformation and (2) our belief that shifting an organization's culture to one that is more inclusive requires a systems approach that is mutually reinforcing across multiple types of measurement, reward, and decision-making processes.

In each section we begin by describing the OD process itself and why it is important for driving change; we then provide recent benchmark data from two different sources regarding the current levels of integration between D&I and OD efforts among Fortune 500 companies; and finally, we explore the integration and evolution of the D&I agenda in these four core people processes as implemented at PepsiCo, a multinational consumer products organization with a long history of highly effective D&I efforts. We then discuss some important observations and challenges associated with practicing inclusive OD effectively.

Integrating Diversity and Inclusion into Key Organization Development Processes

Based on our experience, the organizational survey is one of the most powerful tools of the OD practitioner. Although recent articles (for example, Hansen, 2010) have questioned the movement toward what some would consider the softer aspects, such as the internal measurement of employee engagement as it relates to the construct of D&I efforts, rather than focusing solely on the hard metrics of diversity, we believe this is an important evolution.

We begin this section with a discussion of survey programs and then move into the related data-driven OD methods of 360-degree feedback, performance management, and talent management.

D&I and Organizational or Employee Surveys

Employee surveys began in industry primarily as static attitudinal and opinion-based measures (for example, focused on job satisfaction). However, over the last twenty to thirty years they have evolved into a far more strategic tool for OD practitioners that, when executed correctly, can produce highly actionable and meaningful diagnostic and predictive analytics (Kraut, 2006). Some of the content areas to which employee surveys have been applied over the years include turnover, likelihood of local unionization efforts, potential for health and safety violations, action planning effectiveness, sales, counterproductive work behavior, confidence in strategic direction, process efficiency, manager quality, and bottom-line outcome measures (for example, Church & Waclawski, 2001; Schiemann & Morgan, 2006; Wiley, 2010). Employee surveys have become such a mainstay in the OD practitioner's toolkit that it is hard to imagine an OD intervention without some type of survey involved. This is largely because organizational surveys are one of the best methods for (1) communicating key messages to all employees involved (in those cases in which the questions asked are a clear indication of what is important to management), and (2) measuring the attitudes, opinions, and behaviors of employees both initially at the start of a large scale change effort as well as over time. As a tool for organizational change, the key is the use of the survey data to create meaningful change for the organization by asking the right questions (relative to the change one is trying to drive) and then doing something with the responses. Prior research, for example, has shown that just sharing survey data with employees but taking no action as a result yields the same lower levels of satisfaction over time as doing nothing at all (Church & Oliver, 2006). Taking action against priorities is the key to a successful OD survey-related intervention.

This is why using an organizational survey program to drive culture change in the area of D&I (and particularly the inclusive culture component) is so vital for practitioners. Although for years many organizations have been analyzing their standard survey by comparing results across different groups (such as women of color, men of color, White women, White men) to look for trends, this approach does not leverage the power of an organizational survey for driving an inclusive culture change. Rather, integrating items that specifically address D&I-related aspects of management, organizational culture, training and development processes, senior leadership behaviors, and the like into a standard core organizational survey sends a clear and significant message regarding the importance of the D&I agenda.

Many companies today are following this approach (which was not the case just ten years ago). For example, a recent benchmark study conducted for the MayflowerGroup (a survey consortium) found that 89 percent of member companies responding had integrated *specific* D&I related questions into their primary employee surveys (that is, where the terms diversity and/or inclusion were used in the item wording itself). Although the overall number of items needed might not be that large (for example, this benchmark indicated an average 3.6 items or about 6 percent of the total questions asked), it still demonstrates to employees how management views the importance of diversity and inclusion. A similar benchmark study of The Conference Board's Council of Talent Management Executives (I & II) yielded somewhat lower percentages, at 52 percent of companies with integrated D&I items, but the average number of items was slightly higher, at 4.2 or 7 percent overall (for details regarding these benchmark studies, contact the MayflowerGroup and The Conference Board).

In contrast to this more integrated approach, some companies have elected to develop and administer a special survey focused solely on D&I issues. Although this results in more data (because the survey is entirely D&I-related), our recommendation is to ultimately fully integrate that content into the core employee survey programs so that the D&I agenda does not appear to stand on its own. This also makes it more likely that the D&I content will be sustainable; this is less likely when there two separate survey efforts must be managed over time (which can increase administration and response burden).

The PepsiCo Organizational Health Survey D&I Journey

PepsiCo's global employee survey, called the *Organizational Health Survey* (OHS), is conducted every other year and is administered to all of the organization's three hundred thousand plus employees worldwide. It focuses on employee engagement and the drivers of engagement, capturing attitudes about the company, job and career, compensation and benefits, customer orientation, manager quality, and the work environment. Translated into over forty languages, the OHS survey has become a vital mechanism for driving change throughout the organization.

As the company has transformed the strategy and execution of its D&I initiatives, so too has the OHS evolved over time to support this agenda. Although surveying at PepsiCo was commonplace within each respective business, it wasn't until the 1990s that a consistent enterprise-wide survey program was administered. Initial OHS administrations dedicated little attention in the survey to D&I-specific efforts, other than the usual analyses by demographic groups as noted earlier, as the company was going through tremendous change involving divestitures and acquisitions (Thomas & Creary, 2009). However, by the mid- to late 1990s, the D&I journey was beginning to take shape, and by 2000, with Steve Reinemund as the new CEO and highly visible champion of the D&I agenda, the company began to undergo significant change with regard to how it defined, measured, celebrated, and cultivated diversity and inclusion.

After the results from the more generic 2000 OHS were published, senior leaders realized that the data from the survey did not reflect what they were seeing and hearing from employees, albeit anecdotally. PepsiCo's Ethnic Advisory Board, a group of leaders from both within and outside the company tasked with providing guidance on D&I matters, suggested that PepsiCo conduct a more focused research effort rather than wait for the limited information provided by the current OHS. A series of focus groups and interviews was launched to determine the major issues and barriers toward becoming a more inclusive culture. The output of this research led to a unique sixty-item Inclusion Survey designed specifically to gain a deeper understanding of existing practices, attitudes, and opinions regarding the current state of D&I efforts across the company. What was so unique about this survey at the time was that very few, if any, organizations had embarked on such a highly focused survey program on diversity and inclusion. Exhibit 9.1 provides examples of the questions included in this initial survey.

Exhibit 9.1. Sample Items from the 2001 Diversity and Inclusion Survey at PepsiCo

- A business case for focusing on diversity has been communicated to me.
- I receive regular and consistent messages about the diversity initiatives being implemented in the company.
- I have available to me communication channels where I can openly talk about my diversity related issues and concerns.
- The leaders of this company inspire me to embrace the notion of inclusion.
- I am comfortable with the idea of being managed by someone who's different from me—physically, socially or culturally.
- Everyone in this company is encouraged to develop greater cultural awareness.
- I can bring all of myself into this organization—it's a place for me to grow and develop without being unfairly judged by others.
- My manager is held accountable in his/her performance review for creating an inclusive work environment.
- My manager has the cultural competence (knowledge and skills) to effectively manage a diverse team or workgroup.
- This company's commitment to diversity and inclusion are compelling reasons for me to continue working here.

The Inclusion Survey, which was administered to all domestic exempt (that is, salaried) PepsiCo employees in 2001, was intended to provide a baseline regarding the evolution of the D&I agenda for the organization and could be used to identify "hotspots" that needed to be addressed through targeted action plans in 2002 and beyond. Perhaps more important (and as noted earlier), at the time administering such a survey was also intended to communicate to employees PepsiCo's commitment to developing a more inclusive culture.

Although conducting such a targeted survey was seen by some as a potential risk (for example, the mere act of gathering this information would clearly raise expectations in the eyes of employees to do something with the data), there was sufficient energy and support from senior leadership to move ahead with the project regardless of the outcome. In the end, the learnings from the Inclusion Survey results were immense. The insights derived from the analyses led to several vital actions. First, the 2002 OHS was redesigned to fully integrate the items into the core survey going forward. Second, a new corporate-sponsored multitiered training and D&I development curriculum was developed and launched. Third, in 2003 and again in 2005, quarterly inclusion pulse surveys were administered, focusing on the impact of the company's D&I training agenda and serving as both a Level 2 and 3 training evaluation (Kirkpatrick & Kirkpatrick, 2006) and a means to track progress on the numerous initiatives taking place in the organization. Finally, the D&I messages and content began to be integrated into other core HR development processes as well (there is more on these later in the chapter).

From a survey perspective, the redesigned OHS in 2002 included many more items devoted to D&I than in the past. Questions covered company leadership, culture, career, and manager quality (see Table 9.1 for more examples of the OHS D&I-related items). This allowed senior leaders to better understand the pervasiveness of the issues uncovered in the focus groups and the Inclusion Survey, and allowed the company to track progress regarding its cultural change efforts over time. Many of these same items remain in PepsiCo's ongoing OHS program.

The inclusion pulse surveys, punctuated by the biennial OHS, enabled PepsiCo to track the implementation of the inclusion training as well as to monitor the impact that the initiatives were having on the organization. For example, the item "Since PepsiCo has implemented the Inclusion Training, I have seen improvements in our culture—it is more inclusive than before" gained thirty-nine points over the three years it was tracked. Similarly, the pulse survey item "I receive regular and consistent messages about the diversity initiatives being

Table 9.1. A Sample of Diversity and Inclusion Items Used in PepsiCo's Organizational Health Survey from 2002 to Present

Leadership
- Senior management (your senior leadership team) has taken ownership for the company's diversity and inclusion initiatives.
- I see diversity reflected in the management of this company.

Culture
- Since PepsiCo has implemented the Inclusion Training, I have seen improvements in our culture—it is more inclusive than before.
- I believe we will have a competitive advantage with a more diverse workforce.
- My work group has a climate in which diverse perspectives are valued.
- I am aware of my company's diversity/inclusion initiatives.
- I am comfortable being in this company, even when I am seen as different in some way.
- Win with diversity and inclusion (Values Item).

Career
- There is an equal opportunity for people to have a successful career at my company, regardless of their differences or background.
- Promotions and assignments at my company are based on a fair and objective assessment of people's skills and performance.
- Career advancement opportunities (for example, vacancies, promotions, project teams, etc.) within the organization are clearly communicated to all employees.

Manager
- My manager recognizes diversity as a business imperative and takes specific actions to drive it.
- My manager values people with different perspectives and experiences.
- My manager or supervisor treats me with respect.
- My manager supports and encourages my involvement in diversity- and/or inclusion-related activities.

implemented in the company" gained over fourteen points in the same time period.

The D&I journey was challenging and often met with resistance, as Thomas and Creary (2009) describe in their Harvard Business School case on the change effort. Yet PepsiCo met many of its D&I goals. The OHS was a vital tool in this transformation, as both a means to track progress and provide scorecard information as well as a platform for communicating the importance of D&I in everything the company did.

OHS Today and Beyond

Today, the biennial OHS is still a vital part of organization change at PepsiCo. The pulse inclusion survey, however, has been replaced by a twenty-five-item Engagement Survey that measures the company's engagement index as well as key items known to drive engagement. Although D&I is still a key area in the Engagement Survey, many of the items on the pulse survey no longer pertain (for example, the initial phases I, II and III of Inclusion training were completed in 2008 and remain in maintenance mode primarily for new employees), or are no longer actionable because they consistently obtained a 95 percent favorable or higher response (for example, those items regarding the importance of the business case for D&I). In short, the company decided it no longer needed to measure some of the basics of the construct of D&I.

That said, the OHS remains heavily focused on D&I from a cultural perspective, which is where the company's overall strategy has shifted, particularly with respect to the notion of Talent Sustainability (PepsiCo Inc., 2011). Professional employees taking the 2011 OHS encountered about 11 percent of the total OHS items dedicated to D&I topics (this is not including the many follow-up questions that are asked if the respondent answers neutrally or unfavorably).

In addition to item content, there are two other ways in which PepsiCo is leveraging OHS to aid in the D&I journey. One is its data analytics. Typically, an insights presentation of one hundred pages or more is created for each ethnic group (analyzed within group and by gender), providing a deep dive into issues specific to the particular subgroup. Within these reports (as well as the main overall report), the company uses various statistical analyses to illuminate the relationships between items. For example, we have found that the item "My manager supports and encourages my involvement in diversity and/or inclusion related activities" has a strong positive relationship with almost every other item on the survey. More specifically, employees who answer favorably to this item are also more likely to give favorable ratings in the other areas measured by the OHS. Conversely, employees who are less than favorable on the item are less favorable on the other areas as well. This strong relationship indicates to us how the success of diversity and inclusion initiatives is often predicated on direct and meaningful support from managers and supervisors. This finding has also proven invaluable to other organizations when benchmarking with customers and other business partners in support of their developing or ongoing D&I efforts. Finally, it sends a powerful message to senior leaders and managers about the importance of support for employees in engaging in the D&I agenda.

The second area in which PepsiCo leverages the OHS beyond the typical question set is in the use of Employee Value Propositions or EVPs (Barrow & Mosley, 2005). Although part of OHS, the EVPs do not assess attitudes per se, but rather the relative importance of certain aspects of work based on employee rankings. Employees are asked to examine a list of twenty-three value propositions (such as a relaxed and fun atmosphere, job security, corporate social responsibility) and answer questions about which are most and least important to them. The organization then calculates a score for each EVP (the probability of being in the "most important" list). These scores can then be used for employee segmentation to identify pockets of individuals who share the same value propositions. Where this is helpful, for example, is in understanding differences in perceived importance of various facets of the EVP by different subgroups of employees (such as people of color, females, generational cohorts, and so on). In other words, whereas the main OHS items help us understand *where* employees believe the company is doing well versus not so well, the EVPs allow us to quantitatively get beneath these numbers by examining *what's important* to the individuals providing the ratings. For example, if a group of Latino executives is unfavorable toward items about career orientation, we might find through the EVP analysis that some are more interested in the pay that goes along with the advancement, whereas others are more interested in the power and influence associated with it. Action planning around these two subgroups might be completely different based on this insight.

It should be clear by now that overall there has been a symbiotic relationship between OHS and the D&I agenda at PepsiCo for the last decade. In general, the OHS survey program continues to innovate so that it remains the main vehicle for driving organization change.

D&I and 360-Degree Feedback

Although surveys are extremely important tools, not every individual manager can expect to receive a report, nor are their individual behaviors assessed via this method. This is where multisource or 360-degree feedback plays an important part in the OD and D&I change process. Tools such as 360-degree feedback are the primary means by which organizations tie their corporate values and key competencies to individual behaviors of leaders and managers (Bracken, Timmreck, & Church, 2001), usually via some type of formal leadership model or framework.

The process is similar to a survey program, but the focal target is an individual rather than a group or business unit. One of the strengths of a 360-degree feedback process is that it provides a robust behavioral assessment gathered from a number of different sources with various perspectives on behaviors associated with a given leadership model. The key assumption of 360-degree feedback from an OD perspective is that feedback from multiple sources will enhance self-awareness, which in turn will lead to a change in specific behaviors relative to what is being measured. Research (for example, Church, 1997) has shown that managers with higher self-awareness of what is being measured tend to be better performers. This is where the content of the competency model that forms the basis of a 360-degree feedback program becomes critical, however, because if diversity and inclusion (that is, inclusive behaviors and competencies) are not integrated into the 360-degree feedback process, then they are essentially set apart from what is considered "effective leadership" for a given organization. This disconnect can send an unintended message to employees that leadership means one thing and inclusive behaviors are something else. Moreover, although D&I items may or may not necessarily be determined through statistical analysis to be predictors of specific performance outcomes of interest today, from an OD normative perspective and based on current and future trends in the workplace (for example, Meister & Willyerd, 2010), we believe that D&I-related behaviors should be part of any formal feedback program. Whether real or aspirational in nature, if diversity and inclusion are important to an organization's business and/or people development strategy they should be part of the formal leadership competency model and the subsequent 360-degree feedback process.

In the MayflowerGroup benchmark study noted earlier, about 52 percent of companies responding had currently incorporated specific D&I competencies into their leadership frameworks, and 68 percent of the Conference Board's Council of Talent Management Executives (I & II) reported doing the same. In both studies, many companies indicated that they were heading in this direction but had not yet achieved the goal. It is important to remember that it takes significant time and resources to change something as fundamental to an organization as its leadership competency model. Surveys are far easier to modify within a given year or two than leadership models because the latter tend to become very integrated into other elements of a broader leadership development program (for example, career resources, toolkits, training programs, interview guides, and talent management processes).

However, it is also important to note that simply collecting behavioral information about someone does not necessarily lead to successful change (regardless of the intent of that change). Although it communicates, just as a survey does, what is important to management, from an OD perspective there are several other factors to consider in terms of ensuring that a 360-degree feedback program provides the maximum value to an organization.

First, the feedback itself is critical. Individuals need to be informed about their strengths and development opportunities to understand how to improve their performance in a manner that is easily interpreted and understood. This means that feedback should be provided in a format that increases the individual's ability to interpret and accept it despite potential negative elements. It is also helpful if the feedback is organized around a core set of competencies or key attributes. In the context of driving a D&I agenda, for example, it is far more meaningful and impactful to recipients if the feedback is provided against "creating an inclusive culture" rather than just a generic *inclusion* dimension (that is, a single average score), or rather than just providing a handful of items that combine into some broader concept, such as interpersonal skills or emotional intelligence. The targeted nature of having a specific D&I competency greatly reinforces the importance of that dimension. In contrast, *not* having D&I-specific competencies highlighted in a leadership model or 360-degree feedback process may communicate the message that these practices are not all that important.

Second, when driving a D&I agenda in particular (or any focused organizational change effort more generally), it is far better to have a customized leadership model than one supplied from a feedback vendor as the basis for the 360-degree feedback process. Although off-the-shelf competency assessments can add value at the individual level, the most constructive and valid 360-degree feedback tools for driving D&I-related change are based on an organization-specific leadership model and reflect the unique values and competencies of that model rather than generic leadership behaviors, for several reasons. First, the model itself, like a survey, communicates what is important and is typically connected to and/or embedded in many different development processes beyond the 360-degree feedback process alone. Second, the diagnostic assessment of a behavior gives it significance, because by linking specific behavioral assessments back to corporate values creates individual accountability and reinforcement for positive performance against those stated ideals. Moreover, when implementing a large-scale 360-degree feedback program involving thousands of leaders and managers, the implementation must be considered from an OD systems perspective, because one is now operating at the meso or even macro levels of the organization to drive behavior change (Church, Walker, & Brockner, 2002).

D&I and 360-Degree Feedback at PepsiCo. The effort to include D&I behaviors as part of PepsiCo's 360-degree feedback process has significantly evolved over time in two primary ways to reflect the increased organizational emphasis on diversity and inclusion. The first change focused on the emphasis or weight placed on D&I behaviors relative to the overall assessment framework. The leadership model in place in the 1990s did not include any specific behaviors related to D&I efforts; rather, the items were more generic and focused on building trusting relationships and related concepts. This changed in 2001, when the organization redesigned the model, included three specific items related to D&I, and added *Inclusion* as one of seventeen key competencies of leadership behavior under one of seven Success Factors called *People Development.* Although this was a positive first step, it still placed only marginal emphasis on diversity and inclusion relative to the overall model, which comprised fifty-eight items (that is, only 5 percent focused on D&I).

This changed further in 2006, when the model was redesigned again (using input collected from interviews and focus groups conducted with multiple stakeholders throughout the organization, from senior leaders to individual contributors and including a wide range of subject-matter experts or SMEs) to better align to PepsiCo's newly stated corporate values and the increasing laser-like focus on the D&I agenda. This new Leadership and Individual Effectiveness Model now included "Creating an Inclusive Culture" as one of its nine key dimensions rather than one of seventeen. In addition, the increased emphasis on D&I both in the leadership model and the subsequent 360-degree feedback process was also reflected in the greater representation of items designed to assess D&I related behaviors. The new version of the model included eleven key D&I behaviors (see Table 9.2) under the heading of "Creating an Inclusive Culture" dimension. These behaviors reflect what is expected in this area of all employees, leaders (that is, middle management), and senior leaders.

Table 9.2. "Creating an Inclusive Culture" Items from PepsiCo's Leadership and Individual Effectiveness Model, by Level

All Employees
- Treats all people with respect and fairness
- Demonstrates sensitivity to differences when dealing with people from different cultural backgrounds and/or other differences
- Demonstrates openness to and respect for others' opinions and points of view

Leaders
- Demonstrates a personal commitment to creating a more inclusive work environment
- Values and leverages people with different perspectives and experiences
- Creates a work environment that helps people achieve a healthy balance between work and personal life
- Fosters a positive and inclusive work environment where all people feel respected and valued for their contributions

Senior Leaders
- Champions diversity of thought, style, and perspective
- Demonstrates sensitivity and awareness of cross-cultural implications when conducting business or executing initiatives
- Creates a work environment that helps people achieve a healthy balance between work and personal life
- Fosters a positive and inclusive work environment where all people feel respected and valued for their contributions

The second area of change in PepsiCo's approach to linking D&I to its leadership model and 360-degree feedback process was also related to the newly revised model in 2006 and centered around the importance and level of integration of the D&I perspective for all employees. Although inclusion was incorporated into the 2001 model, the primary target audience for this framework was executives, which suggested that D&I-related behaviors might not be as relevant for a majority of the organization. This changed with the 2006 redesign, when the model was recast as not only a leadership model but also as a "Leadership &

Individual Effectiveness Model." Now there was a set of D&I-specific behaviors that applied to all employees at all levels, in addition to those for more senior-level executives.

D&I and Performance Management

Although 360-degree feedback is a valuable OD tool for individual development and broad scale culture change, there is considerable debate in the field as to whether it should be used for development only or for other administrative purposes. While some organizations use 360-degree feedback as an input into succession planning and even performance management, others prefer to keep the 360-degree feedback as an independent process, leaving accountability for changing behavior up to the individual's own interest in self-awareness and development—a characteristic that can vary considerably among different types of people (see, for example, Church & Rotolo, 2010). This is why many models of organizational change and OD practitioners who apply them have long placed an emphasis on reward systems in a given intervention or social system (see, for example, Burke, 1982; Cummings & Worley, 2009; Lawler, 1981, 1990); doing this is a way to ensure that the right behaviors—and of more importance, in many cases the *outcomes*—are being measured and rewarded appropriately against some key set of objectives or competencies. Although we assume that the "right" behaviors will indeed lead to the desired outcomes, this may not always be the case and requires validation. Consequently, in many organizational settings it is important to ensure that the performance management process is influencing both behavior *and* outcome.

In general, an organization's reward systems (also known as the performance management process or PMP) are vital in defining and shaping its culture, because they convey what is important to employees and their performance against critical organizational goals. Performance management processes are by definition tied to compensation and internal movement decisions. This increases the need and desire for the process to effectively differentiate among various levels of performance. This is true both in terms of dividing a finite number of resources in the most equitable manner and also for helping employees understand what is important for success in their roles. Clearly, then, it is critical from a D&I perspective to include some form of formal diversity or inclusion objective or goal (or one of each) as part of performance management, if the transformation is to be truly effective.

Despite the value of the PMP in making administrative decisions, it is an OD and HR process that is, unfortunately, less focused on emphasizing diversity and inclusion efforts than perhaps it should be. In the recent MayflowerGroup benchmark study, about 59 percent of member organizations responding indicated using formal D&I metrics in their PMPs. Similarly, 61 percent of The Conference Board's Council of Talent Management Executives (I & II) reported the same, suggesting that 39 percent are not leveraging their PMP at all to support their D&I efforts.

Interestingly, the approach to using D&I measures also varied considerably across the two studies, ranging from focusing on individual metrics regarding representation goals relative to U.S. Census Bureau statistics, to incorporating organizational survey results as goals reflective of having an inclusive culture. Other companies were more activity-based in their approach, citing leadership involvement in employee networks or resource groups as their primary method of measurement. Moreover, in many instances it was evident that D&I goals were only a portion of a broader set of performance targets and often included in the "how" category of work gets done versus the actual outcomes being measured.

D&I and PMP at PepsiCo. In many ways PepsiCo's approach to PMP has evolved in a similar manner and is very reflective of the benchmark data just reported. In general, the company's current version of PMP, a version of which was first implemented in 2001 (also in support of the enhanced focus in the D&I agenda), has the common theme of increased emphasis being placed on diversity and inclusion over time. PepsiCo's previous conceptualization of PMP in the late 1990s used a single assessment of performance, based solely on business outcomes, and did not include any assessment of D&I in the evaluation of performance. In 2001, the PMP was divided into two separate categories—business ratings and people ratings—with business objectives weighted more heavily and accounting for 67 percent of the overall evaluation. The people objectives included "creating an inclusive environment" as a specific component, but represented only one of eight possible elements in the overall people ratings (and all were provided initially as suggestions rather than requirements). Over time, the use of people ratings required the need for a more streamlined and defined process for the people objectives. There was also organizational pressure (given the stated values and the increasing emphasis on diversity and inclusion) to enhance the value of people objectives relative to the business objectives. This led to another change in the PMP in 2008, which truly reflected a cultural shift in emphasis, to weight the two categories equally in a noncompensatory design, such that both now represented 50 percent of an employee's individual performance contribution.

Moreover, to ensure further consistency and integrate diversity and inclusion deeper into the process, another change included greater emphasis on D&I initiatives in the people objectives. "Creating an inclusive environment" became one of four areas of accountability that all employees using this PMP were required to address on an annual basis in their objectives. This change in the PepsiCo process increased the accountability and value associated with D&I efforts in the performance evaluation and no doubt contributed to the OHS scores reported earlier regarding manager support for employees engaging in D&I-related activities (as these were now on managers' individual objectives). In addition, the OHS data collected in 2009 indicated that employees had a favorable impression of the performance management process, with 80 percent of employees reporting that managers are held accountable for both their business and people ratings. This strongly suggests that employees see people ratings, and therefore the company's D&I efforts, as measures to which managers are truly held accountable. It also highlights the importance of taking an OD systems perspective with these data-driven tools, whereby the organization links the survey work to its leadership development and performance management agendas—all in synch to support organizational transformation.

Talent Management

The final OD and HR process we discuss—how an organization approaches talent management—is critical to consider in terms of organizational change initiatives and their linkage to D&I efforts. Performance evaluations are critical to understanding the strengths and weaknesses of individual employees; talent management, in contrast, is the process of identifying, assessing, developing, planning, and moving talent throughout the entire employee lifecycle to satisfy critical and strategic business objectives. Although many aspects of talent management as we know it today have been part of the OD and I-O practitioner's toolkit for years (such as succession planning, workplace assessment, selection, development, and an emphasis on learning through experiences), only in recent years has the term *talent management* taken hold (see, for example, Silzer & Dowell, 2010), largely in response to the evident war for talent and other ongoing changes in the demographics of the workplace, including the values that the next generation of employees are perceived to have (Avedon & Scholes, 2010).

Although some might argue that talent management is outside the purview of the OD practitioner (rather, residing with HR generalists or other types of specialists), we contend (as would Jackson & Hardiman, 1994) that it is indeed or should be part of the systems approach for driving organizational change, particularly with respect to enhancing diversity and inclusion. This is because, at its core, talent management uses workforce planning and analytics to identify potential talent gaps, which are addressed through (1) internal development or external hiring and (2) the manner and method with which talent—whether internal or external—is discussed, reviewed, planned for, and ultimately deployed in an organization. Most talent management processes involve some form of organizational review of the current and future capabilities needed, an analysis of the current talent base, a review of what is called a "slate" of potential candidates for given roles (open now or in the future), and reviews and plans for unique individuals that will ultimately build leadership bench and succession pipelines for the organization (for example, Silzer & Dowell, 2010).

If the D&I agenda is not inextricably linked to the talent management review process, it is possible (depending on the culture of the organization, for example) that decisions will be made about capabilities that may reflect future needs of the business, and that specific groups or types of employees may not be reviewed because of inherent biases or blind spots. Thomas and Gabarro's (1999) research clearly indicated that different groups may indeed take different paths in the succession process, and therefore it is critical to keep an emphasis on diversity and inclusion throughout the entire talent management process.

The role of D&I in the talent management process can be conceptualized in two ways. First, organizations can use an individual's degree of D&I capability when making decisions related to talent management, such as providing developmental opportunities, creating slates, or deciding on promotions. The basic argument is that managers who are better at managing in an inclusive manner will be more effective overall. Doing this relies heavily on D&I-related measures and the other OD tools and processes discussed in this chapter (surveys, 360-degree feedback results, performance management ratings), so these need to be in place and working properly for this approach to be effective.

The second role of D&I in talent management is the targeted measurement and tracking of various groups of employees' progression in the organization relative to others. This is critical for two purposes. First, legal considerations based on concerns of adverse impact related to the OD and HR tools or to selection decisions need to be addressed to avoid litigation from protected groups (Cascio & Aguinis, 2008). Second, demographic differences are associated with diversity in experience, knowledge, and abilities that can be critical in creating an adaptive organization that can respond to the needs of a more diverse customer and consumer base. Enhancing the diversity of perspectives, styles, and thinking—if managed effectively and in an inclusive environment—is likely to lead to greater innovation and business success.

Interestingly, the two benchmarking studies (cited earlier) differed somewhat in this regard; 59 percent of the companies responding on the MayflowerGroup study indicated that they incorporated D&I as an explicit part of their talent management process, whereas 82 percent of The Conference Board's Council of Talent Management Executives (I & II) indicated the same. This difference is probably due more than anything else to the fact that the MayflowerGroup is primarily a survey-based consortium, while the Conference Board benchmark is based on individuals who are particularly focused on the talent management process. The key points are that (1) many organizations are indeed integrating D&I efforts into their talent management processes, and (2) this is an important part of completing the systemic framework for integrating the D&I agenda into their OD and organizational transformational efforts.

D&I and Talent Management at PepsiCo. As with many organizations, diversity and inclusion is a critical component of PepsiCo's talent management process. Details of the organization's use of scorecards and the overall people planning process can be found in other published sources (for example, Church & Waclawski, 2010; Thomas & Creary, 2009) and need not be repeated here. It is important to note, however, that the organization has taken a truly integrated and systemic approach to driving inclusive OD across the enterprise, ensuring that the D&I perspective remains linked to each of its core development processes. This was not easy to accomplish, nor did it happen overnight, but it remains at the core of PepsiCo's strategic OD agenda: ensuring that the company has a diverse population and an inclusive culture to support their varied thinking and contributions.

The Challenges of Doing Inclusive Organization Development

Based on the discussion and benchmark data reported here, it is apparent that practitioners have made significant strides in the integration of D&I efforts into their core organization development toolkits (with organizational surveys and talent management being the most common processes). But there is still room to improve in this area as well. Although it might sound easy enough to simply add an inclusion dimension to a leadership model or to include some diversity metrics in a performance management process, many organizations and practitioners are only just starting on this journey. As noted earlier, aside from OD, other fields fully devoted to organizational change and improvement, such as I-O psychology, have only recently begun to embrace diversity and inclusion as a core construct at meetings and in publications. The reason for this is simple: organizational change is never quick or easy, and there are various challenges associated with moving any organization in a given direction, including toward creating a more inclusive culture.

Some of these challenges are part of any change effort; others are perhaps more unique to diversity and inclusion. More specifically, these include integrating D&I into everything we do, including core OD processes and business models (as described earlier—that is, doing inclusive OD); gaining true senior leadership and management support; educating people about D&I for one's specific organization; and, perhaps most important, helping people to think more broadly about diversity and inclusion beyond the standard U.S.-based demographic trends and groups. After all, from an international perspective, diversity and inclusion vary from country to country and even in some cases from region to region. Perhaps the only universal dimension of diversity is gender, but even that varies cross-culturally (Ferdman, 1999). Beyond that, each country outside of the United States must be examined for its unique aspects from a D&I standpoint (culture, class, caste, heritage, and so on). This requires a more global mindset than many practitioners have today and is reflective of what we consider new territory in practice as it relates to D&I. In any case, all of these factors must be addressed by OD practitioners to see successful integration of D&I initiatives into an organization. The rest of this section discusses several of these challenges in more detail, as well as ways in which the practitioner can move the figurative integration needle in the right direction toward an inclusive OD approach.

The Importance of Senior Leadership Support

Many OD professionals and change experts would agree that any transformational change effort requires senior leadership support to be successful. Some have even embedded this as a key component in their models (for example, Burke & Litwin, 1992; Kotter, 1996). Jack Welch's transformation of GE is a perfect example of this (Welch & Byrne, 2001). Driving an organizational change effort towards a D&I agenda is no exception, as in Jackson and Hardiman's (1994) model of MCOD. Clearly, fully integrating D&I into an organization's management and OD practices and processes is a type of true organizational transformation and requires visible senior leadership support.

A good example of senior leadership successfully leading a D&I change agenda (including the concept of shifting from a focus on just diversity to one on inclusion as well) is the former CEO of PepsiCo, Steve Reinemund. From the beginning of Reinemund's presence in PepsiCo's senior leadership team as president and chief operating officer, he ensured that diversity and inclusion were one of the company's primary strategic priorities (as is fully detailed in Thomas & Creary, 2009). Other senior leaders at PepsiCo had tried to make the workforce more inclusive by creating opportunities for diverse groups and developing leaders, but Reinemund was the first PepsiCo senior leader to make efforts to fully integrate D&I into the culture of the organization (Thomas & Creary, 2009). After being promoted to CEO of PepsiCo, one of the first things that he did was to partner with the senior vice presidents of HR and diversity and community affairs and to establish a team of advisors to support him in driving diversity into PepsiCo's culture and performance. Reinemund first added diversity as a business strategy to help stay ahead of shifting demographics in the U.S. markets in 2000. He believed that by seeking new opportunities in ethnic populations where the business had low market penetration, the company could become more competitive. He believed that, to create products and marketing strategies targeted to those populations, the company needed a diversified employee base that reflected its consumer base. PepsiCo formed a new ethnic marketing group in response to Reinemund's strategy.

In PepsiCo's results-oriented culture, Reinemund realized that measuring the progress of his diversity efforts was critical to the success of the overall strategy. He then held senior leaders accountable (through the performance management process noted previously) for achieving their diversity goals (Thomas & Creary, 2009). This is a perfect OD example of senior leadership truly supporting a change agenda, as it is easy to reward people when they meet a goal but much harder to enforce a negative outcome even if it has been communicated that this would occur.

After several years of driving this approach, Reinemund found that he had been successful in achieving his diversity strategy. There were new products and selling strategies for ethnic populations as well as a more diverse workforce at PepsiCo (reflected both in real numbers and in improved employee perceptions via the OHS measure). He realized, however, that he had not yet fully shifted the culture to be more inclusive and engaging of diverse populations. In short, if you just focus on the diversity of your workforce but not on ensuring that you have a culture that is supportive or inclusive of that diversity, it is unlikely that the diverse talent will remain long with the organization, as others have also noted (for example, Holvino et al., 2004). Thus he decided to move the company into a new phase of the D&I agenda by transforming the culture into both a results-oriented *and* an inclusive company (Thomas & Creary, 2009).

From an OD perspective, culturally transforming the company into a more diverse and inclusive one could not have occurred without Reinemund's commitment to the issue. Reinemund himself describes the type of senior leadership commitment that was necessary to accomplish the culture change: "For nearly all of the meetings I attended inside and outside of PepsiCo, I always spoke about diversity as one of the company's three priorities. I was intentional in this because I knew that affecting the culture would be more difficult if I did not deliver a consistent message" (quoted in Thomas & Creary, 2009, p. 10). Reinemund's successor, Indra Nooyi, has continued to drive a diverse and inclusive culture (see, for example, Frankel, 2008; Murray, 2011), and has further integrated the D&I agenda into her overall sustainability strategy (PepsiCo Inc., 2011). The key message here for OD practitioners already engaged in or planning to move toward a more focused D&I-related strategy is to ensure that the seniormost leaders are not only 100 percent behind the initiative, but that they are truly sponsors and advocates, not simply figureheads for that cause. Otherwise it simply will not ring true to people.

The Importance of Training in D&I Efforts

Although we have not discussed formal training and development efforts as a major OD lever for change (as from our perspective OD is a data-driven methodology, and training design and implementation are the purview of other types of HR professionals), it is important to note that training efforts are an important means for sending key messages, learning new behaviors, and reinforcing a change agenda. In short, training is a necessary component of any D&I change agenda, but not sufficient in and of itself. Given changes in technology over the last few years, training delivery methods can also vary widely compared with just a decade ago, when everything required a more resource-intensive face-to-face approach. For example, if funding for centralized training is not available, programs can be cascaded throughout the organization using train-the-trainer techniques (that is, building internally certified resources to deliver the training), or delivered via webinars, cell phone and hand-held device applications, virtual conference rooms, and the like.

Interestingly, from a D&I perspective, the most common type of diversity management program is indeed training (Jayne & Dipboye, 2004; Society for Human Resource Management, 2010), which may include efforts to increase awareness of discrimination and prejudice and to improve skills of employees in relating to members of other cultural groups. Diversity-related training programs have gained increased prominence over the years, yet there are still important issues to consider. According to a recent study by the Society for Human Resource Management (2010), 71 percent of organizations have some form of diversity-related training programs, but there was considerable variability between organizations regarding the areas of focus. For example, organizations differed in terms of who participated in diversity training. Based on that study, roughly 70 percent of executive- or managerial-level employees participated in mandatory diversity-related training, whereas only 58 percent of nonmanagerial employees participated in mandatory D&I-related training. From an OD and culture change perspective this is worrisome, because the majority of staff at any organization other than perhaps a professional services organization will be significantly more nonmanagerial employees than executives or managers. Supporting a culture change through a training agenda needs to reach all levels of employees to be truly effective and take hold.

In sum, although training can help people understand diversity and what it means to have an inclusive culture, it should not be considered the end solution in itself. Because the impact of the training may eventually wear off (particularly if it is not fully sustained over time as employees exit the organization and new ones enter), organizations should not treat training as a stand-alone solution to integrating diversity into a company's culture. Training can solve a necessary educational need, but in order for diversity and inclusion to be effectively integrated into an organization's culture, their importance must continue to be communicated from the senior leaders of the organization as a business priority and embedded into all OD core processes.

The Next Big Thing in D&I

Few would disagree with the statement that globalization has increased the complexity of understanding how organizations in general, and diversity and inclusion in particular, function across different parts of the world. Technological advances, the interconnectedness of global markets, adoption of new recruiting practices, and other changes have shifted the way people around the world interact with one another and will continue to do so in the future (Meister & Willyerd, 2010). Accordingly, OD practitioners will also need to change the ways they approach diversity and inclusion. This globalization is especially important for large multinational companies to consider. Societal culture is changing as well, and it is important that companies adapt to reflect the social environments in which they operate.

Similarly, D&I as a field is slowly moving away from an emphasis on primarily ethnic differences (such as counting members of different racial and gender groups) to more of an inclusive approach to viewing diverse cultures and ways of thinking in general (Hansen, 2010; Holvino et al., 2004). The focus has also shifted to support and reflect a more international perspective on D&I. This shift, however, requires that companies have what Plummer and Jordan (2007) refer to as "cultural competence" (also see Bennett, Chapter 5, this volume), or creating an environment in which diverse groups can learn from each other's differences and leverage those differences for business effectiveness. As a result of this shift in focus from racial or gender diversity to cultural diversity, D&I initiatives must be customized to fit the organizational culture and mission and strategy of each organization. Effective D&I programs must be adapted by OD practitioners to meet the needs of a global workforce.

We offer a few examples of HR and OD programs designed to meet the unique needs of an international employee population. Before executives leave for international assignments, for example, many companies often ask assignees to take preassignment cultural training programs so that they can better integrate with the host country's culture upon arrival. Some organizations are also expressing an interest in measuring how adept their employees are at adapting to and learning about other cultures. Assessments like the Hogan Personality Inventory (Hogan, Hogan, & Warrenfeltz, 2007) and the Prospector survey (Spreitzer, McCall, & Mahoney, 1997) include subscales on learning about other cultures. Spreitzer and colleagues (1997) found that managers who are better at adapting to change may display higher performance and more executive potential than those who do not adapt well to transitions. In addition, Plummer and Jordan (2007) describe a McKinsey study that characterized high-potential talent as including such key competencies as communicating across differences, practicing cross-cultural adaptability, and solving problems collaboratively, to name a few. The concept of learning ability also fits well here and has been incorporated into recent conceptualizations of high potentials (for example, Silzer & Church, 2009).

Upon reflection, two key points for the practitioner are clear: (1) individuals who are more culturally aware and focused on learning are more inclusive than others and may well make better leaders, and (2) the concept of inclusion is indeed broader than just a D&I functional agenda and represents one of the basic fundamentals of organization development and change. Clearly, this is an area in which OD practitioners can add value by incorporating cultural awareness and learning frameworks and measures into OD processes and practices in organizations. In addition, to advance the integration of D&I and OD in the future, practitioners need to pull diverse perspectives into their own work and look at broader cultural dynamics and issues than what traditional OD efforts might have addressed in the past. Some great work has been started in this area already through various outlets, including the *OD Practitioner* in particular, but the journey is far from over.

Conclusion

The purpose of this chapter has been to help OD and related practitioners think about the ways in which they can significantly influence the organizations with which they work (either internally or externally) to drive a more diverse and inclusive environment in everything they do, or, to put it another way, to practice Inclusive OD. We have discussed four key data-driven processes that currently exist in many organizations of any scale, the importance of each of those tools for driving cultural transformation, and some examples of how these have been applied and/or reapplied over the last decade at PepsiCo. Although there are many approaches to doing OD, we contend that data-based feedback tools and processes are the only true way to drive something as deep and systemic as a full-scale D&I agenda. We have also discussed some key challenges and observations related to achieving this integration between the two disciplines—an integration that seems entirely natural but has not yet occurred in many organizations, as shown by some of the benchmark data and anecdotes from colleagues.

The final point we would like to make is also a classic OD and D&I value or construct: the notion of the role of the self in driving an intervention or behaving inclusively toward others. Whether in the form of process consultation (for example, Schein, 1987, 1988) or from the perspective of having different diversity and inclusion lenses (for example, Williams, 2001), it is critical that OD practitioners engaged in this work consider their own identities and what they bring implicitly to diversity and inclusion. This might mean partnering with different types of practitioners to drive a particular change effort or becoming familiar with other perspectives, volunteering, or even getting in touch with one's own unique aspects (see, for example, the work of Bill Proudman on White males, 2001, 2008), but in the end it reflects back to the notion of learning. As OD professionals we need to continue to learn and embrace the D&I perspective, including how it applies across different groups, organizations, and cultures.

References

Avedon, M. J., & Scholes, G. (2010). Building competitive advantage through integrated talent management. In R. Silzer & B. E. Dowell (Eds.), *Strategy-driven talent management: A leadership imperative* (pp. 73–122). San Francisco: Jossey-Bass.

Barrow, S., & Mosely, R. (2005) *The employer brand: Bringing the best of brand management to people at work.* London: Wiley.

Bracken, D. W., Timmreck, C. W., & Church, A. H. (2001). *The handbook of multisource feedback.* San Francisco: Jossey-Bass.

Brazzel, M. (2007). Diversity and social justice practices for OD practitioners. *OD Practitioner, 39*(3), 15–21.

Burke, W. W. (1982). *Organization development: Principles and practices.* Glenview, IL: Scott, Foresman.

Burke, W. W., & Litwin, G. H. (1992). A causal model of organizational performance and change. *Journal of Management, 18*, 523–545.

Cascio, W. E., & Aguinis, H. (2008). Staffing twenty-first-century organizations. *Academy of Management Annals, 2*, 133–165.

Chin, J. L. (2010). Introduction to the special issue on diversity and leadership. *American Psychologist, 65*(3), 150–156.

Church, A. H. (1997). Managerial self-awareness in high performing individuals in organizations. *Journal of Applied Psychology, 82*, 281–292.

Church, A. H. (2001). The professionalization of organization development: The next step in an evolving field. In W. A. Pasmore and R. W. Woodman (Eds.), *Research in organizational change and development* (Vol. 13, pp. 1–42). Greenwich CT: JAI Press.

Church, A. H., Burke, W. W., & Van Eynde, D. F. (1994). Values, motives, and interventions of organization development practitioners. *Group & Organization Management, 19*, 5–50.

Church, A. H., & Oliver, D. H. (2006), The importance of taking action, not just sharing survey feedback. In A. Kraut (Ed.), *Getting action from organizational surveys: New concepts, technologies, and applications* (pp. 102–130). San Francisco: Jossey-Bass.

Church, A. H., & Rotolo, C. T. (2010). The role of the individual in self-assessment for leadership development. In M. G. Rothstein & R. J Burke (Eds.), *Self-management and leadership development* (pp. 25–61). Cheltenham, Glasgow, UK: Edward Elgar Publishing.

Church, A. H., & Waclawski J. (2001). *Designing and using organizational surveys: A seven step process.* San Francisco: Jossey-Bass.

Church, A. H., & Waclawski, J. (2010). Take the Pepsi Challenge: Talent development at PepsiCo. In R. Silzer & B. E. Dowell (Eds.), *Strategy-driven talent management: A leadership imperative* (pp. 617–640). San Francisco: Jossey-Bass.

Church, A. H., Walker, A. G., & Brockner, J. (2002). Multisource feedback for organization development and change. In J. Waclawski & A. H. Church (Eds.), *Organization development: A data-driven approach to organizational change* (pp. 27–54). San Francisco: Jossey-Bass.

Cummings, T. G., & Worley, C. G. (1993). *Organization development and change* (5th ed.). St. Paul, MN: West Publishing Co.

Cummings, T. G., & Worley, C. G. (2009). *Organization development and change* (9th ed.). Mason, OH: South-Western Cengage Learning.

Ferdman, B. M. (1999). The color and culture of gender in organizations: Attending to race and ethnicity. In G. N. Powell (Ed.), *Handbook of gender and work* (pp. 17–34). Thousand Oaks, CA: Sage.

Frankel, B. (2008, May). PepsiCo's Indra Nooyi: "I am a walking example of diversity." *DiversityInc*, 38–43.

French, W. L., & Bell, C. H. Jr. (1990). *Organization development: Behavioral science interventions for organization improvement* (4th ed.). Englewood Cliffs: NJ: Prentice-Hall.

Hankin, H. (2005). *The new workforce: Five sweeping trends that will shape your company's future.* New York: AMACOM.

Hansen, F. (2010). Diversity of a different color. *Workforce Management, 89*(6), 22–26.

Hogan, R., Hogan, J., & Warrenfeltz, R. (2007). *The Hogan guide: Interpretation and use of Hogan inventories.* Tulsa, OK: Hogan Press.

Holvino, E., Ferdman, B. M., & Merrill-Sands, D. (2004). Creating and sustaining diversity and inclusion in organizations: Strategies and approaches. In M. S. Stockdale & F. J. Crosby (Eds.), *The psychology and management of workplace diversity* (pp. 245–276). Malden, MA: Blackwell.

Jackson, B. W., & Hardiman, R. (1994). Multicultural organization development. In E. Cross, J. H. Katz, F. A. Miller, & E. W. Seashore

(Eds.). *The promise of diversity: Over 40 voices discuss strategies for eliminating discrimination in organizations* (pp. 221–239). Burr Ridge, IL: Irwin.

Jackson, S. E., & Associates (Eds.). (1992). *Diversity in the workplace: Human resources initiatives.* New York: Guilford Press.

Jayne, M. E. A., & Dipboye, R. L. (2004). Leveraging diversity to improve business performance: Research findings and recommendations for organizations. *Human Resource Management, 43,* 409–424.

Kanter, R. M. (1977). *Men and women of the corporation.* New York: Basic Books.

Karoly, L. A., & Panis, C. W. A. (2004). *The 21st century at work: Forces shaping the future workforce and workplace in the United States.* Santa Monica, CA: RAND Corporation.

Katz, D., & Kahn, R. L. (1978). *The social psychology of organizations* (2nd ed.). New York: Wiley.

Kirkpatrick, D., & Kirkpatrick, P. (2006). *Evaluating training programs* (3rd ed.). San Francisco: Berrett-Koehler.

Kotter, J. P. (1996). *Leading change.* Boston, MA: Harvard Business School Press.

Kraut, A. I. (2006). *Getting action from organizational surveys: New concepts, technologies, and applications.* San Francisco: Jossey-Bass.

Lawler, E. E. (1981). *Pay and organization development.* Reading, MA: Addison-Wesley.

Lawler, E. E. (1990). *Strategic pay: Aligning organizational strategies and pay systems.* San Francisco: Jossey-Bass.

Levy, P. E. (2010). *Industrial/organizational psychology: Understanding the workplace* (3rd ed.). New York: Worth Publishers.

McLean, G. N. (2006). *Organization development: Principles, processes, and performance.* San Francisco: Berrett-Koehler.

Meister, J. C., & Willyerd, K. (2010). *The 2020 workplace: How innovative companies attract, develop, and keep tomorrow's employees today.* New York: HarperCollins.

Michaels, E., Handfield-Jones, H., & Axelrod, B. (2001). *The war for talent.* Boston, MA: Harvard Business School Press.

Murray, A. (2011, April). View from the top: PepsiCo's Indra Nooyi on the trade-offs she made—and why she hopes her daughters won't have to. *Wall Street Journal Online,* interview transcript obtained at http://online.wsj.com/article/SB10001424052748704013604576247630655985522.html

PepsiCo Inc. (2011). *Performance with purpose: The promise of PepsiCo (2010 annual report).* Purchase, NY: author.

Plummer, D., & Jordan, C. G. (2007). Going plaid: Integrating diversity into business strategy, structure and systems. *OD Practitioner, 39*(2), 35–40.

Proudman, B. (2001). *Understanding American White male culture.* Unpublished manuscript.

Proudman, B. (2008). White men and diversity: An oxymoron? *Natural Gas & Electricity, 24*(12), 11–15.

Royal, C., & Vogelsang, J. (2010). From the editors. Special issue: In our own voices: The contributions and challenges of OD practitioners of color. *OD Practitioner, 42*(2), 1.

Schein, E. H. (1985). *Organizational culture and leadership: A dynamic view.* San Francisco: Jossey-Bass.

Schein, E. H. (1987). *Process consultation* (Vol. 2). Reading, MA: Addison-Wesley.

Schein, E. H. (1988). *Process consultation* (Vol. 1, rev. ed.). Reading, MA: Addison-Wesley.

Schiemann, W. A., & Morgan, B. S. (2006). Strategic surveys: Linking people to business strategy. In A. Kraut (Ed.), *Getting action from organizational surveys: New concepts, technologies, and applications* (pp. 76–101). San Francisco: Jossey-Bass.

Silzer, R., & Church, A. H. (2009). The pearls and perils of identifying potential. *Industrial and Organizational Psychology: Perspectives on Science and Practice, 2,* 377–412.

Silzer, R., & Dowell, B. E. (Eds.). (2010). *Strategy-driven talent management: A leadership imperative.* San Francisco: Jossey-Bass.

Society for Human Resource Management (SHRM). (2010). *Workplace diversity practices: How has diversity and inclusion changed over time? A comparative examination: 2010 and 2005.* Retrieved from http://www.shrm.org/Research/SurveyFindings/Articles/Pages/WorkplaceDiversityPractices.aspx

Spreitzer, G. M., McCall, M. W., & Mahoney, J. D. (1997). Early identification of international executive potential. *Journal of Applied Psychology, 82,* 6–29.

Thomas, D. A., & Creary, S. J. (2009). *Meeting the diversity challenge at PepsiCo: The Steve Reinemund era* (Case: 9–410–024). Boston, MA: Harvard Business School Publishing.

Thomas, D. A., & Gabarro, J. J. (1999). *Breaking through: The making of minority executives in corporate America.* Boston, MA: Harvard Business School Press.

Waclawski, J., & Church, A. H. (2002). Introduction and overview of organization development as a data-driven approach for organizational change. In J. Waclawski & A. H. Church, (Eds.),

Organization development: A data-driven approach to organizational change (pp. 3–26). San Francisco: Jossey-Bass.

Welch, J., & Byrne, J. A. (2001). *Jack: Straight from the gut.* New York: Warner Business.

Wiley, J. (2010). *Strategic employee surveys: Evidence-based guidelines for driving organizational success.* San Francisco: Jossey-Bass.

Williams, M. A. (2001). *The 10 lenses: Your guide to working in a multicultural world.* Herndon, VA: Capital Books.

Zemke, R., Raines, C., & Filipczak, B. (2000). *Generations at work: Managing the clash of veterans, boomers, Xers, and nexters in your workplace.* New York: American Management Association.

CHAPTER TEN

The Development of Inclusive Leadership Practice and Processes

Lize Booysen

This chapter addresses (1) how leaders can be developed to enhance inclusive leadership behavior and practice and (2) how leadership development can be done in an inclusive way.

My interest in leadership development, diversity, and inclusion was piqued during my work on the sixty-two-nation cross-cultural GLOBE leadership project (Booysen & van Wyk, 2008; House, Hanges, Javidan, Dorfman, & Gupta, 2004), my own doctoral research and scholarly work on race, gender, identity, and leadership in South Africa and Sub-Saharan Africa (Booysen, 1999, 2001, 2007b, 2007c; Booysen & Nkomo, 2006, 2007, 2010, 2012), and extended through my subsequent research with the Center for Creative Leadership (CCL) on the Leadership Across Differences project in twelve different countries (Gentry, Booysen, Hannum, & Weber, 2010; Hannum, McFeeters, & Booysen, 2010). Currently my leadership development focus is on inclusive leadership and social justice issues.

I address the following two questions in this chapter:

- What do we know and what can we suggest about how to fully take account of inclusion in leadership development systems?
- How should organizations do leadership development in a way that both develops inclusive leaders and is in itself inclusive?

In exploring these two questions, we can get nearer to identifying effective strategies and practices for inclusive leadership development and inclusive organizations.

This chapter follows a systems approach, which involves understanding how people, structures, and processes influence one another within a whole. To address question one, the *what* of inclusive leadership development, I first give a short overview of inclusion, inclusive workplaces, and inclusive leadership. I then focus briefly on the evolution of leadership development and discuss the difference between leader development and leadership development. I proceed with discussing first the relationship between leadership and leadership development, and then new trends in leadership thinking and inclusive leadership. I conclude this subsection with a definition of inclusive leadership. I then proceed to discuss how inclusive leadership practices and processes can be institutionalized by focusing on individual (micro), group (meso), and organizational (macro) processes and levels. I also focus on the importance of creating an inclusive organizational culture, a climate of respect, and a safe working environment as enabling factors to do leadership development in an inclusive way.

I address question two, the *how* to do inclusive relational-based leadership development, by presenting a process model for inclusive leadership development based on assessment, challenge, and support in the context of a climate of respect, equality, and fairness. I highlight inclusive leadership practices and provide practical examples. Finally, I conclude the chapter with a summary, as well as highlighting current dilemmas and future questions in the arena of inclusive leadership development.

Inclusion, Inclusive Workplaces, and Inclusive Leadership

Inclusive leadership is good leadership practice and essentially an extension of diversity management. Inclusive leadership focuses on valuing diversity and the effective management of diversity and inclusion of all (Hannum, McFeeters, & Booysen, 2010; Mor Barak, 2011; Pless & Maak, 2004). It shifts the focus from affirmative action and equity toward equality, social justice, fairness, and the leveraging of diversity effects in the system (Ferdman, 2010; Roberson, 2006). Ferdman (2010) defines inclusion as follows: "In its most general sense, inclusion involves both being fully ourselves and allowing others to be fully themselves in the context of engaging in common pursuits. It means collaborating in a way in which all parties can be fully engaged and subsumed, and yet, paradoxically, at the same time believe that they have not compromised, hidden, or given up any part of themselves. Thus, for individuals, experiencing inclusion in a group or organization involves being fully part of the whole while retaining a sense of authenticity and uniqueness" (p. 37; see also Ferdman, Chapter 1, this volume).

Inclusive leadership extends our thinking beyond assimilation strategies or organizational demography to empowerment and participation of all, by removing obstacles that cause exclusion and marginalization. Inclusive leadership involves particular skills and competencies for relational practice, collaboration, building inclusion for others, creating inclusive work places and work cultures, partnerships and consensus building, and true engagement of all (Ferdman, 2010; Mor Barak, 2011).

In contrast to exclusive workplaces where individuals or groups need to conform to preestablished "mainstream" value systems and ways of doing things, inclusive workplaces are based on a collaborative, pluralistic, coconstructed, and coevolving value frame that relies on mutual respect, equal contribution, standpoint plurality (multiple viewpoints), and valuing of difference. Feldman, Khademian, Ingram, and Schneider (2006) as well as Mor Barak (2011) discuss inclusion as functioning at a micro level inside the organization, but also as encompassing individuals (internal micro), groups (internal meso), and organizational processes (internal macro level), as well as operating on a larger external macro level outside the organization, involving other stakeholders, communities, societies, and even nations. Mor Barak (2011) incorporates these levels in her definition of an inclusive workplace:

The inclusive workplace is defined as one that

- Values and utilizes individual and intergroup differences within its workforce

- Cooperates with, and contributes to, its surrounding community
- Alleviates the needs of disadvantaged groups in its wider environment
- Collaborates with individuals, groups, and organizations across national and cultural boundaries [p. 8].

In a truly inclusive workplace or environment, all people from diverse backgrounds will feel valued, respected, and recognized. Inclusive organizations function multiculturally and are places where "there is equality, justice, and full participation at both the group and individual levels . . . [and] . . . differences of all types become integrated into the fabric of the business, such that they become a necessary part of doing its everyday work" (Holvino, Ferdman, & Merrill-Sands, 2004, p. 248). In a truly inclusive organization, no one will feel that he or she does not fit in, is not valued, or does not have a place in the organization; no one will ask: "What about me?"

The benefits of inclusion and frameworks for understanding and communicating inclusion, as well as individual and group level perspectives on inclusion and core competencies and skills of inclusive leaders, are addressed in detail in Parts One and Two of this volume, and I do not repeat them in this chapter. Suffice to say that inclusive leadership is good practice, and that *all leaders and leadership should be inclusive.* It follows then that *for leadership development to be truly effective it also should be inclusive.* So the first question to turn to is, what do we know and what can we suggest about how to fully take account of inclusion in leadership development systems?

Inclusive Leadership and Leadership Development

In this chapter, I assume that leadership is a combination of selection and socialization and can be taught, learned, and developed (McCauley, van Velsor, & Ruderman, 2010). Therefore I do not focus on the debate about whether leadership is innate versus learned—as discussed, for instance, by Popper (2005) and Doh (2003). I do, however, briefly focus on the evolution of leadership development and then clarify the distinction between leader development and leadership development.

Hernez-Broome and Hughes (2004) note that the goal of early leader development practice was about producing more and better leaders, and the general approach to and understanding of leadership was transactional and focused on leadership tasks and relationships. Over time, there has been a shift to thinking about transformational leadership, tapping into follower values, supporting a sense of higher purpose and engendering higher-level commitment. Recent leadership thinking has shifted from a leader and leader-follower focus to a focus on relationships and relational practices in the collective and increased inclusion of all the interconnected systems (Komives & Wagner, 2009; McCauley et al., 2010; Riggio, 2008; Uhl-Bien, 2006).

Leadership development programs have also changed from a focus on individual performance to a focus on performance at the organizational level and on the need to develop organizational capacity and individual capacity alongside each other (Collins, 2001; Hernez-Broome & Hughes, 2004; McCauley et al., 2010; Riggio, 2008). This change in focus spotlights the distinction between leader and leadership development.

Leader Development and Leadership Development

Day, Harrison, and Halpin (2008) define *leader development* as enhancing individual human capacity (that is, knowledge, skills, attitudes), and *leadership development* as growth of social capital (such as relationships and networks) between individuals. *Leader development* (also called "human capital development" or "psychological capital development") is aimed at individuals, to expand their capacity to be effective in leadership roles and processes; it focuses on desirable personal attributes and behavior. Leadership development (social capital development), in contrast, is aimed at expanding the organization's capacity to enact the basic leadership tasks needed for collective work, such as setting direction, creating alignment, and maintaining commitment; in other words, it focuses on leadership as a collective process, includes leader development, and focuses on succession of leadership as a norm (Heifetz, Linsky, & Alexander, 2009; McCauley et al., 2010; Popper, 2005).

Leadership development is a continuous systemic process, designed to expand the capabilities, competencies, and awareness of individuals (leaders and followers), groups, and organizations toward attaining shared goals and objectives. Thus leadership development is the broader concept and expands on leader development. This distinction is important for practitioners working to build inclusive organizations, since it places emphasis on two levels of entry for practitioners, one through the leader (and his or her behavioral changes) in leader development and another through leadership development processes, which include behavioral, structural, and cultural changes at an organizational level.

Wasserman, Gallegos, and Ferdman (2008) emphasized the importance of the role of leaders in creating inclusive environments. While the role of the leader and leader development is important, the process of leadership development—as an expansion of leadership capabilities throughout the organization—is equally important. As Day et al. (2008) argue, "the distinction between leader and leadership development . . . is important because enhancing [the] individual . . . does not guarantee that effective leadership will develop" (p. 159). For that to happen, leadership development is needed, not only leader development. (Again, in this chapter the focus is on leadership development, the umbrella term, which encompasses leader development.)

The Relationship Between Leadership and Leadership Development

Anderson and Ackerman-Anderson (2001) argued that what gets developed in leadership development programs depends on how leadership is framed. When leadership is defined as what people do, what gets developed is about "doing" (skill and ability competencies). If the understanding about leadership is directed toward what people know (their level of expert knowledge), then "knowing" gets developed. And if the view of leadership is about "the aggregate expression of one's mindset, emotions, and behavior" or the "way of being," then the emphasis of leadership development will be on becoming (Anderson & Ackerman-Anderson, 2001, p. 189). Inclusive leadership development should incorporate the development of knowing, doing, and being; it should not be seen as a choice of competencies versus knowledge versus mindset, but rather be focused on all three.

Riggio (2008) reminds us that "the practice of leadership, just like the practice of medicine, or law, or any other profession, is a continual learning process" (p. 387). Because leaders are practitioners, they are busy with "doing" all the time, which is contingent on their "knowing" and "being" or "becoming." Or, as Vaill (1996) argued in his book *Learning as a Way of Being*, leadership is learning. In this sense leadership and leadership development actually fold into each other, in the sense that leadership development is also learning leadership. Or, as McCauley et al. (2010) argued: "Participating in leadership roles and processes is often the very source of the challenge needed for leadership development. Leadership roles and processes are full of novelty, difficulty, conflict, and disappointments. In other words, leadership itself is a developmental challenge. Leading is, in and of itself, learning by doing" (p. 14).

Leaders are thus constantly developing, and leadership development and leadership cannot really be distinguished from each other; they are two sides of the same coin, as aptly pointed out by Johnson (2012): "In fact, perhaps because of the application of adult learning theory to leadership development, there is a growing understanding that leader development is a life-long process that entails developmental experiences and the ability to learn from those experiences" (p. 7). The act of doing or practicing leadership is in itself developmental in nature and as such constitutes a key part of leadership development.

The Relationship Between New Trends in Leadership Thinking and Inclusive Leadership

While it is not my aim in this chapter to categorize inclusive leadership or even to speculate about its status as a theory, a model, or a mere framework, it is useful to at least, in a cursory manner, link its practices to some existing leadership thinking.

Jackson and Parry (2008) point out a tension in the dominant and less dominant perspectives in leadership thinking. They maintain that the dominant perspective is leader focused, as an approach that explains individual, group, and organizational performance outcomes by identifying and examining specific leader behaviors directly related to them, while the less dominant perspectives are relationship-based. Relationship-based perspectives focus on how reciprocal social exchanges between leaders and followers evolve, nurture, and sustain dyadic, group, and collective relationships and collaboration (Cunliffe & Eriksen, 2011; Komives & Wagner, 2009; Sinclair, 2007; Uhl-Bien, 2006). Relationship-based leader perspectives are thus more process- and context-focused and emphasize participation, collaboration, follower expectations, inclusion, and implicit leadership models. Inclusive leadership thinking falls squarely in the relationship-based process and follower-focused, less-dominant way of leadership thinking.

In line with recent leadership thinking, leadership development has also shifted from a leader and leader-follower (human capital) focus to also focusing on the social capital, or the relationships and relational practices, in the collective and on increased inclusion of all the interconnected systems (Day, Harrison, & Halpin, 2008; McCauley et al., 2010; Riggio, 2008; Uhl-Bien, 2006). Table 10.1 depicts the key differences between more traditional and less inclusive entity-based views of leadership and more inclusive relational-based views.

To create more inclusive organizations, leadership training needs to be geared toward instilling the values, norms of behavior, mindsets, and processes listed in the right-hand column, "Inclusive Relational-Based Leadership," in organizational systems and processes. Inclusive leadership skills that focus on collective relational practice are more complex than those needed in traditional leader-focused leadership styles, which emphasize the leader's individual or relational identity; they are also more difficult to develop and to attain. It is also conceivable that most of the foundational individual and interpersonal traditional leadership competencies, as depicted in Table 10.1, are prerequisites for the development of the more complex collective relational practices needed for inclusive leadership.

Table 10.1. Differences Between Traditional Entity-Based and Inclusive Relational-Based Leadership

Traditional Entity-Based Leadership	Inclusive Relational-Based Leadership
Focus of the leader: Entity (individual reality) perspective; subject-object understanding of leadership; human capital focus	**Focus of the leader:** Relationships (multiple reality) perspective of leadership; understanding throughout organization; social capital focus
Leader centered; focus on follower-leader exchanges of the leadership process	Relational context and process centered; focus on various forms of relationships and networks of reciprocal social interactions; social constructions made in a process
Focus on me, us, and them Focus on difference, similarity, and common ground	Focus on us and all Value and pursue diversity and multiple viewpoints
Orient to outcomes and business processes	Orient to outcomes, social processes, context, and business processes
The use of power: Power is seen as a commodity, a leadership tool, concentrated in certain individuals	**The use of power:** Power is seen as distributed throughout the system; focus on mutual enabling practices such as collaboration, power sharing, and empowerment
Forceful and controlling	Thoughtful, reflective, transparent, participating, and inclusive
Smooth things over	Set courageous expectations
Hierarchical and positional	Networked
Decision-making processes Direct, tell, and sell	**Decision-making processes** Elicit and facilitate; create space for dialogue
Give marching orders	Set boundaries and frame the intention
Make decisions	Create a process for engagement, decision making, and leading as learning

Table 10.1. Continued

Traditional Entity-Based Leadership	Inclusive Relational-Based Leadership
Engage in directing and delegating	Engage in meaning making and opportunity creating, agency and partnerships
The role of leadership	**The role of leadership**
Leadership seen as a formal role that drives organizational process	Leadership seen as generated in social dynamics
Entity-based process of leading	Collective, consensual process of leading
Positional, formal and informal	Community and collectives of leaders, and leaders in place, formal and informal
The role of the leader	**The role of the leader**
Create and enforce rules and regulations	Question dominant and normative practices; focus on fairness, equality, and civil dissent
Take control and solve problems	Create a holding space for followers to solve problems
Focus on me, us, and them	Focus on we and all
Focus on similarity and common ground	Value and pursue diversity and multiple viewpoints

Sources: Anderson and Ackerman-Anderson (2001); Booysen (2001); Ferdman and Brody (1996); Heifetz, Linsky, and Alexander (2009); Komives and Wagner (2009); McCauley et al. (2010); Pless and Maak (2004); Riggio (2008); Uhl-Bien (2006); Wasserman, Gallegos, and Ferdman (2008).

Inclusive Relational-Based Leadership

Following Vaill's (1996), Riggio's (2008), and McCauley et al.'s (2010) thinking on leadership as learning, coupled with Uhl-Bien's (2006) emphasis on relational practice and collectives, leadership can be viewed as *practicing learning in relations and in context*. It is an ongoing cycle of collective learning: knowing, being, and doing (learning) together with others (relational practice), in a way that is directed, aligned, and committed toward shared outcomes within specific constraints (context).

In the same vein, I define inclusive leadership as follows:

> *inclusive leadership:* an ongoing cycle of learning through collaborative and respectful relational practice that enables individuals and collectives to be fully part of the whole, such that they are directed, aligned, and committed toward shared outcomes, for the common good of all, while retaining a sense of authenticity and uniqueness.

Inclusive leadership development thus needs to focus on these aspects.

This section has examined the context of inclusive leadership and leadership development. Now I turn to the second question: what can be done to develop leaders and collectives to be inclusive, and to create and sustain inclusive workplaces?

Leadership Development: Institutionalizing Inclusive Leadership Practices and Processes

I pointed out earlier that inclusive leadership is good practice; all leaders and leadership should be inclusive, and leadership development should also be inclusive. Senge's (2006) principles of a learning organization are useful as a starting point in framing how leadership development can be done in an inclusive manner at all levels of the organization. Senge (p. 23) pointed out that although individual learning experiences may work best for individual leader development on a micro level, it is possible for individuals to never see the consequences of their behavior or decisions at the organizational level, or sometimes even at the group level.

Therefore, to enable the organization as a system to continually learn and develop, formal and informal learning mechanisms must be established on all three levels: micro (individual: personal mastery and mental models), meso (team/group: team learning), and macro (organizational: shared vision and systems thinking). In this regard, Marsick and Watkins (1994) state: "Learning is a continuous, strategically used process, integrated with and running parallel to work. Learning is continuous, linked to daily work, developmental, strategic, and just in time. Learning is built into work planning, career paths, and performance rewards. Employees at all levels develop a habit of learning, asking questions, and giving feedback. . . . They are empowered to make decisions that affect their jobs. Learning is rewarded, planned for, and supported through a culture open to risk taking, experimentation, and collaboration" (pp. 354–355).

I contend that for leadership development to be done in inclusively, it must be done in such a systemic way. Also, for leadership development to be done effectively and inclusively, the organizational system in which it occurs must itself be inclusive, with an inclusive organizational culture and a climate of respect, equality, and fairness that fosters safe learning and working spaces. In the following two sections I elaborate on how to create an inclusive organizational culture (the underlying assumptions, values, and beliefs that affect the way in which work is done and people behave) and a climate (the mood, prevailing atmosphere, and subjective perceptions of the work environment) of respect, quality, fairness, and safety.

Creating an Inclusive Organizational Culture

Doing leadership development inclusively requires a large-scale, planned social-change effort for instilling an inclusive organizational culture, one in which the underlying assumptions, values, and beliefs that affect the way work is done are based on inclusion (Anderson, 2010; Booysen, 2007a; Holvino et al., 2004; Wasserman et al., 2008). Individual and cultural values need to be changed from a monocultural perspective with an exclusionary, insular, parochial, and ethnocentric focus to ultimately achieve a multicultural perspective or culture of inclusive leadership, based on justice and respect for all, standpoint plurality, valuing and integrating of differences, empowerment, and recognition (Booysen, 2007a; Holvino et al., 2004; Mor Barak, 2011).

To create a culture of inclusion in an organization, a thorough audit and diagnosis of its structure, culture, systems, strategies, and practices should be undertaken. Once this is done, the change process can start to move the organization toward more inclusion. Inclusive leadership training is an important aspect of this process, but it is not enough. More often than not this also requires a revision of all management systems. Key in this process is to pay attention to employment relations (ER) systems. Some ER practices can create systemic exclusion if practitioners are not particularly mindful of inclusive principles: these practices include recruitment, orientation and induction programs, performance appraisals, compensation and benefit packages, promotion, leadership and organizational training and development, and succession planning (Booysen, 2007a; Mor Barak, 2011; see also, in this volume, Church, Rotolo, Shull, & Tuller, Chapter 9; Nishii & Rich, Chapter 11; Offerman & Basford, Chapter 8; and Winters, Chapter 7).

In essence, these practices do not necessarily have to lead to exclusion, provided that authority, policies, rules, and regulations do not favor one group, level, or function above another. If inclusion has been institutionalized, these rules and regulations can actually be valuable tools toward ensuring inclusion and inclusive leadership practice. Examples include policies punishing discrimination and harassment and incentivizing equal treatment; performance management systems based on fairness and equality; formalized conflict-management procedures providing fair systems for complaints and safe spaces for dialogue, apology, and acceptance; and published codes of conduct based on fairness and inclusion (Hannum et al., 2010; Ruderman & Chrobot-Mason, 2010). Nishii and Rich (Chapter 11, this volume) also elaborate on creating organizational climates for inclusion.

A culture of inclusion can be institutionalized by weaving inclusion into the everyday operation and fabric of the organization through translating the values of inclusion into its mission, vision, strategies, policies, structures, and processes as well as its leadership practices. It is thus important to put systems in place that hold everyone, especially management, accountable for achieving inclusion goals and upholding inclusion values. Once a culture of valuing inclusion is established and entrenched, it is imperative to monitor and evaluate it through a process of continuous oversight to ensure that inclusion stays institutionalized. Lastly, a constant auditing feedback loop into the system will ensure continuous improvement in establishing a culture that values inclusion (Booysen, 2007a).

The importance of organizational structures and processes as part of an integrated systemic strategy to institutionalize inclusive leadership development cannot be overemphasized. However, this discussion of leadership development focuses more on relational leadership practices, processes, and strategies than on organizational structural, design, policy, or development issues, which fall more within the scope of organization development and change than leadership development per se. The need for systemic changes to create inclusive organizations is also further discussed in the rest of Part Three of this volume.

Creating a Climate of Respect and a Safe Learning and Working Environment

Alexandre (2010), Essed (2010), Ferdman (2010), and McFeeters, Hannum, & Booysen (2010) offer some guidelines for how to facilitate and create safe learning and working environments—or, in Heifetz's (1994) terms, "holding environments"—in which all individuals feel comfortable and safe expressing themselves, taking risks, and exploring possibilities. To facilitate inclusion, leaders or facilitators need to recognize, respect, and value difference and pay attention to inclusion by holding all participants in positive regard and valuing their contributions—and in this way modeling inclusive leadership. Leaders or facilitators need to listen carefully and be respectful of everyone's humanity, give voice to all, and not make quick judgments or feel pulled or pushed toward a specific group's point of view. Leaders or facilitators must foster inclusion by remaining aware of power dynamics and must not take responsibility for participants' choices. These are some examples of how to do this:

- Use dialogue strategies that provide space for voice, silence, and listening.
- Prevent dominant consensus from silencing numerical minority dissent (regardless of your own convictions).
- Model how to have discussions about "isms" without making it personal.
- Don't pretend to know everything; allow for vulnerability.
- Foster values of respectful dialogue, mindful inquiry, and civil dissent.

The people in an inclusive learning environment have the capacity to reflect on process, both individually and collectively. It is thus important for inclusive leadership development facilitators to create an environment in which everyone is encouraged, but not forced, to actively participate. When working with groups, facilitators should stress the importance of having openness and mutual respect for one another, as this encourages full participation from all, which is valuable to the organization.

How to Fully Take Account of Inclusion in Leadership Development Systems

How to fully take account of inclusion in leadership development systems is integrated in the Leadership Development System of Inclusion model, depicted in Figure 10.1. This model indicates that the enabling systems for doing leadership development in an inclusive way are (1) an inclusive organizational culture, with inclusion institutionalized throughout the organization's practices, systems, and processes; and (2) an organizational climate of respect, equality, and fairness, which creates safe learning and working environments.

The model also specifies that, to develop leaders and collectives to be inclusive and to create and sustain inclusive workplaces, leadership development should be done in a systemic way; it is an ongoing, developmental cycle of continuous learning and not a series of one-shot events. It should focus on the leader-follower, the relationships and relational practices in the collective, and increased inclusion of all the interconnected systems (social

Figure 10.1. A Leadership Development System of Inclusion Model

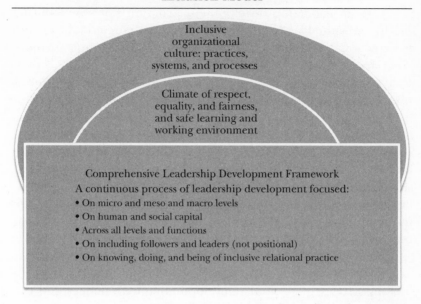

Inclusive organizational culture: practices, systems, and processes

Climate of respect, equality, and fairness, and safe learning and working environment

Comprehensive Leadership Development Framework
A continuous process of leadership development focused:
• On micro and meso and macro levels
• On human and social capital
• Across all levels and functions
• On including followers and leaders (not positional)
• On knowing, doing, and being of inclusive relational practice

capital). It should be done on a micro level inside the organization, including intra- and interpersonal learning of both leaders and followers; on a meso level inside groups and teams; and on a macro organizational process level. Furthermore, it should focus on the knowing, doing, and being of inclusive relational-based leadership, as pointed out in Table 10.1. Lastly, it is important to remember that leadership development also happens in the act of leadership itself. I refer to this all-inclusive continuous process of leadership development as a *comprehensive leadership development framework.*

The discussion up to this point has focused on the *why* and *what* of leadership development as well as the assumptions underlying inclusive leadership development, and culminated in the Leadership Development System of Inclusion (shown in Figure 10.1). The rest of the chapter focuses on *how* to do inclusive relational-based leadership development in an inclusive way, and speaks to question two: How should organizations do leadership development in a way that both develops inclusive leaders and is in itself inclusive?

A good leadership development program starts by focusing on the individual leader (leading the self, with focus on intra- and interpersonal relations); it then progresses to leading in more complex relations (leading other individuals and groups), then to leading organizational functions and projects; finally, it moves into leadership development by focusing on the processes of leading whole organizations, subsidiaries, mergers, and acquisitions, and ultimately leading globally across organizational and country boundaries (McCauley et al., 2010; Riggio, 2008). The focus is thus on progressively maximizing personal leadership and shared leadership, interdependence, and collaboration to accelerate the organization's or collective's direction, alignment, commitment, and, ultimately, results. Allen and Wergin (2009) point out that achieving leadership expertise or mastery requires the "process of outgrowing one system of meaning by integrating it as a subsystem into a new system of meaning" (p. 9). This is a lifelong process that entails developmental experiences and the ability both to learn from them and to acquire new knowledge, skills, and attitudes. Furthermore, the effectiveness of this learning is contingent on how conducive the work team, workplace, culture, and processes are to the integration and implementation of this new learning.

A Process Model for Inclusive Leadership Development

The Center for Creative Leadership (CCL), a well-known and internationally recognized global leadership development institute headquartered in the United States, developed a two-part process model for leadership development (McCauley et al., 2010). Part one includes the elements of assessment, challenge, and support (ACS) to make the learning experience more powerful and developmental. Part two focuses on leadership development as a process "that requires both a variety of development experiences and the ability to learn from experience" (McCauley et al., 2010, p. 6). I believe that inclusive leadership development includes essentially the same type of leader development pro-

Figure 10.2. A Process Model for Inclusive Leadership Development

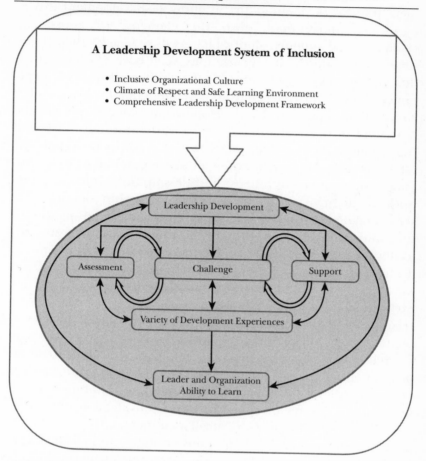

Source: Adapted from McCauley et al., 2010, p. 5.

cesses, but embedded in a system of inclusion (as depicted in Figure 10.1) and focused on relational leadership practices. The CCL process model can be adapted for inclusive leadership development, as depicted in Figure 10.2.

Figure 10.2 shows that inclusive leadership development takes place in a *system of inclusion* (as per Figure 10.1). The leadership development process thus takes place within an inclusive organization culture, a climate of respect, and a safe learning environment, and it follows a comprehensive leadership development framework. It shows that training or development experiences or interventions need the elements of assessment, challenge, and support, all of which feed into each other. It also shows that leaders and organizations need both (1) a variety of development experiences and (2) the ability to learn from experience. This ability to learn from developmental experiences has a reciprocal impact, in that developmental experiences enhance a person's or organization's ability to learn, and individuals and organizations with a high ability to learn will in turn seek out (and may benefit from) a variety of developmental experiences. Finally, since the comprehensive leadership development framework is all-inclusive, it implies that leadership development should take place on a micro, meso, and macro level—across all functions and levels in the organization, with followers and leaders—and it should not be the prerogative of only positional leaders—or worse, only senior leaders. It also follows that the variety of developmental experiences should specifically, but not exclusively, focus on the knowing, doing, and being of inclusive relational-based leadership, along with generic leadership development experiences.

Self-awareness is a key precursor for effective leadership development (Komives & Wagner, 2009; Popper, 2005; Riggio, 2008). On a micro level this means leader awareness. On an organizational level this means not only the individual leader's self-awareness but also organizational self-awareness and organizational learning. Self-awareness also develops through internalizing inclusive leadership values; reflecting on current practice; continuous questioning of normative practices, differential treatment, and assimilation practices; and becoming a community of inclusive practice (Senge, Kleiner, Roberts, Ross, & Smith, 1994). Questions that need to be answered by such a community of inclusive practice are, for instance:

- Who are we as an organization?
- Do we stand for real inclusion? Can that be seen in both our espoused and enacted core values?

- How do our core values, our vision and culture, and our organization's practices, systems, rules, regulations, and policies include and privilege some individuals and groups and exclude and marginalize others?
- How can we be even more inclusive in our leadership practices?

Learning is a key component of leadership development. The capacity for learning is a complex combination of personality and motivational factors and learning experiences. Gaining the ability to turn learning into adaptive practice is even more difficult. It is less complex to learn about inclusion (to have the knowledge, or "knowing") and more complex to translate "knowing" into "being" and "doing"—the practice of inclusive leadership, or leading inclusively. Training interventions should be designed to fit individual and organizational readiness and capacity (McCauley et al., 2010; Riggio, 2008). For inclusive leadership development to be effective, leaders and organizations must both be ready (they must be committed and must intend to be inclusive) and have the capacity to be developed as inclusive leaders or organizations as well as the intent to lead inclusively.

I now take a closer look at how assessment, challenge, and support (ACS) can be applied so as to do leadership development inclusively. My further discussion focuses mainly on the micro level of leadership development. As most of the macro level leadership strategies and some of those at the meso level fall within organization development, they have been discussed already in the section on institutionalizing inclusive leadership practice in this chapter, and they are elaborated on in other chapters (particularly in Part Three) of this volume.

Assessment for Inclusive Leadership Development

The function of assessment is manifold. It gives individuals an understanding of where they are now, functioning as a baseline of their current performance and as a benchmark for future development. It gives information on the gap between current performance or ineffective practices and desired performance or effective practices, and it leads to higher levels of self-awareness. It clarifies what individuals have to learn, change, or improve upon. It provides a means for critical self-reflection; as McCauley et al. (2010) argued, "the result [of assessment feedback] can be an unfreezing of one's current understanding of oneself to facilitate movement toward a broader and more complex understanding" (p. 7). Assessment also creates opportunities to motivate when individuals receive feedback on progress or effective behavior.

There are several sources for individual and organizational assessment, including self-assessment and assessments from family and friends, colleagues, peers, bosses, subordinates in the workplace, customers, coaches, counselors, trainers, facilitators, and organizational consultants. Assessments can be formal or informal. They can be done informally through feedback by others or formally through performance appraisals, 360-degree feedback, employee satisfaction surveys, and evaluations.

Assessment thus helps individuals to fully understand their situation, through reflection, and to become motivated to capitalize on the learning opportunities available to them. The following are some good leader development assessments (McCauley et al., 2010; Riggio, 2008) that can be used in inclusive leader development:

○ **Multirater, multisource feedback**, such as 360-degree feedback, can be adapted to measure specific inclusive leadership competencies, including relational practice, dealing with difference, and appreciation for multiple viewpoints. An example would be designing a 360-degree feedback questionnaire in which peers, teams, subordinates and superiors all can give feedback to each other on their level of inclusiveness in decision making and leading.
○ **Assessments focused on inclusive leadership practices**, such as the Global Competencies Inventory (http://kozaigroup.com/inventories/the-global-competencies-inventory-gci), the Intercultural Effectiveness Scale (http://kozaigroup.com/inventories/the-intercultural-effectiveness-scale), and the Inclusion Measurement Survey (Davis, 2010) (see also Bird,

Mendenhall, Stevens, & Oddou, 2010; Ferdman, Barrera, Allen, & Vuong, 2009).

○ **Other leader development personality and type assessment instruments** can also be used to explore areas for further development, using an "inclusive leadership development lens." Tools for exploration (and associated assessments) can include:

- The Workplace Big 5 Profile (Howard & Howard, 2010), which assesses the degree to which an individual responds to stress, tolerates sensory stimulation from people and situations, is open to new experiences and new ways of doing things, pushes toward goals, and defers to others.
- The FIRO Business assessment tools (Schnell & Hammer, 1997), which assess interpersonal needs such as expressed and wanted involvement, influence and connection.
- The Myers-Briggs Type Indicator (MBTI; Myers & McCaulley, 1985) which assesses thinking style preferences and other individual styles.
- The Belbin Group Profile (Belbin, 1981), which assesses group action role preferences and styles.

The results of such assessments can give leaders (and organizations) more insight into their level of inclusion, leading to better self-awareness and calibration (and reduction) of exclusionary practices. Results can also be discussed in coaching and mentoring conversations and can be very helpful in team building. Leaders can reflect not only on their own results, but also on how those results might interact with those of the team or work group they work in. The results of the interpersonal needs (FIRO Business), cognitive style preferences (MBTI), and group action role preferences (Belbin) assessments can be used with great effect in constructing more diverse and inclusive teams and workgroups.

Challenge for Inclusive Leadership Development

Challenges stretch people and force them out of their comfort zones and habitual ways of doing. Challenges create disequilibrium, or a sense of a "disorienting dilemma," in which known ways of doing are not successful anymore (Mezirow, 2009). These states of disequilibrium cause individuals or collectives to question the appropriateness of their known ways and the adequacy of their existing skills, frameworks, and approaches. They require people to deal with ambiguity and paradox and to find new ways of doing, or to evolve their ways of understanding and learning to be successful. Challenges come in many forms and are dependent on individuals' level of experience and maturity. McCauley et al. (2010) point out that the elements (or sources) of a challenge are usually novelty (new experiences, learning new skills), difficult goals (stretch goals), goal setting, conflict or competing values (intrapersonal, interpersonal, group, or social identity conflict), and dealing with adversity (overcoming difficulty or challenging circumstances).

Challenge can most effectively be practiced in an inclusive way if all people in the organization feel free and safe to participate in decision making and sharing of ideas, and if failure is expected and seen as part of the learning process. The following are some examples of good leadership development challenges (Booysen, 2007b; McCauley et al., 2010) that can be used in inclusive leader development:

○ **Developmental and stretch assignments**, like an expatriate assignment, conflict management resolution between different work teams, or an organizational diagnosis and culture change endeavor can be used to develop inclusive leadership capabilities. These assignments help leaders to test out and develop new inclusive leadership skills and competencies, such as relational practice, and they heighten awareness of marginalization and privilege and promote questioning of dominant and normative thinking styles and practices.
○ **Job rotation and job sharing across and within functions, horizontal job enlargement, or vertical job enrichment** can help leaders to have a deeper understanding of working across different job function levels and of silos in the organization. Leaders will gain more insight into how these different functions, jobs, and processes all work toward shared goals in

the organization, and of how silos can be integrated and boundaries spanned.

∘ **Action learning** (employees learning through working together), **individual talent management** (the process of attracting and retaining high-potential employees), **and career pathing** (charting a course within an organization for an individual's career path and career development) can all be included in this level of development.

∘ **Education, skills training, and development programs** can also be categorized as challenges. These are usually done through a combination of on-site and off-site programs and initiatives and have didactic and experiential components. Inclusive leadership rests on a deep level of consciousness—deep self-awareness as well as an awareness of other perspectives—and an understanding of ethics and social justice issues. To develop these micro-level leadership development strategies in an inclusive manner, the programs need to meet the learners where they are, which may require different approaches even within the same group of participants. Aspects such as participants' different learning styles, social identities, leadership levels, and developmental levels all need to be taken into consideration (Allen & Wergin, 2009; Anderson & Ackerman-Anderson, 2001; McCauley et al., 2010; Riggio, 2008).

To deal effectively with difference and to be inclusive, leaders also need to be aware of the different leader role demands placed on them and to engage in compensatory practices so as not to be caught up in exclusionary practices due to one of these role demands. Hannum et al. (2010) and Ruderman et al. (2010) identify three leader role demands in the context of dealing with difference and exclusion:

1. Leaders are often pulled in many directions between conflicting intergroup values, viewpoints, and beliefs. Inclusive leaders need to be unbiased and not influenced by their own or their group's values and viewpoints, and they need to be respectful of everyone's needs and viewpoints.

2. Leaders are commonly pushed to one side. By definition, a leader is a member of some groups and not others. Groups will form perceptions of a leader based solely on social identities. An inclusive leader will focus on practices of fairness and equity to show that he or she is not partial to his or her own group.

3. Leaders are all too frequently caught out of the loop. This is in part due to information filtering, but also in part due to the leader's lack of critical awareness concerning social identity dynamics. Inclusive leaders need to be sensitive to group dynamics, to create an environment of trust and safety, and to be accessible so as to be in the loop.

Support for Inclusive Leadership Development

Support helps individuals deal with the struggle and pain of development and to find safety and new equilibrium in their growth. The most important sources of support, regardless of experience or challenge, are the other people in an individual's work and life spheres—people who can listen, reassure and empathize, identify with the struggles, give advice for coping strategies, and celebrate the wins. Organizational structural, cultural, and systems support is also critical. Support is also a key motivating factor and a mechanism for providing learning resources, through feedback from others confirming and clarifying the lessons leaders learned from the challenging leadership development experiences. Furthermore, if individuals do not receive support for leadership development from their workplaces or significant others, the challenges inherent in development experiences may overwhelm them rather than foster learning. That is why realistic goal setting is important, because it shifts a classroom or a development event's insights and ideas forward into a process of action outside the classroom into the organization. Goal setting also serves as an individual's own development plan for needed action.

The following are some specific sources of support (Booysen, 2007b; McCauley et al., 2010; McFeeters et al., 2010) that can be used in inclusive leader development:

○ **Mentoring, coaching, and executive coaching for performance development.** For instance, the coach or mentor can raise the coachee's or mentee's awareness levels regarding exclusion or inclusion by focusing on recognizing differences of individuals, while looking for the common bond and/or shared goals among individuals. They can also do this by exploring the coachee's or mentee's personal biases and normative thinking. Cross-cultural coaching and mentoring and role-play during coaching and mentoring can be useful in developing inclusive leadership practices.

○ **Safe learning environments.** Alexandre (2010) maintained that the most important element contributing to a safe learning culture is the establishing of equality through respectful information sharing and mutual growth that empowers all involved. Frank Boyce (2012), the news reporter who worked with Danny Boyle in the creation of the London 2012 Olympic opening ceremony, described such a safe learning space: "Danny created a room where no one was afraid to speak, no one had to stick to their own specialism, no one was afraid of sounding stupid or talking out of turn. He restored us to the people we were before we made career choices—to when we were just wondering" (para. 3).

In summary, the key elements of the Process Model for Inclusive Leadership Development are a variety of learning experiences focused on inclusive relational-based leadership practices, undergone by committed leaders and collectives in a safe learning and working environment, and that include elements of assessment, challenge, and support, in an inclusive organizational context and a climate of respect, equality, and fairness.

Conclusion

This chapter set out to investigate: (1) What do we know and what can we suggest about how to fully take account of inclusion in leadership development systems? (2) How should organizations do leadership development in a way that both develops inclusive leaders and is in itself inclusive?

In addressing these two questions, I first argued that inclusive leadership is good practice: all leaders and leadership should be inclusive and leadership development should also be inclusive. Second, I explained that I use the term *leadership development* as an umbrella term that includes leader development. Third, I argued that the act of doing or practicing leadership is in itself developmental and as such constitutes leadership development. I then showed how recent leadership development thinking has shifted from a leader and leader-follower (human capital- or entity-based) focus to also focus on social capital—the relationships and relational practices in the collective and increased inclusion of all the interconnected systems. I also defined inclusive leadership as an ongoing cycle of learning through collaborative and respectful relational practice that enables individuals and collectives to be fully part of the whole, such that they are directed, aligned, and committed toward shared outcomes, for the common good of all, while retaining a sense of authenticity and uniqueness.

The discussion of question one—the *why* and the *what* of leadership development as well as the assumptions underlying inclusive leadership development—culminated in the Leadership Development System of Inclusion model (Figure 10.1). This figure shows that the enabling systems for doing leadership development are (1) an inclusive organizational culture and (2) an organizational climate of respect, equality, and fairness, which create (3) safe learning and working environments. Furthermore, it shows leadership development as an ongoing cycle of continuous learning and follows a comprehensive leadership development framework. Because this framework is all-inclusive, it implies that leadership development should take place on the micro, meso, and macro level, across all functions and levels in the organization, and should not be only the prerogative of positional leaders. It focuses on both the leader-follower and the relationships and relational practices in the collective and increased inclusion of all the interconnected systems (social capital).

The discussion of question two—how organizations should do leadership development in a way that both develops inclusive leaders and is in itself inclusive—culminated in a Process Model for Inclusive Leadership Development (Figure 10.2). This figure shows that inclusive leadership development takes place in a system of inclusion (as per Figure 10.1). The leadership development process is comprehensive and takes place in an inclusive organization culture, a climate of respect, and a safe learning environment. It shows that leadership training or development experiences or interventions need the elements of assessment, challenge, and support, all of which feed into each other. It also shows that leaders and organizations need both a variety of development experiences and the ability to learn from experience. It follows, then, that the variety of developmental experiences should specifically, but not exclusively, focus on the knowing, doing, and being of inclusive relational-based leadership, as depicted in Table 10.1, alongside generic leadership development experiences.

This chapter focused primarily on the micro level of inclusion in organizations and some macro-level aspects of institutionalizing inclusion in organizations. Although I alluded to some larger systems implications, I did not focus on inclusive practices outside the organization itself (see Mor Barak & Daya, Chapter 13, this volume). So a key question still remains: How can inclusion be effected outside the organization, with stakeholders, communities, societies, and nations, and globally?

Further questions remain unanswered, not only in this chapter but also in the larger debate about inclusion in workplaces: How does one create organizationally sustainable inclusive leadership practices, particularly in multinational corporations? (See Jonsen & Özbilgin, Chapter 12; and Mor Barak & Daya, Chapter 13, this volume.) In what way do historical patterns of exclusion impact the perceptions and efficacy of inclusive leadership practices? What do dominant groups gain from inclusive leadership? Finally, is true inclusion even possible, or is the act of inclusion in organizations invariably still in the hands of those in power? These are questions that should be explored in more depth in future dialogue and research, particularly from a critical perspective problematizing the possible power dynamics still inherent in acts of inclusion. For example, in a forthcoming publication, *The Two Faces of Ubuntu—An Inclusive Positive or Exclusive Parochial Leadership Perspective?* (Booysen, 2013), I explore the inherent exclusionary elements in *Ubuntu*,[1] a concept that is typically seen as an inclusive and generative mechanism and a strength-based perspective. In my opinion, the challenge is to capitalize and to build on the inclusive nondiscriminatory positive practices of *Ubuntu*, while minimizing the possible exclusionary practices, which seem to be more context-bound. Similarly, in developing and implementing inclusive leadership practices, we need to engage in ongoing critique and exploration.

References

Alexandre, L. (2010). Building safe learning environments. In B. B. McFeeters, K. Hannum, & L. Booysen (Eds.), *Leading across differences: Cases and perspectives—Facilitators guide* (pp. 51–61). San Francisco: Pfeiffer.

Allen, S. J., & Wergin, J. F. (2009, Winter). Leadership and adult development theories: Overviews and overlaps. *Leadership Review, 9,* 3–19. Retrieved from http://www.leadershipreview.org/2009winter/article1.pdf

Anderson, D., & Ackerman-Anderson, L. S. (2001). *Beyond change management: Advanced strategies for today's transformational leaders* (pp. 181–197). San Francisco: Jossey-Bass/Pfeiffer.

Anderson, D. L. (2010). *Organization development: The process of leading organizational change.* Thousand Oaks, CA: Sage.

Belbin, M. (1981). *Management teams.* London: Heinemann.

Bird, A., Mendenhall, M. E., Stevens, M. J., & Oddou, G. (2010). Defining the domain of intercultural competence for global leaders. *Journal of Managerial Psychology, 25*(8), 810–828.

Booysen, L. (1999). Male and female managers: Gender influences on South African managers in retail banking. *South African Journal of Labour Relations, 23*(2&3), 25–35.

---

[1]Luthans, van Wyk, and Walumbwa (2004, p. 515) identified *Ubuntu* as a possible "positive strength-based perspective" in South-African organizations. *Ubuntu,* literally translated, means: "I am because we are" and is an expression of collective personhood and collective morality (Kamoche, 2010).

Booysen, L. (2001). The duality in South African leadership: Afrocentric or Eurocentric. *South African Journal of Labour Relations, 25*(3&4), 36–64.

Booysen, L. (2007a). Managing cultural diversity: A South African perspective. In K. April & M. Shockley (Eds.), *Diversity in Africa: The coming of age of a continent* (pp. 51–92). Basingstoke, Hampshire: Palgrave Macmillan.

Booysen, L. (2007b). Social identity changes: Challenges facing leadership. In K. April & M. Shockley (Eds.), *Diversity in Africa: The coming of age of a continent* (pp. 127–156). Basingstoke, Hampshire: Palgrave Macmillan.

Booysen, L. (2007c). Societal power shifts and changing social identities in South Africa: Workplace implications. *Southern African Journal of Economic and Management Sciences, 10*(1), 1–20.

Booysen, L. A. E. (2013) *The two faces of Ubuntu: An inclusive positive or exclusive parochial leadership perspective?* Manuscript in preparation.

Booysen, L., & Nkomo, S. M. (2006). Think manager—think (fe)male: A South African perspective. *International Journal of Interdisciplinary Social Sciences, 1*(2), 23–33.

Booysen, L., & Nkomo, S. M. (2007). The Tea Incident: Racial division at Insurance Incorporated—A teaching case. *International Journal on Diversity in Organisations, Communities & Nations, 7*(5), 97–106.

Booysen, L. A. E., & Nkomo, S. M. (2010). Employment equity and diversity management in South Africa. In A. Klarsfeld (Ed.), *International handbook on diversity management at work: Country perspectives on diversity and equal treatment* (pp. 218–243). Cheltenham: Edward Elgar.

Booysen, L. A. E., & Nkomo, S. M. (2012). The discipline dilemma in Rainbow High School. In D. L. Anderson (Ed.), *Cases & exercises in organization development & change* (pp. 21–30). Thousand Oaks, CA: Sage.

Booysen, L. A., & van Wyk, M. W. (2008). Culture and leadership in South Africa. In J. S. Chhokar, F. C. Brodbeck, & R. J. House (Eds.), *Culture and leadership across the world: The GLOBE Book of in-depth studies of 25 societies* (pp. 433–473). New York: Taylor & Francis.

Boyce, F. C. (2012, July 28). London 2012: Opening ceremony saw all our mad dreams come true. *The Observer.* Retrieved from http://www.guardian.co.uk/commentisfree/2012/jul/29/frank-cottrell-boyce-olympics-opening-ceremony

Collins, D. B. (2001). Organizational performance: The future focus of leadership development programs. *Journal of Leadership & Organizational Studies, 7*(4), 43–54. doi:10.1177/107179190100700404

Cunliffe, L. C., & Eriksen, M. (2011). Relational leadership. *Human Relations, 64*(11), 1425–1449.

Davis, E. (2010, July 14). *Inclusion measurement: Tracking the intangible.* TrendWatcher [Newsletter], Issue 504. Retrieved from http://www.i4cp.com/trendwatchers/2010/07/14/inclusion-measurement-tracking-the-intangible

Day, D. V., Harrison, M. M., & Halpin, S. M. (2008). *An integrative approach to leader development: Connecting adult development, identity, and expertise.* New York: Routledge.

Doh, J. P. (2003). Can leadership be taught? Perspectives from management educators. *Academy of Management Learning and Education, 3*(1), 54–67.

Essed, P. (2010). Social justice and dignity. In K. Hannum, B. B. McFeeters, & L. Booysen (Eds.), *Leading across differences: Cases and perspectives* (pp. 139–146). San Francisco: Pfeiffer.

Feldman, M. S., Khademian, A. M., Ingram, H., & Schneider, A. S. (2006). Ways of knowing and inclusive management practices. *Public Administration Review, 66* (s1), 89–99.

Ferdman, B. M. (2010). Teaching inclusion by example and experience: Creating an inclusive learning environment. In B. B. McFeeters, K. M. Hannum, & L. Booysen (Eds.), *Leading across differences: Cases and perspectives—Facilitator's guide* (pp. 37–50). San Francisco: Pfeiffer.

Ferdman, B. M., Barrera, V., Allen, A., & Vuong, V. (2009, August 11). Inclusive behavior and the experience of inclusion. In B. G. Chung (Chair), *Inclusion in organizations: Measures, HR practices, and climate.* Symposium presented at the 69th Annual Meeting of the Academy of Management, Chicago.

Ferdman, B. M., & Brody, S. E. (1996). *Models of diversity training.* In D. Landis & R. Bhagat (Eds.), *Handbook of intercultural training* (2nd ed., pp. 282–303). Thousand Oaks, CA: Sage.

Gentry, W. A., Booysen, L., Hannum, K., & Weber, T. (2010). Leadership responses to a conflict of gender-based tension: A comparison of responses between men and women in the U.S. and South Africa. *International Journal of Cross Cultural Management, 10,* 285–301.

Hannum, K., McFeeters, B. B., & Booysen, L. (Eds.). (2010). *Leading across differences: Cases and perspectives.* San Francisco: Pfeiffer.

Heifetz, R. A. (1994). *Leadership without easy answers.* Boston, MA: Harvard University Press.

Heifetz, R. A., Linsky, M., & Alexander, G. (2009). *Practice of adaptive leadership: Tools and tactics for changing your organization and the world.* Boston, MA: Harvard Business Press.

Hernez-Broome, G., & Hughes, R. J. (2004). Leadership development: Past, present, and future. *Human Resource Planning, 27*(1), 24–32.

Holvino, E., Ferdman, B. M., & Merrill-Sands, D. (2004). Creating and sustaining diversity and inclusion in organizations: Strategies and approaches. In M. S. Stockdale & F. J. Crosby (Eds.), *The psychology and management of workplace diversity* (pp. 245–276). Malden, MA: Blackwell.

House, R. J., Hanges, P. J., Javidan, M., Dorfman, P. W., & Gupta, V. (Eds.). (2004). *Culture, leadership and organizations: The GLOBE study of 62 societies.* Thousand Oaks, CA: Sage.

Howard, P. J., & Howard, J. M. (2010). *The owner's manual for personality at work: How the Big Five personality traits affect performance, communication, teamwork, leadership, and sales* (2nd ed.). Charlotte, NC: CentACS Press.

Jackson, B., & Parry, K. (2008). *A very short, interesting and reasonably cheap book about studying leadership.* Thousand Oaks, CA: Sage.

Johnson, J. I. (2012). *Museums, leadership, and transfer: An inquiry into organizational supports for learning leadership* (Unpublished doctoral dissertation). Ph.D. Program in Leadership & Change, Antioch University, Yellow Springs, OH.

Kamoche, K. (2010). Contemporary developments in the management of human resources in Africa. *Journal of World Business. 46*, 1–4.

Komives, S. R., & Wagner, W. (Eds.). (2009). *Leadership for a better world: Understanding the social change model of leadership development.* San Francisco: Jossey-Bass.

Luthans, F., van Wyk, R., & Walumbwa, F. O. Recognition and development of hope for South African organizational leaders. *Leadership and Organization Development Journal, 25*(6), 512–527.

Marsick, V. J., & Watkins, K. F. (1994). The learning organization: An integrative vision for HRD. *Human Resource Development Quarterly, 5*(4), 353–360.

McCauley, C., van Velsor, E., & Ruderman, M. (2010). Introduction: Our view of leadership development. In E. van Velsor, C. McCauley, & M. Ruderman (Eds.), *The Center for Creative Leadership handbook of leadership development* (3rd ed., pp. 1–22). San Francisco: Jossey-Bass.

McFeeters, B. B., Hannum, K., & Booysen, L. (Eds.). (2010). *Leading across differences: Cases and perspectives—Facilitator's guide*. San Francisco: Pfeiffer.

Mezirow, J. (2009). *Transformative learning in practice*. San Francisco: Jossey-Bass.

Mor Barak, M. E. (2011). *Managing diversity: Toward a globally inclusive workplace* (2nd ed.). Thousand Oaks, CA: Sage.

Myers, I. B., & McCaulley, M. H. (1985). *Manual: A guide to the development and use of the Myers-Briggs Type Indicator* (2nd ed.). Palo Alto, CA: Consulting Psychologists Press.

Pless, N. M., and Maak, T. (2004). Building an inclusive diversity culture: Principles, processes and practice. *Journal of Business Ethics, 54*(2), 129–147.

Popper, M. (2005). Main principles and practices in leader development. *Leadership & Organization Development Journal, 26*(1), 62–75.

Riggio, R. E. (2008). Leadership development: Current state and future expectations. *Consulting Psychology Journal: Practice and Research, 60*(4), 383–392.

Roberson, Q. M. (2006). Disentangling the meanings of diversity and inclusion in organizations. *Group & Organizational Management, 31*(2), 212–236. doi: 10.1177/1059601104273064

Ruderman, M. N., & Chrobot-Mason, D. (2010). Triggers of social identity conflict. In K. Hannum, B. B. McFeeters, & L. Booysen (Eds.), *Leading across differences: Cases and perspectives* (pp. 81–86). San Francisco: Pfeiffer.

Ruderman, M. N., Glover, S., Chrobot-Mason, D., & Ernst, C. (2010). In K. Hannum, B. B. McFeeters, & L. Booysen (Eds.), *Leading across differences: Cases and perspectives* (pp. 95–114). San Francisco: Pfeiffer.

Schnell, E., & Hammer, A. (1997). *Integrating the FIRO-B with the MBTI: Relationships, case examples, and interpretation strategies. Developing leaders*. Palo Alto, CA: Davies-Black.

Senge, P. M., Kleiner, A., Roberts, C., Ross, R. B., & Smith, B. J. (1994). *The Fifth Discipline fieldbook: Strategies and tools for building a learning organization*. New York: Doubleday.

Senge, P. M. (2006). *The fifth discipline: The art & practice of the learning organization* (Revised ed.). New York: Doubleday.

Sinclair, A. (2007). *Leadership for the disillusioned: Moving beyond myths and heroes to leading that liberates*. Crows Nest, N.S.W.: Allen & Unwin.

Uhl-Bien, M. (2006). Relational leadership theory: Exploring the social processes of leadership and organizing. *Leadership Quarterly, 18*(4), 645–676.

Vaill, P. B. (1996). *Learning as a way of being: Strategies for survival in a world of permanent white water.* San Francisco: Jossey-Bass.

Wasserman, I. C., Gallegos, P. V., & Ferdman, B. M. (2008). Dancing with resistance: Leadership challenges in fostering a culture of inclusion. In K. M. Thomas (Ed.), *Diversity resistance in organizations* (pp. 175–200). New York: Taylor and Francis.

CHAPTER ELEVEN

Creating Inclusive Climates in Diverse Organizations

Lisa H. Nishii and Robert E. Rich

This chapter is the outcome of numerous engaging conversations that the two of us have had about inclusive organizations. What we found was that although we come from different educational and experiential backgrounds—Lisa from the perspective of academic research on climate and diversity, and Robert from the perspective of a practitioner with over twenty years of experience consulting for organizations on the topics of diversity and organizational change—we ultimately agree on the core definition and value of inclusive climates. In our collaborations, Lisa has drawn upon the academic literature to construct and test our theories using reliable and valid measures, and Robert has drawn on experience to help answer practical questions, such as "*How* do we enhance the inclusiveness of our climate?"

Our goal in this chapter is to share our conceptualization of inclusive climates as well as our thoughts on how one might design organizational change efforts for enhancing inclusion. Our focus is on the inclusiveness of work environments, with the assumption that people experience more personal inclusion when they work in an inclusive climate.

Climate for Inclusion Defined

A look at the titles of managers who are responsible for workforce diversity issues quickly reveals a shift that has occurred in many organizations—rather than referring solely to diversity, these titles now refer to inclusion as well. Although a skeptic's view may be that the shift represents a desire to avoid confronting the continuing inequalities that exist within organizations in favor of a broader, more "feel good" focus on inclusion (see, for example, Jayne & Dipboye, 2004), others view inclusion as a fundamental shift in the way that individuals engage across differences. We agree with the latter. By definition, inclusion involves the elimination of marginalization and exclusion. An organization is not inclusive if only the members of select groups are fortunate enough to experience social belongingness and access to the organization's resources. An organization can be considered inclusive to the extent that its policies, practices, and leadership demonstrate that all individuals in the organization have valuable experiences, skills, and ideas to contribute and can integrate their uniqueness without pressure to assimilate in order to be accepted; that is, that they can experience belongingness without sacrificing their uniqueness (Shore, Randel, Chung, Dean, Ehrhart, & Singh, 2010). It is not possible to cultivate such an environment using one-off initiatives and projects. Rather, it requires a fundamental shift in the way an organization thinks about and goes about its work. Unlike many diversity practices that focus specifically on improving the outcomes of disadvantaged groups, inclusion is a general organizing principle that permeates an organization's practices, norms, and operational functioning and that affects employees across the board (Ely & Thomas, 2001; see also Ferdman, Chapter 1, this volume).

We center in our work on inclusive climates. *Climate*, for our purposes, refers to employees' shared perceptions of the formal and informal organizational policies, practices, and procedures with respect to a strategic focus of interest (Reichers & Schneider, 1990)—for example, inclusion, customer service, or safety—in particular the extent to which that focus is a priority in the organization. It is the aggregate of individual climate perceptions that is of greatest theoretical and practical interest, because it reflects the realities that are *shared* by multiple organizational members (James, 1982; James, Joyce, & Slocum, 1984). Thus an organization's climate would not be considered highly inclusive if employees did not share perceptions of its inclusiveness: if only some employees experienced the organization as inclusive, then the aggregate inclusiveness of the environment would suffer.

In our view, there are three primary dimensions that constitute inclusive climates. Consistent with a long tradition of research on climate, we conceptualize climate as emerging from: (1) *organizational practices*, which influence employees' perceptions of what is valued and rewarded in an organization (Ostroff & Bowen, 2000); (2) *interactions* among employees, which give rise to shared meanings and perceptions about the work environment (Schneider & Reichers, 1983); and (3) *objective characteristics of the work setting*, such as the norms and policies that constrain decision making and other behaviors (Payne & Pugh, 1976).

First, it is necessary for organizations to establish a level playing field by fairly implementing employment practices. According to the theories of expectation states (Berger, Fiske, Norman, & Zelditch, 1977; Ridgeway, 1991) and structural ritualization (Knottnerus, 1997), certain groups within society are traditionally treated as being of lower status (Alderfer & Smith, 1982; Alderfer & Thomas, 1988); left unchecked, these societal power imbalances can translate into biased interactions and treatment at work, which not only further perpetuate these societal imbalances and associated negative stereotypes but also make it highly unlikely that lower-status members will be able or willing to contribute meaningfully to organizational processes. However, when an organization's practices and norms delegitimize such societal power imbalances by eliminating the association between favored sociohistorical status and access to resources and opportunities, thereby invalidating the favored status of some groups over others, these status dimensions lose their meaning within that organizational context (Ridgeway & Correll, 2006). Although notions of fairness are complex, with people disagreeing about whether group membership should be taken into account when making organizational decisions (Ferdman,

1997), the important point as far as we are concerned is that the implementation of employment practices leads employees to perceive that arbitrary status differences (based on demographics) are not being perpetuated within a particular context. To the extent that this happens, the intergroup animosity that results from perceptions of favoritism simply is not there to fuel negative interpersonal interactions, and thus individuals are in a better position to engage in constructive and authentic perspective sharing (cf. Ely & Thomas, 2001).

Although we recognize that diversity-specific organizational practices—such as diversity training, targeted recruiting, accountability for diversity goals in performance evaluations, and mentoring programs for women and ethnic minorities—are certainly important, our focus includes the influence that the unfair implementation of HR practices *in general* (like pay, promotions, and access to developmental opportunities) has on the social context. This is because these practices are salient to all employees and serve as important signaling mechanisms about which employees are most supported by their employer (Allen, Shore, & Griffeth, 2003; Shore & Tetrick, 1994). We believe that diversity practices focused on enhancing access—or numerical representation—are not only less effective than originally thought (Kalev, Dobbin, & Kelly, 2006) but also do little to cultivate the organizational conditions that are required for all employees to experience inclusion. Traditional diversity practices may improve opportunities for women and minorities, but such practices on their own are unlikely to significantly alter the more interpersonal, relational sources of discrimination that stifle inclusion (cf. Green & Kalev, 2007–2008). We know from Allport's (1954) classic work on the contact hypothesis that social relations among members of diverse groups will improve and be characterized by inclusion only under certain conditions. First and foremost, perceived equal status is required. This is why the first dimension of climate for inclusion is focused on the messages of equality that employees derive from fair practices consistently applied across the organization.

Equal status is a threshold to inclusion, but it is not enough. Individuals must also have opportunities to get to know each other in more personal ways such that they establish cross-cutting ties and stereotyping is reduced (Allport, 1954; Brewer & Miller, 1988; Ensari & Miller, 2006). Thus our second dimension is focused on the extent to which an organization or unit has adopted an integration strategy (Berry, 1984) that requires adaptation from both dominant and nondominant groups, such that all individuals are able to retain their cultural identities. For employees to feel safe about being authentic at work, there cannot be any palpable pressure for nontraditional employees to assimilate to cultural norms as defined solely by favored employees. If employees perceive that they are being evaluated in terms of their deviance from dominant norms, they are much more likely to constrain their true attitudes and behaviors and construct personas that allow them to blend in with members of favored groups. As long as the psychological safety that people require to express core aspects of their self-identities is lacking, they will carry out their work in a largely scripted and perfunctory manner. We know from research that when people engage in such "surface acting," they experience higher levels of stress and become more disengaged from their work (Hewlin, 2003; Hochschild, 1983; see also Ferdman & Roberts, Chapter 3, this volume).

In contrast, when individuals perceive that it is safe to express core aspects of their self-concept and identity at work and are in fact actively encouraged to do so by their managers and colleagues, they are more likely to infuse their personalities, attitudes, and creativity into their work and to internalize and identify with their work (Argyris, 1964; Brown & Leigh, 1996; Kahn, 1990; Schlenker, 1986). Moreover, they will also be more likely to enjoy the opportunity to be seen by coworkers in ways that are consistent with their own self-views. Such "interpersonal congruence" (Polzer, Milton, & Swann, 2002) results in feelings of connectedness and inclusion (Swann, Milton, & Polzer, 2000). One executive whom we know facilitates opportunities for employees to discover otherwise "unseeable" things about each other by practicing *conocimiento* in team meetings whenever possible. In Spanish, *conocimiento* refers to knowledge or understanding; she operationalizes this by asking team members to each share something from their background or past experiences that has helped inform the way that they approach the task at hand. This, she explains, communicates to her employees that she values their perspectives and individuality, but perhaps more important, it highlights the many previously unknown connections shared among them. Team members then use these connections as a starting point for deeper, more meaningful conversations that allow them to see beyond overly simplistic stereotypes and interact with one another in a more personalized manner. Under such circumstances, mistreatment borne from misunderstanding tends to decline sharply.

Another one of our colleagues told us about how his workplace encouraged employees to connect in more meaningful ways by providing an opportunity for them to share their previously "unseeable" identities. In the main hall of his business school, faculty members were instructed to display a large conference-style poster describing their ongoing research. This stimulated renewed interest among faculty in their colleagues' research, but that wasn't the important change that had been made. On the opposite side of the hallway, faculty were encouraged to display posters that shared details about their nonresearch identities. *This* is what had a transformative impact on the school's culture. By seeing connections with previously distant colleagues (perhaps in other departments), faculty began spontaneous conversations about their hobbies and past experiences, and in so doing, cultivated important cross-boundary ties and genuine camaraderie that previously didn't exist. Faculty reported that cross-department committees functioned more efficiently, territorial divides across departments became less apparent, and new research collaborations sprang up across the faculty.

The development of such meaningful connections that cross traditional demographic and functional boundaries is important not only because these connections promote the experience of social inclusion, but also because they help facilitate informational inclusion. Building on this, the third dimension of inclusive climates focuses on the adoption of mechanisms that facilitate inclusive decision making. The idea underlying this dimension is that an organization's ability to capitalize on the potential benefits associated with increased workforce diversity is contingent on the effectiveness with which diverse perspectives are sought and integrated into decision making, not just from traditionally favored employees but from all employees. Managers can create a climate in which employees are willing to provide their thoughts and ideas about critical work processes by (1) providing multiple channels for upward communication, (2) making a concerted effort to seek informal feedback from employees, (3) being open to alternative ideas about how to go about the organization's work, and (4) actually incorporating the information that they receive into decision making whenever appropriate. Rather than assume that managers know the best way for a group to go about its work, organizations need to exercise what William Foote Whyte described as the "proximity principle," which states that those closest to the work being done are in the best position to design optimal work processes (Rich & Maestro-Scherer, 2001). In addition to using employees' insights to rethink or redefine the work being done by them, it is also important to facilitate productive exchanges about how to improve operations beyond any one individual's specific role. Ideas should be judged based on their quality, not on who is offering them (that is, on the rank or background of the individuals expressing them). Furthermore, rather than being threatened by challenges to the status quo, dissenting opinions need to be sought and reacted to openly, and people must be ready to engage in deep-level processing and integration of the diverse information that emerges from such information sharing.

If, on the other hand, managers are fearful of receiving negative feedback, perceive employees as unknowledgeable or untrustworthy, believe that they themselves know best about most issues, and/or see agreement as healthy but dissent as dangerous, they will quickly create a climate in which employees perceive that contributing one's ideas is not just pointless—it's actually risky (Morrison & Milliken, 2000). Similarly, if they reject, discount, or express annoyance at the input they receive from employees, they will inhibit inclusive decision making and limit decision quality (Milliken, Morrison, & Hewlin, 2003; Tangirala & Ramanujam, 2008) and continuous process improvement (Argyris, 1997), thereby making the organization unable to benefit from diversity.

Of these three dimensions, we view the first as a foundational requirement for the second and third (Nishii, 2008). That is, the creation of work environments that facilitate the full expression of people's true self-concepts (the second dimension) is predicated on the successful implementation of fair employment practices. After all, if employees perceive that some groups are favored over others, or that only employees with certain demographic profiles ascend into senior leadership positions, then they will draw a logical conclusion: in order to have any chance at success within the organization, they should (1) publicly display personas that are organizationally sanctioned and valued, and (2) inhibit any aspects of themselves that diverge from the norms set by the dominant majority. Conversely, by signaling the value of all employees through carefully implemented employment practices, organizations can break down sociohistorical status distinctions and lead employees to reevaluate the perceived legitimacy, permeability, and stability of stereotypes and status differentials (Ellemers, Van Knippenberg, & Wilke, 1990; Elsass & Graves, 1997), thereby paving the way for the interpersonal risk taking and sharing that promote inclusion and quality decision making. Research suggests that one of the biggest obstacles that group members face to effectively build upon, combine, and improve each other's ideas is the fear of being negatively evaluated (Diehl & Stroebe, 1987). This fear can be alleviated when individuals feel supported by others and by the organization, as is the case when equitable HR practices delegitimize sociohistorical status distinctions.

Espoused Versus Experienced Climate for Inclusion

Climate scholars agree that the most appropriate way of assessing the climate of an organization is to solicit the perceptions of employees. Almost all measurement tools ask employees to indicate the extent to which a particular statement about their work environment accurately represents their experiences. While we agree that this is the best way to assess climate, we are concerned that traditional methods don't take into account the possibility that employees' experiences of inclusion diverge from what managers and organizational leaders espouse regarding the organization's climate for inclusion. In the field of diversity and inclusion, perhaps even more so than other areas of management, it is not uncommon to hear employees complain that management does not "walk the talk." That is, employees become accustomed to hearing promises and claims about the importance of fairness, diversity, and inclusion to the organization, but they end up feeling that management does not deliver on their promises. The opposite is possible too, but overpromising and underdelivering are more detrimental to employees than the reverse.

The important point we wish to make here—consistent with arguments in the broader human resource management literature (Bowen & Ostroff, 2004; Nishii & Wright, 2008)—is that espoused practices do not necessarily translate into actual practices and that employee responses to organizational practices are a function of the actual practices, not the espoused ones. Furthermore, the larger the discrepancy between what management claims and what employees actually experience, the worse the outcomes. Indeed, our research supports this idea (Nishii, Leroy, & Simons, 2012). Overall, employees who work in more inclusive climates are more engaged at work and are more willing to engage in citizenship behaviors. However, when considering two units with the same level of experienced climate for inclusion, the bigger the discrepancy between what employees perceive was promised to them with regard to inclusion and what they actually experience, the worse the employee outcomes. The more genuinely the organization is perceived to follow through with its promises of inclusion, the more favorable are employee attitudes and behaviors. These results underscore the need for diversity and inclusion initiatives to be perceived as genuine rather than as window dressing.

Outcomes Associated with Climate for Inclusion

The benefits that accrue to organizations from successfully creating inclusive climates are tremendous. We have developed a measurement scale that includes items measuring each of the three dimensions previously described (Nishii, in press) and have now analyzed data collected from employees working for a range of organizations to understand the individual- and unit-level outcomes associated with a climate for inclusion. Specifically, we ask employees, when answering the items in our climate for inclusion scale, to think about their immediate department or unit; we then aggregate their responses to the unit level of analysis as a representation of employees' collective impression of the inclusiveness of their units. We then use a variety of statistical methods, such as structural equation modeling, to examine how the inclusiveness of a work unit influences the experiences of employees within it.

From these analyses, we see that individuals who work in units with inclusive climates report higher levels of personal inclusion or belongingness within the group, commitment, satisfaction, perceived organizational support, and willingness to engage in citizenship behaviors, and are less likely to leave the organization, compared to individuals working in less inclusive units (Nishii & Langevin, 2009). We have also found that in inclusive climates members of traditionally marginalized groups enjoy much better outcomes. For example, women, members of racial minorities, and people with disabilities report experiencing lower levels of harassment and discrimination. Further, people with disabilities feel more fairly treated during the accommodation process and are more likely to have their accommodation requests granted and receive support from their coworkers for their accommodations (Nishii & Bruyere, 2010). We also see that, although in units that lack an inclusive climate men report more positive work experiences than women (for example, perceived fairness and support, fit and inclusion, engagement) and Whites report more positive experiences than members of ethnic minorities, these demographic-based differences are not evident in inclusive climates. At the unit level, we have found that cohesion is higher and interpersonal conflict is lower among coworkers in inclusive climates, and that, perhaps as a result, these units are able to achieve higher levels of innovation and profits (Nishii, 2011). We have also seen that when interpersonal conflict does occur, employees are better able to resolve that conflict and be more satisfied as a result of having worked through the conflict in inclusive climates (Nishii, in press).

Thus the message is clear: it pays to create inclusive climates. Next, we turn to a discussion of how organizations can go about diagnosing their climates for inclusion and use that information to engage in organizational change efforts to make those climates more inclusive.

Organizational Change Efforts to Become More Inclusive

This section describes how our framework of organizational inclusion and companion assessment tool, combined with participatory action research (PAR) methods, have been used to assist organizations in improving their climates for inclusion. The approach that we describe here is grounded in the tradition of PAR introduced by William Foote Whyte, a pioneer in industrial sociology, author of *Street Corner Society* and other widely known texts, and professor at Cornell University. Whyte was world-renowned for his passion for social reform and change. He strove to empower disenfranchised workers and narrow the gap between those with and without power and wealth. In 1982 Whyte created the extension and community outreach division of Cornell University's Industrial and Labor Relations (ILR) School, known as the Programs for Employment and Workplace Systems (PEWS). His chief motivation was to help organizations to transform by enacting his mantra: "those who know the most about the work are those who do the work." His inclusive approach has been highly influential, both within PEWS and beyond, and the work we present here reflects his influence, particularly since one of us (Robert) worked as an organizational change scholar in PEWS for fourteen years, focusing primarily on increasing inclusion in organizations. The PAR approach is particularly appropriate for change efforts focused on increasing inclusion, because the process itself is highly inclusive and explicitly utilizes many of the principles of inclusive climates. In many ways it is an excellent choice for the participating organization's first adoption of inclusive organizing principles.

Illustrative Example

For pedagogical purposes, we begin with a description of a pilot exercise that we facilitated as a test of the change process design. This was our first experience with an interactive approach to diagnosing ways to reduce discrimination and increase inclusion in an organization. We learned numerous important lessons from this experience:

The image up on the wall is a table of numbers and percentages. It is a cross-tabulation. The table is titled "Perceived Fairness of Pay System." The rows are categories of employees, from frontline to senior management, and in the columns are the different response scales used to assess people's fairness perceptions. About twenty people are assembled to discuss allegations of prejudice and discrimination that had been reported informally and had prompted a formal study. Each person in the room had been recommended by more than one peer to serve on the study group; most were nominated by people in departments other than their own. External nominations were given special consideration, because those individuals who were nominated by people outside of their own departments were considered to be boundary-spanners who would later be very effective at helping to diffuse information quickly.

Although members of the group had suggested that employees be directly interviewed about their perceptions of discrimination, we maintained that direct questioning could elicit socially desirable responses and therefore should be supplemented with more indirect survey methods. Instead, all employees were asked the same questions about their perceptions of the organization's practices, leadership, climate or culture, and everyday experiences. Then, any statistically significant differences among groups in their perceptions could be interpreted as a potential reflection of discrimination and could inform specific recommendations about how the organization's climate for inclusion could be improved. And this is what the chosen group was in the process of trying to do as they "dug into the data," as we refer to it.

Suddenly, someone says, "Oh, no—there's something wrong. I think this says that senior managers see the pay system as more unfair than other employee groups. That can't be right, can it?" Someone else offers, "Maybe they mean their high pay is unfair to others?" Following the laughter, the room falls silent as the group continues to scrutinize the puzzling results before them. The participants, who represent a "diagonal slice" that simultaneously cuts

Continued

across functions and structures of the organization, struggle to interpret the data. Assumptions about management make the finding very improbable to those in the room, many of whom are in hourly positions.

Ultimately, the participants' "local knowledge" about how the integrity of the pay grade system had been compromised when larger, richer departments poached personnel from smaller departments by paying them a couple of grades higher than normal led to hypotheses about how managers in the smaller departments might be disgruntled about the pay system. They tested their hypotheses with data analyses that we ran in real time and projected on a screen so that they had confidence in the data. The process uncovered an actionable area for realignment and an opportunity to improve perceptions of fairness and equal access, both essential elements of inclusion in organizations. From a change perspective, this experience was empowering because it helped participants to see that they had the knowledge necessary to detect and solve problems.

We learned a lot from this exercise. The first lesson we learned was that *PAR techniques are important for maximizing the participation of employees* such that they remain the content and context subject matter experts. We found that the credibility of the change effort was associated with the alignment between the overarching message of inclusion and the methods that were used. Employees themselves identified the research questions, collected data, and then interpreted the data to determine where change was needed, much in keeping with the third dimension of our climate for inclusion conceptualization (inclusion in decision making). Participants in turn related their experiences to coworkers. Because working group members were nominated to represent employees in the change process, it was easy for other employees to identify with them psychologically and to begin to see the world through their eyes (Schein, 1996). Early on, the workforce perceived the change process as empowering and inclusive, and employees started to understand the important role that they would play.

Second, we experienced the *power of grounding the discovery process in data that were unarguably of high quality*. In organizational change efforts, stakeholders who resist the change process or the direction the organization is taking will attempt to discredit the entire effort based on methodological questions. Fairly or unfairly, with or without substantiation, if people question the reliability and validity of the data, they will taint the change process by undercutting the enthusiasm and energy that otherwise materialize when people use data to find out new things about their organization. This may be even more the case in diversity and inclusion efforts, given the backlash and resistance that often accompany such efforts (Thomas & Plaut, 2008). Because of this, it is very important that organizations contract with experts in survey design and data analysis to collect data of unassailable quality. We use only survey scales that have been extensively validated, and we utilize the statistical training of researchers to conduct analyses that ensure the integrity of the data and the confidentiality of people's responses.

We have seen that practitioners often erroneously assume that either (1) anyone can write survey items that can be used to collect such data and run simple descriptive statistics on the data (for example, calculate average scores); or (2) it is prohibitively expensive to administer and analyze a high-quality survey. Both assumptions are faulty. There is an underlying science (psychometrics) to assessing psychological constructs such as employees' perceptions and attitudes. When the assessment is not done properly, it is easy for serious flaws to be introduced—flaws that limit the reliability and validity of the survey instrument. The good news is that a wide range of scales has been published in the research literature, and these can be used in organizational change efforts. The key is to collaborate with someone who has the knowledge and access required to identify these scales. This relates to the second point: although survey administration can be very expensive when contracted through large consulting companies, it often is more affordable when an organization collaborates with an academic researcher, because researchers can be motivated to collaborate in exchange for being able to use collected data for research purposes.

Because they are mandated by their university's Institutional Review Board to guard the confidentiality of the data, organizations can rest assured that they will not be unduly exposed by sharing of the data.

Another lesson that we learned was that it is important to *engage in effective priming.* No amount of reliable or valid data is helpful if the data are not presented to participants in a way that is digestible and therefore capable of stimulating curiosity. We have experimented with various approaches—all the way from beginning a data interpretation session with inch-thick data reports to simply distributing copies of the original survey and asking, "So, what do you want to know? What are you curious about?" We always bring the data on a laptop so that we can run real-time analyses and project them on the screen. From our experience, what works best is to first present participants with a numerical and graphical representation of summative, descriptive information such as overall and subgroup means. Then, as a starting point for the discussion, we highlight survey items on which sociodemographic (such as ethnicity or gender) and/or organizational (such as functional or departmental) groups differed at statistically significant levels. These comparisons always generate intrigue, and as participants discuss their reactions, they end up airing their assumptions and share unique information about the work environment. Indeed, when someone says about a particular finding, "I wonder why that's the case?" the learning process has already started. The facilitator can also help to guide this process if the discussion runs astray by refocusing the group on the potential sources of discrimination or by posing questions that stand out to the facilitator. Although issues of causality cannot be ascertained through this process, it begins the process of inquiry that can lead to subsequent tasks designed specifically to probe more deeply into the main issues of interest. It is this learning that sparks intrinsic motivation to act toward change, which is far more powerful than extrinsic rewards in mobilizing people to invest their attention and energy in change efforts (Pfeffer, 1995).

A fourth lesson that emerged is that it is valuable to *follow structured rules to ensure a feeling of safety and inclusion.* If our methods do not match the message of inclusion, we invite cynicism and withdrawal, so it is important to be hypervigilant about making sure people are not excluded. Every group goes through a process of forming, storming, norming, and performing as they struggle to create structures that will regulate their interpersonal interactions and enable them to achieve their goals (Tuckman, 1965). It is important to facilitate inclusion by providing appropriate structural guidelines; for example: (1) designate a discussion leader who has a defined set of responsibilities; (2) designate a recorder who captures people's ideas (and verifies that they have accurately captured people's intended messages); (3) allow fifteen to twenty minutes of warm-up discussion before calling for a round robin during which every member expresses his or her ideas on the topic; (4) use a multi-voting system to identify which items are the most commonly endorsed by group members; and (5) allow people to self-select the task assignments to which they would like to contribute so that people work on the tasks they personally think are the most important. And it is essential to make sure that every member has a copy of these group rules so that they can hold each other accountable to them.

Finally, this exercise confirmed for us the criticality of *designing the change process in a way that minimizes restraining forces and allows driving forces to gain momentum.* Kurt Lewin's force field theory (1951) highlights how there is often a tension between factors that drive change and those that restrain change from occurring. It is important for participants to begin their group discovery process by identifying the technical, political, and cultural factors that may drive and restrain change. Building on Lewin's work, we have come to see that the role of a good change consultant is to design the change process so that it does not create restraining forces that get in the way of change.

A Step-by-Step Guide to the Change Process

The lessons we learned in this specific exercise, combined with our practical and research experience, led us to make the recommendations summarized in Table 11.1 for how organizations should approach an organizational change effort designed to enhance inclusion in diverse settings. We describe each of these eight steps in the sections that follow.

Table 11.1. Steps Involved in the Change Process

Step	Description
1. Contracting	Educating senior leaders about the PAR approach and about inclusion principles
2. Data Collection	Collecting high-quality data using validated scales as a basis for the change process
3. Peer Reference System	Nominating and selecting members of core working groups
4. Convening of Work Groups	Laying down the ground rules for inclusive processes in groups
5. Data Analysis and Interpretation	Identifying patterns of exclusion and testing explanatory hypotheses through real-time data analysis
6. Identification of Areas for Further Exploration	Converging on interpretations and gathering feedback on them as a means of identifying areas for quick but visible early action
7. Design and Initiation of Improvement Programs	Defining and justifying inclusion initiatives using tools such as From . . . To . . . Because
8. Specification of Expected Outcomes and Related Metrics	Identifying expected outcomes of inclusion initiatives

Contracting

The primary purpose of the contracting phase is to prepare the senior leadership team for what is to come. The assumption is that contracting was initiated by the organization because of some existing dissatisfaction related to diversity and inclusion. However, as noted by scholars such as Edgar Schein (1996), the state of disequilibrium that is brought about by such dissatisfaction is not enough, by itself, to create change, because people can easily dismiss, ignore, or discount the information. For change to occur, leaders first have to be motivated to change by experiencing *survival anxiety* or the fear that if they do not change, they will fail to fulfill their goals or needs. To feel survival anxiety, one must accept the facts that gave rise to the disequilibrium rather than discount them. This can be particularly difficult for leaders, because in the context of inclusion they may perceive that to accept the need for inclusion necessarily requires either admitting that their current leadership style is imperfect or surrendering their power and control. This is not an uncommon reaction; indeed, the belief that managers know best and should be the ones directing and controlling subordinates *does* get in the way of inclusion (Glauser, 1984; Morrison & Milliken, 2000; also see Booysen, Chapter 10, and Gallegos, Chapter 6 this volume).

An important part of this stage, then, is to create some degree of psychological safety (Edmondson, 1999) for leaders so that they are able to accept the proposed change as valid and relevant, thereby internalizing it enough to feel survival anxiety and become motivated to change. Psychological safety can be created by providing positive visions, encouraging leaders, and breaking the learning process into manageable steps. Toward this end, it is helpful to focus on explaining how PAR works, clarifying expectations for the client organization's role in the process, discussing expected timelines, and reviewing the steps listed in Table 11.1. We have also found that providing management with dialogue opportunities that allow them to voice—and thereby relax—their concerns about increasing inclusion can make a big difference. Rather than continuing to harbor their anxieties internally and allow them to get in the way of cognitive and behavioral functioning (Hockey, 1997), facing their fears helps them to feel less vulnerable.

We often focus on helping managers to see that when they adopt a command-and-control form of leadership by delegating and assigning work to subordinates, they maintain control of the work process and therefore have to expend considerable time continually managing the process. Their subordinates are also inhibited from taking initiative and ownership of their work and end up offering little in the way of innovative solutions. But by increasing latitude for decision making and by adopting the proximity principle, managers will benefit from increased efficiencies *and* will end up with more engaged workers who contribute more meaningfully to the manager's goals (Kahn, 1990). We help them see that by increasing inclusion, they will have access to information (from employees) that they did not previously have, which will ultimately make their units more successful. Indeed, inclusive leadership that is characterized by power sharing increases productivity (Hollander, 2009). Our hope is that by sharing with them our own research results—which reveal that the business case for diversity emerges only in inclusive climates—we can at least help them to be open to the possibility that inclusion may benefit them. Usually their attitudes change as they go through the change process.

In this stage, we also train managers on a number of organizing principles that facilitate inclusion. In addition to the proximity principle, we emphasize the rule that no decision should be made about a function without prior consultation with the people who perform that function. Furthermore, we describe the importance of cross-level and cross-department teams. Each team that is constructed within the organization should comprise individuals from one hierarchical layer above and one below the primary members, and whenever possible it should also involve relevant stakeholders in different departments or functions (cf. Brickson, 2000). Such structural changes provide the necessary mechanisms for multidirectional information sharing.

Finally, we emphasize two known principles for human behavior that are critical for managers to understand in order to foster inclusion. The first principle is that perceptions are valid. Rather than evaluating the correctness or validity of others' perceptions, managers need to realize that people's perceptions, and not some objective reality, drive their behavior (Fiske & Taylor, 1991). The second principle is that the felt psychological safety that is derived from interpersonal trust is a prerequisite for inclusion, so managers have to behave in ways that engender employee trust. We find it effective to ask managers to think about all the things that they do to establish and maintain trust with their customers. They usually cite the importance of treating customers with respect and being attuned to customer needs and feedback so that they can provide better service in the future, doing what it takes to coproduce an end product that is maximally useful and satisfying to the customer, and so on. If we then ask managers to what extent they abide by the same principles with their subordinates, they often fall silent. This comparison helps them to appreciate the potential costs associated with an erosion of trust between managers and employees.

Data Collection

The collection of high-quality data from as broad a base of the organization as possible is a must in the PAR approach. As we have already discussed, the process of discovery and learning *must* be grounded in the expressed views of members of the organization. Although people often adopt defensive routines and discount information that they do not want to accept (Lewin, 1951; Schein, 1996), reactions to self-discovered knowledge are different. When people discover things for themselves, that knowledge has immediate credibility. Rather than trigger a fight-or-flight response, it triggers curiosity. They cannot ignore it. We emphasize that no single individual in any organization is capable of accurately representing the views of others, as our own perceptions are clouded by assumptions and biases that are often incorrect. Thus this process needs to be grounded in high-quality data collected from a legitimate and representative sample. What is of most concern to us is that organizations often base major decision making on data that have been collected using sloppy methods: surveys designed by people with no training in psychometrics and analyzed without concern for the reliability or validity of the data, using unsophisticated statistical methods. Academic papers cannot be published in respected journals unless they are based on solid methods that allow alternative hypotheses for the findings to be ruled out; there is absolutely no reason why organizations should not hold themselves accountable to the same high standards, especially as poor-quality data can easily be used to discredit the proposed change.

Peer Reference System

Core working groups that take on the early work in the change process need to be created carefully, such that membership and representation in the groups are inclusive. A key consideration is to achieve broad representation while maintaining comfortable group size. The peer reference system relies on organizational members to nominate the individuals whom they believe will represent them well and participate in rich, productive discussions to better the organization. The procedure begins with the identification of interest groups within the organization (for example, based on race, age, gender, geographic, union, function) and selection criteria for participants. Although the criteria vary based on the local power structure, dynamics of the issues under consideration, and the organizational landscape, common criteria are that group members have a known interest in the topic, demonstrated interest in community activity, and a reputation for open-mindedness. An initial contact person from each of the interest groups is asked to identify several others who fit the criteria, and these people are in turn asked to identify members of the community who fit the criteria. After a master list has been constructed, individuals who have been nominated multiple times and who as a set represent all interest groups are invited to join the working group(s). In the case of groups that are particularly disenfranchised in the organization, it may be important to over-represent them in the working group to facilitate their psychological safety and voice in the process. One of the strengths of the peer reference system is that it ensures that a diagonal slice of the organization is represented in the working groups, sending an early message about the power of working across groups and functions to solve a common problem. Because of the cross-cutting identities that are represented in the groups, the potential for demographic "faultlines" to create subfactions that compete for a voice in the process is greatly reduced (Lau & Murnighan, 1998).

Convening of Working Groups

As working group members convene, they are reminded that it is important that the methods match the message and that they are accountable for operationalizing inclusive methods. As Lewin (1951) suggested, to prompt action the change must have a place and way to begin. When the focus of the change is to increase inclusion, the realization that the methods of change themselves are inclusive provides a starting point for the entire process. As a means of readying the group to operate inclusively, we emphasize their equal status within the group, egalitarian norms, opportunities for self-revealing interactions, and cooperative interdependence (they need each other to solve the problems that emerge). As may be obvious, these prescriptions closely resemble the three dimensions of inclusive climates. We supplement these with the rules for working groups discussed earlier so that at the outset, group interactions are positive and reinforce the value of inclusion.

Data Analysis and Interpretation

The primary objective in this stage is for members of the working group(s) to examine the survey results that have been presented to them in order to identify where exclusion appears to be occurring within the organization. This may be evident in employees' responses to direct questions about bias or exclusion; it may also emerge from subgroup differences in reports of climate for inclusion. For example, the data might show that ethnic minorities experience the organization to be less inclusive than their White counterparts do, or that Asian-Americans working in the Midwest experience lower levels of inclusion than Asian-Americans working on the West Coast. After detecting meaningful patterns, group members share competing theories about what may be causing observed differences; this helps to reveal people's differential lenses and assumptions and also often provides organic opportunities for people to reveal previously "unseeable" aspects of their own backgrounds. As group members test their hypotheses by running additional analyses in real time, they tend to let go of their defensive routines and dive into learning and puzzling together. We also make a point of highlighting group-level results that illustrate how employee experiences differ depending on the inclusiveness of the units within which they work so that participants can begin to derive their own conclusions about the powerful role that inclusive climates play in helping them to achieve the strategic outcomes that they value. This "discovery" helps to sustain the organization's focus on inclusive climates even after the change process ends.

Identification of Areas for Further Exploration

At this point, working groups have formulated their interpretation of what the data say through the lenses of their own experiences, and they begin gathering feedback from other leaders, other working groups, and their peers at large. Once their interpretations have been checked against additional information and feedback, they select candidates for quick but visible early action, using the Action Planning Template (Figure 11.1). After that, group members obtain support from leadership to initiate change in the selected areas. This stage performs two important functions. First, the notable "up-flow" of information that occurs in this process as lower-level employees play an active and important role in decision making attracts a lot of attention regarding the possibility of inclusion. Second, by quickly selecting areas for action, the group is able to reinforce the certainty of change.

Design and Initiation of Improvement Programs

Working groups create a compelling case for each of their chosen action areas by articulating their vision for change, rationale for their vision, and the benefits that are expected to accrue from the change. The tools shown in Figure 11.2 (From . . . To . . . Because) and Figure 11.3 (The Logic Model) are enormously helpful in this process. In the From . . . To . . . Because exercise, group members describe in concrete terms the key differences between the current (From) and the proposed future (To) states, and provide a justification for, or proposed benefit of, each of the proposed changes (Because). After articulating their vision for the changes in ways that can easily be comprehended by others, group members are then ready to identify the activities that logically flow from the "To" box of the From . . . To . . . Because model. An important component of the Logic Model shown in Figure 11.3 is the identification of immediate, intermediate, and long-term outcomes that are expected to result from the activities. This tool helps people to distinguish between measuring actions (what is done) and outcomes of those actions, and to visualize the series of linked effects that ultimately lead to the desired outcome. In the figure,

Figure 11.1. Action Planning Template

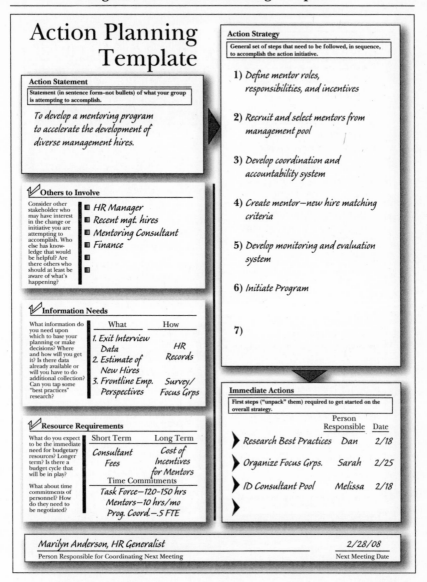

Figure 11.2. From . . . To . . . Because Action Planning Template

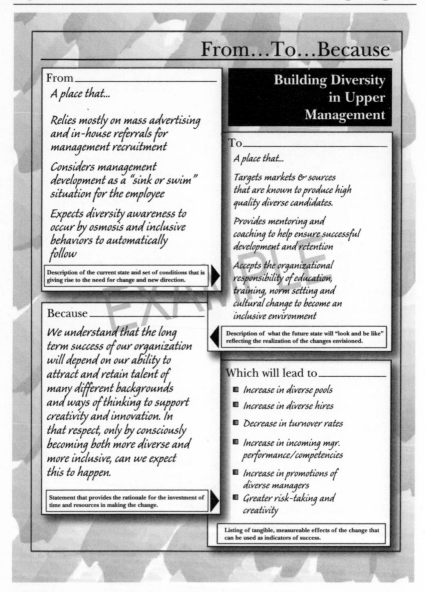

From...To...Because

Building Diversity in Upper Management

From_____
A place that...

Relies mostly on mass advertising and in-house referrals for management recruitment

Considers management development as a "sink or swim" situation for the employee

Expects diversity awareness to occur by osmosis and inclusive behaviors to automatically follow

Description of the current state and set of conditions that is giving rise to the need for change and new direction.

To_____
A place that...

Targets markets & sources that are known to produce high quality diverse candidates.

Provides mentoring and coaching to help ensure successful development and retention

Accepts the organizational responsibility of education, training, norm setting and cultural change to become an inclusive environment

Description of what the future state will "look and be like" reflecting the realization of the changes envisioned.

Because_____

We understand that the long term success of our organization will depend on our ability to attract and retain talent of many different backgrounds and ways of thinking to support creativity and innovation. In that respect, only by consciously becoming both more diverse and more inclusive, can we expect this to happen.

Statement that provides the rationale for the investment of time and resources in making the change.

Which will lead to_____

◼ *Increase in diverse pools*

◼ *Increase in diverse hires*

◼ *Decrease in turnover rates*

◼ *Increase in incoming mgr. performance/competencies*

◼ *Increase in promotions of diverse managers*

◼ *Greater risk-taking and creativity*

Listing of tangible, measureable effects of the change that can be used as indicators of success.

Source: Copyright 2006 Robert E. Rich, The Ithaca Consulting Group, Ithaca, New York.

Figure 11.3. The Logic Model

Activities	Immediate Outcomes	Intermediate Outcomes	Final Outcomes
Assess inclusiveness of climate	(1) Increased awareness of inclusive climates; (2) Identification of problem spots and group differences in experiences of inclusion within organization	(1) Launch efforts to dig deeper into sources of group differences and weaknesses; (2) Design targeted interventions to address sources of identified problems	More inclusive climates, higher felt inclusion among employees
Examine fairness of employment practices	Better understanding of trends and dimensions along which perceptions and experiences of fairness differ within organization	(1) Enhanced managerial sensitivity about these differences; (2) Probing deeper into factors that may account for differential perceptions	Targeted efforts to address sources of differential experience
Create opportunities for employees to share whole selves	Higher levels of sharing, creation of cross-cutting ties, debunking of stereotypes	(1) Better understanding of people's relevant experiences; (2) Improved trust and communication within the organization	(1) Improved perceptions of fit and inclusion; (2) Greater perceived comfort with being true to self at work
Implement mechanisms for increasing inclusion in decision making	More input generated for decision-making	Increased willingness and comfort in sharing one's ideas, even if dissenting	(1) Better-quality decisions made with greater buy-in; (2) Emergence of answers to previously unsolved problems

we have chosen to focus on steps that might logically follow from an assessment of climate for inclusion and from efforts to improve each of the dimensions separately, but the same logic modeling exercise can and should be used to help participants think through the intended outcomes of any intervention. Participants should rely on both professional knowledge and the research literature to formulate the relationships between the action and expected results.

Specification of Expected Outcomes and Related Metrics

By explicating immediate, intermediate, and long-term outcomes in the Logic Model, participants can also identify the metrics that should be examined as a means of evaluating success toward selected goals. This can be done using the Measurement Grid (Figure 11.4). A mid-course correction may be necessary. This should also be verified with data. If an expected intermediary outcome has not been realized, what are the obstacles? By measuring outcomes throughout the linked process to the ultimate goal, the organization has a chance to not only conduct a mid-course correction but also assess progress early on rather than wait (sometimes years) until the entire change process has had a chance to unfold.

Figure 11.4. The Measurement Grid

Activities	Immediate Outcomes	Intermediate Outcomes	Final Outcome
	Expected change	Expected change	Expected change
Assess inclusiveness of climate	(1) Increased awareness of inclusive climates; (2) Identified problem spots and group differences in experiences of inclusion within organization	(1) Launch efforts to dig deeper into sources of group differences and weaknesses; (2) Design targeted interventions to address sources of identified problems	More inclusive climates, higher felt inclusion among employees
	How and When	How and When	How and When
	a) Evidence of enhanced discourse related to inclusion—examined through focus groups and reports from key informants; review of documents and communications from HR to examine whether inclusion principles are more reliably embedded (3–6 months); b) Appropriate analysis of survey data (1–3 months	a) Formation and assessment of progress of diagonal slice task force (6–9 months); b) Review of specific, actionable interventions identified and developed by task force (9–12 months)	Reassessment of organizational inclusion, through survey

Conclusion

Before we end this chapter, we believe it is important to describe how our approach departs from the well-known prescriptions offered by Kotter (1995). In his influential work, Kotter describes the eight steps to transforming an organization: establishing a sense of urgency, forming a powerful guiding coalition, creating a vision, communicating the vision, empowering others to act on the vision, planning for and creating short-term wins, consolidating improvements to produce more change, and institutionalizing new approaches. We agree with the importance of these steps, but we believe that they focus on operational aspects of change and are suggestive of a top-down approach to change management. Without an additional focus on employees' perceptions and reactions to the change process, even change efforts that heed each of Kotter's recommendations could fail to be maximally effective.

As we illustrate in Figure 11.5, the operational factors described by Kotter (1995) are an important part of the change process, but so are the perceptual factors of fairness, trust, and risk taking. Perceptions of fairness are the cornerstone to successful change efforts, because without them employees will not trust the intentions underlying a change effort. Low levels of trust in turn limit the extent to which employees are willing to take risks, share information that is valuable to the success of change efforts, and/or commit to making change happen. Diffusion of the change effort will not gain momentum unless

Figure 11.5. The Change Process: Toward Inclusion

employees perceive the proposed change and the process through which it is enacted to be fair. In other words, "the soft stuff has hard outcomes." We see inclusion itself as the key to making the change process successful. People can get excited about change when they are included in it and own it, but they will almost always resist *being* changed by others, especially those who do not know their work.

In this chapter we have attempted to present both the theoretical case for inclusive climates in organizations and practical methods for achieving them. Our ongoing research has revealed that diversity is associated with better performance outcomes only in inclusive climates (Nishii, 2011), and this logic forms the foundation for our working groups for change, which are focused on understanding how enhanced inclusion can help organizations to develop and achieve better organizational performance. The operationalizing steps outlined here are centered in inclusive mechanisms of change that can transparently introduce the organization, in general, to a new way of perceiving diversity. Beyond being *the right thing to do*, inclusion is the avenue for realizing the vast potential of diversity in organizations.

We should be clear that the steps and methods we proposed here initiate a *process* of building inclusion in organizations. Continuing to maintain a climate of inclusion requires sustained awareness and determination to constantly move in that direction. In the future, we hope to see cultures of inclusion that carry on the assumption of inclusivity in organizational life become more the norm. Our work on climates is intended to help organizations reach that point.

References

Alderfer, C. P., & Smith, K. K. (1982). Studying intergroup relations embedded in organizations. *Administrative Science Quarterly, 27*, 35–65.

Alderfer, C. P., & Thomas, D. A. (1988). The significance of race and ethnicity for understanding organizational behavior. In C. L. Cooper & I. T. Robertson (Eds.), *International review of industrial and organizational psychology* (pp. 1–41). Oxford, England: Wiley.

Allen, D. G., Shore, L. M., & Griffeth, R. W. (2003). The role of perceived organizational support and supportive human resource practices in the turnover process. *Journal of Management, 29,* 99–118.

Allport, G. W. (1954). *The nature of prejudice.* Reading, MA: Addison-Wesley.

Argyris, C. (1964). *Integrating the individual and the organization.* New York: Wiley.

Argyris, C. (1997). Learning and teaching: A theory of action approach. *Journal of Management Education, 21,* 9–26.

Berger, J. M., Fiske, H., Norman, R. Z., & Zelditch, M. (1977). *Status characteristics and social interaction.* New York: Elsevier.

Berry, J. W. (1984). Cultural relations in plural societies: Alternatives to segregation and their socio-psychological implications. In N. Miller & M. Brewer (Eds.), *Groups in contact: The psychology of desegregation* (pp. 11–27). New York: Academic Press.

Bowen, D. E., & Ostroff, C. (2004). Understanding HRM-firm performance linkages: The role of the "strength" of the HRM system. *Academy of Management Review, 29,* 203–221.

Brewer, M. B., & Miller, N. (1988). Contact and cooperation: When do they work? In P. Katz & D. Taylor (Eds.), *Eliminating racism: Profiles in controversy* (pp. 315–326). New York: Plenum.

Brickson, S. (2000). The impact of identity orientation on individual and organizational outcomes in demographically diverse settings. *Academy of Management Review, 25,* 82–101.

Brown, S. P., & Leigh, T. W. (1996). A new look at psychological climate and its relationship to job involvement, effort, and performance. *Journal of Applied Psychology, 81,* 358–368.

Diehl, M., & Stroebe, W. (1987). Productivity loss in brainstorming groups: Toward the solution of a riddle. *Journal of Personality and Social Psychology, 53,* 497–509.

Edmondson, A. (1999). Psychological safety and learning behavior in work teams. *Administrative Science Quarterly, 44,* 350–383.

Ellemers, N., van Knippenberg, D., & Wilke, H. (1990). The influence of permeability of group boundaries and stability of group status on strategies of individual mobility and social change. *British Journal of Social Psychology, 29,* 233–246.

Elsass, P. M., & Graves, L. M. (1997). Demographic diversity in decision-making groups: The experiences of women and people of color. *Academy of Management Review, 22,* 946–973.

Ely, R. J., & Thomas, D. A. (2001). Cultural diversity at work: The effects of diversity perspectives on work group processes and outcomes. *Administrative Science Quarterly, 46,* 229–273.

Ensari, N., & Miller, N. (2006). The application of the personalization model in diversity management. *Group Process & Intergroup Relations, 9,* 589–607.

Ferdman, B. M. (1997). Values about fairness in the ethnically diverse workplace. *Business and the Contemporary World: An International Journal of Business, Economics, and Social Policy, 9,* 191–208.

Fiske, S. T., & Taylor, S. E. (1991). *Social cognition.* New York: McGraw-Hill.

Glauser, M. J. (1984). Upward information flow in organizations: Review and conceptual analysis. *Human Relations, 37,* 613–643.

Green, T. K., & Kalev, A. (2007–2008). Discrimination-reducing measures at the relational level. *Hastings Law Journal, 59,* 1435–1461.

Hewlin, P. F. (2003). And the award for best actor goes to . . . : Facades of conformity in organizational settings. *Academy of Management Review, 28,* 633–642.

Hochschild, A. R. (1983). *The managed heart.* Berkeley: University of California Press.

Hockey, G. R. (1997). Compensatory control in the regulation of human performance under stress and high workload: A cognitive-energetical framework. *Biological Psychology, 45,* 73–93.

Hollander, E. P. (2009). *Inclusive leadership: The essential leader-follower relationship.* New York: Routledge.

James, L. R. (1982). Aggregation bias in estimates of perceptual agreement. *Journal of Applied Psychology, 67,* 219–229.

James, L. R., Joyce, W. F., & Slocum, J. W., Jr. (1984). Collective climate: Agreement as a basis for defining aggregate climates in organizations. *Academy of Management Journal, 27,* 721–742.

Jayne, M. E. A., & Dipboye, R. L. (2004). Leveraging diversity to improve business performance: Research findings and recommendations for organizations. *Human Resource Management, 43,* 409–424.

Kahn, W. A. (1990). Psychological conditions of personal engagement and disengagement at work. *Academy of Management Journal, 33,* 692–724.

Kalev, A., Dobbin, F., & Kelly, E. (2006). Best practices or best guesses? Assessing the efficacy of corporate affirmative action and diversity policies. *American Sociological Review, 71,* 589–617.

Knottnerus, J. D. (1997). The theory of structural ritualization. *Advances in Group Processes, 14,* 257–279.

Kotter, J. P. (1995). Leading change: Why transformational efforts fail. *Harvard Business Review, 73*(2), 59–67.

Lau, D., & Murnighan, J. K. (1998). Demographic diversity and fault-lines: The compositional dynamics of organizational groups. *Academy of Management Review, 23*, 325–340.

Lewin, K. (1951). *Field theory in social science.* New York: Harper.

Milliken, F. J., Morrison, E. W., & Hewlin, P. F. (2003). An exploratory study of employee silence: Issues that employees don't communicate upward and why. *Journal of Management Studies, 40,* 1453–1476.

Morrison, E. W., & Milliken, F. J. (2000). Organizational silence: A barrier to change and development in a pluralistic world. *Academy of Management Review, 25,* 706–725.

Nishii, L. H. (2008, April). Organizational inclusion. In J. Raver & D. van Knippenberg (Chairs), *Diversity mindsets.* Symposium presented at the 23rd Annual Conference of the Society for Industrial and Organizational Psychology, San Francisco, CA.

Nishii, L. H. (2011, August). Eliminating the experiential differences that divide diverse groups through climate for inclusion. In M. Thomas-Hunt (Chair), *Managing status differentials in demographically diverse groups.* Symposium presented at the 71st Annual Meeting of the Academy of Management, San Antonio, TX.

Nishii, L. H. (in press). The benefits of climate for inclusion for gender diverse groups. *Academy of Management Journal,* published online ahead of print October 9, 2012. doi:10.5465/amj.2009.0823

Nishii, L. H., & Bruyere, S. B. (2010, August). Disability harassment and accommodation experiences of employees with disabilities: The role of unit culture and LMX. In D. Stone (Chair), *Emerging issues in research on diversity and unfair discrimination.* Symposium presented at the 70th Annual Meeting of the Academy of Management, Montreal, Quebec.

Nishii, L. H., & Langevin, A. (2009, August). *Climate for inclusion: Unit predictors and outcomes.* Paper presented at the 69th Annual Meeting of the Academy of Management, Chicago.

Nishii, L. H., Leroy, H., & Simons, T. (2012, April). Espoused versus enacted climate: A behavioral integrity lens. In M. Ehrhart (Chair), *Focused organizational climates: New directions and new possibilities.* Symposium presented at the 27th Annual Conference for the Society of Industrial and Organizational Psychology, San Diego.

Nishii, L. H., & Wright, P. (2008). Variability within organizations: Implications for strategic human resource management. In D. B.

Smith (Ed.), *The people make the place* (pp. 225–248). Mahwah, NJ: Erlbaum.

Ostroff, C., & Bowen, D. E. (2000). Moving HR to a higher level: HR practices and organizational effectiveness. In K. J. Klein & S. W. J. Kozlowski (Eds.), *Multilevel theory, research, and methods in organizations: Foundations, extensions, and new directions* (pp. 211–266). San Francisco: Jossey-Bass.

Payne, R. L., & Pugh, D. S. (1976). Organizational structure and climate. In M. Dunnette (Ed.), *Handbook of industrial and organizational psychology* (pp. 1125–1173). Chicago: Rand McNally.

Polzer, J. T., Milton, L. P., & Swann, W. B. Jr. (2002). Capitalizing on diversity: Interpersonal congruence in small work groups. *Administrative Science Quarterly, 47,* 296–324.

Pfeffer, J. (1995). Producing sustainable competitive advantage through the effective management of people. *Academy of Management Executive, 9*(1), 55–69.

Reichers, A. E., & Schneider, B. (1990). Climate and culture: An evolution of constructs. In I. L. Goldstein (Ed.), *Organizational climate and culture* (pp. 5–39). San Francisco: Jossey Bass.

Rich, R., & Maestro-Scherer, J. B. (2001). Self-informing organizational change: A participatory method of data collection, analysis and action planning. *Revue Internationale de Psychosociologie, 16/17,* 1–16.

Ridgeway, C. L. (1991). The social construction of status value: Gender and other nominal characteristics. *Social Forces, 70,* 367–386.

Ridgeway, C. L., & Correll, S. J. (2006). Consensus and the creation of status beliefs. *Social Forces, 85,* 431–453.

Schein, E. H. (1996). Culture: The missing concept in organization studies. *Administrative Science Quarterly, 41,* 229–240.

Schlenker, B. R. (1986). Self-identification: Toward an integration of the private and public self. In R. F. Baumeister (Ed.), *Public self and private self* (pp. 21–56). New York: Springer Verlag.

Schneider, B., & Reichers, A. E. (1983). On the etiology of climates. *Personnel Psychology, 36,* 19–39.

Shore, L. M., Randel, A. E., Chung, B. G., Dean, M. A., Ehrhart, K. H., & Singh, G. (2011). Inclusion and diversity in work groups: A review and model for future research. *Journal of Management, 37,* 1262–1289. doi:10.1177/0149206310385943

Shore, L. M., & Tetrick, L. E. (1994). The psychological contract as an explanatory framework in the employment relationship. In C. L. Cooper & D. M. Rousseau (Eds.), *Trends in organizational behavior* (Vol. 1, pp. 91–109). Chichester, UK: Wiley.

Swann, W. B. Jr., Milton, L. P., & Polzer, J. T. (2000). Should we create a niche or fall in line? Identity negotiation and small group effectiveness. *Journal of Personality and Social Psychology, 79,* 238–250.

Tangirala, S., & Ramanujam, R. (2008). Employee silence on critical work issues: The cross-level effects of procedural justice climate. *Personnel Psychology, 61,* 37–68.

Thmas, K. M., & Plaut, V. C. (2008). The many faces of diversity resistance in the workplace. In K. M. Thomas (Ed.), *Diversity resistance in organizations* (pp. 1–22). Mahwah, NJ: Erlbaum.

Tuckman, B. W. (1965). Developmental sequence in small groups. *Psychological Bulletin, 63,* 384–399.

CHAPTER TWELVE

Models of Global Diversity Management

Karsten Jonsen and Mustafa Özbilgin

Global diversity management (GDM) is an approach to managing diversity in a way that leverages differences in a global workforce. We present models of managing global diversity to aid and inspire practitioners to locate their own organizational practices and reflect on them in the context of academic research. We developed these models drawing on evidence from field studies stretching over a decade. During this time, we have been in close contact with organizations around the globe and executives managing diversity and inclusion departments within their companies. Advocating the use of evidence as a basis for managing global diversity, we identify weaknesses and strengths of each management approach and propose different angles and perspectives on this matter. This chapter brings together different models of GDM that can help frame the rationales, strategy, process, context, interventions, and communications involved in GDM decisions. After presenting models of GDM, the chapter provides examples of how some global corporations systematically approach diversity management. We end up discussing the communication of diversity and inclusion strategies.

Diversity management is a North American concept instigated by the Equal Pay Act of 1963 and the Civil Rights Act of 1964 (Bell, 2012; Ellickson, 2001) and accelerated by scholars who have successfully framed diversity in a business context (Cox, 1993; Ely & Thomas, 2001; Thomas et al., 2002). The concept has been migrating to other regions of the world (Jonsen, Maznevski, & Schneider, 2011; Klarsfeld, 2010; Özbilgin & Syed, 2010; Syed & Özbilgin, 2009). As the concept of diversity management gains new meanings as it travels, it should ideally be reinterpreted according to the demands of the specific context in which it is adopted (see, for example, Boxenbaum, 2006; Glastra, Meerman, Schedler, & de Vries, 2000; Jones, Pringle, & Shepherd, 2000; Klarsfeld, 2009; Omanovic, 2009; Özbilgin, Syed, Ali, & Torunoglu, 2010; Risberg & Soderberg, 2008; Subeliani & Tsogas, 2005; Suss & Kleiner, 2008).

What we learn from the migration experience of the concept of diversity management is that there is neither an agreed-upon definition nor a best method for doing it. Nor should we even take it for granted in corporations, as workforce diversity in many corporations (and societies) across the globe is still being perceived as a *choice*, and some actually choose to say "no" (see Jonsen, Schneider, & Maznevski, 2011). This raises inevitable questions, as suggested by Vedder (2005), of whether diversity management will (1) take off exponentially in number and intensity of organizational adopters and gradually become institutionalized, (2) increase in adoption and intensity in the next few years before losing momentum, or (3) decline over the coming years as a fleeting theme that received unsustainable attention.

For most corporations, however, we are witnessing the emergence of an international repertoire of approaches to managing diversity (Özbilgin & Tatli, 2008). With this chapter, we hope to help decrease the uncertainty in organizations regarding how to manage diversity globally, particularly because uncertainty and lack of knowledge have been identified as barriers for managers to implement diversity management (Jonsen, Schneider, & Maznevski, 2011). In this context, global organizations face a unique challenge to coordinate their diversity management efforts across their national networks, given divergent meanings, starting points, processes, and outcomes for those efforts. Global diversity management (GDM) has emerged out of this unique need for global coordination.

GDM may be defined as a management approach that seeks to leverage diversity in organizations with international, multinational, global, and transnational workforces and operations (Özbilgin & Tatli, 2008). Stumpf, Watson, and Rustogi (1994) explain that GDM is a collection of activities that aim to coordinate diversity management interventions of a global organization across its international branch network (Mor Barak, 2005). Nishii and Özbilgin (2007) point to the dual purpose of GDM: It accommodates local meanings and approaches that diversity management gains when it crosses national borders (see Tatli, Vassilopoulou, Ariss, & Özbilgin, 2012), and it coordinates these disparate approaches toward a coherent global strategy for managing diversity.

Alternative terms are used under the umbrella of global diversity management, with slight variations:

- *Comparative diversity management:* compares and contrasts diversity management across multiple contexts (see, for example, Risberg & Soderberg, 2008).
- *International diversity management:* coordinates diversity management as part of parent and subsidiary relationships in international companies (see, for example, Haq, 2004).
- *Multinational diversity management:* focuses on localizing diversity interventions across branches of a multinational company. In this context, GDM in its more pure form relates to coordination of multiple domestic diversity interventions with a view to giving them global coherence (see Özbilgin & Tatli, 2008; Sippola & Smale, 2007; Wentling & Palma-Rivas, 2000).

Rationales Model of GDM

Before investing in global diversity management, companies need to discuss and decide on their rationales for adoption of diversity, as it is not self-evident that diversity is a critical issue for organizations (Gröschl, 2011). Figure 12.1 shows some of the arguments used inside companies, guided by decades of research. Although many companies do not explicitly state *why* they engage in diversity and its management, these motivations and reasons are, nevertheless, important for how diversity is managed globally and

Figure 12.1. A Model for Organizational Perspectives of Diversity as a Potential Strategic Issue

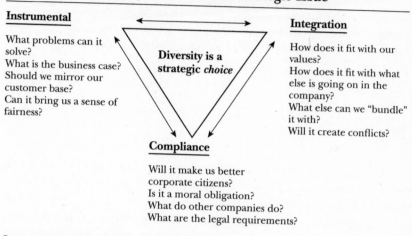

Instrumental

What problems can it solve?
What is the business case?
Should we mirror our customer base?
Can it bring us a sense of fairness?

Diversity is a strategic *choice*

Integration

How does it fit with our values?
How does it fit with what else is going on in the company?
What else can we "bundle" it with?
Will it create conflicts?

Compliance

Will it make us better corporate citizens?
Is it a moral obligation?
What do other companies do?
What are the legal requirements?

Source: Adapted from Jonsen and Jehn, 2009, p. 135.

what interventions are in focus, globally or locally (see also Ely & Thomas, 2001; Ferdman & Brody, 1996; Mor Barak, 2005).

Strategic Model of GDM

Although alternative models are now becoming abundant, in its earlier formulations GDM was about adoption in other regions of the world of domestic approaches developed in North America (Boxenbaum, 2006; Cooke & Saini, 2010; Nishii & Özbilgin, 2007; Özbilgin, 2008; Sippola & Smale, 2007). In addition, multinational and global firms now emerge from developing economies and set up branches in other developing and industrialized countries. Therefore the time is rife to explore how GDM is framed in practice in the new world order, whereby globalization gains a multidirectional form as developing countries enter the global market with their own multinationals. In this new world order, simple unidirectional strategies for managing GD do not work well. The next model, summarized in Table 12.1, illustrates the range of strategic choices available for GDM.

Table 12.1. Three Strategies of GDM

	Localized	*Universal*	*Transversal*
Policy focus	Local branch network policy	Global HQ policy	Global branch network or council policy
Practice	Locally specific	Globally prescribed	Global approach (includes global policies) with national variation

Source: Adapted from Özbilgin, 2009.

Global firms face the challenge of standardizing or localizing their diversity management efforts. The choice between localization and standardization is a false dichotomy, as many global organizations opt for mixed approaches (see Brock and Siscovick, 2007). We identify three strategies for transfer of GDM techniques across branch networks of firms. These are outlined in Table 12.1 as localized, universal, and transversal strategies (Özbilgin & Tatli, 2008).

Localized

Global organizations may choose to localize their diversity management strategies if there is high degree of dissimilarity between home and host country approaches and also little scope for standardization due to differences in regulatory contexts. Alternatively, localization may be an outcome of the readiness of the local context to address diversity issues with preestablished local techniques. However, localization may engender imbalances in the practices of an organization across its headquarters and national branch networks. One prominent example is the fact that gender segregation in occupations is legally enforced in some countries in the Middle East—a practice that would be unlawful in other countries outside the region that have passed gender equality acts. There are similar concerns about use of child labor as a legally acceptable practice in other regions of the world. Lack of coordination from the center may expose the global organization to malpractice and reputational damage if local practices are not sophisticated or congruent with the overall strategic direction of the global organization.

Universal

A universal strategy for GDM overcomes regional and national differences in practice of diversity through a "one best way" approach. The main difficulty in adoption of the universal strategy is that it is blind to differences across national borders, which is problematic when overlooked. For example, ethnic differences are not experienced in the same way globally. While in some countries a majority ethnic group may be dominant, in others minority ethnic groups may hold power. Such historically embedded differences may be disregarded by a universal approach. Evidence from the field suggests that global organizations tend to adopt a mixture of the localized and universal strategies rather than choosing one (Egan and Bendick, 2003; Jonsen, Maznevski, & Schneider, 2010; Mor Barak, 2000).

Transversal

The transversal strategy combines the localized and universal strategies with a view to overcoming their key weaknesses. The transversal strategy involves a commitment to dialogue and negotiation among country representatives of a global organization, in which national priorities for managing diversity are discussed in a bottom-up fashion. In the process, the organization arrives at a set of common principles that all parties may commit to. Karabacakoğlu and Özbilgin (2010) describe a transversal approach that involves active negotiation across the international network of a global firm. Although the transversal approach is sometimes hailed as the holy grail of strategy as it overcomes predicted traps of local and universal approaches, it also may suffer from a weakness of its own. For example, this strategy does not take into account the potential "power struggles" within the organization and how to resolve the potential conflicts between local units and headquarters. A more sophisticated transversal approach would consider power struggles and differences of interest, seeking to provide a truly inclusive platform that tackles inequalities of representation and power.

Nevertheless, for organizations with adequate resources and leadership support, the transversal approach presents a viable way of coordinating diversity management efforts without falling into the above mentioned disadvantages of localization and standardization. Instead, the transversal approach, which involves a global diversity council, made up of local representatives, who intend to develop global policy and practices of diversity, offers extensive possibilities of dialogue, innovation and creativity for effective management of GDM. Karabacakoğlu and Özbilgin (2010) explain that Ericsson adopts this approach in its efforts to manage global diversity.

Process Model of GDM

GDM can be framed as a process in terms of its antecedents, correlates, and consequences. Figure 12.2 presents a framework that illustrates how to manage the process of coordinating global diversity management activities in a global organization. It outlines a number of conditions that make it conducive for organizations to set up a range of GDM activities. If the activities are implemented successfully, they can generate a number of positive organizational outcomes. This model is termed a *process model*, as it depicts inputs, activities, and outputs of managing global diversity across time. The model illustrates that in order to accrue the suggested benefits of diversity management through a set of interventions, an organization should first and foremost have leadership support and other conditions that encourage diversity to flourish. The process model is more suitable for organizations that operate in diversity management contexts, in which the diversity interventions are considered organization-specific concerns, which are not complicated by demands from institutional actors, such as trade unions and other institutions representing collective interests, such as lobbying and network groups.

Contextual Model of GDM

The contextual model of GDM (see Figure 12.3) suggests that activities gain shape through a set of influences at the global, national, sectoral, organizational, and individual levels over time and place (Özbilgin & Tatli, 2008). The contextual model has emerged as a response to studies of GDM from North America that implicitly assumed it would be possible to formulate GDM

Figure 12.2. A Process Model of GDM

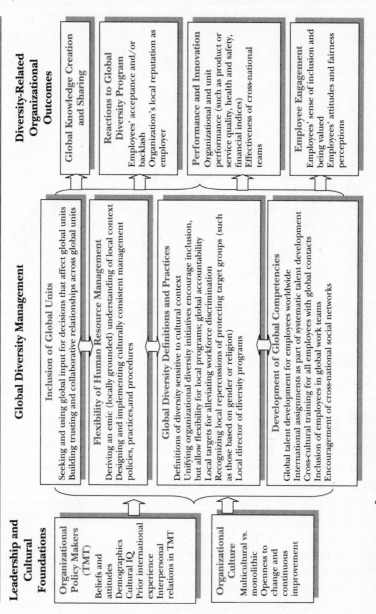

Leadership and Cultural Foundations

Organizational Policy Makers (TMT)

Beliefs and attitudes
Demographics
Cultural IQ
Prior international experience
Interpersonal relations in TMT

Organizational Culture

Multicultural vs. monolithic
Openness to change and continuous improvement

Global Diversity Management

Inclusion of Global Units

Seeking and using global input for decisions that affect global units
Building trusting and collaborative relationships across global units

Flexibility of Human Resource Management

Deriving an emic (locally grounded) understanding of local context
Designing and implementing culturally consistent management policies, practices, and procedures

Global Diversity Definitions and Practices

Definitions of diversity sensitive to cultural context
Unifying organizational diversity initiatives encourage inclusion, but allow flexibility for local programs; global accountability
Local targets for alleviating workforce discrimination
Recognizing local repercussions of protecting target groups (such as those based on gender or religion)
Local director of diversity programs

Development of Global Competencies

Global talent development for employees worldwide
International assignments as part of systematic talent development
Cross-cultural training for all employees with global contacts
Inclusion of employees in global work teams
Encouragement of cross-national social networks

Diversity-Related Organizational Outcomes

Global Knowledge Creation and Sharing

Reactions to Global Diversity Program

Employees' acceptance and/or backlash
Organization's local reputation as employer

Performance and Innovation

Organizational and unit performance (such as product or service quality, health and safety, financial indices)
Effectiveness of cross-national teams

Employee Engagement

Employees' sense of inclusion and being valued
Employees' attitudes and fairness perceptions

Source: Nishii and Özbilgin, 2007, p. 1887.

Figure 12.3. A Contextual Model of GDM

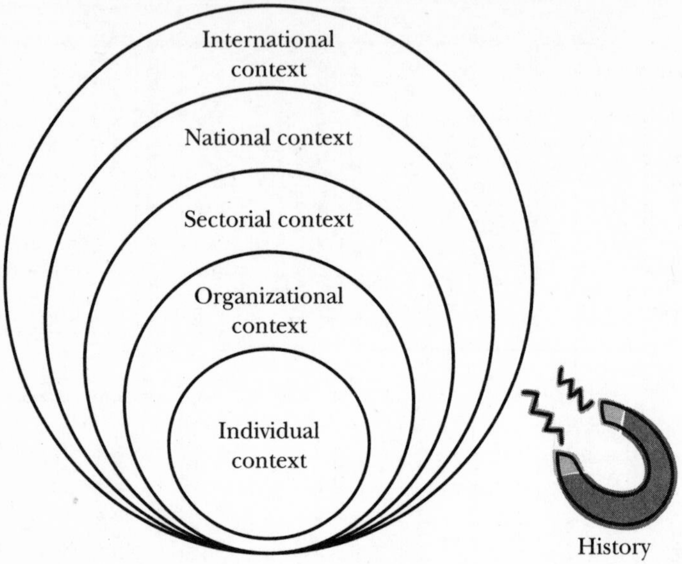

Source: Adapted from Özbilgin and Tatli, 2008, p. 28.

approaches based on the North American context alone. Migration of the GDM formulations to new territories outside North America suggest that in fact contextual influences such as history and human geography account for variations in practices and outcomes (Dameron & Joffre, 2007; Nishii & Özbilgin, 2007; Sippola & Smale, 2007).

Recent evidence (Özbilgin & Tatli, 2011) suggests that divergence of interests and stakes that shape the diversity climate can influence the success and failure of diversity interventions. Global diversity managers need to understand key influences on their diversity activities. These influences may exist at multiple levels, ranging from global to individual. Figure 12.3 shows a contextual model of GDM through a set of layered influences. There is a general tendency in GDM research to ignore the complex influence that layered context can have on how and whether GDM activities are given meaning and provided with resources and leadership support. In contrast, more recently we see recognition of the significance of international, national, and organizational contexts in GDM literature. For example, Joshi and Roh (2009) explain that contextual influences are important in researching GDM (see also Klenke, 2011, for a recent in-depth analysis of context in relation to women in management) and other management and workplace issues (Layder, 1993; Özbilgin, 2005).

The main utility of the contextual model is that it allows practitioners to map out the key influences across international, national, sectoral, organizational, and individual levels. Such an understanding of key stakeholders, individuals, and institutions of influence can help with in-company discussions of why and how GDM is framed and practiced in different ways across these different layers of social and economic life. For example, the European Union acts as a significant supranational power with regulatory influences for organizations that operate across the EU boundaries. However, the main utility of the contextual approach can also become its key weakness, because the relationship between the context and GDM may be envisioned as unidirectional, as the context may be considered to have an effect on the GDM activities. But the impact of GDM practices on the context of the organization often remains unexplored. Indeed, GDM practices can change the context as much as the context can influence GDM strategies.

The first four of the GDM models—rationales, strategic, process, and context—provide only a partial account of GDM activities. We use the word *partial* because these models do not stipulate the range of interventions that GDM activities should involve. Next, we provide intervention models that address some of the stated weaknesses of the three previous models.

Intervention Models of GDM

Most models of GDM do not elaborate how the maturity (age and legitimacy of activity), resources, and strength of support shape the depth of diversity interventions that organizations adopt. To address this gap, we present the intervention model of GDM, which lines up activities in terms of their depth. Some GDM activities remain at a shallow level, as they are limited to a number of interventions that do not change the way organizations embrace diversity and inclusion; others can effect deeper changes in organizations, driving the organization toward an ideal state of full inclusion. However, it is rare to find GDM interventions that seek to address entrenched forms of inequalities or discrimination. Instead, as Martin and Meyerson (2008) write, most interventions suffer from incrementalism, which is sometimes called "softly softly" (small step approaches) among practitioners.

In recognition of the fact that GDM interventions may have different results in different organizations, in this model we divide these interventions into three categories: (1) *informational interventions*, which involve GDM activities that seek to provide information, training, and education to members of staff; (2) *structural interventions*, which seek to change and develop organizational structures and processes; and (3) *cultural interventions*, which challenge the implicit cultural assumptions of the organization with a view to making the organization more welcoming of difference and more inclusive.

If the maturity of GDM in an organization is high, leadership support and resources are strong, and there are high levels of similarity among diversity priorities in the global branch network, we can expect GDM interventions that lead to stronger transformational outcomes, including organization development programs, establishment of diversity councils, and cultural change programs. If, however, these conditions are weak, then we see more surface-level global diversity activities that are limited to awareness raising and basic training. Figure 12.4 depicts how global diversity activities may vary across these three criteria.

Organizations have different starting points on the diagonal line of GDM activities. Some organizations start at the very early steps of the GDM line; others can start from more advanced stages, depending on the strength of their leadership support and resources. Depending on the type, sector, and strategic direction of the organization, GDM may also take small or large steps toward inclusion.

The placement of GDM in the organizational hierarchy can also predict the level of leadership support that it may receive. The GDM office may be centralized in the headquarters or may

Figure 12.4. GDM Activities in Organizational Change

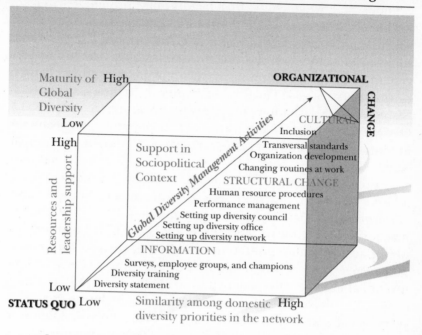

Source: Özbilgin, Jonsen, Tatli, Vassilopoulou, and Surgevil 2013.

have a different headquarters of its own (Karabacakoğlu & Özbilgin, 2010). It can be decentralized or assume a matrix structure with diffuse functions. While in many organizations the GDM function sits close to the human resource management function or is even subsumed under it, other firms have global diversity managers located at the strategic heart of the organization—independent of human resource management—that serve across the institution (Özbilgin & Tatli, 2008). It is possible to centralize, localize, or adopt more complex and distributed positions for diversity management activities. There is also the option of outsourcing diversity management activities to management consultancies, training organizations, or organization development firms.

The intervention model is dynamic, merging the contextual influences with a set of GDM interventions. The model is particularly helpful for GDM practitioners seeking to identify where their organization's activities lie in the trajectory of GDM interventions and what contextual factors may present barriers or enablers for them to move their organizations toward inclusion, which is often the ultimate goal of GDM interventions in more sophisticated and well-resourced organizations. (Inclusion as a goal of diversity interventions is well explained in other chapters of this volume—see Ferdman, Chapter 1; Winters, Chapter 7; Nishii & Rich, Chapter 11; Mor Barak & Daya, chapter 13; O'Mara, Chapter 14—and in the extant literature, for example, Ferdman and Davidson, 2004; Holvino, Ferdman, & Merrill-Sands, 2004).

Roberson (2006) noted that the academic literature did not address inclusion practices; this is unfortunate, because both employees and their organizations can benefit from inclusive climates (Ferdman, Barrera, Allen, & Vuong, 2009). Inclusion is a way of actively valuing differences and using them constructively in all aspects of organizational life, from business issues to organizational climate. Diversity departments in organizations (often called D&I departments) have worked with inclusion for many years, yet the area has only recently drawn scholastic attention, partially through a renewed focus on diversity climate. Consequently, we have only a few proven means of measuring and assessing inclusiveness, primarily based on individual perceptions, with a few exceptions: for example, Ferdman et al. (2009), who studied the relationship of inclusive behaviors by the self, members of workgroups, and the organization with experiences of inclusion. It is important to note that we have limited empirically based knowledge about interventions and how to create an inclusive climate in different cultural contexts (for an exception, see Mor Barak, 2005, and Nishii and Rich, Chapter 11, this volume).

Thus, although managers can look at diversity as a way to *measure* differences, inclusion is seen more as the *how*, for example, as an integrated part of the annual climate surveys made at Dutch Royal Shell. Figure 12.5 presents an example from Shell's global D&I department, in which diversity, as a change initiative, is approached at three different levels: personal, interpersonal, and organizational. Each level requires different thinking and initiatives, and perhaps even different managerial skills, yet they are all

Figure 12.5. Shell's Global D&I

An inclusive environment that respects and values difference is built on our behaviours and systems. For change to be sustainable, efforts must be focused at three levels.

LEVELS OF CHANGE

personal

▲ **LEARN ABOUT YOURSELF**
- Engage in continuous learning
- Understand your attitudes and behaviours

- Identify personal assumptions and beliefs
- Deal with biases you may have

interpersonal

▲ **BUILD DIVERSE / INCLUSIVE RELATIONSHIPS**
- Seek to listen and understand
- Challenge assumptions and behaviours that exclude and limit

- Build inclusive workgroups and teams
- Form productive relationships

organisational

▲ **LEAD THE PROCESS**
- Develop the D&I plan
- Build tools, processes and systems
- Develop goals, measures and accountability

- Model desired behaviour
- Communicate
- Provide resources
- Identify and remove barriers

Source: Royal Dutch Shell plc, "Diversity and Inclusion in Shell" [company brochure], 2011.

equally important. The importance of this model is that it depicts diversity, and inclusion in particular, as change initiatives, and that it "forces" the involved parties to think across levels (see also Ferdman & Brody, 1996; Sucher & Beyersdorfer, 2011; Sucher & Corsi, 2009).

House Model of GDM

The models shown earlier in this chapter work particularly well as reference frames for diversity and inclusion, although managers often do not use the same labels as in the theoretical literature. When it comes to the applied level, several large corporations—such as Hewlett-Packard, Sodexo, and Royal Dutch Shell—have used the pragmatic model depicted in Figure 12.6 for managing their diversity and inclusion. The House Model was built for global organizations with diversity and inclusion departments for their business on a global scale. In many places in the world, there is no legal compliance associated with D&I, so the key question gravitates toward what business value D&I brings, and how D&I supports the overall corporate objectives (see discussions of the rationales behind diversity, earlier in this chapter).

This model is built to design a global strategy, while taking into account national as well as business specific requirements. In Royal Dutch Shell, for example, the global D&I strategy was designed with input from the businesses and regions, and in the end the agreement entailed that all regions and businesses adopt 80 percent from the global D&I strategy and plan while leaving a 20-percent flexibility in their respective D&I plan to add local, national, or business-specific D&I requirements. In essence, the model is managed so that it negotiates national priorities vis-à-vis global "requirements." For example, in the United States, people of color (POC) was a focus area; in Malaysia, local Bumi Putra quotas were added; and in the downstream (retail) business, there was a stronger focus on attracting and developing Asian talent. Called the 80/20 model at Shell, it was embraced by regions and businesses alike. It demonstrated in many ways how truly global the D&I strategy was, and it allowed for aligned focus on key areas, which resulted in progress year over year in both diversity numbers

Figure 12.6. The Diversity and Inclusion House

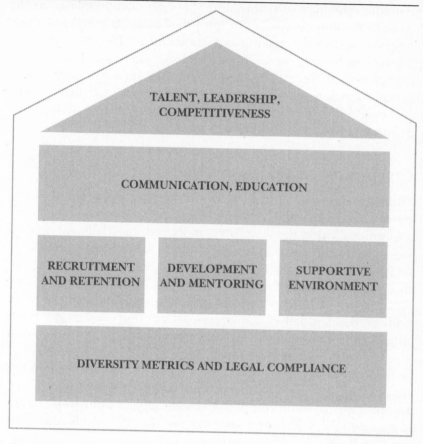

Source: J. van Zanten, former VP of Diversity & Inclusion (2006–2011), Royal Dutch Shell plc; personal communication, October 1, 2010, and July 15, 2011.

and inclusion ratings (J. van Zanten, Global VP of D&I 2006–2011, Royal Dutch Shell; personal communication, October 1, 2010, July 15, 2011).

It so happens that semantics associated with legal compliance— such as "minorities," "quotas," "equal opportunity," and more— create local resistance, as the terms refer to some countries' specific legal requirements but cannot easily be applied, nor do they make sense, across all borders. How then does a chief diversity officer implement D&I change in a corporation that oversees all regions and deals with a multitude of cultures? The model is a simple reflection of reality, and like most change management models, the complexity lies in both the thoughts and discussions prior to the decision making and its execution. The latter requires a seasoned leader, preferably with global diversity management experience, to oversee the implementation. It calls on a broad set of skills—change management, branding, communication, system and process mastery, external focus, customer orientation, intercultural experience, and more.

Communication Models of Diversity

When a company invests resources in diversity management activities such as promoting better relations between diverse members and groups within the workforce, it often does so without classifying its action as such. In essence, many activities that create or facilitate diversity may not be formally labeled as diversity activities, perhaps because in many countries outside of the United States there is little perceived reason to be politically correct, and/or the legislative consequences for "not saying the right thing" are relatively light. We can also speculate that some companies that occasionally embrace diversity do so at the explicit and more rhetorical level, without necessarily reaching or changing more profound levels (such as values, norms, and informal rules). In other words, some companies pay lip service while implementing superficial efforts and favoring the rhetoric of equality over equality itself.

Figure 12.7 encapsulates and summarizes different scenarios, showing what is written down and shown off—the rhetoric—versus what actually goes on—the reality. The upper left quadrant ("Walk the talk") represents companies that are highly committed to diversity in reality in addition to actively sharing information about their diversity activities. Top management team (TMT) commitment means that diversity is on the strategic agenda and significant resources and attention are allocated. The upper right quadrant ("Empty rhetoric") represents companies that talk actively and proactively about diversity and its importance but don't take more than cosmetic action, if any, or perhaps just enough to be politically correct—that is, "window dressing." In

Figure 12.7. Reality Versus Rhetoric: Diversity

| | | Reality (TMT Commitment) | |
		Yes	No
Rhetoric (Espoused Choice)	Yes	Walk the talk	Empty rhetoric
	No	Just do it	Low priority

the lower left quadrant ("Just do it") we find companies that do have a diversity strategy and are undertaking important activities in that area but that do not officially state them or label them as diversity activities. Companies that have rhetorically rejected diversity in one way or another, and have no strategy or dedicated resources, are in the lower right quadrant ("Low priority"). This matrix can serve as a framework for future cross-organizational research, in order to better understand "the state of diversity" and other organizational values in different countries, organizations, and contexts. Organizations that investigate or evaluate diversity and inclusion may reflect on which quadrant they are in and use it for discussions in relation to where they want to be and how they can get there.

Arguably, the four cells are a simplification of reality, which will mostly reside somewhat in between the categories. For example, analyses of oil companies lead to the conclusion that some of them demonstrate strong rhetoric (or intentions) but relatively weak implementation, and vice versa (Säverud & Skjärseth, 2007). Thus a few years ago, Exxon Mobil was "greener" than it indicated in its strategy formulation, while Shell was more proactively rhetorical but allocated fewer resources to back its claims. The biggest problem in both cases is the inconsistency between the walk and the talk, as in the bottom left quadrant or top right quadrant in Figure 12.7. For example, a façade of "empty rhetoric" to impress outsiders, with little action or implementation to follow up, is a risky strategy, because stakeholders and new hires will soon realize the discrepancy. This in turn will hurt the company's integrity and image: if the lived experiences of the employees do not correspond to the rhetoric, this may lead to long-term distrust in the system and its leaders (Fairhurst, Monroe, & Neuwirth, 1997) and potentially to cynicism and apathy (Ledford, Wendenhof, & Strahley, 1995).

When substantial resources are put into diversity and inclusion programs, it would be a shame not to benefit from the potential improvements to the company's reputation with at least some stakeholders. For example, Argyris (1985) argues that values that are not openly articulated or acknowledged lead to defensive routines that inhibit learning and produce nonrational responses. On the other hand, if a company is consistently communicating matters around diversity that are inflated or untrue, this may eventually be revealed by employees or customers and exposed in blogs or websites in ways that damage the company. In essence, it is important to have consistency between the rhetoric of diversity and the reality, as illustrated by Figure 12.8. The consistency path (or integrity path) in Figure 12.8 shows that an alignment is needed between what a company says and what it does, and that the espoused values must be, at least somewhat, close to the lived. If diversity and inclusion is not a demonstrated,

Figure 12.8. Reality Versus Rhetoric: Consistency Path

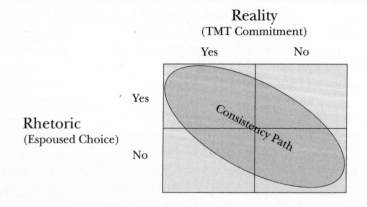

lived value, it should not be proclaimed as one. If, however, it *is* central to a company's culture and identity, it is worthwhile to communicate it.

Concluding Remarks and the Purpose of D&I Models

Diversity is an essential condition for life on earth. Yet, as the evidence of diversity's effects on organizational performance is rich but inconclusive, it can be hard to grasp how to effectively manage it. We need new and multiple ways to frame and advance the intricate relationships among diversity, performance, and business. Research has failed to convincingly deal with how organizations interpret workforce diversity and inclusion, and, more important, how they should go about implementing diversity and inclusion management globally. In fact, we believe that diversity may end up as a *tragedy of the uncommons* (see Jonsen, Tatli, Özbilgin, & Bell, 2013), because society as a whole is losing out as individual organizations either do not use or take advantage of it or disregard it altogether. Thus we argue that, ideally, diversity and inclusion efforts should be not a strategic choice per se but rather a logical consequence of societal reality.

GDM has, nevertheless, become an important field of management in many global organizations. Yet models of GDM are not common in the academic literature. To address this gap, we have presented a variety of GDM models that can help GDM practitioners to locate their organizations in terms of their choices and activities. The fundamental idea behind the models is to develop visual representations or roadmaps. They will help (some of) us organize our thinking and orient development by intended outcomes rather than, for example, limited resources. They can also help us to generate thoughts and discussions about where our starting points are and where we want to go, and to compare this to what others are doing in a simplistic yet meaningful way.

The *rationales model* explains what logic and rationales are used when diversity is discussed as a potential strategic issue in an organization, and thereby create insights into the understanding and interpretation of diversity as a strategic issue. This is intended to increase our understanding of how organizations decide to respond to diversity as a potential strategic issue and which rationales are important to decision makers, also at the individual level. The categories may not be equally important to all people at all times, but in combination they cover the consideration and rationales of the potential adoption of the issue. This may be especially helpful for those organizations that are in the process of adopting or evaluating diversity and inclusion and what resources to devote to it.

The *strategic model* of GDM is about why and how global organizations decide to localize or standardize their GDM policies and interventions. We presented a third alternative that is becoming more common in practice: transversal strategy making, in which global organizations include their local branches or businesses in the strategy making process.

As the strategic model does not account for specific GDM activities, we also present the *process model*, which summarizes the range of GDM activities in terms of their preconditions and outcomes. The process model explains that, provided there is strong leadership support and a positive diversity climate, and a range of GDM activities are performed, a number of positive organizational benefits can accrue. The process model is particularly useful in understanding the connections among the setting, activities, and outcomes of GDM. However, the process model operates only at the organizational level and does not necessarily include an appreciation that GDM decisions, activities, and strategies are affected by layered contextual influences at the international, national, sectoral, organizational, and individual levels that the contextual model takes into account.

The *contextual model* may help GDM practitioners to understand the key influences and influential actors that shape the meanings and processes of GDM across these multiple levels. To do this, it is possible to identify at each level a number of key influences and map out how these influences will shape the GDM approach, interventions, and activities. However, the key weakness of the contextual model is that it does not give GDM practitioners an understanding of the activities from which they may choose to effect changes for the better at work.

To fill this gap, we present the *intervention model* of GDM. The intervention model lines up GDM interventions from weak (informational) to strong (cultural) in terms of their ability to effect organizational changes. The intervention model also connects the context of the organization to the range of GDM activities, suggesting that stronger support for GDM can help organizations to adopt interventions that are more effective in facilitating real and deep changes, including inclusion. Finally, they emphasize the importance of activities (and reflections) at all levels.

The *house model* pulls it together in a simple, manageable format, rooted in a transversal way of thinking wherein some strategic activities and measurements are set universally and some strategic and tactical activities are decentralized, either geographically or sectorally; thus its variation encompasses a matrix-like complexity in which countries and business units have different needs—often shaped by the contextual factors.

We end by discussing a framework for if and when diversity and inclusion activities should be communicated externally, and we present two communication models (thinking frameworks). We have found a large discrepancy between what is said and what is done. We are not trying to moralize here, but rather to effectively provide a tool to understand the need for a balance between rhetoric and reality: in essence, to limit the window-dressing and to augment the communication when reality is in place to support it, as it has great value for communicating to existing and potential stakeholders.

Our contribution in this chapter is important, we hope, as many organizations, especially in regions outside of North America, do not yet have diversity and inclusion management or policies implemented. Researchers, policy makers, consultants, and practitioners are therefore advised to acknowledge the challenging state that some organizations are in, and to help improve conditions by consulting the tools and models described in this chapter.

References

Argyris, C. (1985). *Strategy, change, and defensive routines*. Boston, MA: Pitman.

Bell, M. P. (2012). *Diversity in organizations* (2nd ed.). Mason, OH: South-Western Cengage Learning.

Boxenbaum, E. (2006). Lost in translation? The making of Danish diversity management. *American Behavioral Scientist, 49*, 939–948.

Brock, D. M., & Siscovick, I. C. (2007). Global integration and local responsiveness in multinational subsidiaries: Some strategy, structure, and human resource contingencies. *Asia Pacific Journal of Human Resources, 45*(3), 353–373.

Cooke, F. L., & Saini, D. S. (2010). Diversity management in India: A study of organizations in different ownership forms and industrial sectors. *Human Resource Management, 49*(3), 477–500.

Cox, T. H., Jr. (1993). *Cultural diversity in organizations: Theory, research, and practice.* San Francisco: Berrett-Koehler.

Dameron, S., & Joffre, O. (2007). The good and the bad: The impact of diversity management on cooperative relationships. *International Journal of Human Resource Management, 18*(11), 2037–2056.

Egan, M. L., & Bendick Jr., M. (2003). Workforce diversity initiatives of U.S. multinational corporations in Europe. *Thunderbird International Business Review, 46*, 701–728.

Ellickson, R. C. (2001). The evolution of social norms: A perspective from the legal academy. In M. Hechter & K.-D. Opp (Eds.), *Social norms* (pp. 35–75). New York: Russell Sage Foundation.

Ely, R. J., & Thomas, D. A. (2001). Cultural diversity at work: The effects of diversity perspectives on work group processes and outcomes. *Administrative Science Quarterly, 46*(2), 229–273.

Ferdman, B. M., Barrera, V., Allen, A. A., & Vuong, V. (2009, August 11). Inclusive behavior and the experience of inclusion. In B. G. Chung (Chair), *Inclusion in organizations: Measures, HR practices, and climate.* Symposium presented at the 69th Annual Meeting of the Academy of Management, Chicago.

Ferdman, B. M., & Brody, S. E. (1996). Models of diversity training. In D. Landis & R. Bhagat (Eds.), *Handbook of intercultural training* (2nd ed., pp. 282–303). Thousand Oaks, CA: Sage.

Ferdman, B. M., & Davidson, M. N. (2004). A matter of difference—Some learning about inclusion: Continuing the dialogue. *The Industrial-Organizational Psychologist, 41*(4), 31–37.

Fairhurst, G. T., Monroe J., & Neuwirth, K. (1997). Why are we here? Managing the meaning of an organizational mission statement. *Journal of Applied Communication Research, 25*, 243–263.

Glastra, F., Meerman, M., Schedler, P., & de Vries, S. (2000). Broadening the scope of diversity management: Strategic implications in the case of the Netherlands. *Industrial Relations, 55*, 698–721.

Gröschl, S. (2011). *Diversity in the workplace: Multi-disciplinary and international perspectives.* London, UK: Gower.

Haq, R. (2004). International perspectives on workplace diversity. In M. S. Stockdale & F. J. Crosby (Eds), *The psychology and management of workplace diversity* (pp. 277–298). Malden, MA: Blackwell.

Holvino, E., Ferdman, B. M., & Merrill-Sands, D. (2004). Creating and sustaining diversity and inclusion in organizations: Strategies and approaches. In M. S. Stockdale & F. J. Crosby (Eds.), *The psychology and management of workplace diversity* (pp. 245–276). Malden, MA: Blackwell.

Jones, D., Pringle, J., & Shepherd, D. (2000). Managing diversity meets Aotearoa/New Zealand. *Personnel Review 29*(3), 364–380.

Jonsen, K., & Jehn, K. (2009). Using triangulation to validate themes in qualitative studies. *Qualitative Research in Organizations and Management: An International Journal, 4*(2), 123–150.

Jonsen, K., Maznevski, M. L., & Schneider, S. C. (2010). Gender differences in leadership—Believing is seeing: Implications for managing diversity. *Equal Opportunities: An International Journal, 29*(6), 549–572.

Jonsen, K., Maznevski, M. L., & Schneider, S. C. (2011). Diversity and its not so diverse literature: An international perspective. *International Journal of Cross Cultural Management, 10*(1), 35–62.

Jonsen, K., Schneider, S. C., & Maznevski, M. L. (2011). Diversity as a strategic choice? In S. Gröschl (Ed.), *Diversity in the workplace: Multi-disciplinary and international perspectives.* London, UK: Gower.

Jonsen, K., Tatli, A., Özbilgin, M., & Bell, M. P. (2013). The tragedy of the uncommons: Reframing workforce diversity. *Human Relations, 66,* 271–294. doi 10.1177/0018726712466575

Joshi, A., & Roh, H. (2009). The role of context in work team diversity research: A meta-analytic review. *Academy of Management Journal, 52*(3), 599–627.

Karabacakoğlu, F., & Özbilgin, M. (2010). Global diversity management at Ericsson: The business case. In L. Costanzo. (Ed.), *Cases in strategic management* (pp. 79–91). London, UK: McGraw-Hill.

Klarsfeld, A. (2009). The diffusion of diversity management: The case of France. *Scandinavian Journal of Management, 25,* 363–373.

Klarsfeld, A. (2010). *International handbook on diversity management at work: Country perspectives on diversity and equal treatment.* Cheltenham, UK, and New York: Edward Elgar.

Klenke, K. (2011). *Women in leadership: Contextual dynamics and boundaries.* London, UK: Emerald Group Publishing.

Layder, D. (1993). *New strategies in social research.* Cambridge, UK: Polity Press.

Ledford, G. E. Jr., Wendenhof, J. R., & Strahley, J. T. (1995). Realizing a corporate philosophy. *Organizational Dynamics, 23*(3), 5–19.

Martin, J., & Meyerson, D. (2008). Gender inequity and the need to study change. In D. Barry & H. Hansen (Eds.), *New approaches in management and organization* (pp. 552–553). Thousand Oaks, CA: Sage.

Mor Barak, M. E. (2000). The inclusive workplace: An ecosystems approach to diversity management. *Social Work, 45,* 339–352.

Mor Barak, M. E. (2005). *Managing diversity: Toward a globally inclusive workplace.* Thousand Oaks, CA: Sage.

Nishii, L. H., & Özbilgin, M. F. (2007). Global diversity management: Towards a conceptual framework. *International Journal of Human Resource Management, 18*(11), 1883–1894.

Omanovic, V. (2009). Diversity and its management as a dialectical process: Encountering Sweden and the US. *Scandinavian Journal of Management, 25,* 352–62.

Özbilgin, M. F. (2005). Relational methods in organization studies. In O. Kyriakidou & M. F. Özbilgin (Eds.), *Relational perspectives in organization studies: A research companion* (pp. 244–264). Cheltenham, UK: Edward Elgar.

Özbilgin, M. F. (2008). Global diversity management. In P. Smith, M. F. Peterson, & D. C. Thomas (Eds.), *The handbook of cross-cultural management research* (pp. 379–396). Thousand Oaks, CA: Sage.

Özbilgin, M. F. (Ed.). (2009). *Equality, diversity and inclusion at work: A research companion.* Cheltenham, UK, and New York: Edward Elgar.

Özbilgin, M., Jonsen, K., Tatli, A., Vassilopoulou, J., & Surgevil, O. (2013). Global diversity management. In Q. M. Roberson (Ed.), *The Oxford handbook of diversity and work* (pp. 419–441). New York: Oxford University Press.

Özbilgin, M. F., & Syed, J. (2010). *Managing gender diversity in Asia: A research companion.* Cheltenham, UK, and New York: Edward Elgar.

Özbilgin, M. F., Syed, J., Ali, F., & Torunoglu, D. (2010). International transfer of policies and practices of gender equality in employment to and among Muslim majority countries: A study of Turkey and Pakistan. *Gender, Work and Organization, 19*(4), 345–369.

Özbilgin, M. F., & Tatli, A. (2008). *Global diversity management: An evidence-based approach.* Basingstoke, UK: Palgrave.

Özbilgin, M. F., & Tatli, A. (2011). Mapping out the field of equality and diversity: Rise of individualism and voluntarism. *Human Relations*, *64*(9), 1229–1253.

Risberg, A., & Soderberg, A. M. (2008). Translating a management concept: Diversity management in Denmark. *Gender in Management*, *23*, 426–441.

Roberson, Q. M. (2006). Disentangling the meanings of diversity and inclusion in organizations, *Group & Organization Management*, *31*(2), 212–236. doi: 10.1177/1059601104273064

Säverud, I. A., & Skjärseth, J. B. (2007). Oil companies and climate change: Inconsistencies between strategy formulation and implementation. *Global Environmental Politics*, *7*, 42–62.

Sippola, A., & Smale, A. (2007). The global integration of diversity management: A longitudinal case study. *International Journal of Human Resource Management*, *18*(11), 1895–1916.

Stumpf, S. A., Watson, M. A., & Rustogi, H. (1994). Leadership in a global village: Creating practice fields to develop learning organizations. *Journal of Management Development*, *13*, 16–25.

Subeliani, D., & Tsogas. G. (2005). Managing diversity in The Netherlands: a case study of Rabobank. *International Journal of Human Resource Management*, *16*, 831–851.

Sucher, S. J., & Beyersdorfer, E. (2011, January 11). *Global diversity and inclusion at Royal Dutch Shell (B): The impact of restructuring.* Harvard Business School General Management Unit Case 611–051. Available at SSRN: http://ssrn.com/abstract=2006653

Sucher, S. J., & Corsi, E. (2009, March 9). *Global diversity and inclusion at Royal Dutch Shell (A).* Harvard Business School Case 610–056. Harvard Business School Technology & Operations Mgt. Unit. Available at SSRN: http://ssrn.com/abstract=1628643

Suss, S., & Kleiner, M. (2008). Dissemination of diversity management in Germany: A new institutionalist approach. *European Management Journal*, *26*, 35–47.

Syed, J., & Özbilgin, M. (2009). A relational framework for international transfer of diversity management practices. *International Journal of Human Resource Management*, *20*(12), 2435–2453.

Tatli, A., Vassilopoulou, J., Ariss, A. A., & Özbilgin, M. (2012). The role of regulatory and temporal context in the construction of diversity discourses: The case of the UK, France and Germany. *European Journal of Industrial Relations*, *18*, 293–308. doi: 10.1177/0959680112461092

Thomas, R. R., Jr., Thomas, D. A., Ely, R. J., Meyerson, D., Fletcher, J., Hayashi, A. M., . . . Williamson, A. D. (2002). *Harvard Business Review on managing diversity.* Boston, MA: Harvard Business School Press.

Vedder, G. (2005). Diversity management—quo vadis? *Personal, 57*(5), 20–22.

Wentling, R. M., & Palma-Rivas, N. (2000). Current status of diversity initiatives in selected multinational corporations. *Human Resource Development Quarterly, 11*(1), 35–60.

CHAPTER THIRTEEN

Fostering Inclusion from the Inside Out to Create an Inclusive Workplace

Corporate and Organizational Efforts in the Community and the Global Society

Michàlle E. Mor Barak and Preeya Daya

The world is changing quite rapidly, with unprecedented economic, demographic, social, and legislative trends leading to increased diversity in both our communities and our workplaces. This increased diversity is fertile ground for heightened collaboration and inclusion on one hand, and intergroup conflict and exclusion on the other (Mor Barak & Travis, 2013). The legislative and social policy initiatives undertaken by international organizations (such as the United Nations' Universal Declaration of Human Rights in 1948 and the Charter of Fundamental Rights of the European Union in 2000) and the actions taken by the International Labor Organization (for example, Bureau for Employers' Activities, 2012; Bureau for Gender Equality, 2012), and individual countries (such as the New Zealand Bill of Rights in 1990, the Hong Kong Bill of Rights Ordinance in 1991, and the South Africa Bill of Rights in 1996) can mitigate potential harmful effects of diversity. They also delineate the "rules of the game" for work organizations. However, these legislative and social policy initiatives are more than contextual guidelines for conducting business locally and globally; they define the *scope* of what companies need to consider as their domain when they design diversity policies and programs.

In this chapter, we argue that to avoid the pitfalls and reap the benefits of a diverse workforce, employers need to adopt a *broader vision of inclusion*—a vision that includes not only the organization itself but also its surrounding community and its national and international context. Specifically, this chapter:

- Provides a description of the *inclusive workplace model* (originated and developed by Mor Barak, 2000a, 2005, 2011), highlighting the role of community and society as stakeholders
- Proposes a three-stage continuum of practices that takes inclusion beyond the proverbial corporate walls—from corporate philanthropy through corporate social responsibility to corporate inclusion strategy—treating the community and wider society as true stakeholders
- Demonstrates these policies and practices through case studies, outlining the benefits and obstacles of the expanded scope of inclusion practices and providing implications for corporate strategic vision

The Inclusive Workplace: Community and Society as True Stakeholders

The inclusive workplace model, created by the first author (Mor Barak, 2000b) based on earlier organization-based research (Mor Barak & Cherin, 1998; Mor Barak, Cherin, & Berkman, 1998) and expanded in her later work (Mor Barak, 2005, 2011; Mor Barak & Travis, 2010, 2013), provides a rationale for relating to the local community and society as a whole as stakeholders in any organization.

Contextually, the United States experienced an extraordinary economic crisis as a result of the 2008 economic downturn that reverberated throughout the global economy and had a profound impact on the workforce (International Labour Organization, 2011). Coupled with waves of regional political unrest and continued societal globalization, these events reflect the socioeconomic context that undergirds the need to collaborate with the community and wider society as true partners of business organizations in terms of promoting the well-being of workers, their communities, and beyond.

The concept of the inclusive workplace (Mor Barak, 2000b, 2005, 2011) refers to a work organization that accepts and utilizes the diversity of its workforce—while also being active in the community and in state and federal programs that support immigrants, women, the working poor, and other disadvantaged groups—and that collaborates across cultural and national boundaries. Applying an ecological and systems perspective (Ashford & LeCroy, 2010), the construct of inclusion is used as a cornerstone for expanding the notion of diversity to create a comprehensive way of understanding and managing workforce diversity.

A central proposition of the inclusive workplace model is that work organizations need to expand their notion of diversity to encompass, in addition to the organization itself, the larger systems that constitute their environment (Mor Barak, 2011). According to the model, the inclusive workplace is one that:

- Values and utilizes individual and intergroup differences within its workforce (Level 1)
- Cooperates with, and contributes to, its surrounding community (Level 2)
- Alleviates the needs of disadvantaged groups in its wider environment (Level 3)
- Collaborates with individuals, groups, and organizations across national and cultural boundaries (Level 4) [p. 8]

The model's four levels enhance one another and together form a strategic approach to diversity management. The first level, that of *valuing and utilizing individual and intergroup differences within the organization's workforce*, refers to the organization's relations with its employees. Whereas an exclusionary workplace is based on the perception that all workers need to conform to preestablished organizational values and norms (determined by its "mainstream"), the inclusive workplace is based on a pluralistic value frame that respects all cultural perspectives represented among its employees. It strives to constantly modify its values and norms to accommodate its employees.

The model's second level, *cooperating with, and contributing to, the local community*, refers to the organization's sense of being an integral part of its surrounding community, regardless of whether it derives profits from local institutions and stakeholders. An exclusionary workplace misses the connection between profits and its community because it focuses solely on its short-term responsibility to its financial stakeholders. For example, short-term profits can turn into long-term losses if they affect workers and communities negatively. Many major environmental disasters (for example, Union Carbide's 1984 Bhopal disaster in India, British Petroleum's 2010 oil spill in the Gulf of Mexico) and dis-criminatory policies (for example, Texaco's 1996 discrimination settlement, Walmart's ten-year sex discrimination litigation) have turned into costly lawsuits for companies in the long run. An inclusive workplace, by contrast, maintains a dual focus, simulta-neously internal and external, that results from acknowledging its responsibility to the wider community.

The third level, *alleviating the needs of disadvantaged groups in the organization's wider environment*, refers to the values that drive organizational policies with regard to the disenfranchised (such as the working poor and former welfare recipients). The exclu-sionary workplace views them as disposable labor, but the inclu-sive workplace perceives these groups as a potentially stable and upwardly mobile labor force.

Finally, the fourth level, *collaborating with individuals, groups, and organizations across national and cultural boundaries*, refers to the organization's positions with respect to international collabo-rations. The exclusionary workplace operates from a framework of one culture, is competition-based, and is focused on narrowly defined national interests. The inclusive workplace sees value in collaborating across national borders, being pluralistic, and iden-tifying global mutual interests.

The inclusive workplace model provides a road map for imple-menting organizational inclusion policies and practices both within the organization and beyond its proverbial walls. It empha-sizes the need to collaborate with the local community and to view both the community and society as a whole as true stakeholders in the organization.

Expanding Inclusion Beyond the Traditional Corporate Walls

A truly inclusive workplace recognizes its role in the surrounding community and the reciprocity embedded in this relationship, as well as the economic and noneconomic consequences of its presence in the community. It acknowledges its responsibility to ameliorate adverse effects of this presence and to make a positive contribution to the community's well-being (see also Härtel, Appo, & Hart, Chapter 19, this volume). An exclusionary workplace, on the other hand, has minimal or no connection to its community. For example, an exclusionary organization may view any volunteer work its employees engage in as a private matter that is part of their after-work activities, whereas an inclusive workplace will encourage, support, and finance activities such as teaching computer skills to elementary school students or mentoring inner-city youth.

Relevant terms for examining an organization's role beyond its traditional walls include *corporate social responsibility* (CSR) and *corporate social performance* (CSP), concepts currently used in part to assess the Fortune 500 most-admired companies. Both terms expand an organization's responsibilities beyond its traditional economic shareholders to multiple stakeholders, including the community (Greening & Turban, 2000; Hutchins & Sutherland, 2008; Rowley & Berman, 2000; Valiente, Ayerbe, & Figueras, 2012). Carroll (1979) developed one of the earlier versions of a comprehensive view of corporate social performance and has reiterated his opinion (Carroll, 2000) that social performance review should include a comprehensive assessment of actions related to most social issues and stakeholders.

When first introduced, the notion of corporate social responsibility faced severe criticism. The most well-known critic of corporate social responsibility was Milton Friedman, the Nobel Prize–winning economist who proclaimed in the title of his *New York Times Magazine* article on September 13, 1970, that "the social responsibility of business is to increase its profits" (p. 32). It is important to place Friedman's comment in the proper historical context. In 1970, public expectations for corporations were limited, and employees and consumers alike were not as socially aware and savvy about their power to influence corporate citizenship behavior as they are today. On close examination, Friedman's comment may not be such a contradiction to CSR as it may seem at first. It can be argued that, due to subsequent changes in the social context, corporations are facing more sophisticated publics, who demand that corporations not only cause no harm to their social and physical environment but also contribute to the public welfare. These expectations have made CSR practices vital to creating goodwill among customers and attracting talented employees; both are essential for making a profit. Therefore, such activities are not only in concordance with the responsibility of businesses to make profits—as stated by Milton Friedman—but also often enhance profit-making.

Corporate social performance and corporate social responsibility focus on a direct business-related role vis-à-vis the community, with an emphasis on the strategic and bottom-line implications of socially responsible corporate practices (Heal, 2008; Werther & Chandler, 2011). Both constructs stem from the recognition that the economic actions of business entities have noneconomic consequences and that business organizations have an impact on other societal institutions beyond their economic sphere.

In the past, abiding by the law and exercising fair and honest practices would have been sufficient for a business to be recognized and even celebrated for its integrity. This is no longer the case, as the public is aware of businesses' obligation to society and expects them to have a strategy in place to fulfill this obligation. Today's sophisticated publics expect businesses to be proactive and go beyond government regulations in responding to the needs of the community (Schwartz & Gibb, 1999; Werther & Chandler, 2011). Voluntary activities that benefit the community should extend beyond the corporation's primary role as an economic institution (Greening & Turban, 2000; Johnson, 2009). Such socially responsible actions have the potential to generate goodwill from customers and employees alike. There is accumulating research evidence documenting the connection between a company's social and ethical policies and its financial performance, a connection that has been termed "doing well by doing good" (see, for example, Benioff & Southwick, 2004; Field, 2007; Mor Barak & Travis, 2010).

A Proposed Three-Stage Continuum of Practices: From Philanthropy Through CSR to Corporate Inclusion Strategy

In this section, we propose a three-stage continuum of practices—from corporate philanthropy through corporate social responsibility to corporate inclusion strategy (see Table 13.1). The value-based model of inclusive practice is a multidimensional model that operates alongside corporate philanthropy efforts and corporate social responsibility initiatives. All these practices can have a profound impact on the social and environmental reputation of an organization. Although the primary aim of the inclusive workplace model is to positively influence the experience of stakeholder inclusion, it is likely that outcomes of this model include financial profitability, reputation benefits, and the like, which are the same as many CSR or CSP benefits. This model is therefore not a replacement for CSR, CSP, or corporate philanthropy practices. Rather, it is a strategic practice that can be positioned alongside or in conjunction with such strategies. The best solution is a combined strategy that accounts for the cumulative internal and external social considerations.

Although all three practices have elements in common, the cornerstone of corporate inclusion strategy is unique: treating the community as a stakeholder and as a true partner in determining specific projects, and encouraging employees to actively participate in those initiatives. More specifically, the three guiding principles of corporate inclusion strategy (CIS) are: (1) treating the community as a stakeholder; (2) respecting the community's right to self-determination in identifying projects and initiatives; and (3) involving employees who are local residents in work with the community. Together, these elements will create a natural flow of inclusion both within and outside of the company. Each initiative must include a needs assessment within the community

Table 13.1. A Three-Stage Continuum of Practices: From Corporate Philanthropy Through Corporate Social Responsibility to Value-Based Inclusion

	Corporate Philanthropy (CP) →	*Corporate Social Responsibility (CSR)* →	*Corporate Inclusion Strategy (CIS)* →
Broad Definition	Corporate philanthropy initiatives are typically ad-hoc projects aimed at short-term social impact and long-term financial gain for the company (Zollo, 2004)	Corporate social responsibility initiatives are part of a company's routine operations, with its economic profit serving the long-term goal of contributing to social welfare (Zollo, 2004)	Inclusive workplace initiatives are part of an overall corporate diversity and inclusion strategy, which views the community as a stakeholder and partner in promoting initiatives in the community (Mor Barak, 2011)
Benefits	Sustainable competitive advantage (Zollo, 2004)	Social and environmental sustainability (Zollo, 2004) through such actions as cutting environmental costs, raising productivity, and improving staff recruitment (Clement-Jones, 2005)	Employment opportunities, job training, mentorship, innovative collaborations, improved corporate image and reputation, advantage in recruitment, loyalty, and labor disputes (Mor Barak, 2011)
Associated Practices	Donations and grants to worthy causes that the organization deems important and relevant	Investment in projects that are related to the company's social and economic environment	Engaging the community as a stakeholder, emphasizing the community's right to self-determination, and involving employees in community projects

and the formation of a steering committee that includes community leaders as well as the corporation's employees. The steering committee's responsibilities include identifying and leading relevant initiatives and conducting ongoing and summative evaluations.

The Inclusive Workplace Model in Practice: Global Examples of Corporate Inclusion Strategy

In conjunction with corporate inclusion strategy, and given their economic power, corporations can offer essential resources to groups and communities that would not otherwise be provided by governmental agencies. In this section, we provide some examples of initiatives that demonstrate how the inclusive workplace model can provide a road map for corporate inclusion strategy by identifying "where to invest"—at which of the four levels of the inclusive workplace model—and "what to invest"—how to make the initiatives part of CIS (see Table 13.2).

Snider, Hill, and Martin (2003) explored the community initiatives described on the websites of fifty U.S. companies and forty-three international companies in a qualitative analysis of corporate social responsibility messages. The companies included in the study declared and highlighted a variety of initiatives in both U.S. and global settings. Similarly, a survey of eight multinational corporations revealed that a majority were actively involved in community initiatives aimed at improving the lives of the residents in their communities (Wentling & Palma-Rivas, 2000). These activities included mentor programs for minority students, student internships, sponsorship of local school programs, and participation of company leaders on boards of minority organizations in the community.

For example, in the early 1990s the University of Southern California (USC), the largest private employer in the city of Los Angeles, initiated a series of community outreach programs as part of its strategic plan (University of Southern California, 2011). The university, which is located in downtown Los Angeles—an area that is home to diverse, partly immigrant, and mostly disadvantaged communities—has launched several community-oriented programs. The initiatives aim to create a stronger sense

Table 13.2. A Framework Linking Corporate Inclusion Strategy and the Inclusive Workplace Model

The Inclusive Workplace Model and Corporate Inclusion Strategy	Level 1: Valuing and utilizing individual and intergroup differences within the organization's workforce	Level 2: Cooperating with, and contributing to, the local community	Level 3: Meeting the needs of disadvantaged groups in the organization's wider environment	Level 4: Collaborating with individuals, groups, and organizations across national and cultural boundaries
What to Invest in	**Where to Invest** ⟶			⟶ (arrow pointing up)
1. Treating the community as a stakeholder	As the organization is the stakeholder, it invests in the inclusion of its own employees.	Organizations invest in community projects, such as investment in educational or cultural initiatives; for example, youth mentorship or tutoring children in local schools.	Organizations invest in the social welfare of the wider community, such as investment in treatment and prevention of HIV/AIDS.	Organizations partner with groups to promote social interests, such as companies that manufacture products in developing countries partner with organizations that protect the rights of local employees.

2. Respecting the community's right to self-determination in identifying inclusive projects and initiatives	Employees are encouraged to proactively suggest mechanisms to create inclusive work environments.	Organizations collaborate with community requests for support, such as funding for projects or mentors for scholarly development.	Organizations respond to welfare or social concerns raised at a macro level, such as infrastructure development or disease control.	Organizations respond to international concerns, such as the unfair treatment of a particular group or the exclusion of another group.
3. Involving employees who are local residents in work with the community	Employees are provided with a fixed number of days off work that they should invest in promoting, improving, and uplifting their community.	Employees are allocated to local projects as mentors or subject specialists.	Employees are encouraged to support local projects where possible; for example, engineers could support an infrastructure project.	Employees working in local divisions of companies are encouraged to support projects where possible; for example, an employee could be sent to examine the working conditions of a local supplier.

of inclusion between the diverse employee workforce and the local community (Levels 1 and 2 of the model). These programs included the Family of Five Schools—a public-private partnership that provides special educational, cultural, and developmental opportunities to approximately eight thousand children who live close to USC's University Park campus; the Joint Educational Project—which involves sending 1,200 mentors, teaching assistants, and miniteams into local schools and agencies; and Civic and Community Relations—which encourages more entrepreneurs, and especially minority entrepreneurs, to establish businesses in the immediate vicinity of the university's campuses (Mor Barak, 2011, p. 277; USC Civic and Community Relations, n.d.).

Another example of corporate-community inclusion (Level 2) is the U.S.-based Shell Youth Training Academy (SYTA) and the similar Nigerian Shell Intensive Training Program (SITP), both sponsored by the Royal Dutch/Shell Corporation, a global group of energy and petrochemical companies. The Academy opened in February 1993 to provide high school students in the Los Angeles Unified School District with postsecondary career opportunities and training. The goals of SYTA and SITP also include providing Shell with access to a larger talent pool of prospective employees in the local community (Shell Intensive Training Programme, 2009; Shell Youth Training, 2004). Two similar programs were opened in Chicago and Oakland, with more than a thousand students participating since their inception. Once accepted (based on a minimum grade point average and teacher recommendations), eleventh- and twelfth-grade students attend half-day classes at the SYTA academy for one semester. The program covers consumer service occupations, career planning, job search skills, assessment of personal interests and aptitude, interpersonal skills, effective communication, and other elements of successful career development.

In South Africa, multinationals including BMW, VW, Barloworld, Avis, and Dewey & LeBoeuf have invested in the LoveLife Trust (http://www.lovelife.org.za/corporate/), an organization that raises awareness about HIV/AIDS management and prevention. This is a relevant issue in South Africa, where 11 percent of the working population is HIV positive. In Nigeria, multinational oil companies Shell and Total are also investing to reduce the high prevalence of HIV/AIDS in their operating environment. The companies have built and renovated hospitals, health centers, and clinics; provided equipment for community hospitals; donated ambulances and medications; and funded free community health care programs and local campaigns against HIV/AIDS (Ojo, 2009, p. 404). At a strategic level, Shell has partnered with the National Advisory Council on AIDS through the Nigerian Business Coalition against AIDS to stop the spread of HIV/AIDS in the country (Ojo, 2009). The high prevalence of HIV/AIDS in Africa has a significant impact on organizations and communities. Organizations are increasingly challenged by terminal illness, which results in high absenteeism, low morale, and sometimes death of employees. Employees and their families are severely impacted by the disease, which disrupts lives and affects the livelihood, health, and well-being of entire communities. Given this scenario, it is obvious that these organizations are contributing to inclusion efforts at Levels 2 and 3 of the *inclusive workplace model* through their initiatives and investments.

Microsoft has two initiatives that demonstrate Level 2 corporate–community strategies and Level 3 practices that focus on national programs such as welfare-to-work. The first initiative, the Working Connections partnership with the American Association of Community Colleges (Hogan, 2009), is a project aimed at addressing the shortage of information technology workers by having Microsoft employees conduct needs assessments, design curricula, and create faculty development institutes in collaboration with local community colleges. Although Microsoft supported this investment with a significant financial donation, which the company construed as philanthropic, the direct engagement with the community can be viewed as an example of corporate inclusion strategy at Level 2 of the inclusive workplace model.

The Level 3 initiative relates to support that Microsoft provides to its community in terms of access to technology, training, and support in 115 countries including Costa Rica, where Microsoft officials (P. Leiva, personal communication, August 14, 2006) suggested that beneficiaries have included 3.2 million students. Microsoft achieved this by offering hardware, software, training, support, and maintenance to regions of greatest financial need. Because this project provides learning opportunities and skills to people who otherwise would not have had access to them (Hogan, 2009) and contributes to the social welfare and uplifting of poor people, this is an example of an inclusion strategy at Level 3 of the inclusive workplace model.

In the United Kingdom, large supermarkets such as Tesco, Asda, Sainsbury's, and Morrisons, which stock imported products from less-developed countries, have expressed concern about factory and plantation owners who use unfair labor practices such as poor wages, unacceptable working conditions, and child labor (Idowu, 2009). To mitigate this risk, the supermarkets have partnered with Fairtrade Labelling Organizations International to ensure that producers, farmers, and laborers are remunerated so as to cover their family, business, social, and economic costs (Mor Barak, 2005; Ram, 2002). In France, supermarket Carrefour has implemented similar restrictions on its suppliers by obliging them to respect the International Labour Organization's conventions (Harribey, 2009). In Sweden, the H&M clothing company outsources production of its clothing to approximately two thousand factories in twenty-eight countries. It has partnered with the Global Reporting Initiative to monitor and improve the social conditions of the outsourced companies (Windell, Grafström, & Göthberg, 2009). These alliances demonstrate the companies' commitment to their primary (for example, investors, creditors, employees, management, suppliers, customers, government) and secondary stakeholders (for example, media, the public, nongovernmental organizations, financial analysts) who are not likely to condone the unfair treatment of factory and plantation workers around the world (Idowu, 2009). Further, it protects the actual producers, farmers, and laborers from unfair treatment and abuse. Given that these alliances protect both the community (consumers) and foreign employees, this collaboration is an example of strategies related to both Level 2 and Level 4 of the inclusive workplace model.

These examples demonstrate corporate inclusion strategies that are relevant at different levels of the inclusive workplace model. The conceptual model presented in Table 13.2 provides a framework to link corporate inclusion strategies to the inclusive workplace model, focusing on both where and in what initiatives to invest resources. In particular, it highlights the basic principles of CIS: treating the community as a true stakeholder, respecting the community's right to self-determination in identifying projects and initiatives, and involving employees who are local residents in work with the community.

Conclusion and Implications for Organizational Practice

There is accumulating research evidence documenting the benefits of community involvement for work organizations, including higher productivity, improved talent recruitment, and higher retention rates. Employee productivity is influenced by such community-oriented initiatives because employees are likely to demonstrate discretionary effort when they and their communities are treated well (Misani, 2010). Clement-Jones (2005) asserts that employers who make social contributions are appealing to employees and potential recruits who want to contribute to their communities but do not have time, given their demanding work schedules. A further benefit is derived from new products or ideas created through collaboration with nonmarket partners (Misani, 2010).

On a macro level, companies are likely to decrease litigation costs and reputational risk. Recently, companies such as Nike (Griffin & Vivari, 2009) and Gap (Windell et al., 2009) have come under pressure for the working conditions in the factories in Indonesia and Cambodia where their merchandise is manufactured. Apple has been asked to account for the poor working conditions in the factories in China where the iPhone is manufactured (Barboza & Duhigg, 2012). Companies such as Tesco and Carrefour have sensibly partnered with organizations that ensure the ethical procurement of products (Harribey, 2009; Idowu, 2009).

A barrier to inclusion at the community level is distrust among community members and leaders. If the community does not believe in the sincerity of the organization's plan, the company is not likely to see benefits such as increased productivity and retention. Similarly, it is not likely to benefit from the input of the community. To derive financial benefit and social recognition from social contributions, the organization needs to show genuine social concern for its stakeholders (Velázquez, Marín, Zavala, Bustamante, Esquer, & Munguía, 2009). Businesses need to be proactive in searching for innovative solutions to support their stakeholders. Examples include businesses in the United Kingdom and France (described earlier) that have partnered with organizations to support the ethical procurement of products.

An additional consideration for companies seeking financial benefit from their social contributions is the type of social partnering they choose to undertake. In three recent meta-analytic studies that explored the relationship between social investment and financial performance (Margolis, Elfenbein, & Walsh, 2007; Margolis & Walsh, 2003; Orlitzky, Schmidt, & Rynes, 2003), social investment type emerged as the factor that differentiated companies that garnered a financial benefit from those that were not able to establish this link. This suggests that social investment should be carefully considered and that companies need to be proactive in searching for inclusive and innovative solutions to support their stakeholders.

It is apparent that in countries in which social investment is supported by the government and nongovernmental institutions, companies follow suit and are more likely to invest in their communities. Some companies in Finland are a good example of this—they show high social investment because government and nongovernmental organizations have developed structures to support social investment (Panapanaan & Linnanen, 2009).

In China, investment in social activities is largely undertaken by Western companies operating there, because it is not driven by the Chinese government (Welford & Hills, 2009). Belal and Lubinin (2009) assert that Russia faces the same challenges and suggest that to shift this status quo, greater governmental pressure needs to be placed on businesses to increase their social investment.

Misani (2010) suggests that companies should have a coherent strategy that is unique in its investment approaches, rather than mimicking the activities of other companies out of convenience. Furthermore, the social investment corporate mission needs to be strategically aligned with business philosophy, values, and objectives (Ali, Ibrahim, Mohammad, Zain, & Alwi, 2009) to ensure that the organization is able to derive the desired social and financial benefit.

Panapanaan and Linnanen (2009) suggest that a successful social investment strategy should consider employees, suppliers, the community, and customers. They assert that a social risk assessment should be conducted to determine the organizational vulnerabilities, which in turn form the focus of the strategy. From an employee perspective, the social risk assessment should consider the following points of potential vulnerability: diversity, discrimination, freedom of association, child labor, forced labor, absenteeism, compensation, and flexibility.

From a community perspective, the organization should consider participation in civic action, membership in social forums, and provision of institutional support, grants, donations, or sponsorships. For suppliers, the organization should consider the suppliers' social investment requirements, the purchasing agreement, and information relating to the suppliers' social investment strategy. Finally, organizations should provide customers with product information, alleviate product responsibility concerns, provide social investment information, and provide training and product monitoring. Although risk assessment is a useful diagnostic tool, the social investment strategy should be innovative and include mechanisms to establish a competitive advantage. A single strategy based on these considerations is likely to satisfy CSR, corporate philanthropy, and CIS requirements.

It is quite clear that simply doing good deeds for the community does not constitute an inclusive organization. To be truly inclusive, an organization needs to demonstrate that it views the community as a partner and stakeholder. Only then will it overcome issues of distrust and reap the benefits of its actions. This can be achieved by collaborating with the community to determine the requisite support and by involving company workers in community partnerships to create a fluid inclusion strategy that operates both inside the organization as well as beyond the traditional corporate walls.

References

Ali, M. M., Ibrahim, M. K., Mohammad, R., Zain, M. M., & Alwi, M. R. (2009). Malaysia: Value relevance of accounting numbers. In S. O. Idowu & W. L. Filho (Eds.), *Global practices of corporate social responsibility* (pp. 201–234). Berlin, Germany: Springer.

Ashford, J. B., & LeCroy, C. W. (2010). *Human behavior in the social environment: A multidimensional perspective* (4th ed.). Belmont, CA: Brooks/Cole.

Barboza, D., & Duhigg, C. (2012, September 10). China plant again faces labor issues on iPhones. *New York Times*, p. B1.

Belal, A. R., & Lubinin, V. (2009). Russia: Corporate social disclosures. In S. O. Idowu & W. L. Filho (Eds.), *Global practices of corporate social responsibility* (pp. 165–182). Berlin, Germany: Springer.

Benioff, M., & Southwick, K. (2004). *Compassionate capitalism: How corporations can make doing good an integral part of doing well.* Pompton Plains, NJ: Career Press.

Bureau for Employers' Activities. (2012). *Gender, diversity and equality: Training packages for employers.* Retrieved from International Labour Organization website: http://www.ilo.org/public/english/dialogue/actemp/whatwedo/projects/diversity.htm

Bureau for Gender Equality. (2012). *Gender identity and sexual orientation: Promoting rights, diversity and equality in the world of work (PRIDE).* Retrieved from International Labour Organization website: http://www.ilo.org/gender/Projects/WCMS_184205/lang—en/index.htm

Carroll, A. B. (1979). A three-dimensional conceptual model of corporate performance. *Academy of Management Review, 4,* 497–505. doi:10.5465/AMR.1979.4498296

Carroll, A. B. (2000). A commentary and an overview of key questions on corporate social performance measurement. *Business & Society, 39,* 466–478. doi:10.1177/000765030003900406

Clement-Jones, T. (2005). Corporate social responsibility: Bottom-line issue or public relations exercise? In J. Hancock (Ed.), *Investing in corporate social responsibility. A guide to best practice, business planning & the UK's leading companies* (pp. 5–14). London, England: Kogan Page.

Constitution of the Republic of South Africa, Act 108 of 1996. [South Africa] (1996, December 18). Available at http://www.info.gov.za/documents/constitution/1996/a108-96.pdf

European Union. (2000, December 7). Charter of Fundamental Rights of the European Union. *Official Journal of the European Communities,*

2000(C364). Retrieved from UN Refugee Agency website: http://www.unhcr.org/refworld/docid/3ae6b3b70.html

Field, L. (2007). *Business and the Buddha: Doing well by doing good.* Somerville, MA: Wisdom.

Friedman, M. (1970, September 13). The social responsibility of business is to increase its profits. *New York Times Magazine,* pp. 32–33.

Greening, D. W., & Turban, D. B. (2000). Corporate social performance as a competitive advantage in attracting a quality workforce. *Business & Society, 39,* 254–280. doi:10.1177/000765030003900302

Griffin, J. J., & Vivari, B. (2009). United States of America: Internal commitments and external pressures. In S. O. Idowu & W. L. Filho (Eds.), *Global practices of corporate social responsibility* (pp. 235–250). Berlin, Germany: Springer.

Harribey, L. E. (2009). France. In S. O. Idowu & W. L. Filho (Eds.), *Global practices of corporate social responsibility* (pp. 37–60). Berlin, Germany: Springer.

Heal, G. (2008). *When principles pay: Corporate social responsibility and the bottom line.* New York: Columbia University Press.

Hogan, E. (2009). Costa Rica. In S. O. Idowu & W. L. Filho (Eds.), *Global practices of corporate social responsibility* (pp. 285–308). Berlin, Germany: Springer.

Hong Kong Bill of Rights Ordinance, Cap 383. (1991, June 8). Retrieved from UN Refugee Agency website: http://www.unhcr.org/refworld/docid/3ae6b5350.html

Hutchins, M. J., & Sutherland, J. W. (2008). An exploration of measures of social sustainability and their application to supply chain decisions. *Journal of Cleaner Production, 16,* 1688–1698. doi:10.1016/j.jclepro.2008.06.001

Idowu, S. O. (2009). The United Kingdom of Great Britain and Northern Ireland. In S. O. Idowu & W. L. Filho (Eds.), *Global practices of corporate social responsibility* (pp. 11–36). Berlin, Germany: Springer.

International Labour Organization. (2011). *Key indicators of the labour market (KILM).* Retrieved from http://www.ilo.org/empelm/what/WCMS_114240/lang--en/index.htm

Johnson, H. H. (2009). Corporate social responsibility: Determining your position. In E. Biech (Ed.), *The 2010 Pfeiffer annual: Consulting* (pp. 141–147). San Francisco: Pfeiffer

Margolis, J. D., Elfenbein, H. A., & Walsh, J. P. (2007). *Does it pay to be good? A meta-analysis and redirection of research on the relationship between corporate social and financial performance.* Retrieved from Stakeholder Marketing Consortium website: http://stakeholder.bu

.edu/docs/walsh,%20jim%20does%20it%20pay%20to%20be%20 good.pdf

Margolis, J. D., & Walsh, J. P. (2003). Misery loves companies: Rethinking social initiatives by business. *Administrative Science Quarterly, 48,* 268–305. doi:10.2307/3556659

Misani, N. (2010). Convergent and divergent corporate social responsibility. In C. Louche, S. O. Idowu, & W. L. Filho (Eds.). *Innovative CSR: From risk management to value creation* (pp. 62–83). Sheffield, England: Greenleaf.

Mor Barak, M. E. (2000a). Beyond affirmative action: Toward a model of diversity and organizational inclusion. *Administration in Social Work, 23*(3), 47–68. doi:10.1300/J147v23n03_04

Mor Barak, M. E. (2000b). The inclusive workplace: An ecosystems approach to diversity management. *Social Work, 45,* 339–353. doi:10 .1093/sw/45.4.339

Mor Barak, M. E. (2005). *Managing diversity: Toward a globally inclusive workplace.* Thousand Oaks, CA: Sage.

Mor Barak, M. E. (2011). *Managing diversity: Toward a globally inclusive workplace* (2nd ed.). Thousand Oaks, CA: Sage.

Mor Barak, M. E., & Cherin, D. A. (1998). A tool to expand organizational understanding of workforce diversity: Exploring a measure of inclusion–exclusion. *Administration in Social Work, 22*(1), 47–64. doi:10.1300/J147v22n01_04

Mor Barak, M. E., Cherin, D. A., & Berkman, S. (1998). Organizational and personal dimensions in diversity climate: Ethnic and gender differences in employee perceptions. *Journal of Applied Behavioral Science, 34,* 82–104. doi:10.1177/0021886398341006

Mor Barak, M. E., & Travis, D. J. (2010). Diversity and organizational performance. In Y. Hasenfeld (Ed.), *Human services as complex organizations* (2nd ed., pp. 341–378), Thousand Oaks, CA: Sage.

Mor Barak, M. E., & Travis, D. J. (2013). Socioeconomic trends: Broadening the diversity ecosystem. In Q. M. Roberson (Ed.), *The Oxford handbook of diversity and work* (pp. 393–418). New York: Oxford University Press.

New Zealand Bill of Rights Act 1990. (1990, September 25). Retrieved from UN Refugee Agency website: http://www.unhcr.org/ refworld/docid/3ae6b5198.html

Ojo, O. (2009). Nigeria: CSR as a vehicle for economic development. In S. O. Idowu & W. L. Filho (Eds.), *Global practices of corporate social responsibility* (pp. 393–434). Berlin, Germany: Springer.

Orlitzky, M., Schmidt, F. L., & Rynes, S. L. (2003). Corporate social and financial performance: A meta-analysis. *Organization Studies, 24*, 403–441. doi:10.1177/0170840603024003910

Panapanaan, V., & Linnanen, L. (2009). Finland. In S. O. Idowu & W. L. Filho (Eds.), *Global practices of corporate social responsibility* (pp. 73–102). Berlin, Germany: Springer.

Ram, H. (2002, March 9). The A–Z of fair trade: Harry Ram explains why the decision to make the switch to fair trade produce should be as easy as ABC. *The Independent*, p. 1. Retrieved from http:// www.questia.com/library/1P2-1668301/fair-trade-the-a-z-of-fair -trade-harry-ram-explains#articleDetails

Rowley, T., & Berman, S. (2000). A brand new brand of corporate social performance. *Business & Society, 39*, 397–418. doi:10.1177/00076 5030003900404

Schwartz, P., & Gibb, B. (1999). *When good companies do bad things: Responsibility and risk in an age of globalization.* New York: Wiley.

Shell Intensive Training Programme. (2009). Retrieved from http:// www.shell.com/home/content/nigeria/society_environment/ youth/sitp.html

Shell Youth Training. (2004). Retrieved from http://www.countonshell .com/community/involvement/shell_youth_training.html

Snider, J., Hill, R. P., & Martin, D. (2003). Corporate social responsibility in the 21st century: A view from the world's most successful firms. *Journal of Business Ethics, 48*, 175–187. doi:10.1023/B:BUSI .0000004606.29523.db

UN General Assembly. (1948, December 10). *Universal Declaration of Human Rights.* Retrieved from UN Refugee Agency website: http:// www.unhcr.org/refworld/docid/3ae6b3712c.html

University of Southern California. (2011). *USC strategic vision: Matching deeds to ambition.* Retrieved from http://strategic.usc.edu/USC%20 Strategic%20Vision%20Dec%202011.pdf

USC Civic and Community Relations. (n.d.). Our communities. Retrieved from http://communities.usc.edu/programs/#21

Valiente, J. M. A., Ayerbe, C. G., & Figueras, M. S. (2012). Social responsibility practices and evaluation of corporate social performance. *Journal of Cleaner Production, 35*, 25–38. doi:10.1016/j.jclepro .2012.05.002

Velázquez, L., Marín, A., Zavala, A., Bustamante, C., Esquer, J., & Munguía, N. (2009). Mexico: An overview of CSR programmes. In S. O. Idowu & W. L. Filho (Eds.), *Global practices of corporate social responsibility* (pp. 273–284). Berlin, Germany: Springer.

Welford, R., & Hills, P. (2009). People's Republic of China. In S. O. Idowu & W. L. Filho (Eds.), *Global practices of corporate social responsibility* (pp. 183–200). Berlin, Germany: Springer.

Wentling, R. M., & Palma-Rivas, N. (2000). Current status of diversity initiatives in selected multinational corporations. *Human Resource Development Quarterly, 11,* 35–60. doi:10.1002/1532–1096(200021)11:1<35::AID-HRDQ4>3.0.CO;2-#

Werther, W. B., Jr., & Chandler, D. (2011). *Strategic corporate social responsibility: Stakeholders in a global environment* (2nd ed.). Thousand Oaks, CA: Sage.

Windell, K., Grafström, M., & Göthberg, P. (2009). Sweden. In S. O. Idowu & W. L. Filho (Eds.), *Global practices of corporate social responsibility* (pp. 103–124). Berlin, Germany: Springer.

Zollo, M. (2004). Philanthropy or CSR: A strategic choice. In T. Dickson (Ed.), *EBF on corporate social responsibility* (A Special Report by *European Business Forum,* pp. 18–19). London, UK: European Business Forum. Retrieved from http://www.isc.hbs.edu/Copies%20of%20linked%20articles/ebfoncsr.pdf

Part Four

Key Application Issues and Domains

CHAPTER FOURTEEN

Global Benchmarks for Diversity and Inclusion

Julie O'Mara

> *"What is excellent diversity and inclusion work?" the organizational leader asked the inclusion practitioner.*
> *"It depends," the inclusion practitioner rightly replied.*
> *"On what?" the leader asked.*
> *The inclusion practitioner responded, "Your goals. Your starting point. Challenges. Your culture. Size of your organization. Sector you are in. Like that. One size does not fit all."*
> *The leader sighed.*

Years ago I had a similar exchange with an organizational leader. He was committed to leading his organization in creating a diversity and inclusion initiative, but was not clear about what to do. He knew that he needed to do more than show up at a cultural event, introduce a training program, tell people they need to behave respectfully, or give money to a local organization focused on ethnic minority issues. People had told him to keep it simple, but he figured that if the practice of inclusion was that "simple," it would be ingrained in every organization around the world, and he knew it wasn't. And he was correct. Implementing an effective inclusion initiative is not a simple or quick process.

His query set me on a course of study and practice that resulted in Alan Richter and me, along with seventy-nine expert panelists, publishing *Global Diversity and Inclusion Benchmarks: Standards for*

Organizations Around the World (O'Mara & Richter, 2011), known to many in the field as simply GDIB. GDIB helps leaders and practitioners get clearer about what it takes to be considered a best practice organization in diversity and inclusion. As an organizational manager, professional association volunteer and leader, and external diversity and inclusion consultant, I have been concerned that many managers and leaders advocate for a "simple" approach to inclusion. What many want to do is to select two or three "things" to do. Then they seem to believe that because there is activity and because inclusion is "the right thing to do" that it will just happen.

In my experience, inclusion does not just happen, even with the best of intentions. It is not a matter of asking people to change some behaviors. It is much more complex. It requires adjustments in organizational systems—such as expanding recruiting efforts to reach out to publications that people with disabilities likely read, or instituting flexible work hours to accommodate child- or elder-care challenges—as well as individual behavior changes. I know firsthand that this is not simple. I thought that a tool such as GDIB would be helpful.

This chapter describes the benchmarks, also called standards or outcomes, that can be selected to achieve an inclusion initiative. Benchmarks help people in organizations describe results or aspirations. In a new field like diversity and inclusion, it is important to develop benchmarks to help people know what is considered excellent work. Without benchmarks (or standards or outcomes), there can be a great disparity of opinion over what constitutes quality work.

The GDIB focuses on both diversity and inclusion. In the GDIB document (O'Mara & Richter, 2011), diversity is described as the "variety of differences and similarities/dimensions among people" (p. i). Inclusion "refers to how diversity is leveraged to create a fair, equitable, healthy, and high-performing organization or community where all individuals are respected, feel engaged and motivated, and their contributions toward meeting organizational and societal goals are valued" (p. i).

One way to use GDIB is to first set a target for the outcomes you want to achieve—potentially the best-practice level for most of the thirteen GDIB categories of diversity and inclusion work in organizations. GDIB isn't a "how to" tool; it is a "what" tool. Targeting where you want to be—the outcomes you want to achieve—is a crucial step to take. Once you know where you want to go, using other tools and processes, many of which are described in other chapters in this book, you can determine the strategies and activities needed to reach that desired level.

Knowing the components of an effective initiative for fostering inclusion can be extremely helpful for organizations that either are starting on an inclusion journey or want to improve and sustain their organization's journey. The scope of issues and the dimensions to be considered in doing inclusion work are broader than many leaders and practitioners realize. Using GDIB can help an organization of any size, in any sector, in any region of the world, whether it calls itself "global" or not. In GDIB the use of the term *global* means that the benchmarks apply anywhere in the world.

The GDIB tool can be found on the Internet via a search under its name and the name of the authors. You can download and use it, free of charge. The authors simply require that you ask our permission; this is readily granted, with the agreement that you keep us posted on how you have used the benchmarks.

How the Global Benchmarks Were Developed

This section describes the process for developing the benchmarks and the panel of experts who provided input.

The Methodology

GDIB is the result of a collective opinion of experts. My co-author, Alan Richter, and I drafted the initial collection of global benchmarks based on original work by several practitioners at the Tennessee Valley Authority in the United States (Qirko, Metts, Landon, & Atchley, 1994). Our goal was to make the benchmarks more global in scope and to reflect contemporary practices. Then we identified forty-seven expert panelists to review and critique our work. In round one, using a modified Delphi process, we sent them the first draft inviting feedback on our premise, the categories, the levels, and the benchmarks. In round two we incorporated their comments, created a revised version, and sent that to the expert panelists, inviting their feedback on all aspects of GDIB. We compiled the comments and edited the benchmarks. Richter and I served as the final arbitrators on any disagreements among the expert panelists. We published the first version in 2006 (O'Mara & Richter, 2006; see also O'Mara & Richter, 2009, for a description), and used a similar process to update the document in 2011 (O'Mara & Richter, 2011).

Between publishing the first version in 2006 and beginning the update in 2011, we kept track of user comments and compiled a list of possible changes. Although not all of the original expert panelists were able to work with us on the 2011 version, a total of sixty-two experts, including several new additions, worked on the 2011 version. For the round one review of the 2011 version, Richter and I added an expanded introduction; combined, renamed, and added categories; and added a graphic model emphasizing the systemic and interdependent nature of the categories. We compiled comments and ideas and created a round two version, for which we again received extensive comments. Richter and I then served as the final editors to create the current 2011 version.

GDIB 2011 represents the collective viewpoint of seventy-nine expert panelists plus Alan Richter and me. Included in this number are sixteen panelists who commented on the 2006 version but not on the 2011 version. Although most expert panelists commented on benchmarks in all or most categories, as well as the introduction and the model, some commented on only the few categories of diversity and inclusion work in which they felt they had specific expertise.

Profile of the Seventy-Nine Expert Panelists

We name and thank the expert panelists in the 2011 version. The depth and breadth of GDIB is a testament to the process of including different viewpoints and perspectives. Not all members of our expert panel agreed with all items and statements. Despite all attempts to be as global as possible, the truth is that most people are at least somewhat centric to the countries they know best and, likewise, to the sectors, size, and type of organizations they understand. Therein lies the value in having an expert panel made up of a diverse group of people.

We selected the expert panelists by tapping into our extensive networks. We asked colleagues whom we knew to be outstanding practitioners to identify others who likewise did what we and they considered best-practice work. Our goal was to assemble a group of people highly knowledgeable in many aspects of diversity and inclusion, including, but not limited to, social justice, cultural competence, multiculturalism, and diversity management. We sought panelists with a variety of personal diversity dimensions and experience in various sectors, diversity and inclusion frameworks, types of organizations, size, cultures, regions around the world, and so forth. Most of our panelists are readily identified as diversity and inclusion experts. In a few cases (notably compensation, marketing, and supplier diversity) we identified experts in those specialties whom we believed knew enough about diversity and inclusion to contribute to GDIB.

Because people move across both countries and organizations, and many have extensive global experience not limited to their current affiliation or location, we listed names of the expert panelists without affiliation, title, or location. Although many users have requested a more quantitative profile of the panelists, we resist providing it because many of the expert panelists have been influenced by multiple experiences. For example, a panelist may currently be employed by a small business in France but may have spent the majority of his or her career as a politician in Algeria. Another panelist may currently live in the United States but work mostly in Asia, where she grew up. Most of the panelists are members of LinkedIn or are easy to find using an internet search, if you want to know more about them.

Breadth and Depth of Effective Inclusion Work

Global Diversity and Inclusion Benchmarks (O'Mara & Richter, 2011) identifies benchmarks in thirteen categories of diversity and inclusion work organized into four groups, as follows:

1. The *Foundation Group* includes D&I vision, strategy, and business case; leadership and accountability; and infrastructure and implementation.
2. The *Internal Group* includes recruitment, development, and advancement; benefits, work-life, and flexibility; job design, classification, and compensation; and D&I education and training.
3. The *Bridging Group* includes assessment, measurement, and research; and D&I communications.
4. The *External Group* includes community, government relations, and social responsibility; products and services development; marketing, sales, distribution, and customer service; and supplier diversity.

To create an effective inclusion initiative that meets its goals, an organization needs to set targets and strive to meet the outcomes at the higher levels in most of the GDIB categories. The pace and thoroughness of each organization's inclusion initiative must be determined by that organization based on its commitment, culture, and resources. Important for success is the degree of expertise in understanding how inclusion is both a process and an outcome of related activities.

The GDIB Model

The GDIB model (see Figure 14.1) shows the relationships of the four groups and thirteen categories. The equilateral triangle symbolizes equality and strength—two tenets of diversity and inclusion. The Foundation Benchmarks form the base of the triangle. The Bridging Benchmarks are displayed as a smaller equilateral triangle in the center of the larger triangle, abutting not only the Foundation Benchmarks but also both the Internal Benchmarks on the left side and the External Benchmarks on the right side.

The lines separating the four groups are dashes, symbolizing permeability and the fact that all four groups operate as a system interacting with each other. For example, while recruitment is an Internal Benchmark, some talent is sourced externally; therefore successful recruiting depends on the organization's reputation in

Figure 14.1. GDIB Model

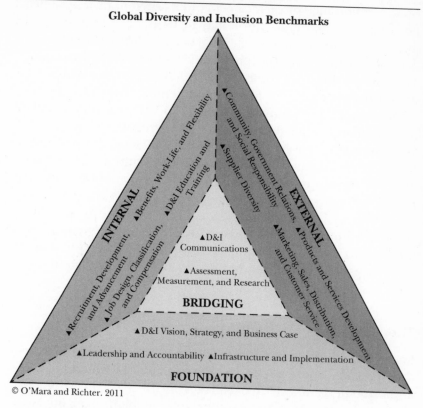

Global Diversity and Inclusion Benchmarks

© O'Mara and Richter. 2011

Source: Global Diversity and Inclusion Benchmarks: Standards for Organizations Around the World, by J. O'Mara and A. Richter, 2011, p. 31. Copyright 2011 by Julie O'Mara and Alan Richter. Reprinted with permission.

the community, which is an External Benchmark. Likewise Customer Service, an External Benchmark, is enhanced by effective training and development, which is an Internal Benchmark. Communications is a Bridging Benchmark because it enables the strategy to be known by all those impacted internally and externally. Strategy, Leadership, and Infrastructure are Foundation Benchmarks because they are necessary to the effective operation of all other benchmarks. Such relationships among the various groups and categories highlight the systemic nature of organizational diversity and inclusion initiatives.

Each organization will need to determine its priorities based on the importance of each category to its current business needs. For example, the organization may be in an economic crisis and may not be able to achieve certain benchmarks for that reason. An example would be the benchmark "Financial resources as well as employee time and labor are provided for a variety of community projects; employees may be compensated for the time they volunteer for community involvement" (O'Mara & Richter, 2011, p. 10), which is a benchmark at the 100-percent level in Category 10: Community, Government Relations, and Social Responsibility. While this benchmark is desirable to meet and is considered a best practice at the 100-percent level, the organization may need to forgo this as a goal until its financial situation is stronger. We do not mean to suggest that all organizations need to achieve every benchmark at the 100- and 75-percent level. Organizations will need to prioritize what they accomplish in diversity and inclusion just as they prioritize what they want to accomplish in other areas.

The Five Levels That Indicate Progress

Each of the thirteen categories presents five levels of benchmarks that indicate progress toward the best practices, which are those at the 100-percent level in each category. In GDIB a best practice is what the expert panelists consider the highest-quality work described as an outcome or standard in that particular category. Based on the descriptions in Table 14.1, the expert panelists, using their judgment and experience, agreed on which level each benchmark best fit into. Although there were differences of opinions as to whether, for example, a certain benchmark belonged at a 50- or 75-percent level, after some discussion and clarification the expert panelists generally came to agreement as to which level each benchmark fell into. Again, we need to emphasize that these decisions are subjective, which is fitting for the intention of GDIB. It is meant to serve as a guide for creating an effective D&I program.

The levels are described as percentages to give the user a numerical label for convenience and as a heuristic to help assess against the current ideal or best practice; however, there is no

Table 14.1. Levels of Progress Toward Diversity and Inclusion Goals

0%	No D&I work has begun; appreciation of differences and a culture of inclusion are not organizational goals.
25%	Compliance mindset at best; symbolic actions only.
50%	Beginning of a programmatic thrust; moving in a healthy direction.
75%	Seeing D&I systemically; a robust D&I approach.
100%	Current best practices in D&I around the world.

Note: Going beyond 100 percent would make the organization a "pioneer"—and probably a model for the next GDIB update.

Source: Adapted from *Global Diversity and Inclusion Benchmarks: Standards for Organizations Around the World,* by J. O'Mara and A. Richter, 2011, p. 13. Copyright 2011 by Julie O'Mara and Alan Richter.

quantitative measurement process to objectively determine at which level an organization falls. To determine your organization's levels, individuals and groups will need to voice their opinions as to which benchmarks are met and which are not. Although the process of individuals and groups voicing their opinion is subjective, the consensus of which levels the organization is in becomes more objective as the number of participants increases. This is useful because it enables the organization to set realistic, objective goals. (See the process described in "How to Use GDIB" later in this chapter.)

Samples of Global Diversity and Inclusion Benchmarks

Exhibit 14.1 shows all the benchmarks at the 100-percent level for Category 7: D&I Training and Education. I selected this category to show in this chapter because education and training are frequent applications for most inclusion initiatives. However, as can be seen from the GDIB Model (Figure 14.1) and gleaned from reading this chapter, even when education and training are executed at the 100-percent level it is not enough to result in an effective initiative. An effective inclusion initiative must include achieving benchmarks in other categories, such as D&I Vision,

> **Exhibit 14.1. Benchmarks at 100 Percent for Category 7: Diversity and Inclusion (D&I) Training and Education**
>
> - D&I training and education include a learning reinforcement, application, and sustainability strategy.
> - D&I training and education involve an ongoing, multiyear, developmental curriculum that takes leaders through various stages of learning, applying, and leading D&I.
> - Learning is customized on an ongoing basis to meet changing local priorities and challenges, ensuring that it is not global at the expense of local relevance.
> - D&I education resources, including an extensive up-to-date library, use a variety of innovative learning methods that are accessible to all, fully supported by the organization, and shared externally.
> - D&I is woven into all training and education and is tied directly to the organization's strategy, vision, and values. The education and training provide employees and leaders at all levels with D&I concepts, knowledge, and skills needed to demonstrate the organization's D&I behaviors and competencies and achieve its vision and goals.
> - Challenging and sometimes controversial issues related to D&I—such as racism, sexism, ageism, homophobia, and unconscious bias—are addressed firmly and with sensitivity, conviction, and compassion.
>
> *Source:* Adapted from *Global Diversity and Inclusion Benchmarks: Standards for Organizations Around the World,* by J. O'Mara and A. Richter, 2011, p. 31. Copyright 2011 by Julie O'Mara and Alan Richter.

Strategy, and Business Case; Leadership and Accountability (also see Gallegos, Chapter 6, and Booysen, Chapter 10, this volume); and D&I Communications (also see Hayles, Chapter 2, this volume), as well as others.

There are a total of 151 benchmarks at the 75- and 100-percent levels. Table 14.2 presents a few samples of benchmarks. Most organizations target benchmarks at the 75- and 100-percent levels, although for organizations just beginning their inclusion journey, the 50-percent level in many categories may be the most reasonable

Table 14.2. Sample Benchmarks in Various Categories

Category	Level	Benchmark
D& I Vision, Strategy, and Business Case	75%	"The spirit, as well as the requirement to embed equity, prevent harassment, reduce discrimination, and so forth is fully supported; violations of diversity-related policies are not tolerated" (p. 19).
Leadership and Accountability	100%	"Leaders and board members understand that the work of D&I is systemic and designed to strengthen the organization's culture. They are owners, not just sponsors, of the organization's D&I work" (p. 22).
Recruitment, Development, and Advancement	75%	"Recruitment and selection panels are representative of the diverse population the organization wants to attract and advance" (p. 26).
Assessment, Measurement, and Research	75%	"Research on specific diversity dimensions, issues, interactions, and systems is conducted for both internal and external purposes. The organization invests in research to study D&I" (p. 32).
Community, Government Relations, and Corporate Responsibility	100%	"The organization leads in supporting and advocating for diversity-related interests in government and societal affairs" (p. 36).
Marketing, Sales, Distribution, and Customer Service	75%	"Diverse groups of customers and potential customers are surveyed on needs and satisfaction. The results shape marketing, sales, distribution, and customer service strategies" (p. 39).

Source: O'Mara and Richter, 2011.

target for the short term. Usually organizations just starting their diversity and inclusion journey tend to be more focused on basic diversity training, cultural events, or meeting legal and compliance regulations, which are generally at or below the 50-percent level. However, that is not always the case. Some organizations may have leaders with expertise in diversity and inclusion, and their initial efforts may be at the more advanced levels.

How to Use GDIB

There are several ways to use GDIB. If you are a novice at diversity and inclusion work, begin by immersing yourself in a course of study and/or seek help from someone who has experience in designing an initiative. Many of the benchmarks at the 75- and 100-percent levels are difficult to achieve. The GDIB model indicates how several benchmarks are related. The success of one benchmark may be dependent on the success of another. Embarking on and sustaining an inclusion initiative require significant competencies on the part of the practitioner. It is best to plan well and avoid mistakes—such as promoting someone before they have the competencies needed, introducing a product or service that has not been reviewed for its suitability for a designated ethnic group, or requiring suppliers to meet terms that are not needed. Mistakes can require damage control that can be costly and embarrassing.

A Suggested Comprehensive Implementation Process

The comprehensive process provided in this section is designed for medium to large organizations in most sectors. The process should be orchestrated by a knowledgeable practitioner. With some modification, it can be used in small organizations. The process is described at a high level and uses techniques and practices that are often identified as group process or organization development. It uses the behaviors of inclusion and collaboration to help achieve a successful implementation.

Step 1: Planning to Plan. A small team of internal and/or external practitioners works with senior organizational leaders to develop and agree on the major steps, key roles of those guiding the process, macro budget, and time parameters.

Step 2: Assemble and Train the Planning and Implementation Team. This is a core group of seven to ten persons who, working with senior organizational leaders and practitioners, will guide the process. It is a working, not an advisory group. As much as possible, it is a diverse group including differences in level, function, work style, skill sets, longevity in the organization, experience, background, and other dimensions of diversity important to the mission of the organization. Training should include familiarity with GDIB, group process, project management, skills needed, inclusive behaviors, and knowledge about the organization's plan from Step 1.

Step 3: Conduct and Analyze a Needs Assessment. Use a combination of interviews, focus groups, and an analysis of employee and customer opinion surveys and organizational and community statistics (hiring and promotion data; sales and service computations to various market segments; opinions of customers, employees, and other stakeholders) to conduct an objective exploration of what factors contribute to inclusion and what factors block inclusion. This may be the step at which to invest in external assistance to ensure that the data compiled are as objective as possible. Consider involving employees in the analysis of the data. In some cases, conducting a needs assessment can be minimized; such cases could include small organizations, organizations where funds are limited, organizations whose leadership and practitioners are confident that few inclusion issues exist, or organizations whose climate is such that the results of a needs assessment could be rejected.

Step 4: Use GDIB to Determine the Organization's Desired Future State. Invite multiple groups of employees and other stakeholders to prioritize which benchmarks the participants want the organization to achieve (or maintain) in approximately three to five years. The groups can be representative of all individual organizational units (divisions or departments), identity groups (for example, gender, sexual orientation, organizational level, job type, nationality, or other groups determined by the Planning and Implementation team), and customers of various service or product lines. Each group is provided with a summary of the needs analysis (if one was conducted) and a copy of the GDIB. The GDIB can be customized or formatted for easy use and made available in hard copy or online. After studying the needs assessment results, respondents are invited to identify up to five benchmarks from the 50-, 75-, or 100-percent level in each of the thirteen categories. Or the planning and implementation team can decide not to use several categories. (However, care should be taken to assure that elimination of some categories does not negatively impact the breadth and depth and therefore the effectiveness of the initiative.) The process can be done through group discussion and consensus-building sessions or through surveys. Results are compiled and analyzed, and the planning and implementation team makes the final determination of the five-year desired future state.

Step 5: Use GDIB to Determine the Organization's Current State. Using groups and a process similar to or the same as those used in Step 4, participants identify up to five benchmarks that indicate the current organizational state on each of the thirteen categories. As in Step 4, the planning and implementation team compiles the information from the various groups and makes the final determination.

Step 6: Determine What Will Be Done to Help the Organization Progress from Its Current State to Its Desired Future State. The planning and implementation team identifies the actions the organization needs to take to move from its current state to its desired state. Ideas for actions can be obtained from other chapters in this book and/or a search of the inclusion literature or discussions with others in the organization. Once those actions are identified, each needs to be assessed for potential effectiveness, cost, and other implementation factors. The planning and implementation team may want to involve others in the organization in determining the actions to take. If others, such as the marketing manager, are involved in determining the actions needed to be taken regarding marketing, then implementation may go more smoothly because the marketing manager would not need to be "sold" on the action. Next, measurable yearly goals need to be set for each action so that progress toward the desired state can be budgeted, prioritized, tracked, measured, and amended or celebrated on an annual basis.

Step 7: Reassess and Revisit the Plan Every Several Years to Ensure It Is on Track. Using a process similar to that used in Steps 4 and 5, GDIB can be used to measure progress.

Other Ways to Use GDIB

Here are several other ways that GDIB can be used to help an organization create or sustain an inclusion initiative:

- *As an educational tool.* Encourage leaders and planners to read GDIB focusing on the GDIB Model and the best practices. Select a few benchmarks from several categories to learn more about and focus on for the first several years.
- *To create an employee diversity and inclusion survey or to mine for items to add to an existing survey.* Scan GDIB, select items of interest, and rewrite them to meet the style and standards of your organizational survey.
- *To identify organizations to study as examples of best practices.* First, study GDIB. Then, by searching your network, the Internet, and other sources, screen organizations to determine if what they consider a best practice compares to what GDIB states is a best practice.
- *To assess one aspect of your existing diversity and inclusion initiative.* For example, if your organization has a supplier diversity program, use Category 13 to determine at what level you are working for that program. The same process can be used for any of the categories.
- *To assist in hiring an internal inclusion practitioner or external inclusion consultant.* Use several of the benchmarks to craft interview questions. Educate interviewers to listen for the level of experience candidates describe as they respond to the questions.

Conclusion

The organizational leader asking the question in the vignette at the opening of this chapter sighed when the practitioner mentioned just a few of the variables to address before knowing exactly what to do and how to do it. By using *Global Diversity and Inclusion*

Benchmarks: Standards for Organizations Around the World, the leader and practitioner can feel confident that they know the standards for high-quality inclusion work and have some suggestions for how to approach the use of these benchmarks. Effective inclusion work is not a simple process. It involves careful, knowledgeable planning and a well-orchestrated implementation effort to put systems in place that create an environment in which inclusive behaviors can thrive.

References

O'Mara, J., & Richter, A. (2006). *Global diversity and inclusion benchmarks.* Retrieved from http://www.workforcediversitynetwork.com/docs/Articles/Article_GDIBenchmarksOct06_revJuly08%5B1%5D.pdf

O'Mara, J., & Richter, A. (2009). Setting standards for organizational diversity work: It's a lot more than culture fairs and ethnic food. In E. Biech (Ed.), *The 2009 Pfeiffer Annual: Consulting* (pp. 157–163). San Francisco, CA: Pfeiffer.

O'Mara, J., Richter, A., et al. (2011). *Global diversity and inclusion benchmarks: Standards for organizations around the world.* Retrieved from http://www.omaraassoc.com/pdf/GDIB_2011.pdf

Qirko, H., Metts, V., Landon, G., & Atchley, K. (1994). *Benchmarks for diversity: A benchmarking and assessment guide.* Knoxville, TN: Tennessee Valley Authority.

CHAPTER FIFTEEN

The Chief Diversity Officer's View of the Diversity and Inclusion Journey at Weyerhaeuser

Effenus Henderson

Human capital is increasingly the critical success factor in achieving desired business outcomes. Companies are recognizing the importance of investing in their human resources and how this investment can help them build competitive advantage in a global economy. Corporate leaders focus on and measure outcomes such as revenue, expenses, profitability, customer satisfaction, productivity of assets, market share, time to market, and stock price. The degree of success in accomplishing these outcomes will depend on how organizations leverage, engage, and deploy the resources with which they are entrusted.

As the world's talent becomes more interconnected, mobile, and diverse, and as society expects more from its corporate citizens, organizations must constantly adapt to survive and prosper. This adaptive capability is dependent on the organization's talent: it must be committed, engaged, and focused on increasing revenue, reducing time to market, increasing shareholder value and stock prices, minimizing costs, maximizing the efficient use of assets, and enhancing customer satisfaction.

To operate successfully in this environment, effective relationships and collaboration are imperative. The stakeholders—employees, investors, customers, regulators, and communities in which we operate—have become much more diverse and as such require much more cultural agility and skill in building relationships. These stakeholders come from different religious, geographic, political, and other demographic backgrounds and value sets; all of these have changed the paradigm for managing these diverse human relationships.

Operating in this new paradigm of cross-cultural and global value sets requires leaders who know how to leverage these differences and thus ensure that key stakeholders are present and participating when decisions are made. Like the other authors in this volume, I refer to this concept as *inclusion*—how to make the mix of so many differences as well as similarities work for the good of the organization as a whole. Inclusion is the process of making sure that diverse perspectives that should be at the table are not only there but also fully engaged. It is based on the belief that performance outcomes can be optimized when we value, respect, and engage a wide arrange of perspectives in problem-solving and decision-making.

At Weyerhaeuser, we recognize that diversity and inclusion are essential to remain competitive and innovative, and key to becoming the best forest products company in the world and a global leader among all industries. Weyerhaeuser's model of inclusion focuses on four behaviors—building trust, expanding circles of influence, demonstrating commitment to diversity, and providing equal opportunity for growth and development.

As a champion of diversity for my company and its chief diversity officer, I have witnessed a growing connection between diversity and inclusion and business outcomes. Embracing diversity has been part of a major change effort linked to building high-performance work systems at our operations. Fostering diversity has at times challenged leaders, as they struggled with short-term profitability, fewer resources, and poor market conditions that required a relentless focus on costs. However, our leadership understands the long-term importance of a diverse and inclusive workplace and has continued to build momentum in that direction.

Organizational Background: Context for the Change

We started our journey at Weyerhaeuser by establishing an Executive Diversity Council composed of a subset of the CEO's direct reports to develop and implement the multiyear strategy aligned with the company's long-term business plan. Previously most of the attention was focused on compliance. We worked on affirmative action plans. We monitored our progress on changing our workforce representation. Yet the broader business imperative was not fully understood or embraced.

Diversity is seen not as simply a compliance issue but rather as a key business imperative. As a result, our managers are held accountable for leading in this area the same way they lead on safety, profitability, ethics, and corporate environmental stewardship.

Weyerhaeuser's strategic direction in diversity and inclusion is set by our CEO, with the active support of his management team, human resources, and the diversity office. Efforts have been focused on establishing a strategic framework for diversity and inclusion with senior leadership sponsorship and implementing a short list of high-impact actions that focus our effort in this important area.

Over the past decade, Weyerhaeuser's CEO and leadership team have increased their emphasis on building a more diverse and inclusive organization to reflect our customers, communities, investors, and other stakeholders.

Reasons for the Initiative: The Business Imperative

Historically, diversity and inclusion efforts have been very heavily focused on workforce representation and driven by a compliance mindset. We wanted to take our efforts to a new level and to describe the true business value of diversity efforts.

We decided to begin by examining the practices of a number of companies, some of whose practices resulted in class action litigation and lawsuits. We wanted to understand practices that led to employees filing discrimination charges and winning extremely large settlements.

What we learned was striking. No company is immune to litigation. An ineffective leader can easily create a condition that leads employees to feel that litigation is the only remedy. We also learned that the most effective companies elevated the conversation so that the business imperative was directly linked and integrated into the values, vision, and strategic framework of the company. We learned that diversity and inclusion cannot be seen as a "set aside" initiative or program. They must be embraced and viewed as a strategic imperative and integrated into business decisions, including how they help the company accomplish the following goals:

- Serve a growing global customer base
- Innovate and design new products for emerging markets so that we can respond to increasing demands of the global customer base
- Deliver products and services to the customer efficiently and rapidly and with an in-depth understanding of their needs and values
- Engage employees, consumers, and other stakeholders in ways that create positive relationships and that focus on critical priorities (product, satisfaction, sustainability)
- Respond expeditiously to opportunities, problems, and challenges brought by employees, customers, and communities
- Examine the growing demographic changes that will take place within the next fifteen to thirty-five years and how inclusion will be involved in responding effectively to these critical changes.

What Was Done: The Change Management Process

At the start of the effort, senior leaders had to decide whether diversity was on the short list of corporate priorities going forward. The human resources group developed an updated business case for diversity and shared it with the senior management team. Based on much discussion and debate, the senior management team decided it was definitely on the short list of priorities, and they helped to shape the initial strategic framework for action.

In initiating the new strategy, the leaders drew upon learning from high-performance, work-system change efforts that had been successful in the past. These previous efforts were led by top HR and business leaders serving as champions and change agents. The following outlines the elements of the change effort used; leaders needed to do each of these.

1. *Understand the Current State.* Meet with organizational leaders to understand the business case and to help further refine it. Discuss and build the business imperative that is owned and supported by the top leadership team, including the head of human resources.

2. *Build the Strategy.* Under senior leadership guidance, work with either an existing project team or diversity council to help hone the strategy. Seek input by gathering data and working with key stakeholders—HR, human capital management, training and education, legal department, and operating units. Ensure a clear line of sight to business and operating strategy. Assess leadership understanding and commitment.

3. *Create a Change Framework for the Strategy.* Focus on developing a multiyear framework for change. Build understanding, shape key indicators and milestones for progress in each area, and build key partnership with internal and external stakeholders in carrying them out.

4. *Bring Clarity to Roles, Responsibilities, and Relationships.* Shape the implementation of the strategy through clear accountabilities and responsibilities. Seek low-cost, valued-added approaches that are bottom-line focused and that show a clear line of sight to the business objectives.

5. *Establish Key Success Factors and Strategic Milestones.* In partnership with organization leaders, establish metrics for improvement: ROI, retention/turnover, workforce representation, leadership scorecard focus areas and targets, employee engagement, and employee satisfaction.

The framework for the change process developed by Weyerhaeuser leaders consists of five high-impact areas accompanied by specific actions, timelines and targeted outcomes monitored annually. In developing the five high-impact areas, we reviewed best practices for driving change as well as some of the actions taken by companies recognized for their excellence in building more diverse and inclusive organizations.

We determined that the most important areas were (1) leadership accountability, (2) a focus on improvement in governance activities (affirmative action, training, risk mitigation), (3) targeted talent acquisition, development, and retention strategies, (4) processes to monitor the culture and climate (engagement surveys, employee resource groups, retention, and the like), and (5) intentional outreach strategies (supplier diversity, community organizations, and so on).

In an effort to ensure transparency, we put in place a process for reviewing our progress annually with the CEO and the board of directors.

Weyerhaeuser's Strategic Framework for Change

The five high-impact action areas that are part of our diversity and inclusion strategic framework (see Table 15.1) are discussed in more detail in this section.

The development and implementation of diversity and inclusion strategies are treated as multiyear change efforts. These efforts are guided by the change management principles we have used in other major organizational change processes.

Our company has faced a number of challenges since the initial framework was created. We have shifted our business model to that of a real estate investment trust, sold a large part of our business portfolio, and updated the company strategies. Our workforce has dropped from fifty thousand employees in 2005 to approximately thirteen thousand in 2011.

Although our diversity and inclusion change process has a long way to go to achieve its desired end state, we are gaining excellent traction in each of our action areas. In spite of the significant amount of downsizing, our workforce representation remained very close to predownsizing levels.

Building the platform for the change strategy was the beginning of the work; however, we became convinced that leadership commitment and effectiveness would be the glue to hold a multiyear strategy together. Our leaders had to have a clear vision of success, they had to be effective communicators of the business

Table 15.1. Weyerhaeuser's Strategic Diversity Framework

Action Area	Key Focus
Leadership Effectiveness and Role Modeling	Setting clear expectations for leaders; establishing metrics and defining inclusive leadership behaviors; measuring results
Diversity Governance and Accountability	Meeting regulatory and compliance requirements, assessing organizational risks in the workplace, and requiring participation in mandatory training such as harassment prevention and inclusion
Talent Management (recruitment, development, retention)	Building the pipeline of diverse talent through recruitment processes, and instituting mentoring programs
Work Climate and Culture	Establishing employee resource groups, tracking satisfaction levels of employees by demographic groups, and monitoring turnover patterns
Supplier, Community, and Customer Outreach	Building proactive outreach efforts in communities of color, targeted associations and colleges, minority suppliers, and the like

imperative, and they had to exercise superior judgment throughout the process as business conditions changed and as the company struggled to perform in a very weak economy.

After additional thought, our senior leaders decided that the initial step was to enhance leader effectiveness by focusing on a short list of behaviors identified by employees as critical to building a sense of engagement and inclusion. In this process, we learned that inclusive leadership is really about leadership effectiveness.

Leadership Effectiveness

We learned that the most critical part of a diversity and inclusion change strategy is ensuring that it is driven by the CEO and the company's senior leadership team. Company leaders must see it as a business imperative, and they must make certain that the diversity and inclusion strategy is reflected in the way business is done and hold their respective organizations accountable for achieving results.

At the start of implementing our change strategy, our senior leaders underwent a self-assessment of their individual effectiveness as leaders in two areas: personal behavior and results in diversity and inclusion. Each leader developed a personal action plan to close any major gaps identified. Performance improvement plans linking a portion of pay to diversity outcomes were implemented and tracked.

We learned that the development and communication of the business case must be given careful consideration. We discovered that we were not communicating enough about diversity throughout the organization, so we enhanced processes and venues for sharing information about our efforts. We learned that we cannot expect leaders and employees to know about progress if they are not informed of progress and opportunities. We discovered that leaders have to communicate often, in a variety of ways, to a wide audience.

To monitor our progress at the business and company levels, we developed a report that updates the organization on our diversity progress annually. Leaders are encouraged to include diversity and inclusion as an ongoing topic on management agendas. We updated our image advertisement and outreach strategies and built diversity and inclusion information into the company's annual sustainability reports.

In 2010, we focused on a strategy for strengthening leader understanding of personal behavior and how it could contribute to building a more inclusive culture. A taskforce was developed to create a new, leader-led learning effort on inclusive behaviors. The taskforce tested our approach with training and development and curriculum development experts to ensure that it would be effective. We received excellent feedback on the design. However, several training consultants preferred instruction led by a skilled trainer. In contrast, the taskforce felt that the leader could learn more by having to teach rather than by being a participant.

Training modules were developed in four areas: (1) building trust, (2) expanding circles of influence, (3) demonstrating commitment to diversity and inclusion, and (4) providing equal opportunity for growth and development. The modules were developed from extensive input from employees throughout the company who shared their thoughts and ideas on inclusive behavior. The implementation of the training was launched in 2011, starting with the CEO and his team. I discuss this program in greater detail later in the chapter.

Governance and Accountability

In examining best practices in diversity and inclusion governance, we learned that governance continues to be a cornerstone of effective diversity and affirmative action efforts. Across industries, diversity is growing in its importance to boards of directors, external advocacy groups, investors, and shareholders. All these stakeholders want to see more transparency in operations, so they are examining the extent of diversity and how it is reflected at all levels in organizations.

Federal contractors are expected to have robust affirmative action plans in place to increase diversity in the workforce. They are also expected to analyze workplace practices and systems that create adverse impact. Gaps in such systems can lead to costly class action lawsuits if not monitored closely.

To strengthen our efforts in this area, we require robust affirmative action plans at all establishments and audit them annually. Using external online resources with up-to-date expertise in compliance and harassment, we provide online antiharassment education programs that all employees are expected to complete. Based on our research, we found that when employees feel disrespected and devalued, they are much more likely to file charges of discrimination. We also learned that regular due diligence of HR policies and practices is an important part of the governance process. As part of our risk mitigation strategies, Weyerhaeuser business and HR leaders are required to review HR systems and practices for diversity implications and make appropriate changes where necessary.

Talent Management

Weyerhaeuser is not as well known as a number of other Fortune 500 companies, so we had to think of creative ways to attract, develop, and retain talent. As mentioned earlier, human capital management is increasing in importance as the demand for highly talented and qualified women and minorities increases. Employment trends underscore the impending shortage of skilled labor in a number of areas and disciplines.

As the pool of talent decreases, the level of diversity in these pools is increasing and becoming more global. We learned that a key driver that guides many applicants' decision whether to accept an employment offer is the level of diversity found in the prospective organization or company.

To become an employer preferred by top talent, leaders need to understand the desires and interests of this diverse job applicant pool. Factors such as the quality of leadership, policies regarding work-life balance, and career development programs are increasingly a part of the decision process. Compensation and benefits are also key factors used by these new entrants when they accept job offers and as they ponder whether they will stay with an employer.

Remaining an employer of choice requires that a company have effective strategies for recruiting, developing, and retaining critical talent. Building strong relationships with key recruiting sources is a critical component of the overall strategy.

Prior to our downsizing efforts, we instituted a Weyerhaeuser Scholars Program in partnership with the United Negro College Fund to fund internships and scholarships to diverse students. Additionally, we supported outreach efforts with the King Center in Atlanta, Georgia; the National Society of Black Engineers; Society of Hispanic Engineers; Catalyst; and the National Urban League, among others. We continue to strengthen relations with a targeted group of diverse organizations.

We also learned that our leaders need to understand the aspirations of the Millennials entering the workplace. Traditional Baby Boomer approaches to management and leadership will not work for this next generation of talent. In discussion with some of our Generation Next employees, we learned that they expect to have greater work-life integration, to be judged on results rather than face time, and to enjoy diverse and inclusive work environments.

Work Climate and Culture

Our goal was to make our culture and climate more inclusive. We learned that corporations around the world are entering an era when there will be more job opportunities than candidates to fill them, particularly in the technical and scientific areas. While the current global economic situation has slowed the numbers entering the workplace, the long-term challenges still exist. Changing jobs will become easier as jobs for high-tech talent become more plentiful.

We learned that organizations will need to examine their work environments to ensure that they are attractive to diverse talent. Processes and tools to gather feedback from employees on their levels of satisfaction with the work environment are very important if we are to understand their preferences and to ensure that they are engaged.

At Weyerhaeuser, we have strengthened our commitment to employee networks and councils and have sponsored several new business support networks, including Generation Next, Women in Action, Hispanic Opportunities for Leadership Achievement (iHOLA), Weyerhaeuser Black Employee Network (W-BEA), Weyerhaeuser Asian Business Network (WABN), ACCESS (focused on people with disabilities), our Veterans Group, and COLORS (our gay, lesbian, bisexual, transgender resource group).

These groups have well-developed charters, missions, and action plans strategically linked to the company's overall diversity and inclusion action plans. The network groups are very helpful in mentoring other employees, conducting educational forums, assisting with external recruiting events, and helping organizational leaders explore ways to retain diverse talent.

Employee satisfaction and engagement levels among diverse employee populations, as well as workforce representation change, attrition, turnover, and related areas are monitored annually. If trends dip, we institute processes to uncover reasons for dissatisfaction and turnover and then develop strategies to close the gaps.

Outreach

As stated earlier, Weyerhaeuser is not a well-known company outside of the communities in which we operate. Many business-to-business companies like ours are not well known in communities of color. Given the talent shortage and the lack of familiarity of the company in these communities, we had to institute proactive strategies to reach out to them. Relationships are critical for attracting diverse talent, and they have to be sustained over time.

Weyerhaeuser continues to build key relationships with targeted minority and woman-owned suppliers, associations, and community groups as an integral part of our strategy. To help maintain our supplier diversity efforts, we examine our programs internally and look for ways to continue our strategic partnerships with key national and regional organizations as a smaller, cost-constrained company.

We have broadened our thinking about diversity and inclusion to consider other stakeholder groups, including customers, investors, regulators, and governments. While diversity and inclusion may be seen as just about numbers and representation in some organizations, we believe it is a fundamental and growing part of our overall value proposition and our strategic imperative across much broader stakeholder groups. Women and minorities represent the majority of the new entrants into the workforce in the United States (Humes, Jones, & Ramirez, 2011), and many customers for our products are increasingly women, people of color, and immigrants. Public policy decisions impacting our industry are reviewed by very diverse local, state, and national government officials. Our ability to build strong relations with local decision makers, leading to fewer zoning restrictions, regulatory requirements, and other licensing requirements, could be at stake.

Markets are becoming more interdependent, global, and sophisticated. Corporate social responsibility and sustainability are emerging as key requirements for doing business in a greener world.

I believe that we cannot achieve our vision of being the best forest products company in the world and a global leader among all industries without a heartfelt commitment to human rights, diversity, and inclusion. I have had the opportunity to work with the United Nations and understand the growing importance of global human rights. We developed a company policy in support of human rights (Weyerhaeuser NR Company, 2012) as part of our corporate social responsibility and sustainability commitments.

Integration

To be sustainable, diversity efforts must have direct linkage to the business outcomes mentioned earlier: increasing revenue, reducing time to market, increasing shareholder value and stock prices, minimizing costs, maximizing the efficient use of assets, and enhancing customer satisfaction. The effort must then be integrated into the fabric of how one does business.

We learned that diversity and inclusion strategies must be aligned with these business goals and objectives and driven by leadership to be effective and sustainable. Inclusion cannot stand alone. Inclusion efforts require leaders to shift their thinking from diversity as "all about numbers" and workforce representation, a compliance-oriented mindset, to one that reinforces and connects the business imperative. We learned that diversity strategies cannot be owned only by the HR function. Diversity and inclusion efforts must be led by the CEO and senior management team, with strong support from the board, HR, business leaders, and the diversity office. These strategies must be linked and integrated with the company's strategic direction. They must be shared with leaders further down in the organization as well. Getting that message down throughout the organization has been a challenge for us.

The dimensions of this integration include understanding the implications of global demographic change on product demands and customer requirements. It also underscores the fact that diverse and inclusive teams often outperform homogeneous teams in terms of productivity and innovation (see Hayles, Chapter 2, this volume).

Global talent is in short supply and increasingly diverse. This talent is motivated by opportunity and the potential to grow, rather than loyalty to company or organization. If this talent is not fully utilized and engaged in helping to solve critical business issues, they will leave—and this is especially true of the Millennial generation.

It is not enough to produce a good product or service; you must operate with integrity and possess a healthy respect for community, environment, and diverse points of view. Your license to operate in many communities can be impacted by the quality of your relationships with diverse sectors of society. Building enduring relationships and collaborating with diverse stakeholders is extremely important and should be integrated into all decision-making processes.

Inclusive Leadership: Twenty-First-Century Strategy

As our diversity journey continued at Weyerhaeuser, we realized that having a diverse workforce, at all organizational levels, was an integral part of the solution. However, understanding and strengthening inclusion practices was even more important.

We defined inclusion as the way an organization configures opportunity, interaction, communication, information, and decision making to realize the potential of diverse employees and other stakeholders. Inclusion involves the organization's culture or environment. Achieving inclusion requires creating the structures, policies, and practices in organizational life that recognize multiple perspectives and signal the importance of learning from those differences. We became convinced that inclusion starts with inclusive leadership.

In 2010, I led a project team to develop learning modules to help leaders understand inclusion and the behaviors that effective leaders display in this area. Inclusion is not necessarily limited to the way an organization deals with employees; it may refer to interactions with other stakeholders: customers, clients, partners, vendors, suppliers and subcontractors as well. As a result of extensive input from our employees, our efforts have been focused on the following outcomes:

1. *Strengthening inclusive leadership behaviors.* Inclusive leadership is effective leadership. Our short list of inclusive behaviors aligns

with our people values and principles. Our goal is to improve leadership skills by providing tools and education to strengthen understanding. We will measure and hold leadership accountable for respectful and inclusive behaviors.

2. *Linking diversity closely to business results.* Leaders will be expected to identify specific actions that are tied to achieving business outcomes and results.

3. *Fostering a respectful work environment.* All employees and leaders will be required to complete harassment prevention and inclusion education every twenty-four months. This Inclusive Leadership training was required for all leaders (anyone directing the work of others) in 2011. Others in nonleadership roles were also in the training session.

A diverse and inclusive workforce enhances and stimulates a more creative and innovative learning organization and contributes to enhanced productivity, satisfaction, engagement, and retention. In that regard, Scott Page, a well-known authority on this topic, writes the following:

> To understand innovation, we must focus on diversity as well as ability. A scan of the intellectual landscape as well as of the policies of successful companies reveals a tacit understanding of diversity's role in innovation. George Mason University professor Richard Florida's work on the creative class, *The Rise of the Creative Class* and *The Flight of the Creative Class,* touches on the link between diversity and innovation, as do Yale University's Barry Nalebuff and Ian Ayres in their book and accompanying website *Why Not?* Some of the innovation policies of Toyota Motor Corp. and Google Inc. illustrate a similar understanding that differences in the composition of their work forces boosts [*sic*] their bottom lines [2007, para. 7].

Inclusive Behavior Is a Cornerstone of Effective Leadership

To build leadership effectiveness in managing an increasingly diverse organization, we wanted to determine the behaviors that were important to our employees. We asked a number of employees from across the company to give us their thoughts, and after tabulating the results, four behavior areas emerged. Inclusive leaders:

- Build trust (through communication, acknowledgement, recognition, respectful behavior, listening to different points of view, and so on).
- Ensure equal opportunity for development and growth (selection, promotion, task force assignments, and so on).
- Demonstrate commitment to diversity and inclusion (hold leaders accountable, set expectations, monitor results, link to performance and pay, and so on).
- Expand their circle of influence (eliminate silos and patterns of exclusivity; seek different perspectives from others not in the department, not like them, and so on).

Using the input from employees, the task force developed a "leader-led" skill-building program to help leaders identify and build strategies for improving personal and team effectiveness in these four behavior areas. Our view is that leaders learn best through personal discovery, reflection, and action planning, so these program features were a key part of our design. We developed an updated self-assessment tool based on the new behaviors that could also be used to gather data from peers and direct reports to help with the self-examination, reflection, and action planning. We created a Microsoft SharePoint website on our intranet to house all the materials needed to conduct the training session.

An overview focused on the business imperative was developed along with a module for each of the behavior areas. Each module contains a scenario in which an example of the behavior was or was not carried out. Participants are asked to discuss the impact of the leader's action on employee engagement, motivation, and productivity, as well as business outcomes.

The Tangible Benefits of Inclusive Leadership

Based on my analysis and review of current literature on the topic, I developed a list of benefits that can be derived from inclusive leadership. My list of benefits was consistent with input that I received from our leaders and our employees. I believe that inclusive leaders help us:

- Attract and retain the best individuals from a shrinking pool of talent
- Satisfy the needs of an increasingly diverse set of stakeholders (communities, investors, regulators, employees, customers, and so on)
- Enhance the productivity, innovation, and engagement of our workforce
- Create a culture that encourages increased candor and risk taking
- Better represent the diversity of our stakeholders
- Enhance our reputation as an employer of choice
- Minimize financial risks in terms of litigation
- Optimize problem solving and product or market development

Exclusive Processes and Practices Can Impact Effectiveness

As we began to develop the inclusive leadership series, we asked employees to identify leaders' behaviors that affected whether they felt included, engaged, and valued. A number of situations were identified (on and off the job) in which employees personally experienced exclusion. Based on this input, we decided to create a learning experience in which leaders could better understand the impact of exclusive behavior on achieving organizational results. We determined that engagement, retention, and satisfaction are all directly related to the quality of the relationship with the supervisor or team leader. As a result, we felt that an action-planning component, which helps the leader incorporate inclusive behaviors into work practices and processes, was needed.

What Effective Leaders Do

We encouraged leaders to examine the culture and climate for diversity as a part of the action-planning process. We then developed a set of focus areas for leaders (listed in Table 15.2), based

Table 15.2. Focus Areas for Inclusive Leaders

Focus Area	Specific Leadership Actions to Consider
General Awareness	Start by gaining a realistic and up-to-date understanding of the organization's diversity profile at all levels (workforce representation).
Action Orientation	Initiate specific and targeted actions to increase the pipeline of women and minorities in your organization (in areas of underutilization); assess satisfaction levels within demographic groups.
Monitoring	Test how well diversity and inclusion are valued within the organization at all levels.
Role Modeling	Demonstrate effective leadership by holding leaders accountable and by initiating specific and compelling actions to build a more diverse and inclusive culture and work environment.
Effectiveness	Understand your own behavior gaps in inclusive leadership and those of other leaders reporting to you. Develop strategies and actions to address these gaps. Review policies and practices that may unintentionally be getting in the way.
Personal Commitment	Display personal commitment to diversity and inclusion by regularly communicating expectations, holding leaders accountable, and regularly inspecting progress.
Business Priority	Build the business case for your unit and business. Set the tone so that the organization understands that creating a more diverse and inclusive culture is a top business priority.
Indicators of Progress	Establish a short list of priorities and monitor progress quarterly. Build into performance management plans. Communicate progress on key goals.
Personal Improvement Plans	Understand personal and team gaps in behavior and develop an action plan to close critical gap areas.

on a review of best practices and my own experience leading change processes. The areas highlighted in Table 15.2 are a helpful framework for examining practices.

I am convinced that the leader must set the tone by understanding personal and team gaps. The leader and team must develop action plans to address organizational shortcomings and institute processes for monitoring improvement.

Effective leaders understand that building and sustaining a diverse and inclusive organization doesn't just happen; it requires a multiyear, systemic approach that is focused on the critical gaps within their unit. Effective leaders start by examining personal behavior but also explore the areas of greatest opportunity within the unit and leadership team.

Effective leaders ensure that their personal behaviors are inclusive. They seek feedback from their employees and peers. They communicate directly, honestly, and courageously. They speak up when others are being excluded and do not tolerate inappropriate or disrespectful behavior.

In Summary

Diversity and inclusion management is a continuous process of improvement and adaptation to changing conditions both inside and outside of the organization. The worldview and mindset of leaders must change to reflect an understanding and appreciation for the power and influence of diversity and inclusion across all stakeholder groups. Failure to understand and appreciate the impact of these global demographic trends will lead to less than optimal results. Organizational sustainability depends on it.

The bottom line is this: to achieve the organizational outcomes desired in the next period of economic growth, business leaders will have to sharpen their understanding of diversity and build their skills in leveraging that diversity through inclusive behavior.

Demonstrations, uprisings, voting blocks—to name a few—clearly point to the growing influence and power diverse populations have, both in the United States and around the world. Building mutually beneficial relationships will be vital to survival and growth.

References

Humes, K. R., Jones, N. A., & Ramirez, R. R. (2011, March). *Overview of race and Hispanic origin: 2010* (2010 Census Brief C2010BR-02). Washington DC: United States Census Bureau. Retrieved from http://www.census.gov/prod/cen2010/briefs/c2010br-02.pdf

Page, S. (2007, January). Diversity powers innovation [Blog post]. Retrieved from http://www.americanprogress.org/issues/economy/news/2007/01/26/2523/diversity-powers-innovation

Weyerhaeuser NR Company (2012, June 20). Human rights [Web page]. Retrieved from http://www.weyerhaeuser.com/Sustainability/People/Employees/HumanRights

CHAPTER SIXTEEN

Creating Diverse and Inclusive Colleges and Universities

Kumea Shorter-Gooden

Colleges and universities are arguably the most important institutions in which to work toward full inclusion, as they are the prime training ground for the future professionals, managers, and leaders in almost all industries. If we can transform higher education such that it is fully inclusive of people of diverse cultures, value systems, and identities, and if we can successfully influence the cultural competence of college graduates, we will have workforce leaders who have at least the rudimentary disposition, knowledge, and skills to lead in the transformation of other societal institutions.

The aim of this chapter is to address the goals and key components in creating diverse and inclusive higher educational settings. I begin with definitions, followed by a brief description of the history of diversity and inclusion initiatives in higher education and the current aims of such efforts. I describe four key components of diversity and inclusion work and provide examples of strategies to address these four areas. Finally, I suggest some considerations for college and university diversity and inclusion initiatives in the next decade. I provide examples from my experience as the chief diversity officer at Alliant International University, a private, non-profit university with campuses in California, Tokyo, Hong Kong, and Mexico City. Alliant has 4,300 students, most of whom are pursuing graduate degrees in psychology, education, or business and management. In 2006, Alliant developed a plan that includes diversity-related institutional objectives and competencies for students, staff, and faculty.

Definitions

In the study of organizations, the term *diversity* typically refers to the demographic composition of groups or workforces (Roberson, 2006). The focus historically has been on demographic differences between members of the workforce; initially, on differences in race, ethnicity, and gender, which are related to differences in power and privilege in the broader society and within organizations (Cox, 1993). Over the years, the definition of diversity has broadened to include similarities and differences based on a broad array of factors—some visible, others hidden or invisible; some based on group characteristics, others on unique individual differences (Thomas, 1996).

In contrast, the term *inclusion*, which has gained in usage and popularity in the last decade (Roberson, 2006; see also Ferdman, Chapter 1, this volume), addresses the extent to which individuals feel like active participants in the organization (Mor Barak, 2005; Roberson, 2006). At times the term *diversity* is used similarly to capture the psychological experiences of organizational members and the impact of these experiences on their work satisfaction, work performance, and progress in the organization (see, for example, Hays-Thomas, 2004). Thus the terms are often used interchangeably, particularly in the field of education; however, inclusion highlights the set of issues—beyond counting heads—that organizations face in working to create equitable environments in which all people feel valued for their perspectives and contributions.

An important foundational step for colleges and universities is to attend to the numbers of people from diverse or underrepresented groups; for example, by asking the question "Is our student body representative of the communities that we serve?" However, the long-term goal is for transformation that ensures active participation and engagement, and thus full inclusion. Both diversity and inclusion require particular attention to historical and contemporary differences in power and privilege (Kivel, 2004); thus assessing and addressing which identity groups are marginalized and which groups are not succeeding or achieving equitable outcomes.

In this chapter, I use the terms *diversity* and *inclusion* to address issues of composition and full engagement, respectively. As Holvino, Ferdman, and Merrill-Sands (2004) assert: "In multicultural, inclusive organizations, members of all groups are treated fairly, feel included and actually are included, have equal opportunities and are represented at all organizational levels and functions" (p. 249).

A Brief History of Diversity and Inclusion in Higher Education

Explicit attention to diversity and inclusion has a forty-plus-year history in U.S. higher education, stemming largely from the social movements of the 1960s and early 1970s, which led the nation and its colleges and universities to begin to address the civil rights of African Americans, other people of color, women, and people who are gay and lesbian (Banks, 2001; Smith, 2009). For example in 1968, after the assassination of Dr. Martin Luther King, Jr. and the subsequent civil rebellion in numerous cities throughout the United States, a number of U.S. colleges and universities opened their doors for the first time to a significant number of African American students (Williams & Wade-Golden, 2007). Additionally, in the 1960s, affirmative action policies and other laws and regulations contributed to greater access to higher education, and to systematic attention to inequitable treatment; for example, sexual harassment of students, staff, and faculty (Hays-Thomas, 2004). In the last couple of decades the "browning of America"— the increase in the number of people of color, in part due to increased immigration—has further fueled the need for change (Kitano, 1997a).

The attention to diversity logically led to a focus on inclusive curricula, as colleges and universities responded to student demands for meaningful and relevant courses; for example, through African American and women's studies, and later through the infusion of multicultural content throughout all academic curricula (Banks, 1999; Kitano, 1997a; Williams & Wade-Golden, 2007). And increasingly, universities are examining the degree to which their research agendas align with diversity and inclusion. They are exploring how they can more effectively serve the greater good by fostering diversity-related research (Williams & Wade-Golden).

Over the years, there has been an evolution from a focus on affirmative action and equity, wherein diversity and inclusion efforts are seen as benefiting only those who have been under-represented and underserved, to a focus on diversity and inclusion as a resource that enhances the learning of all students and the effectiveness and competence of faculty and staff (Williams & Wade-Golden, 2007). In other words, diversity and inclusion are increasingly viewed as critical elements of institutional and academic excellence.

There has been another shift—from a focus on race/ethnicity and gender specifically, a focus only on visible aspects of identity, to a more holistic approach, in which there is attention to visible and invisible (or less visible) differences based on socioeconomic status, sexual orientation, religion, age, ability, and other dimensions for which there are power and privilege differentials. Moreover, there is increasing recognition of the intersectionality and fluidity of identity, acknowledging that identity is not fixed or static and that people have multiple identities and often multiple reference groups (Cole, 2009; see also Ferdman & Roberts, Chapter 3, this volume). Another change has been to a more comprehensive and systematic approach to diversity and inclusion, wherein these issues are not isolated in specific offices, but instead are integrated into all university functions and programs. Notably, in recent years more and more colleges and universities have appointed chief diversity officers as senior administrators who report to the president, chancellor, or chief academic officer and whose job it is to lead the university in becoming a diverse, fully inclusive campus (Williams & Wade-Golden, 2007).

In spite of significant successes in the past four decades, U.S. higher education continues to struggle with diversity and inclusion. For example, wide racial/ethnic gaps persist in college enrollment rates, with Whites making up the highest proportion of eighteen- to twenty-four-year-olds enrolled as well as having the greatest gains in enrollment for ten years beginning in the mid-1990s (Ryu, 2008). In contrast, Latinos have the lowest rates of enrollment and the smallest improvement over the same ten-year span (Ryu). Moreover, the graduation rates of African American and Latino students are consistently lower than those of White and Asian students, with African American students having the lowest persistence rates (Ryu). The number of women faculty and presidents has increased but is still not commensurate with the population (Ryu). And interviews and focus groups with students of color at predominantly White colleges reveal that they often experience feelings of isolation and distrust and do not feel fully integrated into and included in the academy (see, for example, Bourke, 2010; Watson et al., 2002). A recent study found that low-income and poor students experienced less sense of belonging to the university in contrast to their middle class and upper-middle class peers (Chatman, 2008, as cited in Langhout, Drake, & Rosselli, 2009). There is much more work to be done!

Four Key Components of Diversity and Inclusion

A useful framework for considering the degree and depth of diversity and inclusion in colleges and universities is to focus on four components: institutional commitment, access and success, infused programs, and an affirming climate. *Institutional commitment* has to do with the extent to which the institution as a whole, including top leadership, has explicitly committed to creating a diverse, inclusive university. *Access and success* has to do with who is at the table—the diversity and representation of students, staff, faculty, and trustees, and the degree to which diversity is well represented at all levels, not just at the bottom rungs. This component also addresses issues of equity; for example, whether there are equitable outcomes with respect to student graduation rates, faculty tenure rates, staff retention and advancement, and compensation for diverse employees—based on, for example, race, ethnicity, and gender. *Infused programs* refers to the substantive business of higher education—academic programs, course curricula, teaching, and research. The relevant question is: To what extent are diverse perspectives and issues of diversity and inclusion integrated into these core functions of the university?

Table 16.1. Four Components of Diversity and Inclusion in Universities

Institutional Commitment	Access and Success	Infused Programs	Affirming Climate
• Vision and mission statement • Institutional values • Strategic plan for diversity • Words and actions of board members, president, administrators, and faculty leaders	• Recruitment, retention, and graduation of diverse students • Recruitment, retention, advancement, and equitable compensation of diverse faculty and staff • Diverse trustee or governing board	• Academic curricula infused with multicultural content • Pedagogical approaches for diverse learners • Diversity issues central to research and scholarship	• Physical environment that reflects diversity • Policies that support diversity and inclusion • Activities and events that celebrate diversity • Everyday interactions that support diversity and inclusion

Affirming climate refers to how various constituents experience the university: Do they feel welcomed? Affirmed? Supported? Included? These four components overlap and are interactive.

Institutional Commitment

Having a clear, explicit institutional commitment to diversity and inclusion is critical for colleges and universities that are serious about embarking on this work (Smith, 2009). Leadership is important, and the words and actions of the president, provost, deans, and other top leaders send an important message to the rest of the college community (Sue et al., 1998). Optimally, the commitment to diversity and inclusion is part of the university's vision, mission, and/or statement of institutional values—part of the core institutional purpose and raison d'être. The commitment to diversity and inclusion should be evident in the university's strategic plan through diversity-related objectives and action steps. However, if this is not the case, then a separate strategic plan for diversity with specific action steps should be developed.

Ideally, all constituents of the university—faculty, staff at all levels, students, alumni and alumnae, board members, donors, and friends—have the opportunity to shape the institutional pledge to diversity and inclusion. Colleges and universities differ in their purpose and goals, and they exist in different environmental contexts; thus the standpoints from which they view and embrace diversity and inclusion will differ. A public community college in an impoverished inner-city neighborhood is likely to have a different vision of diversity and inclusion from that of a rural Midwestern Christian college, whose view will likely differ from that of a historically Black southern university. Involving all constituents in creating the diversity and inclusion vision and plan helps to ensure that what is developed is realistic and fits the university, and that constituents throughout the university will work to fulfill the plan.

I'll share an example from my previous institution, Alliant International University. Alliant was born in 2001 of the merger of the California School of Professional Psychology (CSPP) and United States International University (USIU). CSPP was a national leader with respect to multicultural psychology—the development of psychological theory, research, and practice that addresses diverse and underserved groups. USIU was a leader in international education—the engagement of students in the United States and abroad in global learning—with a network of international campuses and a substantial number of international scholars and students at its U.S. campus.

A few years after the merger, the provost convened a university-wide committee to consider these multicultural and international legacies and how to advance them. Committee members hosted meetings on their respective campuses and invited students, staff, and faculty to attend and share their perspectives on diversity, on multicultural and international issues, and particularly on whether and how the university might recommit itself to this work.

In 2006, after a year of discussions, the committee developed a university diversity plan, which was approved by the faculty senate, the staff council, student government, and the president's steering committee. This plan includes university objectives for representational diversity, for infusion of diversity content into the curricula, and for the development of welcoming and affirming campus climates. Additionally, it contains overlapping sets of multicultural and international competencies for students, faculty, and staff (see Table 16.2). This diversity plan continues to serve as the framework and guide for Alliant's diversity and inclusion initiatives.

An important ingredient in developing a vision and plan for diversity and inclusion is to conduct an assessment that reveals challenges to diversity and inclusion as well as strengths and resources (García, Hudgins, McTighe Musil, Nettles, Sedlacek, & Smith, 2001; Jackson, 2005; Sue et al., 1998). Data on numerical diversity and equity of outcomes are critical, as are data on student satisfaction and employee perceptions of campus climate. Alliant did not use formal assessment data in developing its plan; however, the informal feedback, perceptions, and perspectives of an array of university community members were vital. Subsequently, Alliant has used assessment data to guide the specific action steps necessary to realize the plan.

Written documents, like vision and mission statements and diversity strategic plans, are necessary but not sufficient. If the vision, plan, and underlying values are not articulated and reinforced in the words and actions of the faculty and administration, then the documents become dusty relics. The reinforcement of the vision should come not only from those administrators who are specifically charged with responsibility for diversity and inclusion, but also from the president, provost, deans, and others, as part of their everyday communications and messages to the college community. Otherwise, the risk is that diversity and inclusion efforts will be marginalized, perhaps viewed as "something over there for those people," rather than as "front and center" on the university's agenda.

Access and Success

There are numerous strategies to address the "access and success" dimension of diversity and inclusion. The key question is: "To what extent do our recruitment, hiring, admissions, orientation,

Table 16.2. Alliant International University's Multicultural/International Competencies

Students	Faculty	Staff
Positive, pro-active and non-judgmental attitude towards diverse cultural and international identities and in their interpersonal and professional interactions.		
Multicultural skill set for understanding oneself and being able to successfully navigate intercultural transactions.		
Ability to engage effectively in difficult dialogues about multicultural and international issues.		
Ability to transfer and apply insights from one's group, region, or nation-state and culture to another to create knowledge and understanding in areas of professional practice.		
General knowledge of various local and international cultures as it relates to one's own field, to include: cultural differences and similarities, the dimensions of privilege and power, identity, social and political issues, communication and personal expression. a. Understanding of at least two cultures, preferably covering at least two countries. b. Understanding of problems and issues related to race, gender, social class, etc. within the two cultures.		
Demonstrate an ability to conceptualize and deliver culturally competent professional services in their respective areas to diverse populations.		
Show respect, affirmation, and adaptability to diverse cultures and nationalities with which they interact.		
Communicate effectively regarding multicultural and international issues.		
Demonstrate skills and abilities in a second language; one of the two languages should be Alliant's language of instruction.		

Continued

Table 16.2. Continued

Students	Faculty	Staff
	Demonstrate familiarity with a different worldview, and demonstrate skills, awareness and knowledge in teaching, international content, and settings.	
	Understand and model multiculturalism and respect for international perspectives in their interactions, teaching, professional practice and research.	
		Be able to recognize that different cultural styles exist and should be taken into account when working with culturally different student, staff, and faculty populations.
		Be able to demonstrate customer service skills in dealing effectively with multicultural/international communities.

Source: Alliant International University's International-Multicultural Plan, 2006.

and human resource policies, practices, formal and informal messages support the full engagement of diverse students and employees and their success?" Here, I briefly describe strategies that can be used with respect to students and faculty and staff.

Students

The first step with respect to students is, of course, to get students from diverse and underrepresented groups in the door. A number of structural strategies have been developed over several decades to address outreach, recruitment, admission, and orientation of diverse students, particularly underrepresented students of color. For example, a number of universities have developed university-community partnerships that create a relationship between the "ivory tower" and surrounding communities (Myers, Caruso, & Birk, 1999), which, for urban institutions, are often home to African American, Latino, poor, and working class families. Other commonly used approaches are early awareness programs—which reach out to high schools, middle schools, and sometimes even elementary schools (Myers et al.)—as well as targeted recruitment programs and targeted scholarship support (see, for example, Stewart, 2004).

Admissions standards have been examined for biases that disadvantage students of color and working class or economically underprivileged students (see, for example, Crisp, Horn, Dizzino, & Wang, 2010) and adjusted to provide a more holistic picture of the applicant's strengths. Sedlacek (2003) argues for the inclusion of more "noncognitive" assessment tools, such as measures of students' adjustment, motivation, and perceptions, which have been found to be particularly relevant factors in the prediction of success for students of color and those from nontraditional backgrounds. Some important questions are: "To what extent do we rely on SAT and GRE scores and what are the data on their utility in predicting academic performance and success?" and "Are we relying too heavily on the quality of writing in the admissions essay, and how do we adjust our requirements and expectations to be inclusive of students for whom English (or standard English) is a second language?"

Because retention and graduation are critical indicators of student success, numerous initiatives have been developed to foster the persistence of underrepresented or historically marginalized students; for example, orientation and transition programs that help students to learn how to navigate the university and mentoring programs with peer or faculty mentors. In addition, cultural centers and women's centers, ethnic affairs offices, and academic support services are often important resources for retention and graduation (Jones, 2004; Langhout et al., 2009; Moody, 2004; Stewart, 2004). These programs often make explicit the rules and the strategies for successfully navigating the academy (Langhout et al., 2009), provide social and academic support to marginalized students (Turner, 2004), and sensitize and educate the broader campus community to the needs and concerns of those who have been historically sidelined (Turner, 2004).

In keeping with this last point, in the course of recruiting, admitting, orienting, and socializing all students, it is important to include attention to diversity and inclusion. It should not come as a surprise to any students, including those from mainstream or privileged groups, that the university wants to engage a student body that is diverse on multiple dimensions, to create a multicultural campus community, and to infuse the curricula with multicultural content. The aim is to create diversity champions in all groups.

Smith (2009) cautions that retaining and graduating diverse students is not simply a matter of developing programs. There is evidence that historically marginalized students thrive when faculty and staff continually convey their belief in students' ability to succeed, help to focus students on the greater purpose of their education, and create a campus environment that is focused on learning. In other words, the university culture and its explicit and implicit messages are important for student success. Thus student access and success is partly or largely contingent on the climate, which will be discussed later.

As mentioned previously, it is important to have data on the diversity of the student population and on educational outcomes, and particularly on disparities in outcomes.

Evaluative data are also important to assess the benefit of policies, programs, and practices that address student diversity and student success. These sorts of data provide important information for directing, targeting, and improving intervention programs. Quantitative data are critical, as are qualitative data; for example, from interviews or focus groups that can provide rich, textured information about students' experiences and about their perceptions of the climate (García et al., 2001).

The Alliant dean of students office includes questions about the climate for diversity and inclusion in its biannual satisfaction survey of all students and its follow-up focus groups with a sample of students. In addition, before I left, there was work on developing an online survey for all graduating students to learn about their experiences, as well as an exit interview with all students who leave the university without graduating. Both the survey and the interview may include questions about students' perceptions of support, feelings of inclusion, and experiences of cultural alienation. The data will be disaggregated by race or ethnicity and gender to understand the experiences of subgroups of students; for example, Latino and Latina students and women. These evaluation strategies represent the integration of the diversity and inclusion agenda into the ongoing processes and functions of the university. This is an example of a structural change that places this important diversity and inclusion function with the dean of students, with support and assistance from the chief diversity officer.

Most students eventually become alumni or alumnae, another important constituency, and the university's capacity to continue to engage them in an inclusive manner has implications for the university's reputation and influence in the broader community, for its capacity to continue to recruit talented students, staff, and faculty from underrepresented groups, and also for its capacity to friend-raise and fund-raise.

Faculty and Staff

In U.S. higher education, diversification of the student body is more advanced than diversification of the faculty and senior administrators (Ryu, 2008). Achieving faculty diversity in U.S. colleges and universities has been particularly slow (Smith, 2009). How do we attract and retain a diverse faculty? How about staff? How do we ensure that employees from marginalized or underserved groups excel, succeed, advance, and thrive in our institution? How do we ensure that all faculty and staff have the cultural competence to educate and serve effectively?

Many universities have launched initiatives to target and recruit underrepresented faculty. The primary approach is to rework faculty search procedures so that they incorporate best practices in the recruitment of people of color and women. The following specific strategies have been used (Glass & Minnotte, 2010; Gordon, 2004; Greene & Harrigan, 2004):

- Assisting departments in distinguishing between required and desirable qualifications
- Diversifying search committees
- Proactive recruitment of candidates from underrepresented groups
- Addressing the hidden biases of search committee members that can prevent underrepresented candidates from being seen as viable
- Providing financial incentives to departments for targeted hires
- Holding department chairs and deans accountable for diversity in hiring

Once underrepresented faculty and staff are on board, another important task is to provide support for them to enhance their opportunity for success. Orientation programs, mentoring programs, and employee affinity groups can all help to create an environment that is welcoming, supportive, and sustaining (Wadsworth, 1999).

It is important to engage all faculty and staff in the diversity and inclusion agenda; thus it is critical that awareness, knowledge, and skills with respect to diversity and inclusion are criteria in the hiring of all faculty and staff, not just those from underrepresented groups. Diversity and inclusion are critical issues in teaching, research, advising, academic support services, residential life services, and all other staff functions, including, for example, serving as a receptionist or an IT technician. Thus all prospective faculty and staff should be screened for, at a minimum, their openness to working with diverse students and colleagues and to becoming more culturally competent. Moreover, all new (and existing) staff and faculty need to be oriented to and acculturated into the university's diversity and inclusion goals and plan.

Systematic faculty and staff development programs should incorporate attention to diversity and inclusion issues that are relevant to the specific faculty or staff functions (Chism & Whitney, 2005). At Alliant, the university's articulated faculty and staff competencies (see Table 16.2) provide a framework for ongoing professional development.

It is, of course, important to ensure equity in salaries and compensation and to ensure that biases do not lead to, for example, women and people of color being paid less than White men. Data on salaries and compensation as well as on retention, advancement, and promotion rates should be routinely reviewed to ascertain whether all faculty and staff are achieving equitable outcomes.

It is also important that the accountability and reward systems for faculty and staff include attention to diversity and inclusion, such that employees are evaluated based in part on their effectiveness with respect to the university's diversity and inclusion action plan and their success in incorporating diversity awareness, knowledge, and skills into their everyday assignments and tasks. As an example, at Alliant, after adoption of the university diversity plan, the provost worked with the faculty senate to amend the criteria for faculty advancement and promotion to include the degree to which faculty incorporate multicultural and international topics and issues in their teaching and scholarship. In their annual self-study, faculty are asked to discuss whether and how their work has integrated multicultural and international issues, and their program directors, deans, and peer reviewers consider this in the evaluation decision.

Additionally, evaluative data should be collected to assess the experiences of diverse staff and faculty. Climate surveys should be administered to all faculty and staff, with data collected carefully and confidentially, including demographic information—such as race, ethnicity, gender, sexual orientation, and ability status—so that findings can be disaggregated by key demographic variables. As with students, it is useful to conduct exit interviews with faculty and staff who leave the university, in order to learn about their experience of the institution with respect to diversity and inclusion (Wadsworth, 1999).

Infused Programs

The wonderful thing about higher education is that its core mission is to teach and to produce scholarship that advances understanding. We have the opportunity, therefore, to integrate teaching, learning, and conducting research on diversity and inclusion into the everyday work of the academy.

Transforming Courses

With respect to academic curricula, although the initial thrust was to develop ethnic studies and women's studies programs, this "separatist" strategy evolved into a far-reaching movement to transform the entire curriculum (Banks, 1999; Kitano, 1997b; Williams & Wade-Golden, 2007). Kitano describes the "transformed" course as one in which the instructor encourages students to critique the traditional perspectives and to reconceptualize what is "truth." The instructor aims to enhance both personal and academic growth of students and to foster classroom interactions that empower students to be both teachers and learners.

There are several models of course transformation (see, for example, Schoem, Frankel, Zúñiga, & Lewis, 1993) and a number of books and chapters that address the process, challenges, and outcome of multicultural course change. Most of the focus has been on the curricular infusion of diverse ethnic and cultural perspectives and the experiences of women; sometimes the focus is on the inclusion of diverse sexual orientation, religious, and ability perspectives, and more recently, on international perspectives (see, for example, Fiol-Matta & Chamberlain, 1994; Mestenhauser & Ellingboe, 1998; Morey & Kitano, 1997; Ouellett, 2005). Although transforming courses in the humanities and social sciences is perhaps easier and more obvious, experts emphasize that all courses in all disciplines, including mathematics and science, can be transformed (Morey & Kitano, 1997).

In Kitano's (1997b) model, there are four components of course transformation: course content, instructional strategies, strategies for assessing student knowledge, and classroom interactions. Morey and Kitano (1997) point out that it is important to change not only the course content but also the teaching methods. Both content and pedagogy are important targets.

Teaching Diverse Learners

The principle of "universal design," which grows out of the literature on persons with disabilities, is useful in transforming instructional strategies, assessment strategies, and classroom interactions—three of Kitano's (1997b) four components. Universal design is "the process of making design decisions to assure that a course, facility, product, or service can be used comfortably by people with a wide variety of characteristics, including those related to gender, race/ethnicity, age, native language, and level of ability to see, hear, move and speak" (Burgstahler, 2004, p. 396). Universal design means incorporating diverse ways for students to engage and to share their knowledge and understanding; for example, using discussion, fieldwork, hands-on projects, online communication, group projects, and oral presentations. The underlying notion is that diverse students have diverse learning styles and varied areas of strength, and that instructors should provide an array of opportunities for students to connect with the material. Cooperative learning approaches, in particular, have been found to facilitate the engagement and success of many students (Smith, 2009).

For faculty to effectively transform their courses, they need to learn the rationale for such change, identify nontraditional content, explore universal design strategies and student-centered classroom interactions, and examine their own biases and preconceptions about students and teaching. Course transformation workshops and other ongoing faculty development strategies are a must!

From Course to Curriculum

The substantial literature on course transformation focuses on the course as the unit of intervention. Notably, there is less attention to how faculty ought to work together to construct student learning outcomes that will support the development of culturally competent students. Courses are not islands; they function collectively to foster the student's education. Program faculty should work as a team to revise student learning outcomes and to determine the role of specific courses in fostering student achievement of these outcomes.

As mentioned previously, at Alliant, diversity-related student competencies have been adopted by the university, and the aim is for all students, regardless of their academic discipline or degree program, to achieve the competencies by graduation. To accomplish this, each academic program is charged with operationalizing the student competencies into specific student learning outcomes. In Exhibit 16.1, I provide an illustrative example of such competencies.

Exhibit 16.1. Diversity-Related Student Learning Outcomes in Alliant's Clinical Ph.D. Program, Fresno Campus

- Students will develop awareness of their own culture and the culture(s) and level of acculturation of others as mediators of one's world view.
- Students will develop skills for determining how those varied world views interact with research, clinical, and teaching processes.
- Students will develop the willingness and ability to seek out culture-specific knowledge, as needed.

In the past decade, the regional associations that accredit U.S. colleges and universities have become more concerned about educational effectiveness—whether the institution can demonstrate that students actually learn what it says they will learn (Allen, 2004). When universities set goals with respect to students gaining awareness, knowledge, and/or skills related to cultural competence, they are also expected to develop assessment strategies to determine whether the goals are being met and to collect feedback for course and curricular revisions. Thus the educational effectiveness agenda provides a leverage point in institutions that have made a commitment to educate students to be culturally competent.

Research and Scholarship

Aside from fostering the development of well-educated students, the other primary "product" of many higher education institutions is scholarship and research that, in the best cases, enhances the world's knowledge and understanding and improves the quality of life. More and more universities are encouraging and supporting a focus on diversity-related topics and issues in the research that is conducted by their faculty and students (Williams & Wade-Golden, 2007). Universities can provide extra research funds and travel funds for faculty who are working on research projects related to multicultural issues, and they can bring faculty together across disciplines to explore these topics (Wadsworth, 1999).

As an example, at Alliant, with support from the associate provost for research and scholarship, my office sponsored a mentoring program in which senior faculty partner with junior faculty to assist the latter in publishing a manuscript that focuses on or substantively engages multicultural or international issues. The mentors were provided a small stipend for their work, and the mentees received a stipend if their manuscript was submitted by a designated deadline. My office provided an orientation and support to the mentors and mentees and gave some structure to the process.

Summary

Because colleges and universities are focused on education, scholarship, and research, there are many opportunities to integrate the diversity and inclusion agenda into the core business of higher education. However, the opportunity also presents a challenge, because a commitment to diversity and inclusion means revamping—perhaps even overhauling—the traditional curriculum, the age-old style of teaching, and the conventional research agenda of the university. Organizational change of this magnitude is not easy, and much has been written about resistance in the academy and about important considerations in multicultural organizational change in higher education (see, for example, Harvey, 2004; Jackson, 2005; Morey, 1997).

Affirming Climate

The fourth component of a university that is committed to diversity and inclusion is the climate. Edgert (1994, as cited in Watson et al., 2002) defines climate as "the interpersonal and group dynamics that comprise the experiences of participants in a collegiate setting" (p. 65). Campus climate tells us the degree to which the campus is welcoming and affirming to students, staff, and faculty from diverse groups. What does it feel like? What is the vibe? What are the differences in people's experiences, based on visible and hidden aspects of their identity? Do underrepresented groups experience the campus differently than those in the mainstream? These are important questions with which to wrestle.

Physical Environment

There are a number of steps that universities can take to address climate. A relatively simple first task is to assess the physical environment of the campus, particularly the degree to which the photos, pictures, and decor reflect diverse faces, images, and cultures. For example, if the art is primarily or exclusively the work of Whites or primarily depicts White people, then it is likely that it is not conveying to those who are members of other groups that the campus is a welcoming and affirming place (see Kivel, 2004).

Policies

A second step is to ask the question: Do we have policies in place that support a healthy climate? For example, is there a policy on bias-related incidents that asserts the university's lack of tolerance for ethnic slurs or homophobic jokes and that provides a mechanism for those who have been victimized to seek redress? In the past decade, many universities have developed such policies as a way of affirming their commitment to an inclusive climate. Another important question is: Do we have a policy on religious and spiritual observances that supports students, staff, and faculty in observing their diverse religious and spiritual traditions?

As an example, a few years ago at Alliant, a flashpoint occurred when an important annual gathering of administrators was "inadvertently" scheduled on Rosh Hashanah, the Jewish High Holy day. My office subsequently convened an ad hoc task force on religious observance to consider our existing university policy with respect to religious observances and the available resources to support the diversity of religious or spiritual expression and observance. We also surveyed Alliant students and employees to learn about their religious, spiritual, and cultural observances and whether they had experienced conflicts with their work or school schedules and expectations. The task force proposed a stronger, more affirming policy, which was ultimately approved by the university. My former office now develops and disseminates an annual calendar of diverse religious, spiritual, and cultural observances to educate the community and assist with scheduling. The task force's plan was to resurvey the community to determine whether these steps have improved the climate for religious diversity.

Activities and Events

Another important step toward enhancing the campus climate is to use cocurricular activities, events, and celebrations as a way of sharing, communicating, and learning about diverse cultures and identities. This can be a way to engage not only students but also staff and faculty. Funding can be provided to the student government association, cultural centers, and employee and student affinity groups to sponsor programs for the campus community.

At Alliant, on each campus, there are diversity committees that have a budget to sponsor cocurricular programs, initiatives, and events for the campus community. The campus committees are composed of students, staff, and faculty. This helps to break down the barriers between these three groups and, as a consequence, to address some of the elitism that is a feature of most higher education institutions (Smith, 2009). Elitism is a rarely addressed "ism," but one that surely can get in the way of campus communities' fully achieving their diversity and inclusion agenda.

Everyday Interactions

In addition to the physical environment, the policies, and the cocurricular programs, the climate is affected by the everyday interactions that students, staff, and faculty have on the campus. Although structural diversity changes and diversity-related initiatives have gotten a fair amount of attention in the literature on higher education, the ordinary interactions that students (and staff and faculty) have with diverse others have gotten short shrift; yet there is evidence that these interactions may powerfully influence the experience of climate (Bourke, 2010; Watson et al., 2002). Derald Sue (2010), for example, talks about the damaging impact of microaggressions, which are small but often frequent instances of experiences of invalidation.

Data are important in determining campus climate. Many universities have instituted campus climate and student and employee satisfaction surveys, focus groups, and/or exit interviews to discern how university constituents experience the campus (see, for example, García et al., 2001). It is, of course, important to disaggregate the data by key demographic variables, such as race, ethnicity, and gender, to determine whether specific groups are experiencing more difficulty than others.

The Challenge of Transforming Climate

In many ways, climate is more difficult to address than access and success and infused programs. It is generally easier to scrutinize the numbers of diverse people or to determine whether the academic and research programs include attention to multicultural issues than it is to get a handle on the campus climate. Assessing and intervening in the climate means focusing on the informal, implicit norms of the organization—its often unspoken assumptions, values, and beliefs—which Holvino et al. (2004, p. 253) call the "cultural level of change." It means going beyond what the university proclaims and purports to be; it means transcending the "structural level of change" (Holvino et al., p. 251), which focuses on the formal policies, practices, and structures of the institution. Because institutional culture is partially invisible and often difficult to acknowledge or name, changes at the cultural level are particularly challenging (Smith, 2009), yet interventions at this level are critically important, as hidden culture can be very powerful (Schein, 1990).

Thus climate is a critically important arena for diversity and inclusion efforts, yet it is perhaps the most elusive area and the least studied. Although structural changes, often created through policies, likely have an impact on climate, addressing the climate also requires attention to cultural changes, which are less obvious and tangible.

Key Issues in Diversity and Inclusion in Higher Education in the Next Decade

In this final section, I highlight some emerging issues in diversity and inclusion in higher education: (1) the role of chief diversity officers, (2) conflicts between identity groups, (3) classism, and (4) globalization and its relationship to diversity and inclusion.

The Role of Chief Diversity Officers

In the past several years, there has been an uptick in the number of chief diversity officers (CDOs) in U.S. colleges and universities. Though the titles vary considerably, the chief diversity officer is defined as a senior administrator, typically reporting to the president or chief academic officer, who provides institution-wide leadership for diversity and inclusion initiatives and strategies (Smith, 2009; Williams & Wade-Golden, 2007). The surge in the number of chief diversity officers parallels the shift in the higher education diversity agenda from a primary focus on affirmative action and equity to a focus on diversity as central to academic excellence. The position of CDO reflects the significance of diversity and inclusion for the university as a whole.

Notably, the National Association of Diversity Officers in Higher Education (NADOHE; www.nadohe.org) was founded in 2006 as a networking and professional development organization to support the work of chief diversity officers. The increase in appointments of CDOs in colleges and universities reflects higher education's following in the footsteps of the corporate world, where issues of diversity and inclusion and a focus on multicultural organization development have been pursued vigorously for some time (Jackson, 2005).

Conflicts Between Identity Groups

An emerging issue on college campuses is conflict between people from different identity groups. Though navigating these conflicts is not new in higher education settings, what is different these days is that often the flashpoints are between two groups that have both been historically marginalized. So, in my experience, students who identify as fundamentalist Christian are increasingly in conflict with those who identify as sexual minorities. (Note that while being Christian in the general U.S. context is not a marginalized identity, in the academy, Christianity and particularly fundamentalist Christianity are sometimes marginalized or stigmatized [Hodge, 2002]).

At Alliant, which aims to be affirming of sexual minorities and of diverse religious perspectives, tensions have developed between instructors who are educating therapists-in-training to be LGBT-affirming and fundamentalist Christian students who believe that engaging in same-gender sexual behavior is sinful. These are not easily reconcilable positions, and Alliant's position, like that of many other universities, is to not pathologize same-gender sexuality but instead support the full equality of LGBT people. Yet how do we do this without simply dismissing and pathologizing some community members' religious beliefs? How do we find a way to stay in dialogue with those whose views on sexual orientation differ from ours? In colleges and universities throughout the United States, we need to work collectively and creatively to better understand these tensions and to find ways to hear and understand multiple viewpoints while staying true to the underlying core values of diversity and inclusion.

Classism

In the pantheon of "isms," classism, defined as "a type of discrimination based on social class, where people with less social class status . . . are treated in ways that serve to exclude, devalue, discount, and separate them based on that status" (Lott, 2002, as quoted in Langhout et al., 2009, p. 167), is an area that has received limited attention. However, classism has a significant impact on the achievement of diversity and full inclusion (Langhout et al., 2009; Smith, 2009). Because the United States is a capitalist society, there appears to be an expectation that people's earnings and assets will vary substantially as well as a general belief that these variations are not inherently unfair. Thus issues of class differences—in education, income, and social and cultural capital—are often not directly addressed or even seen as problems. Moreover, elitism is a prominent feature in the U.S. academy (Smith, 2009).

In my view, one consequence of academic elitism is that front-line and middle management staff are often not valued as highly as faculty and senior administrators, and as a result, the diversity and inclusion agenda often ignores the critical role of staff in the creation of a welcoming climate, in the development of inclusive cocurricular activities, and in the maintenance of an infrastructure that undergirds a diverse and inclusive institution. Langhout et al. (2009) propose the creation of social class studies departments as a way of fostering higher education's (and, I will add, our society's) critical understanding of class.

Globalization and Its Relationship to Diversity and Inclusion

In this dynamic, shrinking world of tremendous dislocation and migration, international and global issues are more and more in the forefront. Historically, higher education has treated international issues as separate from domestic diversity issues, and the offices supporting these respective initiatives—for example, study abroad offices and African American cultural centers—have worked separately and disparately, sometimes even construing themselves as adversaries (Olson, Evans, & Shoenberg, 2007). Olson et al. describe how the different histories and motivations for internationalization and multicultural education have contributed to the divide, with multiculturalists often viewing internationalists as escaping from important social justice issues in the United States by engaging with exotic cultures abroad.

However, international issues are increasingly seen as integrally related to domestic diversity issues; they are being viewed as another important area of diversity in which differences based on power and privilege affect opportunities and outcomes. Over the past decade, the American Council on Education (ACE) has sponsored several initiatives to address the historical divide between multicultural education and internationalization and to foster an exploration of common goals and opportunities, with the ultimate aim of graduating students who are culturally competent citizens of the world (see Olson et al., 2007).

Universities are faced with questions like: How can the internationalization agenda be integrated with the diversity and inclusion agenda without watering down or diminishing the latter? How can the power-and-privilege framework that is central to the diversity and inclusion agenda help to inform the academy's global initiatives? For example, how might the efforts to build partnerships with Chinese universities be guided by diversity and inclusion? Is it reasonable for these entrepreneurial ventures to focus solely on enhancing the reach, stature, and economic stability of the university? To what degree do United States institutions engage in academic imperialism—whereby U.S.-centric knowledge and ways of knowing are privileged, and Chinese knowledge and ways of knowing are devalued? How important is it to teach students in China to be culturally competent; for example, by engaging them around issues of gender and ethnic bias? What if the leaders or students in Chinese institutions do not value this kind of education?

Notably, Alliant is a leader in this arena. Alliant's diversity plan includes attention to both multicultural and international issues and competencies, and in 2011 Alliant was selected by ACE to join its "At Home in the World" Initiative, in which eight U.S. colleges and universities formed a two-year learning community focused on the integration of multicultural education and internationalization in the curricula.

This is clearly an emerging, though still contested, issue. As an example, the Call for Papers for the 2012 Annual Conference of the National Association of Diversity Officers in Higher Education included a session entitled "Integrating International Issues into the Diversity Agenda: Dangerous Distraction or Golden Opportunity?"

Conclusion

In the past forty years, U.S. higher education has come a long way in its journey toward full diversity and inclusion, yet there is still much work to be done in the areas of institutional commitment, access and success, infused programs, and affirming climates. The relatively recent shift to viewing diversity and inclusion as an asset for the entire university bodes well for the future. Similarly, the move to appoint chief diversity officers, which reflects an understanding of the central role of diversity and inclusion in the ultimate success of the institution, suggests that higher education is on the right track. The fact that the business of higher education is teaching and scholarship means that there are ready-made opportunities to engage around issues of diversity and inclusion, to educate the next generation of leaders to be culturally competent, and to produce research that is relevant to diverse populations and problems.

References

Allen, M. J. (2004). *Assessing academic programs in higher education.* Bolton, MA: Anker.

Banks, J. A. (1999). Multicultural education: Development, dimensions, and challenges. In J. Q. Adams & J. R. Welsch (Eds.), *Cultural diversity: Curriculum, classroom, and climate issues* (pp. 3–14). Macomb, IL: Illinois Staff and Curriculum Developers Association.

Banks, J. A. (2001). Multicultural education: Characteristics and goals. In J. A. Banks & C. McGee Banks (Eds.), *Multicultural education: Issues and perspectives* (4th ed., pp. 3–30). New York: Wiley.

Bourke, B. (2010). Experiences of Black students in multiple cultural spaces at a predominantly White institution. *Journal of Diversity in Higher Education, 3*(2), 126–135.

Burgstahler, S. (2004). Faculty development and students with disabilities: Accommodations and universal design. In M. L. Ouellett (Ed.), *Teaching inclusively: Resources for course, department & institutional change in higher education* (pp. 393–404). Stillwater, OK: New Forums Press.

Chatman, S. (2008, March). *Does diversity matter in the education process? An exploration of student interactions by wealth, religion, politics, race, ethnicity and immigrant status at the University of California* (Research and Occasional Paper Series: CSHE. 5.08). Berkeley, CA: University of California, Berkeley, Center for Studies in Higher Education.

Chism, N., & Whitney, K. (2005). It takes a campus: Situating professional development efforts within a campus diversity program. In M. L. Ouellett (Ed.), *Teaching inclusively: Resources for course, department & institutional change in higher education* (pp. 34–45). Stillwater, OK: New Forums Press.

Cole, E. R. (2009). Intersectionality and research in psychology. *American Psychologist, 64*(3), 170–180.

Cox, T. H., Jr. (1993). *Cultural diversity in organizations: Theory, research, and practice.* San Francisco: Berrett-Koehler.

Crisp, G., Horn, C., Dizzino, G., & Wang, D. (2010). Modeling the racial and ethnic implications of admissions policy changes in the pursuit of Tier One status. *Journal of Diversity in Higher Education, 3*(2), 71–84.

Edgert, P. (1994, Spring). Assessing campus climate: Implications for diversity. *New Directions for Institutional Research, 81,* 61.

Fiol-Matta, L., & Chamberlain, M. K. (Eds.) (1994). *Women of color and the multicultural curriculum: Transforming the college classroom.* New York: The Feminist Press at The City University of New York.

García, M., Hudgins, C. A., McTighe Musil, C., Nettles, M. T., Sedlacek, W. E., & Smith, D. G. (2001). *Assessing campus diversity initiatives: A guide for campus practitioners.* Washington, DC: Association of American Colleges and Universities.

Glass, C., & Minnotte, K. L. (2010). Recruiting and hiring women in STEM fields. *Journal of Diversity in Higher Education, 3*(4), 218–229.

Gordon, M. (2004). Diversification of the faculty: Frank talk from the front line about what works. In F. W. Hale, Jr. (Ed.), *What makes racial diversity work in higher education: Academic leaders present successful policies and strategies* (pp. 183–198). Sterling, VA: Stylus.

Greene, L. S., & Harrigan, M. N. (2004). Strategic priorities and strategic funding: Minority faculty hiring at the University of Wisconsin-Madison, 1988–2003. In F. W. Hale, Jr. (Ed.), *What makes racial diversity work in higher education: Academic leaders present successful policies and strategies* (pp. 233–254). Sterling, VA: Stylus.

Harvey, W. B. (2004). Deans as diversity leaders: Modifying attitudes by taking bold actions—Learning lessons and changing cultures. In F. W. Hale, Jr. (Ed.), *What makes racial diversity work in higher education: Academic leaders present successful policies and strategies* (pp. 293–306). Sterling, VA: Stylus.

Hays-Thomas, R. (2004). Why now? The contemporary focus on managing diversity. In M. S. Stockdale & F. J. Crosby (Eds.), *The psychology and management of workplace diversity* (pp. 3–30). Malden, MA: Blackwell.

Hodge, D. R. (2002). Does social work oppress evangelical Christians? A "new class" analysis of society and social work. *Social Work, 47*(4), 401–414.

Holvino, E., Ferdman, B. M., & Merrill-Sands, D. (2004). Creating and sustaining diversity and inclusion in organizations: Strategies and approaches. In M. S. Stockdale & F. J. Crosby (Eds.), *The psychology and management of workplace diversity* (pp. 245–276). Malden, MA: Blackwell.

Jackson, B. W. (2005). The theory and practice of multicultural organization development in education. In M. L. Ouellett (Ed.), *Teaching inclusively: Resources for course, department & institutional change in higher education* (pp. 3–20). Stillwater, OK: New Forums Press.

Jones, L. (2004). The development of a multicultural student services office and retention strategy for minority students: Still miles to go! In F. W. Hale, Jr. (Ed.), *What makes racial diversity work in higher education: Academic leaders present successful policies and strategies* (pp. 125–145). Sterling, VA: Stylus.

Kitano, M. K. (1997a). A rationale and framework for course change. In A. I. Morey & M. K. Kitano (Eds.), *Multicultural course transformation in higher education: A broader truth* (pp. 1–17). Boston: Allyn & Bacon.

Kitano, M. K. (1997b). What a course will look like after multicultural change. In A. I. Morey & M. K. Kitano (Eds.), *Multicultural course transformation in higher education: A broader truth* (pp. 18–34). Boston: Allyn & Bacon.

Kivel, P. (2004). The culture of power. In F. W. Hale, Jr. (Ed.), *What makes racial diversity work in higher education: Academic leaders present successful policies and strategies* (pp. 25–32). Sterling, VA: Stylus.

Langhout, R. D., Drake, P., & Rosselli, F. (2009). Classism in the university setting: Examining student antecedents and outcomes. *Journal of Diversity in Higher Education, 2*(3), 166–181.

Lott, B. (2002). Cognitive and behavioral distancing from the poor. *American Psychologist, 57,* 100–110.

Mestenhauser, J. A., & Ellingboe, B. J. (Eds.). (1998). *Reforming the higher education curriculum: Internationalizing the campus.* Phoenix, AZ: American Council on Education and Oryx Press.

Moody, J. (2004). Departmental good practices for retaining minority graduate students. In F. W. Hale, Jr. (Ed.), *What makes racial diversity work in higher education: Academic leaders present successful policies and strategies* (pp. 165–181). Sterling, VA: Stylus.

Mor Barak, M. E. (2005). *Managing diversity: Toward a globally inclusive workplace.* Thousand Oaks, CA: Sage.

Morey, A. I. (1997). Organizational change and implementation strategies for multicultural infusion. In A. I. Morey & M. K. Kitano (Eds.), *Multicultural course transformation in higher education: A broader truth* (pp. 258–277). Boston: Allyn & Bacon.

Morey, A. I., & Kitano, M. K. (Eds.). (1997). *Multicultural course transformation in higher education: A broader truth.* Boston: Allyn & Bacon.

Myers, K. A., Caruso, R., & Birk, N. A. (1999). The diversity continuum: Enhancing student interest and access, creating a staying environment, and preparing students for transition. In J. Q. Adams & J. R. Welsch (Eds.), *Cultural diversity: Curriculum, classroom, and climate issues* (pp. 429–442). Macomb, IL: Illinois Staff and Curriculum Developers Association.

Olson, C. L., Evans, R., & Shoenberg, R. F. (2007). *At home in the world: Bridging the gap between internationalization and multicultural education.* Washington, DC: American Council on Education.

Ouellett, M. L. (Ed.) (2005). *Teaching inclusively: Resources for course, department & institutional change in higher education.* Stillwater, OK: New Forums Press.

Roberson, Q. M. (2006). Disentangling the meanings of diversity and inclusion in organizations. *Group & Organization Management, 31,* 212–236. doi: 10.1177/1059601104273064

Ryu, M. (2008). *Minorities in higher education 2008: Twenty-third status report.* Washington, DC: American Council on Education.

Schein, E. H. (1990). Organizational culture. *American Psychologist, 45*(2), 109–119.

Schoem, D., Frankel, L., Zúñiga, X., & Lewis, E. A. (1993). The meaning of multicultural teaching: An introduction. In D. Schoem, L. Frankel, X. Zúñiga, & E. A. Lewis (Eds.), *Multicultural teaching in the university* (pp. 1–12). Westport, CT: Praeger.

Sedlacek, W. E. (2003). Alternative admissions and scholarship selection measures in higher education. *Measurement and Evaluation in Counseling & Development, 35*(4), 263–272.

Smith, D. G. (2009). *Diversity's promise for higher education: Making it work.* Baltimore: Johns Hopkins University Press.

Stewart, M. A. (2004). Effective minority programs at the Ohio State University. In F. W. Hale, Jr. (Ed.), *What makes racial diversity work in higher education: Academic leaders present successful policies and strategies* (pp. 147–163). Sterling, VA: Stylus.

Sue, D. W. (2010). *Microaggressions in everyday life: Race, gender, and sexual orientation.* Hoboken, NJ: Wiley.

Sue, D. W., Carter, R. T., Casas, J. M., Fouad, N. A., Ivey, A. E., Jensen, M., . . . Vazquez-Nutall, E. (1998). *Multicultural counseling competencies: Individual and organizational development.* Thousand Oaks, CA: Sage.

Thomas, R. R., Jr. (1996). *Redefining diversity.* New York: AMACOM.

Turner, M. R. (2004). The Office of African-American Affairs: A celebration of success. In F. W. Hale, Jr. (Ed.), *What makes racial diversity work in higher education: Academic leaders present successful policies and strategies* (pp. 113–123). Sterling, VA: Stylus.

Wadsworth, E. B. (1999). Faculty development programs in support of multicultural education. In J. Q. Adams & J. R. Welsch (Eds.), *Cultural diversity: Curriculum, classroom, and climate issues* (pp. 457–462). Macomb, IL: Illinois Staff and Curriculum Developers Association.

Watson, L. W., Terrell, M. C., Wright, D. J., Bonner, F. A., Cuyjet, M. J., Gold, J. A., . . . Person, D. R. (2002). *How minority students experience college: Implications for planning and policy.* Sterling, VA: Stylus.

Williams, D. A., & Wade-Golden, K. C. (2007). *The Chief Diversity Officer: A primer for college and university presidents.* Washington, DC: American Council on Education.

CHAPTER SEVENTEEN

Fostering Inclusion from the Outside In

Engaging Diverse Citizens in Dialogue and Decision Making

Carolyn J. Lukensmeyer, Margaret Yao, and Theo Brown

Imagine a room overflowing with people representing the spectrum of diversity of the community—all ages, races, ethnic groups, income levels, and wide differences in political views. Now imagine these people sitting at round tables, spending all day on a sunny Saturday to talk sincerely about how to solve a tough issue, such as health care reform, reducing the budget deficit, or rebuilding their devastated city.

Do you see arguments? Frustration? Exasperation? Or can you imagine informed, thoughtful dialogue, with people expressing themselves passionately and feeling they have been heard? Can you imagine participants, before long, becoming willing to be influenced by tablemates, some very different from themselves? Can you imagine decision makers willing to listen to the many specific recommendations that emerged from the participants' discussions?

Meetings like this don't exist only in the imagination. Hundreds of them have been organized around the country and around the world during the past couple of decades by a growing movement that promotes improved forms of dialogue and public deliberation. The key groups, organizations, and individuals in this movement are transforming the way that meetings are conducted and providing a range of new resources and tools for those who want to promote inclusive decision making.

At the heart of this movement is a commitment to empowering individuals and making sure that all relevant parties have a chance to give input on the decisions that affect their lives. Practitioners of dialogue and deliberation believe that inclusion is essential to what they are doing, and they build it into every aspect of their work. They see it as one of the bedrock principles of successful citizen engagement.

Our organization, America*Speaks*, is at the forefront of this movement in the United States, and there are many other organizations also doing innovative work to make sure that people are included in the important decisions that affect their lives. A wide range of different organizations are working to engage the general public and empower them to have a greater say in local, regional, and national issues of concern to them. Examples of the work done by some of the more prominent groups in the United States provide a sense of how this movement has grown and what it has to offer to those interested in empowerment and inclusion:

○ *National Issues Forum.* Created in 1981, this was one of the first organizations to use principles of dialogue and deliberation as a way of involving the public on policy issues. The National Issues Forum is a nonpartisan, nationwide network of locally sponsored public forums that consider issues such as health care, immigration, social security, education, or the environment. The forums provide a way for people of diverse views and experiences to seek a shared understanding of the problem and to search for common ground for action. Forums are led by trained, neutral moderators and use an issue discussion guide that frames the issue by presenting the overall situation and then three or four broad approaches to the problem.
○ *Everyday Democracy.* The goal of Everyday Democracy's programs and services is to help create communities that work better for everyone because all voices are included in public

problem solving, and to link that work to creating a stronger democracy. During the past twenty years, they have used a small-group dialogue model in hundreds of communities to help people find ways to think, talk, and work together to solve problems. The core principle of their work is to involve everyone and demonstrate that the whole community is welcome and needed.

° *Public Agenda Foundation.* This innovative public opinion research and public engagement organization works to strengthen our democracy's capacity to tackle tough public policy issues. Their efforts in communities around the United States are all focused on ensuring that the public's views are represented in decision making. They work on a long list of issues but are especially well-known for efforts to engage the public on issues relating to higher education, energy, the federal budget deficit, and foreign policy.

° *Public Conversations Project.* The Public Conversations Project (PCP) works to prevent and transform conflicts driven by deep differences in identity, beliefs, or values. The Public Conversations Project brings disputants together for the kind of dialogue that shifts relationships from ones of mistrust, defense, withdrawal, or attack to those of curiosity, connection, and compassionate understanding of differences. PCP first entered the public eye in the 1990s with a series of citizen dialogues on abortion and since then has worked to help many groups reach agreement on difficult issues. They now give regular trainings for the public on a variety of ways to use dialogue and deliberation to deal with areas of potential conflict.

Representatives of these and many other organizations are part of the National Coalition for Dialogue and Deliberation, which shares information among thousands of professionals and serves as a resource for those who wish to learn more about the growing movement. In addition to the large national organizations just mentioned, there are hundreds of smaller local organizations throughout the country doing innovative work to encourage inclusive citizen engagement. Some practitioners are based at universities, some have started their own local organizations, and others work as independent consultants who help groups apply the principles of dialogue and deliberation to specific projects.

This chapter discusses the principles and practices of interactive deliberation that have been developed by these organizations and individuals, focusing in particular on the experience of America*Speaks*. We explore ways to apply these principles to many different types of decision-making processes and show how they can help people find surprising agreements on highly divisive issues. Such proven principles and practices from the public arena may be useful as an "outside" perspective that will assist leaders striving for inclusion "inside" their organizations.

To understand how these principles and practices can be applied, we closely examine the work of America*Speaks*, which has been a leader in national efforts to create inclusive decision making since 1996. America*Speaks* was founded to serve as a counterweight to the influence of special interest groups, providing opportunities for the general public to express their views on important policy issues. America*Speaks* is grounded in the belief, which we have found to be true in our work, that people want to take responsibility for the decisions that impact their lives and to contribute to the common good. America*Speaks* programs have shown that extremely diverse groups of people can talk together respectfully, learn from each other, and find ways to work together. A fuller explanation of the principles that underlie the work of America*Speaks* can be found in the recent book *Bringing Citizen Voices to the Table: A Guide for Public Managers* (Lukensmeyer, 2012).

Examples of Dialogue and Deliberation

Like the other organizations that are leaders in the field of dialogue and deliberation, America*Speaks* has conducted programs on a wide range of different issues of concern to people in the United States and around the world. America*Speaks* has organized hundreds of meetings in more than thirty states and, under its international name of Global Voices, has worked in eight other countries around the world. Some prominent examples that show how dialogue and deliberation can be used in creative ways include:

○ *Citizen Summits* in Washington, D.C., which brought together thousands of citizens over a six-year period to identify budget and policy priorities for the mayor.

○ *Listening to the City*, a town meeting in Manhattan held months after 9/11, which enabled a broadly diverse group of more than four thousand people who lived and worked in New York to come together and agree on key principles for the rebuilding of Ground Zero.

○ Community Congresses in New Orleans and cities across the country that brought together several thousand current and former New Orleans residents to adopt the *Unified New Orleans Plan* to rebuild the city after Hurricane Katrina.

○ *CaliforniaSpeaks on Health Care*, which brought 3,500 Californians together in seven cities across the state to give recommendations to the governor and legislative leadership about what to do on statewide health care legislation.

○ *Our Budget, Our Economy*, a nationwide electronic town meeting that was attended by an ideologically diverse cross section of Americans in nineteen cities who worked to find solutions to our country's budget stalemate.

○ The *Port Philip Speaks Community Summit*, in Port Philip, Australia, organized by Global Voices, which brought together a representative sample of citizens from many different neighborhoods to fights threats to their quality of life and develop a long-term plan for development of the city.

All of these events are examples of the power of inclusive decision making. Complex problems that have an impact on large numbers of people can be adequately addressed only if all voices are heard and the needs and desires of everyone involved are made known. Each of the meetings just cited was particularly significant because the people who attended were demographically representative of the larger community, and the discussion and recommendations reflected a full range of stakeholder perspectives. Simply bringing together a large number of people to provide input does not guarantee real inclusion. The real test is whether or not the community involved is accurately represented and empowered to fully participate.

America*Speaks* Meetings

A closer look at the America*Speaks* meetings just mentioned provides a clear look at inclusive decision making and the many ways it can be put into practice. These examples are also representative of the many types of issues that the broader dialogue and deliberation movement has worked on through the years. While it can be difficult to create real inclusion and have all of the diverse groups in a community come together, results like those described here show why it is worth the effort.

In the late 1990s, Washington, D.C., was emerging from a time of scandal and corruption that had seen its previous mayor go to jail; confidence in local government had reached an all-time low. The new mayor, Anthony Williams, was faced with the challenge of getting the city moving again, but the public was skeptical about whether anything positive could be done. To overcome this attitude, Mayor Williams turned to the people themselves and created an inclusive decision-making process unprecedented in any large American city. He asked America*Speaks* to organize four Citizen Summits over a six-year period, each bringing together two to three thousand citizens to help set priorities for Washington, D.C. The Washingtonians who participated came from each section of the city and every segment of society. They came together across socioeconomic, racial, and cultural barriers to talk and share their views. These citizen gatherings not only created an inspiring vision for the city's future but also gave very clear input about what city policies and spending priorities should be. Because participants in the Citizen Summits were so representative of the city, the outcomes had a high degree of credibility, and their impact was felt in many different ways. They also helped to alter public attitudes and restore confidence in the government's ability to act effectively.

In the summer of 2002, New York City was still reeling from the devastating effects of 9/11 and badly in need of a successful process to bring the residents together and help them plan for the future. *Listening to the City* was created to give all those who lived and worked in New York an opportunity to do just that, but it could be effective only if the full range of New York's City's incredibly diverse population was represented. America-*Speaks* accomplished this by recruiting participants from New York City's many different neighborhoods, cultures, and ethnic groups and also by making sure that different ages, occupations, and socioeconomic backgrounds were represented. This diversity was impressive, but even more needed to be done to make sure that the right people were included. Special efforts were made to reach out to those who had been most affected by the terrorist attack—survivors, families of the victims and residents of the area around the World Trade Center—to make sure that their voices were heard loud and clear. The result was a day-long gathering that may have been the most diverse and inclusive in New York City's long history. In his column the next day in the *New York Daily News*, Pete Hamill (2002) described the scene: "There were representatives of every race, religion and ethnic group . . . gray haired veterans of civic causes, young artists and people who had lost husbands or wives or children when the terrorists struck. Most of all, there were plain citizens, thousands of them" (p. 8).

After New Orleans was devastated by Hurricane Katrina in 2005, residents of the city faced the daunting task of reaching agreement about how to rebuild the city. The task was complicated by deep economic and racial divides and the fact that half of the city—especially large numbers of low-income African-Americans—had been forced to evacuate and were scattered across the country. Several early attempts to convene groups that could adopt a plan on behalf of the city failed miserably, and for the first year there was no agreement about future direction. America*Speaks* was then brought in to work with city and state officials and create a fair planning process that would include everyone—even those who no longer lived in the city. A massive outreach effort was launched to recruit residents for two

Community Congresses that would present ideas and options and ask participants to identify priorities and specific action steps. Recruitment was done in every part of New Orleans and special attention was paid to getting representation from different neighborhoods, cultures and socioeconomic groups. Since it was essential to have input from those who had still not returned to New Orleans, the Community Congresses also recruited people in cities across the country to participate through video teleconferencing and online links. These efforts culminated in tremendously successful Community Congresses that linked hundreds of people in Dallas, Houston, Baton Rouge, Atlanta, and other cities with more than 1,500 who attended the central meeting at the New Orleans Convention Center.

Not only did thousands of New Orleans residents take part in these Community Congresses, but, most important, the demographics of those who participated almost exactly matched the population of the city before Hurricane Katrina. Previous citywide meetings had not even been close to an accurate representation of the population, and it was essential to have everyone's perspective included if the results were to be meaningful. In particular, low- to moderate income African-Americans, who had been inadequately represented in the early part of the planning process, were present in proportion to their pre-Katrina population. As Carey Shea of the Rockefeller Foundation, who served as a member of the advisory team for the planning process, noted, "You could have had 2,000 people in the room, 5,000 people in the room, but if the demographics weren't right, that would have just tainted the rest of the day" (quoted in Williamson, 2007, p. 20). The key was that the participants mirrored what the city looked like in its entirety, and that gave credibility to the results that emerged. Because the input was truly inclusive, the effort could serve as a guide for city and state officials who were in charge of rebuilding and revitalizing the city.

In California, as in much of the rest of the country, the debate over health care has been difficult and divisive for years. In 2007, the Republican governor, Arnold Schwarzenegger, and the Democratic leaders of the legislature were working to reform the state's existing health care system and seemed close to reaching agreement. However, they were stuck on certain key points and needed to understand what citizens would support before they could break their stalemate and move forward. America-*Speaks* brought together a cross section of 3,500 Californians that closely reflected the state's population so they could talk about what reforms they could support and under which situations. The day-long meetings may have been among the most inclusive discussions in the history of the state, as people of all ages, ethnic backgrounds, income levels, and political ideologies worked together to try and find common ground. As Fabian Nuñez, then speaker of the California Assembly, said: "[California*Speaks*] . . . helped drive the agenda towards a solution, and I think it was incredibly effective. The forum had a direct impact on the policy" (quoted in California*Speaks*, 2008, p. 19). The resulting citizen priorities that were identified played a big role in the intensive legislative discussion that took place, and the state was on the verge of adopting historic reforms until they were derailed at the last minute by new information about the state's budget problems.

Another issue that has created gridlock in the U.S. political system is the question of the federal budget and national debt. In the summer of 2010, America*Speaks* convened a nationwide conversation between citizens of different backgrounds and points of view to see which ideas could gain support from a broad segment of the population. More than three thousand Americans from all walks of life—from conservative groups like the Tea Party to liberal groups like MoveOn—came together to spend an entire day searching for possible solutions to the country's budget problems. To many people's surprise, this extremely diverse group of citizens found many areas of agreement, and the results from the meeting received careful consideration when they were presented to the National Commission on Fiscal Responsibility and Reform (Lukensmeyer, 2010b). The input from *Our Budget, Our Economy* had credibility and impact only because of its inclusive nature. It was not only the largest simultaneous discussion of the country's national budget in history, but also the most diverse—particularly in terms of the political ideologies that were represented.

America*Speaks* has also been active in other countries around the world under its international name, Global Voices. In Port Philip, Australia, residents were concerned about rapid growth in their community and the deterioration of their quality of life. They were divided about how to deal with problems caused by increased population, such as transportation, parking, pollution, noise, and the threatened loss of open space. The Port Philip Community Summit brought together more than 750 residents to set community priorities, identify projects that could be taken on by various groups, and make personal commitments for action. Smaller neighborhood meetings two weeks after the summit further developed the community plan and set the stage for ongoing action.

Meetings like these are not easy to organize and can be successful only if inclusion is in the forefront of all planning, outreach, and program design activities. Inclusion cannot be an afterthought or a secondary concern. Ensuring a demographically representative attendance at a community meeting is labor intensive and requires a larger than customary investment in time and money for outreach and communication. If true inclusive decision making is to take place, it must be a central goal that permeates all aspects of meeting development and resource allocation. It must be a priority from start to finish in everything that is done.

Start with an Inclusive Recruitment Process

Although there is more to inclusion than just having the correct mix of people participate, good recruitment is an essential element of success and the right place to begin. If outreach and recruitment are done poorly, then efforts to create an inclusive meeting are doomed. Unless the true diversity of a community is represented in the room or at the table, there is nothing that can be done to get their views adequately heard.

There are different challenges to getting people involved in different situations. The first step is to analyze who needs to be involved and in what numbers. Before outreach begins, attendance goals need to be set for each target population, and these goals should be the basis for development of strategy and resource allocation. In many situations, the attendance goals may be to simply have proportionate representation of everyone in the general community. At other times, especially when a particular group is more affected by a problem or issue, it may be important to have a somewhat larger representation of that segment of the population. For example, when America*Speaks* conducted meetings in several cities to fight youth obesity, it was important to have a disproportionate number of people who worked with youth attend the event along with other community representatives.

Once participation goals are determined, the next step is to lay out a specific plan for recruiting participants. This involves an assessment of what resources are available, who can be recruited to help, and what outreach methods will be most effective. Another crucial part of the recruitment plan is the development of a clear message about why people should participate. This is important for everyone, but particularly when working with segments of the population that generally do not attend community meetings. Unless these people can be clearly shown why they should participate, then they probably won't. People act differently or do new things only when they see a reason to do so, and that reason must be clearly laid out in a compelling way.

Essential Steps for an Outreach Strategy

Whoever is seeking to create an inclusive decision-making process—whether a government entity, a community organization or a specific workplace—has to develop strategies and specific tactics to make sure that everyone who needs to be included is invited. The exact recruitment efforts will vary in different situations, but there are a few steps America*Speaks* always takes that help make the planning and implementation of an outreach strategy more effective. It is always a good idea to:

○ *Create a strong outreach team that meets regularly.* The key people in charge of recruitment need to be in close touch and work together in a coordinated way. This necessitates

frequent contact, clear communication, and regular
meetings.

○ *Prepare a work plan with detailed weekly tasks.* Effective outreach
efforts need to build on each other and must be designed with
a careful timeline in mind. These efforts must be carried out
with precision and done in very specific ways in order to be
successful.

○ *Produce outreach materials that are simple and easy to use.* The key
to good outreach materials—whether printed or online—is to
make sure that they are easy to understand and easy to use.
Simple materials, accessible to lots of different people, are
always more effective; these also need to be prepared for a
variety of different audiences.

Two Broad Types of Outreach

To find and recruit those who need to be included, it is generally
important to do two broad types of outreach: (1) with existing
groups and organizations in the community and (2) with the
general public. Recruiting participants in these two ways helps to
create the desired balance between those who are already active
in some way and those who are "unaffiliated" and rarely participate in community activities. Both types of outreach are central
to the success that America*Speaks* has had in creating meetings
that are truly inclusive and representative of a community's
diversity.

Working with well-established groups and community organizations to reach their members is an important way to recruit
specific constituencies. Every community has civic associations,
faith-based groups, labor unions, ethnic organizations, professional associations, and dozens of other community groups that
may have members who need to be included. Invitations issued
through these organizations are particularly effective because of
the relationship and trust that already exists. Sometimes a close
working relationship with the right organization can result in the
successful recruitment of almost the entire target population for
a specific demographic group. In New Orleans, it was initially difficult for America*Speaks* to recruit participants from the city's

Vietnamese population because of the language barrier and their lack of trust in local government. However, after a partnership was created with a large Vietnamese Catholic church, the parishioners felt comfortable with the planning process and participated in large numbers. Similar results can be produced with many different segments of the population if invitations are issued through organizations or groups that they know and trust.

At the same time, it isn't possible to focus all outreach efforts on groups and organizations in the community. To have truly inclusive representation from diverse populations, it is necessary to recruit participants who may not be active members of any organized groups. There are large numbers of people who can be reached only through general community outreach that involves calls, letters, or emails to specific lists, canvassing in public places, general advertising, and invitations that are issued through traditional media or social networking. These recruitment methods have a much smaller rate of return than recruitment through established groups and organizations and therefore have to be much broader and more widespread. It is also essential to have a carefully crafted message about why it's important for those being invited to participate.

Five Principles for Recruiting Participants

To achieve diverse participation, the specific strategies vary depending on the situation, the issues involved, and the segments of the community that need to be included. At the same time, there are five key outreach principles that are applicable in almost every setting. The five key principles to keep in mind when recruiting participants for an inclusive meeting are:

1. *Issue direct personal invitations.* Whenever possible, invitations to participate should be issued directly to specific individuals through either one-on-one conversations or personalized written materials. People need to feel that they have a specific role to play, and asking them directly to take part is the best way to communicate that to them.
2. *Make it clear that it's a "different kind of meeting."* Most people have negative images of community meetings as boring or a

waste of time. They need to know that the meeting they are being invited to is important and that it can make a real difference. Similarly, they need to be made aware that this will be an interactive meeting where they will have an opportunity to express their views and have an impact on what is decided.

3. *Give special attention to the "hard to reach."* There are some segments of the population that are much harder to reach than others and therefore are typically underrepresented at community meetings. Although exactly who is "hard to reach" varies depending on the location and subject matter of the meeting, common examples are low-income residents, young people, and representatives of cultural and ethnic minorities. To compensate for the difficulties involved in recruiting some groups, extra effort must be made to build relationships and get the word out to those who are potentially interested. Without the commitment of additional energy and resources, it will not be possible to fully include these hard-to-reach members of the community.

4. *Use preregistration so that outreach strategy can be adjusted as needed.* If it is important for a meeting to be inclusive, then it is essential to know in advance who is planning to attend. Preregistration on a website or by other means provides an opportunity to monitor progress on outreach and determine what else needs to be done to make sure the right people are going to be participating.

5. *Follow up frequently and effectively.* Well-timed follow-up calls and emails may be the most important key to successful recruitment. Once people have expressed interest, it is essential that they get regular information and be reminded of the importance of their participation. Systematic follow-up should continue right up until the time of the meeting.

Following these principles will aid recruitment and make it more likely to get the desired inclusive participation. As interest is being built and people are signing up, it is also important to explain how the meeting they are being asked to attend is part of an ongoing effort. People are more likely to follow through on their commitments to participate if they see that they are part of a clear process that is leading to specific results. This can be done by emphasizing that there is buy-in from key decision makers and that there is some type of plan for sustained involvement.

To Ensure Inclusive Decision Making, Meetings Require Conscious Design

Even after accomplishing the difficult task of getting the right people in the room, inclusive decision making does not just happen. Most groups, institutions, workplaces, and government agencies have tendencies and patterns that limit decision making to only a few people. Inclusive decision making begins with a conscious decision to create new ways for people to be heard and becomes real through a series of specific steps. Only actions taken with a clear intention can create a different type of process that provides an opportunity for everyone affected by an issue to have a say in what should be done.

To create decision making that is truly inclusive, we need to conduct new types of meetings in a wide variety of different settings. Most large public or private meetings do very little to foster inclusion. Most meetings do not ask for input but are designed only to pass on information to those who are present. Even meetings that say they want input often have little diversity of perspective and are more like pep rallies for a particular point of view. When meetings are poorly designed, people who show up to participate do not have an adequate opportunity to express themselves and leave frustrated and disappointed.

It is important to remember that what happens when people get together is just as important for inclusive decision making as getting them there in the first place. Here are some important characteristics of a meeting that is truly inclusive:

- People of different backgrounds and points of view are treated well and feel comfortable.
- Participants know what to expect and how their input will contribute to the decision.

- Everyone has an opportunity to be fully engaged in all aspects of the discussion and deliberation.
- Each person's views are fairly recorded and taken into account.

All of these characteristics can be seen in a 21st Century Town Meeting®, the basic model that America*Speaks* uses in cities across the country. This unique process updates the traditional New England town meeting to address the needs of today's citizens and decision makers. Just like the traditional town meeting, a 21st Century Town Meeting creates an opportunity for all present to openly express their views and also listen to others. This new town meeting model focuses on discussion and deliberation among citizens rather than speeches, question-and-answer sessions, or panel presentations. At the same time, it incorporates the latest technologies and meeting design tools and allows for group deliberation to be taken to a much larger scale. Through the combination of small group discussion and "participation technology," thousands of citizens can be involved simultaneously in discussing public policy issues. During a 21st Century Town Meeting, all participants have access to networked laptop computers as well as to handheld keypads that allow them to cast individual votes on a variety of issues. The computers and keypads work together in a powerful way to generate a very useful combination of quantitative and qualitative data on which to build the day-long conversation. The data are also a rich source of information for post-meeting analysis if desired.

Key Principles of a 21st Century Town Meeting

Six key principles lie at the heart of a 21st Century Town Meeting. These principles are essential to make sure that everyone who attends is really included and has a say in the outcome of the meeting:

1. *Diverse Representation.* As we have already seen, this is the essential first step in making sure there is an inclusive process.

Much thought and effort must go into making sure that those who need to be involved are involved. Tailored outreach strategies need to be used to make sure that those who are impacted by the issue are involved in a demographically representative way.

2. *Informed Participation.* Those who are present need to be provided with highly accessible materials that frame the issue in a fair way and provide a baseline of data on which participants may begin their discussions. These background materials educate participants and create the foundation for a rich, informed table discussion. In addition to the written materials, issue experts also are available to respond to specific questions generated at tables during the discussion period.

3. *Facilitated Deliberation.* Participants engage in small group discussions (ten to twelve people) that are facilitated by trained, experienced facilitators. These table facilitators ensure that everyone has a chance to participate and that the process is democratic. Their job is to balance the voices of those who speak constantly and loudly with those who may have difficulty being heard. They work under the guidance of a lead facilitator who directs the program from the stage and helps participants work through the tough aspects of an issue to develop a common agenda for action.

4. *Shared Priorities.* These emerge during the process of a 21st Century Town Meeting, which is designed to help identify where there are high levels of agreement among participants. This occurs as ideas from table discussions are entered into the networked computers, then "themed" into a list of ideas that were most commonly mentioned. Keypad polling prioritizes these ideas and is also used to measure the group's overall level of support for proposed policies and actions.

5. *Link to Action.* This is a primary goal of citizen deliberation. Involvement of decision makers and key leaders throughout the project is central to the success of the overall effort. Convening a meeting on a large scale (several hundred to several thousand participants) enables the outcomes to have greater visibility and credibility with policy makers, the media, key stakeholders, and the public as a whole.

6. *Sustained Citizen Engagement.* Ongoing involvement of citizens in the policy-making process is crucial to achieving long-lasting results. It develops civic leadership and also enhances implementation of public priorities. The process of organizing a public meeting that features inclusive decision making is a starting point for many different ways that citizens can take effective action on issues they care about.

Outcomes of 21st Century Town Meetings

Meetings that follow these principles have demonstrated a profound impact on public decision making. They significantly improve the quality of citizen input and increase the likelihood that elected officials and other leaders will make good decisions. As Kim Belshé, the former California Secretary of Health and Human Services, commented, ". . . California*Speaks* . . . helped connect both the public to policymakers, and policymakers to the public . . . and in so doing it helped inform policymakers' understanding of what is important to average Californians" (quoted in California*Speaks*, 2008, p. ii).

In many cases, America*Speaks* 21st Century Town Meetings have helped to produce solutions that are more effective, easier to implement, and more sustainable. Comments from some of the public officials who have worked with America*Speaks* give testimony to the results that have been achieved:

○ "I think [the Community Congress] has done more to bring credibility to the table than all of the little individual meetings that people go to. . . . It's brought the people who were displaced into the process" (New Orleans Councilwoman Cynthia Hedge Morrell, quoted in Williamson, 2007, p. 20).
○ "America*Speaks* methodology engages and activates the grassroots so the ideas and concerns and ideals of everyday people throughout America are able to get to the highest levels of government" (John Baldacci, former governor of Maine, quoted in America*Speaks*, 2009).
○ "[The participants in *Our Budget, Our Economy*] have restored my confidence in the ability of citizens to talk civilly about very

hard issues. All of us need to challenge the politicians to do as well as we have done today." (Alice Rivlin, former director of the Congressional Budget Office, quoted in Lukensmeyer, 2012, p. 35).

At the same time, there is another result from this type of meeting that may be even more profound. Inclusive decision making not only changes how communities make decisions, but also changes those who are involved. It provides a meaningful and highly personal experience that causes many people to think of themselves and their role in the community in a different way. One impact is that people begin to see possibilities that they didn't see before. As one participant in the Portland, Oregon meeting of *Our Budget, Our Economy* told evaluators, "The most important thing I learned from this process is that ordinary citizens could tackle a complex issue, filter it civilly through their own perspective, and come up with consensus. I literally did not think this was possible" (quoted in Lukensmeyer, 2010a).

This type of public involvement reduces the alienation people feel from their government and helps them to see how they can have an impact on policy as well as the larger world around them. Joe Williams, the executive director of the New Orleans Recovery Authority, saw this happen during the Community Congresses and observed: "I think that when you have a population that's been actively involved in a planning process, they'll never be docile again . . . I think the citizenry has come to realize its own power" (quoted in Williamson, 2007, p. 32). Similarly, one participant in the New Orleans meetings made a moving observation about how being part of the meetings had changed her life: "We are formidable and willing to go out on a limb with our own resources, our own wit, and our own backbones to accomplish what we believe we need to" (quoted in Wilson, 2009, p. 17).

Another powerful result of inclusive decision making is that participants often alter their views about those whom they had perceived to be "different" or "on the other side of an issue." An essential element of any inclusive decision making process is taking the time to listen to people with different views—and that experience changes people. This has huge implications not only for public policy deliberations but also for how people interact in a wide variety of situations. In a world where people of different backgrounds and cultures are intermingling as never before, the ability to understand and relate to diverse points of view may become the most important skill that anyone can possess (see Bennett, Chapter 5, this volume; Wasserman, Chapter 4, this volume).

Countless participants in America*Speaks* meetings have given testimony to how much they benefited from sitting at a table for several hours with a diverse group of their fellow citizens of different ages, races, cultures, income levels, and political points of view. People are amazed at how much they can learn from people they would rarely meet in their daily lives and, if they did, would never spend time talking with them. Vera Triplett, chair of the New Orleans Community Support Organization, described how powerful it was to observe the discussions that took place: ". . . I saw people sitting at tables together of different socioeconomic backgrounds, different parts of town, having healthy discussions. Not necessarily always agreeing, but actually having conversations. Not just rhetoric, not yelling and screaming, but really just having healthy conversations about what they saw as the issue. . . ." (quoted in Williamson, 2007, p. 21).

Independent evaluators from Harvard and the University of California have studied the impact on participants at California*Speaks*, the New Orleans Community Congresses, and *Our Budget, Our Economy* (California*Speaks*, 2008; Esterling, Fung, & Lee, 2010; Williamson, 2007). They interviewed a wide variety of participants and measured several significant changes in views and attitudes that resulted from working with others of diverse backgrounds. In California*Speaks* and *Our Budget, Our Economy*, both of which were huge multisite events involving thousands of people, researchers found that almost half of all participants agreed with the statement, "I have personally changed my views as a result of what I learned today." Researchers have also found that participants at America*Speaks* events often change their attitudes about their role as citizens and are surprised to see how much they have in common with people who are different. Tarance Davis, another member of the New Orleans Community Support Organization, summarized what often happens when people come together for inclusive decision making on an important issue: "I think that's the greatest part of the UNOP process so far is that it has broken down barriers that have existed for a long time in New Orleans between people who just consider themselves to be different and now have been allowed to come together to explore those differences and those similarities" (quoted in Williamson, 2007, p. 21).

Crucially, researchers have also measured what happens with participants after a 21st Century Town Meeting and, in particular, whether they continue to be involved in trying to make a difference. Their studies have shown that more participants in America*Speaks* events continue to learn about the issues that were the focus of the meeting, discuss them with others, and advocate for their views. For example, five months after California*Speaks*, researchers followed up with many participants and found that, compared to a control group of people who registered for the event but did not attend, three times as many participants had contacted a political official and written a letter to the editor of their newspaper, and significantly more had also volunteered for a political group, attended meetings, and followed issues closely in the media. In short, participants took the increased sense of empowerment that they felt and put it to work in very specific ways.

The changes in attitudes and actions that flow out of inclusive decision making as practiced by America*Speaks*—a greater sense of personal empowerment, more understanding of different points of view, a willingness to embrace new options, and an increased desire to be involved and make a difference—are exactly what is needed to solve the many problems we face in our society today. People who undergo these changes feel better about themselves and want to be more a part of shaping their own future. They have a greater degree of personal satisfaction and shared ownership and want to have a say in decisions that are happening around them.

From the Outside In: Implications for Other Organizations

Inclusive decision making has tremendous implications not only for government but, of course, for other sectors of society as well. Leaders of any large organization, business, or institution need to think through the process they currently use for decision making and reflect on how they could do a better job of listening to the voices of those impacted by their decisions. Businesses and private organizations make many decisions at multiple levels about operational policy, membership guidelines, employee relations, shareholder or membership concerns, and a myriad of other things. For many of these decisions there is an opportunity to create a process that includes more people and provides a better way for their needs and concerns to be heard. Just as inclusive decision making has a positive impact in the broader community, it can also help businesses and organizations by improving both internal functioning and external results. Private groups that practice inclusive decision making see the same benefits as in the public sector: better decisions are made, and the lives of those who participate are enhanced. Indeed, if inclusive decision making is widely practiced in private sector workplaces, there may be even greater benefit than in government. People tend to have more immediate concern for the business, organization, or institution they are part of than they do for public policy issues; not only that, they know more about it. This means that in some ways it is easier to tap into the vast energy, insight, and wisdom that business and private organizations have available to them.

In spite of the many benefits of inclusive decision making, many leaders fear it because it creates uncertainty and makes it harder to control specific outcomes. Elected officials, as well as leaders in business and the private sector, often believe they know what is best and that they do not really need input from others. Some are concerned that if they do seek meaningful input, it will slow them down and make it more difficult to do what needs to be done. While it may take longer to include the input of all segments of a group or community, it makes it easier and not more difficult to plan a path forward. If the views of a decision maker are not in line with what the constituents or members or employees really need and want, then it is important to know that. Also, it is better to learn that sooner rather than later so that the decision maker does not have to deal with the consequences of bad decisions that lack broad support.

America*Speaks*, and other members of the growing dialogue and deliberation movement, have shown repeatedly that it is possible to bring together a representative sample of people who are concerned about a particular issue or problem and get creative input from them to help generate solutions and solve problems. The lessons learned from the work that has been done are important, not only for political leaders but also for all who seek to be leaders in the world's increasingly diverse societies. Principles and practices of inclusive decision making have been developed that, if followed, can have a transformative effect on both those who participate and the outcomes they create. As a result, we are not limited to *imagining* meetings where diverse views are included and exciting new solutions emerge; we can create them to serve our needs in a wide variety of situations.

References

America*Speaks* (2009, April 15). *AmericaSpeaks 21st Century Town Meeting* [Video file]. Retrieved from http://www.youtube.com/watch?v=Rq5EkW0xIw0

California*Speaks*. (2008). *Public impacts: Evaluating the outcomes of the CaliforniaSpeaks statewide conversation on health care reform.* Retrieved from: http://americaspeaks.org/wp-content/uploads/2010/06/CaSpks-Evaluation-Report.pdf

Esterling, K., Fung, A., & Lee, T. (2010). *The difference that deliberation makes: Evaluating the "Our Budget, Our Economy" public deliberation.* Retrieved from: http://usabudgetdiscussion.org/wp-content/uploads/2010/12/OBOEResearcherReport_Final.pdf

Hamill, P. (2002, July 22). Thrilling show of people power. *New York Daily News: Sports Edition Final,* p. 8.

Lukensmeyer, C. J. (2010a, July 23). *What does it take to have a civil conversation these days?* Retrieved from http://www.huffingtonpost.com/carolyn-lukensmeyer/what-does-it-take-to-have_b_656032.html

Lukensmeyer, C. J. (2010b). Written testimony for the National Commission on Fiscal Responsibility and Reform. Retrieved from http://usabudgetdiscussion.org/written-testimony-for-the-national-commission-on-fiscal-responsibility-and-reform

Lukensmeyer, C. J. (2012). *Bringing citizen voices to the table: A guide for public managers.* San Francisco: Jossey-Bass.

Williamson, A. (2007). *Citizen participation in the Unified New Orleans Plan.* Cambridge, MA: Harvard University, Kennedy School of Government. Retrieved from http://www.americaspeaks.org/wp-content/_data/n_0001/resources/live/citizenpartstudy1.pdf

Wilson, P. A. (2009). Deliberative planning for disaster recovery: Re-membering New Orleans. *Journal of Public Deliberation, 5*(1), 1–22.

CHAPTER EIGHTEEN

Building a Culture of Inclusion: The Case of UNAIDS

Alan Richter

This chapter examines the ways in which a particular organization, UNAIDS, has worked on building a culture of inclusion in their workplace and in society at large wherever they operate. UNAIDS is a unique organization in many ways, but it is also part of the broad range of international public-sector organizations that by definition have international workforces and thereby have intercultural and diversity challenges.

I was the consultant hired by UNAIDS to assist in the creation of its new Diversity and Inclusion Policy, having previously delivered global diversity training and train-the-trainer sessions for the organization. I had been doing similar training work at both the United Nations and the World Health Organization (WHO).

The chapter has four parts: (1) an introduction of UNAIDS, (2) the model of inclusion that I used with UNAIDS, (3) the challenges that the organization faced and solutions it devised, and (4) the lessons that it learned.

Introducing UNAIDS

The agency, UNAIDS, is known as the Joint United Nations Programme on HIV/AIDS. It sees itself as "an innovative joint venture of the United Nations family, bringing together the efforts and resources of ten UN system organizations in the AIDS response to help the world prevent new HIV infections, care for people living with HIV, and mitigate the impact of the epidemic" (United Nations Foundation, 2012). The UNAIDS Secretariat is headquartered in Geneva, Switzerland, and has active operations in more than eighty countries. A number of other international agencies cosponsor UNAIDS; these include UNHCR (UN High Commissioner for Refugees), UNICEF (UN Children's Fund), WFP (World Food Program), UNDP (UN Development Program), UNFPA (UN Population Fund), UNODC (UN Office on Drugs and Crime), ILO (International Labour Organization), UNESCO (UN Educational, Scientific and Cultural Organization), WHO (World Health Organization), and the World Bank. UNAIDS works with many organizations, both from government and civil society, to "help mount and support an expanded response to AIDS" (United Nations Foundation, 2012).

Staff at UNAIDS are formally considered international civil servants and follow the International Civil Service Commission (ICSC) standards of conduct, which include the value of *Respect for Diversity*. What makes UNAIDS a uniquely interesting organization with regard to inclusion is that it works in a world in which people living with HIV are routinely stigmatized and excluded from society at large. So unlike other international organizations that focus on a specific field (such as ILO on work, WHO on health, UNICEF on children), UNAIDS is focused on a specific population or group whose members are very often the victims of discrimination and prejudice; thus the challenge of inclusion is paramount.

Model of Inclusion

My approach to inclusion is derived from the Global Diversity Survey® (GDS, 2003–2012), a self-administered, self-scoring tool that aims to help people enhance their competency to manage and value diversity and inclusion in the workplace. In use since 2003, this online tool prepares managers and employees, through a process of introspection, to:

- See beyond differences and work more successfully with people who are different from them.

- Make others feel they are valued members of a group or team.
- Act with openness, fairness, and a spirit of co-operation and generosity towards diverse colleagues.
- Adapt behaviors to better communicate and solve problems with diverse colleagues [Global Diversity Survey, 2003–2012].

The GDS was designed as a global self-assessment tool—global in two senses: it is usable worldwide across cultures, and it addresses the total range of diversity dimensions (age, ethnicity, gender, sexual orientation, culture, language, and so on). At the time it was launched (2003), to our knowledge, although a number of comparable diversity assessments existed, their approach was not usable globally because they were too U.S.-centric. Cultural assessments were available, but they focused solely on cultural dimensions, thereby excluding some of the important diversity dimensions (such as age, gender, sexual orientation, and religion).

One of the key assumptions behind the development of the GDS was to be systemic both psychologically and sociologically. Psychologically, this meant that the GDS, to be comprehensive, had to cover cognitive, emotional, and behavioral components of diversity and inclusion; sociologically, it had to cover individual, organizational, and societal levels.

Consequently, the GDS assesses three main constructs, namely *insight* (head), *inclusion* (heart), and *adaptation* (hands), using the H^3 model (Hayles & Russell, 1997; see also Hayles, Chapter 2, this volume). Insight refers to the ability to see oneself, others, and the world around one in an unbiased way. Inclusion focuses on one's actual efforts in making all people feel that they are included and part of a team. Finally, adaptation looks at one's ability to change one's own behavior so that it meets the needs of people from diverse backgrounds. Furthermore, the assessment measures three levels, namely the Self, Others, and the World, because everyone operates across these three levels—individual, interpersonal, and organizational/societal—and diversity and inclusion challenges are found at all levels. When we place the three constructs (verticals) across the three levels it generates the GDS model, with nine competencies (see Table 18.1). Focusing on the Heart or Inclusion column, we see three competencies—Sensitivity,

Table 18.1. Global Diversity Survey Matrix

	Head *Insight*	Heart *Inclusion*	Hands *Adaptation*
Self	Self-Awareness	Sensitivity	Engagement
Others	Understanding Differences	Openness	Communication
World	Facts/Objectivity	Fairness	Problem Solving

Source: Richter and Mendez-Russell, 2012. Used by permission.

Openness, and Fairness—according to the Self, Others, and World levels, respectively.

The main focus of this chapter is on how UNAIDS builds inclusion as seen through the GDS lens (sensitivity, openness, and fairness). I also discuss another key competency, engagement, which has to do with behavioral adaptation on the part of the individual.

Challenges and Solutions: Inclusion at UNAIDS

Like any international organization, UNAIDS has a broad range of diversity and inclusion challenges. In addition to the standard "isms"—such as racism, sexism, and ageism—that most organizations often face, UNAIDS, because of its unique mission, also addresses the issue of HIV-positive status, which has typically been viewed in most of the world as a stigma and hence as a basis for exclusion. Goffman (1963) defined social stigma in terms of the characteristics or other aspects of individuals that serve to discredit them in the eyes of others, who see the stigmatized person as less than normal. The stigma associated with HIV/AIDS has led to discrimination, but in varied ways, shaped by culture and historical timing; like all forms of discrimination, it breaches fundamental human rights, especially the right to be treated equally and the right of human dignity. Discrimination based on stigma poses a substantial challenge with regard to inclusion: the challenge of how to create an organizational culture that is sensitive and open to people living with HIV as well as to people with same-sex orientation and people with a disability, and that, regardless, treats everyone fairly. UNAIDS has attempted to deal with these challenges in three key areas: its mission, policy, and training, each of which I describe in the following sections. Let's start with the UNAIDS mission.

Mission

In January 2000, the UN Security Council made history when for the first time it debated a health issue—AIDS. By subsequently adopting Resolution 1308, it highlighted the growing impact of AIDS on social instability and emergency situations and the potentially damaging impact of HIV on the health of international peacekeeping personnel. The eight Millennium Development Goals (MDGs, http://www.un.org/millenniumgoals), which range from halving extreme poverty to halting the spread of HIV and providing universal primary education—all by the target date of 2015—form a target agreed to by all the world's countries and all the world's leading development institutions.

In 2001, heads of state and government representatives of 189 nations gathered at the first-ever Special Session of the United Nations General Assembly on HIV/AIDS. They unanimously adopted the Declaration of Commitment on HIV/AIDS (United Nations General Assembly, 2001), acknowledging that the AIDS epidemic constitutes a "global emergency and one of the most formidable challenges to human life and dignity" (United Nations General Assembly, 2001, p. 6). The Declaration of Commitment covers ten priorities, from prevention to treatment to funding. It provides a strong mandate to help move the AIDS response forward, with scaling up toward universal access to HIV prevention, treatment, care, and support. It also supports the particular MDG goal to halt and begin to reverse the spread of AIDS by 2015.

However, as much as the UN had previously addressed the issues of human rights, UNAIDS realized that the Declaration of Human Rights and the subsequent UN Conventions (including one on Persons with Disabilities) were not specific enough to handle the challenges that people with HIV/AIDS faced. So in 2008, the organization set out to write a Diversity and Inclusion Policy that addressed these new challenges to human life and dignity. I was privileged to work with UNAIDS to help draft this policy.

Policy

UNAIDS has developed a Diversity and Inclusion Policy to apply to all its staff and partners. One of the key components of the policy is the application of the GIPA principle: GIPA stands for Greater Involvement of People Living with HIV and AIDS ("The Greater Involvement," 2007). GIPA is an excellent example of the engagement competency in the GDS model. The engagement competency entails creating a basis for real relationships with those who are different from us. Engagement requires a commitment to move out of one's comfort zone and create genuine relationships with others across differences.

The basis for GIPA is that people living with HIV understand each other's situation better than anyone and are often best placed to counsel one another and to represent their needs in decision making and policy making forums. This was described by UNAIDS as follows: "The idea that the personal experiences of people living with HIV could and should be translated into helping to shape a response to the [AIDS] epidemic was first voiced in 1983 at a national AIDS conference in the USA. . . . It was formally adopted as a principle at the Paris AIDS Summit in 1994, where 42 countries declared the Greater Involvement of People Living with HIV and AIDS (GIPA) to be critical to ethical and effective national responses to the epidemic" (Joint United Nations Programme on HIV/AIDS, 2010b, p. 1).

The GIPA principle serves as the foundation of many interventions throughout the world: "People living with, or affected by HIV are involved in a wide variety of activities at all levels of the fight against AIDS; from appearing on posters, bearing personal testimony, and supporting and counseling others with HIV, to participating in major . . . policy-making activities" (GIPA Principle, formalized at the 1994 Paris AIDS Summit, quoted by Gooey, 2006, p. 9).

The UNAIDS Diversity and Inclusion Policy was released in March 2009 (as an internal document). In the following sections, using extracts of the relevant documents, I highlight its purpose, rationale, and key elements.

Purpose of the Policy

"UNAIDS recognizes the importance of a diverse workforce. This diversity is a reflection of a changing world. Diverse work teams bring high value to our work on AIDS, in which we promote the rights of all to a work environment that encourages productivity, while respecting individual differences. We define diversity as acknowledging, seeking to understand, accepting, and valuing differences among people with respect to age, class, ethnicity, sex, physical and mental ability, sexual orientation, etc." The UNAIDS Secretariat is committed to encouraging diversity in its workforce, with the goal of creating "a fair and safe environment where everyone has access to opportunities and benefits" (UNAIDS Diversity and Inclusion Policy, 2009).

The policy is not only a values statement but also the "operational basis for institutional and individual standards of behavior and performance" (UNAIDS Diversity and Inclusion Policy, 2009).

Rationale for the Policy

Respect for Diversity is a UN organizational core value, together with Integrity and Professionalism. These values are consonant with the UN Charter and Article 1 of the Staff Regulations. The Universal Declaration of Human Rights (United Nations, 1948) prohibits discrimination on multiple grounds, including race, color, sex, language, religion, political or other opinion, national or social origin, property, birth, or other status. UNAIDS has articulated "other status" to include sexual orientation; gender; disability; age; parental, marital, and family status; pregnancy; and health status, including HIV status.

In promoting and respecting diversity, UNAIDS upholds these values and rights, as well as key organizational principles including fairness, inclusiveness, and a healthy and productive work environment. Such an environment enables all members of the organization to maximize their contribution to UNAIDS' core mandate and the global AIDS response. Managing and promoting the value of diversity therefore is relevant to all UNAIDS staff members. UNAIDS staff must demonstrate respect for and understanding of diverse points of view and reflect this in all aspects of daily work and decision making. UNAIDS recognizes with this policy that an effective response to the AIDS epidemic necessitates that people from many different parts of society, with wide-ranging perspectives and experiences, collaborate to overcome the barriers to expanding HIV prevention, treatment, care, and support.

Elements of the Policy

This section covers values and behaviors, same-sex partnerships, HIV status, disability and life conditions, and gender parity. The policy is quoted verbatim:

1. Promoting values and behaviors: UNAIDS staff will promote the Respect for Diversity value throughout the UNAIDS family, with counterparts in the UN System, and with other partners. Staff members are expected to demonstrate the following behaviors (from the definition of the value of Diversity in the UN's "Competencies for the Future"):

- Works effectively with people from all backgrounds
- Treats all people with dignity and respect
- Treats men and women equally
- Shows respect for and understanding of diverse points of view and demonstrates this understanding in daily work and decision making
- Examines own biases and behaviors to avoid stereotypical responses
- Does not discriminate against any individual or group

The UNAIDS Secretariat, within the framework of its administrative agencies staff rules and regulations, is committed to the principle of recognizing same sex partnership equality. UNAIDS is also committed to preventing any discrimination including that based on HIV status.

2. Encouraging and attracting diversity: UNAIDS upholds diversity as a key factor in all of its human resources practices and acts to promote an inclusive workplace culture.

Continued

- *Same-sex partnerships:* Under the umbrella of the relevant staff rules, regulations and policies, UNAIDS recognizes same-sex domestic partnership entitlement equality and strives to promote expansion within the UN Common system to extend this recognition beyond current UN Human Resources Policies. UNAIDS has zero tolerance for discrimination toward any individual or group on any basis, and therefore supports all initiatives for the elimination of discrimination against same-sex partnerships by UN staff or by institutional policies at UN Common System level.

- *HIV status:* UNAIDS follows the 1991 UN Personnel Policy on HIV/AIDS, the 2001 ILO Code of Conduct and the World of Work, and the 2008 UN Cares 10 minimum standards. It does not tolerate HIV-related stigma or discrimination based on real or perceived HIV status. To enable the active engagement of people living with HIV, UNAIDS urges all actors to ensure that people living with HIV have the space and the practical support for their greater and more meaningful involvement (GIPA). Also, UNAIDS hosts the UN-wide HIV-Positive Staff Group (UN Plus), which helps to inform both changes to workplace policies and wider UN Reform.

- *Disability and life conditions:* UNAIDS supports the full inclusion of people with disabilities in the workplace. UNAIDS will seek appropriate ways of providing necessary adaptive technologies or reasonable physical adaptation of office space on UNAIDS premises to facilitate access and use.

- *Gender parity:* UNAIDS strives to attain gender equality by creating a culture in which gender balance and diversity are valued as the core of a positive working environment, sensitive to the concerns of all staff, including the specific concerns of female staff. The goal set by the Secretary General is to achieve a 50/50 gender distribution at all levels, but in particular for posts at the P-5 level and above [UNAIDS Diversity and Inclusion Policy, 2009].

Note the special focus on same-sex partnerships, HIV status, and disability. These are issues at the core of the organization and therefore need to be highlighted lest they fade under the general umbrella of diversity. For inclusion to be effective, it cannot be diluted in too generic a context. For UNAIDS, focusing on these key aspects (same sex partnerships, HIV status, and disability) is central to the organization and its culture.

The purpose of the policy is to change the organization and its culture, but organizational change does not come about from simply writing a policy. That leads us to training.

Training

With the approval of the Diversity and Inclusion Policy, UNAIDS has committed resources to promulgate it through training and communication. A half-day diversity and inclusion workshop has been successfully piloted with senior management (buy-in from the top is critical) and with some headquarters staff; train-the-trainer sessions have been held with internal trainers to prepare them to run the workshops across all regions of the world and to enable leaders to communicate and explain the Diversity and Inclusion Policy in every country office in which UNAIDS operates.

The content of the training follows the diversity and inclusion model outlined at the beginning of the chapter: the head, heart, and hands model. Thus the content of the workshop includes "headwork," "heartwork," and "handswork."

"Headwork" starts with the online self-assessment tool, the Global Diversity Survey, taken as prework, followed with coverage of the dimensions of diversity and culture as well as of the "business case" for diversity and inclusion.

"Heartwork" is tackled primarily through a simulation called *Reincarnation* (designed by Thiagarajan, 2002, but adapted for UNAIDS). This simulation has participants imagine being reincarnated into an alternate universe where one dimension of diversity is switched, allowing each person to explore the impact of that dimension on his or her professional and personal life. In light of UNAIDS's key diversity issues, we chose the following four dimensions to explore: gender, sexual orientation, ethnicity, and

HIV status. The debrief of the exercise is designed to acknowledge the "unearned" advantages that exist in the world and the
imperative to build an open, inclusive, and fair organization
(UNAIDS) and larger world.

The "handswork" portion of the training addresses the adaptive skills needed to overcome biases (and stigma) and build
engagement and inclusion. The workshop ends with a review of
the results of each person's preworkshop online self-assessment.
This step provides a foundation for participants to improve their
commitment to diversity and inclusion strategies and actions.

Training and communication alone will not be sufficient to
enable organizational change and the broadening and deepening
of inclusion, but they are a good start. Other conditions, such as
leadership role models and performance management, are key.
Compliance with the UNAIDS Diversity and Inclusion Policy is
mandatory and must be seen as such. In addition, the policy has
a segment on monitoring and evaluation, which states: "A variety
of monitoring tools will be used to allow the comparison of data
and to determine the type of culture we are promoting" (UNAIDS
Diversity and Inclusion Policy, 2009). Such tools may include
benchmarks, staff opinion surveys, staffing reviews, staff association surveys, grievances filed, and results-based tools such as
scorecards and evaluation reports to measure achievements
against set standards.

Human Resources Management is responsible for monitoring
implementation and compliance with the diversity policy, and
monitoring other policies and practices for their impact on diversity. These roles include monitoring and reporting on workplace
composition; recruitment; impact of the mobility and rotation
policy on diversity; implementation of the "UN Cares" HIV in the
workplace program; and implementation of the work/life balance
policy and related measures. Results of such monitoring and
assessment will be used in the revision of policies. In addition,
there will be a continuous monitoring of the number of complaints related to discrimination, with emphasis on those derived
from diversity; for example, discrimination related to gender,
sexual orientation, HIV status, and disability.

Following through on this, and keeping a steady eye on the
data and measures, will be key to UNAIDS' success in continuing

to build a culture of inclusion and being a pioneering organizational role model in the world.

Lessons Learned

Perhaps the most important lesson learned from working with UNAIDS was that inclusion sometimes needs to go beyond the usual dimensions of diversity. Most organizations worldwide deal with gender, ethnic, cultural, disability and generational dimensions, as well as perhaps language, religion, and sexual orientation. What made work with UNAIDS unique was the HIV status dimension, as an addition—not a replacement of—the other dimensions of diversity, and the consequent challenges for inclusion in that context.

A second, related lesson is the realization of intersectionality—meaning, in the UNAIDS context, that HIV status interacts with other components of identity, such as sexual orientation, gender, disability, age or generation, religion, and culture (to name the more obvious ones), and that no one dimension of identity stands alone; they all intersect, therefore each one of us is a unique human being (see Ferdman & Roberts, Chapter 3, in this volume).

Finally, the third lesson learned is the importance of listening to the client and then customizing diversity and inclusion work (consulting, training, communication, and so on) to the particularity of the organization. Just as human beings are all unique but have many things in common, so organizations are unique, despite their commonalities. It is inspiring that within the international public sector arena there is an enormous diversity of organizations addressing such varied topics as health, economic development, sustainability, international justice and human rights, food security, climate change, peacekeeping, and so on, and each must address inclusion in their workforce and workplace in their own unique way.

Update

The UNAIDS Diversity and Inclusion Policy is a few years old now, and much substantive progress has been made. The latest strategic update from the organization spells out its goals for 2015, namely: Zero New Infections, Zero AIDS-Related Deaths, and Zero Discrimination. Under Zero Discrimination, the objectives are to:

- Reduce by half, the number of countries with punitive laws and practices around HIV transmission, sex work, drug use or homosexuality that block effective responses;
- Eliminate by half, the number of countries that have HIV-related restrictions on entry and residence;
- Address in at least half of all national HIV responses, HIV-specific needs of women and girls; and
- Zero tolerance for gender-based violence [Joint United Nations Programme on HIV/AIDS, 2010a].

UNAIDS can rightly consider itself on the forefront of creating a more inclusive world.

The challenges of inclusion go on—how dignified the world would be if we could reach the lofty aim of *zero exclusion worldwide!*

References

Global Diversity Survey (GDS). (2003–2012). http://globaldiversityser vices.com/survey/gdsabout.php

Goffman, E. (1963). *Stigma: Notes on the management of spoiled identity.* New York: Simon & Schuster.

Gooey, S. L. (2006). The greater involvement of people living with and affected by HIV and AIDS (GIPA): NGO experiences and implications for the work of Oxfam International and Oxfam Australia. Retrieved from http://www.hivpolicy.org/Library/HPP 001513.pdf

Hayles, V. R., & Russell, A. M. (1997). *The diversity directive: Why some initiatives fail and what to do about it.* Chicago: Irwin Professional.

Joint United Nations Programme on HIV/AIDS. (2010a). Getting to zero: 2011–2015 strategy Joint United Nations Programme on HIV/AIDS (UNAIDS). Retrieved from http://www.unaids.org/ en/aboutunaids/unaidsstrategygoalsby2015

Joint United Nations Programme on HIV/AIDS. (2010b). Partnerships with people living with HIV. Retrieved from http://www.unaids.org/ en/media/unaids/contentassets/documents/programmes/ janbeagle/civilsociety/cs_B5L1_ptn.pdf

Richter, A., & Mendez Russell, A. (2012). The global diversity survey (GDS). Retrieved from http://globaldiversityservices.com/survey/gdsoutcome.php

The Greater Involvement of People Living with HIV (GIPA). (2007, March). UNAIDS Policy Brief. Retrieved from http://data.unaids.org/pub/Report/2007/JC1299-PolicyBrief-GIPA_en.pdf

Thiagarajan, S. (2002). *Diversity simulation games: Exploring and celebrating differences.* Amherst, MA: HRD Press.

UNAIDS Diversity and Inclusion Policy. (2009). (Internal document).

United Nations. (1948, December 10). Universal Declaration of Human Rights. General Assembly Resolution 217 A (III). Retrieved from http://www.unhcr.org/refworld/docid/3ae6b3712c.html

United Nations Foundation. (2012). What we do: Partners. Retrieved from http://www.unfoundation.org/what-we-do/partners/un-partners/unaids.html

United Nations General Assembly. (2001). Declaration of commitment on HIV/AIDS. Retrieved from http://www.unaids.org/en/media/unaids/contentassets/dataimport/publications/irc-pub03/aidsdeclaration_en.pdf

CHAPTER NINETEEN

Inclusion at Societal Fault Lines: Aboriginal Peoples of Australia

Charmine E. J. Härtel, Dennis Appo, and Bill Hart

In this chapter, we look at the steps that societies and organizations must take to redress the longstanding social and economic exclusion in their midst, focusing on the case in which two societies within one nation collide. We do so by presenting a brief examination of the historical context of Aboriginal peoples in Australian society, followed by a case study of how Rio Tinto Iron Ore pioneered a new organizational approach to advance the social and economic inclusion of Aboriginal contractors in the Pilbara region of Australia. We find evidence for the need to take a community building approach to address the needs of Australian Indigenous communities. Such an approach has the goal of building governance institutions that are culturally appropriate to the community and that are effective in addressing the community's challenges. Developing the capacity to participate in employment opportunities in ways that do not create dependencies, while ensuring that Indigenous peoples retain the sovereignty to choose the type of economic development that meets community needs and values, is key to achieving social inclusion when two of a nation's societies come into conflict.

Introduction

Just as fault lines in the earth indicate places where geological ruptures can occur, Lau and Murnighan's (1998) notion of group fault lines indicates those places where social division can occur in work groups. The likelihood that a work group will split into subgroups, they argue, is predicted by two conditions. The first is the extent to which the context makes an attribute within the group relevant or irrelevant to the work being performed. For example, cultural differences are more likely to be valued, and thus less likely to result in cultural subgrouping, when the group task is to identify marketing campaigns for different cultural market segments (Shaw, 2004). Second, subgrouping is more likely to occur when group members' attributes are visibly discerned or are uniquely linked to other attributes (such as gender and occupation), and when large numbers of potential subgroups could be formed (Shaw, 2004). The fault line concept is a useful way of thinking about workgroup composition—in particular, the social inclusion risks.

We draw on Lau and Murnighan's (1998) fault line concept to propose the notion of societal-level fault lines. Whether examining societies between countries or within countries, we argue that there are visible features that increase the risk of social exclusion and create a unique set of challenges for organizational diversity practices. Examples of societal-level features are physical appearance attributes, norms, beliefs, politics, history, wealth, and behavioral practices. Strong fault lines exist where there are large differences in these attributes between societies. In this chapter, we examine the issue of societal fault lines within a nation. We consider some of the issues of diversity and inclusion that organizations may face when operating in a country in which there are internal societal fault lines.

There are many cases of two societies in conflict within one nation, with tragic societal and economic consequences. To name a few, consider the Tutsis and the Hutus in Rwanda, the Gypsies in the U.K., the Tibetans in China, East and West Germany at the point of reunification, and the Indigenous and non-Indigenous peoples of South America, Canada, the United States, Mexico, and Australia. In this chapter, we critically examine the historical context of Aboriginal peoples in Australian society and Rio Tinto Iron Ore's bold step in pioneering a new organizational approach to advance social inclusion and economic development of the Aboriginal peoples in its areas of operation. Our analysis highlights the challenges while providing optimistic insights into how social justice might be facilitated at the boundaries where two societies in a nation meet. We begin by briefly setting the scene of Aboriginal peoples in Australia, followed by a case study of how Rio Tinto Iron Ore (RTIO) framed and implemented a strategy to enhance the economic and social inclusion of Australian Aboriginal contractors in the Pilbara. In our conclusion, we identify lessons from their framewrk to further advance innovative organizational and societal practices that support social and economic inclusion.

The European colonization of Australia visited on its traditional Aboriginal peoples massacres, separation of families, confiscation of children, displacement from traditional lands, and removal and denial of decision-making rights and self-governance (Appo & Härtel, 2003, 2005; Taylor & Scambary, 2005). The devastation of the Aboriginal peoples' traditional culture and the years of containment, oppression, and paternalistic attitudes underpin the human deprivation that marks many Aboriginal groups today (Appo & Härtel, 2003, 2005). As Foulks (1991) observed, the destruction of a traditional culture has a transgenerational effect, as subsequent generations are exposed to the effects of a *sick culture*, the term Foulks uses to describe the culture arising from the physical and psychosocial damage experienced by those whose culture and social fabric were ripped away. Examples of such artificially induced sick societies abound around the world; all feature the common elements of marginal status, identity confusion, unemployment, and psychopathologies such as despair, suicide, and substance abuse (Foulks, 1991).

In light of the effects of cultural upheaval and disintegration, treatment as children incapable of governing themselves for more than one hundred years, and denial of the full benefits of Australian citizenship until 1967, it is no wonder that Indigenous unemployment has been an ongoing and intractable social, economic, and political problem in Australia (Royal Commission, 1991), even in the presence of employment opportunities (Department of Families, Housing, Community Services and Indigenous

Affairs, 2010). Despite a wide range of initiatives and considerable monetary investment by the private, public, and third sectors (not-for-profit and nongovernment), little has happened over the past two decades to change this situation (Australian Government, 2007). The disadvantages—including high welfare dependency, low literacy, low personal initiative, and poor physical and psychosocial well-being—persist (Appo & Härtel, 2003, 2005; Taylor & Scambary, 2005).

The contemporary situation for the majority of Australian Aboriginals remains one of societal and economic exclusion. The challenge for organizations and governments is to identify ways to turn this situation around. Our aim in this chapter is to highlight the key issues that need to be considered in doing so and to present a case study that provides fertile ground for critiquing and developing organizational solutions to contribute to this agenda.

In the next section, we present a case study of a practical intervention recently implemented in the Pilbara region by RTIO that demonstrates the important practical lessons and solutions regarding social inclusion that can be learned by examining the issues that arise at the boundaries of two societies in a single nation.

Case Study: Rio Tinto Iron Ore

The Pilbara region of Western Australia was once home to thirty-one language groups (clans) who peacefully respected one another's territories at the time of European contact in 1864 (Pilbara History and Cultures, 2009). The Pilbara region was one of the last areas to experience contact between Aboriginal and European society, and this region went through similar colonization experience of massacres and decimation of traditional culture (Bednarik, 2002).

Early work for Aborigines in the Pilbara, as in so many other places in Australia, was on cattle stations. As this work faded with the rise of industry, including the mining sector, most Aborigines were excluded from training and, as a consequence, from employment opportunities (Langton & Mazel, 2008). Many were demoralized and forced into welfare dependency. Some were forcibly relocated to overcrowded camps, and their fringe-dweller status on the edges of towns led to further social marginalization. As noted by Howitt (2005), "each new wave of development, each new layer of investment contributed its characteristic elements to emerging patterns of Aboriginal marginalization and powerlessness" (p. 165).

Today, the Pilbara is a hotbed of mining activity, earning $34.5 billion between 2009 and 2010 alone and providing 29.4 percent of the employment opportunities in the region (Department of Regional Development and Lands, 2011). The Traditional Owners[1] of the Pilbara are legally entitled to receive massive dividends from this boom, but those dividends are not necessarily forthcoming without protracted legal battles or in the amount provided by law (O'Brien, 2011). While non-Indigenous Australia has prospered from the mining boom, considerable debate continues to rage—reminiscent of past paternalistic approaches—regarding the best way to distribute the wealth to the Aboriginal people on whose land 60 percent of mining activities occur. The reality is that in many cases, the Traditional Owners of the land are experiencing further cultural upheaval and little prosperity (Langton & Mazel, 2008).

The case we present emanates from a project undertaken on behalf of Rio Tinto Iron Ore (RTIO). The impetus for the project was a situation not uncommon to industries operating near Indigenous communities: acute labor shortage in the face of high Aboriginal unemployment. In this case, the issue was that many of the Aboriginal contractors in the Pilbara did not have enough work, while at the same time RTIO was having some difficulty in finding enough contractors to satisfy its requirements. We begin the case with a brief discussion of RTIO's orientation toward Aboriginal Traditional Owners in the Pilbara, followed by a description of the steps taken to identify the causal factors underlying the low participation of Aboriginal contractors and discussion of the approach designed and implemented by RTIO to advance the social and economic inclusion of Aboriginal contractors in the Pilbara.

---

[1]The term *Traditional Owner* has a statutory meaning, referring to the land rights an Aboriginal clan has, based on historical ties to the land (Holcombe, 2004).

RTIO: Aboriginal Community Relations

Some background on RTIO is useful in understanding the contemporary philosophy by which the organization relates to the Aboriginal Traditional Owners of the Pilbara. Prior to the appointment of CEO Leon Davis, RTIO dealt with Aboriginal land owners through legal means, as did the mining industry in general. Confronted with this situation, in 1995 Davis gave a speech drawing on the legal concept in his native country, the UK, of *fiat justitia* ("let right be done"), which the British king had used to endorse correcting a wrong. Davis said he saw the reliance on legislation in Aboriginal relations as "a never ending war with no winners" and believed that in spite of the legality of such a route, "right" was not being done (Hart, 2008). Davis's view led to a shift in the RTIO philosophy as well as the industry stance, with most mining organizations moving away from legislation to a model of negotiation and collaboration.

Today, RTIO embraces the tripartite collaborative model posited by Taylor and Scambary (2005) as the foundation for overcoming Aboriginal disadvantage in the Pilbara. This model identifies unique and interdependent roles for government, industry, and Indigenous organizations. In the case of employment, this means capacity building by government organizations, problem identification and decision making by Indigenous organizations, and alignment of industry policies and practices with the realities of the Aboriginal labor pool. A key challenge for a corporation such as RTIO is changing its expectations regarding decision-making time frames because cultural norms for decision making in many Aboriginal communities require ample deliberation involving all members of the community.

RTIO lays out its business practice statement in a document titled, "The Way We Work" (Rio Tinto Iron Ore, n.d.; all subsequent quotations are from that document, unless otherwise indicated). The company asserts: "Wherever we operate, we do our best to accommodate the different cultures, lifestyles, heritage and preferences of our neighbors, particularly in areas where industrial development is little known. Our communities and environment work is closely coordinated and takes account of peoples' perceptions of the effects and consequences of our activities."

RTIO acknowledges that "good management of community relationships is as necessary to our business success as the management of our operations. Good performance requires all of us to accept responsibility for community relationships." The focus on community relations is illustrated by this statement: "We set out to build enduring relationships with our neighbors that are characterized by mutual respect, active partnership and long term commitment." RTIO's Communities policy goes on to say: "Our relationships with communities involve consultation to open new facilities, to run existing ones and to close them at the end of their productive lives. In doing so, we support community based projects that can make a difference in a sustainable way without creating dependency. We also assist regional development and training, employment and small business opportunities. In developing countries, we are often asked to support health, education and agricultural programs and, in collaboration with others, we help where practical."

Competencies in community development and community relations are key to the sustainability of modern mining companies, which require not only a legal license to operate but also a social license, which refers to the permission given by a society for an organization to operate (Harvey, 2011). As expressed by Bruce Harvey, Global Practice Leader— Communities and Social Performance for RTIO, earning a social license to operate means "a direct engagement and a direct broad-based social contract with the host community around what they expect of us . . ." (Harvey, 2011). Regarding RTIO, Harvey goes on to say "We should be earning our social licence through fitting in and adapting to the prevailing social norms and acceptable social norms and the legal requirements are simply a complementary element to that" (Harvey, 2011). Accordingly, RTIO aims to be "the 'developer of choice' for communities and governments" (Harvey & Brereton, 2005, p. 3), which it sees as essential to competitive advantage in securing new resources, attracting and retaining talent, and reducing corporate risk.

From its organizational values to its business practice statement, RTIO appears to adopt a view of social inclusion as incorporating community consultation in corporate activity from preentry to exit, good corporate-community relations, community self-determination, and promotion of community and regional sustainability. In line with this perspective, the first step undertaken in the project was problem identification in consultation with local communities. This phase of the project is summarized next.

Problem Identification

Although RTIO had publicly stated its commitment to working with Aboriginal contractors, there was clear evidence that this commitment was not being translated into practice (Wand, Langton, & McLeish, 2008). As a first step to addressing the limited engagement of Pilbara Aboriginal contractors with RTIO, the Aboriginal Enterprise Development workshop was codesigned and coconvened by one of this chapter's authors (Dennis Appo) in Dampier on August 22, 2007. The purpose of this forum was to consult with Aboriginal contractors to identify the issues and concerns underpinning the unsatisfactory level of engagement. The outcome of the forum discussions indicated that some of the issues related to RTIO organizational practices. The following issues were the drivers for the intervention we designed:

- Start-up environment does not facilitate Aboriginal contractors to grow their business and meet standards—there is a lack of mentoring to get established and meet bond requirements.
- High cost of training to standard Aboriginal people who have never worked before.
- Complicated entry systems (such as police record and reference checks, absence of drug and alcohol issues, use of electronic applications, and literacy requirements) create barriers to recruitment.
- Poaching by big companies of Aboriginal people after Aboriginal businesses had invested funds in training them.

- Big contractors working for RTIO do not make real efforts to recruit Aboriginal subcontractors.
- High cost (money and time) of tendering (bidding) for a contract is a barrier to small Aboriginal businesses.
- Poor coordination between RTIO and Aboriginal businesses, including advising Traditional Owners which companies have received contracts and when tender opportunities are available.
- Lack of business acumen in Aboriginal businesses, including tender writing skills and financial management skills.
- Some organizations claiming Aboriginal Organization status (that is, an organization that represents Aboriginal economic and cultural interests) when they have a low level of Aboriginal participation or ownership.
- Ad hoc approach by RTIO to capacity building, driven by immediate operational needs.

The workshop surfaced a number of issues that needed to be addressed at the policies and procedures level for RTIO to enable the Aboriginal contractors to become more actively engaged in the wider Pilbara economy. Facilitating the development of an intervention to address these issues was RTIO's explicit re-cognition of the need for a holistic and systematic approach to community relations and capacity development. Harvey and Brereton (2005) summarize this approach, saying:

> Clearly, for any corporate capability to be sustainable it must be systemic; that is, it must be built into the organization's standard methods and processes for "doing business" and must be able to sustain changes in personnel. This recognition has led leading companies such as Rio Tinto to focus on developing comprehensive systems in the social arena, with the long term aim of embedding the same level of competency as exists in the corporation's technical and financial systems. . . . Overall, these systems can be usefully imagined as the "architecture" of the corporation; they include clearly articulated values and policies, standards and guidance, communication and reporting systems, and methods of verification [p. 4].

In the next section, we describe the intervention we developed to respond to the issues identified in the workshop as relating to RTIO systems and processes.

The Intervention

The first step we took in formulating possible solutions RTIO could offer to the issues identified in the workshop was to tabulate in detail the identified barriers to engagement for Aboriginal contractors, along with possible ways RTIO could remove these. The result of this undertaking is presented in Table 19.1.

The list of barriers identified demonstrates the complexity of RTIO's relationships with its Aboriginal contractors. Accordingly, the potential solutions identified indicated the need for RTIO to take a holistic and systematic approach to addressing the issues. Two underlying principles were followed in solution identification. First, RTIO required that all contractors meet safety standards, deliver on contracts, and ensure financial accountability. Second, the Traditional Owners required a reversal of the trend of continued economic decline among their people in the midst of an economic boom fueled by resources from their land (Langton & Mazel, 2008).

Keeping these two principles in mind, we examined RTIO's procurement process with the intent of identifying how the process could be modified to open the way for participation by the Aboriginal contractors. The process, depicted by the unshaded steps in Figure 19.1, commenced contact with contractors at the time the call for tenders was issued (step 4) followed by the receipt of submitted tenders (step 9). Comparing this part of the process to the reality of Aboriginal contractors revealed several issues. First, there was a need to understand which businesses qualified as Aboriginal businesses. The Traditional Owners take responsibility for this process, as they are the ones with the history, knowledge, and cultural authority to speak on behalf of all of the families in the Pilbara. Adding this step was essential for a systematic approach to increasing participation and to enable assessment of the true

Table 19.1. Barriers to Aboriginal Contractor Engagement and Potential RTIO Solutions

Barriers to engagement	RTIO's possible solutions
Systems and processes for contractors need to be altered.	Alter the systems and processes.
Prequalification process with government is onerous. Stepping stones to address this process should be put in place.	This is a normal part of doing business. Training and development programs are being provided to upgrade business skills.
RTIO is missing out on good Aboriginal people because of your systems—such as police records and referee checks.	We don't care about work history—we will train people in the operation. If you are fit to work and literate, you will get a job.
Talent—spotting existing employees—to access apprenticeships for potential business development.	We are always looking for good people and will assist with training and development.
EPMS system—we got rid of EPMS system with Woodside contracts.	We will work to refine our procurement system to include evaluation criteria relevant to Aboriginal contractors.
Electronic application excludes some Aboriginal people.	Train all Aboriginal contractors to be proficient with electronic applications.
Health barrier—drug and alcohol.	We work with people to get through these issues.
Literacy.	Numeracy and literacy education is a state government responsibility. We will assist in connecting Aboriginal contractors to these resources.
No flexibility—be innovative, not lenient.	We will work to refine our procurement system to include evaluation criteria relevant to Aboriginal contractors.

Table 19.1. Continued

Barriers to engagement	RTIO's possible solutions
Is there any way that some work need not go to tender?	See AUSAID—training Aboriginal people to participate in projects—six months' notice to give people a chance to prepare themselves. Rather than lowering standards, we are providing training and development for Aboriginal contractors so that they will have the necessary skills to write tender applications.
Putting up 10 percent of the contract as a bond is not realistic for small contractors unless there is some continuity of work (RTIO might be prepared to waive this bond).	The new procurement process (with no bond) should provide a steady flow of work to Aboriginal contractors who are capable of meeting the commercial and operational outcomes sought by the business.
Cost for preparing contract is high and not easily managed by small companies. May require some additional support.	Training and development will be provided for Aboriginal contractors.
Many people have never worked, but we carry the cost of bringing people up to speed.	Use the existing training and development resources from government.
High cost of training to skill people to contract standards.	This is the reality for this industry.
Aboriginal people who don't get into the mainstream get left behind and it becomes harder to get a job.	We agree; that's why we are providing training and development.
EPCM contractors are not approaching Traditional Owners to do joint venture projects or directly employ *local* people.	Provide incentives for EPCM contractors to employ local Aborigines.

Continued

Table 19.1. Continued

Barriers to engagement	RTIO's possible solutions
We are being ignored as potential subcontractors. Head contractors at this level need to be given clear directions from RTIO and there should be follow-up audit from RTIO.	We can't make them do something that is not in their contract, but we can provide them with incentives to employ local Aborigines.
"Best endeavors" is subjective—problematic in performance of contracts.	Where allowable by law, we will make our contracts much less subjective.
Need for consistency in tenders and performance to overcome "the veneer of the Aboriginal organization"—need to test the level of Aboriginal participation and or ownership.	Need to develop a coordinated consistent approach to contracting across RTIO: Guidelines Access Transparency
Not enough weight given to Indigenous employment—what are the weightings? Local Aboriginal people being employed. Local/Traditional Owner joint venture.	Develop transparent performance measures for procurement—roll out trial to all contracts and focus on: Local Aboriginal employees Level of support for entry-level employees Joint venture projects with traditional owners
How can there be real value out of these "head" contracts delivering for Traditional Owners and Indigenous businesses and honoring their commitments to RTIO?	Audit head contractor performance—we need to check levels of Indigenous participation.
Big contractors are locking Aboriginal contractors out.	Get IBA or another big contractor to assist with projects outside RTIO. Contracting steering group inside RTIO would be useful, as would Pilbara Contracting Association. Coordinate across Aboriginal businesses.

Figure 19.1. Aboriginal Contractor Engagement

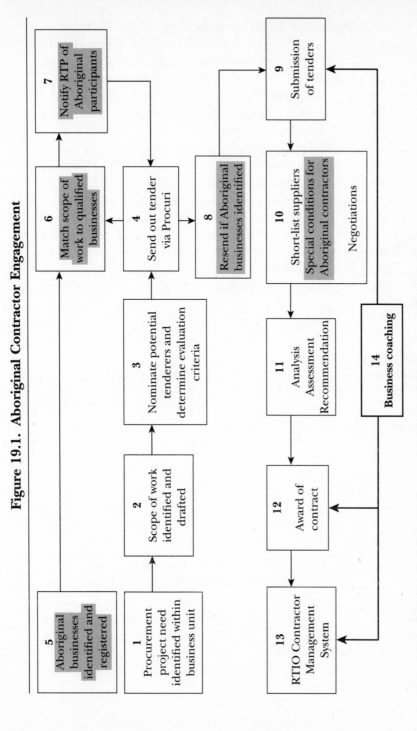

Note: The shaded areas indicate changes to the Rio Tinto Procurement (RTP) system.

Source: Härtel and Fujimoto, 2010, p. 336.

level of participation in RTIO work by Aboriginal contractors. The procurement process for Aboriginal contractors was thus modified to include assessment by Traditional Owners of Aboriginal Organization status, denoted as step 5 in Figure 19.1. One development issue identified for this step was that coaching and training were needed to ensure that Aboriginal contractors could meet prequalification criteria.

The second and related process gap was the need to match work on offer with the capacity and category of qualified Aboriginal contractors. This additional step (denoted as step 6 in Figure 19.1) was necessary to ensure that calls for tenders are distributed to all qualified Aboriginal contractors. One development issue identified for this step was that many Aboriginal contractors require business coaches to help them with writing tender applications (bid proposals). The skills and knowledge that must be evident in the tender application from all contractors include the following:

- Costing
- Time frame
- Health, safety, and environment
- Plant and equipment
- Current work obligations
- Personnel (HR management)
- Insurance
- Demonstrated capacity
- Project management
- Technical skills
- General management
- Cash flow management

The dual aim of business coaching is to help the contractors complete the tender application properly and to develop the contractors' skills in this area. The inclusion of notifying RTIO procurement (see Figure 19.1, step 7) enables RTIO to track Aboriginal participants for the purposes of providing timely support and ensure Aboriginal contractors do not miss out on work opportunities due to inadequately constructed tender applications, a primary point at which many Aboriginal contracts were lost previously. The new step also allows RTIO to resend the call for tenders (step 8) if Aboriginal businesses are identified beyond those determined in step 7.

Once tenders are submitted, short-listing and negotiations begin. Previously this step (step 10) did not incorporate a means for preferential treatment for Aboriginal businesses or businesses with Aboriginal employment initiatives. To address this gap, special conditions were added to Step 10 in the form of key performance indicators (KPIs). The KPIs, shown in Table 19.2, are used not only in the tender selection process but also subsequently in quarterly contract review meetings.

The revised process for Aboriginal contractor engagement highlighting key development areas is depicted in Figure 19.2. The figure illustrates that development does not stop at the point of winning the contract but rather is ongoing until the Aboriginal contractors are established with proficient technical, enterprise, and financial skills. This is important, as most of the Aboriginal contractors are small to medium in size with limited resources. Given the context in which the Aboriginal contractors exist, we concluded that the best results would be achieved through one-on-one mentoring, commencing from the writing of the application to tender through to contract completion. A social inclusion approach in these circumstances would thus be formal and systematic, and based on an individual business development needs assessment. A scaffolding approach is required, which needs to be ongoing until the contractor involved has become independent, supporting the self-determination criteria of social inclusion. Recognizing that organizations are one pillar of the solution, where external resources exist, these should be drawn upon. A wealth of such resources exists, for example from Indigenous-specific commercial organizations (such as Indigenous Business Australia), state government (for example, the Department of Industry and Resources), and not-for-profits (such as the Pilbara Area Consultative Committee); however, no coordination body exists. For this reason, we concluded that RTIO needed to provide a coordination role to ensure development was delivered systematically.

Table 19.2. Key Performance Indicators

Key Performance Indicator	Agreed Target
Support for school-based vocational programs	
Number of school-based apprenticeships and traineeships	X number per year
Number of structured workplace learning opportunities	X number per year
Attendance at Aboriginal education, training, and employment meetings	80 percent of scheduled meetings
Preemployment programs for Aboriginal people	
Number of preemployment programs (structured workplace learning opportunities) conducted for Aboriginal people	X number per year
Number of participants in preemployment programs (structured workplace learning opportunities) conducted for Aboriginal people	X number of participants successfully completing
Entry-level training	
Number of apprentices and trainees employed by the service provider	X apprentices and trainees
Number of Aboriginal apprentices and trainees employed by the service provider	
Number of Aboriginal apprentices and trainees employed by the service provider's subcontractor	
Culturally appropriate working environment	
Proportion of new starters receiving cultural awareness training	100 percent
Proportion of managers and supervisors undertaking appropriate level of cultural awareness training	100 percent
Aboriginal employment	
The number of Aboriginal people working for the service provider and the service provider's subcontractor	Increase of X number of Aboriginal employees
Business development	
Prequalified Aboriginal organizations are invited to bid on subcontracted goods or service requirements	100 percent of subcontracted requirements where possible
Value of subcontracts let to prequalified Aboriginal organizations	$ value

Figure 19.2. Aboriginal Contractor Engagement: Revised Process

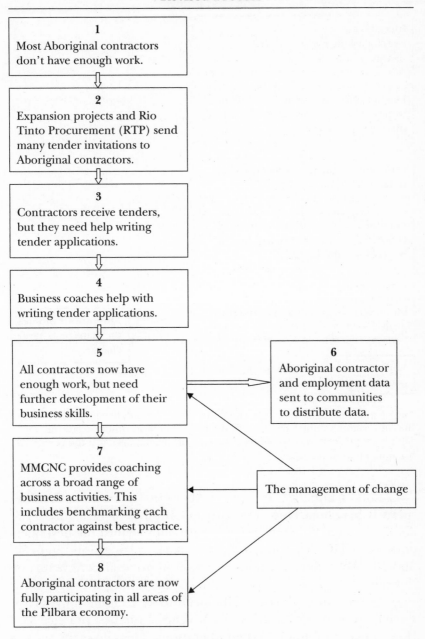

Figure 19.3. Benchmarking to Identify Viable Business Solutions

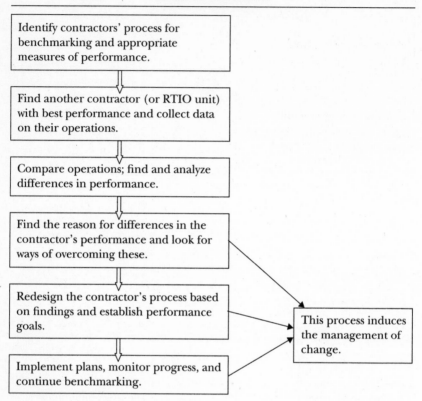

Note: Many aspects of the contractors' businesses were deficient in some way; the most viable solution for most of them is to see how other successful businesses perform the functions. This type of benchmarking is the preferred learning method for most contractors.

Another initiative to support Aboriginal contractor development is benchmarking. This process, illustrated in Figure 19.3, should be used to compare each contractor against the best operations in RTIO. The targeted benchmark organization might be another Aboriginal contractor, a non-Aboriginal contractor, or any one of the RTIO operations. At the beginning, all of the business systems for each contractor need to be examined by RTIO. Each contractor also needs to be advised of the best practice that they can copy or adapt to their operations. This allows the setting of realistic performance targets and shows the contractor how these targets can be met.

Lessons Learned

In this chapter, we looked at the longstanding social and economic exclusion of Aboriginal peoples in Australia, which persists even in the midst of the extraordinary economic boom associated with mining operations undertaken largely on their traditional lands. We introduced the concept of societal fault lines to address the potential for social exclusion on the basis of differences in societal characteristics. We illustrated that societal fault lines can occur across national borders or within, and we identified the situation of Aboriginal peoples in Australia as an example of the latter. We presented a case study of Aboriginal contractors in the Pilbara region of Australia, which showed persistent underrepresentation in work opportunities despite acute labor shortages in the mineral and resources sector in the region. The case outlines a new approach pioneered by Rio Tinto Iron Ore (RTIO) in response to community dissatisfaction with the ongoing economic exclusion.

The case illustrated a number of factors contributing to the social exclusion of local Aboriginal peoples from work opportunities. One of these barriers to engagement was created by RTIO's internal administrative systems and procedures. By modifying its procurement system to take into account the fault line relating to the realities of Aboriginal work history and business and financial skills, the company was able to open doors that had previously been closed.

Another barrier identified was game playing. Analysis of RTIO contractor behavior revealed that some organizations were claiming Indigenous status on the basis of a single Indigenous owner or minimal Aboriginal employment. In consultation with the Traditional Owners, it became clear that the process RTIO used— allowing potential contractors to self-identify as an Aboriginal business—was not only flawed but disrespectful of the sovereignty of Aboriginal communities. This cultural fault line was addressed by turning the identification process over to the Traditional Owners.

A third barrier related to mismatches between claims and actual efforts by RTIO contractors to employ Aboriginal contractors. Two responses were proposed to remove this conflict. First, a clause with special conditions for Aboriginal contractors was introduced into RTIO's procurement process to allow for preferential treatment. Second, key performance indicators for supporting Aboriginal social and economic development were identified and included in quarterly contract review meetings.

A fourth barrier to engagement illustrated in the case was access to skills development. Analysis of tender outcomes revealed that many Aboriginal contractors were losing out on contracts due to skill deficiencies in writing tender applications. Although quite a number of communities and families had formed private companies to provide services under contract to RTIO and other mining companies, most who won contracts were underperforming, and some were encountering difficulties staying commercially viable. What was required was one-on-one mentoring for both new and established Aboriginal contractors to grow sustainable businesses. Additionally, despite a plethora of training resources available from state and commonwealth agencies and not-for-profit agencies, the lack of a coordinated approach to delivery of systematic ongoing training based on individual needs analysis meant few were getting the development they needed. RTIO's response to this fault line issue was to identify the available development resources for different needs, undertake regular needs analysis of Aboriginal contractors, and design a mechanism to coordinate the various agency offerings with its own.

There are a number of broader lessons that can be drawn from the approach developed for RTIO. We present these next, along with some suggestions on how to build on this framework to further advance innovative organizational and societal practices that support social and economic inclusion.

We find evidence that a community-building approach is needed in order to address the needs of Australian Indigenous communities. For organizations, this requires quite a different view of human resource management as traditionally practiced:

as an inward-looking exercise. To achieve a truly diversity-open mindset (Härtel, 2004), organizations need to become intimately familiar with the diversity in the communities in which they operate, recognizing that issues to accessing economic participation do not begin at the point at which individuals respond to a job advertisement. A holistic social inclusion approach takes a lifespan view of the employment process and recognizes the importance of self-determination to individual, community, and organizational well-being (see Härtel, 2008; Härtel & Ashkanasy, 2011). Such an approach has the goal of promoting self-governance, developing the capacity to participate in employment opportunities in ways that do not create dependencies, and allowing flexibility in decision-making practices to enable culturally appropriate consultation processes. Although the approach described in this chapter has this perspective at its heart, it is limited by the fact that the Traditional Owners on whose land mining operations largely occur lack sovereignty to choose the type of economic development they desire and that meets community needs and values. As Morphy (2008) aptly sums up: "But unless change is managed so that people themselves feel ownership of the process, and in a way that speaks to their—rather than the market's—concerns, and that reflects their—rather than the state's—aspirations, we will be gazing in a few years' time on yet another failure in Indigenous policy" (p. 8).

Real social and economic inclusion of Indigenous peoples requires respect for cultural differences and the right to self-determination. In the absence of the ability to choose how to develop a sustainable economy that preserves their distinct heritage, it is likely that the motivation of Indigenous peoples to develop the skills and attitudes germane to an industrial worksite will remain low. It is an economic imperative, therefore, for businesses to identify the ways in which traditional culture can be integrated into their organizational practices, such as in the community consultation processes described in the case presented in this chapter. Not only do organizations require an accurate understanding of the individual culture of each of the Aboriginal clans in their areas of operation, but they also require the intercultural competency to effectively and respectfully relate. While some work has been done in the area of intercultural competency, including some that identifies that the intercultural competencies required in a given cultural setting may differ from those required in another (Härtel, Lloyd, & Singhal, 2010), there is a lack of research on the competencies required of non-Indigenous organizations interacting with local Aboriginal communities. Given the variety of Aboriginal cultural groupings an organization may relate with, it would be more prudent to define a methodology for the relevant intercultural competencies for a given group than to develop a single framework.

Conclusion

Economic and social inclusion of Aboriginal Australians will occur to the extent that a community's cultural, political, economic, and social priorities are part of day-to-day decision making and that these priorities support (1) balancing change with cultural continuity, (2) self-determination of meaning, and (3) notions of prosperity and successful societies. Although organizations cannot address these issues in isolation, a social inclusion approach, as illustrated by the case of RTIO presented in this chapter, enables positive community relations, which have cascading economic effects for both the organization as well as the development and support of Indigenous businesses (see Brereton, 2002; Harvey & Brereton, 2005; Humphreys, 2000, 2001). Focusing on doing right is one way business can contribute to the cultural well-being of the Australian Aboriginal people.

References

Appo, D., & Härtel, C. E. J. (2003). Questioning management paradigms that deal with Aboriginal development programs in Australia. *Asia Pacific Journal of Human Resources, 41*(1), 36–50.

Appo, D., & Härtel, C. E. J. (2005). On the pathogenicity of culture: Questioning the rationality of "development" programs for perpetually dysfunctional Aboriginal groups. *Cross-cultural Management: An International Journal, 12*(1), 4–30.

Australian Government. (2007). *Emergency response to protect Aboriginal children in the NT.* Retrieved from http://www.fahcsia.gov.au

Bednarik, R. G. (2002). *The killing fields of Murujuga.* Retrieved from http://home.vicnet.net.au/~auranet/dampier/shared_files/massacre.pdf

Brereton, D. (2002). *Building the business case for sustainable development.* Minerals Council of Australia 2002 Sustainable Development Conference, Newcastle, Australia.

Department of Families, Housing, Community Services and Indigenous Affairs, Australian Government. (2010). *Closing the gap—Prime minister's report.* Retrieved from http://www.fahcsia.gov.au/our-responsibilities/indigenous-australians/publications-articles/closing-the-gap/closing-the-gap-prime-ministers-report-2010

Department of Regional Development and Lands, Pilbara Development Commission. (2011). *Pilbara: A region in profile.* Retrieved from http://www.pdc.wa.gov.au/publications/

Foulks, E. F. (1991). Transcultural psychiatry and normal behavior. In D. Offer & M. Sabshin (Eds.), *The diversity of normal behavior: Further contributions to normatology* (pp. 207–238). New York: Basic Books.

Hart, B. (2008). Building capability through collaboration in the Pilbara [Transcript]. Unpublished speech.

Härtel, C. E. J. (2004). Towards a multicultural world: Identifying work systems, practices and employee attitudes that embrace diversity. *Australian Journal of Management, 29*(2), 189–200.

Härtel, C. E. J. (2008). How to build a healthy emotional culture and avoid a toxic culture. In C. L. Cooper & N. M. Ashkanasy (Eds.), *Research companion to emotion in organization* (pp. 575–588). Cheltenham, UK: Edward Elgar.

Härtel, C. E. J., & Ashkanasy, N. M. (2011). Healthy human cultures as positive work environments. In N. M. Ashkanasy, C. P. M. Wilderom, & M. F. Peterson (Eds.), *The handbook of organizational culture and climate* (2nd ed., pp. 85–100). Thousand Oaks, CA: Sage.

Härtel, C. E. J., & Fujimoto, Y. (2010). *Human resource management* (2nd ed.). Frenchs Forest, N.S.W.: Pearson Education Australia.

Härtel, C. E. J., Lloyd, S., & Singhal, D. (2010). Intercultural competencies across cultures: Same or different? In J. Syed & M. F. Özbilgin (Eds.), *Managing cultural diversity in Asia: A research companion* (pp. 192–223). Cheltenham & New York: Edward Elgar.

Harvey, B. (Interviewee). (2011). Social licence to operate is good business. *Achieve. The Sinclair Knight Merz Magazine, 4* [Interview transcript]. Retrieved from http://www.skmconsulting.com/Knowledge-and-Insights/Achieve-Magazine/Issue4–2011/cover.aspx

Harvey, B., & Brereton, D. (2005, August). *Emerging models of community engagement in the Australian minerals industry.* Paper presented at the International Conference on Engaging Communities, Brisbane, Australia.

Holcombe, S. (2004). Traditional owners and "community-country" *anangu*: Distinctions and dilemmas. *Australian Aboriginal Studies, 2,* 64–71.

Howitt, R. (2005). Resource development and the Aborigines: The case of Roebourne 1960–1980. *Australian Geographic Studies, 27*(2), 165.

Humphreys, D. (2000). A business case perspective on community relations in mining. *Resources Policy, 26*(3), 127–131.

Humphreys, D. (2001). Sustainable development: Can the mining industry afford it? *Resources Policy, 27*(1), 1–7.

Langton, M., & Mazel, O. (2008). Poverty in the midst of plenty: Aboriginal people, the resource curse and Australia's mining boom. *Journal of Energy & Natural Resources Law, 26*(1), 31–65.

Lau, D., & Murnighan, J. K. (1998). Demographic diversity and faultlines: The compositional dynamics of organizational groups. *Academy of Management Review, 23*(2), 325–340.

Morphy, F. (2008, November). *Re-engaging the economic with the social* (Topical Issue No. 9). Retrieved from Centre for Aboriginal Economic Policy Research website: http://caepr.anu.edu.au/sites/default/files/Publications/topical/Morphy_CDEP.pdf

O'Brien, K. (Producer). (2011, July 18). Iron and dust. *Four Corners* [Television series]. Australian Broadcasting Corporation.

Pilbara History and Cultures. (2009). Retrieved from Wangka Maya Pilbara Aboriginal Language Centre website: http://www.wangkamaya.org.au.

Rio Tinto Iron Ore (n.d.). *The way we work: Our statement of business practice.* (2008). Retrieved from http://www.riotintomadagascar.com/pdf/The_way_we_work.pdf

Royal Commission into Aboriginal Deaths in Custody. (1991). *National Report.* Canberra: Australian Government Publishing Service.

Shaw, J. B. (2004). The development and analysis of a measure of group faultlines. *Organizational Research Methods, 7*(1), 66–100.

Taylor, J., & Scambary, B. (2005). *Indigenous people and the Pilbara mining boom: A baseline for regional participation.* CAEPR Research Monograph No. 25. Retrieved from http://epress.anu.edu.au/caepr _series/no_25/pdf/prelims.pdf

Wand, P., Langton, M., & McLeish, K. (2008). *RTIO independent enquiry into Aboriginal contracting practices.* Retrieved from http://www .aemee.org.au/common/pdf/SME/Session02-PaulWand-RTIO .pdf

Part Five

Moving Forward

CHAPTER TWENTY

Inclusion as a Transformational Diversity and Business Strategy

Michael L. Wheeler

"You are asking people to do what is not natural," an executive once said to me. He was right, in part. He was referring to inclusion. What he was really talking about, though, was inclusion across differences. Inclusion—being included, including others, valuing and respecting, engaging, fully contributing—comes easily for those who perceive themselves as similar, like-minded, and sharing values, perspectives, and experiences. But across differences, inclusion indeed requires attention, intention, and practice.

As a corporate diversity leader, I approach my work with this dilemma in mind—that as desirable as it is to be included, and as important as inclusion is for business, it is not natural across differences. It is a powerful matter of nuance, a subtext that influences everything I do. To address the challenges posed by this dilemma, I find using a cross-disciplinary approach critical to success. The ability to draw upon my knowledge of or research in psychology, group dynamics, organizational behavior, organization development, instructional design, adult learning theory, sociology, and systems theory gives me insight, tools, and tactics for effectively implementing and leading the implicit and explicit elements of a corporate strategy.

This is why I find the arrival of this book, *Diversity at Work: The Practice of Inclusion* (hereinafter referred to as *The Practice of Inclusion*), so timely and valuable. As a diversity leader, I believe it is extremely important to approach strategy and tactics with the individual, interpersonal, and organizational perspectives in mind, which is how the chapters are organized. The chapters in this book provide a systematic framework for thinking about and practicing inclusion in the context of work. While they draw on a wide array of perspectives, disciplines, and models, the authors also offer many practical examples and tactics. I especially appreciate the book's cross-disciplinary approach, its contributions to expand the rationale for inclusion, and the deeper dive into inclusion's myriad complex issues. I can easily say the book models inclusion.

The editors and authors offer a great service to the diversity professional by creating and contributing to an easy-to-use, one-stop shop of in-depth information presented in a cohesive way. Seeking out these perspectives and works separately would be a timely and challenging endeavor. The chapters proactively and substantively address many of the issues I have observed and present below. They reinforce what I know, yet provide me with new insights. This is a book that I believe corporate leaders have needed for a long time.

Inclusion takes ongoing conscious effort and work, a reality completely supported by the authors in this book. It is not the easy route, but it is essential for the workplace and, ultimately, for society. Why? Diversity is a global demographic fact, and we must understand its implications for talent, the workplace, and the marketplace. Moreover, where barriers exist across differences, those same barriers can inhibit performance and success. Inclusion, on the other hand, can enhance performance through greater engagement, stronger teams, and more creativity and innovation.

With twenty-plus years in the field of diversity and a unique background, I have developed some strong opinions about what works, what does not, and what is needed to move the field of diversity and inclusion forward. Drawing on this experience and focusing on my current corporate role with responsibility for building and leading a results-oriented strategy, I want to share what I believe is needed to be effective and successful. Along the way, I indicate how I think this book, *The Practice of Inclusion,* aligns with and supports a corporate leader's work. I include key observations on the field of diversity and inclusion and make recommendations for how professionals and the field of diversity and inclusion (or "D&I" as we practitioners often refer to it) can evolve into the future.

What Needs to Be Either Present or Put in Place to Create Inclusion

To build and drive effective, sustainable, results-oriented, and truly transformational strategy—beyond benchmark practices—there are key considerations, tactics, and competencies that need to be either present or developed and put in place. Before I explain, here is what I mean by some of the words I just used:

- *Effective:* In simple terms, it works; it gets the expected results.
- *Sustainable:* It lasts; it becomes part of the fabric of the business and its way of doing things.
- *Results-oriented:* It provides outcomes, measured qualitatively and/or quantitatively.
- *Transformational:* It enhances the motivation, morale, and performance of people and the organization.
- *Considerations:* It encourages us to think in the broadest sense.
- *Tactics:* It means taking action.
- *Competencies:* It requires personal and organizational capabilities.

I make a point of defining these words because in business we often throw vernacular around as if universally understood or supported by action, when without shared and understood meaning and without behaviorally and process-based application, these words are just words. Hence, my recommendations that follow begin with establishing clear definitions.

Establish Clear Definitions with Shared Understanding, Actionable Behaviors, Processes, and Outcomes

Clear definitions and shared understanding help establish strategy, tactics, expected outcomes, metrics, and more. It is not that every company needs the same definition; rather, it is important that everyone within a company have clarity on what they mean when they say *diversity* and *inclusion*. Throughout *The Practice of Inclusion*, contributors define terms and ensure clarity of purpose and content. Scholarly rigor may seem arduous at times to the business person, but in fact there is much to be learned from the specificity with which scholars operate.

Be Clear on Context

Let's be clear: the first part of this book's title is *Diversity at Work*— we are talking about the workplace! Our definitions of diversity and inclusion, our strategies, and our tactics must be framed in the context of work. I need to use language and definitions that have meaning in the context of what the company is about. Personally, I rarely use the term *inclusion*. (Yes, I'm bucking the trend of most of my colleagues.) I do, however, use the word *diversity*. My infrequent use of *inclusion* does not mean that it is not important to what I do. In fact, I consider inclusion to be mission-critical. Nevertheless, my preference is to use more business-oriented, less altruistic-sounding terms that tend to have more meaning in the business context, such as "engagement," "reducing barriers," "finding new sources of talent," and "unleashing potential." As the concept of inclusion becomes clearer and more connected to work, it will be easier to use and better understood.

Start with the End in Mind

To use Covey's (2004) concept and phrase, I believe starting with the end in mind is absolutely essential. The organization's goals and objectives are critical to accomplishing its mission. Understanding and communicating how diversity can support business objectives (as well as how exclusion can inhibit performance) will help drive a successful strategy, and it will help engage the commitment and support of the organization's leaders, managers, and employees.

Balance the Business Case with the Right Thing to Do

I agree with Hayles's assertion (in Chapter 2) that facts are not enough when communicating about diversity. A business case argument without understanding emotional issues and responses can backfire, stall, and even halt a process. Emotional connections can also be used to leverage progress. Sometimes, when facts do not work, an emotional appeal to altruism may work. The "head, heart, and hand" model that Hayles explains is extremely valuable and influences everything I do. If I consistently consider each, I develop better solutions.

When I wrote my first report on the "Business Case" (Wheeler, 1995) someone said to me, "Michael, there was a business case for slavery." That comment was seared into my memory. That individual was right. The business case, while critical, is limited. There are reasons for laws, checks, and balances. Human rights and dignity and emotional well-being are ultimately critical to healthy businesses and society.

Develop (for Self) and Build (for Others) Cultural Competence

This recommendation applies to leaders, including diversity leaders, employees, teams, and even the organization. I see my job in part as helping these constituencies develop cultural competence. I accomplish this with information, education, training, and dialogue.

Cultural competence is not a separate capability, but a truly integrated intelligence that is part of and woven into every other skill and competency. I consider cultural competence to encompass "multiple types of intelligence—social and emotional" (Wasserman, Chapter 4, this volume). It requires the ability to use "head, heart, and hand" (Hayles, Chapter 2), as well as having "cognitive, affective, and behavioral skills and characteristics that support appropriate and effective interaction in a variety of cultural contexts" (see the definition of intercultural competence in Bennett, Chapter 5).

It is important to call out a critical component of cultural competence that I call *nuance*. Just about any professional who knows how to get things done can implement a diversity strategy. But not everyone is culturally competent or understands nuance enough to do it well. Nuance is seeing what others do not see. It is about understanding the background, history, and complexity of the issues at play in the workplace and in the world. The following are a few examples of understanding nuance:

- Not assuming that because an individual is Asian he or she understands the "Asian marketplace," which encompasses a broad array of countries, cultures, and people.
- Knowing that, although the term *Hispanic* represents a common language—Spanish—the nations and cultures that speak that language are actually quite diverse and that Latinos in the United States are mostly native-born. In Miami, a mariachi band might not be the right choice for a Hispanic or Latino marketing event!
- Knowing why the term *sexual preference* is a hot button for the LGBT community.
- Observing the subtle differences in body language and interactions across a diverse team and how microinequities and microaffirmations are constantly at play (see Offermann & Basford, Chapter 8; Wasserman, Chapter 4; Winters, Chapter 7).
- Recognizing that U.S.-based HR demographic metrics do not apply outside the United States. This one may just be good common sense, but it remains an issue globally (see Jonsen & Özbilgin, Chapter 12; Offermann & Basford, Chapter 8).
- Noticing who is *not* present as well as who is present in the boardroom, in interviews, and on teams across the company (see Gallegos, Chapter 6; Wasserman, Chapter 4).
- Understanding why *diverse people* might actually be an exclusive term (see Ferdman & Roberts, Chapter 3).
- Knowing why, as Hayles (Chapter 2) points out, "fact-based" communication about diversity and inclusion is not enough to support change.

The diversity executive must have radar tuned in to frequencies to which others are not necessarily attending. This comes as a result of experience and education, knowledge acquisition, and practice. And, of course, exposure to, interaction with, and feedback from people different from one's self.

I would also reinforce the importance of the "inherently interdisciplinary" aspect of cultural competence highlighted by Bennett (Chapter 5), spanning "sociology, business, linguistics, intercultural communication, counseling, social work, cultural geography, anthropology, and education" (pp. 157–158). Additionally, systems theory (see, for example, Katz & Kahn, 1978; Parsons, 1977; von Bertalanffy, 1969)—which involves understanding how the components of a larger whole are interconnected and each is influenced by the others—can help one identify and make connections between seemingly disparate fields and disciplines. Specific tasks at hand can help corporate practitioners pull it all together and more effectively determine strategy. *The Practice of Inclusion* conveniently helps us make the connections between scholarly research and its workplace applications, between theory and practice, and among different fields and disciplines. This ability to make connections is itself a key component of cultural competence.

Engage Different Perspectives

As someone who attempts to be constantly aware of inclusion, I often ask myself, "Who is not here?" or "What other perspectives should I seek out?" In the business context it is very important to engage different roles and functions to help create inclusion. I need to talk to marketing, research and development, sales, human resources, and finance to gain better understanding and to garner buy-in. They need to learn to talk to each other. I also need to leverage employees' and leaders' involvement through dialogues, employee resource or affinity groups, and diversity councils. These are structurally integrated ways to ensure inclusion. *The Practice of Inclusion* models the engagement of different perspectives for the practitioner, which significantly enhances our understanding, raises our awareness, and identifies models and tactics to aid in our work to create inclusion. Having interpersonal, organizational, social, and business models of inclusion available to turn to is extremely valuable.

Leverage Benchmark Practices

For as long as I have been doing this work and served as a resource to corporate leaders, I have frequently been asked the question: "What works?" My answer always is, "It depends, but . . ." The "it depends" simply means there is no one-size-fits-all. The "but" means there are some core components of any strong, comprehensive benchmark strategy. O'Mara and Richter (see O'Mara, Chapter 14) have effectively compiled, in their Global Diversity and Inclusion Benchmarks, the core items that I believe are needed for any successful strategy. Hundreds of years of combined experience and insights went into the development of these benchmarks. Every strategy should incorporate as many of the benchmarks as are pertinent, but that does not mean all strategies will look the same.

Observations in the Field of Diversity and Inclusion

In the early 1990s, I was asked by a reporter if diversity was a fad, the "latest flavor of the month." My response was, "No. I don't know what it might be called in twenty years, but diversity is a force of change that will force change." Twenty years later, now that we see how what we call "diversity and inclusion" has become well established, I can say I was right. No brilliant insight on my part! Diversity represents a simple yet powerful global force for change.

We can measure progress, in part, by the large number of chief diversity officers (CDOs) sitting in the C-suite, the fact that most Fortune 500 companies now have some form of D&I strategy, and the creation of an entire diversity industry. Current statistics tell us that employees in corporations reflect much of the diversity of the workforce. Almost everyone in the corporate world in the United States has had some kind of exposure to a diversity initiative. At the same time, the diversity of the population has exceeded prior predictions. Progress on diversity initiatives can be attributed in large part to historical events, key figures in time, corporate diversity pioneers, advocacy groups and organizations, legislation, and customer and business demands resulting from changing demographics.

Amid progress there remain numerous challenges. Despite the fact that many corporations reflect the diversity of the population, distribution and representation across levels and functions remains disproportionate in many cases. Exclusion continues to be easier than inclusion. Systemic forms of discrimination and oppression (such as racism, sexism, heterosexism) still exist. The progression of the field of diversity and our corporations gets stalled for a variety of reasons.

Why We Have Not Made More Progress on Inclusion in Corporations

Considering the context of this book, and from my point of view as a corporate diversity leader, I conclude by focusing on what I see as the key barriers to progress. By no means is this list comprehensive. Rather, it is a focused list of key challenges for which I believe there are solutions. I present these issues as high-level observations and provocative food for thought rather than as in-depth analyses.

Complexity

The challenges of inclusion are complex; they are systemic, personal and professional, economic and social, organizational and political, and simply the result of the increased complexity that comes from more diversity at multiple levels. This complexity can seem overwhelming and may sometimes contribute to the lack of progress. Wasserman (Chapter 4), for example, discusses some of the challenges involved when people are simply trying to make meaning in a diverse workplace and develop their capability to handle complexity. Mor Barak and Daya (Chapter 13) address the complexities of exploring inclusion both inside and outside the walls of the organization with the inclusive workplace model and the corporate inclusion strategy model. Amid complexity, employers and employees often look for simple solutions not quite suited for complex issues.

Competing Issues

At work, people are tasked with deliverables. If diversity and inclusion are perceived as something else to do, without a clear understanding of why it matters to those primary deliverables, diversity and inclusion will fall by the wayside. There is also sometimes competition associated with diversity—within and across groups. There is what I call the "my diversity is more important than your diversity" phenomenon, in which individuals or groups seeking inclusion exclude others. One key to inclusion is integrating it into the fundamental work of the organization and its people; the various chapters in this book provide many examples and frameworks for doing this.

Lack of History and Credentialing for Diversity and Inclusion

The field of diversity and inclusion is not yet afforded the same credence as other business fields. No one asks what the chief marketing officer does, or the chief financial officer, or even the chief information officer or chief legal officer. But people do ask, "What does the chief diversity officer do?" When equipped with the credentials that have been afforded the CDO's peers—formal degrees, licensing, accreditation, governing bodies, and associations—there are fewer questions asked, and clearer models and processes to follow. In comparison, a CDO may come from almost any background or discipline, and thus may travel with an incomplete roadmap. This last statement is not a value judgment; it is simply the current case that a CDO's career credentials may be different from other well-established career paths and institutionalized functions and roles. This can often result in a challenging situation for a leader trying to create change and success in an organization. At the very least, CDOs and their staff, regardless of their backgrounds, must become familiar with the concepts and approaches addressed by the chapters in this book.

Untapped Resources

It is rare to find theories, models, and research under the headings of *diversity* or *diversity and inclusion*—whether in the scholarly or particularly in mainstream business literature—that can directly and immediately benefit leaders; this omission remains a huge missed opportunity. It is not that the information does not exist; rather, it lies hidden in various disciplines, such as psychology, sociology, communication, and others. One of the challenges, then, is access. Diversity at work and the practice of inclusion involve a cross- and inter-disciplinary proposition that leverages theory, research, models, and practices with substantive foundations and actionable tactics and behaviors. This is one of the reasons why this book is so important. It brings under one cover a wealth of research and frameworks written in language accessible to leaders and practitioners. And it opens a window into the field of industrial-organizational psychology, where a great deal of relevant knowledge, ideas, and insight are housed.

Lack of Inclusion

Most everyone wants to be included; no one really wants to be excluded. Yet not everyone wants to include. If we want to be included, we need to be inclusive. In the United States, where many individuals and groups traditionally have been underrepresented in and even excluded from the workplace, and where race has played such a major role in its historical challenges, it is difficult sometimes not to see the world, quite literally, in Black and White. The White majority and disproportionate distribution of diversity in corporations make it difficult for both Whites and people of color to see diversity in any other way. With the need to address key historical issues, it is sometimes difficult to see diversity outside the context of us versus them, or majority versus minority. With an emerging "majority minority," we sometimes see pockets of traditional minorities engaging in exclusion. Exclusion and inclusion play out in a variety of ways.

Equipping people with the concepts and the fundamental tools to be inclusive will go a long way toward improving things across the board now and into the future. For example, see Gallegos's recommendations for developing the relational capacities of inclusive leaders (Chapter 6), Booysen's description of ways to develop leaders inclusively (Chapter 10), and Henderson's account of how Weyerhaeuser developed its inclusive leadership program (Chapter 15). These accounts, together with others in this volume, point to the power of inclusion and its practice as a way to go beyond traditional and often divisive distinctions, while continuing to address historical and persisting challenges.

Programmatic and Simplistic Approaches Rather Than Strategic and Systemic Ones

In the early years of the diversity and inclusion effort, most corporations were training people in D&I. There were mixed results: sometimes it backfired, other times it worked. Training, of course, has a role. But there is good training and bad training. There are matters that training cannot address. In particular, trying to create and sustain inclusion with training alone will not work. Strategic and systemic change requires multiple tactics and a deeper understanding of what it takes to drive change. For excellent and thorough examples, see how Church, Rotolo, Shull, and Tuller (Chapter 9) at PepsiCo are practicing inclusive organization development and changing the way they approach four key practices, as well as Nishii and Rich's (Chapter 11) suggestions for creating inclusive climates and enhancing inclusion.

Lack of Clarity on "It"

Those who have been in this field for any time at all have likely heard, or even said, "She (or he) gets it," or "He (or she) just doesn't get it" with regard to D&I. I have asked people what they mean by "it," and their response has often been a pause or a stammer. We need to be able to answer that question definitively, particularly in our organizations. Although *The Practice of Inclusion* does not provide a definitive "it," the book absolutely provides details of what "it" is for inclusion in many of its forms. In particular, see Ferdman's (Chapter 1) account of the concept and its variations and Winters's (Chapter 7) discussion of the inclusion equation.

Recommendations for Moving Forward

Corporate diversity leaders must innovate and enhance their work to be effective and to create sustainable, results-oriented strategies and tactics. We must always be innovating if we are to create inclusive organizations that work for all employees. I conclude with ten recommendations for moving forward.

First, I reiterate: define your terms, be clear on the context you are addressing, and start with the end in mind.

Second, proactively seek specific solutions for barriers discussed in the prior section. For example, if we use clear definitions, as recommended, we will not have to worry about lack of clarity or understanding of "it." We can work with competing issues by helping to understand that inclusion is a way of doing things, not yet another thing to do. We can help manage complexity by focusing on those things we can manage. We want to instill the idea that "I may not be able to change the world, but I can influence change in my environment."

Third, distill complexity into simplicity. But do not be simplistic. I cannot overwhelm already busy leaders and employees with all the details, historical issues, and dynamics at play in the world. Employees and leaders do not necessarily need all the details. However, I myself must thoroughly understand these issues and their implications for the systems I am trying to influence. I look at my role as akin to that of information technology. I do not have to be a programmer to know how to use my computer effectively. The computer is my tool; someone else takes care of the details behind it. In a sense, I do something similar—I create the tools and leverage my expertise so that people and the organization have what they need to be successful with regard to diversity and inclusion.

Fourth, become true corporate partners. Speak the language of business, know the business, and know how diversity can enhance or inhibit goal achievement for your business.

Fifth, recognize that diversity and inclusion matter to all we do. It is not an HR initiative or a program. It does not and cannot stand alone—it permeates everything.

Sixth, manage dissonance. If we are asking people to do what is not natural to them, then we need to be sensitive to the discomfort that may cause. We should not judge, but rather accept where people and things are and work from there. Härtel, Appo, and Hart (Chapter 19) capture some of the dynamic of dissonance with great insights and applications, particularly in their discussion of societal fault lines.

Seventh, constantly be aware of readiness. There is almost always a disconnect between where the diversity leader wants the company or its individuals and teams to be versus where they actually are. But we must start with where people and companies are and help them get to where they need to be. Understanding the stages and processes that individuals and organizations must go through can help the diversity leader be successful. In this regard, Bennett's (Chapter 5) discussion of the stages of how people experience difference is particularly helpful. Note that dissonance and readiness are different, although they are closely related. Dissonance involves the psychological, sociological, political, and economical tensions that are constantly at play. Readiness is more about willingness and ability to accept change.

Eight, be a global citizen. Bennett (Chapter 5) says it perfectly: "Being 'global souls'—seeing ourselves as members of a world community, knowing that we share the future with others— requires powerful intercultural competence. . . . Such competence embraces globalization and seeks to reconcile the competing commitments to self and others. . . . It is grounded in the certainty that we cannot neglect either side of the equation, domestic or international" (p. 155). The United States and, increasingly, other countries around the world are truly microcosms of the rest of the world; we are international and local and the world is global and local. We must see ourselves and others as an integral part of our global village.

Ninth, do not replicate dysfunction. We all have this potential if we are not careful and self-aware of our own conscious or unconscious biases. I have seen individuals as well as employee resource groups and other groups sometimes replicate the very culture of the organizations in which they are trying to overcome barriers. I have seen people and groups who want to be included be exclusive. I have seen groups frustrated with being excluded from a dominant culture when they in turn are not aware of their own exclusionary practices. The practice of inclusion must be implemented for oneself if it is to be expected of others.

Tenth, include! Leverage differences, include multiple perspectives, and engage many others. I can develop expertise and I can gain knowledge, but I can never know it all. We all need others to complement our skills and competencies, to provide important insights, and to inspire us to be more creative and innovative to accomplish the important work at hand.

References

Covey, S. R. (2004). *The 7 habits of highly effective people: Powerful lessons in personal change* (rev. ed.). New York: Free Press.

Katz, D., & Kahn, R. L. (1978). *The social psychology of organizations* (2nd ed.). New York: Wiley.

Parsons, T. (1977). *Social systems and the evolution of action theory.* New York: Free Press.

von Bertalanffy, L. (1969). *General system theory: Foundations, development, applications* (rev. ed.). New York: George Braziller.

Wheeler, M. L. (1995). Diversity: Business rationale and strategies: A research report. Report 1130–95-RR, The Conference Board, New York.

CHAPTER TWENTY-ONE

An I/O Psychologist's Perspective on Diversity and Inclusion in the Workplace

Angelo S. DeNisi

Although the Civil Rights Act of 1964 was passed when I was in high school, my only real exposure to the law was what I saw on television when students were barred from entering college campuses. Only later, when I was a graduate student, did I come to learn more about all the implications of the law, especially relative to the workplace. But this was the time when I/O psychologists were really getting involved in issues of discrimination at work. Whether they were working with companies trying to defend their hiring practices, with plaintiffs trying to prove they were the victims of discrimination, or explaining what different types of discrimination might look like statistically (see, for example, Cleary, 1968; Darlington, 1971), these issues occupied a lot of the space in which I/O psychologists were working.

By the 1980s, when I had graduated and been working for a while, although these topics still commanded a great deal of attention, the focus began to shift to identifying methods for selection and appraisal that had less disparate impact. Also, during this period, I/O psychologists were spending more time dealing with discrimination on the basis of gender, age, and disabilities, although race discrimination was still seen as an important topic. The point in all of this research, however, was that the United States had laws forbidding discrimination, and that we psychologists (and others) should help organizations to make good employment decisions without violating the law. That is, most of this work was concerned with nondiscrimination—it was all about avoiding something that was wrong. Surely, we were all honorable people, and so avoiding doing something illegal was important, and surely, we could all appreciate that giving everyone in our country equal access to employment opportunities was the "right" thing to do from a moral perspective.

Things were changing, however. As the 1990s began, it became clear that there was more to this issue than nondiscrimination. The relevant laws in the United States dealt with only discrimination, but scholars and practitioners began discussing the potential benefits of increasing diversity in the workplace. Thus the focus had shifted from issues of compliance or noncompliance to arguments that, the law aside, organizations could benefit from having a workforce in which people of different genders, races, religions, nationalities, sexual orientations, backgrounds, and interests all worked together. The discussion had shifted from a legal case for diversity to a business case for diversity. Unfortunately, the empirical support for this case was not very strong. Several authors reported evidence to suggest that diversity could present problems for organizations (see, for example, Michel & Hambrick, 1992; Tsui, Egan, & O'Reilly, 1992), while others reported no significant effects of diversity on organizational outcomes (see, for example, Jackson et al., 1991; Riordan & Shore, 1997). Gonzalez and DeNisi (2009), in a later study, reported that diversity climate moderated several relationships between diversity and outcomes at both the individual and firm levels. This study is interesting, though, because the authors reported almost no negative effects for any type of diversity, in a company in which, overall, there was a great deal of diversity and where, in fact, White, non-Hispanic employees were in a minority.

Thus it is perhaps not surprising that, in a major review of the literature tying diversity to firm-level outcomes, Kochan et al. (2003) found no real evidence for any systematic links, leading them to conclude that "diversity professionals, industry leaders, and researchers might do better to recognize that while there is no reason to believe diversity will naturally translate into better or worse results, diversity is both a labor-market imperative and societal expectation and value. Therefore managers might do better to focus on building an organizational culture, human resource practices, and the managerial and group process skills needed to translate diversity into positive organizational, group, and individual results" (p. 18).

This brings us to the focus of this volume. There is no longer any question about whether we can discriminate in offering employment opportunities (although I am not so naïve as to believe that there is no discrimination anywhere). Furthermore, it is now clear that diversity is a reality in the workplace. In the United States, the workforce is becoming more female, less White, and more Hispanic. If firms want to compete for the best people in the market, they must seek a diverse workforce. If they don't, they will simply be limiting the pool of talent from which they can draw, and they will hurt themselves competitively. Therefore there is no need to argue that diversity is either good or bad—it just "is." As I discuss in this chapter, some authors in this volume note that this may not be the case in every part of the world, which raises some interesting issues. But for the most part, experts agree that building a diverse workforce is largely a business necessity.

Returning to the conclusions from Kochan et al. (2003), and echoing the points raised by most of the authors in this volume, building a diverse workforce is not enough. As already noted, a number of studies have clearly demonstrated some negative effects of diversity in a workplace. The challenge facing organizations today is how to avoid (or minimize) any potential negative effects of workforce diversity, while still enjoying any positive effects. The question then is, how does a firm leverage the various interests, skills, and ideas of all the people who work there and make everyone feel valued and part of the organization? Many scholars, including those associated with this volume, believe that policies and programs designed to increase inclusion are the key to unlocking the potential benefits of diversity for the individual, the firm, and the society.

In this chapter, I discuss some of the implications of these inclusion efforts for I/O psychology and suggest some areas where research and practice might focus in the future. I briefly discuss the content of the specific chapters, all of which provide interesting ideas and insights. Some focus on specific cases; I say less about those, because they largely speak for themselves. I also spend more time discussing chapters that raise issues that might be more controversial, but it is not my intent to "review" or "critique" the chapters, rather simply to summarize what each contains as a basis to describe where I think we can go from here.

The Contents of This Volume

The volume begins with an introduction by one of the editors and ends with an overview by the two co-editors. There are also chapters in which a diversity scholar and a corporate diversity officer offer their own insights from reading this volume. I will comment, very briefly, on Chapter 1, but will not comment, even briefly, on any of these other chapters.

The Preface and Chapter 1 lay out the strategy and structure of this volume. Chapter 1 provides an overview of the construct of inclusion and sets the tone for the rest of the volume, but requires no further comment by me. Thus I begin my commentary focusing on Chapter 2. Here, Robert Hayles introduces a theme that is woven through much of the volume—the critical nature of communications in building inclusion. This is the first of several chapters that deal with interpersonal skills as the key to building inclusion. But Hayles is not suggesting that we simply communicate the facts of how diverse our workforce may be, or what we are doing about inclusion. He notes that simply communicating such facts is not enough. Instead, he is interested in how people communicate with each other in ways designed to reduce prejudice and bias. In this regard, he is the first author in this volume, but by no means the last, who discusses the importance of sensitivity training and even advocates psychotherapeutic ways of helping employees to be more inclusive. He goes further to suggest that top management communicate all the ways in which diversity benefits the firm and even appeal to morals and ideas of fairness in convincing employees to be inclusive, and that training should include information about etiquette and cultural norms regarding communication.

Later, in Chapter 4, Wasserman sounds a similar theme. She emphasizes the importance of developing the interpersonal skills needed to deal effectively with a diverse workforce. Wasserman is the first (chronologically) in this volume who discusses the role of emotional intelligence in this process. I believe that the concept of emotional intelligence (referred to as EQ by some) has been broadened to the point that it is almost useless, but originally it was defined clearly and precisely by Salovey and Mayer (see, for example, Salovey & Mayer, 1990) as "the subset of social intelligence that involves the ability to monitor one's own and others' feelings and emotions, to discriminate among them and to use this information to guide one's thinking and action" (p. 189; italics in original removed). If we keep to this more precise definition, then EQ definitely plays a role in organizational efforts to increase inclusion.

In Chapter 5, Janet Bennett frames some related concerns in terms of dealing with employees across different cultures. This is a useful way of approaching the issue, because inclusion means accepting and reaching out to people who are dissimilar to us in a variety of ways. It is also worth noting here that there is also a role for a construct that is related to EQ, but has been defined and measured more precisely—that of cultural intelligence (CQ: Earley & Ang, 2003). Bennett goes on to discuss training to improve intercultural sensitivity and the Developmental Model of Intercultural Sensitivity (or DMIS; M. J. Bennett, 1986). The model is an interesting one, describing the steps one must take in moving from being ethnocentric to becoming ethnorelative (whereby difference is sought after). According to the model, we move from denial of differences, to defense of our identity relative to others, to minimization of those differences, to acceptance, adaptation, and finally integration—the latter defined as the capability to shift cultural frames of reference. It is also interesting to note how this chapter relates to an earlier (Chapter 3) discussion by Ferdman and Roberts about the need to access one's multiple identities in an effort to become more inclusive at work. It would seem that factors such as EQ and CQ are related to one's ability to access these identities and use them at work.

There are also a number of chapters that stress the need for leadership in this process. Not only should leaders set a good example for inclusion, but leaders are also responsible, to a large extent, for setting the climate for inclusion. Gallegos (Chapter 6) is the first to formally raise the issue of leadership. She draws on Avolio and Gardner's (2005) idea of authentic leadership, stating that authentic leaders demonstrate awareness of self and context, and are seen as "confident, hopeful, optimistic, resilient, and of high moral character" (Avolio, Luthans & Walumbwa, 2004, quoted by Avolio & Gardner, 2005, and by Gallegos). She also calls for greater concern for communal interests and the development of mutual trust and respect to develop a strong collective identity, being flexible as demands shift, and acting ethically. I should also note that Gallegos is pushing a very different agenda for leadership than is typical of leadership scholars, noting that, for true inclusion, we cannot have a single leader who has all the responsibility and a lot of followers who simply carry out directives.

Later (Chapter 10), Booysen returns to the topic of leadership and leader training, raising the related issues of how we can make leadership development more inclusive and how we can train leaders to be more inclusive. She calls for more inclusive models of leadership—models that focus on valuing diversity and effective management and inclusion of all and that move from affirmative action and equity toward equality, fairness, and social justice. Interestingly, Booysen seemed to equate equality with fairness and justice. Although equality of opportunity is clearly something that most people would agree is fair, equality as a rule for determining the fair distribution of outcomes is likely not what they would consider to be fair. In fact, most justice scholars within the United States would equate equity with fairness, and, in other cultures, fairness might be equated to things such as need (see, for example, the discussion in Roch & Shanock, 2006).

But in the end, many of the chapters in this volume really concentrate on ways to improve the climate and the culture for diversity. This is the goal of the chapters already discussed that deal with interpersonal skills and leadership; it is also the focus of several chapters that deal explicitly with ways to improve climate and culture at work.

Winters (Chapter 7) calls for integrated practices and policies, supported at the highest level in the organization, as the keys to establishing an inclusive climate and culture. This chapter is followed by Offermann and Basford's (Chapter 8) discussion of specific HR practices that have been shown to improve the climate for inclusion, citing a number of success stories in which an inclusive climate was created by more enlightened HR practices. Following that, we have Church, Rotolo, Shull, and Tuller's (Chapter 9) discussion on how firms can make inclusion a core element of organization development efforts, citing specific examples from PepsiCo and other large firms. Finally, Nishii and Rich (Chapter 11) provide a specific model of how to build more inclusive cultures, and they report on the success of some efforts to make that happen. It seems clear that many of the authors in this volume see the creation of a climate and culture of inclusion as the most critical aspect of any effort to build inclusion.

Two other chapters from these first three parts of the book do not fit neatly into the framework I have been using. In Chapter 13, Mor Barak and Daya discuss the inclusive workplace model, which highlights the role of the community and society as stakeholders. Basically, this model suggests that organizations should (1) value and utilize individual and intergroup differences in its workforce, (2) cooperate with and contribute to the surrounding community, (3) alleviate the needs of the disadvantaged groups in its wider environment, and (4) collaborate with organizations and groups across national and cultural boundaries. Thus they go beyond notions of corporate social responsibility (CSR), which they say does good and enhances profits but, while they cite many examples from around the world of firms that are profitable and do good for others outside the firm, there are other scholars who do not believe that the link between CSR and firm performance has been established or should even be a goal for organizations (cf. Aupperle, Carroll, & Hatfield, 1985; Friedman, 1970). Personally, I agree that there is evidence to suggest that firms can both do good and be profitable, but it is worth noting that not everyone agrees.

Among those who might disagree are Jonsen and Özbilgin (Chapter 12). They suggest that diversity grows out of the U.S. Civil Rights Act (which may not be the case), and is really a U.S.-based concept that has begun to travel around the world. They worry about the future of global diversity management because in many countries there are no laws fostering diversity. They also argue that "diversity is an essential condition for life on Earth. Yet, as the evidence of diversity's effects on organizational perfor-mance is rich but inconclusive, it can be hard to grasp how to effectively manage it" (p. 383). Research has failed to convinc-ingly deal with how organizations interpret workforce diversity and inclusion, and, more important, how they should go about implementing diversity and inclusion management on a global scale. The authors conclude by stating their concern that diversity may end up as a tragedy of the uncommons (see Jonsen, Tatli, Özbilgin, & Bell, 2013), because society as a whole is losing out, as individual organizations either do not use or take advantage of diversity or simply disregard it. Thus Jonsen and Özbilgin argue that, ideally, diversity and inclusion efforts should not be a strate-gic choice per se but rather a logical consequence of societal reality. I will return to this point shortly.

The remaining chapters in the volume deal with examples of cases in which organizations have successfully become more inclu-sive. These require no comment, nor do they benefit from any attempt on my part to draw out common themes. In fact, these chapters do an excellent job of demonstrating that building diverse and inclusive organizations is in fact a real possibility—notably, when dealing with very old issues regarding the Aborigi-nal peoples in Australia.

What Does an I/O Psychologist Make of This?

It is interesting to note the discussion of basic definitions that flows through these chapters. Although most of the authors agree with the distinctions I made at the beginning of this chapter, not everyone does. The laws in the United States outlaw discrimination, but do not go far beyond that. Thus U.S. lawmakers have assumed that, if firms ceased discriminatory practices, they would become more diverse; however, except in very narrow cases, there is nothing in the U.S. legal system that mandates diversity per se. But it is even more important to recognize that there are probably no legal systems anywhere that mandate inclusion—yet it seems clear to me that nondiscrimination and diversity management do not gain much for anyone without policies that promote inclusion.

Fortunately, though, it seems to me that this is one of the few instances in which everyone involved has aligned interests. Whether or not there is a law forbidding discrimination, the globalization of business in the world and the changing demographics in countries such as the United States mean that increased diversity in the workplace is simply becoming the reality. In many countries, individuals who had been denied access to work now find they are sought out by employers who find it increasingly difficult to find talented employees. This means that everyone will be working with people who look different from them, speak different languages, eat different food, and have different cultural and religious beliefs (among other differences). Given that these changes are already occurring and are inevitable, organizations must find ways to deal with these diverse work forces more effectively, and must find ways to leverage this diversity to produce some competitive advantage.

As noted by many of the authors of the chapters in this volume, making every member of the organization feel valued is a good thing to do for its own sake. Furthermore, it seems only right to acknowledge the unique characteristics of coworkers (or students, or clients, or whomever) and to celebrate those aspects of uniqueness. But it is not only the right thing to do; it is also the road to gaining competitive advantage. As noted earlier, there is sufficient literature to illustrate that diversity can bring problems as well as benefits. The key is to develop practices and policies by which all employees feel valued and contribute. In this way, organizations can minimize the negative effects of diversity and maximize the positive ones. Thus building cultures of inclusion is not only good sense; it is also good business. An organization cannot logically be "against" inclusion, unless it is willing to forego hiring every employee who can be effective on the job. In the United States, such a policy would be illegal, but regardless of the laws, a more diverse workforce brings fresh ideas and fresh approaches to solving problems, and it gives organizations a face that looks like their customer and client base. Thus, in my opinion, the discussion should not be about whether building inclusion is good or not—it should instead be about how to best build cultures and climates for inclusion that allow us to capture the value of every one of our employees.

What Can I/O Psychologists Contribute to This Issue?

In my view, there are several distinct areas in which I/O psychologists can make contributions that are not easy to find elsewhere—areas where I/O psychologists could make a difference. One distinct competency possessed by I/O psychologists is good measurement skills. These skills can be useful in trying to find ways to assess the success or failure of any inclusion policies. Several of the chapters in this volume, in discussing climate, stated that a climate for inclusion is one in which everyone feels valued and free to participate. Is that a goal or is that how inclusion should be evaluated? Perhaps more critically, is there a way to assess perceived inclusion without confounding it with performance or competence? That is, a person may feel undervalued because of some demographic variable, but that perception may arise because he or she is simply not very competent. We must assume that poor performance, like good performance, is equally distributed in every group, but we also know that people tend to attribute their own poor performance to external factors. When we say we want everyone to feel valued, does that mean that someone who cannot generate good ideas is listened to in the same way as someone who *can* generate good ideas? I realize that the definition of a "good idea" could be socially construed by the majority group, but that does not obviate the need to be sure we can separate perceptions of inclusion and real levels of competence. This seems to be an area where I/O psychologists can really help.

Measurement issues seem to also be relevant when assessing the outcomes associated with diversity and inclusion. Reading these chapters, it seems that a fair amount of the evidence supporting the importance of inclusion is anecdotal. Furthermore, noting that several of the authors have firms that specialize in this area and/or instruments that could be used, it seems even more important that we be sure we can reliably measure the outcomes associated with greater inclusion. It is interesting to note that, although I/O psychologists are very good at assessing outcomes such as individual performance, and even group performance, they are less successful in assessing firm performance (cf. DeNisi, 2000), which will be critical going forward.

Another area in which I/O psychologists could help is in establishing reward systems to foster inclusion. I/O psychologists have been studying work teams for many years and have written a great deal about the trade-offs in various team reward schemes (see, for example, Brannick, Salas, & Prince, 1997). Specifically, they have written about the problems of rewarding individuals within groups instead of the entire team (namely, this can foster competition instead of cooperation) and the problems associated with rewarding teams but not individuals (that is, it can foster free-riding). There is no single answer for all the cases involving teams and rewards, but the work of I/O psychologists can certainly contribute to the discussion of designing ideal team reward systems while building inclusion.

Of course, I/O psychologists have been deeply involved in selection and testing, and this may be one of the most important areas in which I/O psychologists can make a contribution. How do we select people to encourage and reinforce inclusion? What kind of person will be able to contribute to an inclusive organization? These are two important questions that I/O psychology may be able to help answer. The answer to the first question seems to lie in research and practice related to affirmative action and selection fairness. For example, there may be less concern for policies of inclusion if an organization's selection system yields only White males from which to choose employees (although even in this case we should be concerned about inclusion in terms of a wide range of social identities, including age and sexual orientation). But even if a firm could defend this outcome, it ignores the potential benefits that can come with a more diverse workforce, and it probably would be difficult to defend such an outcome in court. Affirmative action, although much maligned in some quarters, simply refers to efforts to identify qualified applicants from groups that are underrepresented. It does not have to include any type of preferential hiring, although some firms choose to give preference to members of underrepresented groups.

There is, however, an alternative to traditional selection models that, although quite controversial, provides some insight into what I/O psychologists might be able to contribute. In most selection settings, we give some test to a group of applicants and then select the person (or persons) with the highest test scores. In truth, selection is rarely this simple (as discussed by Murphy, 2004), but a willing suspension of disbelief for a moment will help me explain the notion of "banding." Let us suppose that the test scores of three of the applicants for this job (two men and one woman) are close enough to each other to not make much difference in terms of predicted performance. In this case, why couldn't a firm make a selection decision on the basis of some-thing other than test scores (race, gender, or some other factor altogether)? If, for example, the organization was concerned that women were underrepresented at this job level, the organi-zation could give preference to the woman, hire her, improve diversity, and not really suffer from a decrement in performance (this approach, too is controversial, and there are other ways of forming bands as well). This is a complicated idea that is open to legal as well as logical objections (see Aguinis, 2004, for a wide range of papers on this topic), but it does offer some insight into what I/O psychologists could offer to organizations interested in increasing diversity. More research and discussion of various banding models and their implication could truly make a difference.

The answer to the second question, concerning hiring people who will foster inclusion, seems more difficult to address. Even if an organization has hired a diverse workforce, the challenge is to figure out how to leverage that diversity for competitive advantage; that is where policies of inclusion become important. Several authors have discussed the importance of training and development, but it is also important that we select employees who can appreciate the virtues of inclusion. The proposal that employees higher in emotional intelligence (EQ) or cultural intelligence (CQ) would be more inclusive was raised explicitly by Wasserman and Bennett and alluded to by several other authors. Is this truly the case? Are individuals who are more attuned to their own actions and the cultures of others more likely to foster a climate of inclusion? It seems reasonable, but there are no hard data I know of regarding this. Do we have the best methods available to measure these constructs? This is a related issue that I/O psychologists can weigh in on. There does seem to be an acceptable measure of CQ (see Earley & Ang, 2003), but defining and measuring EQ is more controversial. There are issues concerning how broadly the construct has been defined, and there are issues related to how EQ should be measured and used (see, for example, discussion by Ashkanasy & Daus, 2005). But the resources of I/O psychology could be brought to bear on both of these issues and better definitions and measures developed.

Are there other personality variables or values that might predict support for inclusion? Surely personality constructs such as "openness to experience," from the Big Five personality traits, might be a good predictor, and measures of fairness as a value might also be useful in this regard. I/O psychologists could help here by beginning research programs aimed at identifying individuals more likely to be inclusive at work.

There are surely other areas where research efforts on the part of I/O psychologists could aid in the development of the practice of inclusion. For example, several authors discuss training and development interventions that include providing employees with feedback about their own behavior and its impact on others. But scholars have raised questions about the effectiveness of feedback for changing behavior in all situations (for example, Kluger & DeNisi, 1998). What types of feedback would be most useful for helping employees understand their impact on others? Would any single type of feedback program work equally well for all employees? These are further examples of questions that I/O psychologists could address in future research.

In conclusion, there are a number of areas where I/O psychologists can help the development of practices and policies for inclusion. I hope that this volume will help convince some of them that this is a topic worth devoting themselves to. As I noted earlier, it seems that when it comes to the topic of inclusion, everyone's interests are aligned. If one assumes that the workforce everywhere is becoming more diverse, then we need to develop practices that foster inclusion to allow firms to leverage the advantages offered by these diverse workers. As Winters notes in Chapter 7, "diversity is about counting heads; inclusion is about making heads count" (p. 206). In order to develop an inclusive culture, we need to work on systems (procedures, policies, and so on) managed by people who really believe in inclusion (not people who just say that they do), so that inclusion is part of the strategic vision of the firm. Only then will an organization create a culture in which, as outlined by Nishii and Rich, every employee will be safe in expressing his or her own true identities. I believe that I/O psychologists can help create this type of culture, and I believe that this volume may convince some of them to start.

References

Aguinis, H. (Ed.). (2004). *Test-score banding in human resource selection: Technical, legal, and societal issues.* Westport, CT: Praeger.

Ashkanasy, N. M., & Daus, C. S. (2005). Rumors of the death of emotional intelligence in organizational behavior are vastly exaggerated. *Journal of Organizational Behavior, 26,* 441–452.

Aupperle, K. E., Carroll, A. B., & Hatfield, J. D. (1985). An empirical examination of the relationship between corporate social responsibility and profitability. *Academy of Management Journal, 26,* 446–463.

Avolio, B. J., & Gardner, W. L. (2005). Authentic leadership development: Getting to the root of positive forms of leadership. *Leadership Quarterly, 16,* 315–320.

Bennett, M. J. (1986). A developmental approach to training for intercultural sensitivity. *International Journal of Intercultural Relations, 10,* 179–196.

Brannick, M. T., Salas, E., & Prince, C. (1997). *Team performance assessment and measurement: Theory, methods, and applications.* Mahwah, NJ: Erlbaum.

Cleary, T. A. (1968). Test bias: Prediction of grades of Negro and White students in integrated colleges. *Journal of Educational Measurement, 5*, 115–124.

Darlington, R. B. (1971). Another look at "cultural fairness." *Journal of Educational Measurement, 8*, 71–82.

DeNisi, A. S. (2000). Performance appraisal and performance management: A multilevel analysis. In K. Klein & S. Kozlowski (Eds.), *Multilevel theory, research, and methods in organizations: Foundations, extensions, and new directions* (pp. 121–156). San Francisco: Jossey-Bass.

Earley, P. C., & Ang, S. (2003). *Cultural intelligence: Individual interactions across cultures.* Stanford, CA: Stanford University Press.

Friedman, M. (1970, September 13). The social responsibility of business is to increase its profits. *New York Times Magazine,* pp. 122–126.

Gonzalez, J., & DeNisi, A. S. (2009). Cross-level effects of demography and diversity climate on organizational attachment and firm effectiveness. *Journal of Organizational Behavior, 30*, 21–40.

Jackson, S. E., Brett, J. F., Sessa, V. I., Cooper, D. M., Julinn, J. A., & Peyronnin, K. (1991). Some differences make a difference: Individual dissimilarity and group heterogeneity as correlates of recruitment, promotions, and turnover. *Journal of Applied Psychology, 76*, 675–689.

Jonsen, K., Tatli, A., Özbilgin, M. F., & Bell, M. P. (2013). The tragedy of the uncommons: Reframing workforce diversity. *Human Relations, 66*, 271–294.

Kluger, A. N., & DeNisi, A. S. (1998). Feedback interventions: Toward the understanding of a double-edged sword. *Current Directions in Psychological Science, 7*(3), 67–72.

Kochan, T., Bezrukova, K., Ely, R., Jackson, S., Joshi, A., Jehn, K., . . . Thomas, D. (2003). The effects of diversity on business performance: Report of the Diversity Research Network. *Human Resource Management, 42*, 3–21.

Michel, J., & Hambrick, D. (1992). Diversification posture and top management team characteristics. *Academy of Management Journal, 35*, 9–37.

Murphy, K. R. (2004). Conflicting values and interests in banding research and practice. In H. Aguinis (Ed.), *Test-score banding in human resource selection: Technical, legal, and societal issues* (pp. 175–192). Westport, CT: Praeger.

Riordan, C. M., & Shore, L. M. (1997). Demographic diversity and employee attitudes: An empirical examination of relational demography within work units. *Journal of Applied Psychology, 82*, 342–358.

Roch, S., & Shanock, L. (2006). Organizational justice in exchange frameworks: Clarifying organizational justice distinctions. *Journal of Management, 32,* 299–322.

Salovey, P., & Mayer, J. D. (1990). Emotional intelligence. *Imagination, Cognition, and Personality, 9,* 185–211.

Tsui, A. S., Egan, T. D., & O'Reilly, C. A. (1992). Being different: Relational demography and organizational attachment. *Administrative Science Quarterly, 37,* 549–579.

CHAPTER TWENTY-TWO

Inclusion: Old Wine in New Bottles?

Stella M. Nkomo

An initial reaction to the concept of inclusion is that it may very well be a case of old wine in new bottles, or what Oswick and Noon (in press) argue is a "rhetorical management fashion." Calling for inclusion in opposition to exclusion is a natural theoretical and practical response to the historical barriers to workplace equality in organizations. One might ask whether, indeed, this was not also the aim of diversity management in organizations. To answer this question, it may be useful to examine the evolution of theoretical and practical prescriptions for ending racism, sexism, ableism, and heterosexism in the workplace. Such a review may assist in really understanding how the inclusion approach differs from earlier responses to workplace exclusion. I begin this chapter by tracing the historical evolution of theoretical and practical approaches to dealing with social identity differences in the workplace. The focus is on the United States, as it is the country where research and practical attention began. I am mindful, however, that greater attention has been paid to transnational conceptions of diversity and inequality in the workplace more recently (see, for example, Calás, Holgersson, & Smircich, 2010; Klarsfeld, 2010; Mor Barak, 2011; Özbilgin & Syed, 2010). Next, I critically and reflectively examine the ways in which inclusion is different from or similar to previous approaches, drawing from the contributions in this book. Finally, I conclude with some thoughts about the prospects for inclusion being realized.

Historical Evolution of Approaches to Managing Diversity in the Workplace

The incorporation into the workplace of employees who were not considered members of the dominant White male group has been a consistent challenge dating back to the era of rapid industrialization in the United States (Nkomo & Hoobler, in press). European ethnic immigrants faced exclusion and discrimination as they tried to gain employment in the rising new industrial factories in the United States (Roediger, 1999). Blacks and other racial minorities found themselves totally barred from such employment or confined to the lowest-paying and most dangerous jobs (Foner & Lewis, 1989; Takaki, 1990). Over time, European ethnic minorities who had been denigrated were assimilated into the dominant group by eventually being socially constructed as White—or, simply put, they were incorporated into the White category (Ignatiev, 1995). Because White supremacy was the dominant diversity ideology of the time, Blacks and other racial minorities continued to face widespread exclusion and discrimination in the workplace until the passage of the landmark Civil Rights Act of 1964 and Title VII. Thus, prior to the introduction of legislation, organizations largely practiced what I would call selective exclusion of racial minorities (and White women) from jobs with greater power, authority, and compensation. Although these groups were in the workplace, they were employed mainly in a limited set of occupations and largely absent from the managerial and supervisory ranks of organizations.

There was, at the same time, very little research focused on issues of exclusion and/or race and ethnicity in the workplace (Nkomo, 1992). In a seminal article, Cox and Nkomo (1990) documented the inattention to issues of difference and the invisibility of Blacks in management and organizational scholarship. Although some attention had been given to what was labeled intergroup relations primarily in the work of organization behavior scholars such as Clayton Alderfer (see Alderfer, Alderfer, Tucker, & Tucker, 1980), for the most part there was very little scholarship systematically examining such issues in the U.S. workplace until the passage of Title VII.

To be more accurate, however, the demand for labor during World War II motivated then-President Roosevelt, in 1941, to issue Executive Order 8802, which banned discrimination (Foner & Lewis, 1989). One result of this order was the establishment of the Fair Employment Practices Committee (Delton, 2007). Some organizations responded with a short-lived flurry of activity to rectify the exclusion of Blacks and other racial minorities in the workplace (Delton). For instance, a number of companies hired industrial psychologists who developed workplace interventions consistent with the human relations approach emanating from Elton Mayo's seminal research (Nkomo & Hoobler, in press). At the time, organizations asked for assistance in using human relations as a means of addressing the ways in which race and ethnicity obstructed cooperative working relations, and some research on the topic subsequently appeared (Delton, 2007; Hughes, 1946; Vallas, 2003).

However, it was not until the passage of Title VII and the establishment of the Equal Employment Opportunity Commission that both practitioners and organizational scholars gave serious attention to diverse race and ethnic groups in the workplace, as well as gender. As noted by Kelly and Dobbin (1998), the size and scope of what was then known as personnel management grew, as it became the focal function for determining how to comply with the legislation. The approach to dealing with exclusion at the time can be summarized as compliance. Human resource managers at the time focused their attention not so much on how to leverage the diversity of groups previously excluded but on how to make sure that their organizations did not discriminate or that there was equal opportunity for those previously excluded. It was more of a defensive position rather than really advocating for the value of diverse perspectives in the workplace. Despite the provision through executive orders for affirmative action in the workplace, it too was largely positioned as a corrective mechanism (Kelly & Dobbin, 1998).

The compliance approach to workplace diversity is akin to the discrimination and fairness paradigm in Thomas and Ely's (1996) framework of diversity paradigms. Thomas and Ely (1996) argued that organizations that approach a diverse workforce through a discrimination and fairness paradigm usually focus on equal opportunity, fair treatment, recruitment, and compliance with antidiscrimination legislation. Concomitantly, research also focused on detecting discrimination in selection, promotion, and differences in affective outcomes of primarily Black and White employees (Nkomo, 1992). There was less research into the status of other racial and ethnic minorities as well as women (Nkomo & Cox, 1996).

Diversity emerged as the next turn in the evolution of approaches for addressing exclusion in the workplace, in part in in response to the release of labor market forecasts predicting an increase in the numbers of women and racial and ethnic minorities entering the U.S. workplace (Johnston & Packer, 1987; Lorbiecki & Jack, 2000). Although the release of this data is credited as the main influence, other scholars point to a change in how human resource managers perceived the challenges faced in dealing with resistance to the call for equal opportunity for women and racial and ethnic minorities in the workplace. According to Kelly and Dobbin (1998), human resource practitioners experienced decreasing returns to their calls for incorporation of women and minorities, and they attempted to overcome this by repositioning compliance practices into a call for managing and valuing diversity in the workplace. Thus there was a dramatic shift from a discourse of equal opportunity and compliance to valuing diversity or the business case for the inclusion of minorities and women in the workplace, both in the workplace and in research (Oswick & Noon, in press).

Diversity was positioned as a means of improving organizational effectiveness and, ultimately, the bottom line. The title of Roosevelt Thomas's (1991) seminal book, *Beyond Race and Gender: Unleashing the Power of Your Total Workforce by Managing Diversity*, captures the essence of the diversity approach to exclusion. First, it signaled a change in who constituted the targets for inclusion. Diversity, in contradistinction to the traditional focus on race and gender, moved beyond these so-called primary (surface) categories of difference to include secondary or deep level differences (such as professional identity and personality) (Harrison, Price,

& Bell, 1998). Second, as noted by some scholars at the time, the diversity approach was to be inclusive of all people in the workplace, including White men.

There was a notable proliferation of research and an expansion of the topics during the 1990s and into the early 2000s. Under the rubric of diversity, scholars explored the business case for diversity (for example, Herring, 2009; Richard, 2000), the experiences of racial and ethnic minorities beyond African-Americans (for example, DelCampo & Blancero, 2008; Ferdman & Cortes, 1992; Kawahara & Jang van Kirk, 2010); diversity in work teams (for example, Jackson & Joshi, 2010); sexual identity (for example, Bell, Özbilgin, Beauregard, & Sürgevil, 2011; Ragins, 2001); diversity in countries other than the United States (for example, Klarsfeld, 2010); critical perspectives (for example, Prasad, Mills, Elmes, & Prasad, 1997; Zanoni, Janssens, Benschop, & Nkomo, 2010); and transnational dimensions of diversity (Calás, Holgersson, & Smircich, 2010). The research over several decades moved from defining the concept to demonstrating why diversity should be valued and how to create diversity in the workplace. The creation of positions such as chief diversity officer in organizations and the establishment of a Gender and Diversity in Organizations division of the Academy of Management (the premier association for management scholars) are testimony to the legitimization of diversity management attained in the late 20th century.

The Inclusion Paradigm

It is not entirely clear when the inclusion approach began to emerge as a means of addressing exclusion in the workplace, although it did appear in some works in the 1990s (see, for example, Ferdman & Brody, 1996; see also Ferdman, Chapter 1, this volume). The concept of inclusion has its theoretical roots in social psychology and social work (Shore, Randel, Chung, Dean, Ehrhart, & Singh, 2011). However, similar to the emergence of the diversity approach in the 1990s, it seems to have arisen primarily from practice. Inclusion has been driven by the need to close the gap between the promise of diversity and the current ability of individuals, organizations, groups, and societies to leverage the advantages of diversity (Ferdman, 2010; Mor Barak, 2011). This point is made by Henderson (Chapter 15, this volume) in his discussion of how Weyerhaeuser's former focus on compliance, affirmative action, and representation failed to contribute to the broader business imperative.

How does the inclusion paradigm differ from the diversity paradigm, particularly in terms of what it means for practice? There is a core theme running through all of the chapters in terms of the meaning of inclusion. Inclusion is ultimately a way of being for individuals, groups, organizations, and societies. Inclusion requires a deep understanding of the taken-for-granted ways that organizations and societies create exclusion and how individuals have internalized responses to those who are dissimilar. I like to think of inclusion as creating a "new normal" or changing what organization culture scholar Edgar Schein refers to, in his model of organizational cultures, as *assumptions*. Schein (1990) described organizational cultures as being composed of three layers: artifacts, values, and assumptions. His pioneering work conceptualized assumptions as the deepest level of culture, or what Argyris and Schön (1974) defined as theories-in-use. Assumptions are the deepest and most difficult layer of culture to penetrate, because they are often implicit and unconsciously drive action. Or simply put, theories-in-use are deep rooted assumptions that underpin everyday practices in organizations. It is indeed these everyday practices that often block inclusion. On the surface, these practices may appear to be neutral and nonexclusionary, but in reality they operate to exclude those considered "others" and outside dominant groups.

While the diversity management approach argued for the incorporation of those constructed as different, scholars rarely ventured into probing the fundamental and deeply embedded, taken-for-granted assumptions in organizations that maintain exclusion. Critical diversity scholars, however, raised such questions but were largely a minority voice (for example, Lorbiecki & Jack, 2000; Noon, 2007; Zanoni et al., 2010). All of the authors in this book make clear that inclusion cannot be achieved without addressing the core of culture of our organizations. As Nishii and Rich stress in their chapter, inclusion requires a ındamental shift in the way individuals and organizations think and behave. Karl Weick's (1996) notion of dropping *one's tools* as a proxy for unlearning comes to mind. The tools and assumptions that organizations and individuals assume to be normal or good practice have to be dropped to make room for inclusive tools and assumptions.

For example, at the organizational level several of the chapters in this book point to making organizational climates and cultures more inclusive. Nishii and Rich suggest that a climate for inclusion is created by fair organizational practices, the quality of interaction among employees, and the objective characteristics of the work setting. They further assert that an organization can be said to have an inclusive climate only if all employees experience the climate as inclusive. Additionally, Schein (1990) stresses that climate is a surface manifestation of culture. In a real sense, if organizations want to change their climates they must create an inclusive organization culture.

The authors in this book also make explicit reference to what is required at the level of values with respect to organizational cultures. They stress the need for an organizational value system that explicitly positions inclusion as a critical imperative for organizational effectiveness. But perhaps more important, they assert that inclusion must be embraced as a superordinate value, not merely as part of a long list of values.

In Schein's model artifacts are tangible, observable organizational practices (such as human resource management policies). Achieving an inclusive workplace is not about cosmetic changes in organizational practices but about fundamentally thinking through what it means to design practices that are embedded in inclusivity. A number of chapters discuss various organizational practices and how to transform them to be inclusive. In Chapter 8, Offermann and Basford observe how human resource management did not figure significantly in scholarly work on diversity management but stress its critical role in building inclusive organizations. Their interviews with practitioners from the United States and several other countries reveal a number of human resource management best practices. There are also several contributions that delve into the requirements for inclusive leadership. Booysen, in Chapter 10, argues that organizations must first make sure leadership development is inclusive of all groups but also make sure inclusive leadership is part of the development of all organizations leaders. Gallegos, in Chapter 6, evokes Ferdman's (2010) notion that creating inclusive organizations requires leaders to embrace a complex leadership task: taking on the sacred cows of deeply embedded assumptions and practices. In Chapter 9, Church, Rotolo, Shull, and Tuller focus on prescriptions for inclusive organization development practices, while Hayles writes in Chapter 2 about the importance of communication practices for inclusion.

What then is required of individuals? At the individual level, creating inclusive organizations means dropping all assumptions we hold about differences and changing our behavior. It means letting go of what we believe to be true about men and women. It means letting go of the idea that there is such a thing as races and other fixed notions about social identities. Wasserman, as well as Bennett, provide valuable insights into the interpersonal skills and intercultural competencies required of individuals to practice inclusive interactions in the workplace. In Chapter 4, Wasserman positions inclusive communication as the process of relating to others. Bennett, in Chapter 5, lays out the cognitive, affective, and behavioral skills that help individuals to be competent in cross-cultural interactions.

Mor Barak and Daya, in Chapter 13, argue for removing the barrier between what goes on inside organizations and directly linking the quest for inclusion to the broader society. They urge organizations to adopt a broader vision of inclusion, which includes not only the organization but also its surrounding community. The idea that organizations are embedded in a broader context has been around for a long time in management and organizations studies. Yet rarely have explicit linkages been made between the internal and external issues of difference and diversity, particularly in the U.S. context. A simple example is that much of the literature on gender diversity in U.S. organizations, unlike what is often found in other countries, rarely makes reference to international protocols on gender equality in society. The explicit incorporation of the societal level in the discourse of inclusion represents a departure from the previous compliance and diversity approaches.

In sum, the authors in this book collectively suggest that moving from diversity to an inclusion approach requires what change theorists refer to as *second-order change*. Whereas diversity too often ends up being largely reduced to incremental change, inclusion requires second-order or radical change—the need to break the frame (Nadler & Tushman, 1989). It is difficult to imagine, but what if organizations from the outset had been developed and structured not for a dominant group of White males but for a group of people diverse in all the ways humanity can differ? What if White supremacy and patriarchy had not become embedded ideologies and systems for exclusion? How would organizations operate? How would they practice human resource management? How would individuals in organizations relate to one another? What kinds of organization cultures would exist? How would organizations ensure that the talents of all their employees are utilized? The chapters in this book provide good insight into how these difficult questions might be answered.

Another intriguing aspect of inclusion is the notion that it does not require people to abandon their uniqueness. Shore et al. (2011) employed the concept of optimal distinctiveness to capture this idea at the individual level. That is, inclusion will have been achieved only if individuals are able to bring all that they are to the workplace, without having to suppress or marginalize any aspect of their identities, as Ferdman and Roberts discuss in Chapter 3. At the group level, we might infer the existence of inclusiveness by how the group draws on and uses its diversity to perform tasks, using the talents of all its members (Chatman, 2010). Research on the benefits of heterogeneous groups clearly underscores that the mere presence of diversity does not automatically result in high performance (Jackson & Joshi, 2010). At the societal level, an inclusive approach, as noted by Mor Barak and Daya, implies that organizations have a major role to play in addressing issues of exclusion and inequality in the broader society and the community.

Conclusion

What then are the prospects for achieving inclusion in organizations? Inclusion holds promise for eradicating exclusion as long as its proponents do not lose sight of two key elements in its intent. First, inclusion interventions must tackle the deep-rooted assumptions and practices that result in exclusion and the privileging of some over others. Second, true inclusion can be declared only when no one can say, "What about me?" Although one might read cynical motives into the changes in approaches to exclusion over the last several decades, another reading suggests that these changes in approaches have been motivated largely by the reality that the "isms" have not been erased—sadly, they appear to be able to take the heat. Perhaps the heat has not been of the right intensity or the right kind. Or perhaps we have too quickly thrown out the baby with the bath water. I say this to argue, along with Oswick and Noon (in press) as well as a tendency of authors in this book to write about "diversity and inclusion," that scholars and practitioners probably need to employ a synchronic approach that targets antidiscrimination (making sure that discrimination is not a feature of organizations), diversity (increasing the representation and power throughout the organization of those usually excluded), and inclusion (helping everyone to be able to bring all that they are to the workplace). The interconnection among all of these approaches is their intent to address the historical dominance of some groups at the expense of the marginalization of others in the workplace. The journey to inclusion will not be an easy one, as the inequality regimes and exclusionary practices noted by Acker (2006) are well entrenched. Yet scholars and practitioners have no choice but to strive for the possibility of breaking the frame and transforming our workplaces from places of exclusion to ones of inclusion. Organizations are grappling with talent shortages and the need to be more innovative and creative. These challenges, now more than ever, create a need for all organizations to embrace the diversity of talent available.

References

Acker, J. (2006). Inequality regimes: Gender, race and class in organizations. *Gender and Society, 20,* 441–464.

Alderfer, C. P., Alderfer, C. J., Tucker, R., & Tucker, L. (1980). Diagnosing race relations in management. *Journal of Applied Behavioral Science, 16,* 135–166.

Argyris, M., & Schön, D. (1974). *Theory in practice. Increasing professional effectiveness.* San Francisco: Jossey-Bass.

Bell, M. P., Özbilgin, M. F., Beauregard, A., & Sürgevil, O. (2011). Voice, silence and diversity in 21st century organizations: Strategies for inclusion of gay, lesbian, bisexual and transgender employees. *Human Resource Management, 50,* 131–146.

Calás, M. B., Holgersson, C., & Smircich, L. (2010). Diversity management? Translation? Travel? *Scandinavian Journal of Management, 25,* 349–351.

Chatman, J. A. (2010). Norms in mixed sex and mixed race work groups. *Academy of Management Annals, 4,* 447–484.

Cox, T. H., Jr., & Nkomo, S. M. (1990). Invisible men and women: A status report on race as a variable in organization behavior research. *Journal of Organization Behavior, 11,* 419–431.

DelCampo, R. G., & Blancero, D. M. (2008). Perceptions of psychological contract fairness of Hispanic professionals. *Cross-Cultural Management: An International Journal, 15,* 300–315.

Delton, J. (2007). Before the EEOC: How management integrated the workplace. *Business History Review, 81,* 269–295.

Ferdman, B. M. (2010). Teaching inclusion by example and experience: Creating an inclusive learning environment. In B. B. McFeeters, K. M. Hannum, & L. Booysen (Eds.), *Leading across differences: Cases and perspectives—Facilitator's guide* (pp. 37–50). San Francisco: Pfeiffer.

Ferdman, B. M., & Brody, S. E. (1996). Models of diversity training. In D. Landis & R. Bhagat (Eds.), *Handbook of intercultural training* (2nd ed., pp. 282–303). Thousand Oaks, CA: Sage.

Ferdman, B. M., & Cortes, A. (1992). Culture and identity among Hispanic managers in an Anglo business. In S. B. Knouse, P. Rosenfeld, & A. Culbertson (Eds.), *Hispanics in the workplace* (pp. 246–277). Thousand Oaks, CA: Sage.

Foner, P. S., & Lewis, R. L. (1989). *Black workers: A documentary history from colonial times to the present times.* Philadelphia, PA: Temple University Press.

Harrison, D. A., Price, H. H., & Bell, M. P. (1998). Beyond relational demography: Time and effects of surface- and deep-level diversity on work group cohesion. *Academy of Management Journal, 41,* 96–107.

Herring, C. (2009). Does diversity pay? Race, gender, and the business case for diversity. *American Sociological Review, 74,* 208–224.

Hughes, E. C. (1946). The knitting of racial groups in industry. *American Sociological Review, 11,* 512–519.

Ignatiev, N. (1995). *How the Irish became White*. New York: Routledge.

Jackson, S. E., & Joshi, A. (2010). Work team diversity. In S. Zedeck (Ed.), *APA handbook of industrial and organizational psychology* (Vol. 1, pp. 651–686). Washington, DC: American Psychological Association.

Johnston, W. B., & Packer, A. E. (1987). *Workforce 2000: Work and workers for the twenty-first century*. Indianapolis, IN: Hudson Institute.

Kelly, E., & Dobbin, F. (1998). How affirmative action became diversity management. *American Behavioral Scientist, 41*, 960–985.

Klarsfeld, A. (Ed.). (2010). *International handbook of diversity management at work: Country perspectives on diversity and equal treatment*. Cheltenham, UK: Edward Elgar.

Kawahara, D., & Jang van Kirk, J. (2010). Asian Americans in the workplace: Facing prejudice and discrimination in multiple contexts. In J. L. Chin (Ed.), *The psychology of prejudice and discrimination: A revised and condensed edition* (pp. 39–63). Santa Barbara, CA: Praeger.

Lorbiecki, A., & Jack, G. (2000). Critical turns in the evolution of diversity management. *British Journal of Management, 11*, 17–31.

Mor Barak, M. E. (2011). *Managing diversity: Toward a globally inclusive workplace* (2nd ed.). Thousand Oaks, CA: Sage.

Nadler, D. A., & Tushman, M. L. (1989). Organizational frame bending: Principles for managing reorientation. *Academy of Management Executive, 3*, 194–204.

Nkomo, S. M. (1992). The emperor has no clothes: Rewriting race in the study of organizations. *Academy of Management Review, 17*, 487–513.

Nkomo, S. M., & Cox, T. H., Jr. (1996). Diverse identities in organizations. In S. Clegg, C. Hardy, & W. Nord (Eds.), *Handbook of organization studies* (pp. 338–356). Thousand Oaks, CA: Sage.

Nkomo, S. M., & Hoobler, J. (in press). An historical perspective on diversity ideologies in the United States: Reflections on human resource management research and practice. *Human Resource Management Review*.

Noon, M. (2007). The fatal flaws of diversity and the business case for ethnic minorities. *Work, Employment and Society, 21*, 773–784.

Oswick, C., & Noon, M. (in press). Discourses of diversity, equality and inclusion: Trenchant formulations or transient fashions? *British Journal of Management*, published online ahead of print May 23, 2012. doi: 10.1111/j.1467-8551.2012.00830.x

Özbilgin, M. F., & Syed, J. (2010). *Managing cultural diversity in Asia: A research companion*. Cheltenham, UK: Edward Elgar.

..sad, P., Mills, A. J., Elmes, M., & Prasad, A. (Eds.). (1997). *Managing the organizational melting pot: Dilemmas of workplace diversity*. Thousand Oaks, CA: Sage.

Ragins, B. R. (2001). Pink triangles: Antecedents and consequences of perceived workplace discrimination against gay and lesbian employees. *Journal of Applied Psychology, 86*, 1244–1261.

Richard, O. (2000). Racial diversity, business strategy and firm performance: A resource-based view. *Academy of Management Journal, 43*, 164–177.

Roediger, D. R. (1999). *The wages of whiteness: Race and the making of the American working class* (rev. ed.). London, NY: Versco.

Schein, E. H. (1990). Organization culture. *American Psychologist, 4*, 109–119.

Shore, L. M., Randel, A. E., Chung, B. G., Dean, M. A., Ehrhart, K. H., & Singh, G. (2011). Inclusion and diversity in work groups: A review and model for future research. *Journal of Management, 37*, 1262–1289. doi:10.1177/0149206310385943

Takaki, R. (1990). *Iron cages: Race and culture in 19th century America*. New York: Oxford University Press.

Thomas, D. A., & Ely, R. (1996). Making differences matter: A new paradigm for managing diversity. *Harvard Business Review, 74*(5), 79–90.

Thomas, R. R., Jr. (1991). *Beyond race and gender: Unleashing the power of your total workforce by managing diversity*. New York: AMACOM.

Vallas, S. P. (2003). Rediscovering the color line within work organizations: The "knitting of racial groups" revisited. *Work and Occupations, 30*, 379–400.

Weick, K. E. (1996). Drop your tools: An allegory for organizational studies. *Administrative Science Quarterly, 41*, 301–313.

Zanoni, P., Janssens, M., Benschop, Y., & Nkomo, S. (2010). Unpacking diversity, grasping inequality: Rethinking difference through critical perspectives. *Organization, 17*, 9–29.

CHAPTER TWENTY-THREE

Practicing Inclusion: Looking Back and Looking Ahead

Bernardo M. Ferdman and
Barbara R. Deane

In this final chapter, we reflect on what we believe this book has accomplished and share a few thoughts about both lessons learned and perspectives for the future. Bringing this book to fruition has been a long yet gratifying journey; along the way, we have discovered new insights and new questions about inclusion, both in the content of the pages you have before you (and the multiple drafts that preceded them) as well as in the process of producing and editing them. Because this volume—like all those in SIOP's Professional Practice Series—is geared specifically to practitioners, a guiding editorial principle for us has been to make sure that in each chapter there is value for those who want to apply its insights in their work and life. At the same time, given the particular needs we have observed in the field of diversity and inclusion, we have sought to deepen overall understanding of the concept of inclusion, particularly its expression and practice in organizations seeking to increase, work more effectively with, and benefit from diversity.

In the Preface, series editors Allan Church and Janine Waclawski thoughtfully and aptly highlight the importance of taking a "comprehensive and holistic approach"—as we have sought to do—to link diversity and inclusion (D&I) work with the

.s of organizational psychology, organization development
.D), and human resource management (HRM). Church and
Waclawski also remind us that diversity and inclusion represent
some of the core values of organizational psychology, OD, and
HRM. We wholeheartedly agree, and add that the *practice of
inclusion*, as described and documented throughout this book's
chapters, offers clear guidance for substantively acting on these
core values.

Our goal has been to present a new and larger vision to understand diversity and its benefits at work. To do this, we focused on
inclusion, as a fundamental approach and practice to benefit
from diversity in a way that works for everyone, across multiple
dimensions of difference. The book's chapters provide a state-of-
the-art perspective on inclusion and how to practice it so as to
truly integrate and benefit from diversity throughout organizations. The authors describe and illuminate in much detail what
inclusion is, why it matters to organizations, and how it can be
created and fostered, while emphasizing the lens and grounding
provided by theory and research in organizational psychology,
OD, and HRM. In doing this, the accent has been on the proactive, dynamic, ongoing, and participatory aspects of creating and
sustaining inclusion, a theme that we elaborate in the next section.

The *Practice* of Inclusion: What Have We Learned?

Conceptualizing inclusion as a practice allows for greater understanding of its multiple and complex components and, more
important, how they interact in a dynamic and interdependent
fashion. Indeed, *practicing* inclusion is ongoing and never-ending;
it must be continuously done and attended to in order to achieve
its objectives. It is not a one-time event or action, but rather a set
of ongoing and integrated activities, attitudes, behaviors, mindsets, and approaches to self and others, to work, to leadership,
and even to life.

A Dynamic and Cyclical Process

First, as documented and illustrated in many of the preceding
chapters, practicing inclusion is a dynamic and ongoing process

that involves both what is done by individuals, groups, and organizations to create and sustain it and how people understand and experience these behaviors and policies. These experiences not only are the key to unlocking the benefits of diversity and inclusion, but also help to refuel the overall process of practicing inclusion. The key to practicing inclusion is what individuals, leaders, organizations, and societies actively do to bring this experience and the overall process of inclusion to life. When inclusion is realized, that experience encourages and allows each of us to be fully ourselves, with all of our differences from and similarities to those with whom we interact. Out of that experience come the full contributions of each individual to the collective, whether at work, in the community, or in the greater society as a whole. The process can be seen as a virtuous and self-reinforcing cycle in which benefits accrue to all parties—the individuals and the groups and organizations to which they belong.

A Proactive and Never-Ending Process

Second, the notion of practicing inclusion implies a systematic, proactive, evolving, and perhaps even revolutionary effort on the part of interdependent parties. This intentional, developmental, and transformative aspect of symbiotic action can be compared to the dynamism of love. Once we are *in* love, we are not done with it; in fact, we are just beginning; the true experience of love is derived in the process of actively *loving*, as a verb. The same goes for inclusion: when organizations and individuals decide to practice inclusion, they must engage in an interactive—and often challenging—process that requires ongoing attention and reflection, connection and presence, assessment and calibration, as well as a healthy and growth-promoting balance between comfort and discomfort. Practicing inclusion requires ongoing mindfulness. In other words, effectively practicing inclusion must be situated in the daily realities, needs, interactions, and aspirations, both individual and collective, of all those involved—in every moment and without an ending. Inclusion is not ever *done*!

A Professional Foundation and Framework for Praxis

A third important aspect of the practice of inclusion is the professional framework that permits, supports, and informs it. As documented throughout this book's chapters, practicing inclusion well—especially at the organizational level—should be grounded on and informed by a systematic body of knowledge and expertise: by concepts, models, theories, and research with practical applications. In other words, inclusion is a developing field of professional practice, connected to but going beyond what we have come to know as the field of diversity in organizations (Ferdman & Sagiv, 2012; Roberson, 2013).

The well-known Brazilian educator Paulo Freire (1970/2006) highlighted the critical importance of *praxis*—"reflection and action directed upon the structures to be transformed" (p. 126). As he reminded us, theory and practice must necessarily go hand in hand for change to happen: "Theory without practice would be mere abstract thinking, just as practice without theory would be reduced to naive action" (Freire & Vittoria, 2007, p. 97). Freire (1970a) described it this way: "The action of men without objectives, whether the objectives are right or wrong, mythical or demythologized, naive or critical, is not praxis, though it may be orientation in the world. And not being praxis, it is action ignorant both of its own process and of its aim. The interrelation of the awareness of aim and of process is the basis for planning action, which implies methods, objectives, and value options" (p. 206).

From this perspective and for this reason, grounding the practice of inclusion in clear conceptual frameworks and supporting evidence is not only a professional imperative, but also critical to its success, continuity, and evolution. It can allow practitioners to understand available options regarding what to do, why to do it, and why it may work, and can provide a framework for testing working assumptions. This understanding of practice has important implications for the field, including raising the question of who is qualified to conduct the work of inclusion, particularly at the organizational level. A professional field of practice requires its specialists to have certain knowledge, skills, and abilities. Those doing the work must continually rethink their ideas, test their assumptions, and document what they discover and learn.

At the same time, it cannot be a specialized or an isolated field of practice. In the Freirian spirit, professional work on inclusion must itself be inclusive and involve people across the organization. This is what Freire (1970/2006) wrote about liberation, a far-reaching concept not unlike inclusion: "Authentic liberation—the process of humanization—is not another deposit to be made in men. Liberation is a praxis: the action of men and women upon their world in order to transform it. Those truly committed to the cause of liberation can accept neither the mechanistic concept of consciousness as an empty vessel to be filled, nor the use of banking methods of domination (propaganda, slogans—deposits) in the name of liberation" (p. 79). Inclusion has a similar potential to be a liberatory concept.

Multiple Levels of Analysis and Action

A fourth insight about the practice of inclusion illuminated throughout the book's chapters involves the multiple levels at which inclusion is manifested, experienced, and enacted. Our key premise has been that inclusion is the approach necessary to reap the advantages of diversity at the individual, interpersonal, group, organizational, and societal levels. At each of these levels, there are roles and responsibilities related to inclusion for leaders and employees and for practitioners and scholars alike. These can apply in a range of organizational types—including business organizations, educational institutions, NGOs, and governmental organizations—and can also address the needs of the larger community and society. It is important to maintain a comprehensive perspective on the many facets and components of inclusion, and the combination of chapters in the book certainly helps to illuminate many of the intricacies of the systemic, multilevel approach introduced in Chapter 1.

Questions for the Future

We conclude by briefly raising four sets of questions with implications for the future of the practice of inclusion.

1. Adopting the lens of inclusion for understanding and examining every individual and collective practice presents a learning challenge for all organizational members that will require both developing new knowledge while simultaneously applying it. What is the process of learning how to apply the lens of inclusion and simultaneously supporting the development of collective and new understanding of its complexities, nuances, and challenges? Taken together, the chapters in this book present a strong case for practicing inclusion as a key to diversity's benefits, and they contain a wealth of information about the current state of the art of this relatively young approach and its applications. At the same time, there is a great deal of work yet to be done to further develop the field and validate its working assumptions across a range of settings and circumstances. It is an evolving field that continues to develop, even as its contributions are applied in real time. Those in organizations who are involved in these applications will need to learn how to engage in the work in ways that are yet to be charted, while taking their bearings from the cumulative state of knowledge and experience at present. How will they engage in this learning? How and to what extent will what they learn in this process be fed back into our collective learning about the practice of inclusion and serve to advance the field? How can individuals, groups, and organizations incorporate the processes and attitudes needed to continually practice inclusion at the same time that we continue to develop our collective understanding of both what those processes and attitudes are and inclusion's multiple and complex facets?

2. Engaging inclusion as a practice presents a holistic and systematic approach, yet will it help to unite the wide range of practitioners who are and need to be involved? As documented throughout the book, practicing inclusion—especially across a complex organization, but also in any work group—is unlikely to be done well or systematically if it is simply done intuitively or with a seat-of-the-pants approach. At the same time, specialists in inclusion are insufficient and certainly cannot do it alone; in any case, practicing inclusion requires multiple disciplines, perspectives, and types of expertise. How can we keep and contribute the expertise and unique concerns derived from our particular

vantage points and disciplines, and yet still continue to build and apply a holistic approach to the practice of inclusion? How can we avoid working at cross-purposes, given our particular interests, motivations, and contingencies? How can we join together without losing the potency or nuances of the unique and special contributions made from our particular perspective and specialty, and at the same time avoid each claiming the whole? How can we practice inclusion among all of those seeking to advance the field of inclusion and practice in it?

3. Approaching the practice of inclusion on a multilevel basis provides both conceptual clarity and practical complexity. How can we best combine the need for immediate application with the need to learn about and act at multiple levels and in multiple domains? Is it possible to work on just one part of the puzzle and still make meaningful change? How can we work in a particular section or domain while keeping the whole in mind? These are some of the challenges of practicing inclusion more generally; for example, if I engage inclusively with a particular individual who is quite different from me, but in the process I do not address systemic and intergroup patterns of exclusion, and perhaps even perpetuate certain injustices, am I still being inclusive? How can we make progress (and what even constitutes progress?) when the practice of inclusion is so multilayered and complex? Certainly, ongoing reflection and learning—individually and collectively— are key. Yet the need for action and change is often immediate, and in many cases we must become more able and willing to learn while doing and to do while learning.

4. Advancing the practice of inclusion to greater maturity will require input from and participation by both practitioners and scholars (and scholar-practitioners). What types of interaction and collaboration—and how much—will there be between practitioners and scholars so that both consult each other's work and learn from each other? How can inclusion best be practiced in that conjunction? Although it is true for many areas of professional practice that advancement requires research and theory on the one hand and application and learning from experience on the other, we believe that this is particularly the case for the practice of inclusion.

It seems fitting to end the book with questions. The practice of inclusion is continually evolving. Along with our colleagues who have written the other chapters in this collection, and standing on the shoulders of many pioneers who have taught and inspired us, we have presented what we have learned, understood, and believed about the practice of inclusion. Even as we continue to be passionate about this work and excited to see the further application of the expertise and knowledge presented in these pages, we are also enthusiastic about seeing what new ideas, perspectives, and frameworks will emerge to both challenge and change those for which we have advocated. In the spirit of inclusion, we now let go of our work and hand it off to those who read and are inspired by this book, and invite them to join us in—and even take charge of—this collective process of learning and application, in search of a better world for all of us together.

References

Ferdman, B. M., & Sagiv, L. (2012). Diversity in organizations and cross-cultural work psychology: What if they were more connected? *Industrial and Organizational Psychology: Perspectives on Science and Practice, 5*, 323–345. doi:10.1111/j.1754–9434.2012.01455.x

Freire, P. (1970a). The adult literacy process as cultural action for freedom. *Harvard Educational Review, 40*(2), 205–225.

Freire, P. (2006). *Pedagogy of the oppressed* (30th anniversary ed.). New York: Continuum. (Original work published 1970)

Freire, A. M. A., & Vittoria, P. (2007). Dialogue on Paolo Freire. *Interamerican Journal of Education for Democracy, 1*(1), 96–117.

Roberson, Q. M. (Ed.). (2013). *The Oxford handbook of diversity and work.* New York: Oxford University Press.

Name Index

Subject Index